Philosophic Classics
Volume I

ANCIENT PHILOSOPHY

Walter Kaufmann
Late, of Princeton University

Forrest E. Baird, Editor
Whitworth College

Prentice Hall, Englewood Cliffs, New Jersey 07632

Library of Congress Cataloging-in-Publication Data

Philosophic classics / [compiled by] Walter Kaufmann, Forrest E.
Baird, editor.
p.   cm.
Contents: v. 1. Ancient philosophy   —v. 3. Modern philosophy.
Includes bibliographical references.
ISBN 0-13-091316-2 (v. 1).—ISBN 0-13-097551-6 (v. 3)
1. Philosophy.   I. Kaufmann, Walter Arnold.   II. Baird, Forrest
E.
B21.P39   1994
100—dc20   93-34534
                                                CIP

Acquisitions editor: Ted Bolen
Editorial assistant: Nicole Gray
Editorial/production supervision and
   interior design: Linda B. Pawelchak
Art supervision: Anne Bonanno
Chapter introduction sketches: Don Martinetti
Cover design: Donna Wickes
Photo editor: Lori Morris Nantz
Photo research: Joelle Burrows
Production coordinators: Kelly Behr and Peter Havens

Cover photo: Greek Tomb Painting 490–480 B.C.
   Detail, Museo Nazionale, Paestum.
   Nimatallah/Art Resource, NY.

 © 1994 by Prentice-Hall, Inc.
A Paramount Communications Company
Englewood Cliffs, New Jersey 07632

A revision of *Philosophic Classics* 2/e © 1968

Printed in the United States of America
10   9   8   7   6   5   4   3   2

ISBN 0-13-091316-2

Prentice-Hall International (UK) Limited, *London*
Prentice-Hall of Australia Pty. Limited, *Sydney*
Prentice-Hall Canada Inc., *Toronto*
Prentice-Hall Hispanoamericana, S.A., *Mexico*
Prentice-Hall of India Private Limited, *New Delhi*
Prentice-Hall of Japan, Inc., *Tokyo*
Simon & Schuster Asia Pte, Ltd., *Singapore*
Editora Prentice-Hall do Brasil, Ltda., *Rio de Janeiro*

This volume is dedicated to

Stanley R. Obitts

and

Robert N. Wennberg
Professors of Philosophy
Westmont College

Contents

Preface

Since 1961, *Philosophic Classics* has provided a generation of students with an anthology of quality in the history of Western philosophy. While classics do not change, students who read them do. It is time to give students a fresh version of the late Professor Kaufmann's outstanding work.

One of the major changes in this revision is to split the first volume into two. Accordingly, there are now separate volumes on ancient and medieval philosophy. In addition to allowing for more adequate treatment of the medieval period, this change makes it possible to include more of the Hellenistic and Roman philosophers in this first volume.

In making changes I have tried wherever possible to follow three principles: (1) to use complete works or, where more appropriate, complete sections of works (2) in clear translations (3) of texts central to the thinker's philosophy or widely accepted as part of the "canon." To make the works more accessible to students, most footnotes treating textual matters (variant readings, etc.) have been omitted and all Greek words have been transliterated and put in angle brackets. I have also rewritten the introductions, dividing them into three sections: (1) biographical (a glimpse of the life), (2) philosophical (a résumé of the philosopher's thought), and (3) bibliographical (suggestions for further reading).

Besides moving the medieval thinkers to a separate volume, I have made the following major revisions in this edition of Volume I.

Additions: Plato, *Euthyphro, Crito, Republic* (Book V plus sections of Books IV, VI, and VII); Epicurus, *Letter to Menoeceus;* Lucretius, *On the Nature of Things* (Book III); Marcus Aurelius, *Meditations* (Book VII).

Deletions: Plato, *Phaedrus,* the partial selections from *The Sophist, Timaeus, Laws,* and *Epistle VII;* Aristotle, *Poetics.*

Changes: Two-thirds of the translations have been changed to more up-to-date versions (including three of Plato's dialogues in new translations done specifically for this edition by Tom Griffith); the Aristotle selections have been changed to emphasize whole books or sections rather than bits and pieces; and the section on Hellenistic and Roman philosophers, besides being expanded to include Lucretius and Marcus Aurelius, has added materials from Epicurus, Sextus Empiricus, and Plotinus.

Those who use this first volume in a one-term course in ancient philosophy will find more material here than can easily fit a normal semester. But this embarrassment of riches gives teachers some choice and, for those who offer the same course year after year, an opportunity to change the menu.

*   *   *

I would like to thank the many people who assisted me in this volume, including the library staff of Whitworth College, especially Hans Bynagle, Gail Fielding, Jeanette Langson, and Joan Spanne; my colleagues F. Dale Bruner, who made helpful suggestions on all the introductions, and Barbara Filo, who helped make selections for artwork; Stephen Davis, Claremont McKenna College; Jerry H. Gill, The College of St. Rose; Rex Hollowell, Spokane Falls Community College; Stanley Obitts, Westmont College; and Charles Young, The Claremont Graduate School, who each read some of the introductions and gave helpful advice; my student assistant, Meredith TeGrotenhuis; my secretary, Lorrie Nelson; and Linda B. Pawelchak, production editor, and Ted Bolen of Prentice Hall. I would also like to thank the following reviewers: James W. Allard, Montana State University; Robert C. Bennett, El Centro College; Herbert L. Carson, Ferris State University; Helen S. Lang, Trinity College; Scott MacDonald, University of Iowa; Stephen Scott, Eastern Washington University; Daniel C. Shartin, Worcester State College; Donald Phillip Verene, Emory University; and Robert M. Wieman, Ohio University.

I am especially thankful to my wife, Joy Lynn Fulton Baird, and to our children, Whitney Jaye, Sydney Tev, and Soren David, who have supported me in this arduous enterprise.

Finally, I would like to thank Stanley R. Obitts and Robert N. Wennberg, who first introduced me to the joys of philosophy. It is to them that this volume is dedicated.

Forrest E. Baird
Professor of Philosophy
Whitworth College
Spokane, WA 99251

ANCIENT PHILOSOPHY

Philosophers in This Volume

Thales
  Anaximander
    Anaximenes
      Pythagoras
      Xenophanes

Plato 427--Athens
  Aristotle
  Pyrrho

        Epicurus
        Zeno of Citium
        Cleanthes

Heraclitus
Anaxagoras
Pericles
Protagoras
Parmenides
Empedocles
Gorgias
Antiphon
Socrates
Zeno
Democritus
Melissus

Other Important Figures

Zoroaster
  Lao-Tse
    Ezekial
      Confucius
      Buddha

Nehemiah
    Alexander the Great
    Euclid

Sophocles
Herodotus
Euripides
Thucydides
Hippocrates
Aristophanes
Ezra

A Sampling of Major Events

Jerusalem falls to Babylonians
  Battle of Marathon
    Parthenon built
      Peloponnesian War

Punic Wars and rise of Rome

Wall of China

600 B.C.   500 B.C.   400 B.C.   300 B.C.   200 B.C.

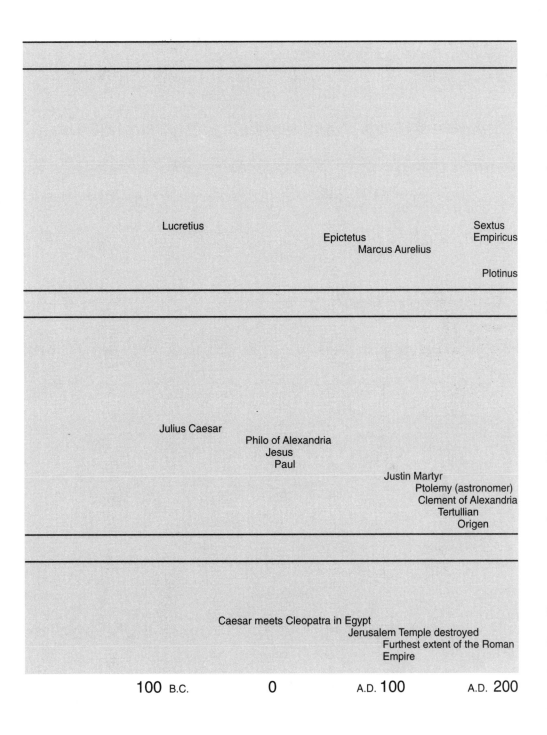

Lucretius

Epictetus
Marcus Aurelius

Sextus
Empiricus

Plotinus

Julius Caesar

Philo of Alexandria
Jesus
Paul

Justin Martyr
Ptolemy (astronomer)
Clement of Alexandria
Tertullian
Origen

Caesar meets Cleopatra in Egypt
Jerusalem Temple destroyed
Furthest extent of the Roman
Empire

100 B.C.   0   A.D. 100   A.D. 200

Before Socrates

Something unusual happened in Greece and the Greek colonies of the Aegean Sea some 2,500 years ago. Whereas the previous great cultures of the Mediterranean had used mythological stories of the gods to explain the operations of the world and of the self, some of the Greeks began to discover new ways of explaining things. Instead of reading their ideas into, or out of, ancient scriptures or poems, they began to use reason, contemplation, and sensory observation to make sense of reality.

It all began with the Greeks living on the coast of Asia Minor (present-day Turkey); colonists such as Thales tried to find the one common element in the diversity of nature. Subsequent thinkers such as Anaximenes sought not only to find this one common element, but also to find the process by which one form changes into another. Other thinkers, such as Pythagoras, turned to the nature of form itself rather than the basic stuff that takes on a particular form. These lovers of wisdom, or *philosophers,* came to very different conclusions and often spoke disrespectfully of one another. Some held the universe to be one, while others insisted that it must be many. Some believed that human knowledge was capable of understanding virtually everything about the world, while others thought that it was not possible to have any knowledge at all. But despite all their differences, there is a thread of continuity, a continuing focus: the *human* attempt to understand the world, using *human* rea-

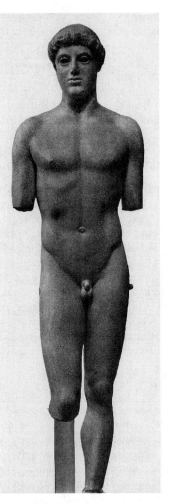

The Kritos Boy, 480 B.C. Just as the philosophers of classical Greece focused on human reason and its ability to know, the artists of the same period examined the human body in its idealized form. *(Acropolis Museum, Athens)*

son. This fact distinguishes these philosophers from the great minds that preceded them.

There are excellent reasons for beginning a study of philosophy with these men and then proceeding to Socrates and Plato. This, after all, is how Western philosophy did begin, and we can still recapture something of the excitement of this new way of thinking as we move from the bald statements of Thales to the all-embracing questions of Socrates, and thence to Plato's efforts to fuse criticism with construction.

If dissatisfaction with facile answers is the starting point of philosophic thought, the fragments of the Pre-Socratics are especially appropriate for a beginning. Not one of their works has survived complete—all we have are scattered quotations and reports from later writers. As a result, Pre-Socratic thought has a mysterious quality. Cryptic passages and forceful aphorisms, whose original context is lost, stimulate the imagination. Instead of looking for "the" answer, one is fascinated by a wealth of possible answers. And in the effort to show why some suggested answers are untenable, one develops critical faculties.

Some fragments may remind readers of archaic statues—heads with broken noses, torsos without heads or arms—pieces so perfect in form that one has no regrets at the loss of the whole and may even feel that the complete work could not have been as fascinating.

For all that, most interest in the Pre-Socratics is motivated by the fact that these thinkers furnish the backdrop for the thought of Socrates, Plato, and Aristotle—that is why one lumps them together as "the Pre-Socratics." But this magnificent succession of thinkers deserves more respect. Though often enigmatic and at times oracular, the Pre-Socratics are distinguished above all by their appeal to reason. And through the appeal to reason, each thinker makes it possible for successors to exercise criticism, to amend, to develop alternatives, to move beyond.

The Pre-Socratics' influence on Plato was so great that a study of their thought is essential to an understanding of many passages in his dialogues and of his intentions—many problems were suggested to him by Heraclitus, the Eleatics, and the Pythagoreans—and, of course, of his originality. Aristotle studied the Pre-Socratics closely and discussed them at length in the first book of his *Metaphysics* (reprinted in this volume). Of the later Greek philosophers, it has often been remarked that the Stoics were particularly influenced by Heraclitus, the Epicureans by Democritus. Elements of Orphism, an early Greek religious movement, also found their way into the ideas of the Pre-Socratics—most obviously, but by no means only, into Pythagoreanism—and hence into Plato and, later, into Christianity. In fact, a few of the fragments survived only as quotations in the works of early Christian writers.

*   *   *

What follows is only a selection. There is no such thing as a complete roster of the Pre-Socratics. The so-called Sophists were Socrates' contemporaries, but Protagoras and Gorgias were older than he and had acquired reputations before he came along and challenged them; and they are included here. After all, it was partly in response to their teaching that his thought was developed. Among the older writers, it is arguable who was, and who was not, a philosopher. Various poets, for example, are occasionally included among the Pre-Socratics. Not counting the Sophists (and a speech of Pericles), the present selection concentrates on twelve major figures. They might conveniently be arranged into four groups of three: (1) the three great Milesians (Thales, Anaximander, and Anaximenes); (2) the three great independents—figures who came from different places and stood for quite different principles (Pythagoras, Xenophanes, and Heraclitus); (3) the three great Eleatics (Parmenides, Zeno, and Melissus); and finally (4) the three great pluralists (Empedocles, Anaxagoras, and Democritus). The only major name missing in this list is Leucippus, founder of the atomistic philosophy, who is included with his better-known follower, Democritus.

If we were to offer all the fragments of the twelve figures, we would have to include such unhelpful items as the following, each given in its entirety: "The joint connects two things"; "as when fig juice binds white milk"; "having kneaded together barley-meal with water"; "nozzle of the bellows" (Empedocles, fragments 32, 33, 34; Anaximander fragment 4). Instead, the following selections were chosen (1) to give an idea of each thinker's main teachings, as far as possible in his own words; and (2) to provide some sense of his way of thinking and feeling. In short, the selections should give us the essence of thinkers who still have the power to astonish students across roughly 2,500 years.

* * *

For a discussion of the primary sources, see the "Sources of the Fragments" section on page 60. For a comprehensive work on the Pre-Socratics, see Volumes I and II of W.K.C. Guthrie's authoritative *The History of Greek Philosophy,* six vols. (Cambridge: Cambridge University Press, 1962–1981). John Burnet, *Early Greek Philosophy* (1892; reprinted New York: Meridian, 1960); John Mansley Robinson, *An Introduction to Early Greek Philosophy* (Boston: Houghton Mifflin, 1968); and Jonathan Barnes, *The Pre-Socratic Philosophers* (London: Routledge & Kegan Paul, 1982) are standard secondary sources, while the relevant sections of W.T. Jones, *The Classical Mind* (New York: Harcourt, Brace, & World, 1969); Frederick Copleston, *A History of Philosophy: Volume I, Greece & Rome, Part I* (Garden City, NY: Doubleday, 1962); and J.V. Luce, *An Introduction to Greek Philosophy* (New York: Thames and Hudson, 1992) provide basic introductions. Robert S. Brumbaugh, *The Philosophers of Greece* (Albany, NY: SUNY Press, 1981), is an accessible introduction with pictures, charts, and maps. Francis MacDonald Cornford, *Principium Sapientiae: The Origins of Greek Philosophical Thought* (Cambridge: Cambridge University Press, 1952), and Werner Jaeger, *The Theology of the Early Greek Philosophers* (Oxford: Clarendon Press, 1947) are both classic works that discuss the movement from mythology to philosophy. For a collection of essays, see David J. Furley and R.E. Allen, eds., *Studies in Presocratic Philosophy,* two vols. (New York: Humanities Press, 1970–1975), and A.P.D. Mourelatos, ed., *The Pre-Socratics* (Garden City, NY: Anchor Books, 1974).

In addition to the general sources listed here, the individual articles in Paul Edwards, ed., *The Encyclopedia of Philosophy* (New York: Macmillan, 1967) are frequently useful.

Consult the following books for these specific thinkers:

ANAXIMANDER—Charles H. Kahn, *Anaximander and the Origins of Greek Cosmology* (New York: Columbia University Press, 1960).

PYTHAGORAS—C.J. De Vogel, *Pythagoras and Early Pythagoreanism* (Assen, The Netherlands: Van Gorcum, 1966); and Walter Burkert, *Lore and Science in Ancient Pythagoreanism,* translated by Edwin L. Minar, Jr. (Cambridge, MA: Harvard University Press, 1972).

HERACLITUS—G.S. Kirk, *Heraclitus: The Cosmic Fragments* (Cambridge: Cambridge University Press, 1954); and Charles H. Kahn, *The Art and Thought of Heraclitus* (Cambridge: Cambridge University Press, 1979).

PARMENIDES—Leonardo Tarán, *Parmenides: A Text with Translation, Commentary, and Critical Essays* (Princeton, NJ: Princeton University Press, 1965); A.P.D. Mourelatos, *The Route of Parmenides* (New Haven, CT: Yale University Press, 1970); and David Gallop, *Parmenides of Elea* (Toronto: University of Toronto Press, 1984).

ZENO OF ELEA—Wesley C. Salmon, ed., *Zeno's Paradoxes* (Indianapolis, IN: Bobbs-Merrill, 1970); and Adolf Grünbaum, *Modern Science and Zeno's Paradoxes* (Middletown, CT: Wesleyan University Press, 1967).

EMPEDOCLES—Denis O'Brien, *Empedocles' Cosmic Cycle* (Cambridge: Cambridge University Press, 1969).

ANAXAGORAS—Malcolm Schofield, *An Essay on Anaxagoras* (Cambridge: Cambridge University Press, 1980).

DEMOCRITUS (ATOMISM)—Cyril Bailey, *The Greek Atomists and Epicurus* (Oxford: Clarendon Press, 1928; reprinted New York: Russell and Russell, 1964).

SOPHISTS—Mario Untersteiner, *The Sophists,* translated by Kathleen Freeman (New York: Philosophical Library, 1954); and G.B. Kerferd, *The Sophistic Movement* (Cambridge: Cambridge University Press, 1981).

Much of the critical work on the Pre-Socratics is found only in journal articles. *The Philosophers' Index* offers a way to locate such articles.

The Milesians

THALES

fl. 585 B.C.

Thales lived in Miletus in Asia Minor (on the east coast of present-day Turkey) and is said to have been so scientifically skilled that he accurately predicted the eclipse of the sun on May 23, 585 B.C. He was a contemporary of the Hebrew prophet Jeremiah, of the Persian prophet Zoroaster, of the Indian sage Siddhartha Gautama (the Buddha), and of the Chinese philosophers Confucius and Lao-tse.

Thales has traditionally been considered the first Western philosopher (though some scholars now claim that this honor belongs to Anaximander). Thales was apparently the first to ask the question, "What is the basic 'stuff' of the universe?" According to Aristotle, Thales claimed that this basic stuff was water. This claim involves three vital assumptions: (1) that the fundamental explanation of the universe must be one in number, (2) that this one reality must be a "thing," and (3) that this one thing must have within itself the ability to move and change. Later thinkers disputed Thales' choice of the universe's basic "stuff," but his bold theory encouraged them and helped them to develop their own philosophical programs.

Like many other Pre-Socratics, Thales was by no means a philosopher only. He was also a statesman, an astronomer, a geometer, and a sage. The first three fragments that follow deal with Thales' life. Number one is probably the world's oldest "absent-minded professor" story, while numbers two and three appear to be defenses designed to show how practical Thales could be. The remaining fragments are reports on Thales' ideas. There are no known writings of Thales, nor, surprisingly, are there any reports of his ever having written.

[1]* A witty and attractive Thracian servant-girl is said to have mocked Thales for falling into a well while he was observing the stars and gazing upwards; declaring that he was eager to know the things in the sky, but that what was behind him and just by his feet escaped his notice.

[2] When they reproached him because of his poverty, as though philosophy were no use, it is said that, having observed through his study of the heavenly bodies that there would be a large olive-crop, he raised a little capital while it was still winter, and paid deposits on all the olive presses in Miletus and Chios, hiring them cheaply because no one bid against him. When the appropriate time came there was a sudden rush of requests for the presses; he then hired them out on his own terms and so made a large profit, thus demonstrating that it is easy for philosophers to be rich, if they wish, but that it is not in this that they are interested.

[3] When he came to the Halys river, Croesus then, as I say, put his army across by the existing bridges; but, according to the common account of the Greeks, Thales the Milesian transferred the army for him. For it is said that Croesus was at a loss how his army should cross the river, since these bridges did not yet exist at this period; and that Thales, who was present in the army, made the river, which flowed on the left hand of the army, flow on the right hand also. He did so in this way; beginning upstream of the army he dug a deep channel, giving it a crescent shape, so that it should flow round the back of where the army was encamped, being diverted in this way from its old course by the channel, and passing the camp should flow into its old course once more. The result was that as soon as the river was divided it became fordable in both of its parts.

*   *   *

[4] Thales . . . says the principle is water (for which reason he declared that the earth rests on water), getting the notion perhaps from seeing that the nutriment of all things is moist, and that heat itself is generated from the moist and kept alive by it . . ., and from the fact that the seeds of all things have a moist nature, and that water is the origin of the nature of moist things.

[5] Moist natural substance, since it is easily formed into each different thing, is accustomed to undergo very various changes: that part of it which is exhaled is made into air, and the finest part is kindled from air into aether, while when water is compacted and changes into slime it becomes earth. Therefore Thales declared that water, of the four elements, was the most active, as it were, as cause.

[6] He [Thales] said that the world is held up by water and rides like a ship, and when it is said to "quake" it is actually rocking because of the water's movement.

[7] Thales, too, seems, from what they relate, to have supposed that the soul was something kinetic, if he said that the [Magnesian] stone possesses soul because it moves iron.

*The numbers in brackets serve the purposes of this volume. See the "Sources of the Fragments" section on page 60 for the source of each fragment.

[8] Some say that it [soul] is intermingled in the universe, for which reason, perhaps, Thales also thought that all things are full of gods.

ANAXIMANDER

ca. 610–ca. 546 B.C.

Anaximander was born in Miletus about 610 B.C., and he died around 546 B.C. During his lifetime, Nebuchadnezzar conquered Jerusalem and the prophet Ezekiel was exiled to Babylon. Anaximander travelled extensively and was so highly regarded by his fellow Milesians that he was honored with the leadership of a new colony. He may have been the first Greek to write a book of prose.

Anaximander seems to have accepted Thales' three basic assumptions (summed up in the statement that the universe must be one changeable thing), but he differed with Thales on the nature of the "stuff" underlying the "many" that we observe. In place of Thales' water, Anaximander introduced the concept of the ⟨apeiron⟩—the unlimited, boundless, infinite, or indefinite—as the fundamental principle of the world. This notion was a step up in philosophical sophistication—a metaphysical principle rather than an empirically observed material thing. This idea of a basic "stuff," with properties different from anything in the observable world, has survived to the present.

Anaximander also developed a rudimentary concept of natural law—the idea that all growing things in the natural world develop according to an identical pattern. He invented the idea of models, drawing what is considered to be the first geographical map. But what has fascinated all subsequent students of philosophy, more than anything else, is the one sentence, or half-sentence, quoted by Simplicius in fragment [3] following. This remark, the oldest known piece of Western philosophy, has elicited a large literature, including a forty-eight-page essay by Martin Heideggger.

[1] Anaximander son of Praxiades, of Miletus, philosopher, was a kinsman, pupil and successor of Thales. He first discovered the equinox and solstices and hour-indicators, and that the earth lies in the center. He introduced the gnomon [a vertical rod whose shadow indicates the sun's direction and height] and in general made known an outline of geometry. He wrote *On Nature, Circuit of the Earth* and *On the Fixed Stars and a Celestial Globe,* and some other works.

[2] [Anaximander] was the first of the Greeks whom we know who ventured to produce a written account on nature.

* * *

[3] Of those who say that it is one, moving, and infinite, Anaximander, son of Praxiades, a Milesian, the successor and pupil of Thales, said that the principle and element of existing things was the ⟨apeiron⟩ [indefinite, or infinite], being the first to introduce

this name of the material principle. He says that it is neither water nor any other of the so-called elements, but some other ⟨apeiron⟩ nature, from which come into being all the heavens and the worlds in them. And the source of coming-to-be for existing things is that into which destruction, too, happens "according to necessity; for they pay penalty and retribution to each other for their injustice according to the assessment of time," as he describes it in these rather poetical terms. It is clear that he, seeing the changing of the four elements into each other, thought it right to make none of these the substratum, but something else besides these; and he produces coming-to-be not through the alteration of the element, but by the separation off of the opposites through the eternal motion.

[4] He says that that which is productive from the eternal of hot and cold was separated off at the coming-to-be of this world, and that a kind of sphere of flame from this was formed round the air surrounding the earth, like bark around a tree. When this was broken off and shut off in certain circles, the sun and moon and stars were formed.

[5] He says that the earth is cylindrical in shape, and that its depth is a third of its width.

[6] Its shape is curved, round, similar to the drum of a column; of its flat surfaces we walk on one, and the other is on the opposite side.

[7] Anaximander [says the sun] is a circle 28 times the size of the earth, like a chariot wheel, with its [rim] hollow and full of fire, and showing the fire at a certain point through an aperture as though through the nozzle of a bellows.

[8] Anaximander said that the first living creatures were born in moisture, enclosed in thorny barks; and that as their age increased they came forth on to the drier part and, when the bark had broken off, they lived a different kind of life for a short time.

[9] Further he says that in the beginning man was born from creatures of a different kind; because other creatures are soon self-supporting, but man alone needs prolonged nursing. For this reason he would not have survived if this had been his original form.

[10] Therefore they [the Syrians] actually revere the fish as being of similar race and nurturing. In this they philosophize more suitably than Anaximander; for he declares, not that fishes and men came into being in the same parents, but that originally men came into being inside fishes, and that, having been nurtured there—like sharks— and having become adequate to look after themselves, they then came forth and took to the land.

ANAXIMENES

fl. 546 B.C.?

Very little is known about the life of Anaximenes, except that he was a Milesian and a younger contemporary of Anaximander. Anaximenes proposed air as the basic world principle. While at first this thesis may seem a step backwards from the more comprehensive (like Anaximander's unlimited) to the less comprehensive particular (like Thales' water), Anaximenes added an important point. He explained a *process* by which the underlying one (air) becomes the observable many: By rarefaction air becomes fire and by condensation air becomes, successively, wind, water, and earth. Observable qualitative differences (fire, wind, water, earth) are the result of quantitative changes, that is, of how densely packed is the basic principle. This view is still held by scientists.

[1] Anaximenes son of Eurystratus, of Miletus, was a pupil of Anaximander . . . He said that the material principle was air and the infinite; and that the stars move, not under the earth, but round it. He used simple and unsuperfluous Ionic speech. He was active, according to what Apollodorus says, around the time of the capture of Sardis [by Cyrus in 546/5 B.C.?], and died in the 63rd Olympiad.

[2] He [Anaximander] left Anaximenes as his disciple and successor, who attributed all the causes of things to infinite air, and did not deny that there were gods, or pass them over in silence; yet he believed not the air was made by them, but that they arose from air.

[3] And all things are produced by a kind of condensation, and again rarefaction, of this [air]. Motion, indeed, exists from everlasting; he says that when the air melts, there first of all comes into being the earth, quite flat—therefore it accordingly rides on the air; and sun and moon and the remaining heavenly bodies have their source of generation from earth. At last, he declares the sun to be earth, but that through the rapid motion it obtains heat in great sufficiency.

Three Solitary Figures

PYTHAGORAS

ca. 571–ca. 497 B.C.

Pythagoras was a contemporary of the Hebrew prophets Haggai and Zechariah, as well as of Siddhartha Gautama, the Buddha, who had his major inspiration about 521 B.C. Born on the island of Samos, just off the coast of Asia Minor and very close to Miletus, Pythagoras moved to southern Italy, where the Greeks had colonies, and settled at Croton, on the Bay of Tarentum.

Pythagoras was soon associated with so many legends that few scholars dare to say much about his life, his personality, or even his teachings, without adding that we cannot be sure our information is accurate. That there was a man named Pythagoras who founded the sect called the Pythagoreans, we need not doubt: Among the witnesses to his historicity was his younger contemporary, Heraclitus, who thought ill of him (see Heraclitus, section D, following). Nevertheless, it is notoriously difficult to distinguish between the teachings of Pythagoras himself and those of his followers, the Pythagoreans.

Today he is best known for the so-called Pythagorean theorem in geometry (fragment [5] following). But his interest in mathematics went far beyond this theorem. While the Egyptians and others had been interested in mathematics for its practical uses in building, commerce, and

11

so on, Pythagoras was interested in mathematics for its own sake. And while the Milesians searched for the *stuff* of all things, Pythagoras (or the Pythagoreans) focused on the *form* of all things. He claimed that "things are numbers," that mathematical formulas and ratios explain the physical world. (Those who think this odd might ponder the contemporary physicist's assertion that an electron is a "probability cloud.")

Pythagoras was also interested in religious salvation and established a proto-monastic religious order with strict rules of conduct (see fragments [10–27] following). His religion and his philosophy might seem disconnected to us, but for Pythagoras the two were inseparable. Like Plato after him, he believed that the study of mathematics could convert the soul from the world of the senses to the contemplation of the eternal. The religious sect Pythagoras founded still existed in Plato's time, 150 years later, and decisively influenced Plato's thought—an influence, in fact, second only to that of Plato's revered teacher, Socrates.

The following Pythagorean ideas especially influenced Plato: the dualism of body and soul and the conception of the body (*soma* in Greek) as the tomb (*sema* in Greek) of the soul; the belief in the immortality of the soul; the doctrine of the transmigration of souls; the idea that knowledge and a philosophic life are required for the salvation of the soul; the notion that one might design a society that would be an instrument of salvation for its members; the admission of women to this society; the suggestion that all members of this society should hold their property in common; and, finally, the division of humankind into three basic types—tradesmen being the lowest class; those in whom the competitive spirit and ambition are highly developed, a little higher; and those who prefer contemplation, the highest. In fact, the whole of Plato's thought, from his earliest to his latest works, can be understood as a gradual and sustained departure from the heritage of Socrates to that of Pythagoras.

[1] As I have heard from the Greeks who live on the Hellespont and the Black Sea, this Salmoxis was a man, who was a slave in Samos, the slave in fact of Pythagoras son of Mnesarchus . . .

[2] Aristoxenus says that at the age of forty, seeing that the tyranny of Polycrates was too intense . . . he made his departure for Italy [to Croton].

[3] Three hundred of the young men [followers of Pythagoras], bound to each other by oath like a brotherhood, lived segregated from the rest of the citizens, as if to form a secret band of conspirators, and brought the city [Croton] under their control.

*   *   *

[4] Ten is the very nature of number. All Greeks and all barbarians alike count up to ten, and having reached ten revert again to the unit. And again, Pythagoras maintains, the power of the number ten lies in the number four, the tetrad. This is the reason: if one starts at the unit and adds the successive numbers up to four, one will make up the number ten; and if one exceeds the tetrad, one will exceed ten, too. If, that is, one takes the unit, adds two, then three, and then four, one will make up the number ten. . . . So the Pythagoreans used to invoke the tetrad as their most binding oath: "Nay, by him that gave to our generation the tetractys, which contains the fount and root of eternal nature."

[5] The square of the hypotenuse of a right-angled triangle is equal to the sum of the squares on the sides enclosing the right angle. [The text of the next sentence is cor-

rupt, but the sense is:] If we pay any attention to those who like to recount ancient history, we may find some of them referring this theorem to Pythagoras, and saying that he sacrificed an ox in honor of his discovery.

[6] On the subject of reincarnation, Xenophanes bears witness in an elegy which begins: "Now I will turn to another tale and show the way." What he says about Pythagoras runs thus: "Once they say that he was passing by when a puppy was being whipped, and he took pity and said: Stop, do not beat it; for it is the soul of a friend that I recognized when I heard it giving tongue."

[7] Moreover, the Egyptians are the first to have maintained the doctrine that the soul of man is immortal and that, when the body perishes, it enters into another animal that is being born at the time, and when it has been the complete round of the creatures of the dry land and of the sea and of the air it enters again into the body of a man at birth; and its cycle is completed in 3,000 years. There are some Greeks who have adopted this doctrine, some in former times and some in later, as if it were their own invention; their names I know but refrain from writing down.

[8] None the less the following became universally known: first that he maintains that the soul is immortal; next, that it changes into other kinds of living things; also that events recur in certain cycles, and that nothing is ever absolutely new; and finally, that all living things should be regarded as akin. Pythagoras seems to have been the first to bring these beliefs into Greece.

[9] If one were to believe the Pythagoreans that events recur in an arithmetical cycle, and that I shall be talking to you again sitting as you are now, with this pointer in my hand, and that everything else will be just as it is now, then it is plausible to suppose that the time, too, will be the same as now.

* * *

[10] Let the rules to be pondered be these:

[11] When you are going out to a temple, worship first, and on your way neither say nor do anything else connected with your daily life. (1)

[12] On a journey neither enter a temple nor worship at all, not even if you are passing the very doors. (2)

[13] Sacrifice and worship without shoes on. (3)

[14] Turn aside from highways and walk by footpaths. . . . (4)

[15] Follow the gods and restrain your tongue above all else. . . . (6)

[16] Stir not the fire with iron. . . . (8)

[17] Help a man who is loading freight, but not one who is unloading. (10)

[18] Putting on your shoes, start with the right foot; washing your feet, with the left. (11)

[19] Speak not of Pythagorean matters without light. (12)

[20] Never step over a cross-bar. (13)

[21] When you are out from home, look not back, for the furies come after you. . . . (14)

[22] Do not wear a ring. . . . (22)

[23] Do not look in a mirror beside a lamp. . . . (23)

[24] Eat not the heart. . . . (30)

[25] Spit upon the trimmings of your hair and finger-nails. . . . (32)

[26] Abstain from beans. . . . (37)

[27] Abstain from living things. (39)

[28] Pythagoras turned geometrical philosophy into a form of liberal education by seeking its first principles in a higher realm of reality.

[29] Life, he said, is like a festival; just as some come to the festival to compete, some to ply their trade, but the best people come as spectators, so in life the slavish men go hunting for fame or gain, the philosophers for the truth.

XENOPHANES

ca. 570–ca. 478 B.C.

A contemporary of Pythagoras, Xenophanes was from Colophon on the mainland of Asia Minor, a few miles inland and approximately fifty miles north of Miletus and about fifteen miles north of Ephesus. He travelled a great deal, reciting his poetry, of which only a few fragments survive. At one time he was thought to have been Parmenides' teacher and the founder of the Eleatic school, no doubt due to his conception of one unmoving god—a notion readily associated with Parmenides' idea of being. But this connection is now generally rejected, and Xenophanes is seen rather as an essentially solitary figure.

Little of his work has come down to us, but the little that has is unforgettable. Xenophanes challenges Homer's and Hesiod's anthropomorphic conception of the gods and invites skepticism about the ability of humans to know the divine.

[1] Xenophanes son of Dexios or, according to Apollodorus, of Orthomenes, of Colophon . . . being expelled from his native land, passed his time in Zancle in Sicily and in Catana. . . . He wrote in epic metre, also elegiacs and iambics, against Hesiod and Homer, reproving them for what they said about the gods. But he himself also recited his own original poems. He is said to have held contrary opinions to Thales and Pythagoras, and to have rebuked Epimenides, too. He had an extremely long life, as he himself somewhere says: "Already there are seven and sixty years tossing my thought up and down the land of Greece; and from my birth there were another twenty-five to add to these, if I know how to speak truly about these things."

[2] Homer and Hesiod ascribed to the gods whatever is infamy and reproach among men: theft and adultery and deceiving each other.

[3] Mortals suppose that the gods are born and have clothes and voices and shapes like their own.

[4] But if oxen, horses, and lions had hands or could paint with their hands and fashion works as men do, horses would paint horse-like images of gods and oxen ox-like ones, and each would fashion bodies like their own.

[5] The Ethiopians consider the gods flat-nosed and black; the Thracians blue-eyed and red-haired.

[6] There is one god, among gods and men the greatest, not at all like mortals in body or mind.

[7] He sees as a whole, thinks as a whole, and hears as a whole.

[8] But without toil he moves everything by the thought of his mind.

[9] He always remains in the same place, not moving at all, nor is it fitting for him to change his position at different times.

[10] Everything comes from earth and returns to earth in the end.

[11] No man knows or ever will know the truth about the gods and about every-thing I speak of: for even if one chanced to say the complete truth, yet oneself knows it not; but seeming is wrought over all things.

[12] Not from the beginning have the gods revealed all things to mortals, but by long seeking men find what is better.

HERACLITUS

fl. 500 B.C.

Little is known about the life of Heraclitus except that he lived in Ephesus (just north of Miletus) and flourished around 500 B.C. He may have come from an aristocratic family, since his writings indicate a clear contempt for common people. The mystery of his life, together with the obscurity of his writings, led the ancients to call him "the dark philosopher." His surviving epigrammatic fragments, though often paradoxical and elusive, are immensely suggestive, invite frequent rereading, and haunt the mind. In the sayings of Heraclitus, as in no previous philosopher, one encounters the personality of the thinker. After twenty-five centuries, he still evokes instant antipathy in some and the highest admiration in others. Influential admirers include Hegel, Nietzsche, and Bergson.

While Thales considered water the basic principle, and Anaximenes believed it was air, Heraclitus saw the fundamental "world stuff" in fire. Fire seems to have been associated in his mind with change, strife, and war. He may also have been influenced by the Persians and their conception of a fiery judgment (see fragment [35], following). Fire, or the process of change itself, is the "one" truth that ⟨Logos⟩ teaches those few who will listen.

Plato referred to Heraclitus frequently and named one of his dialogues after Heraclitus' follower, Cratylus. One of the speakers in the dialogue *Cratylus* speaks of "the opinion of Heraclitus that all things flow," and the phrase, "all things flow" *(panta rhei)* has often been called the quintessence of Heracliteanism. With some slight oversimplification, one can say that Plato was convinced by Heraclitus that in this sensible world all things are in flux and, if this sensible world is all there is, no rational discourse is possible. This led Plato to the conclusion that there must be another world beyond the world of sense experience—a realm utterly free from change, motion, and time. At that point Plato was probably influenced not only by the Pythagoreans but also by Parmenides, the next great Pre-Socratic.

A. THE MAN

[1] Antisthenes, in his *Successions* quotes as a sign of his [Heraclitus'] arrogance that he resigned the hereditary "kingship" to his brother.

[2] The book said to be his is called *On Nature,* from its chief content, and is divided into three discourses: On the Universe, Politics, Theology. He dedicated it and

placed it in the temple of Artemis, as some say, having purposely written it rather obscurely so that only those of rank and influence should have access to it, and it should not be easily despised by the populace. . . . The work had so great a reputation that from it arose disciples, those called Heracliteans.

B. LOGOS* AND SENSES

[3] Those awake have one ordered universe in common, but in sleep every man turns away to one of his own.

[4] The thinking faculty is common to all.

[5] Of the Logos which is as I describe it men always prove to be uncomprehending, both before they have heard it and when once they have heard it. For although all things happen according to this Logos men are like people of no experience, even when they experience such words and deeds as I explain, when I distinguish each thing according to its constitution and declare how it is; but the rest of men fail to notice what they do after they wake up just as they forget what they do when asleep.

[6] Therefore it is necessary to follow the common; but although the Logos is common the many live as though they had a private understanding.

[7] Listening not to me but to the Logos it is wise to agree that all things are one.

[8] The things of which there is seeing and hearing and perception, these do I prefer.

[9] The eyes are more exact witnesses than the ears.

[10] If all existing things turned to smoke, the nose would be the discriminating organ.

[11] Evil witnesses are eyes and ears for men, if they have souls that do not understand their language.

C. COSMOS

[12] The path up and down is one and the same.

[13] The sun is new each day.

[14] In the same river we both step and do not step, we are and are not.

[15] It is not possible to step twice into the same river.

[16] Upon those that step into the same rivers different and different waters flow.

[17] Sea is the most pure and polluted water: for fishes it is drinkable and salutary, but for men undrinkable and deleterious.

[18] Disease makes health pleasant and good, hunger satiety, weariness rest.

[19] What is in opposition is in concert, and from what differs comes the most beautiful harmony.

[20] War is the father of all and king of all, and some he shows as gods, others as men; some he makes slaves, others free.

[21] It is necessary to know that war is common and right is strife and that all things happen by strife and necessity.

---

*The term ⟨Logos⟩, left untranslated in this section, is sometimes rendered as "reason," sometimes as "word" (as in the first sentence of the Gospel of John: "In the beginning was the Word"); and it may also denote a rational principle in the world.

[22] For souls it is death to become water, for water death to become earth; from earth water comes-to-be, and from water, soul.

[23] Immortals are mortal, mortals immortal, living each other's death, dying each other's life.

[24] After death things await men which they do not expect or imagine.

[25] Time is a child playing a game of draughts; the kingship is in the hands of a child.

D. RELIGION AND FIRE

[26] Being a polymath does not teach understanding: else Hesiod would have had it and Pythagoras; also Xenophanes and Hekataeus.

[27] Homer deserves to be thrown out of the contests and whipped, and Archilochus, too.

[28] The most popular teacher is Hesiod. Of him people think he knew most—he who did not even know day and night: they are one.

[29] They purify themselves by staining themselves with other blood, as if one stepped into mud to wash off mud. But a man would be thought mad if one of his fellowmen saw him do that. Also, they talk to statues as one might talk with houses, in ignorance of the nature of gods and heroes.

[30] The consecrations of the mysteries, as practiced among men, are unholy.

[31] Corpses should be thrown away more than dung.

[32] To god all things are beautiful and good and just, but men have supposed some things to be unjust, others just.

[33] Man is called childish compared with divinity, just as a boy compared with a man.

[34] Fire lives the death of earth, and air the death of fire; water lives the death of air, earth that of water.

[35] Fire, having come upon them, will judge and seize upon [condemn] all things.

[36] This world-order [the same of all] did none of gods or men make, but it always was and is and shall be: an ever-living fire, kindling in measures and going out in measures.

E. MEN AND MORALS

[37] Asses prefer chaff to gold.

[38] Dogs bark at those whom they do not recognize.

[39] If happiness lay in bodily pleasures, we should call oxen happy when they find vetch to eat.

[40] It is not good for men to obtain all they wish.

[41] Sane thinking is the greatest virtue, and wisdom is speaking the truth and acting according to nature, paying heed.

[42] All men are granted what is needed for knowing oneself and sane thinking.

[43] A dry soul is wisest and best.

[44] A man when he is drunk is led by an unfledged boy, stumbling and not knowing where he goes, having his soul moist.

[45] The best choose one above all else: everlasting fame above mortals. The majority are contented like well-fed cattle.

[46] The people must fight on behalf of the law as though for the city wall.

[47] One man to me is ten thousand if he is the best.

[48] The Ephesians would do well to hang themselves, every adult man, and leave their city to adolescents, since they expelled Hermodorus, the worthiest man among them, saying: Let us not have even one worthy man; but if we do, let him go elsewhere and live among others!

F. EPILOGUE

[49] I sought myself.

[50] If one does not expect the unexpected one will not find it, for it is not reached by search or trail.

[51] Character is man's fate.

[52] Nature loves hiding.

[53] The Sybil, uttering her unlaughing, unadorned, unincensed words with raving mouth, reaches out over a thousand years with her voice, through the god.

[54] The lord whose oracle is in Delphi neither speaks out nor conceals, but gives a sign.

The Eleatics

PARMENIDES

fl. ca. 485 B.C.?

Parmenides, a younger contemporary of
Heraclitus and an older contemporary of
Socrates, lived in Elea in southern Italy.
According to Plato's dialogue of the
same name (*Parmenides,* reprinted in
part in this volume), Parmenides visited
Athens when he was about sixty-five,
accompanied by his chief pupil, Zeno,
then nearly forty, and conversed with
the still "quite young" Socrates.
Whether the visit to Athens really took
place, we do not know; that Socrates
met Parmenides is not likely; that they
did not have the conversation reported
in the dialogue is absolutely clear, for
that discussion presupposes Plato's earlier work.

According to Parmenides, there are
two ways of inquiry. The first asserts that
whatever is (i.e., being), "is and cannot
not-be" (see fragment [2] following). This
is the path of truth that leads us to see that
being is one and cannot be created, destroyed, or changed. (If any of these alter-
ations in being were possible, being
would no longer be what "is" and would
become what "is not"—but by definition
there *is* no "is not" from which being
could arise or into which being could
change.) Being must be one seamless unchanging whole. The other path of inquiry, the path of opinion, which claims
that something arises from not-being, is
not only impossible, it is unthinkable.

Parmenides, the philosopher of changeless being, has often been contrasted with Heraclitus, the philosopher of change and becoming. But it should not be overlooked that both are one in repudiating the wisdom of tradition and of common sense. Both claim that things may not be what they seem to be. One is as radical as the other.

Plato was greatly impressed by Parmenides' thought and freely acknowledged his debt to the Eleatic philosopher. In the Platonic *Parmenides*, the character "Parmenides" instructs the young Socrates, while in most dialogues Socrates bests or teaches others. Plato's dichotomies—of knowledge/belief and of unchanging, eternal, timeless reality/ever-changing, temporal appearance—were derived from Parmenides. However, Plato did not accept Parmenides' idea that reality is one, devoid of any plurality: Plato occupied the "real" world with a number of unchanging, eternal forms.

The fragments that follow are part of a poem in which, after an imposing prologue, the ways of knowledge and belief, of being and nonbeing, are distinguished.

[1] The mares that carry me as far as my heart ever aspires sped me on, when they had brought and set me on the far-famed road of the god, which bears the man who knows over all cities. On that road was I borne, for that way the wise horses bore me, straining at the chariot, and maidens led the way. And the axle in the naves gave out the whistle of a pipe, blazing, for it was pressed hard on either side by the two well-turned wheels as the daughters of the Sun made haste to escort me, having left the halls of Night for the light, and having thrust the veils from their heads with their hands.

There are the gates of the paths of Night and Day, and a lintel and a stone threshold enclose them. They themselves, high in the air, are blocked with great doors, and avenging Justice holds the alternate bolts. Her the maidens beguiled with gentle words and cunningly persuaded to push back swiftly from the gates the bolted bar. And the gates created a yawning gap in the door frame when they flew open, swinging in turn in their sockets the bronze-bound pivots made fast with dowels and rivets. Straight through them, on the broad way, did the maidens keep the horses and the chariot.

And the goddess greeted me kindly, and took my right hand in hers, and addressed me with these words: "Young man, you who come to my house in the company of immortal charioteers with the mares which bear you, greetings. No ill fate has sent you to travel this road—far indeed does it lie from the steps of men but right and justice. It is proper that you should learn all things, both the unshaken heart of well-rounded truth, and the opinions of mortals, in which there is no true reliance. But nonetheless you shall learn these things too, how what is believed would have to be assuredly, pervading all things throughout."

[2] Come now, and I will tell you (and you must carry my account away with you when you have heard it) the only ways of enquiry that are to be thought of. The one, that [it] is and that it is impossible for [it] not to be, is the path of Persuasion (for she attends upon Truth); the other, that [it] is not and that it is needful that [it] not be, that I declare to you is an altogether indiscernible track: for you could not know what is not—that cannot be done—nor indicate it.

[3] For the same thing is there both to be thought of and to be.

[4] But look at things which, though far off, are securely present to the mind; for you will not cut off for yourself what is from holding to what is, neither scattering everywhere in every way in order [*i.e.* cosmic order] nor drawing together.

Charioteer, 475 B.C. The Charioteer stands in solemn grandeur commemorating the serious nature of competition for the ancient Greeks. This statue comes from the same time and place as Parmenides' poem with its image of a chariot ride to truth. *(Alison Frantz, Athens)*

[5] It is a common point from which I start; for there again and again I shall return.

[6] What is there to be said and thought needs must be; for it is there for being, but nothing is not. I bid you ponder that, for this is the first way of enquiry from which I hold you back, but then from that on which mortals wander knowing nothing, two-headed; for helplessness guides the wandering thought in their breasts, and they are carried along, deaf and blind at once, dazed, undiscriminating hordes, who believe that to be and not to be are the same and not the same, and the path taken by them is backward-turning.

[7] For never shall this be forcibly maintained, that things that are not are, but you must hold back your thought from this way of enquiry, nor let habit, born of much ex-

perience, force you down this way, by making you use an aimless eye or an ear and a tongue full of meaningless sound: judge by reason the strife-encompassed refutation spoken by me.

[8] Only one way remains; that it is. To this way there are very many sign-posts: that being has no coming-into-being and no destruction, for it is whole of limb, without motion, and without end. And it never was, nor will be, because it is now, a whole all together, one, continuous; for what creation of it will you look? How, whence sprung? Nor shall I allow you to speak or think of it as springing from not-being; for it is neither expressible nor thinkable that what-is-not is. Also, what necessity impelled it, if it did spring from nothing, to be produced later or earlier? Thus it must be absolutely, or not at all. Nor will the force of credibility ever admit that anything should come into being, beside being itself, out of not-being. So far as that is concerned, justice has never released *(being)* from its fetters and set it free either to come into being or to perish, but holds it fast. The decision on these matters depends on the following: it is, or it is not. It is therefore decided, as is inevitable: ignore the one way as unthinkable and inexpressible (for it is no true way) and take the other as the way of being and reality. How could being perish? How could it come into being? If it came into being, it is not, and so too if it is about-to-be at some future time. Thus coming-into-being is quenched, and destruction also into the unseen.

Nor is being divisible, since it is all alike. Nor is there anything there which could prevent it from holding together, nor any lesser thing, but all is full of being. Therefore it is altogether continuous; for being is close to being.

But it is motionless in the limits of mighty bonds, without beginning, without cease, since becoming and destruction have been driven very far away, and true conviction has rejected them. And remaining the same in the same place, it rests by itself and thus remains there fixed; for powerful necessity holds it in the bonds of a limit, which constrains it round about, because it is decreed by divine law that being shall not be without boundary. For it is not lacking; but if it were *(spatially infinite)*, it would be lacking everything.

To think is the same as the thought that it is; for you will not find thinking without being to which it refers. For nothing else either is or shall be except being, since fate has tied it down to be a whole and motionless; therefore all things that mortals have established, believing in their truth, are just a name: becoming and perishing, being and not-being, and change of position, and alteration of bright color.

But since there is a *(spatial)* limit, it is complete on every side, like the mass of a well-rounded sphere, equally balanced from its center in every direction; for it is not bound to be at all either greater or less in this direction or that; nor is there not-being which could check it from reaching to the same point, nor is it possible for being to be more in this direction, less in that, than being, because it is an inviolate whole. For, in all directions equal to itself, it reaches its limits uniformly.

At this point I cease my reliable theory ⟨*Logos*⟩ and thought, concerning Truth; from here onwards you must learn the opinions of mortals, listening to the deceptive order of my words.

They have established *(the custom of)* naming two forms, one of which ought not to be *(mentioned):* that is where they have gone astray. They have distinguished them as opposite in form, and have marked them off from another by giving them different signs: on one side the flaming fire in the heavens, mild, very light *(in weight),* the same as itself in every direction, and not the same as the other. This *(other)* also is by itself and opposite: dark night, a dense and heavy body. This world-order I describe to you throughout as it appears with all its phenomena, in order that no intellect of mortal men may outstrip you.

[9] But since all things are named light and night, and names have been given to each class of things according to the power of one or the other, everything is full equally of light and invisible night, as both are equal, because to neither of them belongs any share (of the other).

[10] You shall know the nature of the heavens, and all the signs in the heavens, and the destructive works of the pure bright torch of the sun, and whence they came into being. And you shall learn of the wandering works of the round-faced moon, and its nature; and you shall know also the surrounding heaven, whence it sprang and how necessity brought and constrained it to hold the limits of the stars.

[11] *(I will describe)* how earth and sun and moon, and the aether common to all, and the milky way in the heavens, and outermost Olympus, and the hot power of the stars, hastened to come into being.

[12] For the narrower rings were filled with unmixed fire, and those next to them with night, but between (these) rushes the portion of flame. And in the center of these is the goddess who guides everything; for throughout she rules over cruel birth and mating, sending the female to mate with the male, and conversely again the male with the female.

[13] First of all the gods she devised Love.

[14] *(The moon):* Shining by night with a light not her own, wandering round the earth.

ZENO OF ELEA

fl. ca. 465 B.C.

All the ancient authorities agree that Zeno of Elea was a pupil and associate of Parmenides. Zeno is noted for his writings in defense of Parmenides' concept of the One. Zeno showed the paradoxes that result from the theses of plurality held by philosophers like Pythagoras. Zeno's paradoxes were designed to prove that plurality and change are not possible.

Zeno's puzzles have fascinated philosophers, logicians, and mathematicians ever since, and never more than in our own time: probably more has been written on his paradoxes in the last hundred years than in the preceding two thousand. (See the suggestions for further reading in the introduction to the Pre-Socratics.) Much of this work is cheerfully unconcerned with the connection, if any, between the writers "Zeno" and Zeno. Reading the critics could give one extravagant notions of the reasoning powers of this remote Greek. Hence one will probably be surprised by reading what Zeno actually said in the fragments that follow.

The fragments have been arranged into four broad arguments: against plurality, against motion, against space, and, in a slightly different vein, against the reliability of sense experience (in the paradox of the millet seed). These paradoxes are all designed to show that Parmenides is correct: Being is one seamless unchanging whole.

The four paradoxes against motion are perhaps the most famous—and the most difficult to resolve. These paradoxes clearly bring out the discrepancy between logic and experience. For example, the second of the paradoxes logically concludes that Achilles cannot catch a tortoise—but it *seems* so obvious to experience that he can. Either there is something wrong with Zeno's logic (which is, of course, what modern discussions of the paradox have tried to show) or else experience is illusory. Zeno maintained that his logic was right and that he had demonstrated that Parmenides was right: Change is impossible.

[1] [My] book is in fact a sort of defence of Parmenides' argument against those who try to make fun of it by showing that his supposition, that there is a One, leads to many absurdities and contradictions. This book, then, is a retort against those who assert a plurality. It pays them back in the same coin with something to spare, and aims at showing that, on a thorough examination, their own supposition that there is a plurality leads to even more absurd consequences than the hypothesis of the One.

[2] [Zeno] of Elea has an art of speaking, such that he can make the same things appear to his audience like and unlike, or one and many, or again at rest and in motion. . . .

A. ARGUMENTS AGAINST PLURALITY

[3] He [Zeno] showed earlier [i.e., prior to the parts of the argument constituting B1 and B2] that nothing has size because each of the many is self-identical and one.

[4] For if it [something having no size] were added to another, it would make it [the latter] no larger. For having no size, it could not contribute anything by way of size when added. And thus the thing added would be nothing. If indeed when [something is] subtracted from another, the latter is not reduced, nor again increased when [something is] added [to it], it is clear that what is added or subtracted is nothing.

[5] If there are many, they must be just so many as they are, neither more nor fewer. But if they are just so many as they are, they must be finite [in number]. If there are many, the existents are infinite [in number]: for there are always other [existents] between existents, and again others between these. And thus the existents are infinite [in number].

B. ARGUMENTS AGAINST MOTION

The Race Course

[6] For we have many arguments contrary to (common) beliefs, whose solution is yet difficult, like Zeno's that it is impossible to move or to traverse the race course.

[7] For this reason Zeno's argument too assumes falsely that it is impossible to traverse or to come in contact with each one of an infinite number [of things] in a finite time.

[8] The first [of Zeno's arguments against motion "which cause difficulty to those who try to solve the problems they raise"] says that there is no motion, because the moving [body] must reach the midpoint before it gets to the end.

[9] In the same way one should reply to those who pose [literally, "ask"] Zeno's argument, claiming that it is always necessary to traverse the half [i.e., to traverse any given distance we must first traverse its first half], and these [i.e., half-distances] are infinitely numerous, while it is impossible to traverse an infinity. . . .

[10] If there is motion, the moving object must traverse an infinity in a finite [time]: and this is impossible. Hence motion does not exist. He demonstrates his hypothesis thus: The moving object must move a certain stretch. And since every stretch is infinitely divisible, the moving object must first traverse half the stretch it is moving, and then the whole; but before the whole of the half, half of that and, again, the half of that. If then these halves are infinite, since, whatever may be the given [stretch] it is possible to halve it, and [if, further,] it is impossible to traverse the infinity [of these stretches] in a finite time . . . it follows that it is impossible to traverse any given length in a finite time.

The Achilles

[11] The second [of Zeno's arguments against motion] is what is known as "the Achilles," which purports to show that the slowest will never be overtaken in its course by the swiftest, inasmuch as, reckoning from any given instant, the pursuer, before he can catch the pursued, must reach the point from which the pursued started at that instant, and so the slower will always be some distance in advance of the swifter.

The Arrow

[12] The third [of Zeno's arguments against motion is] that the arrow is stationary while on its flight . . . Since a thing is at rest when it has not shifted in any degree out of a place equal to its own dimensions, and since at any given instant during the whole of its supposed motion the supposed moving thing is in the place it occupies at that instant, the arrow is not moving at any time during its flight.

The Stadium

[13] The fourth [of Zeno's arguments against motion] supposes a number of objects all equal with each other in dimensions, forming two equal trains and arranged so that one train stretches from one end of a racecourse to the middle of it, and the other from the middle to the other end. Then if you let the two trains, moving in opposite directions but at the same rate, pass each other, Zeno undertakes to show that half of the time they occupy in passing each other is equal to the whole of it . . . This is his demonstration. Let there be a number of objects *AAAA*, equal in number and bulk to those that compose the two trains but stationary in the middle of the stadium. Then let the objects *BBBB*, in number and dimension equal to the *A*'s, form one of the trains stretching from the middle of the *A*'s in one direction; and from the inner end of the *B*'s let *CCCC* stretch in the opposite direction, being the equal in number, dimension, and rate of movement to the *B*'s.

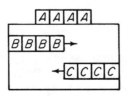

Then when they cross, the first *B* and the first *C* will simultaneously reach the extreme *A*'s in contrary directions.

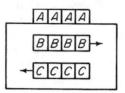

Now during this process the first *C* has passed all the *B*'s, whereas the first *B* has only passed half the *A*'s, and therefore only taken half the time; for it takes an equal time (the minimal time) for the *C* to pass one *B* as for the *B* to pass one *A*. But during this same half-time the first *B* has also passed all the *C*'s (though the first *B* takes as long, says Zeno, to pass a *C* as an *A*) because measured by their progress through the *A*'s the *B*'s and *C*'s have had the same time in which to cross each other. Such is his argument. . . .

C. ARGUMENT AGAINST SPACE

[14] If place is something that exists, where will it be? The difficulty raised by Zeno requires some answer. For if *everything* that exists has a place, it is clear that place too will have a place, and so on without limit.

D. THE PARADOX OF THE MILLET SEED

[15] "Tell me, Protagoras," [Zeno] said, "does a single millet seed, or the ten thousandth part of a seed, make a noise when they fall?" When Protagoras said they did not, he said: "Does the bushel then make a noise when it falls or not?" When Protagoras said this did, Zeno said: "Is there not then some ratio of the bushel to one seed and to a ten thousandth of a seed?" When Protagoras said there was, Zeno said: "But then must not the respective noises stand to one another in the same ratios? For as the sounding bodies are to one another, so must be the sounds they make. This being so, if the bushel of millet makes a noise, then the single millet seed must also make a noise, and so must the ten thousandth of a millet seed."

MELISSUS

fl. ca. 440 B.C.?

Melissus is said to have come from the island of Samos, like Pythagoras, and to have flourished during the fifth century B.C. He is reported to have been a naval commander who led the Samians to victory over the Athenians in 440 B.C. (see fragment [2] following). He wrote a book, *About Nature or Reality,* probably some time after the completion of Zeno's more celebrated work. Melissus, too, attempted to defend Parmenides, and it is therefore convenient to have a single label for the philosophy of these three men—Parmenides, Zeno, and Melissus. They are traditionally called Eleatics, after the small town in southern Italy where Parmenides made his home, Elea.

In addition to two ancient citations about his life, all of his genuine fragments are given here. These fragments show that, like Parmenides, Melissus believed that being is one seamless unchanging whole and, like Zeno, he presented *ad absurdum* arguments to show the impossibility of plurality or change. In particular he argued against the Ionian philosophy of Anaximander that things could change into their opposites.

[1] Melissus son of Ithagenes, a Samian. He was a pupil of Parmenides. . . . He was a statesman, and was held in great honor by the citizens; and later, when he was elected admiral, he won even greater fame for his personal courage. . . .

[2] When Pericles had set sail, Melissus, son of Ithagenes, a philosopher who was then in command of Samos, was so contemptuous of the small number of the Athenian ships or of their commander's inexperience that he persuaded the Samians to attack. A battle took place which the Samians won. They took so many prisoners and destroyed so many ships that they had command of the sea, and they devoted to the prosecution of the war certain supplies which they did not till then possess. Pericles himself, according to Aristotle, had also been defeated by Melissus in an earlier naval battle.

* * *

[3] That which was, always and always will be. For if it had come into being, it necessarily follows that before it came into being, nothing existed. If however nothing existed, in no way could anything come into being out of nothing.

[4] Since therefore it did not come into being, it is and always was and always will be, and has no beginning or end, but it is eternal. For if it had come into being, it would have a beginning (for it would have come into being at some time, and so begun), and an end (for since it had come into being, it would have ended). But since it has neither begun nor ended, it always was and always will be and has no beginning nor end. For it is impossible for anything to be unless it is completely.

[5] But as it is always, so also its size must always be infinite.

[6] Nothing that has a beginning and an end is either everlasting or infinite.

[7] If it were not one, it would form a boundary in relation to something else.

[8] If it were infinite, it would be one; for if it were two, *(these)* could not be *(spatially)* infinite, but each would have boundaries in relation to each other.

[9] (1) Thus therefore it is everlasting and unlimited and one and like throughout *(homogeneous).*

(2) And neither could it perish or become larger or change its *(inner)* arrangement, nor does it feel pain or grief. For if it suffered any of these things, it would no longer be one. For if being alters, it follows that it is not the same, but that that which previously was is destroyed, and that not-being has come into being. Hence if it were to become different by a single hair in ten thousand years, so it must be utterly destroyed in the whole of time.

(3) But it is not possible for it to be rearranged either, for the previous arrangement is not destroyed, nor does a nonexistent arrangement come into being. And since

it is neither increased by any addition, nor destroyed, nor changed, how could it have undergone a rearrangement of what exists? For if it were different in any respect, then there would at once be a rearrangement.

(4) Nor does it feel pain; for it could not be completely if it were in pain; for a thing which is in pain could not always be. Nor has it equal power with what is healthy. Nor would it be the same if it were in pain; for it would feel pain through the subtraction or addition of something, and could no longer be the same.

(5) Nor could that which is healthy feel pain, for the healthy—that which is— would perish, and that which is not would come into being.

(6) And with regard to grief, the same reasoning applies as to pain.

(7) Nor is there any emptiness; for the empty is nothing; and so that which is nothing cannot be. Nor does it move; for it cannot withdraw in any direction, but *(all)* is full. For if there were any empty, it would have withdrawn into the empty; but as the empty does not exist, there is nowhere for it *(being)* to withdraw.

(8) And there can be no dense and rare. For the rare cannot possibly be as full as the dense, but the rare must at once become more empty than the dense.

(9) The following distinction must be made between the full and the not-full: if a thing has room for or admits something, it is not full; if it neither has room for nor admits anything, it is full.

(10) It *(being)* must necessarily be full, therefore, if there is no empty. If therefore it is full, it does not move.

[10] (1) This argument is the greatest proof that it *(being)* is one only; but there are also the following proofs:

(2) If things were many, they would have to be of the same kind as I say the one is. For if there is earth and water and air and fire and iron and gold, and that which is living and that which is dead, and black and white and all the rest of the things which men say are real: if these things exist, and we see and hear correctly, each thing must be of such a kind as it seemed to us to be in the first place, and it cannot change or become different, but each thing must always be what it is. But now, we say we see and hear and understand correctly,

(3) and it seems to us that the hot becomes cold and the cold hot, and the hard soft and the soft hard, and that the living thing dies and comes into being from what is not living, and that all things change, and that what was and what now is are not at all the same, but iron which is hard is worn away by contact with the finger, and gold and stone and whatever seems to be entirely strong *(is worn away)*; and that from water, earth and stone come into being. So that it comes about that we neither see nor know existing things.

(4) So these statements are not consistent with one another. For although we say that there are many things, ever-lasting(?), having forms and strength, it seems to us that they all alter and change from what is seen on each occasion.

(5) It is clear therefore that we have not been seeing correctly, and that those things do not correctly seem to us to be many; for they would not change if they were real, but each would be as it seemed to be. For nothing is stronger than that which is real.

(6) And if it changed, being would have been destroyed, and not-being would have come into being. Thus, therefore, if things are many, they must be such as the one is.

[11] If therefore being is, it must be one; and if it is one, it is bound not to have body. But if it had bulk, it would have parts, and would no longer be.

[12] If being is divided, it moves; and if it moved, it could not be.

The Pluralists

EMPEDOCLES

ca. 484–424 B.C.

The philosophers who came after the Eleatics, down to Plato and Aristotle, were concerned to show how change *was* possible. The first three philosophers to make this attempt are sometimes lumped together as "the Pluralists," for each of them tried to explain change by invoking several ultimate principles.

The first of these was Empedocles from Acragas on the south coast of Sicily. Born of an aristocratic family, he opposed tyranny and reputedly refused the crown of his native town. Like the more legendary Pythagoras, he fused scientific thought with religious concerns and left others with the impression he had performed miracles. Again like Pythagoras, he spoke of both the transmigration of souls and of himself as a god. He is said to have ended his life by leaping into the crater of Mount Etna.

Empedocles wrote two poems, "On Nature" and "Purifications." The former is said to have been divided into two books, totalling two thousand lines, of which fewer than four hundred have survived. According to Diogenes Laertius, the two poems together came to five thousand lines; if so, less than one-fifth of the "Purifications" has come down to us.

Empedocles was the first great synthesizer of the history of philosophy. Around 450 B.C., a full century before Aristotle's summation, Empedocles tried to find a place in his thought for all the major contributions of his predecessors. By explaining generation and destruction, if not all change, in terms of mixture and separation, Empedocles sought to reconcile Heraclitus' insistence on the reality of change with the Eleatic claim that generation and destruction are unthinkable. Going back to the Greeks' traditional belief in four elements, he found a place for Thales' water, Anaximenes' air, and Heraclitus' fire and added earth as the fourth. In addition to these four elements, which Aristotle would later call "material causes," Empedocles postulated two "efficient causes": strife (Heraclitus' great principle) and love. He envisaged four successive ages: an age of love or perfect mixture in the beginning; then gradual separation as strife enters; then complete separation as strife rules; finally, as love enters again, a gradual remixture.

[1] Empedocles of Acragas was born not long after Anaxagoras, and was an emulator and associate of Parmenides, and even more of the Pythagoreans.

[2] Anaxagoras of Clazomenae, though older than Empedocles, was later in his philosophical activity.

* * *

[3] For limited are the means of grasping *(i.e. the organs of sense-perception)* which are scattered throughout their limbs, and many are the miseries that press in and blunt the thoughts. And having looked at (only) a small part of existence during their lives, doomed to perish swiftly like smoke they are carried aloft and wafted away, believing only that upon which as individuals they chance to hit as they wander in all directions; but every man preens himself on having found the Whole: so little are these things to be seen by men or to be heard, or to be comprehended by the mind! But you, since you have come here into retirement, shall learn—not more than mortal intellect can attain.

[4] I shall tell you another thing: there is no creation of substance in any one of mortal existences, nor any end in execrable death, but only mixing and exchange of what has been mixed; and the name "substance" *(⟨Physis⟩, "nature")* is applied to them by mankind. (8)

[5] But men, when these *(the Elements)* have been mixed in the form of a man and come into the light, or in the form of a species of wild animals, or plants, or birds, then say that this has "come into being"; and when they separate, this men call sad fate *(death)*. The terms that right demands they do not use; but through custom I myself also apply these names. (9)

[6] From what in no wise exists, it is impossible for anything to come into being; and for being to perish completely is incapable of fulfillment and unthinkable; for it will always be there, wherever anyone may place it on any occasion. (12)

[7] Nor is there any part of the whole that is empty or overfull. (13)

[8] No part of the whole is empty; so whence could anything additional come? (14)

[9] I shall tell of a double *(process):* at one time it increased so as to be a single one out of many; at another time again it grew apart so as to be many out of one. There is a double creation of mortals and a double decline: the union of all things causes the birth and destruction of the one *(race of mortals),* the other is reared as the elements grow apart, and then flies asunder. And these *(elements)* never cease their continuous exchange, sometimes uniting under the influence of love, so that all become one, at other times again each moving apart through the hostile force of hate. Thus in so far as

they have the power to grow into one out of many, and again, when the one grows apart and many are formed, in this sense they come into being and have no stable life; but in so far as they never cease their continuous exchange, in this sense they remain always unmoved *(unaltered)* as they follow the cyclic process.

But come, listen to my discourse! For be assured, learning will increase your understanding. As I said before, revealing the aims of my discourse, I shall tell you of a double process. At one time it increased so as to be a single one out of many; at another time it grew apart so as to be many out of one—fire and water and earth and the boundless height of air, and also execrable hate apart from these, of equal weight in all directions, and love in their midst, their equal in length and breadth. Observe her with your mind, and do not sit with wondering eyes! She it is who is believed to be implanted in mortal limbs also; through her they think friendly thoughts and perform harmonious actions, calling her joy and Aphrodite. No mortal man has perceived her as she moves in and out among them. But *you* must listen to the undeceitful progress of my argument.

All these *(elements)* are equal and of the same age in their creation; but each presides over its own office, and each has its own character, and they prevail in turn in the course of time. And besides these, nothing else comes into being, nor does anything cease. For if they had been perishing continuously, they would be no more; and what could increase the whole? And whence could it have come? In what direction could it perish, since nothing is empty of these things? No, but these things alone exist, and running through one another they become different things at different times, and are ever continuously the same. (17)

[10] This process is clearly to be seen throughout the mass of mortal limbs: sometimes through love all the limbs which the body has as its lot come together into one, in the prime of flourishing life; at another time again, sundered by evil feuds, they wander severally by the breakers of the shore of life. Likewise too with shrub-plants and fish in their watery dwelling, and beasts with mountain lairs and diver-birds that travel on wings. (20)

[11] But come, observe the following witness to my previous discourse, lest in my former statements there was any substance of which the form was missing. Observe the sun, bright to see and hot everywhere, and all the immortal things *(heavenly bodies)* drenched with its heat and brilliant light; and the rain, dark and chill over everything; and from the earth issue forth things based on the soil and solid. But in *(the reign of)* wrath they are all different in form and separate, while in *(the reign of)* love they come together and long for one another. For from these *(elements)* come all things that were and are and will be; and trees spring up, and men and women, and beasts and birds and water-nurtured fish, and even the long-lived gods who are highest in honor. For these *(elements)* alone exist, but by running through one another they become different; to such a degree does mixing change them. (21)

[12] For all these things—beaming sun and earth and heaven and sea—are connected in harmony with their own parts: all those *(parts)* which have been sundered from them and exist in mortal limbs. Similarly all those things which are suitable for mixture are made like one another and united in affection by Aphrodite. But those things which differ most from one another in origin and mixture and the forms in which they are molded are completely unaccustomed to combine, and are very baneful because of the commands of hate, in that hate has wrought their origin. (22)

[13] . . . Touching on summit after summit, not to follow a single path of discourse to the end. (24)

[14] For what is right can well be uttered even twice. (25)

[15] In turn they get the upper hand in the revolving cycle, and perish into one another and increase in the turn appointed by fate. For they alone exist, but running through one another they become men and the tribes of other animals, sometimes uniting under the influence of love into one ordered whole, at other times again each moving apart through the hostile force of hate, until growing together into the whole which is one, they are quelled. Thus in so far as they have the power to grow into one out of many, and again, when the one grows apart and many are formed, in this sense they come into being and have no stable life; but in so far as they never cease their continuous exchange, in this sense they remain always unmoved *(unaltered)* as they follow the cyclic process. (26)

[16] *(The sphere under the dominion of love):* Therein are articulated neither the swift limbs of the sun, nor the shaggy might of earth, nor the sea: so firmly is it *(the whole)* fixed in a close-set secrecy, a rounded Sphere enjoying a circular solitude. (27)

[17] But he *(god)* is equal in all directions to himself and altogether eternal, a rounded sphere enjoying a circular solitude. (28)

[18] For there do not start two branches from his back; *(he has)* no feet, no swift knees, no organs of reproduction; but he was a sphere, and in all directions equal to himself. (29)

[19] But I will go back to the path of song which I formerly laid down, drawing one argument from another: that *(path which shows how)* when hate has reached the bottommost abyss of the eddy, and when love reaches the middle of the whirl, then in it *(the whirl)* all these things come together so as to be one—not all at once, but voluntarily uniting, some from one quarter, others from another. And as they mixed, there poured forth countless races of mortals. But many things stand unmixed side by side with the things mixing—all those which hate *(still)* aloft checked, since it had not yet faultlessly withdrawn from the whole to the outermost limits of the circle, but was remaining in some places, and in other places departing from the limbs *(of the sphere).* But in so far as it went on quietly streaming out, to the same extent there was entering a benevolent immortal inrush of faultless love. And swiftly those things became mortal which previously had experienced immortality, and things formerly unmixed became mixed, changing their paths. And as they mixed, there poured forth countless races of mortals, equipped with forms of every sort, a marvel to behold. (35)

[20] As they came together, hate returned to the outermost. (36)

[21] There whirls round the earth a circular borrowed light. (45)

[22] It is the earth that makes night by coming in the way of the *(sun's)* rays. (48)

[23] Sea, the sweat of earth. (55)

[24] Limbs wandered alone. (58)

[25] Creatures with rolling gait and innumerable hands. (60)

[26] The way everything breathes in and out is as follows: all have tubes of flesh, empty of blood, which extend over the surface of the body; and at the mouths of these tubes the outermost surface of the skin is perforated with frequent pores, so as to keep in the blood while a free way is cut for the passage of the air. Thus, when the thin blood flows back from here, the air, bubbling, rushes in in a mighty wave; and when the blood leaps up *(to the surface),* there is an expiration of air. As when a girl, playing with a water-catcher of shining brass—when, having placed the mouth of the pipe on her well-shaped hand she dips the vessel into the yielding substance of silvery water, still the volume of air pressing from inside on the many holes keeps out the water, until she uncovers the condensed stream *(of air).* Then at once when the air flows out, the water flows in in an equal quantity. Similarly, when water occupies the depths of the brazen vessel, and the opening or passage is stopped by the human flesh *(hand),* and the air out-

side, striving to get in, checks the water, by controlling the surface at the entrance of the noisy strainer until she lets go with her hand: then again, in exactly the opposite way from what happened before, as the air rushes in, the water flows out in equal volume. Similarly when the thin blood, rushing through the limbs, flows back into the interior, straightway a stream of air flows in with a rush; and when the blood flows up again, again there is a breathing-out in equal volume. (100)

[27] If you press them deep into your firm mind, and contemplate them with good will and a studious care that is pure, these things will all assuredly remain with you throughout your life; and you will obtain many other things from them; for these things of themselves cause each *(element)* to increase in the character, according to the way of each man's nature. But if you intend to grasp after different things such as dwell among men in countless numbers and blunt their thoughts, miserable *(trifles),* certainly these things will quickly desert you in the course of time, longing to return to their own original kind. For all things, be assured, have intelligence and a portion of thought. (110)

[28] You shall learn all the drugs that exist as a defence against illness and old age; for you alone will I accomplish all this. You shall check the force of the unwearying winds which rush upon the earth with their blasts and lay waste the cultivated fields. And again, if you wish, you shall conduct the breezes back again. You shall create a seasonable dryness after the dark rain for mankind, and again you shall create after summer drought the streams that nourish the trees and [which will flow in the sky]. And you shall bring out of Hades a dead man restored to strength. (111)

KATHARMOI (PURIFICATIONS)

[29] Friends, who dwell in the great town on the city's heights, looking down on yellow Agrigentum, you who are occupied with good deeds, who are harbors treating foreigners with respect, and who are unacquainted with wickedness: greeting! I go about among you as an immortal god, no longer a mortal, held in honor by all, as I seem *(to them to deserve),* crowned with fillets and flowing garlands. When I come to them in their flourishing towns, to men and women, I am honored; and they follow me in thousands, to inquire where is the path of advantage, some desiring oracles, while others ask to hear a word of healing for their manifold diseases, since they have long been pierced with cruel pains. (112)

[30] But why do I lay stress on these things, as if I were achieving something as great in that I surpass mortal men who are liable to many forms of destruction? (113)

[31] Friends, I know that truth is present in the story that I shall tell; but it is actually very difficult for men, and the impact of conviction on their minds is unwelcome. (114)

[32] There is an oracle of necessity, an ancient decree of the gods, eternal, sealed fast with broad oaths, that when one of the divine spirits whose portion is long life sinfully stains his own limbs with bloodshed, and following hate has sworn a false oath— these must wander for thrice ten thousand seasons far from the company of the blessed, being born throughout the period into all kinds of mortal shapes, which exchange one hard way of life for another. For the mighty air chases them into the sea, and the sea spews them forth on to the dry land, and the earth *(drives them)* towards the rays of the blazing sun; and the Sun hurls them into the eddies of the Aether. One *(Element)* receives them from the other, and all loathe them. Of this number am I too now, a fugitive from heaven and a wanderer, because I trusted in raging Hate. (115)

[33] For by now I have been born boy, girl, plant, bird, and dumb sea-fish. (117)

[34] I wept and wailed when I saw the unfamiliar land *(at birth)*. (118)

[35] How great the honor, how deep the happiness from which *(I am exiled)!* (119)

[36] Will ye not cease from this harsh-sounding slaughter? Do you not see that you are devouring one another in the thoughtlessness of your minds? (136)

ANAXAGORAS

ca. 500–ca. 428 B.C.

Anaxagoras came from Clazomenae on the coast of Asia Minor, not far north-west of Colophon (Xenophanes' home) and Ephesus (Heraclitus' home). He was the first of the Greek philosophers to move to Athens, where he became a good friend of Pericles, the great statesman, who gave his name to the whole epoch. The dates are uncertain, but Anaxagoras may have been born about 500 B.C. and have come to Athens around 480. He lived in Athens in the time of her greatest glory, a contemporary of the classical tragedians Aeschylus, Sophocles, and Euripides. Anaxagoras was the first philosopher to be tried and condemned on a charge of heresy or impiety. He was saved by Pericles and went into exile at Lampsacus, a Milesian colony on the Hellespont, where he died about 428/7, a year after Pericles.

Anaxagoras taught that everything consists of an infinite number of particles or seeds, and that in all things there is a portion of everything. Hair could not come from what is not hair, nor could flesh come from what is not flesh. The names we apply to things are determined by the preponderance of certain seeds in them—for example, hair seeds or flesh seeds. Like Empedocles, he added to such "material causes" an "efficient cause" to account for the motion and direction of things; however, unlike Empedocles' two, Anaxagoras added only one "efficient cause," which was mind, *nous* in Greek. The introduction of mind led Aristotle to hail Anaxagoras as the only sober man among the Pre-Socratics; yet Aristotle found fault with Anaxagoras for not making more use of this new principle to explain natural events.

[1] He is said to have been twenty years old at the time of Xerxes' crossing, and to have lived to seventy-two. . . . He began to be a philosopher at Athens in the archonship of Callias (456/5), at the age of twenty, as Demetrius Phalereus tells us in his *Register of Archons,* and is said to have spent thirty years there. . . . There are different accounts given of his trial. Sotion, in his *Succession of Philosophers,* says that he was prosecuted by Cleon for impiety, because he claimed that the sun was a red-hot mass of metal, and that after Pericles, his pupil, had made a speech in his defense, he was fined five talents and exiled. Satyrus, in his *Lives,* on the other hand, says that the charge was brought by Thucydides in his political campaign against Pericles; and he adds that the charge was not only for impiety but for Medism [Persian leanings] as well; and he was condemned to death in absence. . . . Finally he withdrew to Lampsacus, and there died. It is said

that when the rulers of the city asked him what privilege he wished to be granted, he replied that the children should be given a holiday every year in the month in which he died. The custom is preserved to the present day. When he died, the Lampsacenes buried him with full honors.

[2] Anaxagoras, the natural philosopher, was a distinguished Clazomenion, an associate of Anaximenes of Miletus; and his own pupils included Archelaus the natural philosopher and Euripides the poet.

[3] Those who wrote only one book include Melissus, Parmenides, and Anaxagoras.

* * *

[4] All Things were together, infinite in number and in smallness. For the Small also was infinite. And since all were together, nothing was distinguishable because of its smallness. For Air and Aether dominated all things, both of them being infinite. For these are the most important *(Elements)* in the total mixture, both in number and in size.

[5] Air and Aether are separated off from the surrounding multiplicity, and that which surrounds is infinite in number.

[6] For in Small there is no Least, but only a Lesser: for it is impossible that Being should Not-Be, and in Great there is always a Greater. And it is equal in number to the small, but each thing is to itself both great and small.

[7] Conditions being thus, one must believe that there are many things of all sorts in all composite products, and the seeds of all Things, which contain all kinds of shapes and colors and pleasant savors. And men too were fitted together, and all other creatures which have life. And the men possessed both inhabited cities and artificial works [cultivated fields] just like ourselves, and they had sun and moon and the rest, just as we have, and the earth produced for them many and diverse things, of which they collected the most useful, and now use them for [or, "in"] their dwellings. This I say concerning Separation, that it must have taken place not only with us, but elsewhere.

Before these things were separated off, all things were together, nor was any color distinguishable, for the mixing of all Things prevented this, *(namely)* the mixing of moist and dry and hot and cold and bright and dark, and there was a great quantity of earth in the mixture, and seeds infinite in number, not at all like one another. For none of the other things either is like any other. And as this was so, one must believe that all Things were present in the Whole.

[8] These things being thus separated off, one must understand that all things are in no wise less or more (for it is not possible for them to be more than All), but all things are forever equal *(in quantity)*.

[9] And since there are equal *(quantitative)* parts of Great and Small, so too similarly in everything there must be everything. It is not possible *(for them)* to exist apart, but all things contain a portion of everything. Since it is not possible for the Least to exist, it cannot be isolated, nor come into being by itself; but as it was in the beginning, so now, all things are together. In all things there are many things, and of the things separated off, there are equal numbers in *(the categories)* Great and Small.

[10] So that the number of the things separated off cannot be known either in thought or in fact.

[11] The things in the one Cosmos are not separated off from one another with an axe, neither the Hot from the Cold, nor the Cold from the Hot.

[12] Thus these things circulate and are separated off by force and speed. The speed makes the force. Their speed is not like the speed of any of the Things now existing among mankind, but altogether many times as fast.

[13] How can hair come from not-hair, and flesh from not-flesh?

[14] In everything there is a portion of everything except Mind; and some things contain Mind also.

[15] Other things all contain a part of everything, but Mind is infinite and self-ruling, and is mixed with no Thing, but is alone by itself. If it were not by itself, but were mixed with anything else, it would have had a share of all Things, if it were mixed with anything; for in everything there is a portion of everything, as I have said before. And the things mixed *(with Mind)* would have prevented it, so that it could not rule over any Thing in the same way as it can being alone by itself. For it is the finest of all Things, and the purest, and has complete understanding of everything, and has the greatest power. All things which have life, both the greater and the less, are ruled by Mind. Mind took command of the universal revolution, so as to make *(things)* revolve at the outset. And at first things began to revolve from some small point, but now the revolution extends over a greater area, and will spread even further. And the things which were mixed together, and separated off, and divided, were all understood by Mind. And whatever they were going to be, and whatever things were then in existence that are not now, and all things that now exist and whatever shall exist—all were arranged by Mind, as also the revolution now followed by the stars, the sun and moon, and the Air and Aether which were separated off. It was this revolution which caused the separation off. And dense separates from rare, and hot from cold, and bright from dark, and dry from wet. There are many portions of many things. And nothing is absolutely separated off or divided the one from the other except Mind. Mind is all alike, both the greater and the less. But nothing else is like anything else, but each individual thing is and was most obviously that of which it contains the most.

[16] And when Mind began the motion, there was a separating-off from all that was being moved; and all that Mind set in motion was separated *(internally);* and as things were moving and separating off *(internally),* the revolution greatly increased this *(internal)* separation.

[17] Mind, which ever Is, certainly still exists also where all other things are, *(namely)* in the multiple surrounding *(mass)* and in the things which were separated off before, and in the things already separated off [things that have been either aggregated or separated].

[18] The dense and moist and cold and dark *(Elements)* collected here, where now is Earth, and the rare and hot and dry went outwards to the furthest part of the Aether.

[19] From these, while they are separating off, Earth solidifies; for from the clouds, water is separated off, and from the water, earth, and from the earth, stones are solidified by the cold; and these rush outward rather than the water.

[20] The Greeks have an incorrect belief on Coming into Being and Passing Away. No Thing comes into being or passes away, but it is mixed together or separated from existing Things. Thus they would be correct if they called coming into being "mixing," and passing away "separation-off."

[21] It is the sun that endows the moon with its brilliance.

[22] We give the name Iris to the reflection of the sun on the clouds. It is therefore the sign of a storm, for the water which flows round the cloud produces wind or forces out rain.

[23] Through the weakness of the sense-perceptions, we cannot judge truth.

DEMOCRITUS   ca. 460–ca. 370 B.C.
and
LEUCIPPUS   fifth century B.C.

Democritus of Abdera, on the coast of Thrace, was probably born in 460 B.C. He wrote over sixty works, of which several hundred fragments survive. Together with Leucippus, a virtually unknown figure who was supposedly his teacher, Democritus was the prime exponent of the philosophy known as *atomism*. While Leucippus' work has perished, we have many reports about the Democritean form of atomistic philosophy.

Atomism accepted Parmenides' idea that being must be one seamless whole, but posited an infinite number of such "one's." According to Democritus, the world is made up of tiny "un-cut-ables" ⟨*atomos*⟩ that move within the "void" (corresponding to Parmenides' non-being). These atoms combine in different patterns to form the material objects of the observable world. Democritus applied this understanding of reality to human beings as well. Both the soul and the body are made up of atoms. Perception occurs when atoms from objects outside the person strike the sense organs inside the person, which in turn strike the atoms of the soul further inside. Death, in turn, is simply the dissipation of the soul atoms when the body atoms no longer hold them together.

Such an understanding of the person seems to eliminate all possibility of freedom of choice and, indeed, the only known saying of Leucippus is "Nothing happens at random; everything happens out of reason and by necessity." Such a position would seem to eliminate all ethics: If you *must* act a certain way, it seems futile to talk about what you *ought* to do (since, as Kant later said, "*ought* implies *can*"). Yet Democritus wrote a great deal on ethics, including a book of ethical maxims called the *Gnomae*.

The fragments that follow have been grouped into four sections: first, the ancient reports about Leucippus and Democritus; then the metaphysical and epistemological fragments; next, the *Gnomae* (complete); and finally, some of the other fragments on ethics.

There are three reasons for allotting so much space to Democritus. First, we have much more material on him than on any of his predecessors. Second, while atomism represents still another pluralistic answer to Parmenides, and while Leucippus was a Pre-Socratic, nevertheless Democritus was actually a slightly younger contemporary of Socrates and an older contemporary of Plato. Hence Democritus' atomistic materialism may be viewed as an important alternative to Plato's idealism. Third, Democritus' thought continued to have an impact, being taken up first by Epicurus and then, in Roman times, by Lucretius.

A.   ANCIENT REPORTS ON ATOMISM

[1] Leucippus of Elea or Miletus (both accounts are current) had associated with Parmenides in philosophy, but in his view of reality he did not follow the same path as Parmenides and Xenophanes but rather, it seems, the opposite path. For while they re-

garded the whole as one, motionless, uncreated, and limited, and forbade even the search for what is not, he posited innumerable elements in perpetual motion—namely the atoms—and held that the number of their shapes was infinite, on the ground that there was no reason why any atom should be of one shape rather than another; for he observed too that coming-into-being and change are incessant in the world. Further he held that not-being exists as well as being, and the two are equally the causes of things coming-into-being. The nature of atoms he supposed to be compact and full; that, he said, was being, and it moved in the void, which he called not-being and held to exist no less than being. In the same way his associate, Democritus of Abdera, posited as principles the full and the void.

[2] Apollodorus in the *Chronicles* says that Epicurus was instructed by Nausiphanes and Praxiphanes; but Epicurus himself denies this, saying in the letter to Eurylochus that he instructed himself. He and Hemarchus both maintain that there never was a philosopher Leucippus, who some (including Apollodorus the Epicurean) say was the teacher of Democritus.

[3] Leucippus postulated atoms and void, and in this Democritus resembled him, though in other respects he was more productive.

[4] Democritus . . . met Leucippus and, according to some, Anaxagoras also, whose junior he was by forty years. . . . As he himself says in the *Little World-system*, he was a young man in the old age of Anaxagoras, being forty years younger.

[5] Demetrius in his *Homonyms* and Antisthenes in his *Successions* say that he [Democritus] travelled to Egypt to visit the priests and learn geometry, and that he went also to Persia to visit the Chaldaeans, and to the Red Sea. Some say that he associated with the "naked philosophers" in India; also that he went to Ethiopia.

[6] Leucippus thought he had arguments which would assert what is consistent sense-perception and not do away with coming into being or perishing or motion, or the plurality of existents. He agrees with the appearances to this extent, but he concedes, to those who maintain the One [the Eleatics], that there would be no motion without void, and says that the void is non-existent, and that no part of what is is non-existent—for what is in the strict sense is wholly and fully being. But such being, he says, is not one; there is an infinite number, and they are invisible because of the smallness of the particles. They move in the void (for there *is* void), and when they come together they cause coming to be, and when they separate they cause perishing.

[7] They [Leucippus, Democritus, and Epicurus] said that the first principles were infinite in number, and thought they were indivisible atoms and impassible owing to their compactness, and without any void in them; divisibility comes about because of the void in compound bodies.

[8] To this extent they differed, that one [Epicurus] supposed that all atoms were very small, and on that account imperceptible; the other, Democritus, that there are some atoms that are very large.

[9] Democritus holds the same view as Leucippus about the elements, full and void . . . he spoke as if the things that are were in constant motion in the void; and there are innumerable worlds which differ in size. In some worlds there is no sun and moon, in others they are larger than in our world, and in others more numerous. The intervals between the worlds are unequal; in some parts there are more worlds, in others fewer; some are increasing, some at their height, some decreasing; in some parts they are arising, in others failing. They are destroyed by collision one with another. There are some worlds devoid of living creatures or plants or any moisture.

[10] Everything happens according to necessity; for the cause of the coming-into-being of all things is the whirl, which he calls necessity.

[11] As they [the atoms] move, they collide and become entangled in such a way as to cling in close contact to one another, but not so as to form one substance of them in reality of any kind whatever; for it is very simple-minded to suppose that two or more could ever become one. The reason he gives for atoms staying together for a while is the intertwining and mutual hold of the primary bodies; for some of them are angular, some hooked, some concave, some convex, and indeed with countless other differences; so he thinks they cling to each other and stay together until such time as some stronger necessity comes from the surrounding and shakes and scatters them apart.

[12] Democritus says that the spherical is the most mobile of shapes; and such is mind and fire.

[13] Democritus and the majority of natural philosophers who discuss perception are guilty of a great absurdity; for they represent all perception as being by touch.

[14] Leucippus, Democritus and Epicurus say that perception and thought arise when images enter from outside; neither occurs to anybody without an image impinging.

[15] Democritus explains sight by the visual image, which he describes in a peculiar way; the visual image does not arise directly in the pupil, but the air between the eye and the object of sight is contracted and stamped by the object seen and the seer; for from everything there is always a sort of effluence proceeding. So this air, which is solid and variously colored, appears in the eye, which is moist (?); the eye does not admit the dense part, but the moist passes through.

B. METAPHYSICAL AND EPISTEMOLOGICAL FRAGMENTS

[16] We know nothing about anything really, but opinion is for all individuals an inflowing (? of the atoms).

[17] It will be obvious that it is impossible to understand how in reality each thing is.

[18] Sweet exists by convention, bitter by convention, color by convention; atoms and void (alone) exist in reality . . . We know nothing accurately in reality, but (only) as it changes according to the bodily condition, and the constitution of those things that flow upon (the body) and impinge upon it.

[19] It has often been demonstrated that we do not grasp how each thing is or is not.

[20] There are two sorts of knowledge, one genuine, one bastard (or "obscure"). To the latter belong all the following: sight, hearing, smell, taste, touch. The real is separated from this. When the bastard can do no more—neither see more minutely, nor hear, nor smell, nor taste, nor perceive by touch—and a finer investigation is needed, then the genuine comes in as having a tool for distinguishing more finely.

[21] Naught exists just as much as Aught.

C. THE SO-CALLED *GNOMAE* (complete)

[22] If any man listens to my opinions, here recorded, with intelligence, he will achieve many things worthy of a good man, and avoid doing many unworthy things.

[23] It is right that men should value the soul rather than the body; for perfection of soul corrects the inferiority of the body, but physical strength without intelligence does nothing to improve the mind.

[24] He who chooses the advantages of the soul chooses things more divine, but he who chooses those of the body, chooses things human.

[25] It is noble to prevent the criminal; but if one cannot, one should not join him in crime.

[26] One must either be good, or imitate a good man.

[27] Men find happiness neither by means of the body nor through possessions, but through uprightness and wisdom.

[28] Refrain from crimes not through fear but through duty.

[29] It is a great thing, when one is in adversity, to think of duty.

[30] Repentance for shameful deeds is salvation in life.

[31] One should tell the truth, not speak at length.

[32] The wrongdoer is more unfortunate than the man wronged.

[33] Magnanimity consists in enduring tactlessness with mildness.

[34] Well-ordered behavior consists in obedience to the law, the ruler, and the man wiser *(than oneself)*.

[35] When inferior men censure, the good man pays no heed.

[36] It is hard to be governed by one's inferior.

[37] The man completely enslaved to wealth can never be honest.

[38] In power of persuasion, reasoning is far stronger than gold.

[39] He who tries to give intelligent advice to one who thinks he has intelligence, is wasting his time.

[40] Many who have not learnt reason, nevertheless live according to reason. [40a] Many whose actions are most disgraceful practice the best utterances.

[41] The foolish learn sense through misfortune.

[42] One should emulate the deeds and actions of virtue, not the words.

[43] Noble deeds are recognized and emulated by those of natural good disposition.

[44] Good breeding in cattle depends on physical health, but in men on a well-formed character.

[45] The hopes of right-thinking men are attainable, but those of the unintelligent are impossible.

[46] Neither skill nor wisdom is attainable unless one learns.

[47] It is better to examine one's own faults than those of others.

[48] Those whose character is well-ordered have also a well-ordered life.

[49] Virtue consists, not in avoiding wrong-doing, but in having no wish thereto.

[50] To pronounce praise on noble deeds is noble; for to do so over base deeds is the work of a false deceiver.

[51] Many much-learned men have no intelligence.

[52] One should practice much-sense, not much-learning.

[53] It is better to deliberate before action than to repent afterwards.

[54] Believe not everything, but only what is approved: the former is foolish, the latter the act of a sensible man.

[55] The worthy and the unworthy man *(are to be known)* not only by their actions, but also their wishes.

[56] For all men, good and true are the same; but pleasant differs for different men.

[57] Immoderate desire is the mark of a child, not a man.

[58] Untimely pleasures produce unpleasantnesses.

[59] Violent desire for one thing blinds the soul to all others.

[60] Virtuous love consists in decorous desire for the beautiful.

[61] Accept no pleasure unless it is beneficial.

[62] It is better for fools to be ruled than to rule.

[63] For the foolish, not reason but advantage is the teacher.

[64] Fame and wealth without intelligence are dangerous possessions.

[65] To make money is not without use, but if it comes from wrong-doing, nothing is worse.

[66] It is a bad thing to imitate the bad, and not even to wish to imitate the good.

[67] It is shameful to be so busy over the affairs of others that one knows nothing of one's own.

[68] Constant delay means work undone.

[69] The false and the seeming-good are those who do all in word, not in fact.

[70] The cause of error is ignorance of the better.

[71] The man who does shameful deeds must first feel shame in his own eyes.

[72] He who contradicts and chatters much is ill-fitted for learning what he ought.

[73] It is greed to do all the talking and not be willing to listen.

[74] One must be on one's guard against the bad man, lest he seize his opportunity.

[75] The envious man torments himself like an enemy.

[76] An enemy is not he who injures, but he who wishes to do so.

[77] The enmity of relatives is much worse than that of strangers.

[78] Be not suspicious towards all, but be cautious and firm.

[79] Accept favors in the foreknowledge that you will have to give a greater return for them.

[80] When you do a favor, study the recipient first, lest he prove a scoundrel and repay evil for good.

[81] Small favors at the right time are greatest to the recipients.

[82] Marks of honor are greatly valued by right-thinking men, who understand why they are being honored.

[83] The generous man is he who does not look for a return, but who does good from choice.

[84] Many who seem friendly are not so, and those who do not seem so, are.

[85] The friendship of one intelligent man is better than that of all the unintelligent.

[86] Life is not worth living for the man who has not even one good friend.

[87] The man whose tested friends do not stay long with him is bad-tempered.

[88] Many avoid their friends when they fall from wealth to poverty.

[89] In all things, equality is fair, excess and deficiency not so, in my opinion.

[90] The man who loves nobody is, I think, loved by no one.

[91] In old age, a man is agreeable if his manner is pleasant and his speech serious.

[92] Physical beauty is *(merely)* animal unless intelligence be present.

[93] In prosperity it is easy to find a friend, in adversity nothing is so difficult.

[94] Not all one's relatives are friends, but only those who agree with us about what is advantageous. It is proper, since we are human beings, not to laugh at the misfortunes of others, but to mourn.

[95] Good things are obtained with difficulty if one seeks; but bad things come without our even seeking.

[96] The censorious are not well-fitted for friendship.

[97] A woman must not practice argument: this is dreadful.

[98] To be ruled by a woman is the ultimate outrage for a man.

[99] It is the mark of the divine intellect to be always calculating something noble.

[100] Those who praise the unintelligent do *(them)* great harm.

[101] It is better to be praised by another than by oneself.

[102] If you do not recognize *(i.e. understand)* praise, believe that you are being flattered.

D. FRAGMENTS ON ETHICS

[103] The man who wishes to have serenity of spirit should not engage in many activities, either private or public, nor choose activities beyond his power and natural capacity. He must guard against this, so that when good fortune strikes him and leads him on to excess by means of *(false)* seeming, he must rate it low, and not attempt things beyond his powers. A reasonable fullness is better than overfullness. (3)

[104] Pleasure and absence of pleasure are the criteria of what is profitable and what is not. (4)

[105] Medicine heals diseases of the body, wisdom frees the soul from passions. (31)

[106] Coition is a slight attack of apoplexy. For man gushes forth from man, and is separated by being torn apart with a kind of blow. (32)

[107] Nature and instruction are similar; for instruction transforms the man, and in transforming, creates his nature. (33)

[108] Man is a universe in little (Microcosm). (34)

[109] *(I would)* rather discover one cause than gain the kingdom of Persia. (118)

[110] If the body brought a suit against the soul, for all the pains it had endured throughout life, and the ill-treatment, and I were to be the judge of the suit, I would gladly condemn the soul, in that it had partly ruined the body by its neglect and dissolved it with bouts of drunkenness, and partly destroyed it and torn it in pieces with its passion for pleasure—as if, when a tool or a vessel were in a bad condition, I blamed the man who was using it carelessly. (159)

[111] *(To live badly is)* not to live badly, but to spend a long time dying. (160)

[112] Do not try to understand everything, lest you become ignorant of everything. (169)

[113] Happiness, like unhappiness, is a property of the soul. (170)

[114] Happiness does not dwell in cattle or gold. The soul is the dwelling-place of the *(good and evil)* genius. (171)

[115] The cheerful man, who is impelled towards works that are just and lawful, rejoices by day and by night, and is strong and free from care. But the man who neglects justice, and does not do what he ought, finds all such things disagreeable when he remembers any of them, and he is afraid and torments himself. (174)

[116] But the gods are the givers of all good things, both in the past and now. They are not, however, the givers of things which are bad, harmful or non-beneficial, either in the past or now, but men themselves fall into these through blindness of mind and lack of sense. (175)

[117] Education is an ornament for the prosperous, a refuge for the unfortunate. (180)

[118] The man who employs exhortation and persuasion will turn out to be a more effective guide to virtue than he who employs law and compulsion. For the man who is prevented by law from wrongdoing will probably do wrong in secret, whereas the man who is led towards duty by persuasion will probably not do anything untoward

either secretly or openly. Therefore the man who acts rightly through understanding and knowledge becomes at the same time brave and upright. (181)

[119] Beautiful objects are wrought by study through effort, but ugly things are reaped automatically without toil. For even one who is unwilling is sometimes so wrought upon by learning. . . . *(? MMS. corrupt.)* (182)

[120] Continuous association with base men increases a disposition to crime. (184)

[121] Similarity of outlook creates friendship. (186)

[122] The criterion of the advantageous and disadvantageous is enjoyment and lack of enjoyment. (188)

[123] One must avoid even speaking of evil deeds. (190)

[124] Cheerfulness is created for men through moderation of enjoyment and harmoniousness of life. Things that are in excess or lacking are apt to change and cause great disturbance in the soul. Souls which are stirred by great divergences are neither stable nor cheerful. Therefore one must keep one's mind on what is attainable, and be content with what one has, paying little heed to things envied and admired, and not dwelling on them in one's mind. Rather must you consider the lives of those in distress, reflecting on their intense sufferings, in order that your own possessions and condition may seem great and enviable, and you may, by ceasing to desire more, cease to suffer in your soul. For he who admires those who have, and who are called happy by other mortals, and who dwells on them in his mind every hour, is constantly compelled to undertake something new and to run the risk, through his desire, of doing something irretrievable among those things which the laws prohibit. Hence one must not seek the latter, but must be content with the former, comparing one's own life with that of those in worse cases, and must consider oneself fortunate, reflecting on their sufferings, in being so much better off than they. If you keep to this way of thinking, you will live more serenely, and will expel those not-negligible curses in life, envy, jealousy and spite. (191)

[125] The great pleasures come from the contemplation of noble works. (194)

[126] The animal needing something knows how much it needs, the man does not. (198)

[127] People are fools who hate life and yet wish to live through fear of Hades. (199)

[128] People are fools who live without enjoyment of life. (200)

[129] People are fools who yearn for long life without pleasure in long life. (201)

[130] People are fools who yearn for what is absent, but neglect what they have even when it is more valuable than what has gone. (202)

[131] Fools want to live to be old because they fear death. (206)

[132] One should choose not every pleasure, but only that concerned with the beautiful. (207)

[133] The self-control of the father is the greatest example for the children. (208)

[134] A rich table is provided by luck, but a sufficient one by wisdom. (210)

[135] Moderation multiplies pleasures, and increases pleasure. (211)

[136] Sleep in the daytime signifies bodily trouble or aberration of mind or laziness or lack of training. (212)

[137] Courage minimizes difficulties. (213)

[138] The brave man is not only he who overcomes the enemy, but he who is stronger than pleasures. Some men are masters of cities, but are enslaved to women. (214)

[139] The reward of justice is confidence of judgement and imperturbability, but the end of injustice is the fear of disaster. (215)

[140] Imperturbable wisdom is worth everything. (216)

[141] The passion for wealth, unless limited by satisfaction, is far more painful than extreme poverty; for greater passions create greater needs. (219)

[142] The excessive accumulation of wealth for one's children is an excuse for covetousness, which thus displays its peculiar nature. (222)

[143] The things needed by the body are available to all without toil and trouble. But the things which require toil and trouble and which make life disagreeable are not desired by the body but by the ill-constitution of the mind. (223)

[144] Freedom of speech is the sign of parties; for both to the conquerors and freedom; but the danger lies in discerning the right occasion. (226)

[145] Misers have the fate of bees: they work as if they were going to live forever. (227)

[146] The right-minded man is he who is not grieved by what he has not, but enjoys what he has. (231)

[147] Men ask in their prayers for health from the gods, but do not know that the power to attain this lies in themselves; and by doing the opposite through lack of control, they themselves become the betrayers of their own health to their desires. (234)

[148] It is hard to fight desire; but to control it is the sign of a reasonable man. (236)

[149] Bad men, when they escape, do not keep the oaths which they make in time of stress. (239)

[150] More men become good through practice than by nature. (242)

[151] All kinds of toil are pleasanter than rest, when men attain that for which they labor, or know that they will attain it. But whenever there is failure to attain, then labor is painful and hard. (243)

[152] Do not say or do what is base, even when you are alone. Learn to feel shame in your own eyes much more than before others. (244)

[153] To a wise man, the whole earth is open; for the native land of a good soul is the whole earth. (247)

[154] Civil war is harmful to both parties; for both to the conquerors and the conquered, the destruction is the same. (249)

[155] Poverty under democracy is as much to be preferred to so-called prosperity under an autocracy as freedom to slavery. (251)

[156] One must give the highest importance to affairs of the state, that it may be well run; one must not pursue quarrels contrary to right, nor acquire a power contrary to the common good. The well-run state is the greatest protection, and contains all in itself; when this is safe, all is safe; when this is destroyed, all is destroyed. (252)

[157] Anyone killing any brigand or pirate shall be exempt from penalty, whether he do it by his own hand, or by instigation, or by vote. (260)

[158] One must punish wrong-doers to the best of one's ability, and not neglect it. Such conduct is just and good, but the neglect of it is unjust and bad. (261)

[159] Those who do what is deserving of exile or imprisonment or other punishment must be condemned and not let off. Whoever contrary to the law acquits a man, judging according to profit or pleasure, does wrong, and this is bound to be on his conscience. (262)

[160] One must not respect the opinion of other men more than one's own; nor must one be more ready to do wrong if no one will know than if all will know. One must

respect one's own opinion most, and this must stand as the law of one's soul, preventing one from doing anything improper. (264)

[161] Men remember one's mistakes rather than one's successes. This is just; for as those who return a deposit do not deserve praise, whereas those who do not do so deserve blame and punishment, so with the official: he was elected not to make mistakes but to do things well. (265)

[162] Use slaves as parts of the body: each to his own function. (270)

[163] The man who is fortunate in his choice of a son-in-law gains a son; the man unfortunate in his choice loses his daughter also. (272)

[164] A woman is far sharper than a man in malign thoughts. (273)

[165] An adornment for a woman is lack of garrulity. Paucity of adornment is also beautiful. (274)

[166] The rearing of children is full of pitfalls. Success is attended by strife and care, failure means grief beyond all others. (275)

[167] I do not think that one should have children. I observe in the acquisition of children many great risks and many griefs, whereas a harvest is rare, and even when it exists, it is thin and poor. (276)

[168] Whoever wants to have children should, in my opinion, choose them from the family of one of his friends. He will thus obtain a child such as he wishes, for he can select the kind he wants. And the one that seems fittest will be most likely to follow on his natural endowment. The difference is that in the latter way one can take one child out of many who is according to one's liking; but if one begets a child of one's own, the risks are many, for one is bound to accept him as he is. (277)

[169] If your desires are not great, a little will seem much to you; for small appetite makes poverty equivalent to wealth. (284)

[170] One should realize that human life is weak and brief and mixed with many cares and difficulties, in order that one may care only for moderate possessions, and that hardship may be measured by the standard of one's needs. (285)

[171] He is fortunate who is happy with moderate means, unfortunate who is unhappy with great possessions. (286)

[172] It is unreasonableness not to submit to the necessary conditions of life. (289)

[173] Cast forth uncontrollable grief from your benumbed soul by means of reason. (290)

[174] To bear poverty well is the sign of a sensible man. (291)

[175] The hopes of the unintelligent are senseless. (292)

[176] Those to whom their neighbors' misfortunes give pleasure do not understand that the blows of fate are common to all; and also they lack cause for personal joy. (293)

[177] The good things of youth are strength and beauty, but the flower of age is moderation. (294)

Three Sophists

PROTAGORAS

ca. 490–ca. 420 B.C.

Protagoras, like Democritus, came from Abdera, on the Thracian coast. An ancient story relates that he was at first a porter and that Democritus of Abdera saw him, admired his poise, and decided to instruct him; but this story's truth is doubtful. Protagoras reflected on language and developed a system of grammar. Having settled in Athens, where he taught the youth, he won the respect of Pericles, who commissioned him to frame laws for the new colony of Thurii, in Italy. At age seventy he was accused and convicted of atheism and is said to have left for Sicily and to have drowned at sea.

Protagoras is primarily known for his claim that "of all things the measure is Man . . ." In the dialogues *Protagoras* and *Theaetetus* (the relevant sections from the latter are reprinted in this volume), Plato takes Protagoras to mean that each person, not humanity as a whole, is the measure of all things and so attacks Protagoras' relativism.

Protagoras was the first of those travelling teachers of philosophy and rhetoric who became known as "Sophists." Sophists were not as interested in metaphysical theories as they were in the skill of ⟨*arete*⟩, or "excellence," in the sense of bettering oneself. Many conservative Greeks, such as Aristophanes, considered proper speech and good manners the inherited characteristics of the upper classes. The Sophists, however, taught such skills for a fee—to the consternation of the aristocracy.

Plato considered it his task to oppose these men, and since his dialogues survived and most of their writings did not, his highly polemical pictures of the Sophists have been widely accepted as fair portraits. The very name "Sophist" has become a reproach. Yet one should not uncritically accept Plato's image of Sophists. While many disagree with Sophist conclusions, nevertheless their questioning of conventions, especially in ethics, and their critique of the limits of knowledge represent a milestone in the history of thought.

[1] Of all things the measure is Man, of the things that are, that they are, and of the things that are not, that they are not.

[2] Teaching needs endowment and practice. Learning must begin in youth.

[3] About the gods, I am not able to know whether they exist or do not exist, nor what they are like in form; for the factors preventing knowledge are many: the obscurity of the subject, and the shortness of human life.

[4] To make the weaker cause the stronger.

[5] When his sons, who were fine young men, died within eight days, he (Pericles) bore it without mourning. For he held on to his serenity, from which every day he derived great benefit in happiness, freedom from suffering, and honor in the people's eyes—for all who saw him bearing his griefs valiantly thought him great-souled and brave and superior to themselves, well knowing their own helplessness in such a calamity.

[6] Art without practice, and practice without art, are nothing.

[7] Education does not take root in the soul unless one goes deep.

GORGIAS

fl. 427 B.C.

After Protagoras, Gorgias was probably the most renowned Sophist. Gorgias came from Leontini, in southern Sicily. His dates are uncertain, but he is said to have died at the age of 108, possibly as late as 375 B.C. He first came to Athens on a mission from his Sicilian countrymen, enlisting (successfully) Athenian help against Syracuse. While in Athens he taught the art of persuasion to Isocrates, the famous rhetorician.

Like Protagoras, Gorgias is a character in Plato's dialogue bearing his name. Also like Protagoras, Gorgias held views—in this case on the impossibility of knowledge—that Plato found unacceptable. The following selections comprise the single philosophic fragment that has come down to us (a long quotation in Sextus Empiricus), a sample speech (the encomium on Helen), and three very short pieces that may help to fill out the picture of Gorgias.

[1] I. Nothing exists.
   (a) Not-Being does not exist.
   (b) Being does not exist.
      i. as everlasting.
      ii. as created.
      iii. as both.
      iv. as One.
      v. as Many.
   (c) A mixture of Being and Not-Being does not exist.
  II. If anything exists, it is incomprehensible.
 III. If it is comprehensible, it is incommunicable.

  I. Nothing exists. If anything exists, it must be either Being or Not-Being, or both Being and Not-Being.
   (a) It cannot be Not-Being, for Not-Being does not exist; if it did, it would be at the same time Being and Not-Being, which is impossible.
   (b) It cannot be Being, for Being does not exist. If Being exists, it must be either everlasting, or created, or both.
      i. It cannot be everlasting; if it were, it would have no beginning, and therefore would be boundless; if it is boundless, then it has no position, for if it had position it would be contained in something, and so it would no longer be boundless, for that which contains is greater than that which is contained, and nothing is greater than the boundless. It cannot be contained by itself, for then the thing containing and the thing contained would be the same, and Being would become two things—both position and body—which is absurd. Hence if Being is everlasting, it is boundless; if boundless, it has no position ("is nowhere"); if without position, it does not exist.
      ii. Similarly, Being cannot be created; if it were, it must come from something, either Being or Not-Being, both of which are impossible.
      iii. Similarly, Being cannot be both everlasting and created, since they are opposite. Therefore Being does not exist.
      iv. Being cannot be one, because if it exists it has size, and is therefore infinitely divisible; at least it is threefold, having length, breadth and depth.
      v. It cannot be many, because the many is made up of an addition of ones, so that since the one does not exist, the many do not exist either.
   (c) A mixture of Being and Not-Being is impossible. Therefore since Being does not exist, nothing exists.
  II. If anything exists, it is incomprehensible. If the concepts of the mind are not realities, reality cannot be thought; if the thing thought is white, then white is thought about; if the thing thought is non-existent, then non-existence is thought about; this is equivalent to saying that "existence, reality, is not thought about, cannot be thought." Many things thought about are not realities: we can conceive of a chariot running on the sea, or a winged man. Also, since things seen are the objects of sight, and things heard are the objects of hearing, and we accept as real things seen without their being heard, and vice versa; so we would have to accept things thought without their being seen or heard; but this would mean believing in things like the chariot racing on the sea. Therefore reality is not the object of thought, and cannot be comprehended by it. Pure mind, as opposed to sense-perception, or even as an equally valid criterion, is a myth.

III. If anything is comprehensible, it is incommunicable. The things which exist are perceptibles; the objects of sight are apprehended by sight, the objects of hearing by hearing, and there is no interchange; so that these sense-perceptions cannot communicate with one another. Further, that with which we communicate is speech, and speech is not the same thing as the things that exist, the perceptibles; so that we communicate not the things which exist, but only speech; just as that which is seen cannot become that which is heard, so our speech cannot be equated with that which exists, since it is outside us. Further, speech is composed from the percepts which we receive from without, that is, from perceptibles; so that it is not speech which communicates perceptibles, but perceptibles which create speech. Further, speech can never exactly represent perceptibles, since it is different from them, and perceptibles are apprehended each by the one kind of organ, speech by another. Hence, since the objects of sight cannot be presented to any other organ but sight, and the different sense-organs cannot give their information to one another, similarly speech cannot give any information about perceptibles. Therefore, if anything exists and is comprehended, it is incommunicable.

[2] (1) The glory *(cosmos)* of a city is courage, of a body, beauty, of a soul, wisdom, of action, virtue, of speech, truth; it is right in all circumstances to praise what is praiseworthy and blame what is blameworthy.

(2) It belongs to the same man both to speak the truth and to refute falsehood. Helen is universally condemned and regarded as the symbol of disasters; I wish to subject her story to critical examination, and so rescue her from ignorant calumny.

(3) She was of the highest parentage: her reputed father Tyndareus was the most powerful of men; her real father, Zeus, was king of all.

(4) From these origins she obtained her divine beauty, by the display of which she inspired love in countless men, and caused the assemblage of a great number of ambitious suitors, some endowed with wealth, others with ancestral fame, others with personal prowess, others with accumulated wisdom.

(5) I shall not relate the story of who won Helen or how: to tell an audience what it knows wins belief but gives no pleasure. I shall pass over this period and come to the beginning of my defence, setting out the probable reasons for her journey to Troy.

(6) She acted as she did either through Fate and the will of the gods and the decrees of Necessity, or because she was seized by force, or won over by persuasion *(or captivated by love)*. If the first, it is her accuser who deserves blame; for no human foresight can hinder the will of God: the stronger cannot be hindered by the weaker, and God is stronger than man in every way. Therefore if the cause was Fate, Helen cannot be blamed.

(7) If she was carried off by force, clearly her abductor wronged her and she was unfortunate. He, a barbarian, committed an act of barbarism, and should receive blame, disgrace and punishment; she, being robbed of her country and friends, deserves pity rather than obloquy.

(8) If it was speech that persuaded her and deceived her soul, her defence remains easy. Speech is a great power, which achieves the most divine works by means of the smallest and least visible form; for it can even put a stop to fear, remove grief, create joy, and increase pity. This I shall now prove:

(9) All poetry can be called speech in metre. Its hearers shudder with terror, shed tears of pity, and yearn with sad longing; the soul, affected by the words, feels as

its own an emotion aroused by the good and ill fortunes of other people's actions and lives.

(10) The inspired incantations of words can induce pleasure and avert grief; for the power of the incantations, uniting with the feeling in the soul, soothes and persuades and transports by means of its wizardry. Two types of wizardry and magic have been invented, which are errors in the soul and deceptions in the mind.

(11) Their persuasions by means of fictions are innumerable; for if everyone had recollection of the past, knowledge of the present, and foreknowledge of the future, the power of speech would not be so great. But as it is, when men can neither remember the past nor observe the present nor prophesy the future, deception is easy; so that most men offer opinion as advice to the soul. But opinion, being unreliable, involves those who accept it in equally uncertain fortunes.

(12) *(Text corrupt.)* Thus, persuasion by speech is equivalent to abduction by force, as she was compelled to agree to what was said, and consent to what was done. It was therefore the persuader, not Helen, who did wrong and should be blamed.

(13) That persuasion, when added to speech, can also make any impression it wishes on the soul, can be shown, firstly, from the arguments of the meteorologists, who by removing one opinion and implanting another, cause what is incredible and invisible to appear before the eyes of the mind; secondly, from legal contests, in which a speech can sway and persuade a crowd, by the skill of its composition, not by the truth of its statements; thirdly, from the philosophical debates, in which quickness of thought is shown easily altering opinion.

(14) The power of speech over the constitution of the soul can be compared with the effect of drugs on the bodily state: just as drugs by driving out different humours from the body can put an end either to the disease or to life, so with speech: different words can induce grief, pleasure or fear; or again, by means of a harmful kind of persuasion, words can drug and bewitch the soul.

(15) If Helen was persuaded by love, defence is equally easy. What we see has its own nature, not chosen by us; and the soul is impressed through sight.

(16) For instance, in war, the sight of enemy forms wearing hostile array is so disturbing to the soul that often men flee in terror as if the coming danger were already present. The powerful habit induced by custom is displaced by the fear aroused by sight, which causes oblivion of what custom judges honorable and of the advantage derived from victory.

(17) People who have seen a frightful sight have been driven out of their minds, so great is the power of fear; while many have fallen victims to useless toils, dreadful diseases and incurable insanity, so vivid are the images of the things seen which vision engraves on the mind.

(18) Painters, however, when they create one shape from many colors, give pleasure to sight; and the pleasure afforded by sculpture to the eyes is divine; many objects engender in many people a love of many actions and forms.

(19) If therefore Helen's eye, delighted with Paris's form, engendered the passion of love in her soul, this is not remarkable; for if a god is at work with divine power, how can the weaker person resist him? And if the disease is human, due to the soul's ignorance, it must not be condemned as a crime but pitied as a misfortune, for it came about through the snares of Fate, not the choice of the will; by the compulsion of love, not by the plottings of art.

(20) Therefore, whichever of the four reasons caused Helen's action, she is innocent.

(21) I have expunged by my discourse this woman's ill fame, and have fulfilled the object set forth at the outset. I have tried to destroy the unjust blame and the ignorant opinion, and have chosen to write this speech as an Encomium on Helen and an amusement for myself.

[3] Not the looks of a woman, but her good reputation should be known to many.

[4] Tragedy, by means of legends and emotions, creates a deception in which the deceiver is more honest than the non-deceiver, and the deceived is wiser than the non-deceived.

[5] Being is unrecognizable unless it succeeds in seeming, and seeming is weak unless it succeeds in being.

ANTIPHON

fifth century B.C.?

Of the many ancient Greeks who bore this name, at least three were put to death. One Antiphon, a poet of Attica who wrote tragedies, epics, and speeches, defied Dionysius the tyrant and was executed for his trouble. Another Antiphon, an orator, promised Philip of Macedonia, the father of Alexander the Great, that he would set fire to the citadel of Athens and so was put to death at the instigation of Demosthenes.

A third Antiphon, born at Rhamnus in Attica about 480 B.C., was one of the great orators of the fifth century. In 411 B.C., during the Peloponnesian War, he helped set up the oligarchy of the 400, but he was condemned to death with the restoration of the democracy.

Most writers distinguish between Antiphon the orator and Antiphon the Sophist, but it is by no means certain the two were not identical. It is generally held that at least some of Antiphon's ideas on the conflict between natural law and human law are reencountered in, and so presumably greatly influenced, first the Cynic school of philosophy and later the Stoics. Some of the material cited here was discovered on Egyptian papyri only in the twentieth century.

[1] [Antiphon was] a man inferior in virtue to none of his contemporaries, and possessed of remarkable powers of thought and gifts of speech. He did not like to come forward in the assembly, or in any other public arena. To the multitude, who were suspicious of his great abilities, he was an object of dislike; but there was no man who could do more for any who consulted him, whether their business lay in the courts of justice or in the assembly. And when the government of the Four Hundred was overthrown and became exposed to the vengeance of the people, and he being accused of taking part in the plot had to speak in his own case, his defense was undoubtedly the best ever made by any man on a capital charge down to my time.

*   *   *

[2] Hence he *(God)* needs nothing and receives no addition from anywhere, but is infinite and lacking nothing.

[3] Justice, then, is not to transgress that which is the law of the city in which one is a citizen. A man therefore can best conduct himself in harmony with justice, if when in the company of witnesses he upholds the laws, and when alone without witnesses he upholds the edicts of nature. For the edicts of the laws are imposed artificially, but those of nature are compulsory. And the edicts of the laws are arrived at by consent, not by natural growth, whereas those of nature are not a matter of consent.

So, if the man who transgresses the legal code evades those who have agreed to these edicts, he avoids both disgrace and penalty; otherwise not. But if a man violates against possibility any of the laws which are implanted in nature, even if he evades all men's detection, the ill is no less, and even if all see, it is no greater. For he is not hurt on account of an opinion, but because of truth. The examination of these things is in general for this reason, that the majority of just acts according to law are prescribed contrary to nature. For there is legislation about the eyes, what they must see and what not; and about the ears, what they must hear and what not; and about the tongue, what it must speak and what not; and about the hands, what they must do and what not; and about the feet, where they must go and where not. Now the law's prohibitions are in no way more agreeable to nature and more akin than the law's injunctions. But life belongs to nature, and death too, and life for them is derived from advantages, and death from disadvantages. And the advantages laid down by the laws are chains upon nature, but those laid down by nature are free. So that the things which hurt, according to true reasoning, do not benefit nature more than those which delight; and things which grieve are not more advantageous than those which please; for things truly advantageous must not really harm, but must benefit. The naturally advantageous things from among these . . .

(According to law, they are justified) who having suffered defend themselves and do not themselves begin action; and those who treat their parents well, even though their parents have treated them badly; and those who give the taking of an oath to others and do not themselves swear. Of these provisions, one could find many which are hostile to nature; and there is in them the possibility of suffering more when one could suffer less; and enjoying less when one could enjoy more; and faring ill when one need not. Now if the person who adapted himself to these provisions received support from the laws, and those who did not, but who opposed them, received damage, obedience to the laws would not be without benefit; but as things are, it is obvious that for those who adapt themselves to these things the justice proceeding from law is not strong enough to help, seeing that first of all it allows him who suffers to suffer, and him who does, to do, and does not prevent the sufferer from suffering or the doer from doing. And if the case is brought up for punishment, there is no advantage peculiar to the sufferer rather than to the doer. For the sufferer must convince those who are to inflict the punishment, that he has suffered; and he needs the ability to win his case. And it is open to the doer to deny, by the same means . . . and he can defend himself no less than the accuser can accuse, and persuasion is open to both parties, being a matter of technique. . . .

We revere and honor those born of noble fathers, but those who are not born of noble houses we neither revere nor honor. In this we are, in our relations with one another, like barbarians, since we are all by nature born the same in every way, both barbarians and Hellenes. And it is open to all men to observe the laws of nature, which are compulsory. Similarly all of these things can be acquired by all, and in none of these things is any of us distinguished as barbarian or Hellene. We all breathe into the air through mouth and nostrils, and we all eat with hands. . . .

[4] Now let life proceed, and let him desire marriage and a wife. This day, this night begin a new destiny; for marriage is a great contest for mankind. If the woman turns out to be incompatible, what can one do about the disaster? Divorce is difficult: it means to make enemies of friends, who have the same thoughts, the same breath, and had been valued and had regarded one with esteem. And it is hard if one gets such a possession, that is, if when thinking to get pleasure, one brings home pain.

However, not to speak of malevolence: let us assume the utmost compatibility. What is pleasanter to a man than a wife after his own heart? What is sweeter, especially to a young man? But in the very pleasure lies near at hand the pain; pleasures do not come alone, but are attended by griefs and troubles. Olympic and Pythian victories and all pleasures are apt to be won by great pains. Honors, prizes, delights, which God has given to men, depend necessarily on great toils and exertions. For my part, if I had another body which was as much trouble to me as I am to myself, I could not live, so great is the trouble I give myself for the sake of health, the acquisition of a livelihood, and for fame, respectability, glory and a good reputation. What then, if I acquired another body which was as much trouble? Is it not clear that a wife, if she is to his mind, gives her husband no less cause for love and pain than he does to himself, for the health of two bodies, the acquisition of two livelihoods, and for respectability and honor? Suppose children are born: then all is full of anxiety, and the youthful spring goes out of the mind, and the countenance is no longer the same.

[5] The whole of life is wonderfully open to complaint, my friend; it has nothing remarkable, great or noble, but all is petty, feeble, brief-lasting, and mingled with sorrows.

[6] There are some who do not live the present life, but prepare with great diligence as if they were going to live another life, not the present one. Meanwhile time, being neglected, deserts them.

[7] There is a story that a man seeing another man earning much money begged him to lend him a sum at interest. The other refused; and being of a mistrustful nature, unwilling to help anyone, he carried it off and hid it somewhere. Another man, observing him, filched it. Later, the man who had hidden it returning, could not find it; and being very grieved at the disaster—especially that he had not lent to the man who had asked him, because then it would have been safe and would have earned increment—he went to see the man who had asked for a loan, and bewailed his misfortune, saying that he had done wrong and was sorry not to have granted his request but to have refused it, as his money was completely lost. The other man told him to hide a stone in the same place, and think of his money as his and not lost: "For even when you had it you completely failed to use it; so that now too you can think you have lost nothing." For when a person has not used and will not use anything, it makes no difference to him either whether he has it or not. For when God does not wish to give a man complete good fortune—when he has given him material wealth but made him poor in right thinking—in taking away one he has deprived him of both.

[8] He is cowardly who is bold in speech concerning absent and future dangers, and hurries on in resolve, but shrinks back when the fact is upon him.

[9] Whoever, when going against his neighbor with the intention of harming him, is afraid lest by failing to achieve his wishes he may get what he does not wish, is wiser. For his fear means hesitation, and his hesitation means an interval in which often his mind is deflected from his purpose. There can be no reversal of a thing that has happened: it is possible only for what is in the future not to happen. Whoever thinks he will ill-treat his neighbors and not suffer himself is unwise. Hopes are not altogether a good thing; such hopes have flung down many into intolerable disaster, and what they

thought to inflict on their neighbors, they have suffered themselves for all to see. Prudence in another man can be judged correctly by no one more than him who fortifies his soul against immediate pleasures and can conquer himself. But whoever wishes to gratify his soul immediately, wishes the worse instead of the better.

[10] Whoever has not desired or touched the base and the bad, is not self-restrained; for there is nothing over which he has gained the mastery and proved himself well-behaved.

[11] The first thing, I believe, for mankind is education. For whenever anyone does the beginning of anything correctly, it is likely that the end also will be right. As one sows, so can one expect to reap. And if in a young body one sows a noble education, this lives and flourishes through the whole of his life, and neither rain nor drought destroys it.

[12] One's character must necessarily grow like that with which one spends the greater part of the day.

Epilogue: Pericles (as reported by Thucydides)

ca. 495–429 B.C.

Neither Pericles, the great statesman, who succumbed to the pestilence that struck Athens in 429 B.C., nor Thucydides, the great historian who died about thirty years later, was a philosopher. But the great speech that Pericles delivered in 431 B.C. at the funeral of those who had been killed in the Peloponnesian War (as reported by Thucydides) still belongs in this volume, for several reasons. In the first place, it is important to recall that the Greek philosophers did not think and write in ivory towers, but were persons deeply involved in the public and cultural life of their day. Secondly, Pericles had a strong influence on subsequent thinkers. There are references to his speeches in several of the selections that follow. This speech is a self-contained unit that does not suffer from being read out of context. Finally, it is often said that Plato's critique of democracy in his time was entirely fitting in relation to the post-Peloponnesian War democracy that put Socrates to death. Pericles' classical defense of Athenian democracy thirty years earlier shows how swiftly political conditions change.

[1] When the remains have been laid in the earth, some man of known ability and high reputation, chosen by the city, delivers a suitable oration over them; after which the people depart. Such is the manner of interment; and the ceremony was repeated from time to time throughout the war. Over those who were the

55

first buried Pericles was chosen to speak. At the fitting moment he advanced from the sepulchre to a lofty stage, which had been erected in order that he might be heard as far as possible by the multitude, and spoke as follows:

FUNERAL ORATION

[2] "Most of those who have spoken here before me have commended the lawgiver who added this oration to our other funeral customs; it seemed to them a worthy thing that such an honor should be given at their burial to the dead who have fallen on the field of battle. But I should have preferred that, when men's deeds have been brave, they should be honored in deed only, and with such an honor as this public funeral, which you are now witnessing. Then the reputation of many would not have been imperilled on the eloquence or want of eloquence of one, and their virtues believed or not as he spoke well or ill. For it is difficult to say neither too little nor too much; and even moderation is apt not to give the impression of truthfulness. The friend of the dead who knows the facts is likely to think that the words of the speaker fall short of his knowledge and of his wishes; another who is not so well informed, when he hears of anything which surpasses his own powers, will be envious and will suspect exaggeration. Mankind are tolerant of the praises of others so long as each hearer thinks that he can do as well or nearly as well himself, but, when the speaker rises above him, jealousy is aroused and he begins to be incredulous. However, since our ancestors have set the seal of their approval upon the practice, I must obey, and to the utmost of my power shall endeavor to satisfy the wishes and beliefs of all who hear me.

[3] "I will speak first of our ancestors, for it is right and becoming that now, when we are lamenting the dead, a tribute should be paid to their memory. There has never been a time when they did not inhabit this land, which by their valor they have handed down from generation to generation, and we have received from them a free state. But if they were worthy of praise, still more were our fathers, who added to their inheritance, and after many a struggle transmitted to us their sons this great empire. And we ourselves assembled here to-day, who are still most of us in the vigor of life, have chiefly done the work of improvement, and have richly endowed our city with all things, so that she is sufficient for herself both in peace and war. Of the military exploits by which our various possessions were acquired, or of the energy with which we or our fathers drove back the tide of war, Hellenic or Barbarian, I will not speak; for the tale would be long and is familiar to you. But before I praise the dead, I should like to point out by what principles of action we rose to power, and under what institutions and through what manner of life our empire became great. For I conceive that such thoughts are not unsuited to the occasion, and that this numerous assembly of citizens and strangers may profitably listen to them.

[4] "Our form of government does not enter into rivalry with the institutions of others. We do not copy our neighbors, but are an example to them. It is true that we are called a democracy, for the administration is in the hands of the many and not of the few. But while the law secures equal justice to all alike in their private disputes, the claim of excellence is also recognized; and when a citizen is in any way distinguished, he is preferred to the public service, not as matter of privilege, but as the reward of

merit. Neither is poverty a bar, but a man may benefit his country whatever be the obscurity of his condition. There is no exclusiveness—in our private intercourse we are not suspicious of one another, nor angry with our neighbor if he does what he likes; we do not put on sour looks at him which, though harmless, are not pleasant. While we are thus unconstrained in our private intercourse, a spirit of reverence pervades our public acts; we are prevented from doing wrong by respect for authority and for the laws, having an especial regard to those which are ordained for the protection of the injured as well as to those unwritten laws which bring upon the transgressor of them the reprobation of the general sentiment.

[5] "And we have not forgotten to provide for our weary spirits many relaxations from toil; we have regular games and sacrifices throughout the year; at home the style of our life is refined; and the delight which we daily feel in all these things helps to banish melancholy. Because of the greatness of our city the fruits of the whole earth flow in upon us; so that we enjoy the goods of other countries as freely as of our own.

[6] "Then, again, our military training is in many respects superior to that of our adversaries. Our city is thrown open to the world, and we never expel a foreigner or prevent him from seeing or learning anything of which the secret if revealed to an enemy might profit him. We rely not upon management or trickery, but upon our own hearts and hands. And in the matter of education, whereas they from early youth are always undergoing laborious exercises which are to make them brave, we live at ease, and yet are equally ready to face the perils which they face. And here is the proof. The Lacedaemonians come into Attica not by themselves, but with their whole confederacy following; we go alone into a neighbor's country; and although our opponents are fighting for their homes and we on a foreign soil, we have seldom any difficulty in overcoming them. Our enemies have never yet felt our united strength; the care of a navy divides our attention, and on land we are obliged to send our own citizens everywhere. But they, if they meet and defeat a part of our army, are as proud as if they had routed us all, and when defeated they pretend to have been vanquished by us all.

"If then we prefer to meet danger with a light heart but without laborious training, and with a courage which is gained by habit and not enforced by law, are we not greatly the gainers? Since we do not anticipate the pain, although, when the hour comes, we can be as brave as those who never allow themselves to rest;

[7] "And thus too our city is equally admirable in peace and in war. For we are lovers of the beautiful, yet simple in our tastes, and we cultivate the mind without loss of manliness. Wealth we employ, not for talk and ostentation, but when there is a real use for it. To avow poverty with us is no disgrace: the true disgrace is in doing nothing to avoid it. An Athenian citizen does not neglect the state because he takes care of his own household; and even those of us who are engaged in business have a very fair idea of politics. We alone regard a man who takes no interest in public affairs, not as a harmless, but as a useless character; and if few of us are originators, we are all sound judges of a policy. The great impediment to action is, in our opinion, not discussion, but the want of that knowledge which is gained by discussion preparatory to action. For we have a peculiar power of thinking before we act and of acting too, whereas other men are courageous from ignorance but hesitate upon reflection. And they are surely to be esteemed the bravest spirits who, having the clearest sense both of the pains and pleasures of life, do not on that account shrink from danger. In doing good, again, we are unlike others; we make our friends by conferring, not by receiving favors. Now he who confers a favor is the firmer friend, because he would fain by kindness keep alive the memory of an obligation; but the recipient is colder in his feelings, because he knows that in requiting another's generosity he will not be winning gratitude, but only paying

a debt. We alone do good to our neighbors not upon a calculation of interest, but in the confidence of freedom and in a frank and fearless spirit.

[8] "To sum up: I say that Athens is the school of Hellas, and that the individual Athenian in his own person seems to have the power of adapting himself to the most varied forms of action with the utmost versatility and grace. This is no passing and idle word, but truth and fact; and the assertion is verified by the position to which these qualities have raised the state. For in the hour of trial Athens alone among her contemporaries is superior to the report of her. No enemy who comes against her is indignant at the reverses which he sustains at the hands of such a city; no subject complains that his masters are unworthy of him. And we shall assuredly not be without witnesses; there are mighty monuments of our power which will make us the wonder of this and of succeeding ages; we shall not need the praises of Homer or of any other panegyrist whose poetry may please for the moment, although his representation of the facts will not bear the light of day. For we have compelled every land and every sea to open a path for our valor, and have everywhere planted eternal memorials of our friendship and of our enmity. Such is the city for whose sake these men nobly fought and died; they could not bear the thought that she might be taken from them; and every one of us who survive should gladly toil on her behalf.

[9] "I have dwelt upon the greatness of Athens because I want to show you that we are contending for a higher prize than those who enjoy none of these privileges, and to establish by manifest proof the merit of these men whom I am now commemorating. Their loftiest praise has been already spoken. For in magnifying the city I have magnified them, and men like them whose virtues made her glorious. And of how few Hellenes can it be said as of them, that their deeds when weighed in the balance have been found equal to their fame! Methinks that a death such as theirs has been given the true measure of a man's worth; it may be the first revelation of his virtues, but is at any rate their final seal. For even those who come short in other ways may justly plead the valor with which they have fought for their country; they have blotted out the evil with the good, and have benefitted the state more by their public services than they have injured her by their private actions. None of these men were enervated by wealth or hesitated to resign the pleasures of life; none of them put off the evil day in the hope, natural to poverty, that a man, though poor, may one day become rich. But, deeming that the punishment of their enemies was sweeter than any of these things, and that they could fall in no nobler cause, they determined at the hazard of their lives to be honorably avenged, and to leave the rest. They resigned to hope their unknown chance of happiness; but in the face of death they resolved to rely upon themselves alone. And when the moment came they were minded to resist and suffer, rather than to fly and save their lives; they ran away from the word of dishonor, but on the battlefield their feet stood fast, and in an instant, at the height of their fortune, they passed away from the scene, not of their fear, but of their glory.

[10] "Such was the end of these men; they were worthy of Athens, and the living need not desire to have a more heroic spirit, although they may pray for a less fatal issue. The value of such a spirit is not to be expressed in words. Any one can discourse to you for ever about the advantages of a brave defence which you know already. But instead of listening to him I would have you day by day fix your eyes upon the greatness of Athens, until you become filled with the love of her; and when you are impressed by the spectacle of her glory, reflect that this empire has been acquired by men who knew their duty and had the courage to do it, who in the hour of conflict had the fear of dishonor always present to them, and who, if ever they failed in an enterprise, would not allow their virtues to be lost to their country, but freely gave their lives to her as the

fairest offering which they could present at her feast. The sacrifice which they collectively made was individually repaid to them; for they received again each one for himself a praise which grows not old, and the noblest of all sepulchres—I speak not of that in which their remains are laid, but of that in which their glory survives, and is proclaimed always and on every fitting occasion both in word and deed. For the whole earth is the sepulchre of famous men; not only are they commemorated by columns and inscriptions in their own country, but in foreign lands there dwells also an unwritten memorial of them, graven not on stone but in the hearts of men. Make them your examples, and, esteeming courage to be freedom and freedom to be happiness, do not weigh too nicely the perils of war. The unfortunate who has no hope of a change for the better has less reason to throw away his life than the prosperous who, if he survive, is always liable to a change for the worse, and to whom any accidental fall makes the most serious difference. To a man of spirit, cowardice and disaster coming together are far more bitter than death, striking him unperceived at a time when he is full of courage and animated by the general hope.

[11] "Wherefore I do not now commiserate the parents of the dead who stand here; I would rather comfort them. You know that your life has been passed amid manifold vicissitudes; and that they may be deemed fortunate who have gained most honor, whether an honorable death like theirs, or an honorable sorrow like yours, and whose days have been so ordered that the term of their happiness is likewise the term of their life. I know how hard it is to make you feel this, when the good fortune of others will too often remind you of the gladness which once lightened your hearts. And sorrow is felt at the want of those blessings, not which a man never knew, but which were a part of his life before they were taken from him. Some of you are of an age at which they may hope to have other children, and they ought to bear their sorrow better; not only will the children who may hereafter be born make them forget their own lost ones, but the city will be doubly a gainer. She will not be left desolate, and she will be safer. For a man's counsel cannot have equal weight or worth, when he alone has no children to risk in the general danger. To those of you who have passed their prime, I say; 'Congratulate yourselves that you have been happy during the greater part of your days; remember that your life of sorrow will not last long, and be comforted by the glory of those who are gone. For the love of honor alone is ever young, and not riches, as some say, but honor is the delight of men when they are old and useless.'

[12] "To you who are the sons and brothers of the departed, I see that the struggle to emulate them will be an arduous one. For all men praise the dead, and, however preeminent your virtue may be, hardly will you be thought, I do not say to equal, but even to approach them. The living have their rivals and detractors, but when a man is out of the way, the honor and good-will which he receives is unalloyed. And, if I am to speak of womanly virtues to those of you who will henceforth be widows, let me sum them up in one short admonition: To a woman not to show more weakness than is natural to her sex is a great glory, and not to be talked about for good or evil among men.

[13] "I have paid the required tribute, in obedience to the law, making use of such fitting words as I had. The tribute of deeds has been paid in part; for the dead have been honorably interred, and it remains only that their children should be maintained at the public charge until they are grown up; this is the solid prize with which, as with a garland, Athens crowns her sons living and dead, after a struggle like theirs. For where the rewards of virtue are greatest, there the noblest citizens are enlisted in the service of the state. And now, when you have duly lamented, every one his own dead, you may depart."

SOURCES OF THE FRAGMENTS

All of the fragments and most of the paraphrases in the preceding texts were collected by a nineteenth-century German scholar, Hermann Diels (and later modified by Walther Kranz), in *Die Fragmente der Vorsokratiker* (Berlin: Weidmann, most recent edition, 1967). Diels assembled the original Greek texts and furnished German translations for all the fragments. He also collected and printed, but did not translate, reports of ancient authors about the lives, works, and ideas of the pre-Socratics.

Kathleen Freeman published *An Ancilla to The Pre-Socratic Philosophers: A complete translation of the Fragments in Diels, Fragmente der Vorsokratiker* (Cambridge, MA: Harvard University Press, 1947). Like Diels-Kranz, she translated only the fragments, not the ancient paraphrases and reports about the philosophers' lives and works. G.S. Kirk, J.E. Raven, and M. Schofield translated many of these previously untranslated items in their discussion of the Greek texts against the background of recent scholarly books and articles in *The Presocratic Philosophers: A Critical History with a Selection of Texts, Second Edition* (Cambridge: Cambridge University Press, 1983). Almost all the translations I have used are either those of Freeman (marked with an F) or those of Kirk, Raven, and Schofield (marked with a K). In a few cases the translation is Kaufmann's (marked with a WK) or the older first edition (1957) of Kirk and Raven (so indicated in the note). Some of the translations have been modified by Kaufmann or myself (and are marked with an *). After direct quotations, the symbols (K, F, and WK) are preceded by the number that the fragment bears in the fifth edition of Diels-Kranz's standard work. (Freeman's numbering is the same as Diels-Kranz.) After paraphrases, the ancient works in which the paraphrases occur are cited briefly (along with the abbreviation and number from one of the above sources). Those interested in an evaluation of the paraphrases will find illuminating discussions in Kirk, Raven, and Schofield.

THALES

1. Plato, *Theaetetus* 174A; K 72.
2. Aristotle, *Politics* A11, 1259a; K 73.
3. Herodotus I, 75; K 66.
4. Aristotle, *Metaphysics* A3, 983b; W.D. Ross's translation.
5. Heraclitus Homericus, *Quaest. Hom.* 22; K 87. These may not really have been Thales' reasons.
6. Seneca, *Qu. Nat.* III, 14; K 88.
7. Aristotle, *De Anima* A2, 405a; K 89.
8. Aristotle, *De Anima* A5, 411a; K91.

ANAXIMANDER

1. Suda s.v.; K 95. Some of this has been disputed.
2. Themistius *Or.* 26; K 96.
3. Simplicius, *Physics* 24; K 101A and 119. Some scholars believe that the quotation begins earlier and comprises the whole sentence.
4. Ps.-Plutarch, *Strom.* 2; K 121.

5. *Ibid.;* K 122A.
6. Hippolytus, *Ref.* I, 6, 3; K 122B.
7. Aetius II, 20; K 126.
8. Aetius V, 19; K 133.
9. Ps.-Plutarch, *Strom.* 2; K 134.
10. Plutarch, *Symp.* VIII, 730E; K 137.

ANAXIMENES

1. Diogenes Laertius II, 3; K 138.
2. Augustine, *City of God,* VIII, 2; K 146.
3. Ps.-Plutarch, *Strom.* 3; K 148.

PYTHAGORAS

1. Herodotus IV, 95; K 257.
2. Porphyry *V.P.* 9; K 266.
3. Iustinus *ap.* Pomp. Trog. *Hist. Phil. Epit.* XX, 4, 14; K 272.
4. Aetius I, 3, 8; 1st edition K 280.
5. Proclus, *In Eucl.,* p. 426 Friedl; 1st edition K 281.
6. Diogenes Laertius VIII, 36; Xenophanes, fragment 7; K 260.
7. Herodotus II, 123; 1st edition K 270.
8. Porphyry, *Vita Pythagorae* 19; 1st edition K 271.
9. Eudemus *ap.* Simplic. *Phys.,* 732, 30; 1st edition K 272. The doctrine of the eternal recurrence of the same events at gigantic intervals was revived in modern times by Friedrich Nietzsche; *cf.* Walter Kaufmann, *Nietzsche* (Princeton: Princeton University Press, 1950; Cleveland: Meridian Books, 1956), Chapter 11, "Overman and Eternal Recurrence."
10–27. Iamblichus, *Protr.* 21; 1st edition K 275. These were some of the rules of the sect founded by Pythagoras. The numbers of the rules in K are given in parentheses after each paragraph.
28. Procl., *In Eucl.,* p. 65 Friedl.; 1st edition K 277.
29. Diogenes Laertius VIII, 8; 1st edition K 278.

XENOPHANES

1. Diogenes Laertius IX, 18; K 161.
2. 11; WK.
3. 14; WK.
4. 15; WK.
5. 16; WK.
6. 23; F*.
7. 24; F.
8. 25; F*.
9. 26; F.

10. 27; F*.
11. 34; K 186.
12. 18; WK.

HERACLITUS

1. Diogenes Laertius IX, 6; K 191.
2. *Ibid.,* IX, 5; 192. Some scholars have questioned the claim about the three parts of his book; indeed, some have doubted that he wrote any book at all.
3. 89; WK.
4. 113; F.
5. 1; K 194.
6. 2; K 195.
7. 50; K 196.
8. 55; K 197.
9. 101a; F.
10. 7; F.
11. 107; K 198.
12. 60; K 200.
13. 6; F.
14. 49a; F*.
15. 91; F.
16. 12; K 214.
17. 61; K 199.
18. 111; K 201.
19. 8; F*.
20. 53; K 212.
21. 80; K 211.
22. 36; K 229.
23. 62; WK.
24. 27; F*.
25. 52; F.
26. 40; WK.
27. 42; WK.
28. 57; WK.
29. 5; F*.
30. 14; WK.
31. 96; WK. To appreciate the full measure of this heresy, one should recall Sophocles' *Antigone* and Homer's *Iliad*.
32. 102; K 206.
33. 79; F.
34. 76; F*.
35. 66; F.
36. 30; K 217.
37. 9; F*.

38. 97; F.
39. 4; F*.
40. 110; F*.
41. 112; F*.
42. 116; WK.
43. 118; K 230.
44. 117; K 231.
45. 29; WK.
46. 44; K 249.
47. 49; F*.
48. 121; F*.
49. 101; WK.
50. 18; WK.
51. 119; WK.
52. 123; WK.
53. 92; F*.
54. 93; K 244.

PARMENIDES

1. 1 (Lines 1–32); K 288.
2. 2; K 291.
3. 3; K 292. K construes the literal meaning as: "the same thing exists for thinking and for being"; Freeman's "For it is the same thing to think and to be" is based on Diels's *Denn (das Seiende) denken und sein ist dasselbe*. This much-discussed sentence seems to be continuous with the preceding two fragments.
4. 4; K 313.
5. 5; K 289.
6. 6; K 293. Freeman renders the final words: "in everything there is a way of opposing stress." Either way, many interpreters believe that Parmenides here alludes to Heraclitus.
7. 7; K 294.
8. 8; F*.
9. 9; Kranz takes ⟨*epei*⟩ with the previous line, and translates: "For nothing is possible which does not come under either of the two" (*i.e.* everything belongs to one or other of the two categories light and night); F*.
10–14. 10–14; F.

ZENO OF ELEA

1. Plato, *Parmenides* 128c; F.M. Cornford translation.
2. Plato, *Phaedrus* 261d; R. Hackforth translation.
3. Simplicius, *Physics* 139, 18–19; WK.
4. Simplicius, *Physics* 109, 34; WK.
5. Simplicius, *Physics* 140, 30; WK.

6. Aristotle, *Topics* 160b 7; WK. Evidently the stage setting of the argument is a race course. On this ground it is better to call the argument by this name, instead of "The Dichotomy," as is often done in the literature, keeping "The Stadium" as the generally accepted name of the fourth argument.

7. Aristotle, *Physics* 233a 21; WK.

8. Aristotle, *Physics* 239b 11; WK.

9. Aristotle, *Physics* 263a 5; WK.

10. Simplicius, *Physics* 1013, 4ff; WK.

11. Aristotle, *Physics* 239b 14; P.H. Wicksteed's translation, edited by F.M. Cornford.

12. Aristotle, *Physics* 239b 1, 30; Wicksteed's translation.

13. Aristotle, *Physics* 239b 33; Wicksteed's translation.

14. Aristotle, *Physics* 209a 23; WK.

15. Simplicius, *Physics* 1108, 18; WK.

MELISSUS

1. Diogenes Laertius, IX, 24; 1st edition K 379.

2. Plutarch, *Pericles* 26; K 519. The great battle referred to took place in 441/40 B.C.

3–12. 1–10; F.

EMPEDOCLES

1. Simplicius, *Physics* 25, 19; K 335.

2. Aristotle, *Metaphysics* A 3, 984a.

3–36. The fragments in this section are all from F. I have numbered them consecutively to make it easier to follow. The Diels/Freeman numbering follows each paragraph.

ANAXAGORAS

1. Diogenes Laertius II, 7–15; K 459.

2. Strabo 14, p. 645 Cas.; K 463.

3. Diogenes Laertius I, 16; K 466.

4–23. 1–19, 21 (Opening sentences from his book *On Natural Science*); F.

DEMOCRITUS

1. Simplicius, *Physics* 28, 4; 1st edition of K 539.

2. Diogenes Laertius X, 13; K 540.

3. Cicero, *Academica* pr. II, 37, 118; K 541.

4. Diogenes Laertius IX, 34; K 542.

5. *Ibid.,* IX, 35; K 544.

6. Aristotle, *De Gen. et Corr.,* A 8, 325a; K 545.

7. Simplicius, *De Caelo* 242, 18; K 557.

8. Dionysius *ap.* Eusebium P.E. XIV, 23, 3; K 561.

9. Hyppolytus *Ref.* I, 13, 2; K 565.

10. Diogenes Laertius IX, 45; K 566; cf. "the only extant saying of Leucippus himself," K 569, Fr. 2, Aetius I, 25, 4: "Nothing occurs at random, but everything for a reason and by necessity."

11. Aristotle *On Democritus ap.* Simplicium *De Caelo* 295, 11; K 583.

12. Aristotle, *De Anima,* A 2, 405a; K 585.

13. Aristotle, *De Sensu* 4, 442a; K 587.

14. Aetius IV, 8; K 588.

15. Theophrastus, *De Sensu* 50; R 589.

16. 7 (from "On the Forms"); F.

17. 8 (from "On the Forms"); F.

18. 9; F.

19. 10; F.

20. 11 (from "The Canon"); F.

21. 156; F.

22–102. 35–115; F.

103–177. The fragments in this section are all from F. I have numbered them consecutively to make it easier to follow. The Diels/Freeman numbering follows each paragraph.

PROTAGORAS

1. 1 (from "Truth" or "Refutatory Arguments"); F.

2. 3 (from a treatise entitled "Great Logus"); F.

3. 4 (from "On the Gods"); F.

4. 6b; F.

5. 9; F.

6. 10; F.

7. 11; F.

GORGIAS

1. 3, Sextus, from *On Not-being or on Nature;* F.

2. 11 ("Encomium on Helen": summary); F.

3. 22; F.

4. 23; F.

5. 26; F.

ANTIPHON

1. Thucydides, VIII. 68; (Jowett's translation).

2. 10 (From "Truth"); F.

3. 44 (Oxyrhynchus papyrus, from "Truth"); F.

4. 49; F.

5. 51; F.
6. 53a; F.
7. 54; F.
8. 56; F.
9. 58; F.
10. 59; F.
11. 60; F.
12. 62; F.

PERICLES

1–13. Thucydides, *Peloponnesian War,* II, 35–46; Benjamin Jowett's translation.

Socrates *470–399 B.C.*
and
Plato *428/7–348/7 B.C.*

Socrates has fascinated and inspired men and women for over two thousand years. All five of the major "schools" of ancient Greece (Academics, Peripatetics, Epicureans, Stoics, and Cynics) were influenced by his thought. Some of the early Christian thinkers, such as Justin Martyr, considered him a "proto-Christian," while others, such as St. Augustine (who rejected this view) still expressed deep admiration for Socrates' ethical life. More recently, existentialists found in Socrates' admonition "know thyself" an encapsulation of their thought, and opponents of unjust laws saw in Socrates' trial a blueprint for civil disobedience. In short, Socrates is one of the most admired men who ever lived.

The Athens into which Socrates was born in 470 B.C. was a city still living in the flush of its epic victory over the Persians, and it was bursting with new ideas. The playwrights Euripides and Sophocles were young boys, and Pericles, the great Athenian democrat, was still a young man. The Parthenon's foundation was laid when Socrates was twenty-two, and its construction completed fifteen years later.

Socrates was the son of Sophroniscus, a sculptor, and of Phaenarete, a midwife. As a boy, Socrates received a classical Greek education in music, gymnastics, and grammar (or the study of language), and he decided early on to become a sculptor like his father. Tradition says he was a gifted artist who fashioned impressively simple statues of the Graces. He married a woman named Xanthippe, and together they had three children. He took an early interest in the developing science of the Milesians, and then he served for a time in the army.

His mature life and noble death are described incomparably in the *Apology,* in the closing pages of the *Phaedo,* and in Alcibiades' climactic speech in the *Symposium.* In 399 B.C., the year of Socrates' execution, Athens was no longer the powerful, self-confident city of 470, the year of his birth. An exhausting succession of wars with Sparta (the Peloponnesian Wars) and an enervating series of political debacles left the city narrow in vision and suspicious of new ideas and of dissent.

Socrates wrote nothing, and our knowledge of his thought comes exclusively from the report of others. The playwright Aristophanes (455–375 B.C.) satirized Socrates in his comedy *The Clouds.* His caricature of Socrates as a cheat and charlatan was apparently so damaging that Socrates felt compelled to offer a rebuttal before the Athenian assembly (see the *Apology,* following). The military general Xenophon (ca. 430–350 B.C.) honored his friend Socrates in his *Apology of Socrates,* his *Symposium,* and, later, in his *Memorabilia* ("Recollections of Socrates"). In an effort to defend his dead friend's memory, Xenophon's writings illumine Socrates' life and character. Though born fifteen years after the death of Socrates, Aristotle (384–322 B.C.) left many fascinating allusions to Socrates in his philosophic works, as did several later Greek philosophers. But the primary source of our knowledge of Socrates is his disciple, Plato.

*   *   *

Plato was probably born in 428/7 B.C. He had two older brothers, Adeimantus and Glaucon, who appear in Plato's *Republic,* and a sister, Potone. Though he may have known Socrates since childhood, Plato was probably nearer twenty when he came under the intellectual spell of Socrates. The death of Socrates made an enormous impression on Plato and contributed to his call to bear witness to posterity of "the best, . . . the wisest and most just" person that he knew (*Phaedo,* 118). Though Plato was from a distinguished family and might have followed his relatives into politics, he chose philosophy.

Following Socrates' execution, the twenty-eight-year-old Plato left Athens and travelled for a time. He is reported to have visited Egypt and Cyrene—though some scholars doubt this. During this time he wrote his early dialogues on Socrates' life and teachings. He also visited Italy and Sicily, where he became the friend of Dion, a relative of Dionysius, the tyrant of Syracuse, Sicily.

On returning to Athens from Sicily, Plato founded a school, which came to be called the Academy. One might say it was the world's first university, and it endured as a center of higher learning for nearly one thousand years, until the Roman emperor Justinian closed it in A.D. 529. Except for two later trips to Sicily where he unsuccessfully sought to institute his political theories, Plato spent the rest of his life at the Athenian Academy. Among his students was Aristotle. Plato died at eighty in 348/7 B.C.

Plato's influence was best described by the twentieth-century philosopher Alfred North Whitehead when he said, "The safest general characterization of the European philosophical tradition is that it consists of a series of footnotes to Plato."

*   *   *

It is difficult to separate the ideas of Plato from those of his teacher, Socrates. In virtually all of Plato's dialogues Socrates is the main character, and, indeed, in the early dialogues there is reason to believe that Plato is recording his teacher's actual words. But in the later dialogues "Socrates" gives Plato's views—views that, in some cases, in fact, the historical Socrates denied.

The first four dialogues presented in this text describe the trial and death of Socrates and are arranged in narrative order. The first, the *Euthyphro,* takes place as Socrates has just learned of an indictment against him. He strikes up a conversation with a "theologian" so sure of his piety that he is prosecuting his own father for murder. The dialogue moves on, unsuccessfully, to find a definition of piety. Along the way, Socrates asks a question that has vexed philosophers and theologians for centuries: Is something good because the gods say it is, or do the gods say it is good because it is? This dialogue is given in the Lane Cooper translation.

The next dialogue, the *Apology,* is generally regarded as one of Plato's first and as eminently faithful to what Socrates said at his trial on charges of impiety and corruption of youth. The speech was delivered in public and heard by a large audience; Plato has Socrates mention that Plato was present; and there is no need to doubt the historical veracity of the speech, at least in essentials. There are two breaks in the narrative: one after Socrates' defense (during which the Athenians vote "guilty") and one after Socrates proposes an alternative to the death penalty (during which the Athenians decide on death). This dialogue includes Socrates' famous characterization of his mission and purpose in life.

In the *Crito,* Plato has Crito visit Socrates in prison to assure him that his escape from Athens has been well prepared and to persuade him to consent to leave. Socrates argues that one has an obligation to obey the state even when it orders one to suffer wrong. That Socrates, in fact, refused to leave is certain; that he used the arguments Plato ascribes to him is less certain. In any case, anyone who has read the *Apology* will agree that after his speech Socrates could not well escape.

The moving account of Socrates' death is given at the end of the *Phaedo,* the last of our group of dialogues. There is common agreement that this dialogue was written much later than the other three and that the earlier part of the dialogue, with its Platonic doctrine of Forms and immortality, uses "Socrates" as a vehicle for Plato's own ideas. These ideas owe much to Pythagoreanism, which exerted an ever-increasing influence on Plato's thought. (See the introduction to the Pythagorean selections, page 11.)

The *Apology, Crito,* and the selections from the beginning and ending of the *Phaedo* are all given in new translations by Tom Griffith. These translations capture the conversational nature of the dialogues while maintaining their literary quality and philosophical depth. I am delighted to use these fresh, readable translations.

Like the *Phaedo,* the *Meno, Symposium,* and *Republic* were written during Plato's "middle period," when he had returned from Sicily to Athens and had established the Academy. The *Meno* gives a fine and faithful picture of Socrates practicing the art of dialogue; it also marks the point where Plato moves beyond his master. This dialogue answers the question, "Can virtue be taught?," and treats the issues of knowledge and belief. The *Meno* is given in W.K.C. Guthrie's authoritative translation.

The *Symposium* represents the high point of Plato's literary skill. In this collection of speeches on love, Plato uses several styles of speaking, including some light-hearted banter. The *Symposium* is a work of art and surely makes no claim to historic accuracy, except for Alcibiades' speech on Socrates: What is said there must be true. As for the rest, we need not believe that Aristophanes, for example, really told the fanciful myth ascribed to him here. (Some commentators see Plato paying Aristophanes back for his earlier ridiculing of Socrates.) Tom Griffith's excellent translation is given here.

Note that when reading the *Symposium* a modern reader should keep in mind that among some—but by no means all—Greek intellectuals, homosexuality was not only accepted, it was considered a superior form of love. Since women were rarely educated, it was thought that only with males could a man move beyond "inferior" physical attraction to reach the heights of love.

There are few books in Western civilization that have had the impact of Plato's *Republic*—aside from the Bible, perhaps none. Like the Bible there are also few books whose interpretation and evaluation have differed so widely. Apparently it is a description of Plato's ideal society: a utopian vision of the just state, possible if only philosophers were kings. But some (see the following suggested readings) claim that its purpose is not to give a model of the ideal state, but to show the impossibility of such a state and to convince aspiring philosophers to shun politics. Evaluations of the *Republic* have also varied widely: from the criticisms of Karl Popper, who denounced the *Republic* as totalitarian, to the admiration of more traditional interpreters such as Cornford and Vlastos.

Given the importance of this work and the diversity of opinions concerning its point and value, it was extremely difficult to decide which sections of the *Republic* to include. I chose to include the important discussions of the virtues and the soul in Book IV, the presentation of the guardians' qualities and lifestyles in Book V, and the key sections on knowledge (including the analogy of the line and the myth of the cave) from the end of Book VI and the beginning of Book VII. I admit that space constraints have forced me to exclude important sections. Ideally, the selections chosen will whet the student's appetite to read the rest of this classic. The selections are given in the translation of Francis MacDonald Cornford.

The *Parmenides* marks a move in the development of Plato's thought—from positive philosophy to critical issues. The *Parmenides* is remarkable for the honesty with which Plato attacks the problems with his own doctrine of Forms. The second half is a lengthy and confusing series of "lessons" designed (apparently) to show that "unity is." This part is omitted because it is the most abstruse and difficult thing Plato ever wrote.

The *Theaetetus* deals with the problem of knowledge and contains an interesting discussion of some of the ideas of Protagoras, the Sophist. Besides much technical philosophy, it also offers some charming digressions, and the conclusion of the dialogue, with its genuinely Socratic spirit, represents a highlight in Plato's work. Both the *Parmenides* and the *Theaetetus* are in the Cornford translation.

The marginal page numbers are those of all scholarly editions, Greek, English, German, or French. They are indispensable for serious students.

*   *   *

For studies of Socrates, see the classic A.E. Taylor, *Socrates: The Man and His Thought* (London: Methuen, 1933); the second half of Volume III of W.K.C. Guthrie, *The History of Greek Philosophy* (Cambridge: Cambridge University

Press, 1969); and N. Gulley, *The Philosophy of Socrates* (New York: St. Martin's Press, 1968). For a collection of essays, see Gregory Vlastos, ed., *The Philosophy of Socrates* (Garden City, NY: Doubleday, 1971). For a discussion of the similarities and differences between the historical Socrates and the "Socrates" of the Platonic dialogues, see Gregory Vlastos, *Socrates: Ironist and Moral Philosopher* (Ithaca, NY: Cornell University Press, 1991), especially chapters two and three.

Books about Plato are legion. Once again the work of W.K.C. Guthrie is sensible, comprehensive, yet readable. See volumes IV and V of his *The History of Greek Philosophy* (Cambridge: Cambridge University Press, 1975 and 1978). A.E. Taylor, *Plato: The Man and His Work* (1926; reprinted New York: Barnes and Noble, 1966), Paul Shorey, *What Plato Said* (Chicago: Chicago University Press, 1933), and G.M.A. Grube, *Plato's Thought* (London: Methuen, 1935) are classic treatments of Plato, while Robert Brumbaugh, *Plato for a Modern Age* (New York: Macmillan, 1964), I.M. Crombie, *An Examination of Plato's Doctrines,* two vols. (New York: Humanities Press, 1963-1969), and R.M. Hare, *Plato* (Oxford: Oxford University Press, 1982) are more recent valuable studies. For a collection of essays see Gregory Vlastos, ed., *Plato: A Collection of Critical Essays,* two vols. (Garden City, NY: Doubleday, 1971). For further reading on the *Republic,* see Nicholas P. White, *A Companion to Plato's Republic* (Indianapolis, IN: Hackett, 1979), and Julia Annas, *An Introduction to Plato's Republic* (Oxford: Clarendon Press, 1981). Finally, for unusual interpretations of Plato and his work, see Werner Jaeger, *Paideia,* Vols. II and III, translated by Gilbert Highet (New York: Oxford University Press, 1939-1943); Karl R. Popper, *The Open Society and Its Enemies, Volume I: The Spell of Plato* (Princeton, NJ: Princeton University Press, 1962); and Allan Bloom's interpretive essay in Plato, *Republic,* translated by Allan Bloom (New York: Basic Books, 1968).

EUTHYPHRO

EUTHYPHRO: This, Socrates, is something new? What has taken you from your haunts   2
in the Lyceum, and makes you spend your time at the royal porch? You surely cannot
have a case at law, as I have, before the Archon-King.

SOCRATES: My business, Euthyphro, is not what is known at Athens as a case at
law; it is a criminal prosecution.

EUTHYPHRO: How is that? You mean that somebody is prosecuting you? I never   b
would believe that you were prosecuting anybody else.

SOCRATES: No indeed.

EUTHYPHRO: Then somebody is prosecuting you?

SOCRATES: Most certainly.

EUTHYPHRO: Who is it?

SOCRATES: I am not too clear about the man myself, Euthyphro. He appears to me
to be a young man, and unknown. I think, however, that they call him Meletus, and his

deme is Pitthos, if you happen to know anyone named Meletus of that deme—a hook-nosed man with long straight hair, and not much beard.

EUTHYPHRO: I don't recall him, Socrates. But tell me, of what does he accuse you?

c   SOCRATES: His accusation? It is no mean charge. For a man of his age it is no small thing to have settled a question of so much importance. He says, in fact, that he knows the method by which young people are corrupted, and knows who the persons are that do it. He is, quite possibly, a wise man, and, observing that my ignorance has

d   led me to corrupt his generation, comes like a child to his mother to accuse me to the city. And to me he appears to be the only one who begins his political activity aright, for the right way to begin is to pay attention to the young, and make them just as good as possible—precisely as the able farmer will give his attention to the young plants first, and afterward care for the rest. And so Meletus no doubt begins by clearing us away, the ones who ruin, as he says, the tender shoots of the young. That done, he obviously will

3   care for the older generation, and will thus become the cause, in the highest and widest measure, of benefit to the state. With such a notable beginning, his chances of success look good.

EUTHYPHRO: I hope so, Socrates, but I'm very much afraid it will go the other way. When he starts to injure you, it simply looks to me like beginning at the hearth to hurt the state. But tell me what he says you do to corrupt the young.

b   SOCRATES: It sounds very queer, my friend, when first you hear it. He says I am a maker of gods; he charges me with making new gods, and not believing in the old ones. These are his grounds for prosecuting me, he says.

EUTHYPHRO: I see it, Socrates. It is because you say that ever and anon you have the spiritual sign! So he charges you in this indictment with introducing novelties in religion, and that is the reason why he comes to court with this slanderous complaint, well knowing how easily such matters can be misrepresented to the crowd. For my own part,

c   when I speak in the Assembly about matters of religion, and tell them in advance what will occur, they laugh at me as if I were a madman, and yet I never have made a prediction that did not come true. But the truth is, they are jealous of all such people as ourselves. No, we must not worry over them, but go to meet them.

SOCRATES: Dear Euthyphro, if we were only laughed at, it would be no serious matter. The Athenians, as it seems to me, are not very much disturbed if they think that so-and-so is clever, so long as he does not impart his knowledge to anybody else. But the moment they suspect that he is giving his ability to others, they get angry, whether

d   out of jealousy, as you say, or, it may be, for some other reason.

EUTHYPHRO: With regard to that, I am not very eager to test their attitude to me.

SOCRATES: Quite possibly you strike them as a man who is chary of himself, and is unwilling to impart his wisdom; as for me, I fear I am so kindly they will think that I pour out all I have to everyone, and not merely without pay—nay, rather, glad to offer something if it would induce someone to hear me. Well then, as I said just now, if they were going to laugh at me, as you say they do at you, it wouldn't be at all unpleasant to spend the time laughing and joking in court. But if they take the matter seriously, then there is no knowing how it will turn out. Only you prophets can tell!

EUTHYPHRO: Well, Socrates, perhaps no harm will come of it at all, but you will carry your case as you desire, and I think that I shall carry mine.

SOCRATES: Your case, Euthyphro? What is it? Are you prosecuting, or defending?

EUTHYPHRO: Prosecuting.

SOCRATES: Whom?

EUTHYPHRO: One whom I am thought a maniac to be attacking.   4

SOCRATES: How so? Is it someone who has wings to fly away with?

EUTHYPHRO: He is far from being able to do that; he happens to be old, a very old man.

SOCRATES: Who is it, then?

EUTHYPHRO: It is my father.

SOCRATES: Your father, my good friend?

EUTHYPHRO: Just so.

SOCRATES: What is the complaint? Of what do you accuse him?

EUTHYPHRO: Of murder, Socrates.

SOCRATES: Good heavens, Euthyphro! Surely the crowd is ignorant of the way   b
things ought to go. I fancy it is not correct for any ordinary person to do that [to prosecute his father on this charge], but only for a man already far advanced in point of
wisdom.

EUTHYPHRO: Yes, Socrates, by heaven! Far advanced!

SOCRATES: And the man your father killed, was he a relative of yours? Of course
he was? You never would prosecute your father, would you, for the death of anybody
who was not related to you?

EUTHYPHRO: You amuse me, Socrates. You think it makes a difference whether
the victim was a member of the family, or not related, when the only thing to watch is
whether it was right or not for the man who did the deed to kill him. If he was justified,
then let him go; if not, you have to prosecute him, no matter if the man who killed him
shares your hearth, and sits at table with you. The pollution is the same if, knowingly,   c
you associate with such a man, and do not cleanse yourself, and him as well, by bringing him to justice. The victim in this case was a laborer of mine, and when we were cul-
tivating land in Naxos, we employed him on our farm. One day he had been drinking,
and became enraged at one of our domestics, and cut his throat; whereupon my father
bound him hand and foot, and threw him into a ditch. Then he sent a man to Athens to
find out from the seer what ought to be done—meanwhile paying no attention to the
man who had been bound, neglecting him because he was a murderer and it would be
no great matter even if he died. And that was just what happened. Hunger, cold, and the
shackles finished him before the messenger got back from visiting the seer. That is why   d
my father and my other kin are bitter at me when I prosecute my father as a murderer.
They say he did not kill the man, and had he actually done it, the victim was himself a
murderer, and for such a man one need have no consideration. They say that for a son to
prosecute his father as a murderer is unholy. How ill they know divinity in its relation,
Socrates, to what is holy or unholy!   e

SOCRATES: But you, by heaven! Euthyphro, you think that you have such an accurate knowledge of things divine, and what is holy and unholy, that, in circumstances
such as you describe, you can accuse your father? You are not afraid that you yourself
are doing an unholy deed?

EUTHYPHRO: Why Socrates, if I did not have an accurate knowledge of all that, I
should be good for nothing, and Euthyphro would be no different from the general run   5
of men.

SOCRATES: Well then, admirable Euthyphro, the best thing I can do is to become
your pupil, and challenge Meletus before the trial comes on. Let me tell him that in the
past I have considered it of great importance to know about things divine, and that now,
when he asserts that I erroneously put forward my own notions and inventions on this
head, I have become your pupil. I could say, Come, Meletus, if you agree that Euthy-   b
phro has wisdom in such matters, you must admit as well that I hold the true belief, and

must not prosecute. If you do not, you must lodge your complaint, not against me, but against my aforesaid master; accuse him of corrupting the elder generation, me and his own father—me by his instruction, his father by correcting and chastising him.

And if he would not yield, would neither quit the suit nor yet indict you rather than myself, then I would say the same in court as when I challenged him!

c   EUTHYPHRO: Yes, Socrates, by heaven! If he undertook to bring me into court, I guess I would find out his rotten spot, and our talk there would concern him sooner by a long shot than ever it would me!

SOCRATES: Yes, my dear friend, that I know, and so I wish to be your pupil. This Meletus, I perceive, along presumably with everybody else, appears to overlook you, but sees into me so easily and keenly that he has attacked me for impiety. So, in the name of heaven, tell me now about the matter you just felt sure you knew quite thor-
d   oughly. State what you take piety and impiety to be with reference to murder and all other cases. Is not the holy always one and the same thing in every action, and, again, is not the unholy always opposite to the holy, and like itself? And as unholiness does it not always have its one essential form, which will be found in everything that is unholy?

EUTHYPHRO: Yes, surely, Socrates.

SOCRATES: Then tell me. How do you define the holy and the unholy?

EUTHYPHRO: Well then, I say that the holy is what I am now doing, prosecuting the wrongdoer who commits a murder or a sacrilegious robbery, or sins in any point like
e   that, whether it be your father, or your mother, or whoever it may be. And not to prose-cute would be unholy. And, Socrates, observe what a decisive proof I will give you that such is the law. It is one I have already given to others; I tell them that the right proce-dure must be not to tolerate the impious man, no matter who. Does not mankind believe that Zeus is the most excellent and just among the gods? And these same men admit that
6   Zeus shackled his own father [Cronus] for swallowing his [other] sons unjustly, and that Cronus in turn had gelded his father [Uranus] for like reasons. But now they are en-raged at me when I proceed against my father for wrongdoing, and so they contradict themselves in what they say about the gods and what they say of me.

SOCRATES: There, Euthyphro, you have the reason why the charge is brought against me. It is because, whenever people tell such stories about the gods, I am prone to take it ill, and, so it seems, that is why they will maintain that I am sinful. Well, now,
b   if you who are so well versed in matters of the sort entertain the same beliefs, then nec-essarily, it would seem, I must give in, for what could we urge who admit that, for our own part, we are quite ignorant about these matters? But, in the name of friendship, tell me! Do you actually believe that these things happened so?

EUTHYPHRO: Yes, Socrates, and things even more amazing, of which the multi-tude does not know.

SOCRATES: And you actually believe that war occurred among the gods, and there were dreadful hatreds, battles, and all sorts of fearful things like that? Such
c   things as the poets tell of, and good artists represent in sacred places; yes, and at the great Panathenaic festival the robe that is carried up to the Acropolis is all inwrought with such embellishments? What is our position, Euthyphro? Do we say that these things are true?

EUTHYPHRO: Not these things only, Socrates, but, as I just now said, I will, if you wish, relate to you many other stories about the gods, which I am certain will astonish you when you hear them.

SOCRATES: I shouldn't wonder. You shall tell me all about them when we have the leisure at some other time. At present try to tell me more clearly what I asked you a little while ago, for, my friend, you were not explicit enough before when I put the

a.

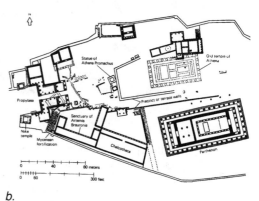

b.

c.

d.

The Acropolis and the Parthenon

a. The *Parthenon,* Athens, built 477–438 B.C. The Parthenon, dedicated
to Athena, patron deity of Athens, was at one period rededicated to the
Christian Virgin Mary and then later became a Turkish mosque. In 1687
a gunpowder explosion created the ruin we see today. The Doric shell
remains as a monument to ancient architectural engineering expertise
and to a sense of classical beauty and order. *(Greek National Tourist
Office Photo)*

b. Restored plan of the Acropolis, 400 B.C. The history of the Acropolis
is as varied as the style and size of the temples and buildings
constructed atop the ancient site.

c. This model of the Acropolis of Athens recreates the complexity of fifth
century B.C. public space, which included centers for worship, public
forum, and entertainment. *(Royal Ontario Museum, Toronto)*

d. Doric, Ionic, and Corinthian columns with their characteristic capitals.
(Library of Congress)

d   question. What is holiness? You merely said that what you are now doing is a holy deed—namely, prosecuting your father on a charge of murder.

EUTHYPHRO: And, Socrates, I told the truth.

SOCRATES: Possibly. But, Euthyphro, there are many other things that you will say are holy.

EUTHYPHRO: Because they are.

SOCRATES: Well, bear in mind that what I asked of you was not to tell me one or two out of all the numerous actions that are holy; I wanted you to tell me what is the essential form of holiness which makes all holy actions holy. I believe you held that there

e   is one ideal form by which unholy things are all unholy, and by which all holy things are holy. Do you remember that?

EUTHYPHRO: I do.

SOCRATES: Well then, show me what, precisely, this ideal is, so that, with my eye on it, and using it as a standard, I can say that any action done by you or anybody else is holy if it resembles this ideal, or, if it does not, can deny that it is holy.

EUTHYPHRO: Well, Socrates, if that is what you want, I certainly can tell you.

SOCRATES: It is precisely what I want.

7   EUTHYPHRO: Well then, what is pleasing to the gods is holy, and what is not pleasing to them is unholy.

SOCRATES: Perfect, Euthyphro! Now you give me just the answer that I asked for. Meanwhile, whether it is right I do not know, but obviously you will go on to prove your statement true.

EUTHYPHRO: Indeed I will.

SOCRATES: Come now, let us scrutinize what we are saying. What is pleasing to the gods, and the man that pleases them, are holy; what is hateful to the gods, and the man they hate, unholy. But the holy and unholy are not the same; the holy is directly opposite to the unholy. Isn't it so?

EUTHYPHRO: It is.

SOCRATES: And the matter clearly was well stated.

b   EUTHYPHRO: I accept it, Socrates; that was stated.

SOCRATES: Was it not also stated, Euthyphro, that the gods revolt and differ with each other, and that hatreds come between them?

EUTHYPHRO: That was stated.

SOCRATES: Hatred and wrath, my friend—what kind of disagreement will produce them? Look at the matter thus. If you and I were to differ about numbers, on the question which of two was the greater, would a disagreement about that make us angry

c   at each other, and make enemies of us? Should we not settle things by calculation, and so come to an agreement quickly on any point like that?

EUTHYPHRO: Yes, certainly.

SOCRATES: And similarly if we differed on a question of greater length or less, we would take a measurement, and quickly put an end to the dispute?

EUTHYPHRO: Just that.

SOCRATES: And so, I fancy, we should have recourse to scales, and settle any question about a heavier or lighter weight?

EUTHYPHRO: Of course.

SOCRATES: What sort of thing, then, is it about which we differ, till, unable to arrive at a decision, we might get angry and be enemies to one another? Perhaps you have

d   no answer ready, but listen to me. See if it is not the following—right and wrong, the noble and the base, and good and bad. Are not these the things about which we differ, till, unable to arrive at a decision, we grow hostile, when we do grow hostile, to each other, you and I and everybody else?

EUTHYPHRO: Yes, Socrates, that is where we differ, on these subjects.

SOCRATES: What about the gods, then, Euthyphro? If, indeed, they have dissensions, must it not be on these subjects?

EUTHYPHRO: Quite necessarily.

SOCRATES: Accordingly, my noble Euthyphro, by your account some gods take   e
one thing to be right, and others take another, and similarly with the honorable and the base, and good and bad. They would hardly be at variance with each other, if they did not differ on these questions. Would they?

EUTHYPHRO: You are right.

SOCRATES: And what each one of them thinks noble, good, and just, is what he loves, and the opposite is what he hates?

EUTHYPHRO: Yes, certainly.

SOCRATES: But it is the same things, so you say, that some of them think right, and others wrong, and through disputing about these they are at variance, and make war   8
on one another. Isn't it so?

EUTHYPHRO: It is.

SOCRATES: Accordingly, so it would seem, the same things will be hated by the gods and loved by them; the same things would alike displease and please them.

EUTHYPHRO: It would seem so.

SOCRATES: And so, according to this argument, the same things, Euthyphro, will be holy and unholy.

EUTHYPHRO: That may be.

SOCRATES: In that case, admirable friend, you have not answered what I asked you. I did not ask you to tell me what at once is holy and unholy, but it seems that what is pleasing to the gods is also hateful to them. Thus, Euthyphro, it would not be strange at all if   b
what you now are doing in punishing your father were pleasing to Zeus, but hateful to Cronus and Uranus, and welcome to Hephaestus, but odious to Hera, and if any other of the gods disagree about the matter, satisfactory to some of them, and odious to others.

EUTHYPHRO: But, Socrates, my notion is that, on this point, there is no difference of opinion among the gods—not one of them but thinks that if a person kills another wrongfully, he ought to pay for it.

SOCRATES: And what of men? Have you never heard a man contending that   c
someone who has killed a person wrongfully, or done some other unjust deed, ought not to pay the penalty?

EUTHYPHRO: Why! There is never any end to their disputes about these matters; it goes on everywhere, above all in the courts. People do all kinds of wrong, and then there is nothing they will not do or say in order to escape the penalty.

SOCRATES: Do they admit wrongdoing, Euthyphro, and, while admitting it, deny that they ought to pay the penalty?

EUTHYPHRO: No, not that, by any means.

SOCRATES: Then they will not do and say quite everything. Unless I am mistaken, they dare not say or argue that if they do wrong they should not pay the penalty. No, I think that they deny wrongdoing. How about it?   d

EUTHYPHRO: It is true.

SOCRATES: Therefore they do not dispute that anybody who does wrong should pay the penalty. No, the thing that they dispute about is likely to be who is the wrongdoer, what he did, and when.

EUTHYPHRO: That is true.

SOCRATES: Well then, isn't that precisely what goes on among the gods, if they really do have quarrels about right and wrong, as you say they do? One set will hold that some others do wrong, and the other set deny it? For that other thing, my friend, I take

e   it no one, whether god or man, will dare to say—that the wrongdoer should not pay the penalty!

EUTHYPHRO: Yes, Socrates, what you say is true—in the main.

SOCRATES: It is the individual act, I fancy, Euthyphro, that the disputants dispute about, both men and gods, if gods ever do dispute. They differ on a certain act; some hold that it was rightly done, the others that it was wrong. Isn't it so?

EUTHYPHRO: Yes, certainly.

9   SOCRATES: Then come, dear Euthyphro, teach me as well, and let me grow more wise. What proof have you that all the gods think that your servant died unjustly, your hireling, who, when he had killed a man, was shackled by the master of the victim, and perished, dying because of his shackles before the man who shackled him could learn from the seers what ought to be done with him? What proof have you that for a man like him it is right for a son to prosecute his father, and indict him on a charge of murder? Come on. Try to make it clear to me beyond all doubt that under these conditions the

b   gods must all consider this action to be right. If you can adequately prove it to me, I will never cease from praising you for your wisdom.

EUTHYPHRO: But, Socrates, that, very likely, would be no small task, although I could indeed make it very clear to you.

SOCRATES: I understand. You think that I am duller than the judges; obviously you will demonstrate to them that what your father did was wrong, and that the gods all hate such deeds.

EUTHYPHRO: I shall prove it absolutely, Socrates, if they will listen to me.

c   SOCRATES: They are sure to listen if they think that you speak well. But while you were talking, a notion came into my head, and I asked myself, Suppose that Euthyphro proved to me quite clearly that all the gods consider such a death unjust; would I have come one whit the nearer for him to knowing what the holy is, and what is the unholy? The act in question, seemingly, might be displeasing to the gods, but then we have just seen that you cannot define the holy and unholy in that way, for we have seen that a given thing may be displeasing, and also pleasing, to gods. So on this point, Euthyphro,

d   I will let you off; if you like, the gods shall all consider the act unjust, and they all shall hate it. But suppose that we now correct our definition, and say what the gods all hate is unholy, and what they love is holy, whereas what some of them love, and others hate, is either both or neither. Are you willing that we now define the holy and unholy in this way?

EUTHYPHRO: What is there to prevent us, Socrates?

SOCRATES: Nothing to prevent me, Euthyphro. As for you, see whether when you take this definition you can quite readily instruct me, as you promised.

e   EUTHYPHRO: Yes, I would indeed affirm that holiness is what the gods all love, and its opposite is what the gods all hate, unholiness.

SOCRATES: Are we to examine this position also, Euthyphro, to see if it is sound? Or shall we let it through, and thus accept our own and others' statement, and agree to an assertion simply when somebody says that a thing is so? Must we not look into what the speaker says?

EUTHYPHRO: We must. And yet, for my part, I regard the present statement as correct.

10   SOCRATES: We shall soon know better about that, my friend. Now think of this. Is

what is holy holy because the gods approve it, or do they approve it because it is holy?

EUTHYPHRO: I do not get your meaning.

SOCRATES: Well, I will try to make it clearer. We speak of what is carried and the carrier, do we not, of led and leader, of the seen and that which sees? And you understand that in all such cases the things are different, and how they differ?

EUTHYPHRO: Yes, I think I understand.

SOCRATES: In the same way what is loved is one thing, and what loves is another?

EUTHYPHRO: Of course.

SOCRATES: Tell me now, is what is carried "carried" because something carries it,   b
or is it for some other reason?

EUTHYPHRO: No, but for that reason.

SOCRATES: And what is led, because something leads it? And what is seen, because something sees it?

EUTHYPHRO: Yes, certainly.

SOCRATES: Then it is not because a thing is seen that something sees it, but just the opposite—because something sees it, therefore it is seen. Nor because it is led, that something leads it, but because something leads it, therefore it is led. Nor because it is carried, that something carries it, but because something carries it, therefore it is carried. Do you see what I wish to say, Euthyphro? It is this. Whenever an effect occurs, or something is effected, it is not the thing effected that gives rise to the effect; no, there is a cause, and   c
then comes this effect. Nor is it because a thing is acted on that there is this effect; no, there is a cause for what it undergoes, and then comes this effect. Don't you agree?

EUTHYPHRO: I do.

SOCRATES: Well then, when a thing is loved, is it not in process of becoming something, or of undergoing something, by some other thing?

EUTHYPHRO: Yes, certainly.

SOCRATES: Then the same is true here as in the previous cases. It is not because a thing is loved that they who love it love it, but it is loved because they love it.

EUTHYPHRO: Necessarily.

SOCRATES: Then what are we to say about the holy, Euthyphro? According to   d
your argument, is it not loved by all the gods?

EUTHYPHRO: Yes.

SOCRATES: Because it is holy, or for some other reason?

EUTHYPHRO: No, it is for that reason.

SOCRATES: And so it is because it is holy that it is loved; it is not holy because it is loved.

EUTHYPHRO: So it seems.

SOCRATES: On the other hand, it is beloved and pleasing to the gods just because they love it?

EUTHYPHRO: No doubt of that.

SOCRATES: So what is pleasing to the gods is not the same as what is holy, Euthyphro, nor, according to your statement, is the holy the same as what is pleasing to the gods. They are two different things.

EUTHYPHRO: How may that be, Socrates?   e

SOCRATES: Because we are agreed that the holy is loved because it is holy, and is not holy because it is loved. Isn't it so?

EUTHYPHRO: Yes.

SOCRATES: Whereas what is pleasing to the gods is pleasing to them just because they love it, such being its nature and its cause. Its being loved of the gods is not the reason of its being loved.

EUTHYPHRO: You are right.

SOCRATES: But suppose, dear Euthyphro, that what is pleasing to the gods and what is holy were not two separate things. In that case if holiness were loved because it was holy, then also what was pleasing to the gods would be loved because it pleased them. And, on the other hand, if what was pleasing to them pleased because they loved it, then also the holy would be holy because they loved it. But now you see that it is just the opposite, because the two are absolutely different from each other, for the one [what is pleasing to the gods] is of a sort to be loved because it is loved, whereas the other [what is holy] is loved because it is of a sort to be loved. Consequently, Euthyphro, it looks as if you had not given me my answer—as if when you were asked to tell the nature of the holy, you did not wish to explain the essence of it. You merely tell an attribute of it, namely, that it appertains to holiness to be loved by all the gods. What it is, as yet you have not said. So, if you please, do not conceal this from me. No, begin again. Say what the holy is, and never mind if gods do love it, nor if it has some other attribute; on that we shall not split. Come, speak out. Explain the nature of the holy and unholy.

EUTHYPHRO: Now, Socrates, I simply don't know how to tell you what I think. Somehow everything that we put forward keeps moving about us in a circle, and nothing will stay where we put it.

SOCRATES: Your statements, Euthyphro, look like the work of Daedalus, founder of my line. If I had made them, and they were my positions, no doubt you would poke fun at me, and say that, being in his line, the figures I construct in words run off, as did his statues, and will not stay where they are put. Meanwhile, since they are your definitions, we need some other jest, for in fact, as you see yourself, they will not stand still.

EUTHYPHRO: But, Socrates, it seems to me that the jest is quite to the point. This tendency in our statements to go in a circle, and not to stay in one place, it is not I who put it there. To my mind, it is you who are the Daedalus; so far as I am concerned, they would have held their place.

SOCRATES: If so, my friend, I must be more expert in his art than he, in that he merely made his own works capable of moving, whereas I give this power not merely to my own, but, seemingly, to the works of other men as well. And the rarest thing about my talent is that I am an unwilling artist, since I would rather see our arguments stand fast and hold their ground than have the art of Daedalus plus all the wealth of Tantalus to boot. But enough of this. And since, to my mind, you are languid, I will myself make bold with you to show how you might teach me about holiness. Do not weaken. See if you do not think that of necessity all that is holy is just.

EUTHYPHRO: Yes, I do.

SOCRATES: Well then, is all justice holy too? Or, granted that all holiness is just, is justice not all holy, but some part of it is holy, and some part of it is not?

EUTHYPHRO: I do not follow, Socrates.

SOCRATES: And yet you surpass me in your wisdom not less than by your youth. I repeat, you are languid through your affluence in wisdom. Come, lucky friend, exert yourself! What I have to say is not so hard to grasp. I mean the very opposite of what the poet wrote.

Zeus, who brought that all to pass, and made it all to grow,
You will not name, for where fear is, there too is reverence.

On that I differ from the poet. Shall I tell you why?

EUTHYPHRO: By all means.

SOCRATES: I do not think that "where fear is, there too is reverence." For it seems to me that there are many who fear sickness, poverty, and all the like, and so are afraid, but have no reverence whatever for the things they are afraid of. Does it not seem so to you?

EUTHYPHRO: Yes, certainly.

SOCRATES: Where, however, you have reverence, there you have fear as well. Is there anybody who has reverence and a sense of shame about an act, and does not at the same time dread and fear an evil reputation? c

EUTHYPHRO: Yes, he will be afraid of it.

SOCRATES: So it is not right to say that "where fear is, there too is reverence." No, you may say that where reverence is, there too is fear—not, however, that where fear is, there always you have reverence. Fear, I think, is wider in extent than reverence. Reverence is a part of fear, as the uneven is a part of number; thus you do not have the odd wherever you have number, but where you have the odd you must have number. I take it you are following me now?

EUTHYPHRO: Yes, indeed.

SOCRATES: Well then, what I asked you was like that. I asked you if wherever justice is, there is holiness as well; or, granted that wherever there is holiness, there is justice too, if where justice is, the holy is not always to be found. Thus holiness would d be a part of justice. Shall we say so, or have you a different view?

EUTHYPHRO: No, that is my opinion. I think that you are clearly right.

SOCRATES: Then see what follows. If holiness is a part of justice, it seems to me that we must find out what part of justice it is. Suppose, for instance, in our case just now, you had asked me what part of number is the even, and which the even number is. I would have said it is the one that corresponds to the isosceles, and not to the scalene. Does it not seem so to you?

EUTHYPHRO: It does.

SOCRATES: Then try to show me in this way what part of the just is holiness, so e that we may tell Meletus to cease from wronging me, and to give up prosecuting me for irreligion, because we have adequately learned from you of piety and holiness, and the reverse.

EUTHYPHRO: Well then, Socrates, I think that the part of justice which is religious and is holy is the part that has to do with the service of the gods; the remainder is the part of justice that has to do with the service of mankind.

SOCRATES: And what you say there, Euthyphro, to me seems excellent. There is one little point, however, on which I need more light. I am not yet quite clear about the 13 thing which you call "service." I suppose you do not mean the sort of care we give to other things. The "service" of the gods is not like that—the sort of thing we have in mind when we assert that it is not everybody who knows how to care for horses. It is the horseman that knows, is it not?

EUTHYPHRO: Yes, certainly.

SOCRATES: I suppose it is the special care that appertains to horses?

EUTHYPHRO: Yes.

SOCRATES: In the same way, it is not everyone who knows about the care of dogs; it is the huntsman.

EUTHYPHRO: True.

SOCRATES: The art of the huntsman is the care of dogs. b

EUTHYPHRO: Yes.

SOCRATES: And that of the herdsman is the care of cattle.

EUTHYPHRO: Yes, certainly.

SOCRATES: And in the same way, Euthyphro, holiness and piety mean caring for the gods? Do you say so?

EUTHYPHRO: I do.

SOCRATES: And so the aim of all this care and service is the same? I mean it thus. The care is given for the good and welfare of the object that is served. You see, for instance, how the horses that are cared for by the horseman's art are benefited and made better. Don't you think so?

EUTHYPHRO: Yes, I do.

SOCRATES: And so no doubt the dogs by the art of the huntsman, the cattle by that
c   of the herdsman, and in like manner all the rest. Unless, perhaps, you think that the care may tend to injure the object that is cared for?

EUTHYPHRO: By heaven, not I!

SOCRATES: The care aims at its benefit?

EUTHYPHRO: Most certainly.

SOCRATES: Then holiness, which is the service of the gods, must likewise aim to benefit the gods and make them better? Are you prepared to say that when you do a holy thing you make some deity better?

EUTHYPHRO: By heaven, not I!

SOCRATES: Nor do I fancy, Euthyphro, that you mean it so—far from it. No, it was on this account that I asked just what you meant by service of the gods, supposing
d   that, in fact, you did not mean that sort of care.

EUTHYPHRO: And, Socrates, you were right. I do not mean it so.

SOCRATES: Good. And now what kind of service of the gods will holiness be?

EUTHYPHRO: Socrates, it is the kind that slaves give to their masters.

SOCRATES: I understand. It seems to be a kind of waiting on the gods.

EUTHYPHRO: Just that.

SOCRATES: See if you can tell me this. The art which serves physicians, what result does it serve to produce? Don't you think that it is health?

EUTHYPHRO: I do.

e   SOCRATES: Further, what about the art that serves the shipwrights? What result does it serve to produce?

EUTHYPHRO: Obviously, Socrates, the making of a ship.

SOCRATES: And that which serves the builders serves the building of a house?

EUTHYPHRO: Yes.

SOCRATES: Now tell me, best of friends, about the service of the gods. What result will this art serve to produce? You obviously know, since you profess to be the best informed among mankind on things divine!

EUTHYPHRO: Yes, Socrates, I say so, and I tell the truth.

SOCRATES: Then tell me, I adjure you, what is that supreme result which the gods produce when they employ our services?

EUTHYPHRO: They do many things and noble, Socrates.

14   SOCRATES: Just as the generals do, my friend. All the same you would have no trouble in summing up what they produce, by saying it is victory in war. Isn't it so?

EUTHYPHRO: Of course.

SOCRATES: And the farmers too, I take it, produce many fine results, but the net result of their production is the food they get from the earth.

EUTHYPHRO: Yes, surely.

SOCRATES: Well now, of the many fine and noble things which the gods produce, what is the sum of their production?

EUTHYPHRO: Just a little while ago I told you, Socrates, that the task is not a light

one to learn precisely how all these matters stand. I will, however, simply tell you this.   b
If anyone knows how to say and do things pleasing to the gods in prayer and sacrifice,
that is holiness, and such behavior saves the family in private life together with the
common interests of the state. To do the opposite of things pleasing to the gods is impious, and this it is that upsets all and ruins everything.

SOCRATES: Surely, Euthyphro, if you had wished, you could have summed up
what I asked for much more briefly. But the fact is that you are not eager to instruct me.   c
That is clear. But a moment since, you were on the very point of telling me—and you
slipped away. Had you given the answer, I would now have learned from you what holiness is, and would be content. As it is—for perforce the lover must follow the loved
one wherever he leads the way—once more, how do you define the holy, and what is
holiness? Don't you say that it is a science of sacrifice and prayer?

EUTHYPHRO: I do.

SOCRATES: Well, and is not sacrifice a giving to the gods, and prayer an asking
them to give?

EUTHYPHRO: Precisely, Socrates.

SOCRATES: By this reasoning, holiness would be the science of asking from the   d
gods and giving to them.

EUTHYPHRO: Quite right, Socrates; you have caught my meaning perfectly.

SOCRATES: Yes, my friend, for I have my heart set on your wisdom, and give my
mind to it, so that nothing you say shall be lost. No, tell me, what is this service to the
gods? You say it is to ask of them and give to them?

EUTHYPHRO: I do.

SOCRATES: And hence to ask aright will be to ask them for those things of which
we stand in need from them?

EUTHYPHRO: What else?

SOCRATES: And, on the other hand, to give aright will be to give them in return   e
those things which they may need to receive from us? I take it there would be no art in
offering anyone a gift of something that he did not need.

EUTHYPHRO: True, Socrates.

SOCRATES: And therefore, Euthyphro, holiness will be a mutual art of commerce
between gods and men.

EUTHYPHRO: An art of commerce, if you like to call it so.

SOCRATES: Well, I do not like it if it is not so. But tell me, what advantage could
come to the gods from the gifts which they receive from us? Everybody sees what they
give us. No good that we possess but is given by them. What advantage can they gain   15
by what they get from us? Have we so much the better of them in this commerce that we
get all good things from them, and they get nothing from us?

EUTHYPHRO: What! Socrates. Do you suppose that the gods gain anything by
what they get from us?

SOCRATES: If not, then what would be the meaning, Euthyphro, of these gifts to
the gods from us?

EUTHYPHRO: What do you think they ought to mean but worship, honor, and, as I
just now said, good will?

SOCRATES: So, Euthyphro, the holy is what pleases them, not what is useful to   b
them, nor yet what the gods love?

EUTHYPHRO: I believe that what gives them pleasure is precisely what they love.

SOCRATES: And so once more, apparently the holy is that which the gods love.

EUTHYPHRO: Most certainly.

SOCRATES: After that, will you be amazed to find your statements walking off,

and not staying where you put them? And will you accuse me as the Daedalus who makes them move, when you are yourself far more expert than Daedalus, and make them go round in a circle? Don't you see that our argument has come full circle to the point where it began? Surely you have not forgotten how in what was said before we
c found that holiness and what is pleasing to the gods were not the same, but different from each other. Do you not remember?

EUTHYPHRO: I do.

SOCRATES: And are you not aware now that you say that what the gods love is holy? But is not what the gods love just the same as what is pleasing to the gods?

EUTHYPHRO: Yes, certainly.

SOCRATES: Well then, either we were wrong in our recent conclusion, or if that was right, our position now is wrong.

EUTHYPHRO: So it seems.

SOCRATES: And so we must go back again, and start from the beginning to find out what the holy is. As for me, I never will give up until I know. Ah! Do not spurn me,
d but give your mind with all your might now at length to tell me the absolute truth, for if anybody knows, of all mankind, it is you, and one must not let go of you, you Proteus, until you tell. If you did not know precisely what is holy and unholy, it is unthinkable that for a simple hireling you ever would have moved to prosecute your aged sire on a charge of murder. No, you would have feared to risk the wrath of the gods on the chance that you were not doing right, and would have been afraid of the talk of men. But now I
e am sure that you think you know exactly what is holy and what is not. So tell me, peerless Euthyphro, and do not hide from me what you judge it to be.

EUTHYPHRO: Another time, then, Socrates, for I am in a hurry, and must be off this minute.

SOCRATES: What are you doing, my friend? Will you leave, and dash me down from the mighty expectation I had of learning from you what is holy and what is not,
16 and so escaping from Meletus' indictment? I counted upon showing him that now I had gained wisdom about things divine from Euthyphro, and no longer out of ignorance made rash assertions and forged innovations with regard to them, but would lead a better life in future.

APOLOGY

17 Well, I don't know what effect the prosecution has had on you, men of Athens. As far as I'm concerned, they made me all but forget the position I am in, they spoke so plausibly. And yet, to all intents and purposes, there was not a word of truth in what they said.

Of their many lies, one in particular filled me with amazement. They said you should be careful to avoid being led astray by my "skill in speaking." They were not in the least embarrassed at the prospect of being immediately proved wrong by my actual
b performance, when it becomes clear that I am not in the least skilled in speaking. That

was what I found the most shameless thing about their behaviour—unless of course they call "skilled in speaking" someone who merely speaks the truth. If *that's* what they mean, then I would agree that I am in a different class from them as an orator.

As I say, they have told you little or nothing that was true, whereas from me you will hear the whole truth—certainly not a piece of polished rhetoric like theirs, men of Athens, with its words and phrases so cleverly arranged. No, the speech you are going to hear from me will use everyday language, arranged in a straightforward way—after all, I have confidence in the justice of what I have to say—so I hope no-one is expecting anything different. And I shall tell the truth, because it wouldn't be appropriate to appear before you at my age making up stories like a schoolboy.

However, there is one important request and concession I am going to ask of you, men of Athens. If you hear me making my defence in the same language I generally use in the city, among people doing business—where many of you have heard me—and elsewhere, do not be surprised on that account, or start interrupting. The reason for it is this. This is the first time I have ever appeared in court, though I am now seventy years of age. The kind of speaking practised here is, quite simply, foreign to me. Imagine I really were a foreigner; you wouldn't hold it against me, presumably, if I spoke in the dialect and manner in which I had been brought up. In the same way now, I make this request—justified, in my view—that you pay no attention to the manner in which I speak, be it inferior or superior. Please consider one point only, and focus your attention on that. Is there any justice in what I have to say, or not? That, after all, is the function of a member of the jury; the speaker's task is to tell the truth.

First of all, then, men of Athens, I am entitled to defend myself against the earliest false accusations made against me, and against my earliest accusers; after that against the more recent falsehoods, and my present accusers. After all, there have been many people, over the years, making accusations about me to you, and speaking not a word of truth. I fear them more than I fear Anytus and his supporters, dangerous though they are as well. But the earlier ones are more dangerous, gentlemen. They took you in hand from childhood, for the most part, and tried to win you over, making accusations every bit as false as these today; they told you there was this man Socrates, an intellectual, a thinker about the heavens, an expert on everything under the earth, a man who could make the weaker argument the stronger.

These people, men of Athens, the ones who have saddled me with this reputation, are my most dangerous accusers, because those who listen to them think that students of these subjects do not recognise the gods. What's more, there are a great many of these accusers, and they have been accusing me for a long time now. And thirdly, they were speaking to you at the age when you were most likely to believe them, when many of you were children and adolescents. Quite simply, they were prosecuting in an uncontested case, since there was no-one there to answer their charges.

What is particularly unfair is that I cannot even know, or tell you, their names—unless maybe one of them is a writer of comedies. But all those who tried to influence you, out of spite and malice, together with those who were trying to influence others because they were genuinely convinced themselves—all these accusers are very hard to deal with. It is not possible to call any of them as a witness here, or cross-examine them; I just have to make my defence like someone shadow-boxing, and conduct my cross-examination with no-one there to answer.

So I hope you will accept my claim that I have two sets of accusers—the ones who have just now brought this case against me, and the ones from way back, the ones I have been telling you about. Please believe also that I must make my defence against this second set first; after all, you heard their accusations at an earlier age, and on many more occasions, than you heard the later ones.

19 Very well. I must make my defence, men of Athens, and try to remove from your minds, in the very brief time available, the prejudice which you have so long held. I hope that is how things will turn out, provided it really *is* the best outcome for you and for me, and that I shall achieve something by my defence. But I think it is difficult, and I am well aware of the magnitude of the task. Still, let it turn out as god wills, I must obey the law, and make my defence.

b Let us go back to the beginning, then, and see what the accusation is which has created this prejudice against me—the prejudice which Meletus was presumably counting on when he brought this case against me. What exactly did the originators of this prejudice say? We ought really to read out a sworn statement from them, just like the prosecution's. "Socrates is guilty of being a busybody. He enquires into things under the earth and in the heavens, and makes the weaker argument the stronger, and he

c teaches these same things to other people." That's roughly how it goes. You saw it for yourselves in Aristophanes' comedy; you saw a Socrates there, swinging round and round, claiming he was walking on air, and spouting a whole lot of other drivel on subjects about which I make not the slightest claim to knowledge. Not that I have anything against knowledge of this kind, if anyone is an expert on such subjects; I hope Meletus will never bring enough cases against me to reduce me to that. No, it's just that I myself have no share in such knowledge.

Once again, I can call most of you as witnesses. I'm sure you can make the posi-
d tion clear to one another, and explain, those of you who have ever heard me talking—and a lot of you come in that category. Tell one another then, if any of you has ever heard me breathe so much as a word on such topics. That will help you to see that the rest of what is generally said about me has as little foundation.

No, there is no truth in these stories. And if anyone has told you that I undertake to educate people, or that I make money out of it, there is equally little truth in that ei-
e ther. Mind you, if anyone *can* educate people—as Gorgias from Leontini can, or Prodicus from Ceos, or Hippias from Elis—then that seems to me to be a fine thing. Any of these men, gentlemen, can go to any city and persuade the young men, who are at liberty to spend their time, free of charge, with whichever of their fellow-citizens they
20 choose, to abandon the company of those fellow-citizens and spend time with him instead—*and* pay money to do so, *and* be grateful into the bargain.

Come to that, there is even one of them here, a wise man from Paros. I found out he was living in Athens when I ran into Callias, the son of Hipponicus, the man who has paid more money to these teachers than everyone else put together. I asked him—you
b know he has two sons—"Callias," I said, "if your sons were colts or calves, we would be able to find and employ someone to look after them, someone who would turn them into outstanding examples of their particular species; and this person would be a trainer or farmer of some kind. But they aren't colts or calves; they are men. Whom do you propose to find to look after them? Who is an expert in this kind of excellence—the excellence of a human being and a citizen? I imagine, since you have sons, you must have thought about this question. Is there someone," I asked him, "or not?"

"There certainly is," he said.

"Who is he?" I said. "Where is he from? What does he charge?"

"Evenus," he said. "He is from Paros, Socrates, and he charges 500 drachmas."

I took my hat off to Evenus, if he really did have this ability, and yet taught for so
c reasonable a fee. I wouldn't. I'd start giving myself airs, and become extremely choosy, if I had this kind of knowledge. But I don't have it, men of Athens.

I can imagine one of you interrupting me, and saying, "That's all very well, Socrates; but what *do* you do? Where have all these prejudices against you come from? I take it all this gossip and rumour about you is not the result of your behaving just like anyone else. You must be doing *something* out of the ordinary. Tell us what it is, so we can avoid jumping to conclusions about you." This seems to me to be a valid point, so   d
I'll try and explain to you what it is that has given me my reputation and created the prejudice against me. Give me a hearing. It may seem to some of you that I am not being serious, but I promise you, every word I say will be the truth.

I have gained this reputation, men of Athens, as a direct result of a kind of wisdom. What sort of wisdom? The sort we might perhaps call human wisdom. In fact, if we are talking about this kind of wisdom, I probably *am* wise. The men I mentioned just   e
now may well be wise with some more-than-human wisdom; I don't know how else to describe it. It's not a wisdom *I* know anything about. Anyone who says I do is lying, and trying to increase the prejudice against me.

Please do not interrupt me, men of Athens, even if you find what I say a little bit boastful. The claim I'm about to make is not *my* claim; I shall appeal to a reliable authority. I shall call the god at Delphi to give evidence to you about my wisdom; he can tell you if I really do possess any, and what it is like.

You remember Chaerephon, I imagine. He was a friend of mine, from an early age, and a friend of most of you. He shared your recent exile, and returned from exile   21
with you. You know what Chaerephon was like, how impetuous he was when he set about something. And sure enough, he went to Delphi one day, and went so far as to put this question to the oracle—I repeat, please do not interrupt, gentlemen—he asked if there was anyone wiser than me; and the priestess of Apollo replied that there was no-one wiser. His brother here will give evidence to you about this, since Chaerephon himself is dead.

Let me remind you of my reason for telling you this. I am trying to show you the   b
origin of the prejudice against me. When I heard the priestess's reply, my reaction was this: "What on earth is the god saying? What is his hidden meaning? I'm well aware that I have no wisdom, great or small. So what can he mean by saying that I am so wise? He can't be lying; he's not allowed to." I spent a long time wondering what he could mean. Finally, with great reluctance, I decided to verify his claim. What I did was this: I approached one of those who seemed to be wise, thinking that there, if anywhere, I could prove the reply wrong, and say quite clearly to the oracle, "This man is wiser than I am,   c
whereas you said that I was the wisest."

So I examined this man—there's no need for me to mention his name, let's just say he was a politician—and the result of my examination, men of Athens, and of my conversations with him, was this. I decided that although the man seemed to many people, and above all to himself, to be wise, in reality he was not wise. I tried to demonstrate to him that he thought he was wise, but actually was not, and as a result I made an enemy of him, and of many of those present. To myself, as I left him, I reflected; "Here   d
is *one* man less wise than I. In all probability neither of us knows anything worth knowing; but he *thinks* he knows when he doesn't, whereas I, given that I don't in fact know, am at least *aware* I don't know. Apparently, therefore, I am wiser than him in just this one small detail, that when I don't know something, I don't *think* I know it either." From him I went to another man, one of those who seemed wiser than the first. I came to exactly the same conclusion, and made an enemy of him and of many others besides.   e

After that I began approaching people in a systematic way. I could see, with regret and alarm, that I was making enemies, yet I thought it was essential to take the god seriously. So on I had to go, in my enquiry into the meaning of the oracle, to everyone

22   who seemed to have any knowledge. And I swear to you, men of Athens—after all, I am
bound to tell you the truth—what I found was this. Those with the highest reputations
seemed to me to be pretty nearly the most useless, if I was trying to find out the meaning of what the god had said, whereas others, who appeared of less account, were a
much better bet when it came to thinking sensibly.

   I can best give an account of my quest by likening it to a set of labours—and all,
as it turned out, to satisfy myself of the accuracy of the oracle. After the politicians I
b   went to the writers—writers of plays, and songs, and the rest of them. That would be an
open-and-shut case, I thought. I should easily show myself up as less wise than them.
So I took to reading their works, the ones which struck me as showing the greatest skill
in composition, and asking them what they meant; I hoped to learn from them.

   Well, I'm embarrassed to tell you the truth, gentlemen; but I must tell you. Practically anyone present could have given a better account than they did of the works they
c   had themselves written. As a result, I quickly came to a decision about the writers too,
in their turn. I realised that their achievements are not the result of wisdom, but of natural talent and inspiration, like fortune-tellers and clairvoyants, who also say many striking things, but have no idea at all of the meaning of what they say. Writers, I felt, were
clearly in the same position. Moreover, I could see that their works encouraged them to
think that they were the wisest of men in other areas where they were not wise. So I left
them too feeling that I had got the better of them, in the same way as I had got the better of the politicians.

   Finally I went to the craftsmen. I was well aware that I knew virtually nothing,
d   and confident that I would find much fine knowledge in them. Nor was I disappointed.
They *did* know things which I didn't know; in this respect they were wiser than I was.
However, our good friends the skilled workmen seemed also to me, men of Athens, to
have the same failing as the writers. Each one, because of his skill in practising his craft,
e   thought himself extremely wise in other matters of importance as well; and this pre-
sumptuousness of theirs seemed to me to obscure the wisdom they did have. So I asked
myself, on behalf of the oracle, whether I should accept being the way I was—without
any of their wisdom, or any of their foolishness—or whether I ought to possess both the
qualities they possessed. The answer I gave myself and the oracle was that it was best
for me to remain as I was.

   This survey, men of Athens, has aroused much hostility against me, of the most
23   damaging and serious kind. The result has been a great deal of prejudice, and in particular, this description of me as being "wise." That is because the people who were present on such occasions think that I am an expert myself on those subjects in which I de-
molish the claims of others. The truth probably is, gentlemen, that in reality god is wise,
and that what he means by his reply to Chaerephon is that human wisdom is of little or
no value. When he refers to the man here before you—to Socrates—and goes out of his
b   way to use my name, he is probably using me as an example, as if he were saying "That
man is the wisest among you, mortals, who realises, as Socrates does, that he doesn't really amount to much when it comes to wisdom."

   That's why, to this day, I go round investigating and enquiring, as the god would
have me do, if I think anyone—Athenian or foreigner—is wise. And when I find he is
not, then, in support of the god, I demonstrate that he is not wise. My preoccupation
with this task has left me no time worth speaking of to take any part in public life or
family life. Instead I live in extreme poverty as a result of my service to the god.

c   Another problem is that young people follow me—the ones with the most time at
their disposal, the sons of the rich—of their own free will; they love listening to people being cross-examined. They often imitate me themselves, and have a go at cross-

examining others. Nor do I imagine they have any difficulty in finding people who think they know something, when in fact they know little or nothing. The result is that the victims of their cross-examination are angry with me, rather than themselves; they say Socrates is some sort of criminal, and that he has a bad influence on the young. When you ask them what I do and what I teach that makes me a criminal, they can't answer; they don't know. But since they don't want to lose face, they come out with the standard accusations made against all philosophers, the stuff about "things in heaven and things under the earth," and "not recognising the gods" and "making the weaker argument stronger." The truth, I think, they would refuse to admit, which is that they have been shown up as pretenders to knowledge who really know nothing. Since, therefore, they are ambitious and energetic, and there are a lot of them, and since they speak forcibly and persuasively about me, they have been filling your ears for some time now, and most vigorously, with their attacks on me.

d

e

That is what Meletus relied on when he brought this charge against me, with Anytus and Lycon—Meletus feeling offended as one of the poets, Anytus as one of the craftsmen and politicians, Lycon as one of the orators. The result, as I said at the beginning, is that it would surprise me if I were able to remove from your minds, in so short a time, a prejudice which has grown so strong. This is the truth, I assure you, men of Athens. I speak with absolutely no concealment or reservation. I'm pretty sure it's this way of speaking which makes me unpopular. My unpopularity is the proof that I am speaking the truth, that this *is* the prejudice against me, and these *are* the reasons for it. You can enquire into these matters—now or later—and you will find them to be so.

24

b

So much for the accusations made by my first group of accusers. I hope you'll find what I've said a satisfactory defence against them. Now let me try and defend myself against Meletus, that excellent patriot (as he claims) and my more recent accusers. Let's treat them as a separate prosecution, and consider in its turn the charge brought by them. It runs something like this: it says that Socrates is guilty of being a bad influence on the young, and of not recognising the gods whom the state recognises, but practising a new religion of the supernatural.

That's what the charge consists of. Let's examine this charge point by point. He says I am guilty of having a bad influence on the young. But *I* claim, men of Athens, that Meletus is guilty of playing games with what is deadly serious; he is too quick to bring people to trial, pretending to be serious and care about things to which he has never given a moment's thought. That this is the truth, I will try to prove to you as well. Come now, Meletus, tell me this. I take it you regard the well-being of the young as of the utmost importance?

c

d

MELETUS: I do.

SOCRATES: In that case, please tell these people who it is who is a good influence on the young. Obviously you must know, since you're so concerned about it. You've tracked down, so you say, the man who is a bad influence—me—and are bringing me here before these people and accusing me. So come on, tell them who is a good influence; point out to them who it is.

You see, Meletus? You are silent; you have nothing to say. Don't you think that's a disgrace, and a sufficient proof of what I am saying—that you haven't given it any thought? Tell us, my friend, who is a good influence?

MELETUS: The laws.

e

SOCRATES: Brilliant! But that's not what I'm asking. The question is what *man*—who will of course start off with just this knowledge, the laws.

MELETUS: These men, Socrates, the members of the jury.

SOCRATES: Really, Meletus? These men are capable of educating the young and being a good influence on them?

MELETUS: They certainly are.

SOCRATES: All of them? Or are some capable, and others not?

MELETUS: All of them.

25   SOCRATES: How remarkably fortunate—no shortage of benefactors there, then. What about the spectators in court? Do they have a good influence, or not?

MELETUS: Yes, they do, as well.

SOCRATES: What about the members of the council?

MELETUS: Yes, the members of the council also.

SOCRATES: But surely, Meletus, the people in the assembly—the citizens meeting *as* the assembly—surely they don't have a bad influence on the young? Don't they too—all of them—have a good influence?

MELETUS: Yes, they do too.

SOCRATES: Apart from me, then, the entire population of Athens, as it appears, makes the young into upright citizens. I alone am a bad influence. Is that what you mean?

MELETUS: Yes, that's exactly what I mean.

b   SOCRATES: That's certainly a great misfortune to charge me with. Answer me this, though: do you think the situation is the same with horses as well? Do the people who are good for them make up the entire population, and is there just one person who has a harmful effect on them? Isn't it the exact opposite? Isn't there just one person, or very few people—trainers—capable of doing them any good? Don't most people, if they spend time with horses, or have anything to do with them, have a harmful effect on them? Isn't that the situation, Meletus, both with horses and with all other living creatures?

It certainly is, whether you and Anytus deny it or admit it. After all, it would be a piece of great good fortune for the young, if only one person has a bad influence on them, and everyone else has a good influence. No, Meletus. You show quite clearly that

c   you have never cared in the slightest for the young; you reveal your own lack of interest quite plainly, since you've never given a moment's thought to the things you're prosecuting me for.

Another point. Tell us honestly, Meletus, is it better to live with good fellow-citizens, or with bad? Answer, can't you? It's not a difficult question. Isn't it true that bad citizens do some harm to those who are their neighbours at any particular time, while good citizens do some good?

MELETUS: Yes, of course.

SOCRATES: That being so, does anyone choose to be harmed by those close to him

d   rather than be helped by them? Answer, there's a good fellow. Besides, the law requires you to answer. Is there anyone who chooses to be harmed?

MELETUS: No, of course not.

SOCRATES: Well, then. You bring me to court for being a bad influence on the young, and making them worse people. Are you saying I do this deliberately, or without realising it?

MELETUS: Deliberately, I'm sure of it.

SOCRATES: Really, Meletus? How odd. Are you, at your age, so much wiser than me at mine? Are *you* aware that bad people generally have a harmful effect on those

e   they come into contact with, and that good people have a good effect? And have *I* reached such a height of stupidity as not even to realise that if I make one of my neighbours a worse man, I'm likely to come to some harm at his hands? And is the result that

I deliberately do such great damage as you describe? On this point I don't believe you, Meletus; and nor, I think, does anyone else. No. Either I'm not a bad influence on the young, or if I do have a bad influence, I do so without realising it. Either way you are wrong. And if I have a bad influence without realising it, it's not our custom to bring people here to court for errors of this sort, but to take them on one side, and instruct them privately, pointing out their mistakes. Obviously, if I'm taught, I shall stop doing what I don't at the moment realise I *am* doing. But you avoided spending time with me and instructing me; you refused to do it. Instead you bring me here to court, where it is our custom to bring those who need punishment, not those who need to learn.

I needn't go on, men of Athens. It must now be clear, as I've said, that Meletus has never given the slightest thought to these matters. All the same, Meletus, tell us this: *in what way* do you claim I'm a bad influence on the young? Isn't it obvious I do it in the way described in the charge you've brought against me—by teaching them not to recognise the gods the city recognises, but to practise this new religion of the supernatural instead? Isn't that your claim, that it's by teaching them these things that I have a bad influence?

MELETUS: Yes, that certainly is exactly what I claim.

SOCRATES: Well then, Meletus, in the name of these gods we are now talking about, make yourself a little clearer, both to me and to these gentlemen here, since *I* at least cannot understand you. Do you mean I teach them to accept that there are *some* gods—not the gods the state accepts, but other gods? In that case I myself must also accept that there are gods, so I am not a complete atheist, and am not guilty on that count. Is this what you charge me with, accepting other gods? Or are you saying that I don't myself recognise any gods at all, and that I teach the same beliefs to others?

MELETUS: Yes, that's what I am saying. You don't recognise any gods at all.

SOCRATES: Meletus, you are beyond belief. What can possess you to say that? Don't I accept that the sun and moon are gods, in the same way as everyone else does?

MELETUS: Good heavens, no, men of the jury. He says the sun is a stone, and the moon is made of earth.

SOCRATES: Is it Anaxagoras you think you're accusing, my dear Meletus? Do you have such contempt for these men here? Do you think them so illiterate as to be unaware that the works of Anaxagoras of Clazomenae are stuffed full of speculations of that sort? And do the young really learn these things from me, when there are often books on sale, for a drachma at the very most, in the Orchestra, in the Agora? They can laugh at Socrates if he claims these views as his own—especially such eccentric views. However, as god is your witness, is that your view of me? Do I not accept the existence of any god at all?

MELETUS: No, in god's name, no god at all.

SOCRATES: What you say is unbelievable, Meletus—even, I think to yourself. This man here, men of Athens, strikes me as an arrogant lout; his prosecution of me is prompted entirely by arrogance, loutishness, and youth. It's as if he were setting a trick question, to test me: "Will Socrates the wise realise that I'm playing with words and contradicting myself, or will I deceive him and the others who hear it?" He certainly seems to me to contradict himself, in his accusation. He might as well say "Socrates is guilty of not recognising the gods, but recognising the gods instead." And that is not a serious proposition.

Please join me, gentlemen, in examining the reasons why I think this is what his accusation amounts to. You, Meletus, answer us. And you *(to the jurymen),* as I asked you at the beginning, remember not to interrupt me if I construct my argument in my usual way.

Is there anyone in the world, Meletus, who accepts the existence of human activity, but not of human beings? He must answer, gentlemen. Don't allow him to keep making all these interruptions. Is there anyone who denies horses, but accepts equine activity? Or denies the existence of flute-players, but accepts flute-playing? No, my very good friend, there isn't. If you refuse to answer, then I'll say it—to you and everyone else present here. But do answer my next question: is there anyone who accepts the

c   activity of the supernatural, but denies supernatural beings?

MELETUS: No, there isn't.

SOCRATES: How kind of you—forced to answer, against your will, by these people here. Very well, then. You claim that I practise and teach a religion of the supernatural—whether of a new or conventional kind—so I do at least, on your own admission, accept the existence of the supernatural. You even swore to it, on oath, in your indictment. But if I accept the supernatural, it follows, I take it, that I must necessarily admit the existence of supernatural beings, must I not? I must; I take your silence for agreement. And don't we regard supernatural beings as either gods or the children of gods?

d   Yes or no?

MELETUS: We certainly do.

SOCRATES: In that case, if I accept supernatural beings—as you admit—and if supernatural beings are gods of some sort, then you can see what I mean when I say that you are setting trick questions, and playing with words, claiming first that I do *not* believe in gods, and then again claiming that I *do* believe in gods, since I do believe in supernatural beings. If, on the other hand, supernatural beings are some form of illegitimate children of gods—born of nymphs or of some of the other mothers they are said to be born from—who on earth could believe that there are children of gods, but no gods?

e   It would be as absurd as saying you believed there were such things as mules, the offspring of horses and donkeys, but didn't believe there were horses and donkeys.

No, Meletus, the only possible explanation for your bringing this accusation against me is that you wanted to test us—or that you didn't have any genuine offence to charge me with. There's no conceivable way you could persuade anyone in the world with a grain of intelligence that belief in the supernatural and the divine does not imply

28   belief in supernatural beings, divine beings and heroes.

So much for that, men of Athens. I don't think it takes much of a defence to show that in the terms of Meletus' indictment I am not guilty. What I have said so far should be enough. There remains what I said in the earlier part of my speech, that there is strong and widespread hostility towards me. Be in no doubt that this is true. It is this which will convict me, if it does convict me—not Meletus, not Anytus, but the preju-

b   dice and malice of the many. What has convicted many other good men before me will, I think, convict me too. There's no danger of its stopping at me.

That being so, you might ask "Well, Socrates, aren't you ashamed of living a life which has resulted in your now being on trial for your life?" I would answer you, quite justifiably, "You are wrong, sir, if you think that a man who is worth anything at all should take into account the chances of life and death. No, the only thing he should think about, when he acts, is whether he is acting rightly or wrongly, and whether this is

c   the behaviour of a good man or a bad man. After all, if we accept your argument, those of the demigods who died at Troy would have been sorry creatures—and none more so than Achilles, the son of Thetis. Compared with the threat of dishonour, he regarded danger as of no importance at all. When he was eager to kill Hector, his mother, who was a goddess, said something like this to him, I imagine: 'My son, if you avenge the death of your friend Patroclus, and kill Hector, you will yourself be killed, since death awaits you immediately after Hector.' When Achilles heard this, he gave no thought to death or danger; what he feared much more was living as a coward, and not avenging his friends. 'Let me die immediately,' he said, 'after making the wrongdoer pay the penalty, rather than remain here by the curved ships, a laughing-stock, like a clod of earth.' You don't imagine *he* gave any thought to death or danger." d

That's the way of things, men of Athens, it really is. Where a man takes up his position—in the belief that it is the best position—or is told to take up a position by his commanding officer, there he should stay, in my view, regardless of danger. He should not take death into account, or anything else apart from dishonour. As for me, when the commanders whom you chose to command me told me to take up position at Potidaea and Amphipolis and Delium, on those occasions I stayed where they posted me, just like anyone else, and risked death. Would it not have been very illogical of me, when *god* deployed me, as I thought and believed, to live my life as a philosopher, examining myself and others, then to be afraid of death—or anything else at all—and abandon my post? e

It would indeed be illogical, and in that case you would certainly be completely justified in bringing me to court for not accepting the existence of the gods, since I disobey their oracle, and am afraid of death, and think I am wise when I am not. After all, the fear of death is just that, gentlemen—thinking one is wise when one is not—since it's a claim to know what one doesn't know. For all anyone knows, death may in fact be the best thing in the world that can happen to a man; yet men fear it as if they had certain knowledge that it is the greatest of all evils. This is without doubt the most reprehensible folly—the folly of thinking one knows what one does not know. 29 b

As for me, gentlemen, perhaps here too I *am* different from most people, in this one particular; and if I did claim to be in any way wiser than anyone else, it would be in this, that lacking any certain knowledge of what happens after death, I am also aware that I have no knowledge. But that it is evil and shameful to do wrong, and disobey one's superiors, divine or human, that I *do* know. Compared therefore with the evils which I know to be evils, I shall never fear, or try to avoid, what for all I know may turn out to be good.

Suppose you now acquit me, rejecting Anytus' argument that either this case should not have been brought in the first place, or, since it *had* been brought, that it was out of the question not to put me to death. He told you that if I got away with it, your sons would all start putting Socrates' teachings into practice, and be totally overwhelmed by my bad influence. And suppose your response were to say to me: "Socrates, on this occasion we will not do what Anytus wants. We acquit you—on this condition, however, that you give up spending your time in this enquiry, and give up the search for wisdom. If you are caught doing it again, you will be put to death." c

Even if, then, to repeat, you were to acquit me on these conditions, I would say to you, "Men of Athens, I have the highest regard and affection for you, but I will obey god rather than you. While I have breath and strength, I will not give up the search for wisdom. I will carry on nagging at you, and pointing out your errors to those of you I meet from day to day. I shall say, in my usual way, 'My very good sir, you are a citizen of Athens, a city which is the greatest and most renowned for wisdom and power. Aren't you ashamed to care about money, and how to make as much of it as possible, and about reputation and public recognition, whereas for wisdom and truth, and making your soul as good as it can possibly be, you do not care, and give no thought to these things at all?' And if any of you objects, and says he does care, I shall not just let him go, or walk away and leave him. No, I shall question him, cross-examine him, try to prove him wrong. And if I find he has not achieved a state of excellence, but still claims d e

30   he has, then I shall accuse him of undervaluing what is most important, and paying too
much attention to what is less important.

"That is what I shall do for anyone I meet, young or old, foreigner or citizen—but
especially for my fellow-citizens, since you are more closely related to me. That is what
god tells me to do, I promise you, and I believe that this service of mine to god is the
most valuable asset you in this city have ever yet possessed. I spend my whole time going round trying to persuade both the young and old among you not to spend your time

b   or energy in caring about your bodies or about money, but rather in making your souls
as good as possible. I tell you, 'Money cannot create a good soul, but a good soul can
turn money—and everything else in private life and public life—into a good thing for
men.' If saying things like this is a bad influence on the young, then things like this must
be harmful. But if anyone claims I say anything different from this, he is wrong. With
that in mind, Athenians," I would say, "either do what Anytus wants, or don't do it; either acquit me, or don't, knowing that I will not behave differently even if I am to be put
to death a thousand times over."

c   Don't interrupt, men of Athens. Please stick to what I asked you to do, which was
not to interrupt what I say, but to give me a hearing. It will be in your interest, I think,
to hear me. I have some more things to say which you could object to quite violently.
Please don't, however.

I have just described the kind of man I am. Take my word for it, if you put me to
death, you will harm yourselves more than you will harm me. As for me, no harm can

d   come to me from Meletus or Anytus, who *cannot* injure me, since I do not think god
ever allows a better man to be injured by a worse. Yes, I know he might put me to death,
possibly, or send me into exile, or deprive me of citizen rights. And perhaps *he* regards
these as great evils—as I suppose others may too. However, *I* do not. I regard it as a
much greater evil to act as he is acting now, attempting to put a man to death unjustly.

It follows, men of Athens, that in this trial I am not by any means defending myself, as you might think. No, I am defending you. I don't want you to fail to recognise

e   god's gift to you, and find me guilty. If you put me to death, you will not easily find another like me. I have, almost literally, settled on the city at god's command. It's as if the
city, to use a slightly absurd simile, were a horse—a large horse, high-mettled, but
which because of its size is somewhat sluggish, and needs to be stung into action by
some kind of horsefly. I think god has caused me to settle on the city as this horsefly, the

31   sort that never stops, all day long, coming to rest on every part of you, stinging each one
of you into action, and persuading and criticising each one of you.

Another like me will not easily come your way, gentlemen, so if you take my advice you will spare me. You may very likely get annoyed with me, as people do when
they are dozing and somebody wakes them up. And you might then swat me, as Anytus
wants you to, and kill me, quite easily. Then you could spend the rest of your lives
asleep, unless god cared enough for you to send you someone else.

b   To convince yourselves that someone like me really is a gift from god to the city,
look at things this way. Behaviour like mine does not seem to be natural. I have completely neglected my own affairs, and allowed my family to be neglected, all these
years, while I devoted myself to looking after your interests—approaching each one of
you individually, like a father or elder brother, and trying to persuade you to consider
the good of your soul.

If I made anything out of it, and charged a fee for this advice, there'd be some
sense in my doing it. As it is, you can see for yourselves that although the prosecution
accused me, in their unscrupulous way, of everything under the sun, there was one point

c   on which they were not so unscrupulous as to produce any evidence. They didn't claim that I ever made any money, or asked for any. I can produce convincing evidence, I think, that I am telling the truth—namely my poverty.

It may perhaps seem odd that in my private life I go round giving people advice like this, and interfering, without having the courage, in public life, to come forward before you, the people, and give advice on matters of public interest. The reason for this is what you have often heard me talking about, in all sorts of places, the kind of divine or supernatural sign that comes to me. This must have been what Meletus was making fun   d
of when he wrote out the charge against me. It started when I was a child, a kind of voice which comes to me, and when it comes, always stops me doing what I'm just about to do; it never tells me what I *should* do. It's this which opposes my taking part in politics, and rightly opposes it, in my opinion. You can be sure, men of Athens, that if I had tried, at any time in the past, to go into politics, I would have been dead long ago, and been no use at all either to you or to myself.

Please don't be annoyed with me for speaking the truth. There is no-one in the   e
world who can get away with deliberately opposing you—or any other popular assembly—or trying to put a stop to all the unjust and unlawful things which are done in pol-   32
itics; it is essential that the true fighter for justice, if he is to survive even for a short time, should remain a private individual, and not go into public life.

I shall give you compelling evidence for this—not words, but what you value, actions. Listen to things which have actually happened to me, and you will realise that I would never obey anyone if it was wrong to do so, simply through fear of dying. No, I would refuse to obey, even if it meant my death. What I am going to say now is the kind of boasting you often hear in the lawcourts; but it is true, for all that.   b

I have never, men of Athens, held any public office in the city, apart from being a member of the Council. It turned out that our tribe, Antiochis, formed the standing committee when you decided, by a resolution of the Council, to put on trial collectively the ten generals who failed to pick up the survivors from the sea battle. This was unconstitutional, as you afterwards all decided. On that occasion I was the only member of the standing committee to argue against you. I told you not to act unconstitutionally, and voted against you. The politicians were all set to bring an immediate action against me, and have me arrested on the spot, and you were encouraging them to do so, and shouting your approval, but still I thought I ought to take my chance on the side of law and justice, rather than side with you, through fear of imprisonment or death, when you   c
were proposing to act unjustly.

That was when the city was still a democracy. When the oligarchy came to power, the junta in its turn sent for me, with four others, and gave me the task of bringing Leon of Salamis from his home in Salamis to the Council chamber, so he could be put to death. They often gave orders of this kind, to all sorts of people; they wanted to impli-   d
cate as many people as possible in their crimes. Again I demonstrated—by what I did this time, rather than what I said—that my fear of death was, if you will pardon my saying so, negligible; what I was afraid of, more than anything, was acting without regard for justice or religion. I was not intimidated by the junta's power—great though it was—into acting unjustly. When we left the Council chamber, the other four went off to Salamis and fetched Leon, but I left, and went home. I might perhaps have been put to death for that, if their power hadn't soon after been brought to an end. Of these events   e
any number of people will give evidence to you.

Do you think I would have survived all these years if I had taken part in public life, and played the part a good man should play, supporting what was just, and attaching the highest importance to it, as is right? Don't you believe it, men of Athens. Nor would anyone else in the world have survived. As for me, it will be clear that, throughout my life, if I have done anything at all in public life, my character is as I have described—and in private life the same. I was never at any time prepared to tolerate injustice in anyone at all—certainly not in any of the people my critics say were my pupils.

33

I have never been anyone's teacher. Equally, I never said no to anyone, young or old, who wanted to listen to me talking and pursuing my quest. Nor do I talk if I am paid, and not talk if I am not paid. I make myself available to rich and poor alike, so they can question me and listen, if anyone feels like it, to what I say in reply. And if any of these people turns out well or badly, I cannot legitimately be held responsible; I neither promised any knowledge, ever, to any of them, nor did I teach them. If anyone ever claims to have learnt or heard anything from me privately, beyond what anyone else learnt or heard, I can assure you he is lying.

b

c

Why then do some people like spending so much of their time with me? You have heard the answer to that, men of Athens; I have told you the whole truth. They like hearing the cross-examination of those who think they are wise when they are not. After all, it is quite entertaining. For me, as I say, this is a task imposed by god, through prophecies and dreams and in every way in which divine destiny has ever imposed any task on a man.

All this is the truth, men of Athens, and easily tested. If I really am a bad influence on some of the young, and have been a bad influence on others in the past, and if some of them, as they have grown older, have realised that I gave them bad advice at some point when they were young, they ought to come forward now, I'd have thought, to accuse me and punish me. And if they weren't prepared to do so themselves, some of the members of their families—fathers, brothers, or other close relatives—ought now to remember, if those close to them came to some harm at my hands, and want to punish me. Certainly I can see plenty of them here today—Crito there, for a start, my contemporary and fellow-demesman, the father of Critobulus, who's here too. Then there's Lysanias from the deme of Sphettos, the father of Aeschines here; or indeed Antiphon over there, from Cephisus, the father of Epigenes.

d

e

Then there are the ones whose brothers have spent their time in my company: Nicostratus the son of Theozotides, the brother of Theodotus—Theodotus of course is dead, so he couldn't have put any pressure on his brother; and I can see Paralius, the son of Demodocus, whose brother was Theages. Then there's Adeimantus I can see, the son of Ariston, whose brother is Plato here; or Aiantodorus, whose brother Apollodorus is present also.

34

There are plenty more I could name for you. Ideally, Meletus would have called some of them himself to give evidence during his speech. However, in case he forgot at the time, let him call them now—I give up my place to him—and let him say if he has any evidence of that kind.

It's the exact opposite, gentlemen. You'll find they're all on my side—although I'm a bad influence, although I harm their relatives, as Meletus and Anytus claim. I can see why the actual victims of my influence might have some reason to be on my side; but those who have not been influenced, the older generation, their relatives, what reason do they have for being on my side, other than the correct and valid reason that they know Meletus is lying, and I am telling the truth?

b

c

Well, there we are, gentlemen. That, and perhaps a bit more along the same lines, is roughly what I might have to say in my defence. There may possibly be those among you who find it irritating, when you remember your own experience; you may, in a trial less important than this one, have begged and pleaded with the jury, with many tears, bringing your own children, and many others among your family and friends, up here to arouse as much sympathy as possible; whereas I refuse to do any of these things—even though I am, as it probably seems to you, in the greatest danger of all.

Thoughts like this could make some of you feel a little antagonistic towards me.   d
For just this reason, you might get angry, and let anger influence your vote. If any of you does feel like this—I am sure you don't, but if you did—I think I might fairly say to you: "Of course I too have a family, my good friend. I do not come, in Homer's famous words, 'from oak or rock.' No, I was born of men, so I do have a family, and sons, men of Athens, three of them. One is not quite grown-up, the other two still boys. All the same, I am not going to bring any of them up here and beg you to acquit me."

Why will I not do any of these things? Not out of obstinacy, men of Athens, nor   e
out of contempt for you. And whether or not I am untroubled by the thought of death is beside the point. No, it's a question of what is fitting—for me, for you, and for the whole city. I don't think it's right for me to do any of these things, at my age and with the reputation I have. It may be justified or unjustified, but there's a prevailing belief   35
that Socrates is in some way different from other people.

If those of you who seem to be outstanding in wisdom or courage, or any other quality, were to behave like this, it would be deplorable. Yet this is just the way I *have* seen men behaving when they are brought to trial. They may seem to be men of some distinction, but still they act in the most extraordinary way; they seem to think it will be a terrible disaster for them if they are put to death—as if they'd be immortal if you *didn't* put them to death. I think they bring disgrace on the city. A visitor to our country might imagine that in Athens people of outstanding character, those whom the Athenians themselves single out from among themselves for positions of office and other dis-   b
tinctions—that these men are no better than women.

Such behaviour, men of Athens, is not right for those of you with any kind of reputation at all; and if we who are on trial behave like that, you should not let us get away with it. You should make one thing absolutely clear, which is that you are much more ready to convict a defendant who stages one of these hysterical scenes, and makes our city an object of ridicule, than a defendant who behaves with decorum.

Quite apart from what is fitting, gentlemen, I think there is no justice, either, in begging favours from the jury, or being acquitted by begging; justice requires instruction and   c
persuasion. The juryman does not sit there for the purpose of handing out justice as a favour; he sits there to decide what justice is. He has not taken an oath to do a favour to anyone he takes a fancy to, but rather to reach a verdict in accordance with the laws. So *we* should not encourage in you the habit of breaking your oath, nor should *you* allow the habit to develop. If we did, we should neither of us be showing any respect for the gods.

Do not ask me, therefore, men of Athens, to conduct myself towards you in a way which I regard as contrary to right, justice and religion—least of all, surely, when I am   d
being accused of impiety by Meletus here. After all, if I did persuade you and coerce you, by my begging, despite your oath, then clearly I *would* be teaching you to deny the existence of the gods; my whole defence would simply amount to accusing myself of not recognising the gods. And that is far from being the case. I do recognise them, men of Athens, as none of my accusers does, and I entrust to you and to god the task of reaching a verdict in my case in whatever way will be best both for me and for you.

*   *   *

If I am not upset, men of Athens, at what has just happened—your finding me guilty—   e
there are a number of reasons. In particular, the result was not unexpected; in fact, I'm surprised by the final number of votes on either side. Personally, I was expecting a large   36

margin, not a narrow one; as it is, if only thirty votes had gone the other way, apparently I would have been acquitted. Indeed, on Meletus' charge, as I see it, I *have* been acquitted, even as things are. And not just acquitted; it's clear to anyone that if Anytus had not come forward, with Lycon, to accuse me, Meletus would have incurred a fine of a thou-
b   sand drachmas for not receiving twenty percent of the votes.

So the man proposes the death penalty for me. Very well. What counter-proposal am I to make to you, men of Athens? What I deserve, obviously. And what is that? What do I deserve to suffer or pay, for . . . for what? For not keeping quiet all through my life, for neglecting the things most people devote their lives to: business, family life, holding office—as general, or as leader of the assembly, or in some other capacity—or the alliances and factions which occur in political life. I thought, quite honestly, that my sense of right and wrong would not allow me to survive in politics; so I did not pursue
c   a course in which I should have been no use either to you or to myself, but rather one in which I could give help to each one of you privately—the greatest help possible, as I claim. That is the direction I took. I tried to persuade each of you not to give any thought at all to his own affairs until he had first given some thought to himself, and tried to make himself as good and wise as possible; not to give any thought to the affairs of the city without first giving some thought to the city itself; and to observe the same priorities in other areas as well.
d   What then do I deserve for behaving like this? Something good, men of Athens, if I am really supposed to make a proposal in accordance with what I deserve. And what's more, a good of a kind which is some use to me. What then *is* of use to a poor man, your benefactor, who needs free time in which to advise you? There can't be anything more useful to a man of this sort, men of Athens, than to be given free meals at the public expense; this is much more use to him than it is to any Olympic victor among you, if one of you wins the horse race, or the two-horse or four-horse chariot race. The Olympic
e   winner makes you *seem* to be happy; I make you really happy. He doesn't need the food; I do need it. So if I must propose a penalty based on justice, on what I deserve,
37   then that's what I propose—free meals at the public expense.

Here again, I suppose, in the same sort of way as when I was talking about appeals to pity and pleas for mercy, you may think I speak as I do out of sheer obstinacy. But it's not obstinacy, men of Athens; it's like this. I myself am convinced that I don't knowingly do wrong to anyone in the world, but I can't persuade you of that; we haven't had enough time to talk to one another. Mind you, if it were the custom here, as it is in other places, to decide cases involving the death penalty over several days rather
b   than in one day, I believe you would have been persuaded. As it is, it was not easy in a short time to overcome the strong prejudice against me.

But if I am convinced that I don't do wrong to anyone else, I am certainly not going to do wrong to myself, or speak against myself—saying I deserve something bad, and proposing some such penalty for myself. Why should I? Through fear of undergoing the penalty Meletus proposes, when I claim not to know whether it is good or bad? Should I, in preference to that, choose one of the things I know perfectly well to be bad, and propose that as a penalty?
c   Imprisonment? What is the point of living in prison, and being the slave of those in the prison service at any particular time? A fine? And be imprisoned until I pay? That's the same as the first suggestion, since I haven't any money to pay a fine. Should I propose exile? I suppose you might accept that. But I'd have to be very devoted to life, men of Athens, to lose the power of rational thought so completely, and not be able to work out what would happen. If you, my fellow-citizens, couldn't stand my talk and my
d   conversation, if you found them too boring and irritating, which is why you now want

to be rid of them, will people in some other country find it any easier to put up with them? Don't you believe it, men of Athens.

A fine life I should lead in exile, a man of my age—moving and being driven from city to city. I've no doubt that wherever I go, the young will listen to me, the way they do here. If I tell them to go away, they will send me into exile of their own accord, bringing pressure to bear on their elders; if I don't tell them to go away, their fathers and relatives will exile me, out of concern for them.

e

I can imagine someone saying, "How about keeping your mouth shut, Socrates, and leading a quiet life? Can't you please go into exile, and live like that?" Of all things, this is the hardest point on which to convince some of you. If I say that it is disobeying god, and that for this reason I can't lead a quiet life, you won't believe me—you'll think I'm using that as an excuse. If on the other hand I say that really the greatest good in a man's life is this, to be each day discussing human excellence and the other subjects you hear me talking about, examining myself and other people, and that the unexamined life isn't worth living—if I say this, you will believe me even less.

38

All the same, the situation is as I describe it, gentlemen—hard though it is to convince you. Equally, for myself, I can't get used to the idea that I deserve anything bad. If I had any money, I would propose as large a fine as I could afford; that wouldn't do me any harm. As it is, I have no money, unless you are willing to have me propose an amount I *could* afford. I suppose I could pay you something like a hundred drachmas of silver, if you like. So that is the amount I propose.

b

Plato here, men of Athens—and Crito and Critobulus and Apollodorus—tell me to propose a penalty of 3000 drachmas; they say they guarantee it. I propose that amount, therefore, and they will offer full security to you for the money.

* * *

For just a small gain in time, men of Athens, you will now have the reputation and responsibility, among those who want to criticise the city, of having put to death Socrates, that wise man—they will *say* I am wise, the people who want to blame you, even though I am not. If you'd waited a little, you could have had what you wanted without lifting a finger. You can see what age I am—far advanced in years, and close to death.

c

I say that not to all of you, but to those who voted for the death penalty. And I have something else to say to the same people. You may think, men of Athens, that I have lost my case through inability to make the kind of speech I *could* have used to persuade you, had I thought it right to do and say absolutely anything to secure my acquittal. Far from it. I have lost my case, not for want of a speech, but for want of effrontery and shamelessness, for refusing to make to you the kind of speech you most enjoy listening to. You'd like to have heard me lamenting and bewailing, and doing and saying all sorts of other things which are beneath my dignity, in my opinion—the kind of things you've grown used to hearing from other people.

d

e

I did not think it right, when I was speaking, to demean myself through fear of danger, nor do I now regret conducting my defence in the way I did. I had much rather defend myself like this, and be put to death, than behave in the way I have described, and go on living. Neither in the courts, nor in time of war, is it right—either for me or for anyone else—to devote one's efforts simply to avoiding death at all costs.

39

In battle it is often clear that death can be escaped, by dropping your weapons and throwing yourself on the mercy of your pursuers—and in any kind of danger there are all sorts of other devices for avoiding death, if you can bring yourself not to mind what you do or say. There's no difficulty in *that*, gentlemen, in escaping death. What is much b   harder is avoiding wickedness, since wickedness runs faster than death. So now, not surprisingly, I, who am old and slow, have been overtaken by the slower of the two. My accusers, being swift and keen, have been overtaken by the faster, by wickedness. Now I am departing, to pay the penalty of death inflicted by you. But they have already incurred the penalty, inflicted by truth, for wickedness and injustice. I accept my sentence, as they do theirs. I suppose that's probably how it was bound to turn out—and I have no complaints.

c   Having dealt with that, I now wish to make you a prophecy, those of you who voted for my condemnation. I am at that point where people are most inclined to make prophecies—which is when they are just about to die. To you gentlemen who have put me to death, I say that retribution will come to you, directly after my death—retribution far worse, god knows, than the death penalty which you have inflicted on me.

You have acted as you have today in the belief that you will avoid having to submit your lives to examination, but you will find the outcome is just the opposite; that is my prediction. There will be more people now to examine you—the ones I have so far been keeping in check without your realising it. They will be harder to deal with, being

d   so much younger, and you will be more troubled by them. If you think that by putting men to death you can stop people criticising you for not living your lives in the right way, you are miscalculating badly. As a way of escape, this is neither effective nor creditable; the best and simplest way lies not in weeding out other people, but in making oneself as good a person as possible.

That is my prophecy to you who voted for my condemnation, and now I am pre-

e   pared to let you go. To those who voted for my acquittal I'd like to make a few remarks about what has just happened, while the magistrates get on with the formalities, and it is not yet time for me to go where I must go to die. Please keep me company, gentlemen, for this little time; there's no reason why we shouldn't talk to one another while it is permitted. I regard you as my friends, and so to you I am prepared to explain the significance of today's outcome.

40   Gentlemen of the jury—since you I properly *can* call jurymen—a remarkable thing has happened to me. The prophetic voice I have got so used to, my supernatural voice, has always in the past been at my elbow, opposing me even in matters of little importance, if I was about to take a false step. You can see for yourselves the situation I'm now in. You might think—and this is how it is generally regarded—it was the ulti-

b   mate misfortune. Yet the sign from god did not oppose my leaving home this morning, nor my appearance here in court, nor was there any point in my speech when it stopped me saying what I was just about to say.

Often in the past, when I have been talking, the sign has stopped me in full flow; this time it has not opposed me at any stage in the whole proceedings—either in what I have done or in what I have said. What do I take to be the reason for this? I'll tell you. The chances are that what has happened to me here is a good thing, and that it is impossible for those of us who think death is an evil to understand it correctly. I have strong evidence for this. The sign I know so well would unquestionably have opposed me, if

c   things had not been going to turn out all right for me.

There is another reason for being confident that death is a good thing. Look at it like this. Death is one of two things; either it is like the dead person being nothing at all, and having no consciousness of anything at all; or, as we are told, it is actually some sort of change, a journey of the soul from this place to somewhere different. Suppose it is a total absence of consciousness—like sleep, when the sleeper isn't even dreaming.

Then death would be a marvellous bonus. At least, I certainly think that if a man had to d
choose the night on which he slept so soundly that he did not even dream, and if he had
to compare all the other nights and days of his life with that night, if he had to think
carefully about it, and then say how many days and nights he had spent in his life that
were better and more enjoyable than that night—I think that not just a private individual, but even the great king of Persia could count these dreamless nights on the fingers e
of one hand compared with the other days and nights. If death is something like that, I
call it a bonus. After all, the whole of time, seen in this way, seems no longer than a single night.

If, on the other hand, death is a kind of journey from here to somewhere different,
and what we're told about all the dead being there is true, what greater good could there
be than that, gentlemen of the jury? Imagine arriving in the other world, getting away 41
from the people here who claim to be judges, and finding real judges, the ones who are
said to decide cases there—Minos, Rhadamanthys, Aeacus, Triptolemus, and others of
the demigods who acted with justice in their own lives. Wouldn't that be a worthwhile
journey?

Or again, what would any of you give to join Orpheus and Musaeus, Hesiod and
Homer? Personally, I am quite prepared to die many times over, if these stories are true.
For me at least, time spent there would be wonderful—I'd keep meeting people like b
Palamedes, or Aias the son of Telamon, or any other of the ancients who died as a result
of an unjust verdict; I could compare my own experience with theirs. That would be entertaining, I imagine. Best of all, I could spend my time questioning and examining people there, just as I do people here, to find out which of them is wise, and which thinks he
is wise but isn't.

What would you give, men of the jury, to interview the man who led the great expedition to Troy—or Odysseus, or Sisyphus, or thousands of others one could mention, c
men and women? It would be an unimaginable pleasure to talk to them there, to enjoy
their company, and question them. They certainly can't put you to death there for asking questions. They are better off than us in many ways—and not least because they are
now immune to death for the rest of time, if what we are told is true.

You too, men of the jury, must not be apprehensive about death. You must regard one thing at least as certain—that no harm can come to a good man either in his
life or after his death; what happens to him is not a matter of indifference to the gods. d
Nor has my present situation arisen purely by chance; it is clear to me that it was better for me to die now and be released from my task. That's why my sign didn't at any
point dissuade me, and why I am not in the least angry with those who voted against
me, or with my accusers. Admittedly that wasn't their reason for voting against me,
and accusing me; they thought they were doing me some harm. We *can* blame them
for that.

However, I do have one request to make. It concerns my sons. When they grow
up, gentlemen, get your own back on them, if you think they are more interested in e
money—or in anything else—than in goodness, by annoying them in exactly the same
way as I annoyed you. If they think they amount to something when they don't, then
criticise them, as I criticised you. Tell them they are not giving any thought to the
things that matter, and that they think they amount to something when they are worth
nothing. If you do this, I shall myself have been fairly treated by you—and so will my 42
sons.

I must stop. It is time for us to go—me to my death, you to your lives. Which of
us goes to the better fate, only god knows.

CRITO

43   SOCRATES: What are you doing here at this time, Crito? Isn't it still early?

CRITO: Yes, it is.

SOCRATES: How early, exactly?

CRITO: It's not yet started to get light.

SOCRATES: I'm surprised the warder didn't refuse to answer your knock.

CRITO: He's become something of a friend of mine, Socrates, what with my coming here so often. Besides, I've done him a bit of a favour.

SOCRATES: Have you just arrived, or have you been here some time?

CRITO: Quite some time.

b   SOCRATES: Then why on earth didn't you wake me up? What were you doing just sitting there beside me in silence?

CRITO: I wouldn't have dreamt of it, Socrates. For my part, I wouldn't choose to be in this state of sleeplessness and misery; and for some time now it has astonished me to see how soundly you sleep. I deliberately didn't wake you because I wanted you to enjoy your rest. It has often struck me in the past, throughout my life in fact, how lucky you are in your temperament—and it strikes me much more forcibly in your present misfortune. You bear it so easily and calmly.

SOCRATES: Yes, Crito, I do. It wouldn't make much sense for a man my age to get upset at the prospect of dying.

c   CRITO: Other people your age, Socrates, find themselves in similar predicaments; *their* age doesn't stop them getting upset at their misfortune.

SOCRATES: That's true. Anyway, why *have* you come so early?

CRITO: To bring news, Socrates, bad news. Not bad for you, as far as I can see, but for me and all your friends it is bad and hard to bear; and I think I shall find it as hard to bear as anybody.

d   SOCRATES: What sort of news? Has the boat from Delos arrived—the one my execution has been waiting for?

CRITO: It hasn't actually arrived, but I think it will today, judging by the reports of some people who've just come from Sunium. It was there when they left. It's clear from what they said that it will arrive today, and so tomorrow, Socrates, you will be forced to end your life.

SOCRATES: Well, Crito, if that is how the gods want it, I hope it will all turn out for the best. All the same, I don't think it will come today.

44   CRITO: What is that based on?

SOCRATES: I'll tell you. My death, I assume, is to take place on the day after the ship arrives.

CRITO: Yes. At least, that's what the prison authorities say.

SOCRATES: Then I think it will come tomorrow, not today. That's based on a dream I had last night, just before I woke up. So perhaps it was lucky you didn't wake me.

CRITO: What was the dream?

SOCRATES: I saw a woman, fair and beautiful, in a white cloak. She came up to b   me, and called my name. "Socrates," she said, "On the third day shall you come to fertile Phthia."

CRITO: A strange dream, Socrates.

SOCRATES: Clear enough, though, I think, Crito.

CRITO: Only too clear, I'm afraid. Now listen, Socrates, it's not too late, even now, to do as I say and escape. For me, if you are put to death, it is a double disaster. Quite apart from losing a friend such as I shall never find again, there will also be many who will think, those who don't know the two of us well, that I had the chance to save   c
you if I'd been prepared to spend some money, and that I wasn't interested in doing so.

Can you think of a worse reputation than being thought to value money more highly than friends? Most people will never believe that it was you yourself who refused to leave here, and that we strongly encouraged you to do so.

SOCRATES: Really, Crito, why should we care so much about what "most people" believe? The best people, who are the ones we should worry about more, will realise that things were done in the way they actually were done.

CRITO: Yet you can see that we have no choice, Socrates, but to care about what   d
most people think as well. The present situation is a clear example of how the many can injure us in ways which are not trivial, but just about as great as can be, if they are given the wrong impression about someone.

SOCRATES: If only the many *could* do us the greatest injuries, Crito. That would mean they were capable of doing us the greatest good as well, which would be excellent. As it is, they're incapable of doing either. They have no power to make a man either wise or foolish; nor do they care what effect they have.

CRITO: I dare say you are right. But tell me something, Socrates. Are you worried   e
about me and the rest of your friends? Do you think, if you leave here, that we shall get into trouble with the people who make a living out of bringing private prosecutions, because we smuggled you out of here? Do you think we shall be forced to   45
forfeit all our property, or pay a very large fine, and possibly undergo some further penalty in addition?

If something like that is what you are afraid of, don't give it another thought. We are in duty bound to run this risk to save you—that goes without saying—and even greater risks, if need be. Listen to me. Don't say "no."

SOCRATES: It *is* something I worry about, Crito. That, and many other things besides.

CRITO: Well then, do not be afraid on that score. There are people prepared, for not a very large sum of money, to save you and get you out of here. And apart from them, can't you see how easily bought they are, the men who make their living out of prosecutions? It wouldn't need a lot of money to take care of them. You have my re-   b
sources at your disposal; that should be plenty, I imagine. And if you're worried about me, and feel you shouldn't spend my money, look at the people we've got here who are not Athenians, who are ready to spend theirs. One of them, Simmias the Theban, has actually brought enough money for just this purpose; Cebes too is fully prepared, and so are many others.

So as I say, you should not let these fears stop you saving yourself; and do not let it be an objection, as you claimed in court, that you would not know what to do with yourself if you went into exile. There are lots of places you can go where they'll be glad to see you; if you want to go to Thessaly, for example, my family has friends there who   c
will be delighted to see you, and who will give you sanctuary. Nobody in Thessaly will give you any trouble.

Apart from that, Socrates, it is actually wrong, in my opinion, to sacrifice yourself, as you are proposing to do, when you could escape. You seem to be voluntarily choosing for yourself the kind of fate your enemies would have chosen for you—and

did choose for you when they were trying to destroy you. Worse still, I think, is the be-
d   trayal of your own sons, when there is nothing to stop you bringing them up and educating them—and yet you are going to go away and leave them, and for all you care
they can turn out how they will. They will have, in all probability, the kind of life orphans generally have when they lose their parents.

No. Either you shouldn't have children, or you should play your part, and go
through with the labour of raising and educating them. You seem to me to be taking the
easy way out. What you should do is choose what a decent and courageous man would
choose—you who claim to have been concerned with human goodness all your life.
e   Personally, I am ashamed both for you and for those of us who are your friends. I think
this whole business of yours will be thought to be the result of some lack of resolution
on our part—first of all the fact that the case came to court when it needn't have done,
then the actual conduct of the case in court, and now this, as the final absurdity of the
46   whole affair, that we shall be thought to have missed the opportunity—through our own
cowardice and lack of resolution, since we didn't save you, nor did you save yourself,
though it was possible, and within your power, with even a modest amount of help from
us. Don't let all this be a humiliation, Socrates, both for you and for us, in addition to
being an evil.

Think it over—or rather, the time for thinking it over is past, you should by
now have thought it over—there is only one course of action. The whole thing must
be done this coming night. If we wait any longer, it will be impossible; it will not be
an option any longer. I cannot urge you too strongly, Socrates. Listen to me. Do as
I say.

SOCRATES: My dear Crito, your enthusiasm is most commendable, so long as
there is some justification for it. Otherwise, the greater your enthusiasm, the more out of
b   place it is. We'd better look into whether this is the right thing to do or not. It has been
my practice, not just now but always, to trust, of all the guides at my disposal, only the
principle which on reflection seems most appropriate. I cannot now throw overboard
principles which I have put forward in the past, simply because of what has happened to
me. They still seem to me very much the same as they always did; I still give pride of
place to, and value, the same principles as before. Unless we can find some better principle than these to put forward on this occasion, you can be quite sure I am not going to
c   agree with you, however many bugbears the power of the many produces to scare us
with—as if we were children—letting loose on us its imprisonments, its death sentences
and its fines.

What then is the best way of looking into this question? Why don't we start by
going back to the argument you put forward based on what people will think? Were we
right or wrong, all those times, when we said we should listen to some opinions, but not
to others? Or were we right before I was sentenced to death, only for it now to become
clear that it was a waste of breath, spoken simply for the sake of having something to
d   say, and that it was really juvenile fantasy? Personally, Crito, I should very much like to
carry out a joint enquiry with you, to see whether the principle will seem rather different to me, now that I am in this situation, or whether it will seem the same—and
whether we are going to forget about it, or follow it.

The principle so often put forward, I think, by those among us who thought they
knew what they were talking about, was the one I referred to just now—that of the opin-
e   ions held by men, we should regard some as important, and others not. Seriously, Crito,
don't you think this is a sound principle? You are, barring accidents, not in the position
47   of having to die tomorrow, so you shouldn't be influenced by the present situation. Examine the question. Don't you think it a sound principle that we should not value all hu-

man opinions equally, but should value some highly, and others not? And the same with the people who hold the opinions. We should not value all of them, but should value some, and not others. What do you think? Isn't this is a sound principle?

CRITO: Yes, it is.

SOCRATES: We should value the good opinions, but not the bad ones?

CRITO: Yes.

SOCRATES: Aren't good opinions the opinions of the wise, whereas bad opinions are those of the foolish?

CRITO: Obviously.

SOCRATES: Well then, what was the kind of analogy we used to employ? If a man   b
is taking physical exercise, and this is what he is interested in, does he listen to the praise and criticism and opinion of just anyone, or only of one person—the person who is in fact a medical expert or a physical training instructor?

CRITO: Only of one person.

SOCRATES: So he should worry about the criticisms, and welcome the praises, of this one person, but not those of the many?

CRITO: Clearly he should.

SOCRATES: In what he does, then—in the exercise he takes, in what he eats and drinks—he should be guided by the one man, the man in charge, the expert, rather than by everyone else.

CRITO: That is so.

SOCRATES: All right. If he defies the one man, and doesn't value his opinion and   c
his recommendations, but does value those of the many, those who are not experts, won't he do himself some harm?

CRITO: Of course he will.

SOCRATES: What is this harm? What is its extent? What part of the man who defies the expert does it attack?

CRITO: His body, obviously. That is what it damages.

SOCRATES: Quite right. Well then, is it the same also in other situations, Crito, to save us going through all the examples—and especially with right and wrong, foul and fair, good and bad, the things we are now discussing? Should we follow the opinion of   d
the many, and fear that, or the opinion of the one man, if we can find an expert on the subject? Should we respect and fear this one man more than all the rest put together? And if we don't follow his advice, we shall injure and do violence to that part which we have often agreed improves with justice and is damaged by injustice. Or is this all wrong?

CRITO: No, I think it is right, Socrates.

SOCRATES: Very well. Take that part of us which improves with health, and is damaged by disease. If we ruin it by following advice other than that of the experts, is life worth living once that part is injured? This is the body, of course, isn't it?   e

CRITO: Yes.

SOCRATES: Is life worth living, then, if our body is in poor condition and injured?

CRITO: Certainly not.

SOCRATES: How about the part of us which is attacked by injustice, and helped by justice? Is life worth living when that is injured? Or do we regard it as less important than the body, this part of us—whichever of our faculties it is—the part to which justice   48
and injustice belong?

CRITO: No, we certainly don't.

SOCRATES: More important, then?

CRITO: Much more important.

SOCRATES: In that case, my dear friend, we should not pay the slightest attention, as you suggested we should, to what most people will say about us. We should listen only to the expert on justice and injustice, to the one man, and to the truth itself. So you were wrong, for a start, in one of your recommendations—when you proposed that we should be concerned about the opinion of the many on the subject of justice, right, good, and their opposites. "Ah!" you might say, "but the many are liable to put us to death."

b   CRITO: That too is obviously true. You might well say that, Socrates. You are quite right.

SOCRATES: All the same, my learned friend, I think the principle we have elaborated still has the same force as it did. And what about this second principle? Tell me, does our belief—that the important thing is not being alive, but living a good life—still hold good, or not?

CRITO: It does still hold good.

SOCRATES: And that when we're talking about a life, good, right and just are one and the same thing—does that still hold good, or not?

CRITO: It does.

c   SOCRATES: Well then, in the light of the points we have agreed, we must look into the question whether it is right, or not right, for me to attempt to leave here without the permission of the Athenians. If it appears to be right, let us make the attempt; otherwise let us forget about it. As for the considerations you raise—questions of expense, public opinion, the upbringing of children—I suspect that these, Crito, are really the concerns of those who readily put people to death, and would as readily bring them back to life again, if they could—for absolutely no reason. I am, of course, talking about the many.

For us, though, the thing is to follow where the argument leads us, and I rather think the only question we need ask is the one we asked just now: shall we act rightly if

d   we give our money, and our thanks, to those who will arrange my escape from here? Shall we ourselves be acting rightly in arranging the escape, and allowing it to be arranged? Or shall we in fact be acting wrongly if we do all these things? If this is clearly the wrong way for us to behave, then I'm pretty sure that compared with the danger of acting wrongly, we should not take into account the certainty either of being put to death if we stay put and accept things quietly, or of suffering anything else at all.

CRITO: I am sure you are right, Socrates. You decide what we should do.

SOCRATES: Let us look into it together, my friend. And if you want to raise an ob-

e   jection at any point while I'm talking, then raise it, and I will listen to you. Otherwise, my fine friend, stop repeating the same thing over and over again—that I should leave here in defiance of the wishes of the Athenians. I attach great importance to acting with your agreement, rather than against your wishes.

Now, think about the starting-point of our enquiry. Do you regard it as satisfac-

49   tory? And when you answer the question, mind you say what you really think.

CRITO: I will try.

SOCRATES: Do we agree that we should never deliberately do wrong, or should we sometimes do wrong, and sometimes not? Is wrongdoing absolutely contrary to what is good and fine, as has often been agreed among us in the past? Or have all those things we once agreed on become, in these last few days, so much water under the

b   bridge? Did we, grown men and at the age we were, Crito, discuss things so enthusiastically with one another, without realising we were no better than children? Or is what we said then more true now than ever? Whether "most people" agree or not, and whether we have to undergo hardships more severe even than these—or possibly less severe—isn't wrongdoing in fact, for the person who does it, wholly evil and bad? Is this what we say, or not?

CRITO: It is.

SOCRATES: A man should never do wrong, then.

CRITO: No, he should not.

SOCRATES: So even if he is wronged, he should not do wrong in return, as most people think, since he ought not *ever* to do wrong.

CRITO: Apparently not.   c

SOCRATES: What about harming people, Crito? Should a man do that, or not?

CRITO: I suppose not, Socrates.

SOCRATES: How about harming people in retaliation, if he is injured by them first—which is what most people say he should do? Is that right or wrong?

CRITO: Completely wrong.

SOCRATES: And that, I imagine, is because injuring people is the same thing as doing them wrong.

CRITO: That is right.

SOCRATES: So he should not do wrong to anyone or injure them, in retaliation, no matter how he has been treated by them. And if you say "yes" to that, Crito, make sure you are not saying "yes" against what you really think. I realise not many people accept   d
this view—or ever will accept it. As a result, there is no common ground between those who do accept it and those who do not; each side necessarily regards the opinions of the other side with contempt. So you too must think very hard about it. Are you on our side? Do you agree with us in accepting this view, and shall we base our argument on the   e
premise that it is never legitimate to do wrong to people, nor do them wrong in retaliation, nor, if one is injured, defend oneself by harming them in return? Or do you disagree? Do you reject the original premise? Personally, I have held this view a long time, and I still hold it now. If you have been holding some other view, tell me; instruct me. But if you stand by what we said earlier, then listen to what follows from it.

CRITO: I do stand by it, and I do agree with you. Tell me what follows.

SOCRATES: Very well, I will tell you. Or rather, I'll ask you. If a man makes an agreement—a fair agreement—with someone, should he fulfil his side of the agreement, or should he try to get out of it?

CRITO: He should fulfil it.

SOCRATES: Then see what follows from that. If we leave here without persuading the city to change its mind, are we doing harm to anyone or anything—those we have   50
least cause to injure—or not? Are we standing by our agreement—our fair agreement—or not?

CRITO: I can't answer your question, Socrates. I don't understand it.

SOCRATES: Look at it like this. Imagine that, just as we were about to run away, or whatever we are supposed to call it, from here, the laws of Athens and the state of Athens appeared before us, and said: "Tell me, Socrates, what are you trying to do? Aren't you simply trying, by this action you are embarking on, to de-   b
stroy both us, the laws, and the entire city, as far as lies within your power? Do you think it possible for a city to continue to exist, and not sink without trace, if the verdicts of its courts have no force, if they are rendered invalid, and nullified, by private citizens?"

What shall we say, Crito, to these questions and others like them? There's a lot that could be said, especially by the public advocate, in defence of this law we are trying to do away with—the law which lays down that verdicts arrived at in the courts should be binding. Shall we say to the laws, "The city wronged us. It did not reach its   c
verdict fairly?" Shall we say that, or what?

CRITO: Yes, we most emphatically should say that, Socrates.

SOCRATES: Suppose then the laws say, "Was *that* what was agreed between us and you, Socrates? Or was it to abide by the verdicts the city arrives at in its courts?" And if we expressed surprise at their question, they might add: "Do not be surprised

d   by our question, Socrates. Answer it. You have had enough practice at question-and-answer. Come on, then. What principle do you appeal to, against us and the city, to allow you to try and destroy us? Did we not bring you into existence, for a start? Was it not through us that your father married your mother, and fathered you? Tell us, then, those of us who are the laws governing marriage, have you some criticism of us? Is there something wrong with us?"

e   "I have no criticism," I should have to reply.

"All right, then. How about your upbringing and education after you were born? How about the laws to do with those? Did we not give your father the right instructions—those of us whose job it is to attend to this—when we told him to educate you by means of the arts and physical training?"

"No, they were the right instructions," I would say.

"Very well. Since you were born, and brought up, and educated, under our protection, you were our offspring and our slave—both you yourself and your parents. Can you deny that, for a start? And if that is so, do you think that justice gives equivalent rights to you and to us? If we decide to do something to you, do you think you have the right to do it to us in return?

"There was no equality of rights as between you and your father or your master,

51   if you had one, entitling you to do to him in retaliation what he did to you—to answer him back if he spoke abusively to you, or beat him in retaliation if he beat you, or anything else like that. Will it then be legitimate for you to retaliate against your country and its laws? And is the result that if we decide to destroy you, because we think it right to do so, you in your turn, to the best of your ability, will set about destroying us, the laws, and your country, in retaliation? Will you claim that in acting like this you are doing what is right, you who are truly so concerned about human excellence? Are you so clever that you fail to realise that your country is an object of greater value, an object of

b   greater respect and reverence, and altogether more important, both among gods and among men, if they have any sense, than your mother and your father and all the rest of your ancestors put together? That you should revere your country, submit to it, mollify it when it is angry with you—more than you would your father—and either persuade it to change its mind, or do what it tells you? That you should quietly accept whatever treatment it ordains you should receive—beating, perhaps, or imprisonment—or if it

c   takes you to war, to be wounded or killed, that is what you should do, and that is what is right? That you should not give way, or retreat, or abandon your position, that in war, in the lawcourts, or anywhere else, you should do what your city and your country tells you, or else convince it where justice naturally lies? And that the use of force, against a mother or a father, is against god's law—still more so the use of force against your country?"

What are we going to say in answer to this, Crito? Shall we say the laws are right, or not?

CRITO: Well, *I* think they are right.

SOCRATES: "Consider, then, Socrates," the laws might perhaps say. "Are we right in saying that you are not justified in embarking on the actions against us which you are

d   now embarking on? We fathered you, brought you up, educated you, gave you and every other citizen a share in every good thing it was in our power to give. And even then, if there is any Athenian who reaches the age of majority, takes a look at his city's constitution, and at us, the laws, and finds we are not to his satisfaction, then by granting him permission we make a public declaration to anyone who wishes that he may take what is his, and go wherever he pleases. If a man chooses to go to one of your colonies, because we and the city are not to his liking, or to leave, emigrate to some other place, and go wherever he wants, with no loss of property, not one of us laws stands in his way, or forbids him.

"To those of you who stay, aware of our way of reaching verdicts in the courts, and of making our other political arrangements, we say that you have now entered into a formal agreement with us, to do what we tell you, and we say that the man who disobeys us is doing wrong in three ways: he is disobeying us who fathered him; he is disobeying those who brought him up; and having made an agreement to obey us, he neither obeys, nor tries to make us change our minds, if we are doing something which is not right. When we make him a fair offer, not harshly demanding that he do whatever we order, but allowing him a straight choice, either to make us change our minds, or to do as we say, he does neither. These are the charges, Socrates, to which we claim that you too will render yourself liable, if you do what you are proposing to do—you in particular, more than any of the Athenians."

If I asked them why me in particular, they might perhaps have a justifiable complaint against me in that I, as much as any of the Athenians, really have entered into this agreement with them. They could say, "Socrates, we have convincing evidence to suggest that we and the city *were* to your liking. You could not possibly have spent more of your time living here in Athens than any other Athenian if the place had not been particularly to your liking; you would not have refused ever to leave the city to see famous places—except Corinth, once—or go anywhere else, unless it was to go somewhere on military service; you never went abroad, as other people do, nor were you seized with a desire to know any other city, or any other laws. No, you were satisfied with us, and with our city. In fact, so strongly did you choose us, and agree to live your life as a citizen under us, that you even produced children in the city. You would not have done that if it had not been to your liking.

"Even at your trial, it was open to you to propose a penalty of exile, if you chose, and do then, with the city's permission, what you are now proposing to do without it. On that occasion you put a brave face on it; you said you didn't mind if you had to die; you preferred, so you said, death to exile. Do not those words now make you feel ashamed? Have you no feeling for us, the laws, as you set about destroying us, and do what the meanest slave might do, trying to run away in breach of the contract and agreement by which you agreed to live your life as a citizen? Answer us this question, for a start: are we right in saying that you have agreed—not just verbally, but by your behaviour—to live your life as a citizen under us? Or are we wrong?"

What are we going to say to this, Crito? Can we do anything but agree?

CRITO: We have no choice, Socrates.

SOCRATES: "Aren't you simply breaking," they might say, "contracts and agreements which you have with us? You did not enter into them under compulsion or false pretences. You were not forced to make up your mind on the spur of the moment, but over a period of seventy years, during which you were at liberty to leave, if we were not to your liking, or if you thought the agreement was unfair. You did not choose Sparta or Crete instead, places which you have always described as well-governed; nor did you choose any other city, inside or outside Greece. Even people who are lame, or blind, or crippled in other ways, spend more time away from Athens than you did. *That* is an indication, quite clearly, of how you, more than any of the Athenians, found the city, and us the laws, to your liking. After all, who could find a city to his liking, and not like its laws? And do you now not stand by what you agreed? You will

e

52

b

c

d

e

53

if you take our advice, Socrates. That way you will avoid making yourself ridiculous by leaving the city.

b   "Think about it. If you break this agreement, and put yourself in the wrong in this way, what good will you do yourself or your friends? That your friends will probably have to go into exile as well, be cut off from their city, and forfeit their property, is reasonably clear. And you? Well for a start, if you go to one of the cities nearby, say Thebes or Megara, both of which have good laws, you will come to them, Socrates, as an enemy of their constitution; those who care for their city will look at you with suspi-

c   cion, believing you to be a subverter of the laws. You will also reinforce the opinion of the jury about you. They will decide they did reach the right verdict. After all, there is a strong presumption that a man who subverts the laws will be a corrupting influence on people who are young and foolish.

           "Will you then keep away from cities with good laws, and the most civilised part of mankind? If you do, will it be worth your while remaining alive? Or will you spend your time with them? And will you have the nerve, in your conversations with them—

d   what sort of conversations, Socrates? The ones you had here, about human excellence and justice being the most valuable things for mankind, together with custom and the laws? Don't you think the whole idea of Socrates will be clearly seen to be a disgrace? You certainly should.

           "Or will you leave this part of the world and go to Thessaly, to Crito's family friends? Up there you will find all sorts of anarchy and self-indulgence. I am sure they would be entertained by the amusing story of your running away from prison in some costume or other—wearing a leather jerkin, perhaps, or one of the other disguises favoured by people running away—and altering your appearance. That an old man, in

e   all probability with a small span of life remaining to him, could bring himself to cling to life in this limpet-like way, by transgressing the most important of the laws—will there be no-one who will say this? Perhaps not, if you can manage not to annoy anyone. Otherwise, Socrates, you will have to listen to a lot of unflattering comments about yourself. Are you going to spend your life ingratiating yourself with everyone, being a slave to them? Oh, yes, you will have a whale of a time up there in Thessaly, as if you had

54   emigrated out to dinner in Thessaly. But what, please tell us, will become of all those conversations about justice and other forms of human excellence?

           "Or do you want to remain alive for your children's sake, so that you can bring them up and educate them? How do you feel about taking them to Thessaly, and bringing them up and educating them there, turning them into foreigners, so you can give them that privilege as well? If not, if they are brought up here, will they be any better brought up and educated because you are alive and separated from them? Your friends will be looking after them. Will they look after them if you go to Thessaly to live, and

b   not look after them if you go to the next world? If those who claim to be your friends are any use at all, of course they will not.

           "No, Socrates, obey us who brought you up. Do not regard your children, or life, or anything at all, as more important than justice; you do not want, when you come to the other world, to have to defend yourself on these charges to the rulers there. Neither in this world does it seem to be better, or more just or more godfearing, for you or any of your friends, if you behave like this; nor, when you come to the next world, will it be

c   better for you there. As it is, you go there, if you do go, as one wronged—not by us, the laws, but by men. If on the other hand you depart, after so shamefully returning wrong for wrong, and injury for injury, breaking your own agreement and contract with us, and injuring those whom you had least cause to injure—yourself, your friends, your country and us—then we shall be angry with you while you are alive, and in the next world our brothers, the laws in Hades, will not receive you kindly, since they will know that you tried, to the best of your ability, to destroy us. So do not let Crito persuade you to follow his advice rather than ours."   d

That, I assure you, Crito, my very dear friend, is what I think I hear them saying, just as those gripped by religious fervour think they hear the pipes; the sound of their words rings in my head, and stops me hearing anything else. Be in no doubt. As far as I can see at the moment, if you disagree with them, you will speak in vain. All the same, though, if you think it will do any good, then speak.

CRITO: Socrates, I have nothing to say.

SOCRATES: Then forget about it, Crito. Let us act in the way god points out to us.   e

PHAEDO (in part)

"My dear Cebes, suppose everything which can share in life were to die, and that dead   72c
things, when they died, were to remain in that state, and not come to life again. Isn't it inevitable that in the end everything would be dead, and nothing would be alive? If liv-   d
ing things came from somewhere other than the dead, and if living things did die, what is to stop everything being used up, and finishing up dead?"

"Nothing, I think, Socrates," said Cebes. "I entirely agree with you."

"Yes, Cebes, in my opinion it is as true as anything can be, and we are not mistaken in our agreement on this point. There really is such a thing as coming to life again; the living really are born from the dead; and the souls of the dead really do go on exist-   e
ing."

"And what's more," put in Cebes, "it necessarily follows, I take it, Socrates, both from the argument you have often used in the past, assuming it's true—that learning for us is in fact simply recollection, or being reminded—and also from this argument this morning, that we must have learnt at some earlier time the things we now recollect, or are reminded of. But this is impossible unless our soul existed somewhere before being born in this human shape; so this too seems to point to the soul being something im-   73
mortal."

At this point Simmias intervened. "What are the proofs of that argument, Cebes? Remind me. I can't quite remember them just at the moment."

"One very convincing argument is that when you ask people questions, if you ask them in the right way, they can give completely accurate answers of their own accord—though if the knowledge and the correct answer were not in fact present in them, they would be incapable of doing this. Secondly, the use of diagrams or visual examples of that kind provides an absolutely clear indication that the theory is true."   b

"And if you don't find that convincing, Simmias," said Socrates, "see if you agree when you look at it in a slightly different way. Are you dubious about what we call learning in fact being recollection?"

"Not exactly dubious. It's just that I need the thing itself, this recollection we are talking about. I can more or less remember from hearing the way Cebes set about the proof, so I am convinced really. All the same, I wouldn't mind hearing how you set about it."

c   "Like this. I imagine we agree that if you are reminded of something, you must have known it at some time in the past."

"Yes."

"Well then, do we also agree that when knowledge comes to us in a particular way, it is recollection, or being reminded? What way do I mean? I'll tell you. If seeing something, or hearing it, or receiving some other perception of it, not only makes you recognise that thing, but also gives you the idea of something else—something the knowledge of which is different—aren't we justified in saying you have been reminded

d   of the second thing you had an idea of?"

"What do you mean?"

"Something like this. Knowing a man is not the same thing as knowing a lyre."

"Of course not."

"Right. You know what lovers are like, when they see a lyre or cloak or anything at all their boyfriend generally uses. They recognise the lyre, and along with that knowledge they get a picture of the boy the lyre belongs to. That is what being reminded is. When you see Simmias, for example, you are often reminded of Cebes. I'm sure you could find thousands of examples of the same kind."

"Yes, thousands," said Simmias.

"So is that kind of thing some sort of recollection? Particularly when it happens

e   with things which the passage of time—and not seeing them—has made you forget about?"

"Yes, it certainly is."

"What about seeing a picture of a horse, or a picture of a lyre, and being reminded of a man? Or a picture of Simmias, and being reminded of Cebes? Is that possible?"

"Very much so."

74   "And also, presumably, seeing a picture of Simmias, and being reminded of Simmias himself?"

"That is certainly possible."

"Doesn't it turn out, in all these examples, that the recollection can arise either from things which are similar, or from things which are dissimilar?"

"Yes, it does."

"When you are reminded of something by what is similar, doesn't something else inevitably happen as well? Don't you decide whether or not it falls short at all, in point of similarity, of the object you were reminded of?"

"Yes. Inevitably."

"See if the next step is valid. I take it we are prepared to talk about equality. I don't mean a stick being equal to a stick, or a stone equal to a stone, or anything of that sort. I mean something else, apart from all these, equality itself. Should we say there is such a thing, or no such thing?"

b   "We should unquestionably say there is," said Simmias. "Most emphatically."

"Do we know just what it is?"

"We certainly do."

"Where did we get our knowledge of it from? Wasn't it from what we were talking about just now—from seeing sticks or stones or other things which were equal? Wasn't it from those that we formed an idea of equality itself, although it is different from them? Or doesn't it seem to you to be different? Look at it like this. Take sticks and stones which are equal. Don't they sometimes, although they don't change, seem to be both equal (to one thing) and unequal (to some other thing)?"

"They certainly do."

"What about the elements which make up absolute equality? Do you think they   c
are ever unequal? Do you think equality is ever inequality?"

"No, Socrates, never."

"So the particular examples of equal things are not the same as equality itself."

"Not at all the same, I think, Socrates."

"Yet it was from these particular examples, although they are different from that
true equality, that you nonetheless conceived and derived a knowledge of it?"

"That is quite true."

"And the equal is either like the particulars, or unlike?"

"Yes."

"In fact it makes no difference. Provided you see one thing, and from seeing that
form a conception of another—whether like it or unlike it—then that, without question,   d
is recollection."

"Yes. That's right."

"What about the equality in sticks, and the examples we were talking about a moment ago? Do we find something like this? Do they strike us as being equal in the same
way as equality itself? Do they to some extent fall short of it, in their resemblance to the
equal? Or do they not fall short at all?"

"They fall a long way short," he said.

"All right, then. Sometimes the sight of something can make you think, 'What I
am now seeing is trying to be like some other existing thing, but it falls short of it, and
cannot be quite like it, only an inferior version.' Do we agree that when you think this,
it necessarily follows that you have in fact previously known the thing you say this ob-   e
ject resembles, though it falls short of it?"

"Yes, necessarily."

"And what about us? Is this what we find with the particular equal things and
equality itself, or isn't it?"

"Yes, that's exactly what we find."

"It must follow, then, that we knew about equality before the time when seeing
the particular equal things first gave us the idea that they were all striving to be like   75
equality, but falling short of it."

"That is true."

"We also agree on one further point. We did not get this idea, nor *could* we have
got it, from anything other than sight, or touch, or one of the other senses. I count all the
senses as the same."

"They are the same, Socrates—for the purposes of this argument, at any rate."

"But of course it must be from the senses that we get the idea that all the objects
of our senses are striving after that equality which is really equal, and falling short of it.   b
Is that what we are saying?"

"Yes."

"So before we ever started to see, or hear, or use our other senses, we must in fact
have gained from somewhere a knowledge of what equality itself really is. Otherwise
we could not have referred to it the particular examples of equality derived from the
senses, or decided that they were all doing their best to be like it, but falling short of it."

"That necessarily follows from the earlier steps in the argument, Socrates."

"Well then, were we able to see and hear, and did we possess our other senses, as
soon as we were born?"

"Of course."

"But we must, didn't we say, have gained our knowledge of equality before our   c
ability to perceive?"

"Yes."

"Before we were born, apparently. That must necessarily be when we gained it."

"Apparently."

"If, in that case, we acquired the knowledge before birth, and were born with it, then did we have the knowledge—both before we were born, and the moment we were born—not only of equality, and of greater and smaller, but also of all other things of the same kind? After all, our present argument is not just about equality. It is also about beauty itself, and good itself, and justice and holiness—in fact everything, as I say, to which we could attach this label 'itself' when we ask our questions or give our answers. We must necessarily, therefore, have acquired our knowledge of all these things before we were born."

"That is true."

"Then if, each time we gain this knowledge, we don't forget it, we must always be born possessing it, and must continue to possess it throughout our lives. After all, knowing something is merely to have acquired the knowledge, and not lost it. Isn't that what we call forgetting, Simmias—the loss of knowledge?"

"Exactly that, I think, Socrates."

"The other possibility, I imagine, is that we acquired it before we were born, but then lost it at birth, and only later, through the use of our senses directed towards particular examples, recovered our former knowledge, the knowledge we had once possessed in the past. If that is what happens, wouldn't what we call learning be the recovery of knowledge which is already ours? And would we be justified in calling this recovery recollection, or being reminded?"

"We certainly would."

"Yes, because earlier on we did establish that it was possible, when we perceive something—either by seeing it, or hearing it, or receiving some other perception—to form from it by association an idea of something else which we had forgotten, something which the first thing reminded us of by its dissimilarity or similarity. So as I say, we have two alternatives: either we are all born with this knowledge, and go on possessing it throughout our lives, or else people are simply reminded of it later, when we say they are learning. Learning would then be this reminding, or recollection."

"That is exactly the position, Socrates."

"Which alternative are you going to choose, then, Simmias? Are we born possessing this knowledge, or are we subsequently reminded of things we once had a knowledge of in the past?"

"I don't know how to decide, Socrates, just at the moment."

"How about a different choice? What is your view on this? If a man knows something, could he give an explanation of what he knows, or not?"

"He must necessarily be able to, Socrates."

"And do you think everyone can give an explanation of the things we've just been discussing?"

"If only they could. But I'm very much afraid that this time tomorrow there will be nobody left in the world capable of doing so properly."

"Then you don't think everyone has a knowledge of them, Simmias?"

"By no means."

"So people *are* reminded of what they once learnt in the past?"

"They must be."

"When did our souls acquire this knowledge? Clearly not after we are born as human beings."

"Clearly not."

"So it must have been before that."

"Yes."

"In that case, Simmias, our souls did exist even before their existence in human shape, separate from our bodies, and they did possess the power of thought."

"Unless of course we gain the knowledge of these things at the actual moment of birth, Socrates. That period of time still remains a possibility."

"Fair enough, my friend. But our loss of this knowledge, when does that happen   d if not at birth? We're not born with it—we've just agreed that. Or do we lose it at the precise moment we acquire it? Or is there some other period of time you can suggest?"

"No, Socrates. I didn't realise I was talking nonsense."

"So is this the position we have reached so far, Simmias? If the originals we keep talking about do exist—a beautiful and a good, and every reality of that kind—if it is to this reality that we refer all particulars derived from the senses, finding it readily available and already in our possession, and if we compare the particulars with this reality, it must follow that just as the originals exist, so too our souls must exist even before we are born. And if they don't exist, the argument we have constructed so far will have   e been a waste of time, won't it? Is that the position? Does the existence of our souls before we were born depend on the existence of those originals? So that if the originals did not exist, then our souls can't have existed either?"

"I think it is overwhelmingly clear, Socrates," said Simmias, "that the one does depend on the other. Luckily for us, the argument comes down to the fact that our soul's existence before we are born is as sure as the reality you are now describing. For my part, I find it as clear as anything can be that the existence of all the things of this type— beauty and goodness and everything else you mentioned just now—is as certain as can   77 be. In my opinion at least, the proof is satisfactory."

"And what about Cebes? We must convince Cebes as well."

"He finds it satisfactory," said Simmias, "at least, I *think* he does, though he's the hardest man in the world when he starts being sceptical about an argument. I think he's fully convinced that our soul existed before we were born. That it will continue to exist even after we die does not seem, even to me, Socrates, to have been proved. Cebes's objection of a short while ago still stands—the common fear that the soul may vanish into   b thin air when a man dies, and that this may be the end of its existence. After all, what is to stop it coming into being from somewhere other than from the dead, coalescing and existing before its arrival in a human body, and when it does arrive, and is separated from the body, then itself dying and being destroyed as well?"

"I agree, Simmias," said Cebes. "We seem to have proved half of what we had to   c prove, by showing that our soul existed before we were born. For the proof to be complete, we must now show also that it will go on existing even after we die, just as much as before we were born."

"We *have* shown that already, Simmias and Cebes," said Socrates, "if you care to combine the argument we have just completed with the one before it, which we all accepted—that everything living comes into being from what is dead. After all, if the soul does exist even before birth, and if, when it enters life and is born, the only place it can possibly come from is death, and from being dead, the inescapable conclusion must be that it goes on existing after it dies as well, given that it has to be born again. So the proof you want has been given already. All the same, I suspect   d you and Simmias would be glad to deal with this argument too in greater detail. I think you have the fear children have, that when the soul leaves the body, the force of the wind really may blow it away in all directions, and cause it to disintegrate— especially if you're unlucky enough to die when there's a strong wind blowing, and   e not on a nice calm day."

Cebes laughed. "Assuming we *are* afraid, Socrates, try and reassure us. Or rather, not that *we* are afraid, but perhaps somewhere, even in us, there is a child who does have fears of this kind. Try and make *him* change his mind, and not fear death as some sort of bogeyman."

"You will have to use enchantments. Sing them to him every day, until you have charmed the fears out of him."

78   "All right, Socrates. But where will we find an enchanter who is any good at dealing with fears of this kind, now that you are leaving us?"

"Greece is a large place, Cebes. There must surely be men who are some good living in it. And there are all the nations of non-Greeks as well. You must investigate all these people in your search for this charmer you want. Don't worry about the expense or the work involved; there's no better investment you could make. You should look for him also in your own conversations with one another; after all, it's quite possible you won't easily find anyone better at it than you are."

b   "Consider it done," said Cebes. "But can we go back to the point where we left off, if you have no objection?"

"Of course I have no objection. Why should I?"

"Good."

"Shouldn't we then," said Socrates, "ask ourselves questions like these? What kind of object is liable to have this happen to it—this process of disintegration? For what kind of object can we be afraid that this *might* happen to it? And what kind of object is not liable? After that shouldn't we look into which kind of object the soul is, and, depending on the answer, be optimistic or apprehensive about our soul?"

"Yes. We should."

c   "Well then, isn't something which is compound, or whose nature is composite, liable to have this happen to it, this separation into the elements of which it is composed? And isn't something which is not composite the one object, if any, which is not liable to have this happen to it?"

"I think it is," said Cebes.

"And things that are always constant and unchanging are most likely not composite, while those that vary from one time to another, and are never constant, are most likely to be composite."

"I think so."

"Take the things we were talking about in the previous argument. Is the actual re-
d   ality whose existence we are defining by our questions and answers always unchanging and constant, or does it vary from one time to another? Surely equality itself, beauty itself, what any given thing in itself is, what is real, surely these don't admit of the slightest change? Since the reality of each of them, taken by itself, has a single form, isn't it always unchanging and constant, never anywhere, in any way, admitting any alteration at all?"

"It must necessarily be unchanging and constant, Socrates."

"What about the many particular examples of beautiful things—such as men, or horses, or clothes, or anything else of the same sort—or the particular examples of equal things, or any of the particulars which go by the same names as the realities we were talking about? Are they constant, or are they just the opposite of those realities?
e   Are they virtually never in any way constant, either in relation to themselves, or to each other?"

"You are right about them, too. They are never constant."

"You can touch the particular examples, can't you, or see them, or perceive them with the other senses, whereas you cannot possibly grasp the things which are constant

with any faculty other than rational thought? Things of this kind cannot be seen, can   79
they? They are not visible."

"You are absolutely right," he said.

"So do you want us to say there are two classes of object—one visible, the other
unseen?"

"Yes."

"Shall we say the unseen is always constant, and the visible never constant?"

"Yes, let's say that as well."

"Well then, isn't one part of us our body, and the other part our soul?"   b

"Yes."

"To which class of objects, then, do we say the body would be more similar, and
more closely related?"

"It's obvious to anyone that it is more similar to the visible class."

"What about the soul? Is that something visible, or something unseen?"

"Well, it's certainly not visible by men, Socrates."

"Surely when we talked of things being 'visible' and 'invisible,' we meant to human eyes. Or did you think we were talking about some other eyes?"

"No. Human eyes."

"All right, then. What is our view of the soul? Do we regard it as something visible, or something invisible?"

"Something invisible."

"Unseen, in fact?"

"Yes."

"So the soul is more similar than the body to what is unseen, while the body is   c
more similar to what is visible."

"They must necessarily be, Socrates."

"Well then, did we also say, a little while back, that when the soul makes use of
the body for the purpose of looking into something, by means of sight, or hearing, or
one of the other senses—after all, examining something using the body simply means
examining it using the senses—it is dragged by the body into the realm of things that are
never constant? That it becomes erratic, confused and dizzy, as if it had had too much to
drink, because of its contact with objects which have these qualities?"

"We did."

"On the other hand, when it looks at things all by itself, the soul goes to the home   d
of what is pure, everlasting, immortal and unchanging. Because of their close kinship, it
stays there with it all the time—when it is all by itself, that is, and it is allowed to. Its
wanderings are over, and when it is with the objects in that realm it remains all the time
constant and unchanging, because of its contact with objects which have these qualities.
Don't we call this state of the soul wisdom?"

"You are right, Socrates. Absolutely right."

"Once again, then, on the strength of our previous discussion and of this present
discussion, which class of objects do you think the soul more closely resembles, and is   e
more closely related to?"

"On this line of argument, Socrates, I think anyone would agree—however slow
on the uptake—that in every way possible the soul more closely resembles the class
which is always constant than the class which is not."

"What about the body?"

"The body is more like the other class."

"Now for a third argument. When the soul and body are united, nature ordains
that the body should serve and be subject, the soul rule and be master. This being so,   80

again, which of them do you think is like what is divine, and which like what is mortal? Don't you think what is divine is a natural ruler and leader, and what is mortal a natural subject and servant?"

"Yes, I do."

"Which of them, then, is the soul like?"

"Obviously, Socrates, the soul is like what is divine, the body like what is mortal."

"What do you think, Cebes? Is the conclusion of our whole discussion so far that the soul most resembles what is divine, immortal, susceptible to thought, unvarying in shape, indestructible, and always remaining constant and true to itself? And that the body, on the other hand, most resembles what is human, mortal, varying in shape, not susceptible to thought, destructible, and never remaining true to itself? Have we any objection to this account of things, my dear Cebes?"

"No, we haven't."

"All right, then. If this is how things are, isn't the body liable to be easily destroyed, while the soul, by contrast, is liable to be altogether indestructible—or very nearly so?"

"Of course."

"Think about what happens when a man dies. The visible part of him, his body, which is located in the visible world, and which we call the corpse, is liable to destruction, decay and dissolution. All the same, though, these things do not start happening to it straight away. The corpse is likely to last for a reasonable while, even if a man's body is in the peak of condition when he dies, and he is in the prime of life; and it *can* last for a very long time. If the body is reduced and embalmed, the way people are embalmed in Egypt, it can remain more or less complete for an incredible time; and even if the body decays, still some parts of it—bones, sinews, things like that—are virtually everlasting, aren't they?"

"Yes."

"What about the soul, then, the unseen part of him, which goes to a different place, a place like itself—noble, pure and invisible, the house of Hades in the true sense of the word—to the good and wise god, which is where, god willing, my soul too is shortly going to have to make its way? Does this soul of ours, whose character and nature are as we have described, get blown in all directions and destroyed as soon as it is released from the body, as most people say? Don't you believe it, my dear Cebes and Simmias.

"No, what really happens is much more like this. Either the soul is released in a state of purity, unencumbered by any part of the body, since it had no more to do with the body in its life than it could help; it avoided it and kept itself to itself, since this moment was what it spent all its time rehearsing for. Its life amounted simply to the pursuit of wisdom in the right way, and a genuine rehearsal for dying without regret. Or wouldn't this be a rehearsal for death?"

"It certainly would."

"Does a soul of this type, then, go to the place which is like it, to what is invisible—the divine, the everlasting, the realm of thought? When it gets there, does it have the chance to be happy, now that it has been released from its wandering and folly, its fears and wild desires, and from the rest of the evils men are subject to? Does it, as they say of those who have been initiated, truly spend the rest of time in the company of the gods? Should that be our view, Cebes? Or something different?"

"That, most emphatically."

"Alternatively, I imagine, the soul may be in a polluted state, and unpurified,   b
when it is released from the body; it may have spent all its time in the company of the
body, serving it, in love with it, bewitched by it and by its desires and pleasures. As a result, only what is corporeal seems real to it—things it can touch, or see, or drink, or eat,
or use for sexual enjoyment. What is hidden from the eyes and invisible, what can be
thought or grasped by philosophy, this it has come to hate and fear and avoid. Do you
believe a soul of this type will get away all by itself, pure and unalloyed?"

"Impossible."   c

"Yes. I should imagine it will have patches of what is corporeal, won't it, which
have been grafted on to it by the fellowship and company of the body, through their
constant association, and through the habits of a lifetime?"

"It certainly will."

"Yes. And we should regard what is corporeal as being a burden, my friend—as
heavy, earthbound, and visible. A soul of this type, with this corporeal element, is
weighed down and dragged back to the visible world by fear of the invisible and of
Hades, so the stories go. It haunts tombstones and graves. That is where the shadowy
phantoms of souls are actually seen, the kind of apparitions produced by souls of this
type, souls which have not been set free in a pure state, but still have some element of   d
what is visible—which is why they can be seen."

"Quite likely, Socrates."

"Extremely likely, Cebes. And it won't be the souls of the good, but those of the
wicked, that are compelled to wander round places of that sort, paying the penalty for
their previous evil life. They go on wandering up to the point when their desire for the
element which accompanies them, the corporeal, causes them to go back and be chained   e
to a body again. They are chained, as you would expect, to characters matching their actual habits during their life."

"What sort of characters do you mean, Socrates?"

"Well, for example, if they have made a habit of gluttony, lust and drunkenness,
rather than avoiding them, they will probably be born in the guise of donkeys, or some
animal like that. Don't you think so?"   82

"Very probably."

"And those who have set the highest value on injustice, tyranny and robbery, in
the guise of wolves, or hawks, or kites. Where else can we say souls like this go?"

"Naturally," said Cebes, "that's the kind of form they will take."

"Is it obvious, then," he said, "that the destination of every other class of soul will
depend on how appropriate it is to its previous way of life?"

"Yes, it is obvious. Of course it is."

"The most fortunate among them, then, and the ones who go to the best home,
aren't they those who have made a habit of excellence in public and political life—what
is known as self-control and justice—when these are the result of their disposition or   b
way of life, but not of philosophy and reason?"

"In what way the most fortunate?"

"Because they will probably return as members of an organised and civilised
species like themselves—bees, I should think, or wasps, or ants—and from those back
again to the same, human, species, to become decent men."

"They probably will."

"But to join the company of the gods is not granted to the man who has not practised philosophy, and departed this life in a state of perfect purity—only to the lover of
wisdom. That is why, my dear Simmias and Cebes, true philosophers abstain from all   c
bodily desires; they stand firm, and do not give in to them. It is not because they have

some fear of losing the family fortune, and being poor, as most people have, in their obsession with money. Nor again do they abstain from bodily pleasures through fear of notoriety or the reputation of living an evil life, like those who are eager for public office or public recognition."

"No, that would not be the right motive, Socrates," said Cebes.

d   "Indeed it would not. That is why those who care at all for their own soul, and do not spend their life moulding it to fit the body, forget about all these people. They regard them as not knowing where they are going, and so they themselves set out by a different route. They believe they must not oppose philosophy, or the release and purification it brings; and so, in their pursuit of it, they follow the direction in which it leads."

"How do they do that, Socrates?"

e   "I'll tell you. Philosophers realise that philosophy finds their soul literally imprisoned in the body, and glued to it, unable to look at reality all by itself, but compelled to look at it through the body, as if through prison bars; philosophy finds the soul wallowing in total ignorance. It can see that the cleverness of the prison is the way it uses desire to make the prisoner, as far as possible, his own jailer. . . ."

*   *   *

112e–end*

112e   "There are many rivers, large and varied. And among these many rivers there are four in particular, of which the greatest, which flows in a circle round the perimeter, is the river called Oceanus. Diametrically opposite to this, flowing in the opposite direction, is the river Acheron, which flows through barren countryside, and then flowing under-

113   ground comes out into the Acherusian lake. This is where the souls of the dead come to, most of them, and after waiting their appointed time—some longer, some shorter—are sent back again to be born as living creatures.

"The third river issues from a point between these first two. Near its source it flows into a vast expanse blazing all over with fire; there it creates a lake bigger than our sea, a boiling mixture of water and mud. From there it comes round in a circle, foul and muddy, and as it winds itself round inside the earth, it passes a number of places, among

b   them the margin of the Acherusian lake, though it does not mingle with the water. And when it has wound itself round many times, it emerges underground at a lower point in Tartarus. This is the river they call Pyriphlegethon; its streams belch forth fragments at various places on the earth's surface.

"Opposite this river, in turn, issues the fourth river—into a land which in the first place is strange and wild, as the story goes, and which is entirely the colour of lapis

c   lazuli. They call this the Stygian land, and the lake created by the river's outflow they call the Styx. The water of the river, in its descent, acquires strange properties; finally it disappears below the ground, and winds about, flowing in the opposite direction to Pyriphlegethon, and meets it at the Acherusian lake, coming from the other side. Nor does the water of this river mingle with any other, but it too goes round in a circle and comes out into Tartarus opposite Pyriphlegethon. The name of this river, according to the poets, is Cocytus.

---

*Socrates is giving his imaginative description of the afterlife of the Underworld.

"That is the nature of the landscape there. When the dead arrive at the place to which the spirit conveys each one, they first submit themselves to judgment—those d who have lived a good and holy life, and those who have not. Those who are found to have lived a middling sort of life make their way to the river Acheron. Using the transport which is available to them, of course, they travel to the lake. There they dwell, and are absolved from their wrongdoings by being purified and paying the penalty for them, those who have done any wrong, while for their good deeds they gain reward, each in e proportion to his deserts.

"Those who are judged to be beyond redemption because of the enormity of their crimes—those who are guilty of wholesale robbery from holy places, or of numerous unjust and unlawful killings, or other crimes which are really the equivalent of these— meet the fate they deserve. They are hurled into Tartarus, whence they nevermore emerge.

"Those who are found guilty of crimes which, though great, are redeemable—for example committing an act of violence in a fit of anger against a father or mother, but then living out one's life in a state of repentance; or becoming a killer in some similar 114 way—these too must of necessity be thrown into Tartarus. But after they have been thrown in and remained there a year, the flood washes them back again, those guilty of homicide down Cocytus, those who have killed a father or mother down Pyriphlegethon. And when in their journey they pass the Acherusian lake, there they shout and call out, some to those they have killed, others to those they have treated with b violence. They call out beseeching them, begging them to let them escape into the lake, and to accept them. If they can persuade them, they do escape, and are released from their punishment; otherwise they are borne once more to Tartarus, and from there back again to the rivers. This goes on happening to them until they do persuade those they have wronged, since this is the penalty assigned to them by the judges.

"Those whose lives are judged to have been distinguished by their sanctity are the ones who are released and set free from these places below the ground, as if from prison. They rise, and come to the pure dwelling-place, where they live above the c ground. Of this group, those who have been fully cleansed by philosophy live entirely without their bodies for all time thereafter, and they come to dwellings finer still than those I have mentioned; it is not easy to give you a clear idea of them, nor is there time just at the moment. But for the reasons we have described, we should do everything we can, Simmias, to share in human excellence and wisdom while we are alive. The reward d is a good one, and our hopes high.

"No sensible man would think it right to state dogmatically that the underworld is exactly as I have described it; but to say that either this or something like it is how things are for our souls and their dwellings, since the soul is clearly something immortal, that I do think is right—and worth taking a chance on, for the man who thinks that is how things are, since there is every chance of being proved right. He should recite to himself stories of the kind we have just told, like enchantments; and this, of course, is why I have been giving this account at such length.

"Those are the grounds for optimism about his soul, for anyone who in his life has rejected, as alien to him, the pleasures of the body and the ways of making it beautiful, e believing they do more harm than good. Instead he will have taken seriously the pleasures of learning; he will have beautified his soul with beauties which are its own, and not alien: self-control, justice, courage, freedom and truth. Thus prepared, he now awaits his journey to the underworld. You, Simmias and Cebes, and the rest of you, will 115 all journey there at some time in the future. As for me, my destiny is even now calling me, as the character in the play says, and it's about time for me to be thinking about a bath. I'm sure it's better to have a bath before drinking the poison, and save the women the trouble of washing the corpse."

b   When he said this, Crito asked him, "Well, Socrates, what instructions do you want to give these people here, or me—about your children, or anything else? What can we do for you that will be most welcome to you?"

"The same as I always say, Crito. Nothing unfamiliar. Take care of yourselves, and whatever you do will be welcome to me, to my family, and to you yourselves, even if you make no promises here and now. If you don't care for yourselves, and refuse to spend your lives on the trail of the things we've been talking about today and in the
c   past, then however many solemn promises you make today, it will get you nowhere."

"We'll try our hardest, then," said Crito, "to do as you say. What about burying you? How do you want us to do that?"

"However you like. Provided you can catch me, that is, and I don't get away from you." He glanced at us, laughing to himself, and said, "Gentlemen, I cannot convince Crito that I am Socrates, here, the person discussing things with you and setting out all these arguments. He thinks I am the body he is shortly going to see, and asks how I
d   would like him to bury me. This whole argument I have spent so much time putting together, to show that when I drink the poison I shall not remain with you, but depart—leaving I trust for that happy region of the blessed—all this encouragement, both of you and of myself, was I think wasted on him. So you must give Crito the opposite undertaking, on my behalf, to the one he wanted to give the jury. His was that I would certainly remain. Yours must be that I shall certainly *not* remain, when I die, but depart and
e   go away. Then Crito will be able to bear it more easily, and will not grieve for me when he sees my body being burnt or buried, as if something terrible were happening to me; he won't say, at my funeral, that he is laying out Socrates, or carrying him out, or burying him.

"Take my word for it, my good friend Crito, saying what is wrong is not only disturbing in itself, but is also damaging to the soul. You must cheer up. Tell yourself you are burying my body, and bury it in a way which is pleasing to you, and which you be-
116   lieve to be most in keeping with tradition."

With these words he got up, and went into a room to take a bath. Crito followed him, telling us to stay where we were. We waited, discussing the arguments among ourselves, examining them closely, and then again repeating to ourselves the great misfortune which had befallen us. We thought, quite simply, that we were losing a father, and that we would be spending the rest of our lives as orphans.

After he had had his bath, his children were taken in to him—he had two young
b   sons, and one fully grown—and the women of his household (you probably know them) went in. He spoke to them in Crito's presence, telling them his last wishes, then told the women and children to leave, and himself came back to us.

It was now close to sunset. He had spent a long time inside. He came and sat down, fresh from his bath. There was not much conversation after this. The officer of
c   the prison authorities came and stood close to him. "Socrates," he said, "I am sure I shall not have the same complaint against you that I often have against others. They get angry with me, and curse me when I tell them to drink the poison, though I am only carrying out the orders of the magistrates. But you, I have come to realise during your time here, are altogether the most generous man, the most gentle, and the best, of all those who have ever come here. And now in particular, I am sure you are angry, not with me, since you know the people responsible, but with them. So now, since you know what I
d   have come to say, farewell, and try to endure what must be as willingly as possible." With this he burst into tears, turned, and left us.

Socrates looked after him. "Farewell to you too. We will do as you say." And then to us, "What a charming man. He has kept coming to see me all this time, and sometimes he has stopped to chat; in fact, he has been altogether the best of men. See how generously now he sheds tears for me. Come, Crito, let us do as he tells us. Let someone bring in the poison, if it has been ground. Otherwise, let the man get on with grinding it."

"If you ask me, Socrates," Crito said, "there is still sun on the mountain-tops; it   e has not set yet. Besides, I know of people who have drunk the poison long after they were told to. They have had dinner, and plenty to drink; some of them have even had sex with the people they most wanted. There is no hurry. We still have some time."

"They have their reasons, Crito, the people you are talking about, for acting as they do. They think they gain something by it. And I have my reasons for not acting like   117 that, since I do not think I shall gain anything by drinking the poison a little later—apart from making myself ridiculous in my own eyes by clutching on to life, and trying to save the last drops when the cup is already empty. Go on. Believe me. Do as I say."

Crito, hearing this, nodded to his slave who was standing nearby. The slave went out, and after quite a while came back with the man who was going to administer the poison; he brought it, already ground, in a cup. When Socrates saw the man, he said, "Well, my good fellow, you know about these things. What do we have to do?"

"Just drink it and walk about," he replied, "until you feel a heaviness in your legs. Then lie down. If you do that, it will work of its own accord." As he said this, he handed the cup to Socrates.

He took it quite cheerfully, Echecrates, with no hesitation, and no change in his   b colour or facial expression. Then he gave the man one of his usual quizzical looks, and

The Death of Socrates, 1787, by Jacques-Louis David (1748–1825).
(The Metropolitan Museum of Art, Wolfe Fund, 1931. Catharine Lorillard Wolfe Collection. [31.45])

asked him, "What is your policy about this drink—I mean about pouring a libation to someone? Is it permitted, or not?"

"Socrates, we grind only what we think is the right amount for the person to drink."

c   "I understand. But a prayer to the gods, I take it, is both permitted and right. Let us hope the move from this world to the next may be a good one. That is what I am praying for, and may that be how it turns out."

Saying this he raised the cup to his lips and drained it, quite unperturbed and with every appearance of enjoyment. Most of us, up to that point, had been reasonably successful in controlling our tears, but when we saw him drinking, saw that he had drunk, we could do so no longer. I found the tears coming despite myself, in a flood, so that I covered my face and wept—not for him, but for my own misfortune, and for the kind of

d   man I was losing as a friend.

Crito collapsed sooner than I did. Unable to hold back his tears any longer, he got up and left. Apollodorus had been crying incessantly even before this, but now he started roaring aloud, upsetting us and making us all break down—apart from Socrates himself.

"Really! What an extraordinary way to behave!" he said. "The main reason I sent the women away was so they would not disturb us like this. I have heard it said that one

e   should die in silence. So keep quiet, and be brave."

When we heard this, we were ashamed, and stopped crying. He walked around, and then, when he said his legs were getting heavy, lay down on his back, as the man had told him to. As he did so, the man who had given him the poison put his hands on him, and after a little time tried his feet and legs; then he squeezed his foot hard, and asked him if he could feel it. He said he could not. After that, again, the man tried his shins. Moving his hand up, he showed us that he was getting cold and stiff. Then the

118   man touched him, and said that when the coldness reached his heart, at that point he would be gone.

The chill had just about reached his abdomen when he uncovered his face—he had covered it up—and said, and these were the last words he uttered, "Crito, we owe a cock to Asclepius. Pay the debt. Don't forget."

"It shall be done," Crito replied. "Is there anything else you want to say?"

To this question Socrates made no reply, but shortly afterwards he gave a start, and the man uncovered his face. His eyes were fixed. Seeing this, Crito pressed his lips and eyelids together.

That, Echecrates, was the death of our friend. Of the men of his time that we knew, he was the best, we would claim, and in general the wisest and most just.

MENO

PERSONS OF THE DIALOGUE:

MENO, A SLAVE OF MENO, SOCRATES, ANYTUS

MENO: Can you tell me Socrates—is virtue something that can be taught? Or does it   70
come by practice? Or is it neither teaching nor practice that gives it to a man but natural
aptitude or something else?

SOCRATES: Well Meno, in the old days the Thessalians had a great reputation
among the Greeks for their wealth and their horsemanship. Now it seems they are   b
philosophers as well—especially the men of Larissa, where your friend Aristippus
comes from. It is Gorgias who has done it. He went to that city and captured the hearts
of the foremost of the Aleuadae for his wisdom (among them your own admirer Aristippus), not to speak of other leading Thessalians. In particular he got you into the
habit of answering any question you might be asked, with the confidence and dignity   c
appropriate to those who know the answers, just as he himself invites questions of every kind from anyone in the Greek world who wishes to ask, and never fails to answer
them. But here at Athens, my dear Meno, it is just the reverse. There is a dearth of wis-   71
dom, and it looks as if it had migrated from our part of the country to yours. At any rate
if you put your question to any of our people, they will all alike laugh and say: "You
must think I am singularly fortunate, to know whether virtue can be taught or how it is
acquired. The fact is that far from knowing whether it can be taught, I have no idea what
virtue itself is."

That is my own case. I share the poverty of my fellow-countrymen in this respect,   b
and confess to my shame that I have no knowledge about virtue at all. And how can I
know a property of something when I don't even know what it is? Do you suppose that
somebody entirely ignorant who Meno is could say whether he is handsome and rich
and well-born or the reverse? Is that possible, do you think?

MENO: No. But is this true about yourself, Socrates, that you don't even know
what virtue is? Is this the report that we are to take home about you?   c

SOCRATES: Not only that; you may say also that, to the best of my belief, I have
never yet met anyone who did know.

MENO: What! Didn't you meet Gorgias when he was here?

SOCRATES: Yes.

MENO: And you still didn't think he knew?

SOCRATES: I'm a forgetful sort of person, and I can't say just now what I thought
at the time. Probably he did know, and I expect you know what he used to say about it.
So remind me what it was, or tell me yourself if you will. No doubt you agree with him.   d

MENO: Yes I do.

SOCRATES: Then let's leave him out of it, since after all he isn't here. What do
you yourself say virtue is? I do ask you in all earnestness not to refuse me, but to speak
out. I shall be only too happy to be proved wrong if you and Gorgias turn out to know
this, although I said I had never met anyone who did.

MENO: But there is no difficulty about it. First of all, if it is manly virtue you are   e
after, it is easy to see that the virtue of a man consists in managing the city's affairs ca-

From *Protagoras and Meno*, translated with an introduction by W.K.C. Guthrie (Harmondsworth, Middlesex,
England: Penguin Classics, 1956). Reprinted by permission of Penguin Books Ltd.

pably, and so that he will help his friends and injure his foes while taking care to come to no harm himself. Or if you want a woman's virtue, that is easily described. She must be a good housewife, careful with her stores and obedient to her husband. Then there is another virtue for a child, male or female, and another for an old man, free or slave as you like; and a great many more kinds of virtue, so that no one need be at a loss to say what it is. For every act and every time of life, with reference to each separate function, there is a virtue for each one of us, and similarly, I should say, a vice.

72

SOCRATES: I seem to be in luck. I wanted one virtue and I find that you have a whole swarm of virtues to offer. But seriously, to carry on this metaphor of the swarm, suppose I asked you what a bee is, what is its essential nature, and you replied that bees were of many different kinds, what would you say if I went on to ask: "And is it in being bees that they are many and various and different from one another? Or would you agree that it is not in this respect that they differ, but in something else, some other quality like size or beauty?"

b

MENO: I should say that in so far as they are bees, they don't differ from one another at all.

SOCRATES: Suppose I then continued: "Well, this is just what I want you to tell me. What is that character in respect of which they don't differ at all, but are all the same?" I presume you would have something to say?

c

MENO: I should.

SOCRATES: Then do the same with the virtues. Even if they are many and various, yet at least they all have some common character which makes them virtues. That is what ought to be kept in view by anyone who answers the question: "What is virtue?" Do you follow me?

d

MENO: I think I do, but I don't yet really grasp the question as I should wish.

SOCRATES: Well, does this apply in your mind only to virtue, that there is a different one for a man and a woman and the rest? Is it the same with health and size and strength, or has health the same character everywhere, if it is health, whether it be in a man or any other creature?

e

MENO: I agree that health is the same in a man or in a woman.

SOCRATES: And what about size and strength? If a woman is strong, will it be the same thing, the same strength, that makes her strong? My meaning is that in its character as strength, it is no different, whether it be in a man or in a woman. Or do you think it is?

MENO: No.

73

SOCRATES: And will virtue differ, in its character as virtue, whether it be in a child or an old man, a woman or a man?

MENO: I somehow feel that this is not on the same level as the other cases.

SOCRATES: Well then, didn't you say that a man's virtue lay in directing the city well, and a woman's in directing her household well?

MENO: Yes.

SOCRATES: And is it possible to direct anything well—city or household or anything else—if not temperately and justly?

MENO: Certainly not.

b

SOCRATES: And that means with temperance and justice?

MENO: Of course.

SOCRATES: Then both man and woman need the same qualities, justice and temperance, if they are going to be good.

MENO: It looks like it.

SOCRATES: And what about your child and old man? Could they be good if they were incontinent and unjust?

MENO: Of course not.

SOCRATES: They must be temperate and just?

MENO: Yes.

SOCRATES: So everyone is good in the same way, since they become good by possessing the same qualities.

MENO: So it seems.

SOCRATES: And if they did not share the same virtue, they would not be good in the same way.

MENO: No.

SOCRATES: Seeing then that they all have the same virtue, try to remember and tell me what Gorgias, and you who share his opinion, say it is.

MENO: It must be simply the capacity to govern men, if you are looking for one quality to cover all the instances.

SOCRATES: Indeed I am. But does this virtue apply to a child or a slave? Should a slave be capable of governing his master, and if he does, is he still a slave?

MENO: I hardly think so.

SOCRATES: It certainly doesn't sound likely. And here is another point. You speak of "capacity to govern." Shall we not add "justly but not otherwise"?

MENO: I think we should, for justice is virtue.

SOCRATES: Virtue, do you say, or a virtue?

MENO: What do you mean?

SOCRATES: Something quite general. Take roundness, for instance. I should say that it is a shape, not simply that it is shape, my reason being that there are other shapes as well.

MENO: I see your point, and I agree that there are other virtues besides justice.

SOCRATES: Tell me what they are. Just as I could name other shapes if you told me to, in the same way mention some other virtues.

MENO: In my opinion then courage is a virtue and temperance and wisdom and dignity and many other things.

SOCRATES: This puts us back where we were. In a different way we have discovered a number of virtues when we were looking for one only. This single virtue, which permeates each of them, we cannot find.

MENO: No, I cannot yet grasp it as you want, a single virtue covering them all, as I do in other instances.

SOCRATES: I'm not surprised, but I shall do my best to get us a bit further if I can. You understand, I expect, that the question applies to everything. If someone took the example I mentioned just now, and asked you: "What is shape?" and you replied that roundness is shape, and he then asked you as I did, "Do you mean it is shape or *a* shape?" you would reply of course that it is *a* shape.

MENO: Certainly.

SOCRATES: Your reason being that there are other shapes as well.

MENO: Yes.

SOCRATES: And if he went on to ask you what they were, you would tell him.

MENO: Yes.

SOCRATES: And the same with colour—if he asked you what it is, and on your replying "White," took you up with: "Is white colour or *a* colour?" you would say that it is *a* colour, because there are other colours as well.

MENO: I should.

SOCRATES: And if he asked you to, you would mention other colours which are just as much colours as white is.

MENO: Yes.

SOCRATES: Suppose then he pursued the question as I did, and objected: "We always arrive at a plurality, but that is not the kind of answer I want. Seeing that you call these many particulars by one and the same name, and say that every one of them is a shape, even though they are the contrary of each other, tell me what this is which embraces round as well as straight, and what you mean by shape when you say that
e straightness is a shape as much as roundness. You do say that?"

MENO: Yes.

SOCRATES: "And in saying it, do you mean that roundness is no more round than straight, and straightness no more straight than round?"

MENO: Of course not.

SOCRATES: "Yet you do say that roundness is no more a shape than straightness, and the other way about."

MENO: Quite true.

SOCRATES: "Then what is this thing which is called 'shape'? Try to tell me." If
75 when asked this question either about shape or colour you said: "But I don't understand what you want, or what you mean," your questioner would perhaps be surprised and say: "Don't you see that I am looking for what is the same in all of them?" Would you even so be unable to reply, if the question was: "What is it that is common to roundness and straightness and the other things which you call shapes?"

Do your best to answer, as practice for the question about virtue.
b MENO: No, you do it, Socrates.

SOCRATES: Do you want me to give in to you?

MENO: Yes.

SOCRATES: And will you in your turn give me an answer about virtue?

MENO: I will.

SOCRATES: In that case I must do my best. It's in a good cause.

MENO: Certainly.

SOCRATES: Well now, let's try to tell you what shape is. See if you accept this definition. Let us define it as the only thing which always accompanies colour. Does
c that satisfy you, or do you want it in some other way? I should be content if your definition of virtue were on similar lines.

MENO: But that's a naïve sort of definition, Socrates.

SOCRATES: How?

MENO: Shape, if I understand what you say, is what always accompanies colour. Well and good—but if somebody says that he doesn't know what colour is, but is no better off with it than he is with shape, what sort of answer have you given him, do you think?

SOCRATES: A true one; and if my questioner were one of the clever, disputatious and quarrelsome kind, I should say to him: "You have heard my answer. If it is wrong,
d it is for you to take up the argument and refute it." However, when friendly people, like you and me, want to converse with each other, one's reply must be milder and more conducive to discussion. By that I mean that it must not only be true, but must em-
e ploy terms with which the questioner admits he is familiar. So I will try to answer you like that. Tell me therefore, whether you recognize the term "end"; I mean limit or boundary—all these words I use in the same sense. Prodicus might perhaps quarrel with us, but I assume you speak of something being bounded or coming to an end. That is all I mean, nothing subtle.

MENO: I admit the notion, and believe I understand your meaning.

SOCRATES: And again, you recognize "surface" and "solid," as they are used in   76
geometry?

MENO: Yes.

SOCRATES: Then with these you should by this time understand my definition of
shape. To cover all its instances, I say that shape is that in which a solid terminates, or
more briefly, it is the limit of a solid.

MENO: And how do you define colour?

SOCRATES: What a shameless fellow you are, Meno. You keep bothering an old
man to answer, but refuse to exercise your memory and tell me what was Gorgias's def-   b
inition of virtue.

MENO: I will, Socrates, as soon as you tell me this.

SOCRATES: Anyone talking to you could tell blindfolded that you are a handsome
man and still have your admirers.

MENO: Why so?

SOCRATES: Because you are forever laying down the law as spoilt boys do, who
act the tyrant as long as their youth lasts. No doubt you have discovered that I can never   c
resist good looks. Well, I will give in and let you have your answer.

MENO: Do by all means.

SOCRATES: Would you like an answer *à la* Gorgias, such as you would most readily follow?

MENO: Of course I should.

SOCRATES: You and he believe in Empedocles's theory of effluences, do you not?

MENO: Whole-heartedly.

SOCRATES: And passages to which and through which the effluences make their
way?

MENO: Yes.

SOCRATES: Some of the effluences fit into some of the passages, whereas others   d
are too coarse or too fine.

MENO: That is right.

SOCRATES: Now you recognize the term "sight"?

MENO: Yes.

SOCRATES: From these notions, then, "grasp what I would tell," as Pindar says.
Colour is an effluence from shapes commensurate with sight and perceptible by it.

MENO: That seems to me an excellent answer.

SOCRATES: No doubt it is the sort you are used to. And you probably see that it
provides a way to define sound and smell and many similar things.

MENO: So it does.   e

SOCRATES: Yes, it's a high-sounding answer, so you like it better than the one on
shape.

MENO: I do.

SOCRATES: Nevertheless, son of Alexidemus, I am convinced that the other is
better; and I believe you would agree with me if you had not, as you told me yesterday,
to leave before the mysteries, but could stay and be initiated.*

MENO: I would stay, Socrates, if you gave me more answers like this.   77

---

*Evidently the Athenians are about to celebrate the famous rites of the Eleusinian Mysteries, but
Meno has to return to Thessaly before they fall due. Plato frequently plays upon the analogy between religious initiation, which bestows a revelation of divine secrets, and the insight that comes from initiation into
the truths of philosophy.

SOCRATES: You may be sure I shan't be lacking in keenness to do so, both for your sake and mine; but I'm afraid I may not be able to do it often. However, now it is your turn to do as you promised, and try to tell me the general nature of virtue. Stop making many out of one, as the humorists say when somebody breaks a plate. Just leave virtue whole

b and sound and tell me what it is, as in the examples I have given you.

MENO: It seems to me then, Socrates, that virtue is, in the words of the poet, "to rejoice in the fine and have power," and I define it as desiring fine things and being able to acquire them.

SOCRATES: When you speak of a man desiring fine things, do you mean it is good things he desires?

MENO: Certainly.

SOCRATES: Then do you think some men desire evil and others good? Doesn't ev-

c eryone, in your opinion, desire good things?

MENO: No.

SOCRATES: And would you say that the others suppose evils to be good, or do they still desire them although they recognize them as evil?

MENO: Both, I should say.

SOCRATES: What? Do you really think that anyone who recognizes evils for what they are, nevertheless desires them?

MENO: Yes.

SOCRATES: Desires in what way? To possess them?

MENO: Of course.

d SOCRATES: In the belief that evil things bring advantage to their possessor, or harm?

MENO: Some in the first belief, but some also in the second.

SOCRATES: And do you believe that those who suppose evil things bring advantage understand that they are evil?

MENO: No, that I can't really believe.

SOCRATES: Isn't it clear then that this class, who don't recognize evils for what

e they are, don't desire evil but what they think is good, though in fact it is evil; those who through ignorance mistake bad things for good obviously desire the good.

MENO: For them I suppose that is true.

SOCRATES: Now as for those whom you speak of as desiring evils in the belief that they do harm to their possessor, these presumably know that they will be injured by them?

MENO: They must.

78 SOCRATES: And don't they believe that whoever is injured is, in so far as he is injured, unhappy?

MENO: That too they must believe.

SOCRATES: And unfortunate?

MENO: Yes.

SOCRATES: Well, does anybody want to be unhappy and unfortunate?

MENO: I suppose not.

SOCRATES: Then if not, nobody desires what is evil; for what else is unhappiness but desiring evil things and getting them?

b MENO: It looks as if you are right, Socrates, and nobody desires what is evil.

SOCRATES: Now you have just said that virtue consists in a wish for good things plus the power to acquire them. In this definition the wish is common to everyone, and in that respect no one is better than his neighbour.

MENO: So it appears.

SOCRATES: So if one man is better than another, it must evidently be in respect of the power, and virtue, according to your account, is the power of acquiring good things.   c

MENO: Yes, my opinion is exactly as you now express it.

SOCRATES: Let us see whether you have hit the truth this time. You may well be right. The power of acquiring good things, you say, is virtue?

MENO: Yes.

SOCRATES: And by good do you mean such things as health and wealth?

MENO: I include the gaining both of gold and silver and of high and honourable office in the State.

SOCRATES: Are these the only classes of goods that you recognize?

MENO: Yes, I mean everything of that sort.

SOCRATES: Right. In the definition of Meno, hereditary guest-friend of the Great   d
King, the acquisition of gold and silver is virtue. Do you add "just and righteous" to the word "acquisition," or doesn't it make any difference to you? Do you call it virtue all the same even if they are unjustly acquired?

MENO: Certainly not.

SOCRATES: Vice then?

MENO: Most certainly.

SOCRATES: So it seems that justice or temperance or piety, or some other part of virtue, must attach to the acquisition. Otherwise, although it is a means to good things,   e
it will not be virtue.

MENO: No, how could you have virtue without these?

SOCRATES: In fact lack of gold and silver, if it results from failure to acquire it—either for oneself or another—in circumstances which would have made its acquisition unjust, is itself virtue.

MENO: It would seem so.

SOCRATES: Then to have such goods is no more virtue than to lack them. Rather we may say that whatever is accompanied by justice is virtue, whatever is without qual-   79
ities of that sort is vice.

MENO: I agree that your conclusion seems inescapable.

SOCRATES: But a few minutes ago we called each of these—justice, temperance, and the rest—a part of virtue?

MENO: Yes, we did.

SOCRATES: So it seems you are making a fool of me.

MENO: How so, Socrates?

SOCRATES: I have just asked you not to break virtue up into fragments, and given you models of the type of answer I wanted, but taking no notice of this you tell me that virtue consists in the acquisition of good things with justice; and justice, you agree, is a   b
part of virtue.

MENO: True.

SOCRATES: So it follows from your own statements that to act with a part of virtue is virtue, if you call justice and all the rest parts of virtue. The point I want to make is that whereas I asked you to give me an account of virtue as a whole, far from telling me what it is itself you say that every action is virtue which exhibits a part of virtue, as if you had already told me what the whole is, so that I should recognize it even   c
if you chop it up into bits. It seems to me that we must put the same old question to you, my dear Meno—the question: "What is virtue?"—if every act becomes virtue when combined with a part of virtue. That is, after all, what it means to say that every act performed with justice is virtue. Don't you agree that the same question needs to be put? Does anyone know what a part of virtue is, without knowing the whole?

MENO: I suppose not.

d   SOCRATES: No, and if you remember, when I replied to you about shape just now, I believe we rejected the type of answer that employs terms which are still in question and not yet agreed upon.

MENO: We did, and rightly.

SOCRATES: Then please do the same. While the nature of virtue as a whole is still under question, don't suppose that you can explain it to anyone in terms of its parts, or by any similar type of explanation. Understand rather that the same question remains to

e   be answered; you say this and that about virtue, but what *is* it? Does this seem nonsense to you?

MENO: No, to me it seems right enough.

SOCRATES: Then go back to the beginning and answer my question. What do you and your friend say that virtue is?

MENO: Socrates, even before I met you they told me that in plain truth you are a

80   perplexed man yourself and reduce others to perplexity. At this moment I feel you are exercising magic and witchcraft upon me and positively laying me under your spell until I am just a mass of helplessness. If I may be flippant, I think that not only in outward appearance but in other respects as well you are exactly like the flat stingray that one

b   meets in the sea. Whenever anyone comes into contact with it, it numbs him, and that is the sort of thing that you seem to be doing to me now. My mind and my lips are literally numb, and I have nothing to reply to you. Yet I have spoken about virtue hundreds of times, held forth often on the subject in front of large audiences, and very well too, or so I thought. Now I can't even say what it is. In my opinion you are well advised not to leave Athens and live abroad. If you behaved like this as a foreigner in another country, you would most likely be arrested as a wizard.

SOCRATES: You're a real rascal, Meno. You nearly took me in.

MENO: Just what do you mean?

c   SOCRATES: I see why you used a simile about me.

MENO: Why, do you think?

SOCRATES: To be compared to something in return. All good-looking people, I know perfectly well, enjoy a game of comparisons. They get the best of it, for naturally handsome folk provoke handsome similes. But I'm not going to oblige you. As for myself, if the stingray paralyses others only through being paralysed itself, then the comparison is just, but not otherwise. It isn't that, knowing the answers myself, I perplex other people. The truth is rather that I infect them also with the perplexity I feel myself.

d   So with virtue now. I don't know what it is. You may have known before you came into contact with me, but now you look as if you don't. Nevertheless I am ready to carry out, together with you, a joint investigation and inquiry into what it is.

MENO: But how will you look for something when you don't in the least know what it is? How on earth are you going to set up something you don't know as the object of your search? To put it another way, even if you come right up against it, how will you know that what you have found is the thing you didn't know?

e   SOCRATES: I know what you mean. Do you realize that what you are bringing up is the trick argument that a man cannot try to discover either what he knows or what he does not know? He would not seek what he knows, for since he knows it there is no need of the inquiry, nor what he does not know, for in that case he does not even know what he is to look for.

81   MENO: Well, do you think it a good argument?

SOCRATES: No.

MENO: Can you explain how it fails?

SOCRATES: I can. I have heard from men and women who understand the truths of religion—

[Here he presumably pauses to emphasize the solemn change of tone which the dialogue undergoes at this point.]

MENO: What did they say?

SOCRATES: Something true, I thought, and fine.

MENO: What was it, and who were they?

SOCRATES: Those who tell it are priests and priestesses of the sort who make it their business to be able to account for the functions which they perform. Pindar speaks of it too, and many another of the poets who are divinely inspired. What they say is this—see whether you think they are speaking the truth. They say that the soul of man is immortal: at one time it comes to an end—that which is called death—and at another is born again, but is never finally exterminated. On these grounds a man must live all his days as righteously as possible. For those from whom

> Persephone receives requital for ancient doom,
> In the ninth year she restores again
> Their souls to the sun above.
> From whom rise noble kings
> And the swift in strength and greatest in wisdom;
> And for the rest of time
> They are called heroes and sanctified by men.*

Thus the soul, since it is immortal and has been born many times, and has seen all things both here and in the other world, has learned everything that is. So we need not be surprised if it can recall the knowledge of virtue or anything else which, as we see, it once possessed. All nature is akin, and the soul has learned everything, so that when a man has recalled a single piece of knowledge—*learned* it, in ordinary language—there is no reason why he should not find out all the rest, if he keeps a stout heart and does not grow weary of the search; for seeking and learning are in fact nothing but recollection.

We ought not then to be led astray by the contentious argument you quoted. It would make us lazy, and is music in the ears of weaklings. The other doctrine produces energetic seekers after knowledge; and being convinced of its truth, I am ready, with your help, to inquire into the nature of virtue.

MENO: I see, Socrates. But what do you mean when you say that we don't learn anything, but that what we call learning is recollection? Can you teach me that it is so?

SOCRATES: I have just said that you're a rascal, and now you ask me if I can teach you, when I say there is no such thing as teaching, only recollection. Evidently you want to catch me contradicting myself straight away.

MENO: No, honestly, Socrates, I wasn't thinking of that. It was just habit. If you can in any way make clear to me that what you say is true, please do.

SOCRATES: It isn't an easy thing, but still I should like to do what I can since you ask me. I see you have a large number of retainers here. Call one of them, anyone you like, and I will use him to demonstrate it to you.

MENO: Certainly. *(To a slave-boy.)* Come here.

---

*The quotation is from Pindar.

SOCRATES: He is a Greek and speaks our language?

MENO: Indeed yes—born and bred in the house.

SOCRATES: Listen carefully then, and see whether it seems to you that he is learning from me or simply being reminded.

MENO: I will.

SOCRATES: Now boy, you know that a square is a figure like this?

[Socrates begins to draw figures in the sand at his feet. He points to the square ABCD.]

BOY: Yes.

c   SOCRATES: It has all these four sides equal?

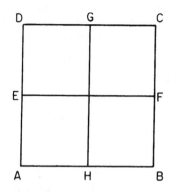

BOY: Yes.

SOCRATES: And these lines which go through the middle of it are also equal? (*The lines* EF, GH.)

BOY: Yes.

SOCRATES: Such a figure could be either larger or smaller, could it not?

BOY: Yes.

SOCRATES: Now if this side is two feet long, and this side the same, how many feet will the whole be? Put it this way. If it were two feet in this direction and only one in that, must not the area be two feet taken once?

BOY: Yes.

d   SOCRATES: But since it is two feet this way also, does it not become twice two feet?

BOY: Yes.

SOCRATES: And how many feet is twice two? Work it out and tell me.

BOY: Four.

SOCRATES: Now could one draw another figure double the size of this, but similar, that is, with all its sides equal like this one?

BOY: Yes.

SOCRATES: It is on this line then, according to you, that we shall make the eight-feet square, by taking four of the same length?

BOY: Yes.

SOCRATES: How many feet will its area be?

BOY: Eight.

SOCRATES: Now then, try to tell me how long each of its sides will be. The present figure has a side of two feet. What will be the side of the double-sized one?   e

BOY: It will be double, Socrates, obviously.

SOCRATES: You see, Meno, that I am not teaching him anything, only asking. Now he thinks he knows the length of the side of the eight-feet square.

MENO: Yes.

SOCRATES: But does he?

MENO: Certainly not.

SOCRATES: He thinks it is twice the length of the other.

MENO: Yes.

SOCRATES: Now watch how he recollects things in order—the proper way to recollect.

You say that the side of double length produces the double-sized figure? Like this I mean, not long this way and short that. It must be equal on all sides like the first figure,   83 only twice its size, that is eight feet. Think a moment whether you still expect to get it from doubling the side.

BOY: Yes, I do.

SOCRATES: Well now, shall we have a line double the length of this *(AB)* if we add another the same length at this end *(BJ)*?

BOY: Yes.

SOCRATES: It is on this line then, according to you, that we shall make the eight-feet square, by taking four of the same length?

BOY: Yes.

SOCRATES: Let us draw in four equal lines (*i.e. counting* AJ, *and adding* JK, KL, *and* LA *made complete by drawing in its second half* LD), using the first as a base. Does   b this not give us what you call the eight-feet figure?

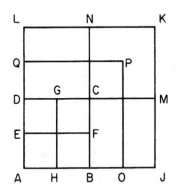

BOY: Certainly.

SOCRATES: But does it contain these four squares, each equal to the original four-feet one?

[Socrates has drawn in the lines CM, CN *to complete the squares that he wishes to point out.]*

BOY: Yes.

SOCRATES: How big is it then? Won't it be four times as big?

BOY: Of course.

SOCRATES: And is four times the same as twice?

BOY: Of course not.

c   SOCRATES: So doubling the side has given us not a double but a fourfold figure?

BOY: True.

SOCRATES: And four times four are sixteen, are they not?

BOY: Yes.

SOCRATES: Then how big is the side of the eight-feet figure? This one has given us four times the original area, hasn't it?

BOY: Yes.

SOCRATES: And a side half the length gave us a square of four feet?

BOY: Yes.

SOCRATES: Good. And isn't a square of eight feet double this one and half that?

BOY: Yes.

SOCRATES: Will it not have a side greater than this one but less than that?

d   BOY: I think it will.

SOCRATES: Right. Always answer what you think. Now tell me: was not this side two feet long, and this one four?

BOY: Yes.

SOCRATES: Then the side of the eight-feet figure must be longer than two feet but shorter than four?

BOY: It must.

e   SOCRATES: Try to say how long you think it is.

BOY: Three feet.

SOCRATES: If so, shall we add half of this bit (*BO*, half of *BJ*) and make it three feet? Here are two, and this is one, and on this side similarly we have two plus one; and here is the figure you want.

[Socrates completes the square AOPQ.*]*

BOY: Yes.

SOCRATES: If it is three feet this way and three that, will the whole area be three times three feet?

BOY: It looks like it.

SOCRATES: And that is how many?

BOY: Nine.

SOCRATES: Whereas the square double our first square had to be how many?

BOY: Eight.

SOCRATES: But we haven't yet got the square of eight feet even from a three-feet side?

BOY: No.

84   SOCRATES: Then what length will give it? Try to tell us exactly. If you don't want to count it up, just show us on the diagram.

BOY: It's no use, Socrates, I just don't know.

SOCRATES: Observe, Meno, the stage he has reached on the path of recollection. At the beginning he did not know the side of the square of eight feet. Nor indeed does he know it now, but then he thought he knew it and answered boldly, as was appropriate—he felt no perplexity. Now however he does feel perplexed. Not only does he not know the answer; he doesn't even think he knows.

MENO: Quite true.   b

SOCRATES: Isn't he in a better position now in relation to what he didn't know?

MENO: I admit that too.

SOCRATES: So in perplexing him and numbing him like the sting-ray, have we done him any harm?

MENO: I think not.

SOCRATES: In fact we have helped him to some extent towards finding out the right answer, for now not only is he ignorant of it but he will be quite glad to look for it. Up to now, he thought he could speak well and fluently, on many occasions and before large audiences, on the subject of a square double the size of a given square, maintaining that it must have a side of double the length.   c

MENO: No doubt.

SOCRATES: Do you suppose then that he would have attempted to look for, or learn, what he thought he knew (though he did not), before he was thrown into perplexity, became aware of his ignorance, and felt a desire to know?

MENO: No.

SOCRATES: Then the numbing process was good for him?

MENO: I agree.

SOCRATES: Now notice what, starting from this state of perplexity, he will discover by seeking the truth in company with me, though I simply ask him questions without teaching him. Be ready to catch me if I give him any instruction or explanation instead of simply interrogating him on his own opinions.   d

[Socrates here rubs out the previous figures and starts again.]

Tell me, boy, is not this our square of four feet? *(ABCD.)* You understand?

BOY: Yes.

SOCRATES: Now we can add another equal to it like this? *(BCEF.)*

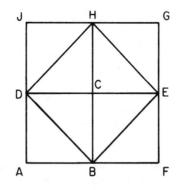

BOY: Yes.

SOCRATES: And a third here, equal to each of the others? *(CEGH.)*

BOY: Yes.

SOCRATES: And then we can fill in this one in the corner? *(DCHJ.)*

BOY: Yes.

SOCRATES: Then here we have four equal squares?

BOY: Yes.

e

SOCRATES: And how many times the size of the first square is the whole?

BOY: Four times.

SOCRATES: And we want one double the size. You remember?

BOY: Yes.

85

SOCRATES: Now does this line going from corner to corner cut each of these squares in half?

BOY: Yes.

SOCRATES: And these are four equal lines enclosing this area? *(BEHD.)*

BOY: They are.

SOCRATES: Now think. How big is this area?

BOY: I don't understand.

SOCRATES: Here are four squares. Has not each line cut off the inner half of each of them?

BOY: Yes.

SOCRATES: And how many such halves are there in this figure? *(BEHD.)*

BOY: Four.

SOCRATES: And how many in this one? *(ABCD.)*

BOY: Two.

b

SOCRATES: And what is the relation of four to two?

BOY: Double.

SOCRATES: How big is this figure then?

BOY: Eight feet.

SOCRATES: On what base?

BOY: This one.

SOCRATES: The line which goes from corner to corner of the square of four feet?

BOY: Yes.

SOCRATES: The technical name for it is "diagonal"; so if we use that name, it is your personal opinion that the square on the diagonal of the original square is double its area.

BOY: That is so, Socrates.

SOCRATES: What do you think, Meno? Has he answered with any opinions that were not his own?

c

MENO: No, they were all his.

SOCRATES: Yet he did not know, as we agreed a few minutes ago.

MENO: True.

SOCRATES: But these opinions were somewhere in him, were they not?

MENO: Yes.

SOCRATES: So a man who does not know has in himself true opinions on a subject without having knowledge.

MENO: It would appear so.

SOCRATES: At present these opinions, being newly aroused, have a dream-like quality. But if the same questions are put to him on many occasions and in different ways, you can see that in the end he will have a knowledge on the subject as accurate as anybody's.

d

MENO: Probably.

SOCRATES: This knowledge will not come from teaching but from questioning. He will recover it for himself.

MENO: Yes.

SOCRATES: And the spontaneous recovery of knowledge that is in him is recollection, isn't it?

MENO: Yes.

SOCRATES: Either then he has at some time acquired the knowledge which he now has, or he has always possessed it. If he always possessed it, he must always have known; if on the other hand he acquired it at some previous time, it cannot have been in this life, unless somebody has taught him geometry. He will behave in the same way   e
with all geometrical knowledge, and every other subject. Has anyone taught him all these? You ought to know, especially as he has been brought up in your household.

MENO: Yes, I know that no one ever taught him.

SOCRATES: And has he these opinions, or hasn't he?

MENO: It seems we can't deny it.

SOCRATES: Then if he did not acquire them in this life, isn't it immediately clear that he possessed and had learned them during some other period?   86

MENO: It seems so.

SOCRATES: When he was not in human shape?

MENO: Yes.

SOCRATES: If then there are going to exist in him, both while he is and while he is not a man, true opinions which can be aroused by questioning and turned into knowledge, may we say that his soul has been forever in a state of knowledge? Clearly he always either is or is not a man.

MENO: Clearly.

SOCRATES: And if the truth about reality is always in our soul, the soul must be   b
immortal, and one must take courage and try to discover—that is, to recollect—what one doesn't happen to know, or (more correctly) remember, at the moment.

MENO: Somehow or other I believe you are right.

SOCRATES: I think I am. I shouldn't like to take my oath on the whole story, but one thing I am ready to fight for as long as I can, in word and act: that is, that we shall be better, braver and more active men if we believe it right to look for what we don't know than if we believe there is no point in looking because what we don't know we   c
can never discover.

MENO: There too I am sure you are right.

SOCRATES: Then since we are agreed that it is right to inquire into something that one does not know, are you ready to face with me the question: what is virtue?

MENO: Quite ready. All the same, I would rather consider the question as I put it at the beginning, and hear your views on it; that is, are we to pursue virtue as something that can be taught, or do men have it as a gift of nature or how?   d

SOCRATES: If I were your master as well as my own, Meno, we should not have inquired whether or not virtue can be taught until we had first asked the main question—what it is; but not only do you make no attempt to govern your own actions—you prize your freedom, I suppose—but you attempt to govern mine. And you succeed too, so I shall let you have your way. There's nothing else for it, and it seems we must inquire into a single property of something about whose essential nature we are still in the   e
dark. Just grant me one small relaxation of your sway, and allow me, in considering whether or not it can be taught, to make use of a hypothesis—the sort of thing, I mean, that geometers often use in their inquiries. When they are asked, for example, about a given area, whether it is possible for this area to be inscribed as a triangle in a given cir-   87
cle, they will probably reply: "I don't know yet whether it fulfils the conditions, but I think I have a hypothesis which will help us in the matter. It is this. If the area is such that, when one has applied it [*e.g., as a rectangle*] to the given line [*i.e., the diameter*]

of the circle, it is deficient by another rectangle similar to the one which is applied, then, I should say, one result follows; if not, the result is different. If you ask me, then, about the inscription of the figure in the circle—whether it is possible or not—I am ready to answer you in this hypothetical way."*

Let us do the same about virtue. Since we don't know what it is or what it resembles, let us use a hypothesis in investigating whether it is teachable or not. We shall say: "What attribute of the soul must virtue be, if it is to be teachable or otherwise?" Well, in the first place, if it is anything else but knowledge, is there a possibility of anyone teaching it—or, in the language we used just now, reminding someone of it? We needn't worry about which name we are to give to the process, but simply ask: will it be teachable? Isn't it plain to everyone that a man is not taught anything except knowledge?

MENO: That would be my view.

SOCRATES: If on the other hand virtue is some sort of knowledge, clearly it could be taught.

MENO: Certainly.

SOCRATES: So that question is easily settled; I mean, on what condition virtue would be teachable.

MENO: Yes.

SOCRATES: The next point then, I suppose, is to find out whether virtue is knowledge or something different.

MENO: That is the next question, I agree.

SOCRATES: Well then, do we assert that virtue is something good? Is that assumption a firm one for us?

MENO: Undoubtedly.

SOCRATES: That being so, if there exists any good thing different from, and not associated with, knowledge, virtue will not necessarily be any form of knowledge. If on the other hand knowledge embraces everything that is good, we shall be right to suspect that virtue is knowledge.

MENO: Agreed.

SOCRATES: First then, is it virtue which makes us good?

MENO: Yes.

SOCRATES: And if good, then advantageous. All good things are advantageous, are they not?

MENO: Yes.

SOCRATES: So virtue itself must be something advantageous?

MENO: That follows also.

SOCRATES: Now suppose we consider what are the sort of things that profit us. Take them in a list. Health, we may say, and strength and good looks, and wealth—these and their like we call advantageous, you agree?

MENO: Yes.

SOCRATES: Yet we also speak of these things as sometimes doing harm. Would you object to that statement?

MENO: No, it is so.

SOCRATES: Now look here: what is the controlling factor which determines whether each of these is advantageous or harmful? Isn't it right use which makes them advantageous, and lack of it, harmful?

---

*The geometrical illustration here adduced by Socrates is very loosely and obscurely expressed. Sir Thomas Heath in his *History of Greek Mathematics* (1921, vol. i, p. 298) says that C. Blass, writing in 1861, already knew of thirty different interpretations, and that many more had appeared since then. Fortunately it is not necessary to understand the example in order to grasp the hypothetical method Socrates is expounding.

MENO: Certainly.

SOCRATES: We must also take spiritual qualities into consideration. You recognize such things as temperance, justice, courage, quickness of mind, memory, nobility of character and others?

MENO: Yes of course I do.

SOCRATES: Then take any such qualities which in your view are not knowledge   b
but something different. Don't you think they may be harmful as well as advantageous? Courage for instance, if it is something thoughtless, is just a sort of confidence. Isn't it true that to be confident without reason does a man harm, whereas a reasoned confidence profits him?

MENO: Yes.

SOCRATES: Temperance and quickness of mind are no different. Learning and discipline are profitable in conjunction with wisdom, but without it harmful.

MENO: That is emphatically true.

SOCRATES: In short, everything that the human spirit undertakes or suffers will   c
lead to happiness when it is guided by wisdom, but to the opposite, when guided by folly.

MENO: A reasonable conclusion.

SOCRATES: If then virtue is an attribute of the spirit, and one which cannot fail to be beneficial, it must be wisdom; for all spiritual qualities in and by themselves are neither advantageous nor harmful, but become advantageous or harmful by the presence   d
with them of wisdom or folly. If we accept this argument, then virtue, to be something advantageous, must be a sort of wisdom.

MENO: I agree.

SOCRATES: To go back to the other class of things, wealth and the like, of which we said just now that they are sometimes good and sometimes harmful, isn't it the same with them? Just as wisdom when it governs our other psychological impulses turns them to advantage, and folly turns them to harm, so the mind by its right use and control of these material assets makes them profitable, and by wrong use renders them   e
harmful.

MENO: Certainly.

SOCRATES: And the right user is the mind of the wise man, the wrong user the mind of the foolish.

MENO: That is so.

SOCRATES: So we may say in general that the goodness of non-spiritual assets depends on our spiritual character, and the goodness of that on wisdom. This argument shows that the advantageous element must be wisdom; and virtue, we agree, is advantageous, so that amounts to saying that virtue, either in whole or in part, is wisdom.   89

MENO: The argument seems to me fair enough.

SOCRATES: If so, good men cannot be good by nature.

MENO: I suppose not.

SOCRATES: There is another point. If they were, there would probably be experts   b
among us who could recognize the naturally good at an early stage. They would point them out to us and we should take them and shut them away safely in the Acropolis, sealing them up more carefully than bullion to protect them from corruption and ensure that when they came to maturity they would be of use to the State.

MENO: It would be likely enough.

SOCRATES: Since then goodness does not come by nature, is it got by learning?   c

MENO: I don't see how we can escape the conclusion. Indeed it is obvious on our assumption that, if virtue is knowledge, it is teachable.

SOCRATES: I suppose so. But I wonder if we were right to bind ourselves to that.

MENO: Well, it seemed all right just now.

SOCRATES: Yes, but to be sound it has got to seem all right not only "just now" but at this moment and in the future.

d   MENO: Of course. But what has occurred to you to make you turn against it and suspect that virtue may not be knowledge?

SOCRATES: I'll tell you. I don't withdraw from the position that if it is knowledge, it must be teachable; but as for its being knowledge, see whether you think my doubts on this point are well founded. If anything—not virtue only—is a possible subject of instruction, must there not be teachers and students of it?

MENO: Surely.

e   SOCRATES: And what of the converse, that if there are neither teachers nor students of a subject, we may safely infer that it cannot be taught?

MENO: That is true. But don't you think there are teachers of virtue?

SOCRATES: All I can say is that I have often looked to see if there are any, and in spite of all my efforts I cannot find them, though I have had plenty of fellow-searchers, the kind of men especially whom I believe to have most experience in such matters. But look, Meno, here's a piece of luck. Anytus has just sat down beside us. We couldn't do better than make him a partner in our inquiry. In the first place he is the son of

90 Anthemion, a man of property and good sense, who didn't get his money out of the blue or as a gift—like Ismenias of Thebes who has just come into the fortune of a Croesus—but earned it by his own brains and hard work. Besides this he shows himself a decent, modest citizen with no arrogance or bombast or offensiveness about him. Also he brought up his son well and had him properly educated, as the Athenian people appre-

b   ciate: look how they elect him into the highest offices in the State. This is certainly the right sort of man with whom to inquire whether there are any teachers of virtue, and if so who they are.

Please help us, Anytus—Meno, who is a friend of your family, and myself—to find out who may be the teachers of this subject. Look at it like this. If we wanted Meno

c   to become a good doctor, shouldn't we send him to the doctors to be taught?

ANYTUS: Of course.

SOCRATES: And if we wanted him to become a shoemaker, to the shoemakers?

ANYTUS: Yes.

SOCRATES: And so on with other trades?

ANYTUS: Yes.

SOCRATES: Now another relevant question. When we say that to make Meno a doctor we should be right in sending him to the doctors, have we in mind that the sensi-

d   ble thing is to send him to those who profess the subject rather than to those who don't, men who charge a fee as professionals, having announced that they are prepared to teach whoever likes to come and learn?

ANYTUS: Yes.

SOCRATES: The same is surely true of flute-playing and other accomplishments.

e   If you want to make someone a performer on the flute it would be very foolish to refuse to send him to those who undertake to teach the art and are paid for it, but to go and bother other people instead and have him try to learn from them—people who don't set up to be teachers or take any pupils in the subject which we want our young man to learn. Doesn't that sound very unreasonable?

ANYTUS: Sheer stupidity I should say.

SOCRATES: I agree. And now we can both consult together about our visitor

91 Meno. He has been telling me all this while that he longs to acquire the kind of wisdom and virtue which fits men to manage an estate or govern a city, to look after their par-

ents, and to entertain and send off guests in proper style, both their own countrymen and foreigners. With this in mind, to whom would it be right to send him? What we have just said seems to show that the right people are those who profess to be teachers of b virtue and offer their services freely to any Greek who wishes to learn, charging a fixed fee for their instruction.

ANYTUS: Whom do you mean by that, Socrates?

SOCRATES: Surely you know yourself that they are the men called Sophists.

ANYTUS: Good heavens, what a thing to say! I hope no relative of mine or any of c my friends, Athenian or foreign, would be so mad as to go and let himself be ruined by those people. That's what they are, the manifest ruin and corruption of anyone who comes into contact with them.

SOCRATES: What, Anytus? Can they be so different from other claimants to useful knowledge that they not only don't do good, like the rest, to the material that one puts in their charge, but on the contrary spoil it—and have the effrontery to take money for doing so? I for one find it difficult to believe you. I know that one of them alone, d Protagoras, earned more money from being a Sophist than an outstandingly fine craftsman like Phidias and ten other sculptors put together. A man who mends old shoes or restores coats couldn't get away with it for a month if he gave them back in worse condition than he received them; he would soon find himself starving. Surely it is incredi- e ble that Protagoras took in the whole of Greece, corrupting his pupils and sending them away worse than when they came to him, for more than forty years. I believe he was nearly seventy when he died, and had been practising for forty years, and all that time— indeed to this very day—his reputation has been consistently high; and there are plenty of others besides Protagoras, some before his time and others still alive. Are we to sup- 92 pose from your remark that they consciously deceive and ruin young men, or are they unaware of it themselves? Can these remarkably clever men—as some regard them—be mad enough for that?

ANYTUS: Far from it, Socrates. It isn't they who are mad, but rather the young men who hand over their money, and those responsible for them, who let them get into the Sophists' hands, are even worse. Worst of all are the cities who allow them in, or b don't expel them, whether it be a foreigner or one of themselves who tries that sort of game.

SOCRATES: Has one of the Sophists done you a personal injury, or why are you so hard on them?

ANYTUS: Heavens, no! I've never in my life had anything to do with a single one of them, nor would I hear of any of my family doing so.

SOCRATES: So you've had no experience of them at all?

ANYTUS: And don't want any either.

SOCRATES: You surprise me. How can you know what is good or bad in some- c thing when you have no experience of it?

ANYTUS: Quite easily. At any rate I know *their* kind, whether I've had experience or not.

SOCRATES: It must be second sight, I suppose; for how else you know about them, judging from what you tell me yourself, I can't imagine. However, we are not asking whose instruction it is that would ruin Meno's character. Let us say that d those are the Sophists if you like, and tell us instead about the ones we want. You can do a good turn to a friend of your father's house if you will let him know to whom in our great city he should apply for proficiency in the kind of virtue I have just described.

ANYTUS: Why not tell him yourself?

SOCRATES: Well, I did mention the men who in my opinion teach these things, but apparently I was talking nonsense. So you say, and you may well be right. Now it is your turn to direct him; mention the name of any Athenian you like.

ANYTUS: But why mention a particular individual? Any decent Athenian gentleman whom he happens to meet, if he follows his advice, will make him a better man than the Sophists would.

SOCRATES: And did these gentlemen get their fine qualities spontaneously—self-taught, as it were, and yet able to teach this untaught virtue to others?

ANYTUS: I suppose they in their turn learned it from forebears who were gentlemen like themselves. Would you deny that there have been many good men in our city?

SOCRATES: On the contrary, there are plenty of good statesmen here in Athens and have been as good in the past. The question is, have they also been good teachers of their own virtue? That is the point we are discussing now—not whether or not there are good men in Athens or whether there have been in past times, but whether virtue can be taught. It amounts to the question whether the good men of this and former times have known how to hand on to someone else the goodness that was in themselves, or whether on the contrary it is not something that can be handed over, or that one man can receive from another. That is what Meno and I have long been puzzling over. Look at it from your own point of view. You would say that Themistocles was a good man?

ANYTUS: Yes, none better.

SOCRATES: And that he, if anyone, must have been a good teacher of his own virtue?

ANYTUS: I suppose so, if he wanted to be.

SOCRATES: But don't you think he must have wanted others to become worthy men—above all, surely, his own son? Do you suppose he grudged him this and purposely didn't pass on his own virtue to him? You must have heard that he had his son Cleophantus so well trained in horsemanship that he could stand upright on horseback and throw a javelin from that position; and many other wonderful accomplishments the young man had, for his father had him taught and made expert in every skill that a good instructor could impart. You must have heard this from older people?

ANYTUS: Yes.

SOCRATES: No one, then, could say that there was anything wrong with the boy's natural powers?

ANYTUS: Perhaps not.

SOCRATES: But have you ever heard anyone, young or old, say that Cleophantus the son of Themistocles was a good and wise man in the way that his father was?

ANYTUS: Certainly not.

SOCRATES: Must we conclude then that Themistocles' aim was to educate his son in other accomplishments, but not to make him any better than his neighbours in his own type of wisdom—that is, supposing that virtue could be taught?

ANYTUS: I hardly think we can.

SOCRATES: So much then for Themistocles as a teacher of virtue, whom you yourself agree to have been one of the best men of former times. Take another example, Aristides son of Lysimachus. You accept him as a good man?

ANYTUS: Surely.

SOCRATES: He too gave his son Lysimachus the best education in Athens, in all subjects where a teacher could help; but did he make him a better man than his neighbour? You know him, I think, and can say what he is like. Or again there is Pericles, that great and wise man. He brought up two sons, Paralus and Xanthippus, and had them taught riding, music, athletics, and all the other skilled pursuits till they were as good as any in Athens. Did he then not want to make them good men? Yes, he wanted that, no doubt, but I am afraid it is something that cannot be done by teaching. And in case you should think that only very few, and those the most insignificant, lacked this power, consider that Thucydides also had two sons, Melesias and Stephanus, to whom he gave an excellent education. Among other things they were the best wrestlers in Athens, for c he gave one to Xanthias to train and the other to Eudoxus—the two who, I understand, were considered the finest wrestlers of their time. You remember?

ANYTUS: I have heard of them.

SOCRATES: Surely then he would never have had his children taught these expen- d sive pursuits and yet refused to teach them to be good men—which would have cost nothing at all—if virtue could have been taught? You are not going to tell me that Thucydides was a man of no account, or that he had not plenty of friends both at Athens and among the allies? He came of an influential family and was a great power both here and in the rest of Greece. If virtue could have been taught, he would have found the man to make his sons good, either among our own citizens or abroad, supposing his political duties left him no time to do it himself. No, my dear Anytus, it looks as if it cannot be e taught.

ANYTUS: You seem to me, Socrates, to be too ready to run people down. My ad- vice to you, if you will listen to it, is to be careful. I dare say that in all cities it is easier to do a man harm than good, and it is certainly so here, as I expect you know yourself. 95

SOCRATES: Anytus seems angry, Meno, and I am not surprised. He thinks I am slandering our statesmen, and moreover he believes himself to be one of them. He doesn't know what slander really is: if he ever finds out he will forgive me.

However, tell me this yourself: are there not similar fine characters in your coun- try?

MENO: Yes, certainly.

SOCRATES: Do they come forward of their own accord to teach the young? Do b they agree that they are teachers and that virtue can be taught?

MENO: No indeed, they don't agree on it at all. Sometimes you will hear them say that it can be taught, sometimes that it cannot.

SOCRATES: Ought we then to class as teachers of it men who are not even agreed that it can be taught?

MENO: Hardly, I think.

SOCRATES: And what about the Sophists, the only people who profess to teach it? Do you think they do?

MENO: The thing I particularly admire about Gorgias, Socrates, is that you will c never hear him make this claim; indeed he laughs at the others when he hears them do so. In his view his job is to make clever speakers.

SOCRATES: So you too don't think the Sophists are teachers?

MENO: I really can't say. Like most people I waver—sometimes I think they are and sometimes I think they are not.

SOCRATES: Has it ever occurred to you that you and our statesmen are not alone in this? The poet Theognis likewise says in one place that virtue is teachable and in an- d other that it is not.

MENO: Really? Where?

SOCRATES: In the elegiacs in which he writes:

Eat, drink, and sit with men of power and weight,
Nor scorn to gain the favour of the great.
For fine men's teaching to fine ways will win thee:
Low company destroys what wit is in thee.

There he speaks as if virtue can be taught, doesn't he? e

MENO: Clearly.

SOCRATES: But elsewhere he changes his ground a little:

> Were mind by art created and instilled
> Immense rewards had soon the pockets filled

of the people who could do this. Moreover

> No good man's son would ever worthless be,
> Taught by wise counsel. But no teacher's skill
> Can turn to good what is created ill.

96

Do you see how he contradicts himself?

MENO: Plainly.

SOCRATES: Can you name any other subject, in which the professed teachers are not only not recognized as teachers of others, but are thought to have no understanding of it themselves, and to be no good at the very subject they profess to teach; whereas those who are acknowledged to be the best at it are in two minds whether it can be taught or not? When people are so confused about a subject, can you say that they are in a true sense teachers?

b

MENO: Certainly not.

SOCRATES: Well, if neither the Sophists nor those who display fine qualities themselves are teachers of virtue, I am sure no one else can be, and if there are no teachers, there can be no students either.

c

MENO: I quite agree.

SOCRATES: And we have also agreed that a subject of which there were neither teachers nor students was not one which could be taught.

MENO: That is so.

SOCRATES: Now there turn out to be neither teachers nor students of virtue, so it would appear that virtue cannot be taught.

d

MENO: So it seems, if we have made no mistake; and it makes me wonder, Socrates, whether there are in fact no good men at all, or how they are produced when they do appear.

SOCRATES: I have a suspicion, Meno, that you and I are not much good. Our masters Gorgias and Prodicus have not trained us properly. We must certainly take ourselves in hand, and try to find someone who will improve us by hook or by crook. I say this with our recent discussion in mind, for absurdly enough we failed to perceive that it is not only under the guidance of knowledge that human action is well and rightly conducted. I believe that may be what prevents us from seeing how it is that men are made good.

e

MENO: What do you mean?

SOCRATES: This. We were correct, were we not, in agreeing that good men must be profitable or useful? It cannot be otherwise, can it?

MENO: No.

SOCRATES: And again that they will be of some use if they conduct our affairs aright—that also was correct?

97

MENO: Yes.

SOCRATES: But in insisting that knowledge was a *sine qua non* for right leadership, we look like being mistaken.

MENO: How so?

SOCRATES: Let me explain. If someone knows the way to Larissa, or anywhere else you like, then when he goes there and takes others with him he will be a good and capable guide, you would agree?

MENO: Of course.

SOCRATES: But if a man judges correctly which is the road, though he has never b been there and doesn't know it, will he not also guide others aright?

MENO: Yes, he will.

SOCRATES: And as long as he has a correct opinion on the points about which the other has knowledge, he will be just as good a guide, believing the truth but not knowing it.

MENO: Just as good.

SOCRATES: Therefore true opinion is as good a guide as knowledge for the purpose of acting rightly. That is what we left out just now in our discussion of the nature of virtue, when we said that knowledge is the only guide to right action. There was also, c it seems, true opinion.

MENO: It seems so.

SOCRATES: So right opinion is something no less useful than knowledge.

MENO: Except that the man with knowledge will always be successful, and the man with right opinion only sometimes.

SOCRATES: What? Will he not always be successful so long as he has the right opinion?

MENO: That must be so, I suppose. In that case, I wonder why knowledge should be so much more prized than right opinion, and indeed how there is any difference be- d tween them.

SOCRATES: Shall I tell you the reason for your surprise, or do you know it?

MENO: No, tell me.

SOCRATES: It is because you have not observed the statues of Daedalus. Perhaps you don't have them in your country.

MENO: What makes you say that?

SOCRATES: They too, if no one ties them down, run away and escape. If tied, they stay where they are put.   e

MENO: What of it?

SOCRATES: If you have one of his works untethered, it is not worth much: it gives you the slip like a runaway slave. But a tethered specimen is very valuable, for they are magnificent creations. And that, I may say, has a bearing on the matter of true opinions. True opinions are a fine thing and do all sorts of good so long as they stay in their place; but they will not stay long. They run away from a man's mind, so they are not worth 98 much until you tether them by working out the reason. That process, my dear Meno, is recollection, as we agreed earlier. Once they are tied down, they become knowledge, and are stable. That is why knowledge is something more valuable than right opinion. What distinguishes one from the other is the tether.

MENO: It does seem something like that, certainly.

SOCRATES: Well of course, I have only been using an analogy myself, not knowl- b edge. But it is not, I am sure, a mere guess to say that right opinion and knowledge are different. There are few things that I should claim to know, but that at least is among them, whatever else is.

MENO: You are quite right.

SOCRATES: And is this right too, that true opinion when it governs any course of action produces as good a result as knowledge?

MENO: Yes, that too is right, I think.

c   SOCRATES: So that for practical purposes right opinion is no less useful than knowledge, and the man who has it is no less useful than the one who knows.

MENO: That is so.

SOCRATES: Now we have agreed that the good man is useful.

MENO: Yes.

SOCRATES: To recapitulate then: assuming that there are men good and useful to the community, it is not only knowledge that makes them so, but also right opinion, and

d   neither of these comes by nature but both are acquired—or do you think either of them *is* natural?

MENO: No.

SOCRATES: So if both are acquired, good men themselves are not good by nature.

MENO: No.

SOCRATES: That being so, the next thing we inquired was whether their goodness was a matter of teaching, and we decided that it would be, if virtue were knowledge, and conversely, that if it could be taught, it would be knowledge.

MENO: Yes.

e   SOCRATES: Next, that if there were teachers of it, it could be taught, but not if there were none.

MENO: That was so.

SOCRATES: But we have agreed that there are no teachers of it, and so that it cannot be taught and is not knowledge.

MENO: We did.

SOCRATES: At the same time we agreed that it is something good, and that to be useful and good consists in giving right guidance.

MENO: Yes.

99   SOCRATES: And that these two, true opinion and knowledge, are the only things which direct us aright and the possession of which makes a man a true guide. We may except chance, because what turns out right by chance is not due to human direction, and say that where human control leads to right ends, these two principles are directive, true opinion and knowledge.

MENO: Yes, I agree.

SOCRATES: Now since virtue cannot be taught, we can no longer believe it to be

b   knowledge, so that one of our two good and useful principles is excluded, and knowledge is not the guide in public life.

MENO: No.

SOCRATES: It is not then by the possession of any wisdom that such men as Themistocles, and the others whom Anytus mentioned just now, became leaders in their cities. This fact, that they do not owe their eminence to knowledge, will explain why they are unable to make others like themselves.

MENO: No doubt it is as you say.

SOCRATES: That leaves us with the other alternative, that it is well-aimed conjec-

c   ture which statesmen employ in upholding their countries' welfare. Their position in relation to knowledge is no different from that of prophets and tellers of oracles, who under divine inspiration utter many truths, but have no knowledge of what they are saying.

MENO: It must be something like that.

SOCRATES: And ought we not to reckon those men divine who with no conscious thought are repeatedly and outstandingly successful in what they do or say?

MENO: Certainly.

SOCRATES: We are right therefore to give this title to the oracular priests and the

d   prophets that I mentioned, and to poets of every description. Statesmen too, when by their speeches they get great things done yet know nothing of what they are saying, are to be considered as acting no less under divine influence, inspired and possessed by the divinity.

MENO: Certainly.

SOCRATES: Women, you know, Meno, do call good men "divine," and the Spartans too, when they are singing a good man's praises, say "He is divine."

MENO: And it looks as if they are right—though our friend Anytus may be annoyed with you for saying so.   e

SOCRATES: I can't help that. We will talk to him some other time. If all we have said in this discussion, and the questions we have asked, have been right, virtue will be acquired neither by nature nor by teaching. Whoever has it gets it by divine dispensation without taking thought, unless he be the kind of statesman who can create another like himself. Should there be such a man, he would be among the living practically what   100 Homer said Tiresias was among the dead, when he described him as the only one in the underworld who kept his wits—"the others are mere flitting shades." Where virtue is concerned such a man would be just like that, a solid reality among shadows.

MENO: That is finely put, Socrates.

SOCRATES: On our present reasoning then, whoever has virtue gets it by divine dispensation. But we shall not understand the truth of the matter until, before asking how men get virtue, we try to discover what virtue is in and by itself. Now it is time for me to go; and my request to you is that you will allay the anger of your friend Anytus by convincing him that what you now believe is true. If you succeed, the Athenians may have cause to thank you.

SYMPOSIUM

THE SPEAKERS IN THE DIALOGUE

AGATHON a writer of tragedies
SOCRATES a truth-loving eccentric
PHAEDRUS an idealist
PAUSANIAS a realist—Agathon's lover
ARISTOPHANES a writer of comedies
ERYXIMACHUS a doctor
ALCIBIADES politician and playboy

PROLOGUE—APOLLODORUS AND A FRIEND

APOLLODORUS: You couldn't have asked anyone better. I live in Phalerum, and the day   172 before yesterday I was going up to town when a man I know caught sight of me disappearing in the distance. He gave me a shout, calling me (a little facetiously) "You there! Citizen of Phalerum! Hey, Apollodorus! Wait a moment."

So I stopped and waited.

"Apollodorus," he said, "I've been looking for you for ages. I wanted to ask you about the time when Agathon and Socrates and Alcibiades and the others all met for
b   dinner. I want to know what was said about love. I was told about it by a man who had talked to Phoenix, son of Philippus; he said you knew about it as well. He wasn't much help—couldn't remember anything very definite. Can you give me your version? After all, who better than you to talk about Socrates' conversations? For instance, were you at the dinner-party yourself, or not?"

"You must have been given a pretty garbled account, if you think the party you're
c   asking about took place recently enough for me to have been at it."

"Oh! I thought you were."

"Really, Glaucon, how could I have been? It's ages since Agathon last lived in Athens, and less than three years since I became friends with Socrates, and got into the
173   habit of keeping up with what he says and does every day. Before that my life was just a random whirl of activity. I thought I was extremely busy, but in fact I was the most pathetic creature imaginable, just as you are now, doing anything to avoid philosophical thought."

"Very funny. When *did* the party happen, then?"

"It was when we were still children, when Agathon won the prize with his first tragedy, the day after he and the members of the chorus made the usual winners' thanksgivings."

"Oh, I see. It was a long time ago, then. Who told you about it? Was it Socrates himself?"

b   "God, no. I got it from the man who told Phoenix, a man called Aristodemus, from Cydathenaeum. Small man, never wears shoes. He'd been at the party; in fact, I think he must have been one of Socrates' keenest admirers in those days. But I've also asked Socrates about some of the things he told me, and his version agreed with Aristodemus'."

"You must tell me all about it, and walking into town is an ideal opportunity. You can talk, and I will listen."

c   So we discussed the party as we went along, and that's why, as I said originally, I'm a good person to ask about it. And if I've got to tell it to you as well, I'd better get on with it. In any case, I get tremendous pleasure out of talking about philosophy myself, or listening to other people talk about it, quite apart from thinking it's good for me. Other conversation, especially your kind, about money or business,
d   bores me stiff. You're my friends, but I feel sorry for you, because you think you're getting somewhere, when you're not. You in turn probably think me misguided, and you may well be right. However, I don't *think* you are misguided; I know for certain you are.

FRIEND: Still the old Apollodorus we know and love. Never a good word for
e   yourself or anyone else. As far as I can see, you regard absolutely everyone, starting with yourself, as a lost cause—except for Socrates, that is. I don't know where you picked up the nickname "softy"; it certainly doesn't fit your conversation—always full of fury against yourself, and everyone else apart from Socrates.

APOLLODORUS: And if that's my opinion of myself and the rest of you, then obviously I'm crazy, or mistaken, I suppose.

FRIEND: Let's not argue about that now, Apollodorus. Just do as I ask, and tell me what was said at Agathon's party.

174   APOLLODORUS: The conversation went something like this . . . or better, let me try to tell it to you right from the beginning, as Aristodemus told it to me.

ARISTODEMUS' ACCOUNT

I met Socrates, all washed and brushed, and wearing shoes (a thing he hardly ever did). I asked him where he was going looking so elegant.

"I'm going to dinner with Agathon. I avoided the first celebration last night; I couldn't face the crowd. But I said I'd come this evening. I'm looking elegant, because   b
Agathon always looks elegant. What about you? How do you feel about coming to dinner uninvited?"

"I'll do anything you tell me."

"Come on then. Let's ignore the proverb, 'good men come uninvited to lesser men's feasts,' or rather let's change it, to 'good men come uninvited to Agathon's feast.' After all, Homer does worse than ignore it; he completely contradicts it. His   c
Agamemnon is an outstanding warrior, while his Menelaus is a man of straw. But when Agamemnon is sacrificing and feasting Homer lets Menelaus come to the feast without an invitation, though that's a case of a lesser man coming to dinner with a better."

"I'm afraid, in my case, that Homer is likely to be nearer the mark than you, Socrates. It'll be a question of a nonentity coming to dinner uninvited with a wise man. You'd better decide what you'll say if you do take me. I'm not coming uninvited—only   d
as your guest."

"Two heads are better than one. We'll think of something to say. Come on."

So off we went. But Socrates, absorbed in his own thoughts, got left behind on the way. I was going to wait for him, but he told me to go on ahead. So I turned up at   e
Agathon's house by myself, and found the door open. In fact, it was slightly embarrassing, because one of the house-slaves met me, and took me straight in, where I found the others had just sat down to dinner. Agathon saw me come in, and at once said, "Aristodemus, you're just in time to have dinner with us. I hope that's what you've come for. If not, it'll have to wait for another time. I tried to get hold of you yesterday, to ask you, but could not find you. How come you haven't brought Socrates with you?"

I turned round and looked behind me, and couldn't see Socrates anywhere. So I explained that I had come with Socrates. In fact, but for his invitation, I wouldn't have come at all.

"I'm glad you did. But where is he?"

"He was right behind me just now. I've no more idea than you where he could   175
have got to."

Agathon turned to a slave. "Could you go and look for Socrates, please, and ask him in? Aristodemus, why don't you sit over there by Eryximachus?"

While one slave was giving me a wash, so I could sit down to dinner, another slave came in: "That Socrates you asked me to look for has gone wandering up to the front door of the wrong house. He's just standing there. I asked him to come in, but he won't."

"How odd. Still, don't give up. Keep on asking him."   b

But I said, "No, leave him alone. He's always doing this. It doesn't matter where he is. He just wanders off and stands there. I don't think he'll be long. Don't badger him; just leave him."

"Well, if you say so, I suppose we'd better." He turned to the slaves. "The rest of us will eat now. Serve the meal just as you like. No-one's going to tell you how to do it, any more than I ever tell you. Imagine we're all your guests, and try to give us a meal we'll enjoy."

c   So we started having dinner, though still no sign of Socrates. Agathon kept wanting to send people to look for him, but I wouldn't let him. When he did turn up, he hadn't been long by his standards, but even so we were about halfway through dinner. Agathon, who'd sat down last, at a table on his own, said "Come and sit next to me, Socrates. Then perhaps I shall absorb whatever it was you were thinking about outside.
d   You must have found the answer, or you wouldn't have come in to join us."

Socrates sat down. "Wouldn't it be marvellous, Agathon," he said, "if ideas were the kind of things which could be imparted simply by contact, and those of us who had few could absorb them from those who had a lot—in the same sort of way that liquid can flow from a full container to an empty one, if you put a piece of string between
e   them? If that's the nature of ideas, then I think I'm lucky to be sitting next to you, and getting a nice, substantial transfusion. My ideas aren't much use. They have an ambiguous, dreamlike quality, whereas yours are brilliant, and with so much scope for further improvement. You're only young, and yet they were particularly brilliant the day before yesterday, as more than thirty thousand Greeks can testify."

"Don't be sarcastic, Socrates. And let's settle this question of ideas a bit later. We'll give Dionysus the casting vote. But you'd better have dinner first."

176   So Socrates sat down and ate, with the others. We poured offerings, sang hymns, and did all the usual things. Then our thoughts turned to drinking, and Pausanias made a suggestion. "Well, gentlemen, how can we make things as painless for ourselves as possible? I must admit to feeling rather frail after yesterday evening. I need a breather, and I expect most of you do, too. After all, you were there as well. So, how can we make
b   our drinking as painless as possible?"

ARISTOPHANES: I couldn't agree more, Pausanias. Whatever else we do, we don't want to let ourselves in for another evening's hard drinking. I'm one of those who sank without trace last night.

ERYXIMACHUS: I'm glad you both feel like that. But we ought also to consider how strong Agathon is feeling.

AGATHON: Not at all strong.

c   ERYXIMACHUS: It would certainly be a stroke of luck for people like Aristodemus and Phaedrus and me, if you hard drinkers are prepared to take an evening off. We're not in your league. I'm not worried about Socrates—he's equally happy either way, so he won't mind what we do. But as far as I can see, no-one here is all that keen on drinking a lot, so perhaps I can tell you the truth about getting drunk without causing too
d   much offence. My experience as a doctor leaves me in no doubt that getting drunk is bad for you. I'm not keen on drinking to excess myself, and I wouldn't advise anyone else to, especially anyone who still had a hangover from yesterday.

PHAEDRUS: Well, I generally follow your advice, especially on medical matters. So will the others, if they have any sense.

e   So we all agreed just to drink what we felt like, rather than treating it as an opportunity to get drunk.

ERYXIMACHUS: Good, that's settled then. We'll all drink as much as we feel like, and there's no compulsion on anyone. And since we've got that sorted out, I've another suggestion to make. I don't think we need this flute girl who's just started playing. She can play to herself, or to the women upstairs, if she feels like it, but for this evening I
177   suggest we stick to conversation. And I've an idea what we might talk about, if you want to hear it.

Everyone said they did want to hear it, and urged him to make his suggestion.

ERYXIMACHUS: Well, it arises out of Euripides' *Melanippe*. And it isn't really my idea. It's Phaedrus'. He gets quite worked up about it. "Don't you think it's odd, Eryximachus," he says, "that most of the other gods have had hymns and songs of praise written to them by the poets, but never a word in praise of Eros, the oldest and greatest   b god? And it's not for want of good poets, either. Or think of the great teachers—they've recorded the exploits of Heracles and other heroes, in prose. Prodicus, for example, does that sort of thing beautifully. Now maybe that's not very surprising, but I came across a book the other day, by a well-known writer, with an extraordinary eulogy in it on the value of salt. You can find any number of things singled out for praise in this way. What is surprising is that there should be so much enthusiasm for that kind of   c thing, and yet no-one, up to the present day, has ever found himself able to praise Eros as he deserves. He is a remarkable god, but he has been totally neglected."

I agree with Phaedrus. I'd like to do him a favour and make my contribution. What's more, the present gathering seems an ideal opportunity to praise the god. So, if you agree, we can quite happily spend our time in talk. I propose that each of us in turn,   d going round anticlockwise, should make a speech, the best he can, in praise of Eros. Phaedrus can start, since he is in the position of honour, and since the whole thing was his idea.

SOCRATES: I don't think anyone will vote against you, Eryximachus. I'm certainly not going to refuse, since love is the only thing I ever claim to know anything about. Agathon and Pausanias won't mind—still less Aristophanes, since his only inter-   e ests in life are Dionysus and Aphrodite. In fact I can't see anyone here who *will* object. It's a little unfair on those of us sitting here in the last positions. Still, if you first speakers speak well enough, we shan't have to worry. Good luck, Phaedrus. You go first, and make your speech in praise of Eros.

They all agreed with Socrates, and told Phaedrus to start. Aristodemus couldn't   178 remember the exact details of everybody's speech, nor in turn can I remember precisely what he said. But I can give you the gist of those speeches and speakers which were most worth remembering.

Phaedrus, as I said, began—something like this.

PHAEDRUS

Eros is a great god, a marvel to men and gods alike. This is true in many ways, and it is especially true of his birth. He is entitled to our respect, as the oldest of the gods—as I can prove. Eros has no parents, either in reality or in works of prose and poetry. Take Hesiod,   b for example. All he says is that in the beginning there was Chaos. ". . . and then came the full-breasted Earth, the eternal and immovable foundation of everything, and Eros." Acusilaus agrees with Hesiod, that after Chaos there were just these two, Earth and Eros. And then there's Parmenides' theory about his birth, that "Eros was created first of the Gods." So there is widespread agreement that Eros is of great antiquity. And being very   c old he also brings us very great benefits. I can see nothing better in life for a young boy, as soon as he is old enough, than finding a good lover, nor for a lover than finding a boy friend. Love, more than anything (more than family, or position, or wealth), implants in men the thing which must be their guide if they are to live a good life. And what is that? It is a horror of what is degrading, and a passionate desire for what is good. These qualities   d are essential if a state or an individual is to accomplish anything great or good. Imagine a man in love being found out doing something humiliating, or letting someone else do something degrading to him, because he was too cowardly to stop it. It would embarrass him more to be found out by the boy he loved than by his father or his friends, or anyone.

Eros and Psyche, a Roman copy ca. 150 B.C. after a Greek statue. Caught in a tender embrace, the two youthful figures, Eros and Psyche, symbolize both love and the human soul. While his friends describe Eros as a young, beautiful god (like this statue depicts), Socrates presents a very different picture. (© Archivi Alinari, 1991/Art Resource)

And you can see just the same thing happening with the boy. He is more worried about be- e
ing caught behaving badly by his admirers than by anyone else. So if there were some
way of arranging that a state, or an army, could be made up entirely of pairs of lovers, it is
impossible to imagine a finer population. They would avoid all dishonour, and compete
with one another for glory: in battle, this kind of army, though small, fighting side by side   179
could conquer virtually the whole world. After all, a lover would sooner be seen by anyone deserting his post or throwing away his weapons, rather than by his boyfriend. He
would normally choose to die many times over instead. And as for abandoning the boy, or
not trying to save him if he is in danger—no-one is such a coward as not to be inspired
with courage by Eros, making him the equal of the naturally brave man. Homer says, and   b
rightly, that god breathes fire into some of his heroes. And it is just this quality, whose origin is to be found within himself, that Eros imparts to lovers.

What is more, lovers are the only people prepared to die for others. Not just men,
either; women also sometimes. A good example is Alcestis, the daughter of Pelias. She
alone was willing to die for her husband. He had a father and mother but she so far sur-   c
passed them in devotion, because of her passion for him, that she showed them to be
strangers to their son, relations in name only. In so doing she was thought, by men and
gods alike, to have performed a deed of supreme excellence. Indeed the gods were so
pleased with her action that they brought her soul back from the underworld—a privilege they granted to only a fortunate handful of the many people who have done good
deeds. That shows how highly even the gods value loyalty and courage in love. Or-   d
pheus, the son of Oeagrus, on the other hand, was sent away from the underworld empty
handed; he was shown a mere phantom of the woman he came to find, and not given the
woman herself. Of course Orpheus was a musician, and the gods thought he was a bit of
a coward, lacking the courage to die for his love, as Alcestis did, but trying to find a way
of getting into the underworld alive. They punished him further for that, giving him
death at the hands of women.

In contrast, the man whom the gods honoured above all was Achilles, the son of   e
Thetis. They sent him to the Islands of the Blessed. His mother had warned him that if
he killed Hector he would himself be killed, but if he didn't, he would return home and
live to a ripe old age. Nevertheless out of loyalty to his lover Patroclus he chose without
hesitation to die—not to save him, but to avenge him; for Patroclus had already been
killed. The gods were full of admiration, and gave him the highest possible honour, because he valued his lover so highly.

Incidentally, Aeschylus' view, that it was Achilles who was in love with Patro-   180
clus, is nonsense. Quite apart from the fact that he was more beautiful than Patroclus
(and than all the other Greek heroes, come to that) and had not yet grown a beard, he
was also, according to Homer, much younger. And he must have been younger because
it is an undoubted fact that the gods, though they always value courage which comes
from love, are most impressed and pleased, and grant the greatest rewards, when the
younger man is loyal to his lover, than when the lover is loyal to him. That's because
the lover is a more divine creature than the younger man, since he is divinely inspired.
And that's why they honoured Achilles more than Alcestis, and sent him to the Islands   b
of the Blessed.

There you are then. I claim that Eros is the oldest of the gods, the most deserving
of our respect, and the most useful, for those men, past and present, who want to attain
excellence and happiness.

That was the gist of Phaedrus' speech. After him, several other people spoke, but   c
Aristodemus couldn't really remember what they said. So he left them out and re-
counted Pausanias' speech.

PAUSANIAS

Phaedrus, I don't think we've been very accurate in defining our subject for discussion. We've simply said that we must make a speech in praise of Eros. That would be fine, if there were just one Eros. In fact, however, there isn't. And since there isn't, we would

d   do better to define first which Eros we are to praise. I am going to try to put things straight—first defining which Eros we are supposed to be praising, and then trying to praise the god as he deserves.

We are all well aware, I take it, that without Eros there is no Aphrodite. If there were only one Aphrodite, there would be one Eros. However, since there are in fact two Aphrodites, it follows that Eros likewise must be two. There's no doubt about there being two Aphrodites; the older has no mother, and is the daughter of Heaven. We call her Heavenly Aphrodite. The younger is the daughter of Zeus and Dione, and we call her

e   Common Aphrodite. It follows that the Eros who assists this Aphrodite should also, properly speaking, be called Common Eros, and the other Heavenly Eros. We certainly ought to praise all the gods, but we should also attempt to define what is the proper province of each.

181   It is in general true of any activity that, simply in itself, it is neither good nor bad. Take what we're doing now, for example—that is to say drinking, or singing, or talking. None of these is good or bad in itself, but each becomes so, depending on the way it is done. Well and rightly done, it is good; wrongly done, it is bad. And it's just the same with loving, and Eros. It's not all good, and doesn't all deserve praise. The Eros we should praise is the one which encourages people to love in the right way.

b   The Eros associated with Common Aphrodite is, in all senses of the word, common, and quite haphazard in his operation. This is the love of the man in the street. For a start, he is as likely to fall in love with women as with boys. Secondly, he falls in love with their bodies rather than their minds. Thirdly, he picks the most unintelligent people he can find, since all he's interested in is the sexual act. He doesn't care whether it's done in the right way or not. That is why the effect of this Eros is haphazard—sometimes good, sometimes the reverse. This love derives its existence from the much

c   younger Aphrodite, the one composed equally of the female and male elements.

The other Eros springs from Heavenly Aphrodite, and in the first place is composed solely of the male element, with none of the female (so it is the love of boys we are talking about), and in the second place is older, and hence free from lust. In consequence, those inspired by this love turn to the male, attracted by what is naturally stronger and of superior intelligence. And even among those who love boys you can tell

d   the ones whose love is purely heavenly. They only fall in love with boys old enough to think for themselves—in other words, with boys who are nearly grown up.

Those who start a love affair with boys of that age are prepared, I think, to be friends, and live together, for life. The others are deceivers, who take advantage of

e   youthful folly, and then quite cheerfully abandon their victims in search of others. There ought really to be a law against loving young boys, to stop so much energy being expended on an uncertain end. After all, no-one knows how good or bad, in mind and body, young boys will eventually turn out. Good men voluntarily observe this

182   rule, but the common lovers I am talking about should be compelled to do the same, just as we stop them, so far as we can, falling in love with free women. They are actually the people who have brought the thing into disrepute, with the result that some people even go so far as to say that it is wrong to satisfy your lover. It is the common lover they have in mind when they say this, regarding his demands as premature and

unfair to the boy. Surely nothing done with restraint and decency could reasonably incur criticism.

What is more, while sexual conventions in other states are clear-cut and easy to understand, here and in Sparta, by contrast, they are complex. In Elis, for example, or Boeotia, and places where they are not sophisticated in their use of language, it is laid down, quite straightforwardly, that it is right to satisfy your lover. No-one, old or young, would say it was wrong, and the reason, I take it, is that they don't want to have all the trouble of trying to persuade them verbally, when they're such poor speakers. On the other hand, in Ionia and many other places under Persian rule, it is regarded as wrong. That is because the Persians' system of government (dictatorships) makes them distrust it, just as they distrust philosophy and communal exercise. It doesn't suit the rulers that their subjects should think noble thoughts, nor that they should form the strong friendships or attachments which these activities, and in particular love, tend to produce. Dictators here in Athens learnt the same lesson, by experience. The relationship between Harmodius and his lover, Aristogeiton, was strong enough to put an end to the dictators' rule.

In short, the convention that satisfying your lover is wrong is a result of the moral weakness of those who observe the convention—the rulers' desire for power, and their subjects' cowardice. The belief that it is always right can be attributed to mental laziness. Our customs are much better but, as I said, not easy to understand. Think about it—let's take the lover first. Open love is regarded as better than secret love, and so is love of the noblest and best people, even if they are not the best-looking. In fact, there is remarkable encouragement of the lover from all sides. He is not regarded as doing anything wrong; it is a good thing if he gets what he wants, and a shame if he doesn't. And when it comes to trying to get what he wants, we give the lover permission to do the most amazing things, and be applauded for them—things which, if he did them with any other aim or intention, would cover him in reproach. Think of the way lovers behave towards the boys they love—think of the begging and entreating involved in their demands, the oaths they swear, the nights they spend sleeping outside the boys' front doors, the slavery they are prepared to endure (which no slave would put up with). If they behaved like this for money, or position, or influence of any kind, they would be told to stop by friends and enemies alike. Their enemies would call their behaviour dependent and servile, while their friends would censure them sharply, and even be embarrassed for them. And yet a lover can do all these things, and be approved of. Custom attaches no blame to his actions, since he is reckoned to be acting in a wholly honourable way. The strangest thing of all is that, in most people's opinion, the lover has a unique dispensation from the gods to swear an oath and then break it. Lovers' vows, apparently, are not binding.

So far, then, gods and men alike give all kinds of licence to the lover, and an observer of Athenian life might conclude that it was an excellent thing, in this city, both to be a lover and to be friendly to lovers. But when we come to the boy, the position is quite different. Fathers give their sons escorts, when men fall in love with them, and don't allow them to talk to their lovers—and those are the escort's instructions as well. The boy's peers and friends jeer at him if they see anything of the kind going on, and when their elders see them jeering, they don't stop them, or tell them off, as they should if the jeers were unjustified. Looking at this side of things, you would come to the opposite conclusion—that this kind of thing is here regarded as highly reprehensible.

The true position, I think, is this. Going back to my original statement, there isn't one single form of love. So love is neither right nor wrong in itself. Done rightly, it is right; done wrongly, it is wrong. It is wrong if you satisfy the wrong person, for the e   wrong reasons, and right if you satisfy the right person, for the right reasons. The wrong person is the common lover I was talking about—the one who loves the body rather than the mind. His love is not lasting, since *what* he loves is not lasting either. As soon as the youthful bloom of the body (which is what he loves) starts to fade, he "spreads his wings and is off," as they say, making a mockery of all his speeches and promises. On the other hand, the man who loves a boy for his good character will stick to him for life, since he has attached himself to what is lasting.

184   Our customs are intended to test these lovers well and truly, and get the boys to satisfy the good ones, and avoid the bad. That's why we encourage lovers to chase after boys, but tell the boys not to be caught. In this way we set up a trial and a test, to see which category the lover comes in, and which category the boy he loves comes in. This explains a number of things—for instance, why it's thought wrong for a boy to let him-
b   self be caught too quickly. It is felt that some time should elapse, since time is a good test of most things. Also why it is wrong to be caught by means of money or political in-fluence—whether it's a case of the boy being threatened, and yielding rather than hold-ing out, or a case of being offered some financial or political inducement, and not turn-ing it down. No affair of this kind is likely to be stable or secure, quite apart from the fact that it is no basis for true friendship.

c   There is just one way our customs leave it open for a boy to satisfy his lover, and not be blamed for it. It is permissible, as I have said, for a lover to enter upon any kind of voluntary slavery he may choose, and be the slave of the boy he loves. This is not regarded as self-seeking, or in any way demeaning. Similarly there is one other kind of voluntary slavery which is not regarded as demeaning. This is the slavery of the boy, in his desire for improvement. It can happen that a boy chooses to serve a man, because he thinks that by association with him he will improve in wisdom in some way, or in some other form of goodness. This kind of voluntary slavery, like the other, is widely held among us not to be wrong, and not to be self-seeking.

d   So it can only be regarded as right for a boy to satisfy his lover if both these con-ditions are satisfied—both the lover's behaviour, and the boy's desire for wisdom and goodness. Then the lover and the boy have the same aim, and each has the approval of convention—the lover because he is justified in performing any service he chooses for a boy who satisfies him, the boy because he is justified in submitting, in any way he will, to the man who can make him wise and good. So if the lover has something to of-
e   fer in the way of sound judgment and moral goodness, and if the boy is eager to accept this contribution to his education and growing wisdom, then, and only then, this favourable combination makes it right for a boy to satisfy his lover. In no other situation is it right.

Nor, in this situation, is there any disgrace in making a mistake, whereas in all
185   other situations it is equally a disgrace to be mistaken or not. For example, suppose a boy satisfies his lover for money, taking him to be rich. If he gets it wrong, and doesn't get any money, because the lover turns out to be poor, it is still regarded as immoral, be-cause the boy who does this seems to be revealing his true character, and declaring that he would do anything for anyone in return for money. And that is not a good way to be-have. Equally, a boy may satisfy a man because he thinks he is a good man, and that he himself will become better through his friendship. If he gets it wrong, and his lover
b   turns out to be a bad man, of little moral worth, still there is something creditable about his mistake. He too seems to have revealed his true character—namely, that he is eager to do anything for anyone in return for goodness and self-improvement. And this is the finest of all qualities.

So it is absolutely correct for boys to satisfy their lovers, if it is done in pursuit of goodness. This is the love which comes from the heavenly goddess; it is itself heavenly, and of great value to state and individual alike, since it compels both lover and boy to   c
devote a lot of attention to their own moral improvement. All other sorts of love derive from the other goddess, the common one.

Well, Phaedrus, that's the best I can offer, without preparation, on the subject of Eros.

Pausanias paused (sorry about the pun—sophistic influence). After that it was Aristophanes' turn to speak. But he had just got hiccups. I don't know if it was from eating too much, or for some other reason; anyway he was unable to make his speech. All he could say, since Eryximachus, the doctor, happened to be sitting just below him, was   d
this: "Eryximachus, you're just the man. Either get rid of my hiccups, or speak instead of me until they stop."

"I'll do both. I'll take your turn to speak, and when you get rid of your hiccups, you can take mine. While I'm speaking, try holding your breath for a long time, to see if they stop. Failing that, gargle with some water. And if they are very severe, tickle   e
your nose and make yourself sneeze. Do that once or twice, and they'll stop, however severe."

"Will you please speak first, then?" said Aristophanes. "And I'll do as you suggest."

ERYXIMACHUS

Pausanias made an impressive start to his speech, but I do not think he brought it to a very satisfactory conclusion. So I think it is important that I should try to complete his   186
account. His analysis of the twofold nature of Eros seems to me to be a valuable distinction. But I cannot accept his implication that Eros is found only in human hearts, and is aroused only by human beauty. I am a doctor by profession, and it has been my observation, I would say, throughout my professional career, that Eros is aroused by many other things as well, and that he is found also in nature—in the physical life of all animals, in plants that grow in the ground, and in virtually all living organisms. My conclusion is that he is great and awe-inspiring, this god, and that his influence is un-   b
bounded, both in the human realm and in the divine.

I will begin by talking about my medical experience, to show my respect for my profession. The nature of the human body shows this twofold Eros, since it is generally agreed that health and sickness in the body are separate and unalike, and that unlike is attracted to unlike, and desires it. So there is one force of attraction for the healthy, and another for the sick. Pausanias was talking just now about it being right to satisfy men, if they are good men, but wrong if all they are interested in is physical pleasure. It is just   c
the same with the body. It is right to satisfy the good and healthy elements in the body, and one should do so. We call this "medicine." Conversely it is wrong to satisfy the bad, unhealthy elements, and anyone who is going to be a skilled doctor should deny these elements.

Medical knowledge is thus essentially knowledge of physical impulses or desires for ingestion or evacuation. In this, the man who can distinguish healthy desires from   d
unhealthy is the best doctor. Moreover he needs the ability to change people's desires, so that they lose one and gain another. There are people who lack desires which they should have. If the doctor can produce these desires, and remove the existing ones, then

he is a good doctor. He must, in fact, be able to reconcile and harmonise the most disparate elements in the body. By "the most disparate" I mean those most opposed to one another—cold and hot, bitter and sweet, dry and wet, and so forth. It was by knowing
e   how to produce mutual desire and harmony among these that our forerunner Asclepius, as the poets say (and I believe) established this art of ours.

187   Medicine, then, as I say, is completely governed by this god. Likewise physical training, and farming. Music too is no exception, as must be clear to anyone who gives the matter a moment's thought. Perhaps that is what Heraclitus means, though he does not actually express it very clearly, when he says that "the One" is "in conflict and harmony with itself," "like the stringing of a bow or lyre." Clearly there is a contradiction in saying that a harmony is in conflict, or is composed of conflicting elements. Perhaps
b   what he meant was that, starting from initially discordant high and low notes, the harmony is only created when these are brought into agreement by the skill of the musician. Clearly there could be no harmony between high and low, if they were still in conflict. For harmony is a consonance, and consonance is a kind of agreement. Thus it is impossible that there should be a harmony of conflicting elements, in which those elements still conflict, nor can one harmonise what is different, and incapable of agree-
c   ment. Or take rhythm as another example; it arises out of the conflict of quick and slow, but only when they cease to conflict. Here it is the art of music which imposes harmony on all the elements, by producing mutual attraction and agreement between them, whereas in the body it is the art of medicine. So music, again, is a knowledge of Eros applied to harmony and rhythm.

        In the actual formation of harmony and rhythm it is a simple matter to detect the hand of Eros, which at this stage is not the twofold Eros. It is altogether more complicated when we come to apply rhythm and harmony to human activity, either to the mak-
d   ing of music, which we call composing, or to the correct use of melody and tempo in what we call education. This really does demand a high degree of skill. And the same argument again holds good, that one should satisfy the most well-ordered people, in the interests of those as yet less well-ordered; one should pay due regard to their desires, which are in fact the good, heavenly Eros, companion of the heavenly muse, Ourania.
e   Common Eros, by contrast, goes with the common muse, Polymnia. The greatest caution is called for in its employment, if one is to gain enjoyment from it without encouraging pure self-indulgence. Similarly, in my profession, there is a great art in the correct treatment of people's desire for rich food, so that they can enjoy it without ill effects.

        Thus in music and medicine, and in all other spheres of activity, human and di-
188 vine, we must keep a careful eye, so far as is practicable, on both forms of Eros. For both are present. The seasons of the year likewise fully illustrate their joint operation. When all the things I was talking about just now (such as hot and cold, wet and dry) hit upon the right Eros in their relation to one another, and consequently form the right sort of mixture and harmony, then they bring what is seasonable and healthy, to men and to the rest of the world of animals and plants; and all is as it should be. But when the other
b   Eros, in violence and excess, takes over in the natural seasons of the year, it does all sorts of damage, and upsets the natural order. When that happens the result, generally, is plague and a variety of diseases—for animals and plants alike. Frost, hail and mildew are the result of this kind of competition and disorder involving Eros. Knowledge of Eros in connection with the movements of the stars and the seasons of the year is called astronomy.

        Then again, all sacrifices, and everything which comes under the direction of the
c   prophetic arts (that is to say, the whole relationship of gods and men to one another), have as their sole concern the observance and correct treatment of Eros. If, in their be-

haviour towards their parents, the living and the dead, or the gods, people stop satisfying the good, well-ordered Eros, if they stop honouring him and consulting him in
every enterprise, and start to follow the other Eros, then the result is all kinds of
wickedness. So the prophetic arts have to keep an eye on, and treat, the two forms of
Eros. Their knowledge of Eros in human affairs, the Eros who is conducive to piety   d
and correct observance, makes them the architects of friendship between gods and
men.

So great and widespread—in fact, universal—is the power possessed, in general
by all Eros, but in particular by the Eros which, in the moral sphere, acts with good
sense and justice both among us and among the gods. And not only does it possess absolute power; it also brings us complete happiness, enabling us to be companions and
friends both of each other and of our superiors, the gods.

Well, I too may have left a lot out in my praise of Eros, but I have not done so de-   e
liberately. And if I have left anything out, it is up to you, Aristophanes, to fill the gap.
Or if you intend to praise the god in some other way, go ahead and do that, now that you
have got rid of your hiccups.

ARISTOPHANES: Yes, they've stopped, but not without resort to the sneezing treat-   189
ment. I wondered if it was the "well-ordered" part of my body which demanded all the
noise and tickling involved in sneezing. Certainly the hiccups stopped the moment I
tried sneezing.

ERYXIMACHUS: Careful, my dear friend. You haven't started yet, and already
you're playing the fool. You'll force me to act as censor for your speech, if you start   b
fooling around as soon as you get a chance to speak in peace.

ARISTOPHANES (laughing): Fair enough, Eryximachus. Regard my remarks so
far as unsaid. But don't be too censorious. I'm worried enough already about what I'm
going to say—not that it may arouse laughter (after all, there would be some point in
that, and it would be appropriate to my profession), but that it may be laughed out of
court.

ERYXIMACHUS: Aristophanes, you're trying to eat your cake and have it. Come
on, concentrate. You'll have to justify what you say, but perhaps, if I see fit, I will ac-   c
quit you.

ARISTOPHANES

Well, Eryximachus, I do intend to make a rather different kind of speech from the kind
you and Pausanias made. It's my opinion that mankind is quite unaware of the power of
Eros. If they were aware of it, they would build vast temples and altars to him, and
make great offerings to him. As it is, though it is of crucial importance that this observance should be paid to him, none of these things is done.

Of all the gods, Eros is the most friendly towards men. He is our helper, and cures   d
those evils whose cure brings the greatest happiness to the human race. I'll try to explain his power to you, and then you can go off and spread the word to others.

First of all you need to know about human nature and what has happened to it.
Our original nature was not as it is now, but quite different. For one thing there were
three sexes, rather than the two (male and female) we have now. The third sex was a
combination of these two. Its name has survived, though the phenomenon itself has dis-   e
appeared. This single combination, comprising both male and female, was, in form and
name alike, hermaphrodite. Now it survives only as a term of abuse.

Secondly, each human being formed a complete whole, spherical, with back and ribs forming a circle. They had four hands, four legs, and two faces, identical in every way, on a circular neck. They had a single head for the two faces, which looked in opposite directions; four ears, two sets of genitals, and everything else as you'd expect from the description so far. They walked upright, as we do, in whichever direction they wanted. And when they started to run fast, they were just like people doing cartwheels. They stuck their legs straight out all round, and went bowling along, supported on their eight limbs, and rolling along at high speed.

The reason for having three sexes, and of this kind, was this: the male was originally the offspring of the sun, the female of the earth, and the one which was half-and-half was the offspring of the moon, because the moon likewise is half-sun and half-earth. They were circular, both in themselves and in their motion, because of their similarity to their parents. They were remarkable for their strength and vigour, and their ambition led them to make an assault upon the gods. The story which Homer tells of the giants, Ephialtes and Otus, is told of them—that they tried to make a way up to heaven, to attack the gods. Zeus and the other gods wondered what to do about them, and couldn't decide. They couldn't kill them, as they had the giants—striking them with thunderbolts and doing away with the whole race—because the worship and sacrifices they received from men would have been done away with as well. On the other hand, they couldn't go on allowing them to behave so outrageously.

In the end Zeus, after long and painful thought, came up with a suggestion. "I think I have an idea. Men could go on existing, but behave less disgracefully, if we made them weaker. I'm going to cut each of them in two. This will have two advantages: it will make them weaker, and also more useful to us, because of the increase in their numbers. They will walk upright, on two legs. And if it's clear they still can't behave, and they refuse to lead a quiet life, I'll cut them in half again and they can go hopping along on one leg."

That was his plan. So he started cutting them in two, like someone slicing vegetables for pickling, or slicing eggs with a wire. And each time he chopped one up, he told Apollo to turn the face and the half-neck round towards the cut side (so that the man could see where he'd been split, and be better behaved in future), and then to heal the rest of the wound. So Apollo twisted the faces round and gathered up the skin all round to what is now called the stomach, like a purse with strings. He made a single outlet, and tied it all up securely in the middle of the stomach; this we now call the navel. He smoothed out most of the wrinkles, and formed the chest, using a tool such as cobblers use for smoothing out wrinkles in a hide stretched over a last. He left a few wrinkles, however, those around the stomach itself and the navel, as a reminder of what happened in those far-off days.

When man's natural form was split in two, each half went round looking for its other half. They put their arms round one another, and embraced each other, in their desire to grow together again. They started dying of hunger, and also from lethargy, because they refused to do anything separately. And whenever one half died, and the other was left, the survivor began to look for another, and twined itself about it, either encountering half of a complete woman (i.e. what we now call a woman) or half a complete man. In this way they kept on dying.

Zeus felt sorry for them, and thought of a second plan. He moved their genitals to the front—up till then they had had them on the outside, and had reproduced, not by copulation, but by discharge on to the ground, like grasshoppers. So, as I say, he moved their genitals to the front, and made them use them for reproduction by insemination, the male in the female. The idea was that if, in embracing, a man chanced upon a woman, they could produce children, and the race would increase. If man chanced upon man, they could get full satisfaction from one another's company, then separate, get on with their work, and resume the business of life.

That is why we have this innate love of one another. It brings us back to our orig-   d
inal state, trying to reunite us and restore us to our true human form. Each of us is a mere fragment of a man (like half a tally-stick); we've been split in two, like filleted plaice [a kind of fish]. We're all looking for our "other half." Men who are a fragment of the common sex (the one called hermaphrodite), are womanisers, and most adulter-ers are to be found in this category. Similarly, women of this type are nymphomaniacs and adulteresses. On the other hand, women who are part of an original woman pay very little attention to men. Their interest is in women; Lesbians are found in this class. And those who are part of a male pursue what is male. As boys, because they are slices   192
of the male, they are fond of men, and enjoy going to bed with men and embracing them. These are the best of the boys and young men, since they are by nature the most manly. Some people call them immoral—quite wrongly. It is not immorality, but bold-ness, courage and manliness, since they take pleasure in what is like themselves. This is proved by the fact that, when they grow up and take part in public life, it's only this kind who prove themselves men. When they come to manhood, they are lovers of boys, and don't naturally show any interest in marriage or producing children; they have to be   b
forced into it by convention. They're quite happy to live with one another, and not get married.

People like this are clearly inclined to have boy friends or (as boys) inclined to have lovers, because they always welcome what is akin. When a lover of boys (or any sort of lover) meets the real thing (i.e. his other half), he is completely overwhelmed by friendship and affection and desire, more or less refusing to be separated for any time at all. These are the people who spend their whole lives together, and yet they cannot find   c
words for what they want from one another. No one imagines that it's simply sexual in-tercourse, or that sex is the reason why one gets such enormous pleasure out of the other's company. No, it's obvious that the soul of each has some other desire, which it cannot express. It can only give hints and clues to its wishes.   d

Imagine that Hephaestus came and stood over them, with his smith's tools, as they lay in bed together. Suppose he asked them, "What is it you want from one an-other, mortals?" If they couldn't tell him, he might ask again, "Do you want to be to-gether as much as possible, and not be separated, day or night? If that's what you want,   e
I'm quite prepared to weld you together, and make you grow into one. You can be united, the two of you, and live your whole life together, as one. Even down in Hades, when you die, you can be a single dead person, rather than two. Decide whether that's what you want, and whether that would satisfy you." We can be sure that no-one would refuse this offer. Quite clearly, it would be just what they wanted. They'd simply think they'd been offered exactly what they'd always been after, in sexual intercourse, trying to melt into their lovers, and so be united.

So that's the explanation; it's because our original nature was as I have described,   193
and because we were once complete. And the name of this desire and pursuit of com-pleteness is Eros, or love. Formerly, as I say, we were undivided, but now we've been split up by god for our misdeeds—like the Arcadians by the Spartans. And the danger is that, if we don't treat the gods with respect, we may be divided again, and go round looking like figures in a bas-relief, sliced in half down the line of our noses. We'd be like torn-off counterfoils. That's why we should all encourage the utmost piety towards the gods. We're trying to avoid this fate, and achieve the other. So we take Eros as our guide and leader. Let no-one oppose this aim—and incurring divine displeasure is op-   b

posing this aim—since if we are friends with god, and make our peace with him, we shall find and meet the boys who are part of ourselves, which few people these days succeed in doing.

I hope Eryximachus won't misunderstand me, and make fun of my speech, and
c   say it's about Pausanias and Agathon. Perhaps they do come in this class, and are both males by nature. All I'm saying is that in general (and this applies to men and women) this is where happiness for the human race lies—in the successful pursuit of love, in finding the love who is part of our original self, and in returning to our former state. This is the ideal, but in an imperfect world we must settle for the nearest to this we can
d   get, and this is finding a boy friend who is mentally congenial. And if we want to praise the god who brings this about, then we should praise Eros, who in this predicament is our great benefactor, attracting us to what is part of ourselves, and gives us great hope for the future that he will reward respect for the gods by returning us to our original condition, healing us, and making us blessed and perfectly happy.

There you are then, Eryximachus. There is my speech about Eros. A bit different from yours, I'm afraid. So please, again, don't laugh at it, and let's hear what all the oth-
e   ers have to say—or rather, both the others, since only Agathon and Socrates are left.

ERYXIMACHUS: All right, I won't laugh. In any case, I thought it was a most enjoyable speech. In fact, if I did not know Socrates and Agathon to be experts on love, I would be very worried that they might have nothing to say, so abundant and varied have been the speeches so far. But knowing them as I do, I have no such anxiety.

194   SOCRATES: It's fine for you, Eryximachus. You've already made an excellent speech. If you were in my shoes—or rather, perhaps, the shoes I will be in when Agathon has made a good speech as well—then you might well be alarmed, and be in precisely the state that I am in now.

AGATHON: Ah! Trying a little black magic, are you, Socrates? Are you hoping it'll make me nervous if I think the audience is expecting a great speech from me?

b   SOCRATES: Agathon, I've seen your nerve and courage in going up on the platform with the actors, to present your plays, before the eyes of that vast audience. You were quite unperturbed by that, so it'd be pretty stupid of me to imagine that you'd be nervous in front of the few people here.

AGATHON: I may be stagestruck, Socrates, but I'm still aware that, to anyone with any sense, a small critical audience is far more daunting than a large uncritical one.

c   SOCRATES: It would be quite wrong for me, of all people, to suggest that you are lacking in taste or judgement. I'm well aware that in all your contacts with those you consider discriminating, you value their opinion more highly than that of the public. But don't put us in that category—after all, we were there, we were part of "the public." Anyway, let's pursue this: if you came across truly discriminating people (not us), you would perhaps be daunted by them, if you thought you were producing something second-rate. Is that right?

AGATHON: It is.

SOCRATES: Whereas offering the public something second-rate would not worry you, would it?

d   PHAEDRUS: Agathon, if you answer Socrates, he won't give a thought to the rest of us, so long as he has someone to talk to, particularly someone good-looking. For myself, I love hearing Socrates talk, but it's my job to supervise the progress of the speeches in praise of Eros, and get a speech out of each of you. When you've both paid your tribute to the god, then the two of you can get on with your discussion.

e   AGATHON: Quite right, Phaedrus. There's no reason why I shouldn't make my speech. I shall have plenty of other opportunities to talk to Socrates.

AGATHON

I want first to talk about *how* I should talk, and then talk. All the speakers so far have given me the impression that they were not so much praising the god as congratulating   195 mankind on the good things the god provides. No-one has told us what the giver of these benefits is really like, in himself. And yet, in any speech of praise on any subject, the only correct procedure is to work systematically through the subject under discussion, saying what its nature is, and what benefits it gives. That is how we too should by rights be praising Eros, describing first his nature, then his gifts.

I claim, then, that though all the gods are blessed, Eros, if I may say this without offending the other gods, is the most blessed, since he is the most beautiful and the best. The most beautiful? Well, for a start, Phaedrus, he is the youngest of the gods. He proves this himself, by running away at top speed from old age. Yet old age is swift   b enough, and swifter than most of us would like. It is Eros' nature to hate old age, and steer well clear of it. He lives and exists always with the young. "Birds of a feather," and all that. So, though there was much in Phaedrus' speech with which I agreed, I didn't agree with his claim that Eros was older than Cronus or Iapetus. I would say he's the youngest of the gods—eternally young, in fact. The earliest troubles among the   c gods, which Hesiod and Parmenides write about, were, if those writers are correct, the work of Necessity, not of Eros. If Eros had been there, there would have been none of this cutting, or tying, each other up, or any of the other acts of violence. There would have been friendship and peace, as there has been since Eros became king of the gods.

So, he is young. And not only young, but delicate. You need a poet like Homer to   d show how delicate. Homer describes Ate as a god and as delicate (or at any rate, with delicate feet): "delicate are her feet; she walks not upon the ground, but goes upon the heads of men." Presumably he's giving an example here to show how delicate—she goes not on what is hard, but on what is soft. We too can use a similar argument to show   e how delicate Eros is. He does not walk upon the ground, nor yet on men's heads (which aren't that soft anyway); he lives and moves among the softest of all things, making his home in the hearts and minds of gods and men. And not in all hearts equally. He avoids any hard hearts he comes across, and settles among the tender-hearted. He must therefore be extremely delicate, since he only ever touches (either with his feet or in any other way) the softest of the soft.

Very young, then, and very delicate. Another thing about him is that he's very   196 supple. He can't be rigid and unyielding, because he wouldn't be able to insinuate himself anywhere he likes, entering and leaving men's hearts undetected. Eros' outstanding beauty is universally agreed, and this again suggests that he is well-proportioned and supple. Ugliness and Eros are ever at odds with one another. Finally, the beauty of his skin is attested by his love of flowers. He will not settle in a man's body, or heart, or anywhere else, if it is past the first flower and bloom of youth. But he does settle down,   b and remain, in any flowery and fragrant place.

So much for the god's beauty, though I've left out more than I've said. Now I must say something about his goodness. The main thing about Eros is that no-one, god or man, wrongs him or is wronged by him. Nothing is done to him, when it is done, by force. Force cannot touch Eros. When he acts, he acts without force, since everyone serves Eros quite willingly, and it's agreed by "our masters, the laws" that where there   c is mutual consent and agreement, there is justice. Moreover, he is a paragon of virtue as well as justice. After all, virtue is agreed to be control of pleasures and desires, and no pleasure is stronger than love. But if they are weaker than love, then he has control over them, and if he has control over pleasures and desires, he must be highly virtuous.

d   And what about courage? "Ares himself cannot hold his ground" against Eros. Ares does not take Eros prisoner; it is Eros—the love of Aphrodite, so the story goes—who takes Ares prisoner, and the captor is stronger than the captive. He who overcomes the bravest is himself the bravest of all.

So much for the god's justice, virtue and courage. Now for his wisdom. I must try as hard as I can not to leave anything out, and so I too, in my turn, will start with a trib-

e   ute to my own profession, following Eryximachus' example. Eros is an accomplished poet, so accomplished that he can turn others into poets. Everyone turns to poetry, "however philistine he may have been before," when moved by Eros. We should take this as an indication that, in general, Eros is master of all forms of literary or artistic creation. After all, no-one can impart, or teach, a skill which he does not himself possess or know. And who will deny that the creation of all living things is the work of Eros' wis-

197   dom, which makes all living things come into being and grow?

It's the same with any skilled activity. It is common knowledge that those who have this god for their teacher win fame and reputation; those he passes by remain in obscurity. For example, Apollo's discoveries (archery, medicine and prophecy) were all

b   guided by desire and love, so he too can be called a disciple of Eros. Likewise with the Muses and the arts, Hephaestus and metalworking, Athene and weaving, and Zeus and "the governance of gods and men." And if we ask why the quarrels of the gods were settled as soon as Eros appeared, without doubt the reason was love of beauty (there being no love of ugliness). In earlier times, as I said originally, there were many violent quarrels among the gods—or so we are told—because they were in the grip of Necessity. But since Eros' birth, all manner of good has resulted, for gods and men, from the love of beauty.

c   Such, Phaedrus, is my view of Eros. He stands out as beautiful and excellent in himself; and secondly, he is the origin of similar qualities in others. I am tempted to speak in verse, and say he brings

> Sweet peace to men, and calm o'er all the deep,
> Rest to the winds, to those who sorrow, sleep.

d   He gives us the feeling, not of longing, but of belonging, since he is the moving spirit behind all those occasions when we meet and gather together. Festivals, dances, sacrifices—in these he is the moving spirit. Implanter of gentleness, supplanter of fierceness; generous with his kindness, ungenerous with unkindness; gracious, gentle; an example to the wise, a delight to the gods; craved by those without him, saved by those who have him; of luxury, delicacy, elegance, charm, yearning and desire he is the father; heedful

e   of the good, heedless of the bad; in hardship and in fear, in need and in argument, he is the best possible helmsman, comrade, ally, and saviour; the glory of gods and men; the best and finest guide, whom every man should follow, singing glorious praises to him, and sharing in the song which he sings to enchant the minds of gods and men.

That is my speech, Phaedrus, in part fun, in part (as far as I could make it) fairly serious. Let it be an offering to the god.

198   When Agathon finished speaking, we all burst into applause. We thought the young man had done full justice both to himself and to the god.

SOCRATES (to Eryximachus): Well, son of Acumenus, do you still think my earlier fear unfounded? Wasn't I right when I predicted Agathon would make a brilliant speech, and there would be nothing left for me to say?

ERYXIMACHUS: Your prediction was half-true. Agathon did make a good speech. But I don't think you will find nothing to say.

SOCRATES: My dear fellow, what is there left for me or anyone else to say, after   b
such a fine and varied speech? Maybe it wasn't all equally brilliant, but that bit at the
end was enough to silence anyone with the beauty of its language and phraseology.
When I realised I wasn't going to be able to make anything like such a good speech, I
nearly ran away and disappeared, in embarrassment, only there was nowhere to go. The
speech reminded me of Gorgias, and put me in exactly the position described by   c
Homer. I was afraid, at the end of his speech there, that Agathon was going to brandish
the head of Gorgias, the great speaker, at my speech, turning me to stone and silencing
me. I realised then how fatuous it was to have agreed to take my turn with you in praising Eros, and to have claimed to be an expert on love. It turns out now that I know nothing at all about making speeches of praise. I was naive enough to suppose that one
should speak the truth about whatever it was that was being praised, and that from this   d
raw material one should select the most telling points, and arrange them as pleasingly as
possible. I was pretty confident I would make a good speech, because I thought I knew
about speeches of praise. However, it now seems that praising things well isn't like that;
it seems to be a question of hyperbole and rhetoric, regardless of truth or falsehood.   e
And if it's false, that's immaterial. So our original agreement, as it now seems, was that
each of us should pretend to praise Eros, rather than really praise him.

That, I imagine, is why you credit Eros with all the good points you have dug out
in his favour. You say his nature is this, and the blessings he produces are these; your
object is to make him appear as noble and fine as possible (in the eyes of the ignorant,   199
presumably, since those who know about Eros clearly aren't going to believe you). Certainly your praise of him looks very fine and impressive, but I didn't realise this was
what was called for; if I had known I wouldn't have agreed to take my turn in praising
him. "My tongue promised, not my heart." Anyway, it can't be helped, but I don't propose to go on praising him like that—I wouldn't know how to. What I am prepared to
do, if you like, is tell the truth, in my own way, and not in competition with your   b
speeches. I don't want to make a complete fool of myself. What do you think, Phaedrus? Do you want a speech of that sort? Do you want to hear the truth told about Eros?
And may I use whatever language and forms of speech come naturally?

Phaedrus and the others told him to make his speech, in whatever way he thought   c
best.

SOCRATES: One other point before I start, Phaedrus. Will you let me ask Agathon
a few brief questions? I'd like to get his agreement before I begin.

PHAEDRUS: Yes, I'll let you. Ask away.

So Socrates began his speech, something like this.

SOCRATES

Well, my dear Agathon, I liked the beginning of your speech. You said the first thing to
do was to reveal the nature of Eros; after that his achievements. I think that was an excellent starting point. And since you've explained everything else about the nature of
Eros so impressively and so well, can you tell me one more thing? Is Eros' nature such   d
that he is love produced by something, or by nothing? I don't mean, is he *the son of* a father or a mother—it would be an absurd question, to ask whether Eros is son of a father
or mother. But suppose I asked you, about this thing "father," whether a father is father
of something or not? If you wanted to give an accurate answer, you would say, presumably, that a father is father of a son or a daughter, wouldn't you?

AGATHON: Yes, I would.

SOCRATES: And the same with a mother?

AGATHON: Yes, the same.

e   SOCRATES: Let's take a few more questions, so you can be quite clear what I mean. Suppose I ask, "What about a brother, simply as a brother? Is he someone's brother, or not?"

AGATHON: Yes, he is.

SOCRATES: His brother's or sister's, I take it?

AGATHON: Yes.

SOCRATES: Try, then, to answer my question about Eros. Is Eros love of nothing, or of something?

AGATHON: Of something, certainly.

200   SOCRATES: Good. Hold on to that answer. Keep it in mind, and make a mental note what it is that Eros is love of. But first tell me this; this thing which Eros is love of, does he desire it, or not?

AGATHON: Certainly.

SOCRATES: And does he possess that which he desires and loves, or not?

AGATHON: Probably not.

SOCRATES: I'm not interested in probability, but in certainty. Consider this propo-

b   sition: anything which desires something desires what it does not have, and it only desires when it is lacking something. This proposition, Agathon, seems to me to be absolutely certain. How does it strike you?

AGATHON: Yes, it seems certain to me too.

SOCRATES: Quite right. So would a big man want to be big, or a strong man want to be strong?

AGATHON: No, that's impossible, given what we have agreed so far.

SOCRATES: Because if he possesses these qualities, he cannot also lack them.

AGATHON: True.

SOCRATES: So if a strong man wanted to be strong, or a fast runner to be fast, or a healthy man to be healthy—but perhaps I'd better explain what I'm on about. I'm a bit worried that you may think that people like this, people having these qualities, can also

c   want the qualities which they possess. So I'm trying to remove this misapprehension. If you think about it, Agathon, people cannot avoid possession of whichever of these qualities they do possess, whether they like it or not. So obviously there's no point in desiring to do so. When anyone says, "I'm in good health, and I also desire to be in good health," or "I am rich and also desire to be rich," i.e. "I desire those things which I al-

d   ready have," then we should answer him: "What you want is to go on possessing, in the future, the wealth, health, or strength you possess now, since you have them now, like it or not. So when you say you desire what you've already got, are you sure you don't just mean you want to continue to possess in the future what you possess now?" Would he deny this?

AGATHON: No, he would agree.

SOCRATES: But isn't this a question of desiring what he doesn't already have in his possession—i.e. the desire that what he does have should be safely and permanently

e   available to him in the future?

AGATHON: Yes, it is.

SOCRATES: So in this, or any other, situation, the man who desires something desires what is not available to him, and what he doesn't already have in his possession. And what he neither has nor himself is—that which he lacks—this is what he wants and desires.

AGATHON: Absolutely.

SOCRATES: Right then, let's agree on the argument so far. Eros has an existence of his own; he is in the first place love of something, and secondly, he is love of that which he is without.

AGATHON: Yes.

SOCRATES: Keeping that in mind, just recall what you said were the objects of Eros, in your speech. I'll remind you, if you like. I think what you said amounted to this: trouble among the gods was ended by their love of beauty, since there could be no love of what is ugly. Isn't that roughly what you said?

AGATHON: Yes, it is.

SOCRATES: And a very reasonable statement, too, my friend. And this being so, Eros must have an existence as love of beauty, and not love of ugliness, mustn't he?

AGATHON: Yes.

SOCRATES: But wasn't it agreed that he loves what he lacks, and does not possess?

AGATHON: Yes, it was.

SOCRATES: So Eros lacks, and does not possess, beauty.

AGATHON: That is the inevitable conclusion.

SOCRATES: Well then, do you describe as beautiful that which lacks beauty and has never acquired beauty?

AGATHON: No.

SOCRATES: If that is so, do you still maintain that Eros is beautiful?

AGATHON: I rather suspect, Socrates, that I didn't know what I was talking about.

SOCRATES: It sounded marvellous, for all that, Agathon. Just one other small point. Would you agree that what is good is also beautiful?

AGATHON: Yes, I would.

SOCRATES: So if Eros lacks beauty, and if what is good is beautiful, then Eros would lack what is good also.

AGATHON: I can't argue with you, Socrates. Let's take it that it is as you say.

SOCRATES: What you mean, Agathon, my very good friend, is that you can't argue with the truth. Any fool can argue with Socrates. Anyway, I'll let you off for now, because I want to pass on to you the account of Eros which I once heard given by a woman called Diotima, from Mantinea. She was an expert on this subject, as on many others. In the days before the plague she came to the help of the Athenians in their sacrifices, and managed to gain them a ten-years' reprieve from the disease. She also taught me about love.

I'll start from the position on which Agathon and I reached agreement, and I'll give her account, as best I can, in my own words. So first I must explain, as you rightly laid down, Agathon, what Eros is and what he is like; then I must describe what he does. I think it'll be easiest for me to explain things as she explained them when she was questioning me, since I gave her pretty much the same answers Agathon has just been giving me. I said Eros was a great god, and a lover of beauty. Diotima proved to me, using the same argument by which I have just proved it to Agathon, that, according to my own argument, Eros was neither beautiful nor good.

"What do you mean, Diotima," I said, "Is Eros then ugly or bad?"

"Careful what you say. Do you think what is not beautiful must necessarily be ugly?"

"Obviously."

"And that what is not wise is ignorant? Don't you realise there is an intermediate state, between wisdom and ignorance?"

"And what is that?"

"Think of someone who has a correct opinion, but can give no rational explanation of it. You wouldn't call this knowledge (how can something irrational be knowledge?), yet it isn't ignorance either, since an opinion which accords with reality cannot be ignorance. So correct opinion is the kind of thing we are looking for, between understanding and ignorance."

b   "That's true."

"So don't insist that what is not beautiful must necessarily be ugly, nor that what is not good must be bad. The same thing is equally true of Eros; just because, as you yourself admit, he is not good or beautiful, you need not regard him as ugly and bad, but as something between these extremes."

"Yet he is universally agreed to be a great god."

"By those who don't know what they are talking about, do you mean? Or those who do?"

"I mean by absolutely everyone."

c   Diotima laughed. "How can Eros be agreed to be a great god by people who don't even admit that he's a god at all?"

"What people?"

"Well, you, for one. And me, for another."

"What do you mean?"

"Quite simple. The gods are all happy and beautiful, aren't they? You wouldn't go so far as to claim that any of the gods is not happy and beautiful?"

"Good Lord, no."

"And you agree that 'happy' means 'possessing what is good and beautiful'?"

"Certainly."

d   "But you have already admitted that Eros lacks what is good and beautiful, and that he desires them because he lacks them."

"Yes, I have."

"How can he be a god, then, if he is without beauty and goodness?" "He can't, apparently."

"You see, even you don't regard Eros as a god."

"What can Eros be, then? A mortal?"

"Far from it."

"What, then?"

"As in the other examples, something between a mortal and an immortal."

"And what is that, Diotima?"

e   "A great spirit, Socrates. Spirits are midway between what is divine and what is human."

"What power does such a spirit possess?"

"He acts as an interpreter and means of communication between gods and men. He takes requests and offerings to the gods, and brings back instructions and benefits in return. Occupying this middle position he plays a vital role in holding the world together. He is the medium of all prophecy and religion, whether it concerns sacrifice,

203   forms of worship, incantations, or any kind of divination or sorcery. There is no direct contact between god and man. All association and communication between them, waking or sleeping, takes place through Eros. This kind of knowledge is knowledge of the spirit; any other knowledge (occupational or artistic, for example) is purely utilitarian. Such spirits are many and varied, and Eros is one of them."

"Who are his parents?"

"That is not quite so simple, but I'll tell you, all the same. When Aphrodite was   b
born, the gods held a banquet, at which one of the guests was Resource, the son of In-
genuity. When they finished eating, Poverty came begging, as you would expect (there
being plenty of food), and hung around the doorway. Resource was drunk (on nectar,
since wine hadn't been invented), so he went into Zeus' garden, and was overcome by
sleep. Poverty, seeing here the solution to her own lack of resources, decided to have a
child by him. So she lay with him, and conceived Eros. That's why Eros is a follower
and servant of Aphrodite, because he was conceived at her birthday party—and also be-   c
cause he is naturally attracted to what is beautiful, and Aphrodite is beautiful.

So Eros' attributes are what you would expect of a child of Resource and Poverty.
For a start, he's always poor, and so far from being soft and beautiful (which is most
people's view of him), he is hard, unkempt, barefoot, homeless. He sleeps on the
ground, without a bed, lying in doorways or in the open street. He has his mother's na-   d
ture, and need is his constant companion. On the other hand, from his father he has inherited an eye for beauty and the good. He is brave, enterprising and determined—a
marvellous huntsman, always intriguing. He is intellectual, resourceful, a lover of wisdom his whole life through, a subtle magician, sorcerer and thinker.

His nature is neither that of an immortal nor that of a mortal. In one and the same   e
day he can be alive and flourishing (when things go well), then at death's door, later still
reviving as his father's character asserts itself again. But his resources are always running out, so that Eros is never either totally destitute or affluent. Similarly he is midway
between wisdom and folly, as I will show you. None of the gods searches for wisdom,
or tries to become wise—they are wise already. Nor does anyone else wise search for
wisdom. On the other hand, the foolish do not search for wisdom or try to become wise
either, since folly is precisely the failing which consists in not being fine and good, or   204
intelligent—and yet being quite satisfied with the way one is. You cannot desire what
you do not realise you lack."

"Who then are the lovers of wisdom, Diotima, if they are neither the wise nor the
foolish?"

"That should by now be obvious, even to a child. They must be the intermediate   b
class, among them Eros. We would classify wisdom as very beautiful, and Eros is love
of what is beautiful, so it necessarily follows that Eros is a lover of wisdom (lovers of
wisdom being the intermediate class between the wise and the foolish). The reason for
this, too, is to be found in his parentage. His father is wise and resourceful, while his
mother is foolish and resourceless.

"Such is the nature of this spirit, Socrates. Your views on Eros revealed a quite   c
common mistake. You thought (or so I infer from your comments) that Eros was what
was loved, rather than the lover. That is why you thought Eros was beautiful. After all,
what we love really *is* beautiful and delicate, perfect and delightful, whereas the lover
has the quite different character I have outlined."

"Fair enough, my foreign friend, I think you're right. But if that's what Eros is
like, what use is he to men?"

"That's the next point I want to explain to you, Socrates. I've told you what Eros   d
is like, and what his parentage is; he is also love of what is beautiful, as you say. Now
let's imagine someone asking us, 'Why is Eros love of the beautiful, Socrates and Dio-   e
tima?' Let me put it more clearly: what is it that the lover of beauty desires?"

"To possess it."

"That prompts the further question, what good does it do someone to possess
beauty?"

"I don't quite know how to give a quick answer to that question."

"Well, try a different question, about goodness rather than beauty: Socrates, what does the lover of goodness want?"

"To possess it."

"What good will it do him to possess it?"

"That's easier. It will make him happy."

205   "Yes, because those who are happy are happy because they possess what is good. The enquiry seems to have reached a conclusion, and there is no need to ask the further question, 'If someone wants to be happy, why does he want to be happy?'"

"True."

"Do you think this wish and this desire are common to all mankind, and that everyone wants always to possess what is good? Or what do you think?"

"I think it is common to all men."

"In that case, Socrates, why do we not describe all men as lovers, if everyone always loves the same thing? Why do we describe some people as lovers, but not others?"

b

"I don't know. I agree with you, it *is* surprising."

"Not really. We abstract a part of love, and call it by the name of the whole—love—and then for the other parts we use different names."

"What names? Give me an example."

"What about this? Take a concept like creation, or composition. Composition means putting things together, and covers a wide range of activities. Any activity which brings anything at all into existence is an example of creation. Hence the exercise of any skill is composition, and those who practise it are composers."

c

"True."

"All the same, they aren't all called composers. They all have different names, and it's only one subdivision of the whole class (that which deals with music and rhythm) which is called by the general name. Only this kind of creation is called composing, and its practitioners composers."

"True."

d

"Well, it's the same with love. In general, for anyone, any desire for goodness and happiness is love—and it is a powerful and unpredictable force. But there are various ways of pursuing this desire—through money-making, through physical fitness, through philosophy—which do not entitle their devotees to call themselves lovers, or describe their activity as loving. Those who pursue one particular mode of loving, and make that their concern, have taken over the name of the whole (love, loving and lovers)."

"You may well be right."

e

"There is a theory that lovers are people in search of their other half. But according to my theory, love is not love of a half, nor of a whole, unless it is good. After all, men are prepared to have their own feet and hands cut off, if they think there's something wrong with them. They're not particularly attached to what is their own, except in

206   so far as they regard the good as their own property, and evil as alien to them. And that's because the good is the only object of human love, as I think you will agree."

"Yes, I certainly do agree."

"Can we say, then, quite simply, that men love the good?"

"Yes."

"And presumably we should add that they want to possess the good?"

"Yes, we should."

"And not merely to possess it, but to possess it forever."

"That also."

"In short, then, love is the desire for permanent possession of the good."

"Precisely."

"If this is always the object of our desire, what is the particular manner of pursuit,   b
and the particular sphere of activity, in which enthusiasm and effort qualify for the title
'love'? What is this activity? Do you know?"

"No, I don't. That's why I find your knowledge so impressive. In fact, I've kept
coming to see you, because I want an answer to just that question."

"Very well, I'll tell you. The activity we're talking about is the use of what is
beautiful for the purpose of reproduction, whether physical or mental."

"I'm no good at riddles. I don't understand what you mean."   c

"I'll try to make myself clearer. Reproduction, Socrates, both physical and mental, is a universal human activity. At a certain age our nature desires to give birth. To do
so, it cannot employ an ugly medium, but insists on what is beautiful. Sexual intercourse between man and woman is this reproduction. So there is the divine element, this
germ of immortality, in mortal creatures—i.e. conception and begetting. These cannot
take place in an uncongenial medium, and ugliness is uncongenial to everything divine,
while beauty is congenial. Therefore procreation has Beauty as its midwife and its des-   d
tiny, which is why the urge to reproduce becomes gentle and happy when it comes near
beauty: then conception and begetting become possible. By contrast, when it comes
near ugliness it becomes sullen and offended, it contracts, withdraws, and shrinks away
and does not beget. It stifles the reproductive urge, and is frustrated. So in anyone who
is keen (one might almost say bursting) to reproduce, beauty arouses violent emotion,
because beauty can release its possessor from the agony of reproduction. Your opinion,
Socrates, that love is desire for beauty, is mistaken."   e

"What is the correct view, then?"

"It is the desire to use beauty to beget and bear offspring."

"Perhaps."

"Certainly! And why to beget? Because begetting is, by human standards, something eternal and undying. So if we were right in describing love as the desire always to
possess the good, then the inevitable conclusion is that we desire immortality as well as
goodness. On this argument, love must be desire for immortality as much as for   207
beauty."

Those were her teachings, when she talked to me about love. And one day she
asked me, "What do you think is the reason for this love and this desire? You know how
strangely animals behave when they want to mate. Animals and birds, they're just the   b
same. Their health suffers, and they get all worked up, first over sexual intercourse, and
then over raising the young. For these ends they will fight, to the death, against far
stronger opponents. They will go to any lengths, even starve themselves, to bring up
their offspring. We can easily imagine human beings behaving like this from rational
motives, but what can be the cause of such altruistic behaviour in animals? Do you   c
know?"

"No, I don't."

"Do you think you can become an expert on love without knowing?"

"Look, Diotima, I know I have a lot to learn. I've just admitted that. That's why
I've come to you. So please tell me the cause of these phenomena, and anything else I
should know about love."

"Well, if you believe that the natural object of love is what we have often agreed
it to be, then the answer is not surprising, since the same reasoning still holds good.   d
What is mortal tries, to the best of its ability, to be everlasting and immortal. It does this
in the only way it can, by always leaving a successor to replace what decays. Think of

what we call the life-span and identity of an individual creature. For example, a man is said to be the same individual from childhood until old age. The cells in his body are always changing, yet he is still called the same person, despite being perpetually reconstituted as parts of him decay—hair, flesh, bones, blood, his whole body, in fact. And not just his body, either. Precisely the same happens with mental attributes. Habits, dispositions, beliefs, opinions, desires, pleasures, pains and fears are all varying all the time for everyone. Some disappear, others take their place. And when we come to knowledge, the situation is even odder. It is not just a question of one piece of knowledge disappearing and being replaced by another, so that we are never the same people, as far as knowledge goes: the same thing happens with each individual piece of knowledge. What we call studying presupposes that knowledge is transient. Forgetting is loss of knowledge, and studying preserves knowledge by creating memory afresh in us, to replace what is lost. Hence we have the illusion of continuing knowledge.

"All continuous mortal existence is of this kind. It is not the case that creatures remain always, in every detail, precisely the same—only the divine does that. It is rather that what is lost, and what decays, always leaves behind a fresh copy of itself. This, Socrates, is the mechanism by which mortal creatures can taste immortality—both physical immortality, and other sorts. (For immortals, of course, it's different). So it's not surprising that everything naturally values its own offspring. They all feel this concern, and this love, because of their desire for immortality."

I found these ideas totally novel, and I said, "Well, Diotima, that's a very clever explanation. Is it really all true?" And she, in her best lecturer's manner, replied, "There can be no question of it. Take another human characteristic, ambition. It seems absurdly irrational until you remember my explanation. Think of the extraordinary behaviour of those who, prompted by Eros, are eager to become famous, and 'amass undying fame for the whole of time to come.' For this they will expose themselves to danger even more than they will for their children. They will spend money, endure any hardship, even die for it. Think of Alcestis' willingness to die for Admetus, or Achilles' determination to follow Patroclus in death, or your Athenian king Codrus and his readiness to give up his life for his children's right to rule. Would they have done these things if they hadn't thought they were leaving behind them an undying memory—which we still possess—of their courage? Of course not. The desire for undying nobility, and the good reputation which goes with it, is a universal human motive. The nobler people are, the more strongly they feel it. They desire immortality.

"Those whose creative urge is physical tend to turn to women, and pursue Eros by this route. The production of children gains them, as they imagine, immortality and a name and happiness for themselves, for all time. In others the impulse is mental or spiritual—people who are creative mentally, much more than physically. They produce what you would expect the mind to conceive and produce. And what is that? Thought, and all other human excellence. All poets are creators of this kind, and so are those artists who are generally regarded as inventive. However, under the general heading 'thought,' by far the finest and most important item is the art of political and domestic economy, what we call good judgment, and justice.

"Someone who, right from his youth, is mentally creative in these areas, when he is ready, and the time comes, feels a strong urge to give birth, or beget. So he goes around, like everyone else, searching, as I see it, for a medium of beauty in which he can create. He will never create in an ugly medium. So in his desire to create he is attracted to what is physically beautiful rather than ugly. But if he comes across a beautiful, noble, well-formed mind, then he finds the combination particularly attractive. He'll drop everything and embark on long conversations about goodness, with such a companion, trying to teach him about the nature and behaviour of the good man. Now c that he's made contact with someone beautiful, and made friends with him, he can produce and bring to birth what he long ago conceived. Present or absent, he keeps it in mind, and joins with his friends in bringing his conception to maturity. In consequence such people have a far stronger bond between them than there is between the parents of children; and they form much firmer friendships, because they are jointly responsible for finer, and more lasting, offspring.

"We would all choose children of this kind for ourselves, rather than human children. We look with envy at Homer and Hesiod, and the other great poets, and the mar- d vellous progeny they left behind, which have brought them undying fame and memory: or, if you like, at children of the kind which Lycurgus left in Sparta, the salvation of Sparta and practically all Greece. In your city, Solon is highly thought of, as the father of your laws, as are many other men in other states, both Greek and foreign. They have published to the world a variety of noble achievements, and created goodness of every e kind. There are shrines to such people in honour of their offspring, but none to the producers of ordinary children.

"You, too, Socrates, could probably be initiated this far into knowledge of Eros. But all this, rightly pursued, is a mere preliminary to the full rites, and final revelation, 210 which might well be beyond you. Still, I'll tell you about it, so that if I fail, it won't be for want of trying. Try to follow, if you can.

"The true follower of this subject must begin, as a young man, with the pursuit of physical beauty. In the first place, if his mentor advises him properly, he should be attracted, physically, to one individual; at this stage his offspring are beautiful discussions and conversations. Next he should realise that the physical beauty of one body is akin to that of any other body, and that if he's going to pursue beauty of appearance, it's the height of folly not to regard the beauty which is in all bodies as one and the same. This insight will convert him into a lover of all physical beauty, and he will become less obsessive in his pursuit of his one former passion, as he realises its unimportance. b

"The next stage is to put a higher value on mental than on physical beauty. The right qualities of mind, even in the absence of any great physical beauty, will be enough to awaken his love and affection. He will generate the kind of discussions which are im- c proving to the young. The aim is that, as the next step, he should be compelled to contemplate the beauty of customs and institutions, to see that all beauty of this sort is related, and consequently to regard physical beauty as trivial.

"From human institutions his teacher should direct him to knowledge, so that he may, in turn, see the beauty of different types of knowledge. Whereas before, in servile d and contemptible fashion, he was dominated by the individual case, loving the beauty of a boy, or a man, or a single human activity, now he directs his eyes to what is beautiful in general, as he turns to gaze upon the limitless ocean of beauty. Now he produces many fine and inspiring thoughts and arguments, as he gives his undivided attention to philosophy. Here he gains in strength and stature until his attention is caught by that one special knowledge—the knowledge of a beauty which I will now try to describe to you. So pay the closest possible attention. e

"When a man has reached this point in his education in love, studying the different types of beauty in correct order, he will come to the final end and goal of this education. Then suddenly he will see a beauty of a breathtaking nature, Socrates, the beauty 211 which is the justification of all his efforts so far. It is eternal, neither coming to be nor passing away, neither increasing nor decreasing. Moreover it is not beautiful in part, and ugly in part, nor is it beautiful at one time, and not at another; nor beautiful in some respects, but not in others; nor beautiful here and ugly there, as if beautiful in some peo- b ple's eyes, but not in others. It will not appear to him as the beauty of a face, or hands, or anything physical—nor as an idea or branch of knowledge, nor as existing in any determinate place, such as a living creature, or the earth, or heaven, or anywhere like that. It exists for all time, by itself and with itself, unique. All other forms of beauty derive from it, but in such a way that their creation or destruction does not strengthen or weaken it, or affect it in any way at all. If a man progresses (as he will do, if he goes about his love affairs in the right way) from the lesser beauties, and begins to catch sight of this beauty, then he is within reach of the final revelation. Such is the experience of

c   the man who approaches, or is guided towards, love in the right way, beginning with the particular examples of beauty, but always returning from them to the search for that one beauty. He uses them like a ladder, climbing from the love of one person to love of two; from two to love of all physical beauty; from physical beauty to beauty in human behaviour; thence to beauty in subjects of study; from them he arrives finally at that branch of knowledge which studies nothing but ultimate beauty. Then at last he understands what true beauty is.

d   "That, if ever, is the moment, my dear Socrates, when a man's life is worth living, as he contemplates beauty itself. Once seen, it will not seem to you to be a good such as gold, or fashionable clothes, or the boys and young men who have such an effect on you now when you see them. You, and any number of people like you, when you see your boyfriends and spend all your time with them, are quite prepared (or would be, if it were possible) to go without food and drink, just looking at them and being with them. But suppose it were granted to someone to see beauty it-

e   self quite clearly, in its pure, undiluted form—not clogged up with human flesh and colouring, and a whole lot of other worthless and corruptible matter. No, imagine he

212   were able to see the divine beauty itself in its unique essence. Don't you think he would find it a wonderful way to live, looking at it, contemplating it as it should be contemplated, and spending his time in its company? It cannot fail to strike you that only then will it be possible for him, seeing beauty as it should be seen, to produce, not likenesses of goodness (since it is no likeness he has before him), but the real thing (since he has the real thing before him); and that this producing, and caring for, real goodness earns him the friendship of the gods and makes him, if anyone, immortal."

b   There you are, then, Phaedrus and the rest of you. That's what Diotima said to me, and I, for one, find it convincing. And it's because I'm convinced that I now try to persuade other people as well that man, in his search for this goal, could hardly hope to find a better ally than Eros. That's why I say that everyone should honour Eros, and why I myself honour him, and make the pursuit of Eros my chief concern, and encourage others to do the same. Now, and for all time, I praise the power and vigour of Eros, to the limits of my ability.

     That's my speech, Phaedrus. You can take it, if you like, as a formal eulogy of

c   Eros. Or you can call it by any other name you please.

     This speech was greeted with applause, and Aristophanes started saying something about Socrates' reference to his speech, when suddenly there was a tremendous sound of hammering at the front door—people going home from a party, by the sound of it. You could hear the voice of a flute-girl.

d   AGATHON (to his slaves): Could you see who that is? If it's one of my friends, ask him in. Otherwise, say we've stopped drinking and are just going to bed.

     Almost at once we heard Alcibiades' voice from the courtyard. He was very drunk, and shouting at the top of his voice, asking "where Agathon was," and demanding "to be taken to Agathon." So in he came, supported by the girl, and some of his fol-

lowers. He stood there in the doorway, wearing a luxuriant garland of ivy and violets,   e
with his head covered in ribbons.

ALCIBIADES: Greetings, gentlemen. Will you allow me to join your gathering completely drunk? Or shall we just crown Agathon (which is what we've come for) and go away? I couldn't come yesterday, but now here I am, with ribbons in my hair, so that I can take a garland from my own head, and crown the man whom I hereby proclaim the cleverest and handsomest man in Athens. Are you going to laugh at me for being drunk? Well, you may laugh, but I'm sure I'm right, all the same. Anyway, those are my   213
terms. So tell me right away: should I come in? Will you drink with me, or not?

Then everyone started talking at once, telling him to come in and sit down. And Agathon called him over. So over he came, assisted by his companions. He was taking off his ribbons, getting ready to put the garland on Agathon, and with the ribbons in front of his eyes he didn't see Socrates. So he sat down next to Agathon, between him and Socrates, Socrates moving aside, when he saw him, to make room. As he sat down he greeted Agathon, and put the garland on his head.   b

AGATHON (to his slaves): Take Alcibiades' shoes off. He can make a third at this table.

ALCIBIADES: Excellent, but who is the other person drinking at our table? (Turning and seeing Socrates, and leaping to his feet.) My God, what's this? Socrates here? You've been lying in wait here for me, just as you used to do. You were always turning   c
up unexpectedly, wherever I least expected you. What are you doing here this time? And come to that, how've you managed to get yourself a place next to the most attractive person in the room? You ought to be next to someone like Aristophanes; he sets out to make himself ridiculous, and succeeds. Shouldn't you be with him?

SOCRATES: I'm going to need your protection, Agathon. I've found the love of this man a bit of a nightmare. From the day I took a fancy to him, I haven't been al-   d
lowed to look at, or talk to, anyone attractive at all. If I do he gets envious and jealous, and starts behaving outrageously. He insults me, and can barely keep his hands off me. So you make sure he doesn't do anything now. You reconcile us, or defend me if he resorts to violence. His insane sexuality scares me stiff.

ALCIBIADES: There can be no reconciliation between you and me. However, I'll get my revenge another time. For the moment, give me some of those ribbons, Agathon,   e
so I can make a garland for this remarkable head of his as well. I don't want him complaining that I crowned you, and not him, though he is the international grandmaster of words—and not just the day before yesterday, like you, but all the time. (As he said this he took some of the ribbons, made a garland for Socrates, and sat down.) Well, gentlemen, you seem to me to be pretty sober. We can't have that. You'll have to drink. After all, that's what we agreed. So I'm going to choose a Master of Ceremonies, to see you all get enough to drink. I choose myself. Agathon, let them bring a large cup, if you've got one. No, wait! (Suddenly catching sight of an ice-bucket holding upwards of half a gallon.) No need for that. Boy, bring me that ice-bucket. (He filled it, and started off by   214
draining it himself. Then he told the slave to fill it up again for Socrates.) A useless ploy against Socrates, gentlemen. It doesn't matter how much you give him to drink, he'll drink it and be none the worse for wear. (So the slave filled the bucket for Socrates, who drank it.)

ERYXIMACHUS: What's the plan, Alcibiades? Are we just going to sit here and   b
drink as if we were dying of thirst? Aren't we going to talk, or sing, at all while we drink?

ALCIBIADES: Ah, Eryximachus. Most excellent scion of a most excellent and sensible father. Good evening.

ERYXIMACHUS: Good evening to you too. But what *do* you want us to do?

ALCIBIADES: Whatever you recommend. We must do as you say. After all, "a doctor is worth a dozen ordinary men." So you tell us your prescription.

c   ERYXIMACHUS: Very well, listen. We had decided, before you came, that going round anticlockwise, each of us in turn should make the best speech he could about Eros, in praise of him. We've all made our speeches. You've drunk but you haven't spoken. So it's only fair that you should speak now; after that you can give any instructions you like to Socrates, and he can do the same to the man on his right, and so on all the way round.

ALCIBIADES: That's a good idea, Eryximachus. But it's grossly unfair to ask me, drunk, to compete with you sober. Also, my dear friend, I hope you didn't pay any attention to Socrates' remarks just now. Presumably you realise the situation is the exact opposite of what he said. He's the one who will resort to violence, if I praise anyone else, god or man, in his presence.

d

SOCRATES: Can't you hold your tongue?

ALCIBIADES: Don't worry, I wouldn't dream of praising anyone else if you're here.

ERYXIMACHUS: Well, that'll do, if you like. Praise Socrates.

e   ALCIBIADES: Really? You think I should, Eryximachus? Shall I set about him, and get my own back on him, here in front of you all?

SOCRATES: Hey! What are you up to? Are you trying to make a fool of me by praising me. Or what?

ALCIBIADES: I'm going to tell the truth. Do you mind that?

SOCRATES: Of course not. In fact, I'm all in favour of it.

ALCIBIADES: I can't wait to start. And here's what you can do. If I say anything that's not true, you can interrupt me, if you like, and tell me I'm wrong. I shan't get anything wrong on purpose, but don't be surprised if my recollection of things is a bit higgledy-piggledy. It's not easy, when you're as drunk as I am, to give a clear and orderly account of someone as strange as you.

ALCIBIADES

215   Gentlemen, I'm going to try and praise Socrates using similes. He may think I'm trying to make a fool of him, but the point of the simile is its accuracy, not its absurdity. I think he's very like one of those Silenus-figures sculptors have on their shelves. They're made with flutes or pipes. You can open them up, and when you do you find little figures of the gods inside. I also think Socrates is like the satyr Marsyas. As far as your appearance goes, Socrates, even you can't claim these are poor comparisons; but I'll tell you how the likeness holds good in other ways: just listen. You're a troublemaker, aren't you? Don't deny it, I can bring witnesses. You may not play the pipes, like Marsyas, but what you do is much more amazing. He had only to open his mouth to delight men, but he needed a musical instrument to do it. The same goes for anyone nowadays who plays his music—I count what Olympus played as really Marsyas', since he learnt from him. His is the only music which carries people away, and reveals those who have a desire for the gods and their rites. Such is its divine power, and it makes no difference whether it's played by an expert, or by a mere flute-girl.

b

c

You have the same effect on people. The only difference is that you do it with words alone, without the aid of any instrument. We can all listen to anyone else talking,

and it has virtually no effect on us, no matter what he's talking about, or how good a   d
speaker he is. But when we listen to you, or to someone else using your arguments, even
if he's a hopeless speaker, we're overwhelmed and carried away. This is true of men,
women and children alike.

For my own part, gentlemen, I would like to tell you on my honour (only you
would certainly think I was drunk) the effect what he says has had on me in the past—
and still does have, to this day. When I hear him, it's like the worst kind of religious
hysteria. My heart pounds, and I find myself in floods of tears, such is the effect of his   e
words. And I can tell lots of other people feel the same. I used to listen to Pericles and
other powerful speakers, and I thought they spoke well. But they never had the effect on
me of turning all my beliefs upside down, with the disturbing realisation that my whole
life is that of a slave. Whereas this Marsyas here has often made me feel that, and decide
that the kind of life I lead is just not worth living. You can't deny it, Socrates.   216

Even now I know in my heart of hearts that if I were to listen to him, I couldn't resist him. The same thing would happen again. He forces me to admit that with all my
faults I do nothing to improve myself, but continue in public life just the same. So I tear
myself away, as if stopping my ears against the Sirens; otherwise I would spend my
whole life there sitting at his feet. He's the only man who can appeal to my better nature   b
(not that most people would reckon I *had* a better nature), because I'm only too aware I
have no answer to his arguments. I know I should do as he tells me, but when I leave
him I have no defence against my own ambition and desire for recognition. So I run for
my life, and avoid him, and when I see him, I'm embarrassed, when I remember conclusions we've reached in the past. I would often cheerfully have seen him dead, and   c
yet I know that if that did happen, I should be even more upset. So I just can't cope with
the man.

I'm by no means the only person to be affected like this by his satyr's music, but
that isn't all I have to say about his similarity to those figures I likened him to, and
about his remarkable powers. Believe me, none of you really knows the man. So I'll en-
lighten you, now that I've begun.

Your view of Socrates is of someone who fancies attractive men, spends all his   d
time with them, finds them irresistible—and you know how hopelessly ignorant and
uncertain he is. And yet this pose is extremely Silenus-like. It's the outward mask he
wears, like the carved Silenus. Open him up, and he's a model of restraint—you
wouldn't believe it, my dear fellow-drinkers. Take my word for it, it makes no differ-   e
ence at all how attractive you are, he has an astonishing contempt for that kind of thing.
Similarly with riches, or any of the other so-called advantages we possess. He regards
all possessions as worthless, and us humans as insignificant. No, I mean it—he treats
his whole life in human society as a game or puzzle.

But when he's serious, when he opens up and you see the real Socrates—I don't
know if any of you has ever seen the figure inside. I saw it once, and it struck me as utterly godlike and golden and beautiful and wonderful. In fact, I thought I must simply   217
do anything he told me. And since I thought he was serious about my good looks, I congratulated myself on a fantastic stroke of luck, which had given me the chance to satisfy
Socrates, and be the recipient, in return, of all his knowledge. I had, I may say, an extremely high opinion of my own looks.

That was my plan, so I did what I had never done up to then—I sent away my at-   b
tendant, and took to seeing him on my own. You see, I'm going to tell you the whole
truth, so listen carefully, and you tell them, Socrates, if I get anything wrong. Well, gentlemen, I started seeing him—just the two of us—and I thought he would start talking to
me as lovers do to their boyfriends when they're alone together. I was very excited. But

c   nothing like that happened at all. He spent the day talking to me as usual, and then left. I invited him to the gymnasium with me, and exercised with him there, thinking I might make some progress that way. So he exercised and wrestled with me, often completely on our own, and (needless to say) it got me nowhere at all. When that turned out to be no good, I thought I'd better make a pretty determined assault on the man, and not give up, now that I'd started. I wanted to find out what the trouble was. So I asked him to dinner, just like a lover with designs on his boyfriend.

d   He took some time to agree even to this, but finally I did get him to come. The first time he came, he had dinner, and then got up to go. I lost my nerve, that time, and let him go. But I decided to try again. He came to dinner, and I kept him talking late into the night. When he tried to go home, I made him stay, saying it was too late to go. So he stayed the night on the couch next to mine. There was no-one else sleeping in the room.

e   What I've told you so far I'd be quite happy to repeat to anyone. The next part I'm only telling you because (a) I'm drunk—"in vino veritas," and all that—and (b) since I've started praising Socrates, it seems wrong to leave out an example of his superior behaviour. Besides, I'm like someone who's been bitten by an adder. They say that a man who's had this happen to him will only say what it was like to others who've been

218   bitten; they're the only people who will understand, and make allowances for, his willingness to say or do anything, such is the pain. Well, I've been bitten by something worse than an adder, and in the worst possible place. I've been stung, or bitten, in my heart or soul (whatever you care to call it) by a method of philosophical argument, whose bite, when it gets a grip on a young and intelligent mind, is sharper than any

b   adder's. It makes one willing to say or do anything. I can see all these Phaedruses and Agathons, Eryximachuses, Pausaniases, Aristodemuses and Aristophaneses here, not to mention Socrates himself and the rest of you. You've all had a taste of this wild passion for philosophy, so you'll understand me, and forgive what I did then, and what I'm telling you now. As for the servants, and anyone else who's easily shocked, or doesn't know what I'm talking about, they'll just have to put something over their ears.

c   There we were, then, gentlemen. The lamp had gone out, the slaves had gone to bed. I decided it was time to abandon subtlety, and say plainly what I was after. So I nudged him. "Socrates, are you asleep?" "No." "Do you know what I've decided?" "What?" "I think you're the ideal person to be my lover, but you seem to be a bit shy about suggesting it. So I'll tell you how I feel about it. I think I'd be crazy not to satisfy

d   you in this way, just as I'd do anything else for you if it was in my power—or in my friends' power. Nothing matters more to me than my own improvement, and I can't imagine a better helper than you. Anyone with any sense would think worse of me for not giving a man like you what he wants than most ignorant people would if I did give you what you want."

Socrates listened to this. Then, with characteristic irony, he replied. "My dear

e   Alcibiades, you're certainly nobody's fool, if you're right in what you say about me, and I do have some power to improve you. It must be remarkable beauty you see in me, far superior to your own physical beauty. If that's the aim of your deal with me, to exchange beauty for beauty, then you're trying to get much the better of the bargain. You want to get real beauty in exchange for what is commonly mistaken for it, like Diomedes getting gold armour in return for his bronze. Better think again, however.

219   You might be wrong about me. Judgment begins when eyesight starts to fail, and you're still a long way from that."

I listened, then said: "Well, as far as I am concerned, that's how things stand. I've told you my real feelings. You must decide what you think best for yourself and for me."

"That's good advice. We must think about it some time, and act as seems best to us, in this matter as in others."   b

After this exchange, thinking my direct assault had made some impact, I got up, before he could say anything more, wrapped my cloak around him (it was winter), and lay down with him under his rough cloak. I put my arms round him. I spent the whole night with him, remarkable, superhuman being that he is—still telling the truth, Socrates, you can't deny it—but he was more than equal to my advances. He rejected them, laughed at my good looks, and treated them with contempt; and I must admit that, as far as looks went, I thought I was quite something, members of the jury. (I call you that, since I'm accusing Socrates of contempt.) In short, I promise you faithfully, I fell asleep, and when I woke up in the morning I'd slept with Socrates all night, but absolutely nothing had happened. It was just like sleeping with one's father or elder brother.   d

Imagine how I felt after that. I was humiliated and yet full of admiration for Socrates' character—his restraint and strength of mind. I'd met a man whose equal, in intelligence and control, I didn't think I should ever meet again. I couldn't have a row with him; that would just lose me his friendship. Nor could I see any way of attracting him. I knew money would make as little impression on him as Trojan weapons on Ajax, and he'd already escaped my one sure means of ensnaring him. I didn't know what to do, and I went around infatuated with the man. No-one's ever been so infatuated.   e

That was the background to our military service together in Potidaea, where we were messmates. In the first place there was his toughness—not only greater than mine, but greater than anyone else's. Sometimes we were cut off and had to go without food, as happens on campaign. No-one could match him for endurance. On the other hand, he was the one who really made the most of it when there was plenty. He wouldn't drink for choice, but if he had to, he drank us all under the table. Surprising as it may seem, no man has ever seen Socrates drunk. I've no doubt you'll see confirmation of that this evening. As for the weather (they have pretty savage winters up there), his indifference to it was always astonishing, but one occasion stands out in particular. There was an incredibly severe frost. No-one went outside, or if they did, they went muffled up to the eyeballs, with their feet wrapped up in wool or sheepskin. In these conditions Socrates went out in the same cloak he always wore, and walked barefoot over the ice with less fuss than the rest of us who had our feet wrapped up. The men didn't like it at all; they thought he was getting at them.   220   b

So much for that. But there's another exploit of this "conquering hero" during that campaign, which I ought to tell you about. He was studying a problem one morning, and he stood there thinking about it, not making any progress, but not giving up either—just standing there, trying to find the answer. By midday people were beginning to take notice, and remark to one another in some surprise that Socrates had been standing there thinking since dawn. Finally, in the evening after supper, some of the Ionians brought out their mattresses (this was in summer), and slept in the open, keeping an eye on him to see if he'd stand there all night. And sure enough he did stand there, until dawn broke and the sun rose. Then he said a prayer to the sun and left.   c   d

Should I say something about his conduct in action? Yes, I think he's earned it. In the battle in which the generals gave me a decoration, my own life was saved by none other than Socrates. He refused to leave me when I was wounded, and saved both me and my weapons. So I recommended that the generals should give you the decoration. Isn't that true, Socrates? You can't object to that, or say I'm lying, can you? In fact the generals were inclined to favour me, because of my social position, and wanted to give it to me, but you were keener than they were that I should get it, rather than you.   e

221   And you should have seen him, gentlemen, on the retreat from Delium. I was with him, but I was on horseback, and he was on foot. He was retreating, amid the general rout, with Laches. I came upon them, and when I saw them I told them not to panic, and said I'd stick by them. This time I got a better view of Socrates than I had at Potidaea, since I was on horseback, and less worried about my own safety. For a start, he was much more composed than Laches. And then I thought your description of him, Aristo-

b   phanes, was as accurate there as it is here in Athens, "marching along with his head in the air, staring at all around him," calmly contemplating friend and foe alike. It was per-fectly clear, even from a distance, that any attempt to lay a finger on him would arouse vigorous resistance. So he and his companion escaped unhurt. On the whole, in battle, you don't meddle with people like that. You go after the ones in headlong flight.

c   I could go on praising Socrates all night, and tell you some surprising things. Many of his qualities can be found in other people, and yet it's remarkable how unlike he is to anyone in the past or present. You can compare Brasidas, or someone like that, with Achilles; Pericles with Nestor or Antenor (for example); and make other similar

d   comparisons. But you could go a long way and not find a match, dead or living, for Socrates. So unusual are the man himself and his arguments. You have to go back to my original comparison of the man and his arguments, to Silenuses and satyrs. I didn't say this at the beginning, but his arguments, when you really look at them, are also just like

e   Silenus-figures. If you decided to listen to one, it would strike you at first as ludicrous. On the face of it, it's just a collection of irrelevant words and phrases; but those are just the outer skin of this trouble-making satyr. It's all donkeys and bronzesmiths, shoe-

222   makers and tanners. He always seems to be repeating himself, and people who haven't heard him before, and aren't too quick on the uptake, laugh at what he says. But look beneath the surface, and get inside them, and you'll find two things. In the first place, they're the only arguments which really make any sense; on top of that they are supremely inspiring, because they contain countless models of excellence and pointers towards it. In fact, they deal with everything you should be concerned about, if you want to lead a good and noble life.

That's my speech, gentlemen, in praise of Socrates—though I've included a bit of blame as well for his outrageous treatment of me. And I'm not the only sufferer.

b   There's Charmides, the son of Glaucon, and Euthydemus, the son of Diocles, and lots of others. He seduces them, like a lover seducing his boyfriend, and then it turns out he's not their lover at all; in fact, they're his lovers. So take my advice, Agathon, and don't be seduced. Learn from our experience, rather than at first hand, like Homer's "fool who learnt too late." Don't trust him an inch.

c   Alcibiades' candour aroused some amusement. He seemed to be still in love with Socrates.

SOCRATES: Not so drunk after all, Alcibiades; or you wouldn't have avoided, so elegantly and so deviously, revealing the real object of your speech, just slipping it in at the end, as if it were an afterthought. What you're really trying to do is turn Agathon and me against one another. You think that I should be your lover, and no-one else's;

d   and that you, and no-one else, should be Agathon's. Well, it hasn't worked. All that stuff about satyrs and Silenuses is quite transparent. You mustn't let him get away with it, my dear Agathon; you must make sure no-one turns us against each other.

AGATHON: You may be right, Socrates. His sitting between us, to keep us apart,

e   bears that out. But it won't work. I'll come round and sit next to you.

SOCRATES: Good idea. Sit here, round this side.

ALCIBIADES: Ye gods. What I have to put up with from the man. He has to keep scoring off me. Look, at least let Agathon sit in the middle.

SOCRATES: Out of the question. You've just praised me, and now I must praise the person on my right. If Agathon sits next to you, he can't be expected to make *another* speech in praise of me. I'd better make one in praise of him instead. No, you'll have to admit defeat, my good friend, and put up with me praising the boy. I look forward to it.

223

AGATHON: What a bit of luck. I'm certainly not staying here, Alcibiades. I'd much rather move, and get myself praised by Socrates.

ALCIBIADES: That's it, the same old story. Whenever Socrates is around, no-one else can get near anyone good looking. Like now, for example. Look how easily he finds plausible reasons why Agathon should sit next to him.

Agathon got up to come and sit by Socrates. Suddenly a whole crowd of people on their way home from a party turned up at the door, and finding it open (someone was just leaving), they came straight in, and sat down to join us. Things became incredibly noisy and disorderly, and we couldn't avoid having far too much to drink. Eryximachus and Phaedrus and some others went home. I fell asleep, and slept for some time, the nights being long at that time of year. When I woke up it was almost light, and the cocks were crowing. I could see that everyone had gone home or to sleep, apart from Agathon, Aristophanes, and Socrates. They were still awake and drinking (passing a large bowl round anticlockwise). Socrates was holding the floor. I've forgotten most of what he

b

c

A Seated Man at a Greek Symposium, Red-figure vase, 460–450 B.C. Today the term "symposium" usually means a scholarly meeting; in ancient Greece it meant a drinking party (as depicted on this vase—and in the dialogue). *(Smithsonian Institution)*

d   was saying, since I missed the beginning of it, and was still half-asleep anyway. The gist of it was that he was forcing them to admit that the same man could be capable of writing comedy and tragedy, and hence that a successful tragedian must also be able to write comedy. As they were being driven to this conclusion, though not really following the argument, they dropped off. Aristophanes went to sleep first, and then, as it was getting light, Agathon. Socrates made them both comfortable, and got up to leave himself. I followed him, as usual. He went to the Lyceum, had a bath, spent the rest of the day as he normally would, and then, towards evening, went home to bed.

REPUBLIC (in part)

BOOK IV

* * *

427c   So now at last, son of Ariston, said I, your commonwealth is established. The next
  d   thing is to bring to bear upon it all the light you can get from any quarter, with the help of your brother and Polemarchus and all the rest, in the hope that we may see where justice is to be found in it and where injustice, how they differ, and which of the two will bring happiness to its possessor, no matter whether gods and men see that he has it or not.

  e   Nonsense, said Glaucon; you promised to conduct the search yourself, because it would be a sin not to uphold justice by every means in your power.
        That is true; I must do as you say, but you must all help.
        We will.
        I suspect, then, we may find what we are looking for in this way. I take it that our state, having been founded and built up on the right lines, is good in the complete sense of the word.
        It must be.
        Obviously, then, it is wise, brave, temperate, and just.
428   Obviously.
        Then if we find some of these qualities in it, the remainder will be the one we have not found. It is as if we were looking somewhere for one of any four things: if we detected that one immediately, we should be satisfied; whereas if we recognized the other three first, that would be enough to indicate the thing we wanted; it could only be the remaining one. So here we have four qualities. Had we not better follow that method in looking for the one we want?
        Surely.

  b   To begin then: the first quality to come into view in our state seems to be its wisdom; and there appears to be something odd about this quality.
        What is there odd about it?

The Republic of Plato (427c–480a, 502c–521b), translated with introduction and notes by Francis MacDonald Cornford (Oxford: Oxford University Press, 1945). Reprinted by permission of Oxford University Press.

I think the state we have described really has wisdom; for it will be prudent in counsel, won't it?

Yes.

And prudence in counsel is clearly a form of knowledge; good counsel cannot be due to ignorance and stupidity.

Clearly.

But there are many and various kinds of knowledge in our commonwealth. There is the knowledge possessed by the carpenters or the smiths, and the knowledge how to   c
raise crops. Are we to call the state wise and prudent on the strength of these forms of skill?

No; they would only make it good at furniture-making or working in copper or agriculture.

Well then, is there any form of knowledge, possessed by some among the citizens of our new-founded commonwealth, which will enable it to take thought, not for some   d
particular interest, but for the best possible conduct of the state as a whole in its internal and external relations?

Yes, there is.

What is it, and where does it reside?

It is precisely that art of guardianship which resides in those Rulers whom we just now called Guardians in the full sense.

And what would you call the state on the strength of that knowledge?

Prudent and truly wise.

And do you think there will be more or fewer of these genuine Guardians in our   e
state than there will be smiths?

Far fewer.

Fewer, in fact, than any of those other groups who are called after the kind of skill they possess?

Much fewer.

So, if a state is constituted on natural principles, the wisdom it possesses as a whole will be due to the knowledge residing in the smallest part, the one which takes the lead and governs the rest. Such knowledge is the only kind that deserves the name of wisdom, and it appears to be ordained by nature that the class privileged to possess it should be the smallest of all.   429

Quite true.

Here then we have more or less made out one of our four qualities and its seat in the structure of the commonwealth.

To my satisfaction, at any rate.

Next there is courage. It is not hard to discern that quality or the part of the community in which it resides so as to entitle the whole to be called brave.

Why do you say so?

Because anyone who speaks of a state as either brave or cowardly can only be   b
thinking of that part of it which takes the field and fights in its defence; the reason being, I imagine, that the character of the state is not determined by the bravery or cowardice of the other parts.

No.

Courage, then, is another quality which a community owes to a certain part of itself. And its being brave will mean that, in this part, it possesses the power of preserving, in all circumstances, a conviction about the sort of things that it is right to be afraid   c
of—the conviction implanted by the education which the law-giver has established. Is not that what you mean by courage?

I do not quite understand. Will you say it again?

I am saying that courage means preserving something.

Yes, but what?

The conviction, inculcated by lawfully established education, about the sort of things which may rightly be feared. When I added "in all circumstances," I meant preserving it always and never abandoning it, whether under the influence of pain or of

d   pleasure, of desire or of fear. If you like, I will give an illustration.

Please do.

You know how dyers who want wool to take a purple dye, first select the white wool from among all the other colours, next treat it very carefully to make it take the dye in its full brilliance, and only then dip it in the vat. Dyed in that way, wool gets a

e   fast colour, which no washing, even with soap, will rob of its brilliance; whereas if they choose wool of any colour but white, or if they neglect to prepare it, you know what happens.

Yes, it looks washed-out and ridiculous.

That illustrates the result we were doing our best to achieve when we were choos-

430   ing our fighting men and training their minds and bodies. Our only purpose was to contrive influences whereby they might take the colour of our institutions like a dye, so that, in virtue of having both the right temperament and the right education, their convictions about what ought to be feared and on all other subjects might be indelibly fixed,

b   never to be washed out by pleasure and pain, desire and fear, solvents more terribly effective than all the soap and fuller's earth in the world. Such a power of constantly preserving, in accordance with our institutions, the right conviction about the things which ought, or ought not, to be feared, is what I call courage. That is my position, unless you have some objection to make.

None at all, he replied; if the belief were such as might be found in a slave or an animal—correct, but not produced by education—you would hardly describe it as in accordance with our institutions, and you would give it some other name than courage.

c   Quite true.

Then I accept your account of courage.

You will do well to accept it, at any rate as applying to the courage of the ordinary citizen; if you like we will go into it more fully some other time. At present we are in search of justice, rather than of courage; and for that purpose we have said enough.

I quite agree.

d   Two qualities, I went on, still remain to be made out in our state, temperance and the object of our whole inquiry, justice. Can we discover justice without troubling ourselves further about temperance?

I do not know, and I would rather not have justice come to light first, if that means that we should not go on to consider temperance. So if you want to please me, take temperance first.

e   Of course I have every wish to please you.

Do go on then.

I will. At first sight, temperance seems more like some sort of concord or harmony than the other qualities did.

How so?

Temperance surely means a kind of orderliness, a control of certain pleasures and appetites. People use the expression, "master of oneself," whatever that means, and various other phrases that point the same way.

Quite true.

Is not "master of oneself" an absurd expression? A man who was master of him-   431
self would presumably be also subject to himself, and the subject would be master; for
all these terms apply to the same person.

No doubt.

I think, however, the phrase means that within the man himself, in his soul, there
is a better part and a worse; and that he is his own master when the part which is better
by nature has the worse under its control. It is certainly a term of praise; whereas it is
considered a disgrace, when, through bad breeding or bad company, the better part is
overwhelmed by the worse, like a small force outnumbered by a multitude. A man in   b
that condition is called a slave to himself and intemperate.

Probably that is what is meant.

Then now look at our newly founded state and you will find one of these two conditions realized there. You will agree that it deserves to be called master of itself, if temperance and self-mastery exist where the better part rules the worse.

Yes, I can see that is true.

It is also true that the great mass of multifarious appetites and pleasures and pains
will be found to occur chiefly in children and women and slaves, and, among free men   c
so called, in the inferior multitude; whereas the simple and moderate desires which,
with the aid of reason and right belief, are guided by reflection, you will find only in a
few, and those with the best inborn dispositions and the best educated.

Yes, certainly.

Do you see that this state of things will exist in your commonwealth, where the
desires of the inferior multitude will be controlled by the desires and wisdom of the su-   d
perior few? Hence, if any society can be called master of itself and in control of pleasures and desires, it will be ours.

Quite so.

On all these grounds, then, we may describe it as temperate. Furthermore, in our
state, if anywhere, the governors and the governed will share the same conviction on the
question of who ought to rule. Don't you think so?

I am quite sure of it.

Then, if that is their state of mind, in which of the two classes of citizens will temperance reside—in the governors or in the governed?   e

In both, I suppose.

So we were not wrong in divining a resemblance between temperance and some
kind of harmony. Temperance is not like courage and wisdom, which made the state
wise and brave by residing each in one particular part. Temperance works in a different   432
way; it extends throughout the whole gamut of the state, producing a consonance of all
its elements from the weakest to the strongest as measured by any standard you like to
take—wisdom, bodily strength, numbers, or wealth. So we are entirely justified in identifying with temperance this unanimity or harmonious agreement between the naturally
superior and inferior elements on the question which of the two should govern, whether
in the state or in the individual.

I fully agree.   b

Good, said I. We have discovered in our commonwealth three out of our four
qualities, to the best of our present judgment. What is the remaining one, required to
make up its full complement of goodness? For clearly this will be justice.

Clearly.

Now is the moment, then, Glaucon, for us to keep the closest watch, like hunts-
men standing round a covert, to make sure that justice does not slip through and vanish

c   undetected. It must certainly be somewhere hereabouts; so keep your eyes open for a view of the quarry, and if you see it first, give me the alert.

I wish I could, he answered; but you will do better to give me a lead and not count on me for more than eyes to see what you show me.

Pray for luck, then, and follow me.

I will, if you will lead on.

The thicket looks rather impenetrable, said I; too dark for it to be easy to start up
d   the game. However, we must push on.

Of course we must.

Here I gave the view halloo. Glaucon, I exclaimed, I believe we are on the track and the quarry is not going to escape us altogether.

That is good news.

Really, I said, we have been extremely stupid. All this time the thing has been under our very noses from the start, and we never saw it. We have been as absurd as a per-
e   son who hunts for something he has all the time got in his hand. Instead of looking at the thing, we have been staring into the distance. No doubt that is why it escaped us.

What do you mean?

I believe we have been talking about the thing all this while without ever understanding that we were giving some sort of account of it.

Do come to the point. I am all ears.

433   Listen, then, and judge whether I am right. You remember how, when we first began to establish our commonwealth and several times since, we have laid down, as a universal principle, that everyone ought to perform the one function in the community for which his nature best suited him. Well, I believe that that principle, or some form of it, is justice.

We certainly laid that down.

Yes, and surely we have often heard people say that justice means minding one's
b   own business and not meddling with other men's concerns; and we have often said so ourselves.

We have.

Well, my friend, it may be that this minding of one's own business, when it takes a certain form, is actually the same thing as justice. Do you know what makes me think so?

No, tell me.

I think that this quality which makes it possible for the three we have already considered, wisdom, courage, and temperance, to take their place in the commonwealth, and so long as it remains present secures their continuance, must be the remaining one.
c   And we said that, when three of the four were found, the one left over would be justice.

It must be so.

Well now, if we had to decide which of these qualities will contribute most to the excellence of our commonwealth, it would be hard to say whether it was the unanimity of rulers and subjects, or the soldier's fidelity to the established conviction about what is, or is not, to be feared, or the watchful intelligence of the Rulers; or whether its excellence were not above all due to the observance by everyone, child or woman, slave
d   or freeman or artisan, ruler or ruled, of this principle that each one should do his own proper work without interfering with others.

It would be hard to decide, no doubt.

It seems, then, that this principle can at any rate claim to rival wisdom, temperance, and courage as conducing to the excellence of a state. And would you not say that the only possible competitor of these qualities must be justice?

Yes, undoubtedly.

Here is another thing which points to the same conclusion. The judging of lawsuits is a duty that you will lay upon your Rulers, isn't it?   e

Of course.

And the chief aim of their decisions will be that neither party shall have what belongs to another or be deprived of what is his own.

Yes.

Because that is just?

Yes.

So here again justice admittedly means that a man should possess and concern   434
himself with what properly belongs to him.

True.

Again, do you agree with me that no great harm would be done to the community by a general interchange of most forms of work, the carpenter and the cobbler exchanging their positions and their tools and taking on each other's jobs, or even the same man undertaking both?

Yes, there would not be much harm in that.

But I think you will also agree that another kind of interchange would be disastrous. Suppose, for instance, someone whom nature designed to be an artisan or   b
tradesman should be emboldened by some advantage, such as wealth or command of votes or bodily strength, to try to enter the order of fighting men; or some member of that order should aspire, beyond his merits, to a seat in the council-chamber of the Guardians. Such interference and exchange of social positions and tools, or the attempt to combine all these forms of work in the same person, would be fatal to the commonwealth.

Most certainly.

Where there are three orders, then, any plurality of functions or shifting from one order to another is not merely utterly harmful to the community, but one might fairly   c
call it the extreme of wrongdoing. And you will agree that to do the greatest of wrongs to one's own community is injustice.

Surely.

This, then, is injustice. And, conversely, let us repeat that when each order—tradesman, Auxiliary, Guardian—keeps to its own proper business in the commonwealth and does its own work, that is justice and what makes a just society.

I entirely agree.   d

We must not be too positive yet, said I. If we find that this same quality when it exists in the individual can equally be identified with justice, then we can at once give our assent; there will be no more to be said; otherwise, we shall have to look further. For the moment, we had better finish the inquiry which we began with the idea that it would be easier to make out the nature of justice in the individual if we first tried to study it in   e
something on a larger scale. That larger thing we took to be a state, and so we set about constructing the best one we could, being sure of finding justice in a state that was good. The discovery we made there must now be applied to the individual. If it is confirmed,   435
all will be well; but if we find that justice in the individual is something different, we must go back to the state and test our new result. Perhaps if we brought the two cases into contact like flint and steel, we might strike out between them the spark of justice, and in its light confirm the conception in our own minds.

A good method. Let us follow it.

Now, I continued, if two things, one large, the other small, are called by the same name, they will be alike in that respect to which the common name applies. Accord-b   ingly, in so far as the quality of justice is concerned, there will be no difference between a just man and a just society.

No.

Well, but we decided that a society was just when each of the three types of human character it contained performed its own function; and again, it was temperate and brave and wise by virtue of certain other affections and states of mind of those same types.

True.

c   Accordingly, my friend, if we are to be justified in attributing those same virtues to the individual, we shall expect to find that the individual soul contains the same three elements and that they are affected in the same way as are the corresponding types in society.

That follows.

Here, then, we have stumbled upon another little problem: Does the soul contain these three elements or not?

Not such a very little one, I think. It may be a true saying, Socrates, that what is worthwhile is seldom easy.

Apparently; and let me tell you, Glaucon, it is my belief that we shall never reach
d   the exact truth in this matter by following our present methods of discussion; the road leading to that goal is longer and more laborious. However, perhaps we can find an answer that will be up to the standard we have so far maintained in our speculations.

Is not that enough? I should be satisfied for the moment.

Well, it will more than satisfy me, I replied.

Don't be disheartened, then, but go on.

e   Surely, I began, we must admit that the same elements and characters that appear in the state must exist in every one of us; where else could they have come from? It would be absurd to imagine that among peoples with a reputation for a high-spirited character, like the Thracians and Scythians and northerners generally, the states have not derived that character from their individual members; or that it is otherwise with the love of knowledge, which would be ascribed chiefly to our own part of the world, or
436   with the love of money, which one would specially connect with Phoenicia and Egypt.

Certainly.

So far, then, we have a fact which is easily recognized. But here the difficulty begins. Are we using the same part of ourselves in all these three experiences, or a different part in each? Do we gain knowledge with one part, feel anger with another, and with
b   yet a third desire the pleasures of food, sex, and so on? Or is the whole soul at work in every impulse and in all these forms of behaviour? The difficulty is to answer that question satisfactorily.

I quite agree.

Let us approach the problem whether these elements are distinct or identical in this way. It is clear that the same thing cannot act in two opposite ways or be in two opposite states at the same time, with respect to the same part of itself, and in relation to
c   the same object. So if we find such contradictory actions or states among the elements concerned, we shall know that more than one must have been involved.

Very well.

Consider this proposition of mine, then. Can the same thing, at the same time and with respect to the same part of itself, be at rest and in motion?

Certainly not.

We had better state this principle in still more precise terms, to guard against misunderstanding later on. Suppose a man is standing still, but moving his head and arms.

We should not allow anyone to say that the same man was both at rest and in motion at the same time, but only that part of him was at rest, part in motion. Isn't that so?   d

Yes.

An ingenious objector might refine still further and argue that a peg-top, spinning with its peg fixed at the same spot, or indeed any body that revolves in the same place, is both at rest and in motion as a whole. But we should not agree, because the parts in respect of which such a body is moving and at rest are not the same. It contains an axis   e and a circumference; and in respect of the axis it is at rest inasmuch as the axis is not inclined in any direction, while in respect of the circumference it revolves; and if, while it is spinning, the axis does lean out of the perpendicular in all directions, then it is in no way at rest.

That is true.

No objection of that sort, then, will disconcert us or make us believe that the same thing can ever act or be acted upon in two opposite ways, or be two opposite things, at the same time, in respect of the same part of itself, and in relation to the same object.   437

I can answer for myself at any rate.

Well, anyhow, as we do not want to spend time in reviewing all such objections to make sure that they are unsound, let us proceed on this assumption, with the understanding that, if we ever come to think otherwise, all the consequences based upon it will fall to the ground.

Yes, that is a good plan.

Now, would you class such things as assent and dissent, striving after something   b and refusing it, attraction and repulsion, as pairs of opposite actions or states of mind—no matter which?

Yes, they are opposites.

And would you not class all appetites such as hunger and thirst, and again willing and wishing, with the affirmative members of those pairs I have just mentioned? For instance, you would say that the soul of a man who desires something is striving after it,   c or trying to draw to itself the thing it wishes to possess, or again, in so far as it is willing to have its want satisfied, it is giving its assent to its own longing, as if to an inward question.

Yes.

And, on the other hand, disinclination, unwillingness, and dislike, we should class on the negative side with acts of rejection or repulsion.

Of course.

That being so, shall we say that appetites form one class, the most conspicuous   d being those we call thirst and hunger?

Yes.

Thirst being desire for drink, hunger for food?

Yes.

Now, is thirst, just in so far as it is thirst, a desire in the soul for anything more than simply drink? Is it, for instance, thirst for hot drink or for cold, for much drink or for little, or in a word for drink of any particular kind? Is it not rather true that you will have a desire for cold drink only if you are feeling hot as well as thirsty, and for hot   e drink only if you are feeling cold; and if you want much drink or little, that will be because your thirst is a great thirst or a little one? But, just in itself, thirst or hunger is a desire for nothing more than its natural object, drink or food, pure and simple.

Yes, he agreed, each desire, just in itself, is simply for its own natural object. When the object is of such and such a particular kind, the desire will be correspondingly qualified.

438   We must be careful here, or we might be troubled by the objection that no one desires mere food and drink, but always wholesome food and drink. We shall be told that what we desire is always something that is good; so if thirst is a desire, its object must be, like that of any other desire, something—drink or whatever it may be—that will be good for one.

Yes, there might seem to be something in that objection.

b   But surely, wherever you have two correlative terms, if one is qualified, the other must always be qualified too; whereas if one is unqualified, so is the other.

I don't understand.

Well, "greater" is a relative term; and the greater is greater than the less; if it is much greater, then the less is much less; if it is greater at some moment, past or future, then the less is less at that same moment. The same principle applies to all such correl-
c   atives, like "more" and "fewer," "double" and "half"; and again to terms like "heavier" and "lighter," "quicker" and "slower," and to things like hot and cold.

Yes.

Or take the various branches of knowledge: is it not the same there? The object of knowledge pure and simple is the knowable—if that is the right word—without any qualification; whereas a particular kind of knowledge has an object of a particular kind.
d   For example, as soon as men learnt how to build houses, their craft was distinguished from others under the name of architecture, because it had a unique character, which was itself due to the character of its object; and all other branches of craft and knowledge were distinguished in the same way.

True.

This, then, if you understand me now, is what I meant by saying that, where there
e   are two correlatives, the one is qualified if, and only if, the other is so. I am not saying that the one must have the same quality as the other—that the science of health and disease is itself healthy and diseased, or the knowledge of good and evil is itself good and evil—but only that, as soon as you have a knowledge that is restricted to a particular kind of object, namely health and disease, the knowledge itself becomes a particular kind of knowledge. Hence we no longer call it merely knowledge, which would have for its object whatever can be known, but we add the qualification and call it medical science.

I understand now and I agree.

439   Now, to go back to thirst: is not that one of these relative terms? It is essentially thirst for something.

Yes, for drink.

And if the drink desired is of a certain kind, the thirst will be correspondingly qualified. But thirst which is just simply thirst is not for drink of any particular sort—much or little, good or bad—but for drink pure and simple.

Quite so.

We conclude, then, that the soul of a thirsty man, just in so far as he is thirsty,
b   has no other wish than to drink. That is the object of its craving, and towards that it is impelled.

That is clear.

Now if there is ever something which at the same time pulls it the opposite way, that something must be an element in the soul other than the one which is thirsting and driving it like a beast to drink; in accordance with our principle that the same thing cannot behave in two opposite ways at the same time and towards the same object with the same part of itself. It is like an archer drawing the bow: it is not accurate to say that his hands are at the same time both pushing and pulling it. One hand does the pushing, the other the pulling.

Exactly.   c

Now, is it sometimes true that people are thirsty and yet unwilling to drink?

Yes, often.

What, then, can one say of them, if not that their soul contains something which urges them to drink and something which holds them back, and that this latter is a distinct thing and overpowers the other?

I agree.

And is it not true that the intervention of this inhibiting principle in such cases always has its origin in reflection; whereas the impulses driving and dragging the soul are   d engendered by external influences and abnormal conditions?

Evidently.

We shall have good reason, then, to assert that they are two distinct principles. We may call that part of the soul whereby it reflects, rational; and the other, with which it feels hunger and thirst and is distracted by sexual passion and all the other desires, we will call irrational appetite, associated with pleasure in the replenishment of certain wants.

Yes, there is good ground for that view.   e

Let us take it, then, that we have now distinguished two elements in the soul. What of that passionate element which makes us feel angry and indignant? Is that a third, or identical in nature with one of those two?

It might perhaps be identified with appetite.

I am more inclined to put my faith in a story I once heard about Leontius, son of Aglaion. On his way up from the Piraeus outside the north wall, he noticed the bodies of some criminals lying on the ground, with the executioner standing by them. He wanted to go and look at them, but at the same time he was disgusted and tried to turn away. He struggled for some time and covered his eyes, but at last the desire was too   440 much for him. Opening his eyes wide, he ran up to the bodies and cried, "There you are, curse you; feast yourselves on this lovely sight!"

Yes, I have heard that story too.

The point of it surely is that anger is sometimes in conflict with appetite, as if they were two distinct principles. Do we not often find a man whose desires would force him   b to go against his reason, reviling himself and indignant with this part of his nature which is trying to put constraint on him? It is like a struggle between two factions, in which indignation takes the side of reason. But I believe you have never observed, in yourself or anyone else, indignation make common cause with appetite in behaviour which reason decides to be wrong.

No, I am sure I have not.

Again, take a man who feels he is in the wrong. The more generous his nature, the   c less can he be indignant at any suffering, such as hunger and cold, inflicted by the man he has injured. He recognizes such treatment as just, and, as I say, his spirit refuses to be roused against it.

That is true.

But now contrast one who thinks it is he that is being wronged. His spirit boils with resentment and sides with the right as he conceives it. Persevering all the more for the hunger and cold and other pains he suffers, it triumphs and will not give in until its   d gallant struggle has ended in success or death; or until the restraining voice of reason, like a shepherd calling off his dog, makes it relent.

An apt comparison, he said; and in fact it fits the relation of our Auxiliaries to the Rulers: they were to be like watch-dogs obeying the shepherds of the commonwealth.

Yes, you understand very well what I have in mind. But do you see how we have changed our view? A moment ago we were supposing this spirited element to be   e something of the nature of appetite; but now it appears that, when the soul is divided into factions, it is far more ready to be up in arms on the side of reason.

Quite true.

Is it, then, distinct from the rational element or only a particular form of it, so that the soul will contain no more than two elements, reason and appetite? Or is the soul like 441 the state, which had three orders to hold it together, traders, Auxiliaries, and counsellors? Does the spirited element make a third, the natural auxiliary of reason, when not corrupted by bad upbringing?

It must be a third.

Yes, I said, provided it can be shown to be distinct from reason, as we saw it was from appetite.

That is easily proved. You can see that much in children: they are full of passion-b ate feelings from their very birth; but some, I should say, never become rational, and most of them only late in life.

A very sound observation, said I, the truth of which may also be seen in animals. And besides, there is the witness of Homer in that line I quoted before: "He smote his breast and spoke, chiding his heart." The poet is plainly thinking of the two elements as c distinct, when he makes the one which has chosen the better course after reflection rebuke the other for its unreasoning passion.

I entirely agree.

And so, after a stormy passage, we have reached the land. We are fairly agreed that the same three elements exist alike in the state and in the individual soul.

That is so.

d Does it not follow at once that state and individual will be wise or brave by virtue of the same element in each and in the same way? Both will possess in the same manner any quality that makes for excellence.

That must be true.

Then it applies to justice: we shall conclude that a man is just in the same way that a state was just. And we have surely not forgotten that justice in the state meant that each of the three orders in it was doing its own proper work. So we may henceforth bear e in mind that each one of us likewise will be a just person, fulfilling his proper function, only if the several parts of our nature fulfil theirs.

Certainly.

And it will be the business of reason to rule with wisdom and forethought on behalf of the entire soul; while the spirited element ought to act as its subordinate and ally. The two will be brought into accord, as we said earlier, by that combination of mental 442 and bodily training which will tune up one string of the instrument and relax the other, nourishing the reasoning part on the study of noble literature and allaying the other's wildness by harmony and rhythm. When both have been thus nurtured and trained to know their own true functions, they must be set in command over the appetites, which form the greater part of each man's soul and are by nature insatiably covetous. They must keep watch lest this part, by battening on the pleasures that are called bodily, b should grow so great and powerful that it will no longer keep to its own work, but will try to enslave the others and usurp a dominion to which it has no right, thus turning the whole of life upside down. At the same time, those two together will be the best of guardians for the entire soul and for the body against all enemies from without: the one will take counsel, while the other will do battle, following its ruler's commands and by its own bravery giving effect to the ruler's designs.

Yes, that is all true.

And so we call an individual brave in virtue of this spirited part of his nature,   c
when, in spite of pain or pleasure, it holds fast to the injunctions of reason about what
he ought or ought not to be afraid of.

True.

And wise in virtue of that small part which rules and issues these injunctions, possessing as it does the knowledge of what is good for each of the three elements and for
all of them in common.

Certainly.

And, again, temperate by reason of the unanimity and concord of all three, when   d
there is no internal conflict between the ruling element and its two subjects, but all are
agreed that reason should be ruler.

Yes, that is an exact account of temperance, whether in the state or in the
individual.

Finally, a man will be just by observing the principle we have so often stated.

Necessarily.

Now is there any indistinctness in our vision of justice, that might make it seem
somehow different from what we found it to be in the state?

I don't think so.

Because, if we have any lingering doubt, we might make sure by comparing it
with some commonplace notions. Suppose, for instance, that a sum of money were en-   e
trusted to our state or to an individual of corresponding character and training, would   443
anyone imagine that such a person would be specially likely to embezzle it?

No.

And would he not be incapable of sacrilege and theft, or of treachery to friend or
country; never false to an oath or any other compact; the last to be guilty of adultery or
of neglecting parents or the due service of the gods?

Yes.

And the reason for all this is that each part of his nature is exercising its proper   b
function, of ruling or of being ruled.

Yes, exactly.

Are you satisfied, then, that justice is the power which produces states or individuals of whom that is true, or must we look further?

There is no need; I am quite satisfied.

And so our dream has come true—I mean the inkling we had that, by some happy   c
chance, we had lighted upon a rudimentary form of justice from the very moment when
we set about founding our commonwealth. Our principle that the born shoemaker or
carpenter had better stick to his trade turns out to have been an adumbration of justice;
and that is why it has helped us. But in reality justice, though evidently analogous to this   d
principle, is not a matter of external behaviour, but of the inward self and of attending
to all that is, in the fullest sense, a man's proper concern. The just man does not allow
the several elements in his soul to usurp one another's functions; he is indeed one who
sets his house in order, by self-mastery and discipline coming to be at peace with himself, and bringing into tune those three parts, like the terms in the proportion of a musical scale, the highest and lowest notes and the mean between them, with all the inter-   e
mediate intervals. Only when he has linked these parts together in well-tempered harmony and has made himself one man instead of many, will he be ready to go about
whatever he may have to do, whether it be making money and satisfying bodily wants,
or business transactions, or the affairs of state. In all these fields when he speaks of just
and honourable conduct, he will mean the behaviour that helps to produce and to preserve this habit of mind; and by wisdom he will mean the knowledge which presides

444 over such conduct. Any action which tends to break down this habit will be for him unjust; and the notions governing it he will call ignorance and folly.

That is perfectly true, Socrates.

Good, said I. I believe we should not be thought altogether mistaken, if we
claimed to have discovered the just man and the just state, and wherein their justice consists.

Indeed we should not.

Shall we make that claim, then?

Yes, we will.

So be it, said I. Next, I suppose, we have to consider injustice.

Evidently.

b This must surely be a sort of civil strife among the three elements, whereby they
usurp and encroach upon one another's functions and some one part of the soul rises up
in rebellion against the whole, claiming a supremacy to which it has no right because its
nature fits it only to be the servant of the ruling principle. Such turmoil and aberration
we shall, I think, identify with injustice, intemperance, cowardice, ignorance, and in a
word with all wickedness.

Exactly.

c And now that we know the nature of justice and injustice, we can be equally clear
about what is meant by acting justly and again by unjust action and wrongdoing.

How do you mean?

Plainly, they are exactly analogous to those wholesome and unwholesome activities which respectively produce a healthy or unhealthy condition in the body; in the

d same way just and unjust conduct produce a just or unjust character. Justice is produced
in the soul, like health in the body, by establishing the elements concerned in their natural relations of control and subordination, whereas injustice is like disease and means
that this natural order is inverted.

Quite so.

e It appears, then, that virtue is as it were the health and comeliness and well-being
of the soul, as wickedness is disease, deformity, and weakness.

True.

And also that virtue and wickedness are brought about by one's way of life, honourable or disgraceful.

That follows.

445 So now it only remains to consider which is the more profitable course: to do right
and live honourably and be just, whether or not anyone knows what manner of man you
are, or to do wrong and be unjust, provided that you can escape the chastisement which
might make you a better man.

But really, Socrates, it seems to me ridiculous to ask that question now that the
nature of justice and injustice has been brought to light. People think that all the luxury

b and wealth and power in the world cannot make life worth living when the bodily constitution is going to rack and ruin; and are we to believe that, when the very principle
whereby we live is deranged and corrupted, life will be worth living so long as a man
can do as he will, and wills to do anything rather than to free himself from vice and
wrong doing and to win justice and virtue?

Yes, I replied, it is a ridiculous question.

Nevertheless, I continued, we are now within sight of the clearest possible proof
of our conclusions, and we ought not to slacken our efforts.

No, anything rather than that.

If you will take your stand with me, then, on this point of vantage to which we   c
have climbed, you shall see all the forms that evil takes, or at least all that it seems
worthwhile to look at.

Lead the way and tell me what you see.

What I see is that, whereas there is only one form of excellence, imperfection exists in innumerable shapes, of which there are four that specially deserve notice.

What do you mean?

It looks as if there were as many types of character as there are distinct varieties
of political constitution.

How many?   d

Five of each.

Will you define them?

Yes, I said. One form of constitution will be the form we have been describing,
though it may be called by two names: monarchy, when there is one man who stands
out above the rest of the Rulers; aristocracy, when there are more than one.

True.

That, then, I regard as a single form; for, so long as they observe our principles of
upbringing and education, whether the Rulers be one or more, they will not subvert the   e
important institutions in our commonwealth.

Naturally not.

BOOK V

Such, then, is the type of state or constitution that I call good and right, and the corre-   449
sponding type of man. By this standard, the other forms in which a state or an individual character may be organized are depraved and wrong. There are four of these vicious
forms.

What are they?

Here I was going on to describe these forms in the order in which, as I thought,   b
they develop one from another, when Polemarchus, who was sitting a little way from
Adeimantus, reached out his hand and took hold of his garment by the shoulder. Lean-
ing forward and drawing Adeimantus towards him, he whispered something in his ear,
of which I only caught the words: What shall we do? Shall we leave it alone?

Certainly not, said Adeimantus, raising his voice.

What is this, I asked, that you are not going to leave alone?

You, he replied.

Why, in particular? I inquired.   c

Because we think you are shirking the discussion of a very important part of the
subject and trying to cheat us out of an explanation. Everyone, you said, must of course
see that the maxim "friends have all things in common" applies to women and children.
You thought we should pass over such a casual remark!

But wasn't that right, Adeimantus? said I.

Yes, he said, but "right" in this case, as in others, needs to be defined. There may
be many ways of having things in common, and you must tell us which you mean. We   d
have been waiting a long time for you to say something about the conditions in which
children are to be born and brought up and your whole plan of having wives and children held in common. This seems to us a matter in which right or wrong management

will make all the difference to society; and now, instead of going into it thoroughly, you
450   are passing on to some other form of constitution. So we came to the resolution which
you overheard, not to let you off discussing it as fully as all the other institutions.

I will vote for your resolution too, said Glaucon.

In fact, Socrates, Thrasymachus added, you may take it as carried unanimously.

You don't know what you are doing, I said, in holding me up like this. You want
to start, all over again, on an enormous subject, just as I was rejoicing at the idea that we
had done with this form of constitution. I was only too glad that my casual remark
b   should be allowed to pass. And now, when you demand an explanation, you little know
what a swarm of questions you are stirring up. I let it alone, because I foresaw no end of
trouble.

Well, said Thrasymachus, what do you think we came here for—to play pitch-
and-toss or to listen to a discussion?

A discussion, no doubt, I replied; but within limits.

No man of sense, said Glaucon, would think the whole of life too long to spend on
questions of this importance. But never mind about us; don't be faint-hearted yourself.
Tell us what you think about this question: how our Guardians are to have wives and
c   children in common, and how they will bring up the young in the interval between their
birth and education, which is thought to be the most difficult time of all. Do try to explain how all this is to be arranged.

I wish it were as easy as you seem to think, I replied. These arrangements are even
more open to doubt than any we have so far discussed. It may be questioned whether the
d   plan is feasible, and even if entirely feasible, whether it would be for the best. So I have
some hesitation in touching on what may seem to be an idle dream.

You need not hesitate, he replied. This is not an unsympathetic audience; we are
neither incredulous nor hostile.

Thank you, I said; I suppose that remark is meant to be encouraging.

Certainly it is.

Well, I said, it has just the opposite effect. You would do well to encourage me, if
e   I had any faith in my own understanding of these matters. If one knows the truth, there
is no risk to be feared in speaking about the things one has most at heart among intelligent friends; but if one is still in the position of a doubting inquirer, as I am now, talk-
451   ing becomes a slippery venture. Not that I am afraid of being laughed at—that would be
childish—but I am afraid I may miss my footing just where a false step is most to be
dreaded and drag my friends down with me in my fall. I devoutly hope, Glaucon, that
no nemesis will overtake me for what I am going to say; for I really believe that to kill
a man unintentionally is a lighter offence than to mislead him concerning the goodness
b   and justice of social institutions. Better to run that risk among enemies than among
friends; so your encouragement is out of place.

Glaucon laughed at this. No, Socrates, he said, if your theory has any untoward
effect on us, our blood shall not be on your head; we absolve you of any intention to
mislead us. So have no fear.

Well, said I, when a homicide is absolved of all intention, the law holds him clear
of guilt; and the same principle may apply to my case.

Yes, so far as that goes, you may speak freely.

We must go back, then, to a subject which ought, perhaps, to have been treated
c   earlier in its proper place; though, after all, it may be suitable that the women should
have their turn on the stage when the men have quite finished their performance, especially since you are so insistent. In my judgement, then, the question under what condi-

tions people born and educated as we have described should possess wives and children, and how they should treat them, can be rightly settled only by keeping to the course on which we started them at the outset. We undertook to put these men in the position of watch-dogs guarding a flock. Suppose we follow up the analogy and imagine them bred and reared in the same sort of way. We can then see if that plan will suit our   d
purpose.

How will that be?

In this way. Which do we think right for watch-dogs: should the females guard the flock and hunt with the males and take a share in all they do, or should they be kept within doors as fit for no more than bearing and feeding their puppies, while all the hard work of looking after the flock is left to the males?

They are expected to take their full share, except that we treat them as not quite so strong.   e

Can you employ any creature for the same work as another, if you do not give them both the same upbringing and education?

No.

Then, if we are to set women to the same tasks as men, we must teach them the same things. They must have the same two branches of training for mind and body and   452
also be taught the art of war, and they must receive the same treatment.

That seems to follow.

Possibly, if these proposals were carried out, they might be ridiculed as involving a good many breaches of custom.

They might indeed.

The most ridiculous—don't you think?—being the notion of women exercising naked along with the men in the wrestling-schools; some of them elderly women too,   b
like the old men who still have a passion for exercise when they are wrinkled and not very agreeable to look at.

Yes, that would be thought laughable, according to our present notions.

Now we have started on this subject, we must not be frightened of the many witticisms that might be aimed at such a revolution, not only in the matter of bodily exercise but in the training of women's minds, and not least when it comes to their bearing arms and riding on horseback. Having begun upon these rules, we must not draw back from the harsher provisions. The wits may be asked to stop being witty and try to be serious; and we may remind them that it is not so long since the Greeks, like most foreign nations of the present day, thought it ridiculous and shameful for men to be seen naked. When gymnastic exercises were first introduced in Crete and later at Sparta, the humorists had their chance to make fun of them; but when experience had shown that   d
nakedness is better uncovered than muffled up, the laughter died down and a practice which the reason approved ceased to look ridiculous to the eye. This shows how idle it is to think anything ludicrous but what is base. One who tries to raise a laugh at any spectacle save that of baseness and folly will also, in his serious moments, set before   e
himself some other standard than goodness of what deserves to be held in honour.

Most assuredly.

The first thing to be settled, then, is whether these proposals are feasible; and it   453
must be open to anyone, whether a humorist or serious-minded, to raise the question whether, in the case of mankind, the feminine nature is capable of taking part with the other sex in all occupations, or in none at all, or in some only; and in particular under which of these heads this business of military service falls. Well begun is half done, and would not this be the best way to begin?

Yes.

Shall we take the other side in this debate and argue against ourselves? We do not want the adversary's position to be taken by storm for lack of defenders.

b   I have no objection.

Let us state his case for him. "Socrates and Glaucon," he will say, "there is no need for others to dispute your position; you yourselves, at the very outset of founding your commonwealth, agreed that everyone should do the one work for which nature fits him." Yes, of course; I suppose we did. "And isn't there a very great difference in nature between man and woman?" Yes, surely. "Does not that natural difference imply a corresponding difference in the work to be given to each?" Yes. "But if so, surely you must be mistaken now and contradicting yourselves when you say that men and women, having such widely divergent natures, should do the same things? What is your answer to that, my ingenious friend?

It is not easy to find one at the moment. I can only appeal to you to state the case on our own side, whatever it may be.

d   This, Glaucon, is one of many alarming objections which I foresaw some time ago. That is why I shrank from touching upon these laws concerning the possession of wives and the rearing of children.

It looks like anything but an easy problem.

True, I said; but whether a man tumbles into a swimming-pool or into mid-ocean, he has to swim all the same. So must we, and try if we can reach the shore, hoping for some Arion's dolphin or other miraculous deliverance to bring us safe to land.

e   I suppose so.

Come then, let us see if we can find the way out. We did agree that different natures should have different occupations, and that the natures of man and woman are different; and yet we are now saying that these different natures are to have the same occupations. Is that the charge against us?

Exactly.

454   It is extraordinary, Glaucon, what an effect the practice of debating has upon people.

Why do you say that?

Because they often seem to fall unconsciously into mere disputes which they mistake for reasonable argument, through being unable to draw the distinctions proper to their subject; and so, instead of a philosophical exchange of ideas, they go off in chase of contradictions which are purely verbal.

I know that happens to many people; but does it apply to us at this moment?

b   Absolutely. At least I am afraid we are slipping unconsciously into a dispute about words. We have been strenuously insisting on the letter of our principle that different natures should not have the same occupations, as if we were scoring a point in a debate; but we have altogether neglected to consider what sort of sameness or difference we meant and in what respect these natures and occupations were to be defined as different or the same. Consequently, we might very well be asking one another whether there is not an opposition in nature between bald and long-haired men, and, when that was admitted, forbid one set to be shoemakers, if the other were following that trade.

That would be absurd.

Yes, but only because we never meant any and every sort of sameness or difference in nature, but the sort that was relevant to the occupations in question. We meant, for instance, that a man and a woman have the same nature if both have a talent for medicine; whereas two men have different natures if one is a born physician, the other a born carpenter.

Yes, of course.

If, then, we find that either the male sex or the female is specially qualified for any particular form of occupation, then that occupation, we shall say, ought to be assigned to one sex or the other. But if the only difference appears to be that the male begets and the female brings forth, we shall conclude that no difference between man and woman   e
has yet been produced that is relevant to our purpose. We shall continue to think it proper for our Guardians and their wives to share in the same pursuits.

And quite rightly.

The next thing will be to ask our opponent to name any profession or occupation in civic life for the purposes of which woman's nature is different from man's.   455

That is a fair question.

He might reply, as you did just now, that it is not easy to find a satisfactory answer on the spur of the moment, but that there would be no difficulty after a little reflection.

Perhaps.

Suppose, then, we invite him to follow us and see if we can convince him that there is no occupation concerned with the management of social affairs that is peculiar   b
to women. We will confront him with a question: When you speak of a man having a natural talent for something, do you mean that he finds it easy to learn, and after a little instruction can find out much more for himself; whereas a man who is not so gifted learns with difficulty and no amount of instruction and practice will make him even re-member what he has been taught? Is the talented man one whose bodily powers are readily at the service of his mind, instead of being a hindrance? Are not these the marks   c
by which you distinguish the presence of a natural gift for any pursuit?

Yes, precisely.

Now do you know of any human occupation in which the male sex is not superior to the female in all these respects? Need I waste time over exceptions like weaving and watching over saucepans and batches of cakes, though women are supposed to be good at such things and get laughed at when a man does them better?   d

It is true, he replied, in almost everything one sex is easily beaten by the other. No doubt many women are better at many things than many men; but taking the sexes as a whole, it is as you say.

To conclude, then, there is no occupation concerned with the management of so-cial affairs which belongs either to woman or to man, as such. Natural gifts are to be found here and there in both creatures alike; and every occupation is open to both, so far as their natures are concerned, though woman is for all purposes the weaker.   e

Certainly.

Is that a reason for making over all occupations to men only?

Of course not.

No, because one woman may have a natural gift for medicine or for music, an-other may not.

Surely.

Is it not also true that a woman may, or may not, be warlike or athletic?   456

I think so.

And again, one may love knowledge, another hate it; one may be high-spirited, another spiritless?

True again.

It follows that one woman will be fitted by nature to be a Guardian, another will not; because these were the qualities for which we selected our men Guardians. So for the purpose of keeping watch over the commonwealth, woman has the same nature as man, save in so far as she is weaker.

So it appears.

b   It follows that women of this type must be selected to share the life and duties of Guardians with men of the same type, since they are competent and of a like nature, and the same natures must be allowed the same pursuits.

Yes.

We come round, then, to our former position, that there is nothing contrary to nature in giving our Guardians' wives the same training for mind and body. The prac-
c   tice we proposed to establish was not impossible or visionary, since it was in accordance with nature. Rather, the contrary practice which now prevails turns out to be unnatural.

So it appears.

Well, we set out to inquire whether the plan we proposed was feasible and also the best. That it is feasible is now agreed; we must next settle whether it is the best.

Obviously.

d   Now, for the purpose of producing a woman fit to be a Guardian, we shall not have one education for men and another for women, precisely because the nature to be taken in hand is the same.

True.

What is your opinion on the question of one man being better than another? Do you think there is no such difference?

Certainly I do not.

And in this commonwealth of ours which will prove the better men—the Guardians who have received the education we described, or the shoemakers who have been trained to make shoes?

It is absurd to ask such a question.

e   Very well. So these Guardians will be the best of all the citizens?

By far.

And these women the best of all the women?

Yes.

Can anything be better for a commonwealth than to produce in it men and women of the best possible type?

No.

457   And that result will be brought about by such a system of mental and bodily training as we have described?

Surely.

We may conclude that the institution we proposed was not only practicable, but also the best for the commonwealth.

Yes.

The wives of our Guardians, then, must strip for exercise, since they will be clothed with virtue, and they must take their share in war and in the other social duties of guardianship. They are to have no other occupation; and in these duties the lighter part must fall to the women, because of the weakness of their sex. The man who laughs
b   at naked women, exercising their bodies for the best of reasons, is like one that "gathers fruit unripe," for he does not know what it is that he is laughing at or what he is doing. There will never be a finer saying than the one which declares that whatever does good should be held in honour, and the only shame is in doing harm.

That is perfectly true.

So far, then, in regulating the position of women, we may claim to have come
c   safely through with one hazardous proposal, that male and female Guardians shall have all occupations in common. The consistency of the argument is an assurance that the

plan is a good one and also feasible. We are like swimmers who have breasted the first wave without being swallowed up.

Not such a small wave either.

You will not call it large when you see the next.

Let me have a look at the next one, then.

Here it is: a law which follows from that principle and all that has gone before, namely that, of these Guardians, no one man and one woman are to set up house together privately: wives are to be held in common by all; so too are the children, and no parent is to know his own child, nor any child his parent.   d

It will be much harder to convince people that that is either a feasible plan or a good one.

As to its being a good plan, I imagine no one would deny the immense advantage of wives and children being held in common, provided it can be done. I should expect dispute to arise chiefly over the question of whether it is possible.

There may well be a good deal of dispute over both points.   e

You mean, I must meet attacks on two fronts. I was hoping to escape one by running away: if you agreed it was a good plan, then I should only have had to inquire whether it was feasible.

No, we have seen through that manoeuvre. You will have to defend both positions.

Well, I must pay the penalty for my cowardice. But grant me one favour. Let me indulge my fancy, like one who entertains himself with idle day-dreams on a solitary   458
walk. Before he has any notion how his desires can be realized, he will set aside that question, to save himself the trouble of reckoning what may or may not be possible. He will assume that his wish has come true, and amuse himself with settling all the details of what he means to do then. So a lazy mind encourages itself to be lazier than ever; and I am giving way to the same weakness myself. I want to put off till later that question,   b
how the thing can be done. For the moment, with your leave, I shall assume it to be possible, and ask how the Rulers will work out the details in practice; and I shall argue that the plan, once carried into effect, would be the best thing in the world for our commonwealth and for its Guardians. That is what I shall now try to make out with your help, if you will allow me to postpone the other question.

Very good; I have no objection.

Well, if our Rulers are worthy of the name, and their Auxiliaries likewise, these latter will be ready to do what they are told, and the Rulers, in giving their commands,   c
will themselves obey our laws and will be faithful to their spirit in any details we leave to their discretion.

No doubt.

It is for you, then, as their lawgiver, who has already selected the men, to select for association with them women who are so far as possible of the same natural capacity.   d
Now since none of them will have any private home of his own, but they will share the same dwelling and eat at common tables, the two sexes will be together; and meeting without restriction for exercise and all through their upbringing, they will surely be drawn towards union with one another by a necessity of their nature—necessity is not too strong a word, I think?

Not too strong for the constraint of love, which for the mass of mankind is more persuasive and compelling than even the necessity of mathematical proof.

Exactly. But in the next place, Glaucon, anything like unregulated unions would be a profanation in a state whose citizens lead the good life. The Rulers will not allow   e
such a thing.

No, it would not be right.

Clearly, then, we must have marriages, as sacred as we can make them; and this sanctity will attach to those which yield the best results.

Certainly.

459   How are we to get the best results? You must tell me, Glaucon, because I see you keep sporting dogs and a great many game birds at your house; and there is something about their mating and breeding that you must have noticed.

What is that?

In the first place, though they may all be of good stock, are there not some that turn out to be better than the rest?

There are.

And do you breed from all indiscriminately? Are you not careful to breed from the best so far as you can?

Yes.

b   And from those in their prime, rather than the very young or the very old?

Yes.

Otherwise, the stock of your birds or dogs would deteriorate very much, wouldn't it?

It would.

And the same is true of horses or of any animal?

It would be very strange if it were not.

Dear me, said I; we shall need consummate skill in our Rulers, if it is also true of the human race.

c   Well, it is true. But why must they be so skilful?

Because they will have to administer a large dose of that medicine we spoke of earlier. An ordinary doctor is thought good enough for a patient who will submit to be dieted and can do without medicine; but he must be much more of a man if drugs are required.

True, but how does that apply?

It applies to our Rulers: it seems they will have to give their subjects a consider-
d   able dose of imposition and deception for their good. We said, if you remember, that such expedients would be useful as a sort of medicine.

Yes, a very sound principle.

Well, it looks as if this sound principle will play no small part in this matter of marriage and child-bearing.

How so?

It follows from what we have just said that, if we are to keep our flock at the high-
e   est pitch of excellence, there should be as many unions of the best of both sexes, and as few of the inferior, as possible, and that only the offspring of the better unions should be kept. And again, no one but the Rulers must know how all this is being effected; other-wise our herd of Guardians may become rebellious.

Quite true.

We must, then, institute certain festivals at which we shall bring together the brides and the bridegrooms. There will be sacrifices, and our poets will write songs be-
460   fitting the occasion. The number of marriages we shall leave to the Rulers' discretion. They will aim at keeping the number of the citizens as constant as possible, having re-gard to losses caused by war, epidemics, and so on; and they must do their best to see that our state does not become either great or small.

Very good.

I think they will have to invent some ingenious system of drawing lots, so that, at each pairing off, the inferior candidate may blame his luck rather than the Rulers.

Yes, certainly.

Moreover, young men who acquit themselves well in war and other duties, should   b
be given, among other rewards and privileges, more liberal opportunities to sleep with
a wife, for the further purpose that, with good excuse, as many as possible of the children may be begotten of such fathers.

Yes.

As soon as children are born, they will be taken in charge by officers appointed   c
for the purpose, who may be men or women or both, since offices are to be shared by
both sexes. The children of the better parents they will carry to the creche to be reared
in the care of nurses living apart in a certain quarter of the city. Those of the inferior
parents and any children of the rest that are born defective will be hidden away, in some
appropriate manner that must be kept secret.

They must be, if the breed of our Guardians is to be kept pure.

These officers will also superintend the nursing of the children. They will bring
the mothers to the creche when their breasts are full, while taking every precaution
that no mother shall know her own child; and if the mothers have not enough milk,   d
they will provide wet-nurses. They will limit the time during which the mothers will
suckle their children, and hand over all the hard work and sitting up at night to nurses
and attendants.

That will make child-bearing an easy business for the Guardians' wives.

So it should be. To go on with our scheme: we said that children should be born
from parents in the prime of life. Do you agree that this lasts about twenty years for a   e
woman, and thirty for a man? A woman should bear children for the commonwealth
from her twentieth to her fortieth year; a man should begin to beget them when he has
passed "the racer's prime in swiftness," and continue till he is fifty-five.

Those are certainly the years in which both the bodily and the mental powers of   461
man and woman are at their best.

If a man either above or below this age meddles with the begetting of children for
the commonwealth, we shall hold it an offence against divine and human law. He will
be begetting for his country a child conceived in darkness and dire incontinence, whose
birth, if it escape detection, will not have been sanctioned by the sacrifices and prayers
offered at each marriage festival, when priests and priestesses join with the whole community in praying that the children to be born may be even better and more useful citizens than their parents.   b

You are right.

The same law will apply to any man within the prescribed limits who touches a
woman also of marriageable age when the Ruler has not paired them. We shall say that
he is foisting on the commonwealth a bastard, unsanctioned by law or by religion.

Perfectly right.

As soon, however, as the men and the women have passed the age prescribed for
producing children, we shall leave them free to form a connexion with whom they will,
except that a man shall not take his daughter or daughter's daughter or mother or   c
mother's mother, nor a woman her son or father or her son's son or father's father; and
all this only after we have exhorted them to see that no child, if any be conceived, shall
be brought to light, or, if they cannot prevent its birth, to dispose of it on the understanding that no such child can be reared.

That too is reasonable. But how are they to distinguish fathers and daughters and   d
those other relations you mentioned?

They will not, said I. But, reckoning from the day when he becomes a bride-
groom, a man will call all children born in the tenth or the seventh month sons and

daughters, and they will call him father. Their children again he will call grandchildren, and they will call his group grandfathers and grandmothers; and all who are born within the period during which their mothers and fathers were having children will be called

e   brothers and sisters. This will provide for those restrictions on unions that we mentioned; but the law will allow brothers and sisters to live together, if the lot so falls out and the Delphic oracle also approves.

Very good.

This, then, Glaucon, is the manner in which the Guardians of your commonwealth are to hold their wives and children in common. Must we not next find arguments to establish that it is consistent with our other institutions and also by far the best plan?

462   Yes, surely.

We had better begin by asking what is the greatest good at which the lawgiver should aim in laying down the constitution of a state, and what is the worst evil. We can then consider whether our proposals are in keeping with that good and irreconcilable with the evil.

By all means.

Does not the worst evil for a state arise from anything that tends to rend it asun-

b   der and destroy its unity, while nothing does it more good than whatever tends to bind it together and make it one?

That is true.

And are not citizens bound together by sharing in the same pleasures and pains, all feeling glad or grieved on the same occasions of gain or loss; whereas the bond is broken when such feelings are no longer universal, but any event of public or personal concern fills some with joy and others with distress?

c   Certainly.

And this disunion comes about when the words "mine" and "not mine," "another's" and "not another's" are not applied to the same things throughout the community. The best ordered state will be the one in which the largest number of persons use these terms in the same sense, and which accordingly most nearly resembles a single person. When one of us hurts his finger, the whole extent of those bodily connexions

d   which are gathered up in the soul and unified by its ruling element is made aware and it all shares as a whole in the pain of the suffering part; hence we say that the man has a pain in his finger. The same thing is true of the pain or pleasure felt when any other part of the person suffers or is relieved.

Yes; I agree that the best organized community comes nearest to that condition.

e   And so it will recognize as a part of itself the individual citizen to whom good or evil happens, and will share as a whole in his joy or sorrow.

It must, if the constitution is sound.

It is time now to go back to our own commonwealth and see whether these conclusions apply to it more than to any other type of state. In all alike there are rulers and common people, all of whom will call one another fellow citizens.

Yes.

463   But in other states the people have another name as well for their rulers, haven't they?

Yes; in most they call them masters; in democracies, simply the government.

And in ours?

b   The people will look upon their rulers as preservers and protectors.

And how will our rulers regard the people?

As those who maintain them and pay them wages.

And elsewhere?

As slaves.

And what do rulers elsewhere call one another?

Colleagues.

And ours?

Fellow Guardians.

And in other states may not a ruler regard one colleague as a friend in whom he has an interest, and another as a stranger with whom he has nothing in common?

Yes, that often happens.

But that could not be so with your Guardians? None of them could ever treat a fellow Guardian as a stranger.

Certainly not. He must regard everyone whom he meets as brother or sister, father or mother, son or daughter, grandchild or grandparent.

Very good; but here is a further point. Will you not require them, not merely to use these family terms, but to behave as a real family? Must they not show towards all whom they call "father" the customary reverence, care, and obedience due to a parent, if they look for any favour from gods or men, since to act otherwise is contrary to divine and human law? Should not all the citizens constantly reiterate in the hearing of the children from their earliest years such traditional maxims of conduct towards those whom they are taught to call father and their other kindred?

They should. It would be absurd that terms of kinship should be on their lips without any action to correspond.

In our community, then, above all others, when things go well or ill with any individual everyone will use that word "mine" in the same sense and say that all is going well or ill with him and his.

Quite true.

And, as we said, this way of speaking and thinking goes with fellow-feeling; so that our citizens, sharing as they do in a common interest which each will call his own, will have all their feelings of pleasure or pain in common.

Assuredly.

A result that will be due to our institutions, and in particular to our Guardians' holding their wives and children in common.

Very much so.

But you will remember how, when we compared a well-ordered community to the body which shares in the pleasures and pains of any member, we saw in this unity the greatest good that a state can enjoy. So the conclusion is that our commonwealth owes to this sharing of wives and children by its protectors its enjoyment of the greatest of all goods.

Yes, that follows.

Moreover, this agrees with our principle that they were not to have houses or lands or any property of their own, but to receive sustenance from the other citizens, as wages for their guardianship, and to consume it in common. Only so will they keep to their true character; and our present proposals will do still more to make them genuine Guardians. They will not rend the community asunder by each applying that word "mine" to different things and dragging off whatever he can get for himself into a private home, where he will have his separate family, forming a centre of exclusive joys and sorrows. Rather they will all, so far as may be, feel together and aim at the same ends, because they are convinced that all their interests are identical.

Quite so.

Again, if a man's person is his only private possession, lawsuits and prosecutions will all but vanish, and they will be free of those quarrels that arise from ownership of
e property and from having family ties. Nor would they be justified even in bringing actions for assault and outrage; for we shall pronounce it right and honourable for a man to defend himself against an assailant of his own age, and in that way they will be compelled to keep themselves fit.

That would be a sound law.

465 And it would also have the advantage that, if a man's anger can be satisfied in this way, a fit of passion is less likely to grow into a serious quarrel.

True.

But an older man will be given authority over all younger persons and power to correct them; whereas the younger will, naturally, not dare to strike the elder or do him any violence, except by command of a Ruler. He will not show him any sort of
b disrespect. Two guardian spirits, fear and reverence, will be enough to restrain him— reverence forbidding him to lay hands on a parent, and fear of all those others who as sons or brothers or fathers would come to the rescue.

Yes, that will be the result.

So our laws will secure that these men will live in complete peace with one another; and if they never quarrel among themselves, there is no fear of the rest of the community being divided either against them or against itself.

No.

c There are other evils they will escape, so mean and petty that I hardly like to mention them: the poor man's flattery of the rich, and all the embarrassments and vexations of rearing a family and earning just enough to maintain a household; now borrowing and now refusing to repay, and by any and every means scraping together money to be handed over to wife and servants to spend. These sordid troubles are familiar and not worth describing.

d Only too familiar.

Rid of all these cares, they will live a more enviable life than the Olympic victor, who is counted happy on the strength of far fewer blessings than our Guardians will enjoy. Their victory is the nobler, since by their success the whole commonwealth is preserved; and their reward of maintenance at the public cost is more complete, since their
e prize is to have every need of life supplied for themselves and for their children; their country honours them while they live, and when they die they receive a worthy burial.

Yes, they will be nobly rewarded.

Do you remember, then, how someone who shall be nameless reproached us for
466 not making our Guardians happy: they were to possess nothing, though all the wealth of their fellow citizens was within their grasp? We replied, I believe, that we would consider that objection later, if it came in our way: for the moment we were bent on making our Guardians real guardians, and moulding our commonwealth with a view to the greatest happiness, not of one section of it, but of the whole.

Yes, I remember.

Well, it appears now that these protectors of our state will have a life better and more honourable than that of any Olympic victor; and we can hardly rank it on a level
b with the life of a shoemaker or other artisan or of a farmer.

I should think not.

However, it is right to repeat what I said at the time: if ever a Guardian tries to make himself happy in such a way that he will be a guardian no longer; if, not content with the moderation and security of this way of living which we think the best, he becomes possessed with some silly and childish notion of happiness, impelling him to make his power a means to appropriate all the citizens' wealth, then he will learn the wisdom of Hesiod's saying that the half is more than the whole.

My advice would certainly be that he should keep to his own way of living.

You do agree, then, that women are to take their full share with men in education, in the care of children, and in the guardianship of the other citizens; whether they stay at home or go out to war, they will be like watch-dogs which take their part either in guarding the fold or in hunting and share in every task so far as their strength allows. Such conduct will not be unwomanly, but all for the best and in accordance with the natural partnership of the sexes.

Yes, I agree.

It remains to ask whether such a partnership can be established among human beings, as it can among animals, and if so, how.

I was just going to put that question.

So far as fighting is concerned, it is easy to see how they will go out to war.

How?

Men and women will take the field together and moreover bring with them the children who are sturdy enough, to learn this trade, like any other, by watching what they will have to do themselves when they are grown up; and besides looking on, they will fetch and carry for their fathers and mothers and see to all their needs in time of war. You must have noticed how, in the potter's trade for example, the children watch their fathers and wait on them long before they may touch the wheel. Ought our Guardians to be less careful to train theirs by letting them look on and become familiar with their duties?

No, that would be absurd.

Moreover, any creature will fight better in the presence of its young.

That is so. But in case of defeat, which may always happen in war, there will be serious danger of their children's lives being lost with their own, so that the country could never recover.

True; but, in the first place, do you think we must make sure that they never run any risk?

No, far from it.

Well, if they are ever to take their chance, should it not be on some occasion when, if all goes well, they will be the better for it?

No doubt.

And is it of no importance that men who are to be warriors should see something of war in childhood? Is that not worth some danger?

Yes; it is important.

Granted, then, that the children are to go to war as spectators, all will be well if we can contrive that they shall do so in safety. To begin with, their fathers will not be slow to judge, so far as human foresight can, which expeditions are hazardous and which are safe; and they will be careful not to take the children into danger. Also they will put them in charge of officers qualified by age and experience to lead and take care of them.

Yes, that would be the proper way.

All the same, the unexpected often happens; and to guard against such chances we must see that they have, from their earliest years, wings to fly away with if need be.

What do you mean by wings?

Horses, which they must be taught to ride at the earliest possible age; then, when they are taken to see the fighting, their mounts must not be spirited chargers but the swiftest we can find and the easiest to manage. In that way they will get a good view of their future business, and in case of need they will be able to keep up with their older leaders and escape in safety.

That seems an excellent plan.

468   Now, as to the conduct of war and your soldiers' relations to one another and to the enemy: am I right in thinking that anyone guilty of an act of cowardice, such as deserting his post or throwing away his arms, should be reduced to the artisan or farmer class; while if any fall alive into the enemy's hands, we shall make them a present of him, and they may do what they like with their prey?

b   Certainly.

And what shall be done to the hero who has distinguished himself by his valour? First, should he not be crowned on the field by the youths and children each in turn?

Surely.

And they might shake his hand?

Yes.

c   But you would stop there, no doubt. I am sure you would not approve of his exchanging kisses with them all?

I am all for that; indeed I would add to the law the provision that, so long as they are on the campaign, no one whom he wishes to kiss may refuse. That would make any soldier who chanced to be in love with a youth or a girl all the more eager to win the prize of valour.

Very well. We have already said that the brave man is to be selected for marriage more frequently than the rest, so that as many children as possible may have such a man for their father. But besides that, these valiant youths may well be rewarded in the

d   Homeric manner. When Ajax distinguished himself in the war, he was "honoured with slices of the chine's full length," a suitable compliment to a lusty young hero, and one that would at the same time strengthen his muscles.

An excellent idea.

Then here at any rate we will follow Homer. At sacrificial feasts and all such occasions, we shall reward the brave, in proportion to their merit, not only with songs and

e   those privileges we mentioned but "with seats of honour, meat, and cups brimful"; and so at once pay tribute to the bravery of these men and women and improve their physique.

Nothing could be better.

Good. And of those who are slain in the field, we shall say that all who fell with honour are of that Golden Race, who, when they die,

469   Dwell here on earth, pure spirits, beneficent.
Guardians to shield us mortal men from harm.

Shall we not believe those words of Hesiod?

We shall.

Then we shall ask the Oracle with what special rites these men of more than human mould should be buried, and we shall do as it prescribes. And for all time to come

b   we shall reverence their tombs and worship them as demigods. Others, too, who die in the natural course of old age or otherwise shall be honoured in the same way, if they are judged to have led an exceptionally noble life.

That is but fair.

And next, how will our soldiers deal with enemies?

In what respect?

First take slavery. Is it right that Greek states should sell Greeks into slavery? Ought they not rather to do all they can to stop this practice and substitute the custom of sparing their own race, for fear of falling into bondage to foreign nations?

c

That would be better, beyond all comparison.

They must not, then, hold any Greek in slavery themselves, and they should advise the rest of Greece not to do so.

Certainly. Then they would be more likely to keep their hands off one another and turn their energies against foreigners.

Next, is it well to strip the dead, after a victory, of anything but their arms? It only gives cowards an excuse for not facing the living enemy, as if they were usefully employed in poking about over a dead body. Many an army has been lost through this pillaging. There is something mean and greedy in plundering a corpse; and a sort of womanish pettiness in treating the body as an enemy, when the spirit, the real enemy, has flown, leaving behind only the instrument with which he fought. It is to behave no better than a dog who growls at the stone that has hit him and leaves alone the man who threw it.

d

e

True.

So we will have no stripping of the slain and we shall not prevent their comrades from burying them. Nor shall we dedicate in the temples trophies of their weapons, least of all those of Greeks, if we are concerned to show loyalty towards the rest of Hellas. We shall rather be afraid of desecrating a sanctuary by bringing to it such spoils of our own people, unless indeed the Oracle should pronounce otherwise.

470

That is very right.

And what of ravaging Greek lands and burning houses? How will your soldiers deal with their enemies in this matter?

I should like to hear your own opinion.

I think they should do neither, but only carry off the year's harvest. Shall I tell you why?

b

Please do.

It seems to me that war and civil strife differ in nature as they do in name, according to the two spheres in which disputes may arise: at home or abroad, among men of the same race or with foreigners. War means fighting with a foreign enemy; when the enemy is of the same kindred, we call it civil strife.

That is a reasonable distinction.

Is it not also reasonable to assert that Greeks are a single people, all of the same kindred and alien to the outer world of foreigners?

Yes.

c

Then we shall speak of war when Greeks fight with foreigners, whom we may call their natural enemies. But Greeks are by nature friends of Greeks, and when they fight, it means that Hellas is afflicted by dissension which ought to be called civil strife.

d

I agree with that view.

Observe, then, that in what is commonly known as civil strife, that is to say, when one of our Greek states is divided against itself, it is thought an abominable outrage for either party to ravage the lands or burn the houses of the other. No lover of his country would dare to mangle the land which gave him birth and nursed him. It is thought fair that the victors should carry off the others' crops, but do no more. They should remember that the war will not last forever; some day they must make friends again.

e

That is a much more civilized state of mind.

Well then, is not this commonwealth you are founding a Greek state, and its citizens good and civilized people?

Very much so.

And lovers of Greece, who will think of all Hellas as their home, where they share in one common religion with the rest?

Most certainly.

471   Accordingly, the Greeks being their own people, a quarrel with them will not be called a war. It will only be civil strife, which they will carry on as men who will some day be reconciled. So they will not behave like a foreign enemy seeking to enslave or destroy, but will try to bring their adversaries to reason by well-meant correction. As b Greeks they will not devastate the soil of Greece or burn the homesteads; nor will they allow that all the inhabitants of any state, men, women, and children, are their enemies, but only the few who are responsible for the quarrel. The greater number are friends, whose land and houses, on all these accounts, they will not consent to lay waste and destroy. They will pursue the quarrel only until the guilty are compelled by the innocent sufferers to give satisfaction.

For my part, I agree that our citizens should treat their adversaries in that way, and deal with foreigners as Greeks now deal with one another.

We will make this a law, then, for our Guardians: they are not to ravage lands or c burn houses.

Yes, we will; it is as satisfactory as all our other laws.

But really, Socrates, Glaucon continued, if you are allowed to go on like this, I am afraid you will forget all about the question you thrust aside some time ago: whether a society so constituted can ever come into existence, and if so, how. No doubt, if it did exist, all manner of good things would come about. I can even add some that you have passed over. Men who acknowledged one another as fathers, sons, or brothers and al- d ways used those names among themselves would never desert one another; so they would fight with unequaled bravery. And if their womenfolk went out with them to war, either in the ranks or drawn up in the rear to intimidate the enemy and act as a reserve in case of need, I am sure all this would make them invincible. At home, too, I can see e many advantages you have not mentioned. But, since I admit that our commonwealth would have all these merits and any number more, if once it came into existence, you need not describe it in further detail. All we have now to do is to convince ourselves that it can be brought into being and how.

472   This is a very sudden onslaught, said I; you have no mercy on my shilly-shallying. Perhaps you do not realize that, after I have barely escaped the first two waves, the third, which you are now bringing down upon me, is the most formidable of all. When you have seen what it is like and heard my reply, you will be ready to excuse the very natural fears which made me shrink from putting forward such a paradox for discussion.

b   The more you talk like that, he said, the less we shall be willing to let you off from telling us how this constitution can come into existence; so you had better waste no more time.

Well, said I, let me begin by reminding you that what brought us to this point was our inquiry into the nature of justice and injustice.

True; but what of that?

Merely this: suppose we do find out what justice is, are we going to demand that a man who is just shall have a character which exactly corresponds in every respect to the ideal of justice? Or shall we be satisfied if he comes as near to the ideal as possible c and has in him a larger measure of that quality than the rest of the world?

That will satisfy me.

If so, when we set out to discover the essential nature of justice and injustice and what a perfectly just and a perfectly unjust man would be like, supposing them to exist, our purpose was to use them as ideal patterns: we were to observe the degree of happiness or unhappiness that each exhibited, and to draw the necessary inference that our own destiny would be like that of the one we most resembled. We did not set out to   d
show that these ideals could exist in fact.

That is true.

Then suppose a painter had drawn an ideally beautiful figure complete to the last touch, would you think any the worse of him, if he could not show that a person as beautiful as that could exist?

No, I should not.   e

Well, we have been constructing in discourse the pattern of an ideal state. Is our theory any the worse, if we cannot prove it possible that a state so organized should be actually founded?

Surely not.

That, then, is the truth of the matter. But if, for your satisfaction, I am to do my best to show under what conditions our ideal would have the best chance of being realized, I must ask you once more to admit that the same principle applies here. Can theory ever be fully realized in practice? Is it not in the nature of things that action should   473
come less close to truth than thought? People may not think so; but do you agree or not?

I do.

Then you must not insist upon my showing that this construction we have traced in thought could be reproduced in fact down to the last detail. You must admit that we shall have found a way to meet your demand for realization, if we can discover how a   b
state might be constituted in the closest accordance with our description. Will not that content you? It would be enough for me.

And for me too.

Then our next attempt, it seems, must be to point out what defect in the working of existing states prevents them from being so organized, and what is the least change that would effect a transformation into this type of government—a single change if possible, or perhaps two; at any rate let us make the changes as few and insignificant as may be.

By all means.   c

Well, there is one change which, as I believe we can show, would bring about this revolution—not a small change, certainly, nor an easy one, but possible.

What is it?

I have now to confront what we called the third and greatest wave. But I must state my paradox, even though the wave should break in laughter over my head and drown me in ignominy. Now mark what I am going to say.

Go on.

Unless either philosophers become kings in their countries or those who are now   d
called kings and rulers come to be sufficiently inspired with a genuine desire for wisdom; unless, that is to say, political power and philosophy meet together, while the many natures who now go their several ways in the one or the other direction are forcibly debarred from doing so, there can be no rest from troubles, my dear Glaucon, for states, nor yet, as I believe, for all mankind; nor can this commonwealth which we   e
have imagined ever till then see the light of day and grow to its full stature. This it was that I have so long hung back from saying; I knew what a paradox it would be, because

it is hard to see that there is no other way of happiness either for the state or for the individual.

Socrates, exclaimed Glaucon, after delivering yourself of such a pronouncement as that, you must expect a whole multitude of by no means contemptible assailants to fling off their coats, snatch up the handiest weapon, and make a rush at you, breathing fire and slaughter. If you cannot find arguments to beat them off and make your escape, you will learn what it means to be the target of scorn and derision.

Well, it was you who got me into this trouble.

Yes, and a good thing too. However, I will not leave you in the lurch. You shall have my friendly encouragement for what it is worth; and perhaps you may find me more complaisant than some would be in answering your questions. With such backing you must try to convince the unbelievers.

I will, now that I have such a powerful ally.

Now, I continued, if we are to elude those assailants you have described, we must, I think, define for them whom we mean by these lovers of wisdom who, we have dared to assert, ought to be our rulers. Once we have a clear view of their character, we shall be able to defend our position by pointing to some who are naturally fitted to combine philosophic study with political leadership, while the rest of the world should accept their guidance and let philosophy alone.

Yes, this is the moment for a definition.

Here, then, is a line of thought which may lead to a satisfactory explanation. Need I remind you that a man will deserve to be called a lover of this or that, only if it is clear that he loves that thing as a whole, not merely in parts?

You must remind me, it seems; for I do not see what you mean.

That answer would have come better from someone less susceptible to love than yourself, Glaucon. You ought not to have forgotten that any boy in the bloom of youth will arouse some sting of passion in a man of your amorous temperament and seem worthy of his attentions. Is not this your way with your favourites? You will praise a snub nose as piquant and a hooked one as giving a regal air, while you call a straight nose perfectly proportioned; the swarthy, you say, have a manly look, the fair are children of the gods; and what do you think is that word "honey-pale," if not the euphemism of some lover who had no fault to find with sallowness on the cheek of youth? In a word, you will carry pretence and extravagance to any length sooner than reject a single one that is in the flower of his prime.

If you insist on taking me as an example of how lovers behave, I will agree for the sake of argument.

Again, do you not see the same behaviour in people with a passion for wine? They are glad of any excuse to drink wine of any sort. And there are the men who covet honour, who, if they cannot lead an army, will command a company, and if they cannot win the respect of important people, are glad to be looked up to by nobodies, because they must have someone to esteem them.

Quite true.

Do you agree, then, that when we speak of a man as having a passion for a certain kind of thing, we mean that he has an appetite for everything of that kind without discrimination?

Yes.

So the philosopher, with his passion for wisdom, will be one who desires all wisdom, not only some part of it. If a student is particular about his studies, especially while he is too young to know which are useful and which are not, we shall say he is no lover of learning or of wisdom; just as, if he were dainty about his food, we should say he was not hungry or fond of eating, but had a poor appetite. Only the man who has a taste for every sort of knowledge and throws himself into acquiring it with an insatiable curiosity will deserve to be called a philosopher. Am I not right?

That description, Glaucon replied, would include a large and ill assorted com-   d pany. It is curiosity, I suppose, and a delight in fresh experience that gives some people a passion for all that is to be seen and heard at theatrical and musical performances. But they are a queer set to reckon among philosophers, considering that they would never go near anything like a philosophical discussion, though they run round at all the Dionysiac festivals in town or country as if they were under contract to listen to every company of performers without fail. Will curiosity entitle all these enthusiasts, not to mention amateurs of the minor arts, to be called philosophers?   e

Certainly not; though they have a certain counterfeit resemblance.

And whom do you mean by the genuine philosophers?

Those whose passion it is to see the truth.

That must be so; but will you explain?

It would not be easy to explain to everyone; but you, I believe, will grant my premise.

Which is—?

That since beauty and ugliness are opposite, they are two things; and conse-   476 quently each of them is one. The same holds of justice and injustice, good and bad, and all the essential Forms: each in itself is one; but they manifest themselves in a great variety of combinations, with actions, with material things, and with one another, and so each seems to be many.

That is true.

On the strength of this premise, then, I can distinguish your amateurs of the arts and men of action from the philosophers we are concerned with, who are alone worthy of the name.   b

What is your distinction?

Your lovers of sights and sounds delight in beautiful tones and colours and shapes and in all the works of art into which these enter; but they have not the power of thought to behold and to take delight in the nature of Beauty itself. That power to approach Beauty and behold it as it is in itself, is rare indeed.

Quite true.   c

Now if a man believes in the existence of beautiful things, but not of Beauty itself, and cannot follow a guide who would lead him to a knowledge of it, is he not living in a dream? Consider: does not dreaming, whether one is awake or asleep, consist in mistaking a semblance for the reality it resembles?

I should certainly call that dreaming.

Contrast with him the man who holds that there is such a thing as Beauty itself   d and can discern that essence as well as the things that partake of its character, without ever confusing the one with the other—is he a dreamer or living in a waking state?

He is very much awake.

So may we say that he knows, while the other has only a belief in appearances; and might we call their states of mind knowledge and belief?

Certainly.

But this person who, we say, has only belief without knowledge may be aggrieved and challenge our statement. Is there any means of soothing his resentment and   e converting him gently, without telling him plainly that he is not in his right mind?

We surely ought to try.

Come then, consider what we are to say to him. Or shall we ask him a question, assuring him that, far from grudging him any knowledge he may have, we shall be only too glad to find that there is something he knows? But, we shall say, tell us this: When a man knows, must there not be something that he knows? Will you answer for him, Glaucon?

My answer will be, that there must.

Something real or unreal?

477   Something real; how could a thing that is unreal ever be known?

Are we satisfied, then, on this point, from however many points of view we might examine it: that the perfectly real is perfectly knowable, and the utterly unreal is entirely unknowable?

Quite satisfied.

Good. Now if there is something so constituted that it both *is* and *is not,* will it not lie between the purely real and the utterly unreal?

It will.

Well then, as knowledge corresponds to the real, and absence of knowledge necessarily to the unreal, so, to correspond to this intermediate thing, we must look for
b   something between ignorance and knowledge, if such a thing there be.

Certainly.

Is there not a thing we call belief?

Surely.

A different power from knowledge, or the same?

Different.

Knowledge and belief, then, must have different objects, answering to their respective powers.

Yes.

And knowledge has for its natural object the real—to know the truth about reality. However, before going further, I think we need a definition. Shall we distinguish under
c   the general name of "faculties" those powers which enable us—or anything else—to do what we can do? Sight and hearing, for instance, are what I call faculties, if that will help you to see the class of things I have in mind.

Yes, I understand.

Then let me tell you what view I take of them. In a faculty I cannot find any of those qualities, such as colour or shape, which, in the case of many other things, enable me to distinguish one thing from another. I can only look to its field of objects and the
d   state of mind it produces, and regard these as sufficient to identify it and to distinguish it from faculties which have different fields and produce different states. Is that how you would go to work?

Yes.

Let us go back, then, to knowledge. Would you class that as a faculty?

Yes; and I should call it the most powerful of all.

e   And is belief also a faculty?

It can be nothing else, since it is what gives us the power of believing.

But a little while ago you agreed that knowledge and belief are not the same thing.

Yes; there could be no sense in identifying the infallible with the fallible.

478   Good. So we are quite clear that knowledge and belief are different things?

They are.

If so, each of them, having a different power, must have a different field of objects.

Necessarily.

The field of knowledge being the real; and its power, the power of knowing the real as it is.

Yes.

Whereas belief, we say, is the power of believing. Is its object the same as that which knowledge knows? Can the same things be possible objects both of knowledge and of belief?

Not if we hold to the principles we agreed upon. If it is of the nature of a different faculty to have a different field, and if both knowledge and belief are faculties and, as   b we assert, different ones, it follows that the same things cannot be possible objects of both.

So if the real is the object of knowledge, the object of belief must be something other than the real.

Yes.

Can it be the unreal? Or is that an impossible object even for belief? Consider: if a man has a belief, there must be something before his mind; he cannot be believing nothing, can he?

No.

He is believing something, then; whereas the unreal could only be called nothing at all.   c

Certainly.

Now we said that ignorance must correspond to the unreal, knowledge to the real. So what he is believing cannot be real nor yet unreal.

True.

Belief, then, cannot be either ignorance or knowledge.

It appears not.

Then does it lie outside and beyond these two? Is it either more clear and certain than knowledge or less clear and certain than ignorance?

No, it is neither.

It rather seems to you to be something more obscure than knowledge, but not so dark as ignorance, and so to lie between the two extremes?   d

Quite so.

Well, we said earlier that if some object could be found such that it both *is* and at the same time *is not,* that object would lie between the perfectly real and the utterly unreal; and that the corresponding faculty would be neither knowledge nor ignorance, but a faculty to be found situated between the two.

Yes.

And now what we have found between the two is the faculty we call belief.

True.

It seems, then, that what remains to be discovered is that object which can be said   e both to be and not to be and cannot properly be called either purely real or purely unreal. If that can be found, we may justly call it the object of belief, and so give the intermediate faculty the intermediate object, while the two extreme objects will fall to the extreme faculties.

Yes.

On these assumptions, then, I shall call for an answer from our friend who denies the existence of Beauty itself or of anything that can be called an essential Form of   479 Beauty remaining unchangeably in the same state forever, though he does recognize the existence of beautiful things as a plurality—that lover of things seen who will not listen to anyone who says that Beauty is one, Justice is one, and so on. I shall say to him, Be so good as to tell us: of all these many beautiful things is there one which will not appear ugly? Or of these many just or righteous actions, is there one that will not appear unjust or unrighteous?

b   No, replied Glaucon, they must inevitably appear to be in some way both beautiful and ugly; and so with all the other terms your question refers to.

And again the many things which are doubles are just as much halves as they are doubles. And the things we call large or heavy have just as much right to be called small or light.

Yes; any such thing will always have a claim to both opposite designations.

Then, whatever any one of these many things may be said to be, can you say that it absolutely *is* that, any more than that it *is not* that?

They remind me of those punning riddles people ask at dinner parties, or the
c   child's puzzle about what the eunuch threw at the bat and what the bat was perched on. These things have the same ambiguous character, and one cannot form any stable conception of them either as being or as not being, or as both being and not being, or as neither.

Can you think of any better way of disposing of them than by placing them between reality and unreality? For I suppose they will not appear more obscure and so less real than unreality, or clearer and so more real than reality.

d   Quite true.

It seems, then, we have discovered that the many conventional notions of the mass of mankind about what is beautiful or honourable or just and so on are adrift in a sort of twilight between pure reality and pure unreality.

We have.

And we agreed earlier that, if any such object were discovered, it should be called the object of belief and not of knowledge. Fluctuating in that half-way region, it would be seized upon by the intermediate faculty.

Yes.

e   So when people have an eye for the multitude of beautiful things or of just actions or whatever it may be, but can neither behold Beauty or Justice itself nor follow a guide who would lead them to it, we shall say that all they have is beliefs, without any real knowledge of the objects of their belief.

That follows.

But what of those who contemplate the realities themselves as they are forever in the same unchanging state? Shall we not say that they have, not mere belief, but knowledge?

That too follows.

480   And, further, that their affection goes out to the objects of knowledge, whereas the others set their affections on the objects of belief; for it was they, you remember, who had a passion for the spectacle of beautiful colours and sounds, but would not hear of Beauty itself being a real thing.

I remember.

So we may fairly call them lovers of belief rather than of wisdom—not philosophical, in fact, but philodoxical. Will they be seriously annoyed by that description?

Not if they will listen to my advice. No one ought to take offence at the truth.

The name of philosopher, then, will be reserved for those whose affections are set, in every case, on the reality.

By all means.

BOOK VI

* * *

One difficulty, then, has been surmounted. It remains to ask how we can make sure of 502^c having men who will preserve our constitution. What must they learn, and at what age should they take up each branch of study? 502^c d

Yes, that is the next point.

I gained nothing by my cunning in putting off those thorny questions of the possession of wives and children and the appointment of Rulers. I knew that the ideal plan would give offence and be hard to carry out; none the less I have had to discuss these e matters. We have now disposed of the women and children, but we must start all over again upon the training of the Rulers. You remember how their love for their country 503 was to be proved, by the tests of pain and pleasure, to be a faith that no toil or danger, no turn of fortune could make them abandon. All who failed were to be rejected; only the man who came out flawless, like gold tried in the fire, was to be made a Ruler with privileges and rewards in life and after death. So much was said, when our argument turned aside, as if hoping, with veiled face, to slip past the danger that now lies in our path. b

Quite true, I remember.

Yes, I shrank from the bold words which have now been spoken; but now we have ventured to declare that our Guardians in the fullest sense must be philosophers. So much being granted, you must reflect how few are likely to be available. The natural gifts we required will rarely grow together into one whole; they tend to split apart.

How do you mean? c

Qualities like ready understanding, a good memory, sagacity, quickness, together with a high-spirited, generous temper, are seldom combined with willingness to live a quiet life of sober constancy. Keen wits are apt to lose all steadiness and to veer about in every direction. On the other hand, the steady reliable characters, whose impassivity is proof against the perils of war, are equally proof against instruction. Confronted with d intellectual work, they become comatose and do nothing but yawn.

That is true.

But we insist that no one must be given the highest education or hold office as Ruler, who has not both sets of qualities in due measure. This combination will be rare. e So, besides testing it by hardship and danger and by the temptations of pleasure, we may now add that its strength must be tried in many forms of study, to see whether it has the courage and endurance to pursue the highest kind of knowledge, without flinching as others flinch under physical trials. 504

By all means; but what kinds of study do you call the highest?

You remember how we deduced the definitions of justice, temperance, courage, and wisdom by distinguishing three parts of the soul?

If I had forgotten that, I should not deserve to hear any more.

Do you also remember my warning you beforehand that in order to gain the clear- b est possible view of these qualities we should have to go round a longer way, although we could give a more superficial account in keeping with our earlier argument. You said that would do; and so we went on in a way which seemed to me not sufficiently exact; whether you were satisfied, it is for you to say.

We all thought you gave us a fair measure of truth.

No measure that falls in the least degree short of the whole truth can be quite c fair in so important a matter. What is imperfect can never serve as a measure;

though people sometimes think enough has been done and there is no need to look further.

Yes, indolence is common enough.

But the last quality to be desired in the Guardian of a commonwealth and its laws. So he will have to take the longer way and work as hard at learning as at training his body; otherwise he will never reach the goal of the highest knowledge, which most of all concerns him.

Why, are not justice and the other virtues we have discussed the highest? Is there something still higher to be known?

There is; and of those virtues themselves we have as yet only a rough outline, where nothing short of the finished picture should content us. If we strain every nerve to reach precision and clearness in things of little moment, how absurd not to demand the highest degree of exactness in the things that matter most.

Certainly. But what do you mean by the highest kind of knowledge and with what is it concerned? You cannot hope to escape that question.

I do not; you may ask me yourself. All the same, you have been told many a time; but now either you are not thinking or, as I rather suspect, you mean to put me to some trouble with your insistence. For you have often been told that the highest object of knowledge is the essential nature of the Good, from which everything that is good and right derives its value for us. You must have been expecting me to speak of this now, and to add that we have no sufficient knowledge of it. I need not tell you that, without that knowledge, to know everything else, however well, would be of no value to us, just as it is of no use to possess anything without getting the good of it. What advantage can there be in possessing everything except what is good, or in understanding everything else while of the good and desirable we know nothing?

None whatever.

Well then, you know too that most people identify the Good with pleasure, whereas the more enlightened think it is knowledge.

Yes, of course.

And further that these latter cannot tell us what knowledge they mean, but are reduced at last to saying, "knowledge of the Good."

That is absurd.

It is; first they reproach us with not knowing the Good, and then tell us that it is knowledge of the Good, as if we did after all understand the meaning of that word "Good" when they pronounce it.

Quite true.

What of those who define the Good as pleasure? Are they any less confused in their thoughts? They are obliged to admit that there are bad pleasures; from which it follows that the same things are both good and bad.

Quite so.

Evidently, then, this is a matter of much dispute. It is also evident that, although many are content to do what seems just or honourable without really being so, and to possess a mere semblance of these qualities, when it comes to good things, no one is satisfied with possessing what only seems good: here all reject the appearance and demand the reality.

Certainly.

A thing, then, that every soul pursues as the end of all her actions, dimly divining its existence, but perplexed and unable to grasp its nature with the same clearness and assurance as in dealing with other things, and so missing whatever value those other things might have—a thing of such supreme importance is not a matter about which those chosen Guardians of the whole fortunes of our commonwealth can be left in the dark.

Most certainly not.

At any rate, institutions or customs which are desirable and right will not, I imagine, find a very efficient guardian in one who does not know in what way they are good. I should rather guess that he will not be able to recognize fully that they are right and desirable.

No doubt.

So the order of our commonwealth will be perfectly regulated only when it is watched over by a Guardian who does possess this knowledge.   b

That follows. But, Socrates, what is your own account of the Good? Is it knowledge, or pleasure, or something else?

There you are! I exclaimed; I could see all along that you were not going to be content with what other people think.

Well, Socrates, it does not seem fair that you should be ready to repeat other people's opinions but not to state your own, when you have given so much thought to this subject.

And do you think it fair of anyone to speak as if he knew what he does not know?   c

No, not as if he knew, but he might give his opinion for what it is worth.

Why, have you never noticed that opinion without knowledge is always a shabby sort of thing? At the best it is blind. One who holds a true belief without intelligence is just like a blind man who happens to take the right road, isn't he?

No doubt.

Well, then, do you want me to produce one of these poor blind cripples, when   d others could discourse to you with illuminating eloquence?

No, really, Socrates, said Glaucon, you must not give up within sight of the goal. We should be quite content with an account of the Good like the one you gave us of justice and temperance and the other virtues.

So should I be, my dear Glaucon, much more than content! But I am afraid it is beyond my powers; with the best will in the world I should only disgrace myself and be laughed at. No, for the moment let us leave the question of the real meaning of good; to   e arrive at what I at any rate believe it to be would call for an effort too ambitious for an inquiry like ours. However, I will tell you, though only if you wish it, what I picture to myself as the offspring of the Good and the thing most nearly resembling it.

Well, tell us about the offspring, and you shall remain in our debt for an account of the parent.

I only wish it were within my power to offer, and within yours to receive, a set-   507 tlement of the whole account. But you must be content now with the interest only; and you must see to it that, in describing this offspring of the Good, I do not inadvertently cheat you with false coin.

We will keep a good eye on you. Go on.

First we must come to an understanding. Let me remind you of the distinction we   b drew earlier and have often drawn on other occasions, between the multiplicity of things that we call good or beautiful or whatever it may be and, on the other hand, Goodness itself or Beauty itself and so on. Corresponding to each of these sets of many things, we postulate a single Form or real essence, as we call it.

Yes, that is so.

Further, the many things, we say, can be seen, but are not objects of rational thought; whereas the Forms are objects of thought, but invisible.

Yes, certainly.

And we see things with our eyesight, just as we hear sounds with our ears and, to
c   speak generally, perceive any sensible thing with our sense-faculties.

Of course.

Have you noticed, then, that the artificer who designed the senses has been exceptionally lavish of his materials in making the eyes able to see and their objects visible?

That never occurred to me.

d   Well, look at it in this way. Hearing and sound do not stand in need of any third
thing, without which the ear will not hear nor sound be heard; and I think the same is
true of most, not to say all, of the other senses. Can you think of one that does require
anything of the sort?

No, I cannot.

But there is this need in the case of sight and its objects. You may have the power
of vision in your eyes and try to use it, and colour may be there in the objects; but sight
will see nothing and the colours will remain invisible in the absence of a third thing pe-
e   culiarly constituted to serve this very purpose.

By which you mean—?

Naturally I mean what you call light; and if light is a thing of value, the sense of
sight and the power of being visible are linked together by a very precious bond, such as
unites no other sense with its object.

508   No one could say that light is not a precious thing.

And of all the divinities in the skies is there one whose light, above all the rest, is
responsible for making our eyes see perfectly and making objects perfectly visible?

There can be no two opinions: of course you mean the Sun.

And how is sight related to this deity? Neither sight nor the eye which contains it
b   is the Sun, but of all the sense-organs it is the most sun-like; and further, the power it
possesses is dispensed by the Sun, like a stream flooding the eye. And again, the Sun is
not vision, but it is the cause of vision and also is seen by the vision it causes.

Yes.

It was the Sun, then, that I meant when I spoke of that offspring which the Good
has created in the visible world, to stand there in the same relation to vision and visible
things as that which the Good itself bears in the intelligible world to intelligence and to
c   intelligible objects.

How is that? You must explain further.

You know what happens when the colours of things are no longer irradiated by
the daylight, but only by the fainter luminaries of the night: when you look at them, the
eyes are dim and seem almost blind, as if there were no unclouded vision in them. But
when you look at things on which the Sun is shining, the same eyes see distinctly and it
d   becomes evident that they do contain the power of vision.

Certainly.

Apply this comparison, then, to the soul. When its gaze is fixed upon an object irradiated by truth and reality, the soul gains understanding and knowledge and is manifestly in possession of intelligence. But when it looks towards that twilight world of
things that come into existence and pass away, its sight is dim and it has only opinions
and beliefs which shift to and fro, and now it seems like a thing that has no intelligence.

That is true.

e   This, then, which gives to the objects of knowledge their truth and to him who
knows them his power of knowing, is the Form or essential nature of Goodness. It is the
cause of knowledge and truth; and so, while you may think of it as an object of knowl-
509   edge, you will do well to regard it as something beyond truth and knowledge and, precious as these both are, of still higher worth. And, just as in our analogy light and vision

were to be thought of as like the Sun, but not identical with it, so here both knowledge and truth are to be regarded as like the Good, but to identify either with the Good is wrong. The Good must hold a yet higher place of honour.

You are giving it a position of extraordinary splendour, if it is the source of knowledge and truth and itself surpasses them in worth. You surely cannot mean that it is pleasure.

Heaven forbid, I exclaimed. But I want to follow up our analogy still further.   b
You will agree that the Sun not only makes the things we see visible, but also brings them into existence and gives them growth and nourishment; yet he is not the same thing as existence. And so with the objects of knowledge: these derive from the Good not only their power of being known, but their very being and reality; and Goodness is not the same thing as being, but even beyond being, surpassing it in dignity and power.

Glaucon exclaimed with some amusement at my exalting Goodness in such ex-   c
travagant terms.

It is your fault, I replied; you forced me to say what I think.

Yes, and you must not stop there. At any rate, complete your comparison with the Sun, if there is any more to be said.

There is a great deal more, I answered.

Let us hear it, then; don't leave anything out.

I am afraid much must be left unspoken. However, I will not, if I can help it, leave out anything that can be said on this occasion.

Please do not.

Conceive, then, that there are these two powers I speak of, the Good reigning   d
over the domain of all that is intelligible, the Sun over the visible world—or the heaven as I might call it; only you would think I was showing off my skill in etymology. At any rate you have these two orders of things clearly before your mind: the visible and the intelligible?

I have.

Now take a line divided into two unequal parts, one to represent the visible order, the other the intelligible; and divide each part again in the same proportion, symboliz-ing degrees of comparative clearness or obscurity. Then (A) one of the two sections in   e
the visible world will stand for images. By images I mean first shadows, and then re-flections in water or in close-grained, polished surfaces, and everything of that kind, if   510
you understand.

Yes, I understand.

Let the second section (B) stand for the actual things of which the first are like-nesses, the living creatures about us and all the works of nature or of human hands.

So be it.

Will you also take the proportion in which the visible world has been divided as corresponding to degrees of reality and truth, so that the likeness shall stand to the orig-inal in the same ratio as the sphere of appearances and belief to the sphere of knowl-edge?

Certainly.   b

Now consider how we are to divide the part which stands for the intelligible world. There are two sections. In the first (C) the mind uses as images those actual things which themselves had images in the visible world; and it is compelled to pursue its inquiry by starting from assumptions and travelling, not up to a principle, but down to a conclusion. In the second (D) the mind moves in the other direction, from an as-sumption up towards a principle which is not hypothetical; and it makes no use of the

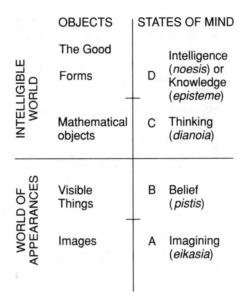

images employed in the other section, but only of Forms, and conducts its inquiry solely by their means.

I don't quite understand what you mean.

c   Then we will try again; what I have just said will help you to understand. (C) You know, of course, how students of subjects like geometry and arithmetic begin by postulating odd and even numbers, or the various figures and the three kinds of angle, and other such data in each subject. These data take as known; and, having adopted them as assumptions, they do not feel called upon to give any account of them to themselves or to anyone else, but treat them as self-evident. Then, starting from these as-

d   sumptions, they go on until they arrive, by a series of consistent steps, at all the conclusions they set out to investigate.

Yes, I know that.

You also know how they make use of visible figures and discourse about them, though what they really have in mind is the originals of which these figures are images: they are not reasoning, for instance, about this particular square and diagonal which they have drawn, but about *the* Square and *the* Diagonal; and so in all cases. The dia-

e   grams they draw and the models they make are actual things, which may have their shadows or images in water; but now they serve in their turn as images, while the stu-

511   dent is seeking to behold those realities which only thought can apprehend.

True.

This, then, is the class of things that I spoke of as intelligible, but with two qualifications: first, that the mind, in studying them, is compelled to employ assumptions, and, because it cannot rise above these, does not travel upwards to a first principle; and second, that it uses as images those actual things which have images of their own in the section below them and which, in comparison with those shadows and reflections, are reputed to be more palpable and valued accordingly.

b   I understand: you mean the subject-matter of geometry and of the kindred arts.

(D) Then by the second section of the intelligible world you may understand me to mean all that unaided reasoning apprehends by the power of dialectic, when it treats its assumptions, not as first principles, but as *hypotheses* in the literal sense, things "laid down" like a flight of steps up which it may mount all the way to something that is not hypothetical, the first principle of all; and having grasped this, may turn back and, holding on to the consequences which depend upon it, descend at last to a conclusion, never c making use of any sensible object, but only of Forms, moving through Forms from one to another, and ending with Forms.

I understand, he said, though not perfectly; for the procedure you describe sounds like an enormous undertaking. But I see that you mean to distinguish the field of intelligible reality studied by dialectic as having a greater certainty and truth than the subject-matter of the "arts," as they are called, which treat their assumptions as first principles. The students of these arts are, it is true, compelled to exercise thought in contemplating objects which the senses cannot perceive; but because they start from assumptions with- d out going back to a first principle, you do not regard them as gaining true understanding about those objects, although the objects themselves, when connected with a first principle, are intelligible. And I think you would call the state of mind of the students of geometry and other such arts, not intelligence, but thinking, as being something between intelligence and mere acceptance of appearances.

You have understood me quite well enough, I replied. And now you may take, as corresponding to the four sections, these four states of mind: *intelligence* for the highest, *thinking* for the second, *belief* for the third, and for the last *imagining*. These you e may arrange as the terms in a proportion, assigning to each a degree of clearness and certainty corresponding to the measure in which their objects possess truth and reality.

I understand and agree with you. I will arrange them as you say.

BOOK VII

Next, said I, here is a parable to illustrate the degrees in which our nature may be en- 514 lightened or unenlightened. Imagine the condition of men living in a sort of cavernous chamber underground, with an entrance open to the light and a long passage all down the cave. Here they have been from childhood, chained by the leg and also by the neck, so that they cannot move and can see only what is in front of them, because the chains will not let them turn their heads. At some distance higher up is the light of a fire burn- b ing behind them; and between the prisoners and the fire is a track with a parapet built along it, like the screen at a puppet-show, which hides the performers while they show their puppets over the top.

I see, said he.

Now behind this parapet imagine persons carrying along various artificial objects, including figures of men and animals in wood or stone or other materials, which project c above the parapet. Naturally, some of these persons will be talking, others silent. 515

It is a strange picture, he said, and a strange sort of prisoners.

Like ourselves, I replied; for in the first place prisoners so confined would have seen nothing of themselves or of one another, except the shadows thrown by the firelight on the wall of the Cave facing them, would they?

Not if all their lives they had been prevented from moving their heads. b

And they would have seen as little of the objects carried past.

Of course.

Now, if they could talk to one another, would they not suppose that their words referred only to those passing shadows which they saw?

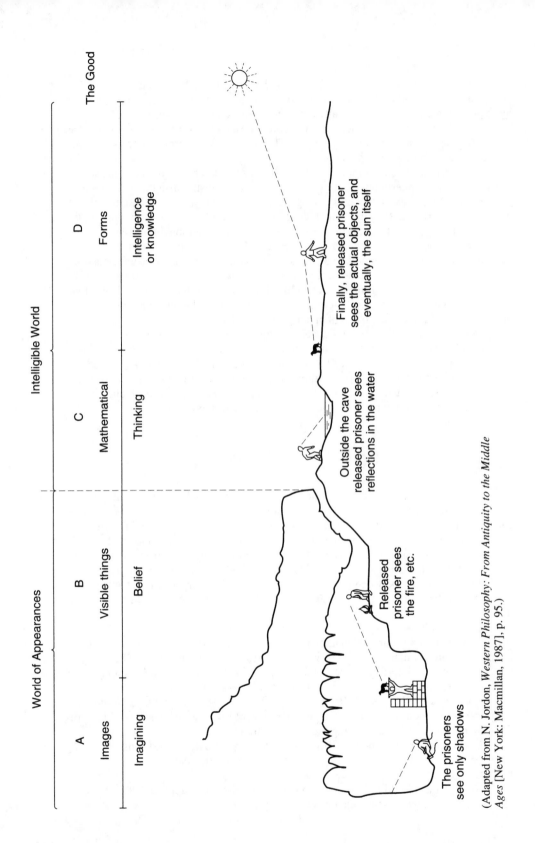

World of Appearances

A	B
Images	Visible things
Imagining	Belief

Intelligible World

C	D
Mathematical	Forms
Thinking	Intelligence or knowledge

The Good

The prisoners see only shadows

Released prisoner sees the fire, etc.

Outside the cave released prisoner sees reflections in the water

Finally, released prisoner sees the actual objects, and eventually, the sun itself

(Adapted from N. Jordon, *Western Philosophy: From Antiquity to the Middle Ages* [New York: Macmillan, 1987], p. 95.)

Necessarily.

And suppose their prison had an echo from the wall facing them? When one of the people crossing behind them spoke, they could only suppose that the sound came from the shadow passing before their eyes.

No doubt.

In every way, then, such prisoners would recognize as reality nothing but the   c
shadows of those artificial objects.

Inevitably.

Now consider what would happen if their release from the chains and the healing of their unwisdom should come about in this way. Suppose one of them were set free and forced suddenly to stand up, turn his head, and walk with eyes lifted to the light; all these movements would be painful, and he would be too dazzled to make out the objects whose shadows he had been used to seeing. What do you think he would say, if some-one told him that what he had formerly seen was meaningless illusion, but now, being   d
somewhat nearer to reality and turned towards more real objects, he was getting a truer view? Suppose further that he were shown the various objects being carried by and were made to say, in reply to questions, what each of them was. Would he not be per-plexed and believe the objects now shown him to be not so real as what he formerly saw?

Yes, not nearly so real.

And if he were forced to look at the firelight itself, would not his eyes ache, so   e
that he would try to escape and turn back to the things which he could see distinctly, convinced that they really were clearer than these other objects now being shown to him?

Yes.

And suppose someone were to drag him away forcibly up the steep and rugged ascent and not let him go until he had hauled him out into the sunlight, would he not suffer pain and vexation at such treatment, and, when he had come out into the light,   516
find his eyes so full of its radiance that he could not see a single one of the things that he was now told were real?

Certainly he would not see them all at once.

He would need, then, to grow accustomed before he could see things in that upper world. At first it would be easiest to make out shadows, and then the images of men and things reflected in water, and later on the things themselves. After that, it would be eas-ier to watch the heavenly bodies and the sky itself by night, looking at the light of the   b
moon and stars rather than the Sun and the Sun's light in the day-time.

Yes, surely.

Last of all, he would be able to look at the Sun and contemplate its nature, not as it appears when reflected in water or any alien medium, but as it is in itself in its own domain.

No doubt.

And now he would begin to draw the conclusion that it is the Sun that produces the seasons and the course of the year and controls everything in the visible world, and moreover is in a way the cause of all that he and his companions used to see.   c

Clearly he would come at last to that conclusion.

Then if he called to mind his fellow prisoners and what passed for wisdom in his former dwelling-place, he would surely think himself happy in the change and be sorry for them. They may have had a practice of honouring and commending one another, with prizes for the man who had the keenest eye for the passing shadows and the best memory for the order in which they followed or accompanied one another, so that he d   could make a good guess as to which was going to come next. Would our released prisoner be likely to covet those prizes or to envy the men exalted to honour and power in the Cave? Would he not feel like Homer's Achilles, that he would far sooner "be on earth as a hired servant in the house of a landless man" or endure anything rather than go back to his old beliefs and live in the old way?

e   Yes, he would prefer any fate to such a life.

        Now imagine what would happen if he went down again to take his former seat in the Cave. Coming suddenly out of the sunlight, his eyes would be filled with darkness.

517   He might be required once more to deliver his opinion on those shadows, in competition with the prisoners who had never been released, while his eyesight was still dim and unsteady; and it might take some time to become used to the darkness. They would laugh at him and say that he had gone up only to come back with his sight ruined; it was worth no one's while even to attempt the ascent. If they could lay hands on the man who was trying to set them free and lead them up, they would kill him.

        Yes, they would.

        Every feature in this parable, my dear Glaucon, is meant to fit our earlier analy-

b   sis. The prison dwelling corresponds to the region revealed to us through the sense of sight, and the firelight within it to the power of the Sun. The ascent to see the things in the upper world you may take as standing for the upward journey of the soul into the region of the intelligible; then you will be in possession of what I surmise, since that is what you wish to be told. Heaven knows whether it is true; but this, at any rate, is how it appears to me. In the world of knowledge, the last thing to be perceived and

c   only with great difficulty is the essential Form of Goodness. Once it is perceived, the conclusion must follow that, for all things, this is the cause of whatever is right and good; in the visible world it gives birth to light and to the lord of light, while it is itself sovereign in the intelligible world and the parent of intelligence and truth. Without having had a vision of this Form no one can act with wisdom, either in his own life or in matters of state.

        So far as I can understand, I share your belief.

        Then you may also agree that it is no wonder if those who have reached this height are reluctant to manage the affairs of men. Their souls long to spend all their time in that upper world—naturally enough, if here once more our parable holds true. Nor,

d   again, is it at all strange that one who comes from the contemplation of divine things to the miseries of human life should appear awkward and ridiculous when, with eyes still dazed and not yet accustomed to the darkness, he is compelled, in a law-court or else-

e   where, to dispute about the shadows of justice or the images that cast those shadows, and to wrangle over the notions of what is right in the minds of men who have never beheld Justice itself.

        It is not at all strange.

518   No; a sensible man will remember that the eyes may be confused in two ways— by a change from light to darkness or from darkness to light; and he will recognize that the same thing happens to the soul. When he sees it troubled and unable to discern anything clearly, instead of laughing thoughtlessly, he will ask whether, coming from a brighter existence, its unaccustomed vision is obscured by the darkness, in which case

b   he will think its condition enviable and its life a happy one; or whether, emerging from the depths of ignorance, it is dazzled by excess of light. If so, he will rather feel sorry for it; or, if he were inclined to laugh, that would be less ridiculous than to laugh at the soul which has come down from the light.

        That is a fair statement.

If this is true, then, we must conclude that education is not what it is said to be by some, who profess to put knowledge into a soul which does not possess it, as if they could put sight into blind eyes. On the contrary, our own account signifies that the soul   c
of every man does possess the power of learning the truth and the organ to see it with; and that, just as one might have to turn the whole body round in order that the eye should see light instead of darkness, so the entire soul must be turned away from this changing world, until its eye can bear to contemplate reality and that supreme splendour   d
which we have called the Good. Hence there may well be an art whose aim would be to effect this very thing, the conversion of the soul, in the readiest way; not to put the power of sight into the soul's eye, which already has it, but to ensure that, instead of looking in the wrong direction, it is turned the way it ought to be.

Yes, it may well be so.

It looks, then, as though wisdom were different from those ordinary virtues, as they are called, which are not far removed from bodily qualities, in that they can be produced by habituation and exercise in a soul which has not possessed them from the first. Wisdom, it seems, is certainly the virtue of some diviner faculty, which never loses its   e
power, though its use for good or harm depends on the direction towards which it is turned. You must have noticed in dishonest men with a reputation for sagacity the   519
shrewd glance of a narrow intelligence piercing the objects to which it is directed. There is nothing wrong with their power of vision, but it has been forced into the service of evil, so that the keener its sight, the more harm it works.

Quite true.

And yet if the growth of a nature like this had been pruned from earliest childhood, cleared of those clinging overgrowths which come of gluttony and all luxurious pleasure and, like leaden weights charged with affinity to this mortal world, hang upon   b
the soul, bending its vision downwards; if, freed from these, the soul were turned round towards true reality, then this same power in these very men would see the truth as keenly as the objects it is turned to now.

Yes, very likely.

Is it not also likely, or indeed certain after what has been said, that a state can never be properly governed either by the uneducated who know nothing of truth or by men who are allowed to spend all their days in the pursuit of culture? The ignorant have no single mark before their eyes at which they must aim in all the conduct of their own lives and of affairs of state; and the others will not engage in action if they can help it,   c
dreaming that, while still alive, they have been translated to the Islands of the Blest.

Quite true.

It is for us, then, as founders of a commonwealth, to bring compulsion to bear on the noblest natures. They must be made to climb the ascent to the vision of Goodness, which we called the highest object of knowledge; and, when they have looked upon it   d
long enough, they must not be allowed, as they now are, to remain on the heights, refusing to come down again to the prisoners or to take any part in their labours and rewards, however much or little these may be worth.

Shall we not be doing them an injustice, if we force on them a worse life than they might have?

You have forgotten again, my friend, that the law is not concerned to make any   e
one class specially happy, but to ensure the welfare of the commonwealth as a whole. By persuasion or constraint it will unite the citizens in harmony, making them share   520
whatever benefits each class can contribute to the common good; and its purpose in forming men of that spirit was not that each should be left to go his own way, but that they should be instrumental in binding the community into one.

True, I had forgotten.

You will see, then, Glaucon, that there will be no real injustice in compelling our philosophers to watch over and care for the other citizens. We can fairly tell them that their compeers in other states may quite reasonably refuse to collaborate: there they have
b   sprung up, like a self-sown plant, in despite of their country's institutions; no one has fostered their growth, and they cannot be expected to show gratitude for a care they have never received. "But," we shall say, "it is not so with you. We have brought you into existence for your country's sake as well as for your own, to be like leaders and king-bees in a hive; you have been better and more thoroughly educated than those others and hence you are more capable of playing your part both as men of thought and as men of action.
c   You must go down, then, each in his turn, to live with the rest and let your eyes grow accustomed to the darkness. You will then see a thousand times better than those who live there always; you will recognize every image for what it is and know what it represents, because you have seen justice, beauty, and goodness in their reality; and so you and we shall find life in our commonwealth no mere dream, as it is in most existing states, where
d   men live fighting one another about shadows and quarrelling for power, as if that were a great prize; whereas in truth government can be at its best and free from dissension only where the destined rulers are least desirous of holding office."

Quite true.

Then will our pupils refuse to listen and to take their turns at sharing in the work of the community, though they may live together for most of their time in a purer air?
e   No; it is a fair demand, and they are fair-minded men. No doubt, unlike any ruler of the present day, they will think of holding power as an unavoidable necessity.

Yes, my friend; for the truth is that you can have a well-governed society only if
521 you can discover for your future rulers a better way of life than being in office; then only will power be in the hands of men who are rich, not in gold, but in the wealth that brings happiness, a good and wise life. All goes wrong when, starved for lack of anything good in their own lives, men turn to public affairs hoping to snatch from thence the happiness they hunger for. They set about fighting for power, and this internecine
b   conflict ruins them and their country. The life of true philosophy is the only one that looks down upon offices of state; and access to power must be confined to men who are not in love with it; otherwise rivals will start fighting. So whom else can you compel to undertake the guardianship of the commonwealth, if not those who, besides understanding best the principles of government, enjoy a nobler life than the politician's and look for rewards of a different kind?

There is indeed no other choice.

PARMENIDES (in part)

127 According to Antiphon, then, this was Pythodorus' account. Zeno and Parmenides once
b   came to Athens for the Great Panathenaea. Parmenides was a man of distinguished appearance. By that time he was well advanced in years, with hair almost white; he may

Plato, *Parmenides* (127–135), translated by F.M. Cornford from *The Collected Dialogues of Plato,* edited by Edith Hamilton and Huntington Cairns. Copyright © 1961 by PUP. Reprinted by permission of Princeton University Press.

have been sixty-five. Zeno was nearing forty, a tall and attractive figure. It was said that he had been Parmenides' favourite. They were staying with Pythodorus outside the walls in the Ceramicus. Socrates and a few others came there, anxious to hear a reading   c of Zeno's treatise, which the two visitors had brought for the first time to Athens. Socrates was then quite young. Zeno himself read it to them; Parmenides at the moment had gone out. The reading of the arguments was very nearly over when Pythodorus himself came in, accompanied by Parmenides and Aristoteles, the man who was after-   d wards one of the Thirty; so they heard only a small part of the treatise. Pythodorus himself, however, had heard it read by Zeno before.

When Zeno had finished, Socrates asked him to read once more the first hypothesis of the first argument. He did so, and Socrates asked: What does this statement mean, Zeno? "If things are many," you say, "they must be both like and unlike. But that is impos-   e sible: unlike things cannot be like, nor like things unlike." That is what you say, isn't it?

Yes, replied Zeno.

And so, if unlike things cannot be like or like things unlike, it is also impossible that things should be a plurality; if many things did exist, they would have impossible attributes. Is this the precise purpose of your arguments—to maintain, against everything that is commonly said, that things are not a plurality? Do you regard every one of your arguments as evidence of exactly that conclusion, and so hold that, in each argument in your treatise, you are giving just one more proof that a plurality does not exist?   128 Is that what you mean, or am I understanding you wrongly?

No, said Zeno, you have quite rightly understood the purpose of the whole treatise.

I see, Parmenides, said Socrates, that Zeno's intention is to associate himself with you by means of his treatise no less intimately than by his personal attachment. In a way, his book states the same position as your own; only by varying the form he tries to delude us into thinking that his thesis is a different one. You assert, in your poem, that   b the All is one; and for this you advance admirable proofs. Zeno, for his part, asserts that it is not a plurality; and he too has many weighty proofs to bring forward. You assert unity, he asserts no plurality; each expresses himself in such a way that your arguments seem to have nothing in common, though really they come to very much the same thing. That is why your exposition and his seem to be rather over the heads of outsiders like ourselves.

Yes, Socrates, Zeno replied; but you have not quite seen the real character of my   c book. True, you are as quick as a Spartan hound to pick up the scent and follow the trail of the argument; but there is a point you have missed at the outset. The book makes no pretence of disguising from the public the fact that it was written with the purpose you describe, as if such deception were something to be proud of. What you have pointed out is only incidental; the book is in fact a sort of defence of Parmenides' argument against those who try to make fun of it by showing that his supposition, that there is a   d One, leads to many absurdities and contradictions. This book, then, is a retort against those who assert a plurality. It pays them back in the same coin with something to spare, and aims at showing that, on a thorough examination, their own supposition that there is a plurality leads to even more absurd consequences than the hypothesis of the One. It was written in that controversial spirit in my young days; and someone copied it surreptitiously, so that I had not even the chance to consider whether it should see the light or not. That is where you are mistaken Socrates; you imagine it was inspired, not by a   e youthful eagerness for controversy, but by the more dispassionate aims of an older man; though, as I said, your description of it was not far wrong.

I accept that, said Socrates, and I have no doubt it is as you say. But tell me this. Do you not recognise that there exists, just by itself, a Form of Likeness and again an-

129   other contrary Form, Unlikeness itself, and that of these two Forms you and I and all the things we speak of as "many" come to partake? Also, that things which come to partake of Likeness come to be alike in that respect and just in so far as they do come to partake of it, and those that come to partake of Unlikeness come to be unlike, while those which come to partake of both come to be both? Even if all things come to partake of both, contrary as they are, and by having a share in both are at once like and unlike one an-

b   other, what is there surprising in that? If one could point to things which are simply "alike" or "unlike" proving to be unlike or alike, that no doubt would be a portent; but when things which have a share in both are shown to have both characters, I see nothing strange in that, Zeno; nor yet in a proof that all things are one by having a share in unity and at the same time many by sharing in plurality. But if anyone can prove that what is simply Unity itself is many or that Plurality itself is one, then I shall begin to be

c   surprised.

And so in all other cases; if the kinds or Forms themselves were shown to have these contrary characters among themselves, there would be good ground for astonishment; but what is there surprising in someone pointing out that I am one thing and also many? When he wants to show that I am many things, he can say that my right side is a different thing from my left, my front from my back, my upper parts from my lower, since no doubt I do partake of plurality. When he wants to prove that I am one thing, he

d   will say that I am one person among the seven of us, since I partake also of unity. So both statements are true. Accordingly, if anyone sets out to show about things of this kind—sticks and stones, and so on—that the same thing is many and one, we shall say that what he is proving is that *something* is many and one, not that Unity is many or that Plurality is one; he is not telling us anything wonderful, but only what we should all admit. But, as I said just now, if he begins by distinguishing the Forms apart just by them-

e   selves—Likeness, for instance, and Unlikeness, Plurality and Unity, Rest and Motion, and all the rest—and then shows that these Forms among themselves can be combined with, or separate from, one another, then, Zeno, I should be filled with admiration. I am sure you have dealt with this subject very forcibly; but, as I say, my admiration would

130   be much greater if anyone could show that these same perplexities are everywhere involved in the Forms themselves—among the objects we apprehend in reflection, just as you and Parmenides have shown them to be involved in the things we see.

While Socrates was speaking, Pythodorus said he was expecting every moment that Parmenides and Zeno would be annoyed; but they listened very attentively and kept on exchanging glances and smiles in admiration of Socrates. When he ended, Parmenides expressed this feeling.

b   Socrates, he said, your eagerness for discussion is admirable. And now tell me: have you yourself drawn this distinction you speak of and separated apart on the one side Forms themselves and on the other the things that share in them? Do you believe that there is such a thing as Likeness itself apart from the likeness that we possess, and so on with Unity and Plurality and all the terms in Zeno's argument that you have just been listening to?

Certainly I do, said Socrates.

And also in cases like these, asked Parmenides: is there, for example, a Form of Rightness or of Beauty or of Goodness, and of all such things?

Yes.

c   And again, a Form of Man, apart from ourselves and all other men like us—a Form of Man as something by itself? Or a Form of Fire or of Water?

I have often been puzzled about those things, Parmenides, whether one should say that the same thing is true in their case or not.

Are you also puzzled, Socrates, about cases that might be thought absurd, such as hair or mud or dirt or any other trivial and undignified objects? Are you doubtful whether or not to assert that each of these has a separate Form distinct from things like those we handle?

d

Not at all, said Socrates; in these cases, the things are just the things we see; it would surely be too absurd to suppose that they have a Form. All the same, I have sometimes been troubled by a doubt whether what is true in one case may not be true in all. Then, when I have reached that point, I am driven to retreat, for fear of tumbling into a bottomless pit of nonsense. Anyhow, I get back to the things which we were just now speaking of as having Forms, and occupy my time with thinking about them.

That, replied Parmenides, is because you are still young, Socrates, and philosophy has not yet taken hold of you so firmly as I believe it will some day. You will not despise any of these objects then; but at present your youth makes you still pay attention to what the world will think. However that may be, tell me this. You say you hold that there exist certain Forms, of which these other things come to partake and so to be called after their names: by coming to partake of Likeness or Largeness or Beauty or Justice, they become like or large or beautiful or just?

e

131

Certainly, said Socrates.

Then each thing that partakes receives as its share either the Form as a whole or a part of it? Or can there be any other way of partaking besides this?

No, how could there be?

Do you hold, then, that the Form as a whole, a single thing, is in each of the many, or how?

Why should it not be in each, Parmenides?

If so, a Form which is one and the same will be at the same time, as a whole, in a number of things which are separate, and consequently will be separate from itself.

b

No, it would not, replied Socrates, if it were like one and the same day, which is in many places at the same time and nevertheless is not separate from itself. Suppose any given Form is in them all at the same time as one and the same thing in that way.

I like the way you make out that one and the same thing is in many places at once, Socrates. You might as well spread a sail over a number of people and then say that the one sail as a whole was over them all. Don't you think that is a fair analogy?

Perhaps it is.

Then would the sail as a whole be over each man, or only a part over one, another part over another?

c

Only a part.

In that case, Socrates, the Forms themselves must be divisible into parts, and the things which have a share in them will have a part for their share. Only a part of any given Form, and no longer the whole of it, will be in each thing.

Evidently, on that showing.

Are you, then, prepared to assert that we shall find the single Form actually being divided? Will it still be one?

Certainly not.

No, for consider this. Suppose it is Largeness itself that you are going to divide into parts, and that each of the many large things is to be large by virtue of a part of Largeness which is smaller than Largeness itself. Will not that seem unreasonable?

d

It will indeed.

And again, if it is Equality that a thing receives some small part of, will that part, which is less than Equality itself, make its possessor equal to something else?

No, that is impossible.

Well, take Smallness: is one of us to have a portion of Smallness, and is Smallness to be larger than that portion, which is a part of it? On this supposition again Smallness itself will be larger, and anything to which the portion taken is added will be
smaller, and larger, than it was before.

That cannot be so.

Well then, Socrates, how are the other things going to partake of your Forms, if
they can partake of them neither in part nor as wholes?

Really, said Socrates, it seems no easy matter to determine in any way.

Again, there is another question.

What is that?

How do you feel about this? I imagine your ground for believing in a single Form
in each case is this: when it seems to you that a number of things are large, there seems,
I suppose, to be a certain single character which is the same when you look at them all;
hence you think that Largeness is a single thing.

True, he replied.

But now take Largeness itself and the other things which are large. Suppose you
look at all these in the same way in your mind's eye, will not yet another unity make its
appearance—a Largeness by virtue of which they all appear large?

So it would seem.

If so, a second Form of Largeness will present itself, over and above Largeness itself and the things that share in it; and again, covering all these, yet another, which will
make all of them large. So each of your Forms will no longer be one, but an indefinite
number.

But, Parmenides, said Socrates, may it not be that each of these Forms is a
thought, which cannot properly exist anywhere but in a mind. In that way each of them
can be one and the statements that have just been made would no longer be true of it.

Then, is each Form one of these thoughts and yet a thought of nothing?

No, that is impossible.

So it is a thought of something?

Yes.

Of something that is, or of something that is not?

Of something that is.

In fact, of some one thing which that thought observes to cover all the cases, as
being a certain single character?

Yes.

Then will not this thing that is thought of as being one and always the same in all
cases be a Form?

That again seems to follow.

And besides, said Parmenides, according to the way in which you assert that the
other things have a share in the Forms, must you not hold either that each of those
things consists of thoughts, so that all things think, or else that they are thoughts which
nevertheless do not think?

That too is unreasonable, replied Socrates. But, Parmenides, the best I can make
of the matter is this: that these Forms are as it were patterns fixed in the nature of things;
the other things are made in their image and are likenesses; and this participation they
come to have in the Forms is nothing but their being made in their image.

Well, if a thing is made in the image of the Form, can that Form fail to be like the
image of it, in so far as the image was made in its likeness? If a thing is like, must it not
be like something that is like it?

It must.

And must not the thing which is like share with the thing that is like it in one and   e
the same thing [character]?

Yes.

And will not that in which the like things share, so as to be alike, be just the Form
itself that you spoke of?

Certainly.

If so, nothing can be like the Form, nor can the Form be like anything. Otherwise
a second Form will always make its appearance over and above the first Form; and if
that second Form is like anything, yet a third; and there will be no end to this emergence   133
of fresh Forms, if the Form is to be like the thing that partakes of it.

Quite true.

It follows that the other things do not partake of Forms by being like them; we
must look for some other means by which they partake.

So it seems.

You see then, Socrates, said Parmenides, what great difficulties there are in asserting their existence as Forms just by themselves?

I do indeed.

I assure you, then, you have as yet hardly a notion of how great they will be, if
you are going to set up a single Form for every distinction you make among things.   b

How so?

The worst difficulty will be this, though there are plenty more. Suppose someone
should say that the Forms, if they are such as we are saying they must be, cannot even
be known. One could not convince him that he was mistaken in that objection, unless he
chanced to be a man of wide experience and natural ability, and were willing to follow
one through a long and remote train of argument. Otherwise there would be no way of
convincing a man who maintained that the Forms were unknowable.   c

Why so, Parmenides?

Because, Socrates, I imagine that you or anyone else who asserts that each of
them has a real being "just by itself," would admit, to begin with, that no such real being exists in our world.

True; for how could it then be just by itself?

Very good, said Parmenides. And further, those Forms which are what they are
with reference to one another, have their being in such references among themselves,
not with reference to those likenesses, or whatever we are to call them, in our world,   d
which we possess and so come to be called by their several names. And, on the other
hand, these things in our world which bear the same names as the Forms are related
among themselves, not to the Forms; and all the names of that sort that they bear have
reference to one another, not to the Forms.

How do you mean? asked Socrates.

Suppose, for instance, one of us is master or slave of another; he is not, of course,
the slave of Master itself, the essential Master, nor, if he is a master, is he master of   e
Slave itself, the essential Slave, but, being a man, is master or slave of another man;
whereas Mastership itself is what it is [mastership] of Slavery itself, and Slavery itself
is slavery to Mastership itself. The significance of things in our world is not with reference to things in that other world, nor have these their significance with reference to us;
but as I say, the things in that world are what they are with reference to one another and   134
towards one another; and so likewise are the things in our world. You see what I mean?

Certainly I do.

And similarly Knowledge itself, the essence of Knowledge, will be knowledge of
that Reality itself, the essentially real.

Certainly.

And again any given branch of Knowledge in itself will be knowledge of some department of real things as it is in itself, will it not?

Yes.

b   Whereas the knowledge in our world will be knowledge of the reality in our world; and it will follow again that each branch of knowledge in our world must be knowledge of some department of things that exist in our world.

Necessarily.

But, as you admit, we do not possess the Forms themselves, nor can they exist in our world.

No.

And presumably the Forms, just as they are in themselves, are known by the Form of Knowledge itself?

Yes.

The Form which we do not possess.

True.

Then, none of the Forms is known by us, since we have no part in Knowledge itself.

Apparently not.

c   So Beauty itself or Goodness itself and all the things we take as Forms in themselves, are unknowable to us.

I am afraid that is so.

Then here is a still more formidable consequence for you to consider.

What is that?

You will grant, I suppose, that if there is such a thing as a Form, Knowledge itself, it is much more perfect than the knowledge in our world; and so with Beauty and all the rest.

Yes.

And if anything has part in this Knowledge itself, you would agree that a god has a better title than anyone else to possess the most perfect knowledge?

Undoubtedly.

d   Then will the god, who possesses Knowledge itself, be able to know the things in our world?

Why not?

Because we have agreed that those Forms have no significance with reference to things in our world, nor have things in our world any significance with reference to them. Each set has it only among themselves.

Yes, we did.

Then if this most perfect Mastership and most perfect Knowledge are in the gods' world, the gods' Mastership can never be exercised over us, nor their Knowledge know

e   us or anything in our world. Just as we do not rule over them by virtue of rule as it exists in our world and we know nothing that is divine by our knowledge, so they, on the same principle, being gods, are not our masters nor do they know anything of human concerns.

But surely, said Socrates, an argument which would deprive the gods of knowledge, would be too strange.

135   And yet, Socrates, Parmenides went on, these difficulties and many more besides are inevitably involved in the Forms, if these characters of things really exist and one is going to distinguish each Form as a thing just by itself. The result is that the hearer is perplexed and inclined either to question their existence, or to contend that, if they do

exist, they must certainly be unknowable by our human nature. Moreover, there seems to be some weight in these objections, and, as we were saying, it is extraordinarily difficult to convert the objector. Only a man of exceptional gifts will be able to see that a Form, or essence just by itself, does exist in each case; and it will require someone still   b
more remarkable to discover it and to instruct another who has thoroughly examined all these difficulties.

I admit that, Parmenides; I quite agree with what you are saying.

But on the other hand, Parmenides continued, if, in view of all these difficulties and others like them, a man refuses to admit that Forms of things exist or to distinguish   c
a definite Form in every case, he will have nothing on which to fix his thought, so long as he will not allow that each thing has a character which is always the same; and in so doing he will completely destroy the significance of all discourse. But of that consequence I think you are only too well aware.

True.

What are you going to do about philosophy, then? Where will you turn while the answers to these questions remain unknown?

I can see no way out at the present moment.

That is because you are undertaking to define "Beautiful," "Just," "Good," and other particular Forms, too soon, before you have had a preliminary training. I noticed   d
that the other day when I heard you talking here with Aristoteles. Believe me, there is something noble and inspired in your passion for argument; but you must make an effort and submit yourself, while you are still young, to a severer training in what the world calls idle talk and condemns as useless. Otherwise, the truth will escape you.

THEAETETUS (in part)

SOCRATES: Do you fancy it is a small matter to discover the nature of knowledge? Is it   148c
not one of the hardest questions?

THEAETETUS: One of the very hardest, I should say.

SOCRATES: You may be reassured, then, about Theodorus' account of you, and set your mind on finding a definition of knowledge, as of anything else, with all the zeal   d
at your command.

THEAETETUS: If it depends on my zeal, Socrates, the truth will come to light.

SOCRATES: Forward, then, on the way you have just shown so well. Take as a model your answer about the roots: just as you found a single character to embrace all that multitude, so now try to find a single formula that applies to the many kinds of knowledge.

THEAETETUS: But I assure you, Socrates, I have often set myself to study that   e
problem, when I heard reports of the questions you ask. But I cannot persuade myself that I can give any satisfactory solution or that anyone has ever stated in my hearing the sort of answer you require. And yet I cannot get the question out of my mind.

Plato, *Theaetetus,* translated by F.M. Cornford from *The Collected Dialogues of Plato,* edited by Edith Hamilton and Huntington Cairns. Copyright © 1961 by PUP. Reprinted by permission of Princeton University Press.

SOCRATES: My dear Theaetetus, that is because your mind is not empty or barren. You are suffering the pains of travail.

THEAETETUS: I don't know about that, Socrates. I am only telling you how I feel.

149   SOCRATES: How absurd of you, never to have heard that I am the son of a midwife, a fine buxom woman called Phaenarete!

THEAETETUS: I have heard that.

SOCRATES: Have you also been told that I practise the same art?

THEAETETUS: No, never.

SOCRATES: It is true, though; only don't give away my secret. It is not known that I possess this skill; so the ignorant world describes me in other terms as an eccentric

b   person who reduces people to hopeless perplexity. Have you been told that too?

THEAETETUS: I have.

SOCRATES: Shall I tell you the reason?

THEAETETUS: Please do.

SOCRATES: Consider, then, how it is with all midwives; that will help you to understand what I mean. I dare say you know that they never attend other women in childbirth so long as they themselves can conceive and bear children, but only when they are too old for that.

THEAETETUS: Of course.

SOCRATES: They said that is because Artemis, the patroness of childbirth, is herself childless; and so, while she did not allow barren women to be midwives, because it

c   is beyond the power of human nature to achieve skill without any experience, she assigned the privilege to women who were past childbearing, out of respect to their likeness to herself.

THEAETETUS: That sounds likely.

SOCRATES: And it is more than likely, is it not, that no one can tell so well as a midwife whether women are pregnant or not?

THEAETETUS: Assuredly.

SOCRATES: Moreover, with the drugs and incantations they administer, midwives

d   can either bring on the pains of travail or allay them at their will, make a difficult labour easy, and at an early stage cause a miscarriage if they so decide.

THEAETETUS: True.

SOCRATES: Have you also observed that they are the cleverest matchmakers, having an unerring skill in selecting a pair whose marriage will produce the best children?

THEAETETUS: I was not aware of that.

SOCRATES: Well, you may be sure they pride themselves on that more than on

e   cutting the umbilical cord. Consider the knowledge of the sort of plant or seed that should be sown in any given soil; does not that go together with skill in tending and harvesting the fruits of the earth? They are not two different arts?

THEAETETUS: No, the same.

SOCRATES: And so with a woman; skill in the sowing is not to be separated from skill in the harvesting?

150   THEAETETUS: Probably not.

SOCRATES: No; only, because there is that wrong and ignorant way of bringing together man and woman which they call pandering, midwives, out of self-respect, are shy even of matchmaking, for fear of falling under the accusation of pandering. Yet the genuine midwife is the only successful matchmaker.

THEAETETUS: That is clear.

SOCRATES: All this, then, lies within the midwife's province; but her performance falls short of mine. It is not the way of women sometimes to bring forth real children,

sometimes mere phantoms, such that it is hard to tell the one from the other. If it were   b
so, the highest and noblest task of the midwife would be to discern the real from the unreal, would it not?

THEAETETUS: I agree.

SOCRATES: My art of midwifery is in general like theirs; the only difference is
that my patients are men, not women, and my concern is not with the body but with the
soul that is in travail of birth. And the highest point of my art is the power to prove by   c
every test whether the offspring of a young man's thought is a false phantom or instinct
with life and truth. I am so far like the midwife, that I cannot myself give birth to wisdom; and the common reproach is true, that, though I question others, I can myself
bring nothing to light because there is no wisdom in me. The reason is this: heaven constrains me to serve as a midwife, but has debarred me from giving birth. So of myself I   d
have no sort of wisdom, nor has any discovery ever been born to me as the child of my
soul. Those who frequent my company at first appear, some of them, quite unintelligent; but, as we go further with our discussions, all who are favoured by heaven make
progress at a rate that seems surprising to others as well as to themselves, although it is
clear that they have never learnt anything from me; the many admirable truths they
bring to birth have been discovered by themselves from within. But the delivery is
heaven's work and mine.

The proof of this is that many who have not been conscious of my assistance but   e
have made light of me, thinking it was all their own doing, have left me sooner than
they should, whether under others' influence or of their own motion, and thenceforward
suffered miscarriage of their thoughts through falling into bad company; and they have
lost the children of whom I had delivered them by bringing them up badly, caring more
for false phantoms than for the true; and so at last their lack of understanding has become apparent to themselves and to everyone else. Such a one was Aristides, son of   151
Lysimachus, and there have been many more. When they come back and beg for a re-
newal of our intercourse with extravagant protestations, sometimes the divine warning
that comes to me forbids it; with others it is permitted, and these begin again to make
progress. In yet another way, those who seek my company have the same experience as
a woman with child: they suffer the pains of labour and, by night and day, are full of
distress far greater than a woman's; and my art has power to bring on these pangs or to
allay them. So it fares with these; but there are some, Theaetetus, whose minds, as I   b
judge, have never conceived at all. I see that they have no need of me and with all good-
will I seek a match for them. Without boasting unduly, I can guess pretty well whose
society will profit them. I have arranged many of these matches with Prodicus, and with
other men of inspired sagacity.

And now for the upshot of this long discourse of mine. I suspect that, as you yourself believe, your mind is in labour with some thought it has conceived. Accept, then,
the ministration of a midwife's son who himself practises his mother's art, and do the
best you can to answer the questions I ask. Perhaps when I examine your statements I   c
may judge one or another of them to be an unreal phantom. If I then take the abortion
from you and cast it away, do not be savage with me like a woman robbed of her first
child. People have often felt like that towards me and been positively ready to bite me
for taking away some foolish notion they have conceived. They do not see that I am doing them a kindness. They have not learnt that no divinity is ever ill-disposed towards
man, nor is such action on my part due to unkindness; it is only that I am not permitted   d
to acquiesce in falsehood and suppress the truth.

So, Theaetetus, start again and try to explain what knowledge is. Never say it is
beyond your power; it will not be so, if heaven wills and you take courage.

THEAETETUS: Well, Socrates, with such encouragement from a person like you, it
e   would be a shame not to do one's best to say what one can. It seems to me that one who
knows something is perceiving the thing he knows, and, so far as I can see at present,
knowledge is nothing but perception.

SOCRATES: Good; that is the right spirit in which to express one's opinion. But
now suppose we examine your offspring together, and see whether it is a mere wind-
egg or has some life in it. Perception, you say, is knowledge?

THEAETETUS: Yes.

SOCRATES: The account you give of the nature of knowledge is not, by any
152   means, to be despised. It is the same that was given by Protagoras, though he stated it in
a somewhat different way. He says, you will remember, that "man is the measure of all
things—alike of the being of things that are and of the not-being of things that are not."
No doubt you have read that.

THEAETETUS: Yes, often.

SOCRATES: He puts it in this sort of way, doesn't he?—that any given thing "is to
me such as it appears to me, and is to you such as it appears to you," you and I being
men.

THEAETETUS: Yes, that is how he puts it.

b   SOCRATES: Well, what a wise man says is not likely to be nonsense. So let us follow up his meaning. Sometimes, when the same wind is blowing, one of us feels chilly,
the other does not; or one may feel slightly chilly, the other quite cold.

THEAETETUS: Certainly.

SOCRATES: Well, in that case are we to say that the wind in itself is cold or not
cold? Or shall we agree with Protagoras that it is cold to the one who feels chilly, and
not to the other?

THEAETETUS: That seems reasonable.

SOCRATES: And further that it so "appears" to each of us?

THEAETETUS: Yes.

SOCRATES: And "appears" means that he "perceives" it so?

THEAETETUS: True.

c   SOCRATES: "Appearing," then, is the same thing as "perceiving," in the case of
what is hot or anything of that kind. They *are* to each man such as he *perceives* them.

THEAETETUS: So it seems.

SOCRATES: Perception, then, is always of something that is, and, as being knowledge, it is infallible.

THEAETETUS: That is clear.

* * *

155b   SOCRATES: . . . When we say that I, being of the height you see, without gaining or
losing in size, may within a year be taller (as I am now) than a youth like you, and later
on be shorter, not because I have lost anything in bulk, but because you have grown. For
apparently I am later what I was not before, and yet have not become so; for without the
c   process of becoming the result is impossible, and I could not be in process of becoming
shorter without losing some of my bulk. I could give you countless other examples, if
we are to accept these. For I think you follow me, Theaetetus; I fancy, at any rate, such
puzzles are not altogether strange to you.

THEAETETUS: No; indeed it is extraordinary how they set me wondering whatever
they can mean. Sometimes I get quite dizzy with thinking of them.

d   SOCRATES: That shows that Theodorus was not wrong in his estimate of your nature. This sense of wonder is the mark of the philosopher. Philosophy indeed has no

other origin, and he was a good genealogist who made Iris [philosophy] the daughter of Thaumas [wonder]. Do you now begin to see the explanation of all this which follows from the theory we are attributing to Protagoras? Or is it not yet clear?

THEAETETUS: I can't say it is yet.

SOCRATES: Then perhaps you will be grateful if I help you to penetrate to the truth concealed in the thoughts of a man—or, I should say, of men—of such distinction.

THEAETETUS: Of course I shall be very grateful.   e

SOCRATES: Then just take a look round and make sure that none of the uninitiate overhears us. I mean by the uninitiate the people who believe that nothing is real save what they can grasp with their hands and do not admit that actions or processes or anything invisible can count as real.

THEAETETUS: They sound like a very hard and repellent sort of people.

* * *

SOCRATES: You have an absolute passion for discussion, Theodorus. I like the way you   161a
take me for a sort of bag full of arguments, and imagine I can easily pull out a proof to
show that our conclusion is wrong. You don't see what is happening: the arguments   b
never come out of me, they always come from the person I am talking with. I am only
at a slight advantage in having the skill to get some account of the matter from another's
wisdom and entertain it with fair treatment. So now, I shall not give any explanation
myself, but try to get it out of our friend.

THEODORUS: That is better, Socrates; do as you say.

* * *

SOCRATES: Let us look at it in this way, then—this question whether knowledge and   163a
perception are, after all, the same thing or not. For that, you remember, was the point to
which our whole discussion was directed, and it was for its sake that we stirred up all
this swarm of queer doctrines, wasn't it?

THEAETETUS: Quite true.   b

SOCRATES: Well, are we going to agree that, whenever we perceive something by sight or hearing, we also at the same time know it? Take the case of a foreign language we have not learnt. Are we to say that we do not hear the sounds that foreigners utter, or that we both hear and know what they are saying? Or again, when we don't know our letters, are we to maintain that we don't see them when we look at them, or that, since we see them, we do know them?

THEAETETUS: We shall say, Socrates, that we know just so much of them as we do see or hear. The shape and colour of the letters we both see and know; we hear and   c
at the same time know the rising and falling accents of the voice; but we neither perceive by sight and hearing nor yet know what a schoolmaster or an interpreter could tell us about them.

SOCRATES: Well done, Theaetetus. I had better not raise objections to that, for fear of checking your growth. But look, here is another objection threatening. How are we going to parry it?

THEAETETUS: What is that?

SOCRATES: It is this. Suppose someone were to ask: "Is it possible for a man who   d
has once come to know something and still preserves a memory of it, not to know just that thing that he remembers at the moment when he remembers it?" This is, perhaps, rather a long-winded way of putting the question. I mean: Can a man who has become acquainted with something and remembers it, not know it?

THEAETETUS: Of course not, Socrates; the supposition is monstrous.

SOCRATES: Perhaps I am talking nonsense, then. But consider: you call seeing "perceiving," and sight "perception," don't you?

THEAETETUS: I do.

SOCRATES: Then, according to our earlier statement, a man who sees something
e   acquires from that moment knowledge of the thing he sees?

THEAETETUS: Yes.

SOCRATES: Again, you recognise such a thing as memory?

THEAETETUS: Yes.

SOCRATES: Memory of nothing, or of something?

THEAETETUS: Of something, surely.

SOCRATES: Of what one has become acquainted with and perceived—that sort of thing?

THEAETETUS: Of course.

SOCRATES: So a man sometimes remembers what he has seen?

THEAETETUS: He does.

SOCRATES: Even when he shuts his eyes? Or does he forget when he shuts them?
164   THEAETETUS: No, Socrates; that would be a monstrous thing to say.

SOCRATES: All the same, we shall have to say it, if we are to save our former statement. Otherwise, it goes by the board.

THEAETETUS: I certainly have a suspicion that you are right, but I don't quite see how. You must tell me.

SOCRATES: In this way. One who sees, we say, acquires knowledge of what he sees, because it is agreed that sight or perception and knowledge are the same thing.

THEAETETUS: Certainly.

SOCRATES: But suppose this man who sees and acquires knowledge of what he has seen, shuts his eyes; then he remembers the thing, but does not see it. Isn't that so?

THEAETETUS: Yes.

b   SOCRATES: But "does not see it" means "does not know it," since "sees" and "knows" mean the same.

THEAETETUS: True.

SOCRATES: Then the conclusion is that a man who has come to know a thing and still remembers it does not know it, since he does not see it; and we said that would be a monstrous conclusion.

THEAETETUS: Quite true.

SOCRATES: Apparently, then, if you say that knowledge and perception are the same thing, it leads to an impossibility.

THEAETETUS: So it seems.

SOCRATES: Then we shall have to say they are different.

THEAETETUS: I suppose so.

* * *

165e   SOCRATES: And now, perhaps, you may wonder what argument Protagoras will find to defend his position. Shall we try to put it into words?

THEAETETUS: By all means.

SOCRATES: No doubt, then, Protagoras will make all the points we have put for-
166   ward in our attempt to defend him, and at the same time will come to close quarters with the assailant, dismissing us with contempt. Your admirable Socrates, he will say, finds a little boy who is scared at being asked whether one and the same person can remem-

ber and at the same time not know one and the same thing. When the child is frightened into saying No, because he cannot foresee the consequence, Socrates turns the conversation so as to make a figure of fun of my unfortunate self. You take things much too easily, Socrates. The truth of the matter is this: when you ask someone questions in order to canvass some opinion of mine and he is found tripping, then I am refuted only if his answers are such as I should have given; if they are different, it is he who is refuted, not I. For instance, do you think you will find anyone to admit that one's present memory of a past impression is an impression of the same character as one had during the original experience, which is now over? It is nothing of the sort. Or again, will anyone shrink from admitting that it is possible for the same person to know and not to know the same thing? Or, if he is frightened of saying that, will he ever allow that a person who is changed is the *same* as he was before the change occurred; or rather, that he is *one* person at all, and not several, indeed an infinite succession of persons, provided change goes on happening—if we are really to be on the watch against one another's attempts to catch at words?

No, he will say; show a more generous spirit by attacking what I actually say; and prove, if you can, that we have not, each one of us, his peculiar perceptions, or that, granting them to be peculiar, it would not follow that what appears to each becomes— or is, if we may use the word "is"—for him alone to whom it appears. With this talk of pigs and baboons, you are behaving like a pig yourself, and, what is more, you tempt your hearers to treat my writings in the same way, which is not fair. For I do indeed assert that the truth is as I have written: each one of us is a measure of what is and of what is not; but there is all the difference in the world between one man and another just in the very fact that what is and appears to one is different from what is and appears to the other. And as for wisdom and the wise man, I am very far from saying they do not exist. By a wise man I mean precisely a man who can change any one of us, when what is bad appears and is to him, and make what is good appear and be to him. In this statement, again, don't set off in chase of words, but let me explain still more clearly what I mean. Remember how it was put earlier in the conversation: to the sick man his food appears sour and is so; to the healthy man it is and appears the opposite. Now there is no call to represent either of the two as wiser—that cannot be—nor is the sick man to be pronounced unwise because he thinks as he does, or the healthy man wise because he thinks differently. What is wanted is a change to the opposite condition, because the other state is better.

And so too in education a change has to be effected from the worse condition to the better; only, whereas the physician produces a change by means of drugs, the sophist does it by discourse. It is not that a man makes someone who previously thought what is false think what is true (for it is not possible either to think the thing that is not or to think anything but what one experiences, and all experiences are true); rather, I should say, when someone by reason of a depraved condition of mind has thoughts of a like character, one makes him, by reason of a sound condition, think other and sound thoughts, which some people ignorantly call true, whereas I should say that one set of thoughts is better than the other, but not in any way truer. And as for the wise, my dear Socrates, so far from calling them frogs, I call them, when they have to do with the body, physicians, and when they have to do with plants, husbandmen. For I assert that husbandmen too, when plants are sickly and have depraved sensations, substitute for these sensations that are sound and healthy; and moreover that wise and honest public speakers substitute in the community sound for unsound views of what is right. For I hold that whatever practices seem right and laudable to any particular State are so, for that State, so long as it holds by them. Only, when the practices are, in any particular

b

c

d

e

167

b

c

case, unsound for them, the wise man substitutes others that are and appear sound. On the same principle the sophist, since he can in the same manner guide his pupils in the

d way they should go, is wise and worth a considerable fee to them when their education is completed. In this way it is true both that some men are wiser than others and that no one thinks falsely; and you, whether you like it or not, must put up with being a measure, since by these considerations my doctrine is saved from shipwreck.

Now if you can dispute this doctrine in principle, do so by argument stating the case on the other side, or by asking questions, if you prefer that method, which has no terrors for a man of sense; on the contrary it ought to be specially agreeable to him.

e Only there is this rule to be observed: do not conduct your questioning unfairly. It is very unreasonable that one who professes a concern for virtue should be constantly guilty of unfairness in argument. Unfairness here consists in not observing the distinction between a debate and a conversation. A debate need not be taken seriously and one may trip up an opponent to the best of one's power; but a conversation should be taken in earnest; one should help out the other party and bring home to him only those slips

168 and fallacies that are due to himself or to his earlier instructors. If you follow this rule, your associates will lay the blame for their confusions and perplexities on themselves and not on you; they will like you and court your society, and disgusted with themselves, will turn to philosophy, hoping to escape from their former selves and become different men. But if, like so many, you take the opposite course, you will reach the opposite result: instead of turning your companions to philosophy, you will make them

b hate the whole business when they get older. So, if you will take my advice, you will meet us in the candid spirit I spoke of, without hostility or contentiousness, and honestly consider what we mean when we say that all things are in motion and that what seems also is, to any individual or community. The further question whether knowledge is, or is not, the same thing as perception, you will consider as a consequence of these

c principles, not (as you did just now) basing your argument on the common use of words and phrases, which the vulgar twist into any sense they please and so perplex one another in all sorts of ways.

* * *

169d SOCRATES: Let us begin, then, by coming to grips with the doctrine at the same point as before. Let us see whether or not our discontent was justified, when we criticised it as making every individual self-sufficient in wisdom. Protagoras then conceded that some people were superior in the matter of what is better or worse, and these, he said, were wise. Didn't he?

THEODORUS: Yes.

SOCRATES: If he were here himself to make that admission, instead of our con-

e ceding it for him in our defence, there would be no need to reopen the question and make sure of our ground; but, as things are, we might be said to have no authority to make the admission on his behalf. So it will be more satisfactory to come to a more complete and clear agreement on this particular point; for it makes a considerable difference, whether this is so or not.

THEODORUS: That is true.

170 SOCRATES: Let us, then, as briefly as possible, obtain his agreement, not through any third person, but from his own statement.

THEODORUS: How?

SOCRATES: In this way. He says—doesn't he?—that what seems true to anyone is true for him to whom it seems so?

THEODORUS: He does.

SOCRATES: Well now, Protagoras, we are expressing what seems true to a man, or rather to all men, when we say that everyone without exception holds that in some respects he is wiser than his neighbours and in others they are wiser than he. For instance, in moments of great danger and distress, whether in war or in sickness or at sea, men regard as a god anyone who can take control of the situation and look to him as a saviour, when his only point of superiority is his knowledge. Indeed, the world is full of people looking for those who can instruct and govern men and animals and direct their doings, and on the other hand of people who think themselves quite competent to undertake the teaching and governing. In all these cases what can we say, if not that men do hold that wisdom and ignorance exist among them?

THEODORUS: We must say that.

SOCRATES: And they hold that wisdom lies in thinking truly, and ignorance in false belief?

THEODORUS: Of course.

SOCRATES: In that case, Protagoras, what are we to make of your doctrine? Are we to say that what men think is always true, or that it is sometimes true and sometimes false? From either supposition it results that their thoughts are not always true, but both true and false. For consider, Theodorus. Are you, or is any Protagorean, prepared to maintain that no one regards anyone else as ignorant or as making false judgments?

THEODORUS: That is incredible, Socrates.

SOCRATES: That, however, is the inevitable consequence of the doctrine which makes man the measure of all things.

THEODORUS: How so?

SOCRATES: When you have formed a judgment on some matter in your own mind and express an opinion about it to me, let us grant that, as Protagoras' theory says, it is true for you; but are we to understand that it is impossible for us, the rest of the company, to pronounce any judgment upon your judgment; or, if we can, that we always pronounce your opinion to be true? Do you not rather find thousands of opponents who set their opinion against yours on every occasion and hold that your judgment and belief are false?

THEODORUS: I should just think so, Socrates; thousands and tens of thousands, as Homer says; and they give me all the trouble in the world.

SOCRATES: And what then? Would you have us say that in such a case the opinion you hold is true for yourself and false for these tens of thousands?

THEODORUS: The doctrine certainly seems to imply that.

SOCRATES: And what is the consequence for Protagoras himself? Is it not this: supposing that not even he believed in man being the measure and the world in general did not believe it either—as in fact it doesn't—then this *Truth* which he wrote would not be true for anyone? If, on the other hand, he did believe it, but the mass of mankind does not agree with him, then, you see, it is more false than true by just so much as the unbelievers outnumber the believers.

THEODORUS: That follows, if its truth or falsity varies with each individual opinion.

SOCRATES: Yes, and besides that it involves a really exquisite conclusion. Protagoras, for his part, admitting as he does that everybody's opinion is true, must acknowledge the truth of his opponents' belief about his own belief, where they think he is wrong.

THEODORUS: Certainly.

b   SOCRATES: That is to say, he would acknowledge his own belief to be false, if he admits that the belief of those who think him wrong is true?

THEODORUS: Necessarily.

SOCRATES: But the others, on their side, do not admit to themselves that they are wrong.

THEODORUS: No.

SOCRATES: Whereas Protagoras, once more, according to what he has written, admits that this opinion of theirs is as true as any other.

THEODORUS: Evidently.

SOCRATES: On all hands, then, Protagoras included, his opinion will be disputed, or rather Protagoras will join in the general consent—when he admits to an opponent

c   the truth of his contrary opinion, from that moment Protagoras himself will be admitting that a dog or the man in the street is not a measure of anything whatever that he does not understand. Isn't that so?

THEODORUS: Yes.

SOCRATES: Then, since it is disputed by everyone, the *Truth* of Protagoras is true to nobody—to himself no more than to anyone else.

THEODORUS: We are running my old friend too hard, Socrates.

SOCRATES: But it is not clear that we are outrunning the truth, my friend. Of

d   course it is likely that, as an older man, he was wiser than we are; and if at this moment he could pop his head up through the ground there as far as to the neck, very probably he would expose me thoroughly for talking such nonsense and you for agreeing to it, before he sank out of sight and took to his heels. However, we must do our best with such lights as we have and continue to say what we think.

* * *

174   THEODORUS: What do you mean, Socrates?

SOCRATES: The same thing as the story about the Thracian maidservant who exercised her wit at the expense of Thales, when he was looking up to study the stars and tumbled down a well. She scoffed at him for being so eager to know what was happening in the sky that he could not see what lay at his feet. Anyone who gives his life to phi-

b   losophy is open to such mockery. It is true that he is unaware what his next-door neighbour is doing, hardly knows, indeed, whether the creature is a man at all; he spends all his pains on the question, what man is, and what powers and properties distinguish such a nature from any other. You see what I mean, Theodorus?

THEODORUS: Yes; and it is true.

SOCRATES: And so, my friend, as I said at first, on a public occasion or in private

c   company, in a law court or anywhere else, when he is forced to talk about what lies at his feet or is before his eyes, the whole rabble will join the maidservants in laughing at him, as from inexperience he walks blindly and stumbles into every pitfall. His terrible clumsiness makes him seem so stupid. He cannot engage in an exchange of abuse, for, never having made a study of anyone's peculiar weaknesses, he has no personal scan-

d   dals to bring up; so in his helplessness he looks a fool. When people vaunt their own or other men's merits, his unaffected laughter makes him conspicuous and they think he is frivolous. When a despot or king is eulogised, he fancies he is hearing some keeper of swine or sheep or cows being congratulated on the quantity of milk he has squeezed out of his flock; only he reflects that the animal that princes tend and milk is more given than sheep or cows to nurse a sullen grievance, and that a herdsman of this sort, penned

e   up in his castle, is doomed by sheer press of work to be as rude and uncultivated as the shepherd in his mountain fold. He hears of the marvellous wealth of some landlord who owns ten thousand acres or more; but that seems a small matter to one accustomed to think of the earth as a whole. When they harp upon birth—some gentleman who can point to seven generations of wealthy ancestors—he thinks that such commendation must come from men of purblind vision, too uneducated to keep their eyes fixed on the whole or to reflect that any man has had countless myriads of ancestors and among them any number of rich men and beggars, kings and slaves, Greeks and barbarians. To pride oneself on a catalogue of twenty-five progenitors going back to Heracles, son of Amphitryon, strikes him as showing a strange pettiness of outlook. He laughs at a man who cannot rid his mind of foolish vanity by reckoning that before Amphitryon there was a twenty-fifth ancestor, and before him a fiftieth, whose fortunes were as luck would have it. But in all these matters the world has the laugh of the philosopher, partly because he seems arrogant, partly because of his helpless ignorance in matters of daily life,

175

b

THEODORUS: Yes, Socrates, that is exactly what happens.

SOCRATES: On the other hand, my friend, when the philosopher drags the other upwards to a height at which he may consent to drop the question "What injustice have I done to you or you to me?" and to think about justice and injustice in themselves, what each is, and how they differ from one another and from anything else; or to stop quoting poetry about the happiness of kings or of men with gold in store and think about the meaning of kingship and the whole question of human happiness and misery, what their nature is, and how humanity can gain the one and escape the other—in all this field, when that small, shrewd, legal mind has to render an account, then the situation is reversed. Now it is he who is dizzy from hanging at such an unaccustomed height and looking down from mid-air. Lost and dismayed and stammering, he will be laughed at, not by maidservants or the uneducated—they will not see what is happening—but by everyone whose breeding has been the antithesis of a slave's.

c

d

Such are the two characters, Theodorus. The one is nursed in freedom and leisure, the philosopher, as you call him. He may be excused if he looks foolish or useless when faced with some menial task, if he cannot tie up bedclothes into a neat bundle or flavour a dish with spices and a speech with flattery. The other is smart in the dispatch of all such services, but has not learnt to wear his cloak like a gentleman, or caught the accent of discourse that will rightly celebrate the true life of happiness for gods and men.

e

176

THEODORUS: If you could convince everyone, Socrates, as you convince me, there would be more peace and fewer evils in the world.

SOCRATES: Evils, Theodorus, can never be done away with, for the good must always have its contrary; nor have they any place in the divine world; but they must needs haunt this region of our mortal nature. That is why we should make all speed to take flight from this world to the other; and that means becoming like the divine so far as we can, and that again is to become righteous with the help of wisdom. But it is no such easy matter to convince men that the reasons for avoiding wickedness and seeking after goodness are not those which the world gives. The right motive is not that one should seem innocent and good—that is no better, to my thinking, than an old wives' tale—but let us state the truth in this way. In the divine there is no shadow of unrighteousness, only the perfection of righteousness; and nothing is more like the divine than any one of us who becomes as righteous as possible. It is here that a man shows his true spirit and power or lack of spirit and nothingness. For to know this is wisdom and excellence of the genuine sort; not to know it is to be manifestly blind and base. All other forms of seeming power and intelligence in the rulers of society are as mean and vulgar as the mechanic's skill in handicraft. If a man's words and deeds are unrighteous and profane,

b

c

d

he had best not persuade himself that he is a great man because he sticks at nothing, glorying in his shame as such men do when they fancy that others say of them: They are no fools, no useless burdens to the earth, but men of the right sort to weather the storms of public life.

Let the truth be told: they are what they fancy they are not, all the more for deceiving themselves; for they are ignorant of the very thing it most concerns them to know—the penalty of injustice. This is not, as they imagine, stripes and death, which do not always fall on the wrong-doer, but a penalty that cannot be escaped.

e

THEODORUS: What penalty is that?

SOCRATES: There are two patterns, my friend, in the unchangeable nature of things, one of divine happiness, the other of godless misery—a truth to which their folly makes them utterly blind, unaware that in doing injustice they are growing less like one of these patterns and more like the other. The penalty they pay is the life they lead, answering to the pattern they resemble. But if we tell them that, unless they rid themselves of their superior cunning, that other region which is free from all evil will not receive them after death, but here on earth they will dwell for all time in some form of life resembling their own and in the society of things as evil as themselves, all this will sound like foolishness to such strong and unscrupulous minds.

177

THEODORUS: So it will, Socrates.

b

SOCRATES: I have good reason to know it, my friend. But there is one thing about them: when you get them alone and make them explain their objections to philosophy, then, if they are men enough to face a long examination without running away, it is odd how they end by finding their own arguments unsatisfying; somehow their flow of eloquence runs dry, and they become as speechless as an infant.

All this, however, is a digression; we must stop now, and dam the flood of topics that threatens to break in and drown our original argument. With your leave, let us go back to where we were before.

c

THEODORUS: For my part, I rather prefer listening to your digressions, Socrates; they are easier to follow at my time of life. However, let us go back, if you like.

* * *

189e

SOCRATES: Do you accept my description of the process of thinking?

THEAETETUS: How do you describe it?.

SOCRATES: As a discourse that the mind carries on with itself about any subject it is considering. You must take this explanation as coming from an ignoramus; but I have a notion that, when the mind is thinking, it is simply talking to itself, asking questions and answering them, and saying Yes or No. When it reaches a decision—which may come slowly or in a sudden rush—when doubt is over and the two voices affirm the same thing, then we call that its "judgment." So I should describe thinking as discourse, and judgment as a statement pronounced, not aloud to someone else, but silently to oneself.

190

THEAETETUS: I agree.

SOCRATES: It seems, then, that when a person thinks of one thing as another, he is affirming to himself that the one is the other.

* * *

210

SOCRATES: So, apparently, to the question, What is knowledge? our definition will reply: "Correct belief together with knowledge of a differentness," for, according to it, "adding an account" will come to that.

THEAETETUS: So it seems.

SOCRATES: Yes; and when we are inquiring after the nature of knowledge, nothing could be sillier than to say that it is correct belief together with a *knowledge* of differentness or of anything whatever.

So, Theaetetus, neither perception, nor true belief, nor the addition of an "account" to true belief can be knowledge.   b

THEAETETUS: Apparently not.

SOCRATES: Are we in labour, then, with any further child, my friend, or have we brought to birth all we have to say about knowledge?

THEAETETUS: Indeed we have; and for my part I have already, thanks to you, given utterance to more than I had in me.

SOCRATES: All of which our midwife's skill pronounces to be mere wind eggs and not worth the rearing?

THEAETETUS: Undoubtedly.

SOCRATES: Then supposing you should ever henceforth try to conceive afresh, Theaetetus, if you succeed, your embryo thoughts will be the better as a consequence of   c
today's scrutiny; and if you remain barren, you will be gentler and more agreeable to your companions, having the good sense not to fancy you know what you do not know. For that, and no more, is all that my art can effect; nor have I any of that knowledge possessed by all the great and admirable men of our own day or of the past. But this midwife's art is a gift from heaven; my mother had it for women, and I for young men of a generous spirit and for all in whom beauty dwells.   d

Now I must go to the portico of the King-Archon to meet the indictment which Meletus has drawn up against me. But tomorrow morning, Theodorus, let us meet here again.

Aristotle
384–322 B.C.

Aristotle was born in Stagira, on the border of Macedonia. His mother, Phaestis, was from a family of doctors, and his father, Nicomachus, was the court physician to the king of Macedonia. At seventeen Aristotle was sent to Athens. There he studied in Plato's Academy for two decades, but, as he later wrote, he loved the truth more than he loved Plato, and so he had no mind to remain a mere disciple. In 347, after Plato's death, he left Athens and spent the next four years conducting zoological investigations on the islands of Assos and Lesbos.

About 343 he was called to Macedonia by King Philip to tutor the king's son—the future Alexander the Great. Upon Alexander's ascension to the throne seven years later, Aristotle returned to Athens to set up the Lyceum, a rival to the Academy. Aristotle did much of his teaching walking up and down the colonnades with advanced students. As a result, his school and philosophy came to be called by the Greek word for walking around: "peripatetic." Tradition has it that as Alexander the Great moved east, conquering Persia and moving into India, he would send back biological specimens for Aristotle's school. While most scholars doubt this popular story, it is nevertheless clear that under Alexander's patronage, the Lyceum flourished.

However, the connection to Alexander proved a liability in the end. On Alexander's death in 323 B.C., the Athenians went on a rampage against any or all associated with him. Indicted on charges of impiety, Aristotle fled Athens, "lest," as he put it, "the Athenians sin twice against philosophy" (referring, of course, to the unjust trial and death of Socrates). Aristotle died a year later. A popular but again highly questionable story says he drowned investigating marine life.

There is no doubt that after Plato, Aristotle is the most influential philosopher of all time. In the early Middle Ages his thought was preserved and commented upon by the great Arab philosophers. He dominated later medieval philosophy to such an extent that St. Thomas referred to him simply as *philosophus*, "the philosopher." Logic, as taught until about the time of the Second World War, was essentially Aristotle's logic. His *Poetics* is still a classic of literary criticism, and his dicta on tragedy are widely accepted even today. Criticism of Aristotle's metaphysical and epistemological views has spread ever since Bacon and Descartes inaugurated modern philosophy; but for all that, the problems Aristotle saw, the distinctions he introduced, and the terms he defined are still central in many, if not most, philosophical discussions. His influence and prestige, like Plato's, are international and beyond all schools.

* * *

Aristotle found Plato's theory of Forms unacceptable. Like Plato, he wanted to discover universals, but he did not believe they existed apart from particulars. The form of a chair, for instance, can be thought of apart from the matter out of which the chair is made, but the form does not subsist as a separate invisible entity. The universal of "chairness" exists only in particular chairs—there is no otherworldly "Form of Chairness." Accordingly, Aristotle began his philosophy not with reflection on or dialogue about eternal Forms but with observations of particular objects.

In observing the world, Aristotle saw four "causes" that are responsible for making an object what it is: the material, formal, efficient, and final. In the case of a chair, for example, the chair's material cause would be its wood and cloth, its formal cause would be the structure or form given in its plan or blueprint, its efficient cause would be the worker who made it, and its final cause would be sitting. The material cause, then, is that *out of which* a thing is made, the formal cause is that *into which* a thing is made, the efficient cause is that *by which* a thing is made, and the final cause is that *for which* a thing is made. It is the last of these, the final cause, that Aristotle held to be most important, for it determined the other three. The goal or end (*telos* in Greek), the final cause, of any given substance is the key to its understanding. This means that all nature is to be understood in terms of final causes or purposes. This is known as a "teleological" explanation of reality.

As Aristotle applied these insights to human beings, he asked what the *telos* of a person could be. By observing what is unique to persons and what they, in fact, do seek, Aristotle came to the conclusion that the highest good or end for humans is *eudaimonia*. While this word is generally translated as "happiness," one must be careful to acknowledge that Aristotle's understanding of "happiness" is rather different from ours. *Eudaimonia* happiness is not a feeling of euphoria—in fact, it is not a feeling at all. It is rather "activity in accordance with virtue." Much of the material from the *Nicomachean Ethics* presented here is devoted both to clarifying the word and to discovering how this kind of "happiness" is to be achieved.

* * *

Aristotle's works lack the literary grace of Plato's. Like Plato, Aristotle is said to have written popular dialogues—the "exoteric" writings intended for those who were not students at the Lyceum—but they have not survived. What we have instead are the difficult "esoteric" works: lecture notes for classes at school. According to some scholars, these are not even Aristotle's notes, but the notes of students collected by editors. In any case, the writings as we have them contain much overlapping, repetition, and apparent contradiction.

The first five chapters of the *Categories,* with which we begin, help clear up a number of questions about Aristotle's conception of substance. Written as a treatise on language, the *Categories* makes clear why Aristotle rejected Plato's approach to knowledge of the Forms. The selection is given in J.L. Ackrill's translation.

The *Posterior Analytics,* which deals with the forms of argument and inquiry, is divided into two books. The selection from Book I included here deals with the nature of knowledge, demonstration, and truth and defines several key terms. The material from Book II considers the four possible forms of inquiry and explains how the individual mind comes to know the basic truths. The translation is by Jonathan Barnes.

Books I and II of the *Physics* deal with some of the main questions of physical science. After establishing the nature of first principles, Aristotle uses actuality and potentiality to explain being and change. And making a distinction between physics and mathematics, he discusses the four causes. This work is translated by R.P. Hardie and R.K. Gaye.

The *Metaphysics* probably consists of several independent treatises. Book I *(Alpha)* of this collection develops Aristotle's four causes and reviews the history of philosophy to his time. Book XII *(Lambda)* employs many of the concepts previously introduced, such as substance, actuality, and potency, and then moves to Aristotle's theology of the Unmoved Mover. The work concludes with Aristotle's rejection of Platonic Forms as separate, mathematical entities. Apparently Aristotle was responding to Plato's successors who emphasized the mathematical nature of the Forms. W.D. Ross is the translator.

The first part of the selection presented from Aristotle's *On the Soul (De Anima)* gives a definition of the soul and distinguishes its faculties. The second part discusses the passive and the active mind. As this selection makes clear, Aristotle rejected Plato's view of a soul separate from the body. The selection is given in the translation by J.A. Smith.

Our final selection, the *Nicomachean Ethics,* is still considered one of the greatest works in ethics. Named for Aristotle's son, Nicomachus, it discusses the nature of the good and of moral and intellectual virtues, as well as investigating specific virtues. The lengthy selection presented here (about one-half of the complete work) reflects this vast range of topics and includes discussions of the subject matter and nature of ethics; of the good for an individual; of moral virtue; of the mean; of the conditions of responsibility for an action; of pride, vanity, humility, and the great-souled man (Aristotle's ideal); of the superiority of loving over being loved; and finally, of human happiness. The translation is W.D. Ross's, revised by J.O. Urmson.

The marginal page numbers, with their "a" and "b," are those of all scholarly editions—Greek, English, German, French, and others.

* * *

W.K.C. Guthrie, *A History of Greek Philosophy, VI: Aristotle: An Encounter* (Cambridge: Cambridge University Press, 1981), gives clear guidance to students, as does the classic W.D. Ross, *Aristotle* (1923; reprinted New York: Meridian Books, 1959). A.E. Taylor, *Aristotle* (New York: Dover, 1955); John Herman Randall, Jr., *Aristotle* (New York: Columbia University Press, 1960); Marjorie Grene, *A Portrait of Aristotle* (Chicago: University of Chicago Press, 1963); J.L. Ackrill, *Aristotle the Philosopher* (Oxford: Oxford University Press, 1981); and Jonathan Barnes, *Aristotle* (Oxford: Oxford University Press, 1982) also provide helpful overviews of Aristotle's thought; while Werner Jaeger, *Aristotle: Fundamentals of the History of His Development,* translated by Richard Robinson (Oxford: Clarendon Press, 1934) is a standard biography. For general collections of essays, see R. Bambrough, ed., *New Essays on Plato and Aristotle* (London: Routledge & Kegan Paul, 1965); J.M.E. Moravcsik, ed., *Aristotle: A Collection of Critical Essays* (New York: Anchor Doubleday, 1967); and J. Barnes, M. Schofield, and R. Sorabji, eds., *Articles on Aristotle: Ethics and Politics* (London: Duckworth, 1979). For help with specific works (besides the *Nicomachean Ethics*), see Helen S. Lang, *Aristotle's Physics and Its Medieval Varieties* (Albany: SUNY Press, 1992); Martha C. Nussbaum and Amelie O. Rorty, eds., *Essays on Aristotle's De Anima* (Oxford: Oxford University Press, 1992); and W.D. Ross, ed., *Aristotle's Metaphysics* (Oxford: Clarendon Press, 1924). The *Nichomachean Ethics* has been such an influential book that many commentaries and essays have been written about it. Among these are H.H. Joachim, *Aristotle: The Nicomachean Ethics,* edited by D.A. Rees (Oxford: Clarendon Press, 1951); W.F.R. Hardie, *Aristotle's Ethical Theory,* 2nd ed. (Oxford: Oxford University Press, 1980); Amelie O. Rorty, ed., *Essays on Aristotle's Ethics* (Berkeley: University of California Press, 1980); J.O. Urmson, *Aristotle's Ethics* (Oxford: Basil Blackwell, 1988); and Sarah Brodie, *Ethics with Aristotle* (Oxford: Oxford University Press, 1991). Alasdair C. MacIntyre's pair of books, *After Virtue: A Study in Moral Theory* (Notre Dame, IN: University of Notre Dame Press, 1981), and *Whose Justice? Which Rationality?* (Notre Dame, IN: University of Notre Dame Press, 1988), are interesting examples of recent attempts to apply Aristotle's ethics to contemporary moral problems.

CATEGORIES (in part)

CHAPTER 1

When things have only a name in common and the definition of being which corresponds to the name is different, they are called *homonymous.* Thus, for example, both a man and a picture are animals. These have only a name in common and the definition of being which corresponds to the name is different; for if one is to say what being an animal is for each of them, one will give two distinct definitions.   1a

5

Aristotle, *Categories,* Chapters 1–5 from *Aristotle's Categories and De Interpetatione,* translated by J.L. Ackrill (Oxford: Oxford University Press, 1963). Reprinted by permission of Oxford University Press.

When things have the name in common and the definition of being which corresponds to the name is the same, they are called *synonymous*. Thus, for example, both a man and an ox are animals. Each of these is called by a common name, "animal," and
10 the definition of being is also the same; for if one is to give the definition of each—what being an animal is for each of them—one will give the same definition.

When things get their name from something, with a difference of ending, they are called *paronymous*. Thus, for example, the grammarian gets his name from grammar,
15 the brave get theirs from bravery.

CHAPTER 2

Of things that are said, some involve combination while others are said without combination. Examples of those involving combination are "man runs," "man wins"; and of those without combination "man," "ox," "runs," "wins."
20 Of things there are: *(a)* some are *said of* a subject but are not *in* any subject. For example, man is said of a subject, the individual man, but is not in any subject. *(b)* Some are in a subject but are not said of any subject. (By "in a subject" I mean what is in something, not as a part, and cannot exist separately from what it is in.) For example,
25 the individual knowledge-of-grammar is in a subject, the soul, but is not said of any subject; and the individual white is in a subject, the body (for all colour is in a body), but is not said of any subject. *(c)* Some are both said of a subject and in a subject. For
1ᵇ example, knowledge is in a subject, the soul, and is also said of a subject, knowledge-of-grammar. *(d)* Some are neither in a subject nor said of a subject, for example, the in-
5 dividual man or individual horse—for nothing of this sort is either in a subject or said of a subject. Things that are individual and numerically one are, without exception, not said of any subject, but there is nothing to prevent some of them from being in a subject—the individual knowledge-of-grammar is one of the things in a subject.

CHAPTER 3

10 Whenever one thing is predicated of another as of a subject, all things said of what is predicated will be said of the subject also. For example, man is predicated of the indi-
15 vidual man, and animal of man; so animal will be predicated of the individual man also—for the individual man is both a man and an animal.

The differentiae of genera which are different and not subordinate one to the other are themselves different in kind. For example, animal and knowledge: footed, winged,
20 aquatic, two-footed, are differentiae of animal, but none of these is a differentia of knowledge; one sort of knowledge does not differ from another by being two-footed. However, there is nothing to prevent genera subordinate one to the other from having the same differentiae. For the higher are predicated of the genera below them, so that all differentiae of the predicated genus will be differentiae of the subject also.

CHAPTER 4

25 Of things said without any combination, each signifies either substance or quantity or qualification or a relative or where or when or being-in-a-position or having or doing or being-affected. To give a rough idea, examples of substance are man, horse; of quantity:

four-foot, five-foot; of qualification: white, grammatical; of a relative: double, half, 2ᵃ
larger; of where: in the Lyceum, in the market-place; of when: yesterday, last-year; of
being-in-a-position: is-lying, is-sitting, of having: has-shoes-on, has-armour-on; of doing: cutting, burning; of being-affected: being-cut, being-burned.

None of the above is said just by itself in any affirmation, but by the combination 5
of these with one another an affirmation is produced. For every affirmation, it seems, is
either true or false; but of things said without any combination none is either true or
false (e.g. "man," "white," "runs," "wins").   10

CHAPTER 5

A *substance*—that which is called a substance most strictly, primarily, and most of
all—is that which is neither said of a subject nor in a subject, e.g. the individual man or 15
the individual horse. The species in which the things primarily called substances are,
are called *secondary substances,* as also are the genera of these species. For example,
the individual man belongs in a species, man, and animal is a genus of the species; so
these—both man and animal—are called secondary substances.

It is clear from what has been said that if something is said of a subject both its
name and its definition are necessarily predicated of the subject. For example, man is 20
said of a subject, the individual man, and the name is of course predicated (since you
will be predicating man of the individual man), and also the definition of man will be
predicated of the individual man (since the individual man is also a man). Thus both the 25
name and the definition will be predicated of the subject. But as for things which are in
a subject, in most cases neither the name nor the definition is predicated of the subject.
In some cases there is nothing to prevent the name from being predicated of the subject, 30
but it is impossible for the definition to be predicated. For example, white, which is in a
subject (the body), is predicated of the subject; for a body is called white. But the definition of white will never be predicated of the body.

All the other things are either said of the primary substances as subjects or in 35
them as subjects. This is clear from an examination of cases. For example, animal is
predicated of man and therefore also of the individual man; for were it predicated of
none of the individual men it would not be predicated of man at all. Again, colour is in
body and therefore also in an individual body; for were it not in some individual body it 2ᵇ
would not be in body at all. Thus all the other things are either said of the primary substances as subjects or in them as subjects. So if the primary substances did not exist it 5
would be impossible for any of the other things to exist.

Of the secondary substances the species is more a substance than the genus,
since it is nearer to the primary substance. For if one is to say of the primary substance what it is, it will be more informative and apt to give the species than the 10
genus. For example, it would be more informative to say of the individual man that he
is a man than that he is an animal (since the one is more distinctive of the individual
man while the other is more general); and more informative to say of the individual
tree that it is a tree than that it is a plant. Further, it is because the primary substances 15
are subjects for all the other things and all the other things are predicated of them or
are in them, that they are called substances most of all. But as the primary substances
stand to the other things, so the species stands to the genus: the species is a subject for 20
the genus (for the genera are predicated of the species but the species are not predicated reciprocally of the genera). Hence for this reason too the species is more a substance than the genus.

But of the species themselves—those which are not genera—one is no more a substance than another: it is no more apt to say of the individual man that he is a man
25 than to say of the individual horse that it is a horse. And similarly of the primary substances one is no more a substance than another: the individual man is no more a substance than the individual ox.

It is reasonable that, after the primary substances, their species and genera should
30 be the only other things called (secondary) substances. For only they, of things predicated, reveal the primary substance. For if one is to say of the individual man what he is, it will be in place to give the species or the genus (though more informative to give man than animal); but to give any of the other things would be out of place—for exam-
35 ple, to say "white" or "runs" or anything like that. So it is reasonable that these should be the only other things called substances. Further, it is because the primary substances are subjects for everything else that they are called substances most strictly. But as the
3ᵃ primary substances stand to everything else, so the species and genera of the primary substances stand to all the rest: all the rest are predicated of these. For if you will call the individual man grammatical it follows that you will call both a man and an animal
5 grammatical; and similarly in other cases.

It is a characteristic common to every substance not to be in a subject. For a pri-
10 mary substance is neither said of a subject nor in a subject. And as for secondary substances, it is obvious at once that they are not in a subject. For man is said of the individual man as subject but is not in a subject: man is not *in* the individual man. Similarly,
15 animal also is said of the individual man as subject but animal is not in the individual man. Further, while there is nothing to prevent the name of what is in a subject from being sometimes predicated of the subject, it is impossible for the definition to be predicated. But the definition of the secondary substances, as well as the name, is predicated
20 of the subject: you will predicate the definition of man of the individual man, and also that of animal. No substance, therefore, is in a subject.

This is not, however, peculiar to substance; the differentia also is not in a subject.
25 For footed and two-footed are said of man as subject but are not in a subject; neither two-footed nor footed is *in* man. Moreover, the definition of the differentia is predicated of that of which the differentia is said. For example, if footed is said of man the definition of footed will also be predicated of man; for man is footed.

30 We need not be disturbed by any fear that we may be forced to say that the parts of a substance, being in a subject (the whole substance), are not substances. For when we spoke of things *in a subject* we did not mean things belonging in something as *parts*.

It is a characteristic of substances and differentiae that all things called from them
35 are so called synonymously. For all the predicates from them are predicated either of the individuals or of the species. (For from a primary substance there is no predicate, since it is said of no subject; and as for secondary substances, the species is predicated of the individual, the genus both of the species and of the individual. Similarly, differ-
3ᵇ entiae too are predicated both of the species and of the individuals.) And the primary substances admit the definition of the species and of the genera, and the species admits
5 that of the genus; for everything said of what is predicated will be said of the subject also. Similarly, both the species and the individuals admit the definition of the differentiae. But synonymous things were precisely those with both the name in common and the same definition. Hence all the things called from substances and differentiae are so called synonymously.

10 Every substance seems to signify a certain "this." As regards the primary substances, it is indisputably true that each of them signifies a certain "this"; for the thing

revealed is individual and numerically one. But as regards the secondary substances, though it appears from the form of the name—when one speaks of man or animal— 15 that a secondary substance likewise signifies a certain "this," this is not really true; rather, it signifies a certain qualification, for the subject is not, as the primary substance is, one, but man and animal are said of many things. However, it does not signify simply a certain qualification, as white does. White signifies nothing but a quali- 20 fication, whereas the species and the genus mark off the qualification of substance— they signify substance of a certain qualification. (One draws a wider boundary with the genus than with the species, for in speaking of animal one takes in more than in speaking of man.)

Another characteristic of substances is that there is nothing contrary to them. For what would be contrary to a primary substance? For example, there is nothing contrary 25 to an individual man, nor yet is there anything contrary to man or to animal. This, however, is not peculiar to substance but holds of many other things also, for example, of quantity. For there is nothing contrary to four-foot or to ten or to anything of this kind— unless someone were to say that many is contrary to few or large to small; but still there 30 is nothing contrary to any *definite* quantity.

Substance, it seems, does not admit of a more and a less. I do not mean that one substance is not more a substance than another (we have said that it is), but that any 35 given substance is not called more, or less, than that which it is. For example, if this substance is a man, it will not be more a man or less a man either than itself or than another man. For one man is not more a man than another, as one pale thing is more pale 4ᵃ than another and one beautiful thing more beautiful than another. Again, a thing is called more, or less, such-and-such than itself; for example, the body that is pale is called more pale now than before, and the one that is hot is called more, or less, hot. Substance, however, is not spoken of thus. For a man is not called more a man now than 5 before, nor is anything else that is a substance. Thus substance does not admit of a more and a less.

It seems most distinctive of substance that what is numerically one and the same 10 is able to receive contraries. In no other case could one bring forward anything, numerically one, which is able to receive contraries. For example, a colour which is numerically one and the same will not be black and white, nor will numerically one and the same action be bad and good; and similarly with everything else that is not substance. A 15 substance, however, numerically one and the same, is able to receive contraries. For example, an individual man—one and the same—becomes pale at one time and dark at another, and hot and cold, and bad and good. 20

Nothing like this is to be seen in any other case, unless someone might object and say that statements and beliefs are like this. For the same statement seems to be both true and false. Suppose, for example, that the statement that somebody is sitting is true; after he has got up this same statement will be false. Similarly 25 with beliefs. Suppose you believe truly that somebody is sitting; after he has got up you will believe falsely if you hold the same belief about him. However, even if we were to grant this, there is still a difference in the way contraries are re- 30 ceived. For in the case of substances it is by themselves changing that they are able to receive contraries. For what has become cold instead of hot, or dark instead of pale, or good instead of bad, has changed (has altered); similarly in other cases too it is by itself undergoing change that each thing is able to receive contraries. Statements and beliefs, on the other hand, themselves remain completely 35 unchangeable in every way; it is because the *actual thing* changes that the contrary comes to belong to them. For the statement that somebody is sitting remains the 4ᵇ

Diskobolos, by Myron. A Roman copy after a bronze original of ca. 450 B.C. Myron's athlete epitomizes the ideal Olympian goals of godlike perfection and rational beauty. (Museo del Terme, Rome)

same; it is because of a change in the actual thing that it comes to be true at one time and false at another. Similarly with beliefs. Hence at least the *way* in which it is able to receive contraries—through a change in itself—would be distinctive of substance, even if we were to grant that beliefs and statements are able to receive
5   contraries. However, this is not true. For it is not because they themselves receive anything that statements and beliefs are said to be able to receive contraries, but because of what has happened to something else. For it is because the actual thing
10   exists or does not exist that the statement is said to be true or false, not because it is able itself to receive contraries. No statement, in fact, or belief is changed at all by anything. So, since nothing happens in them, they are not able to receive contraries. A substance, on the other hand, is said to be able to receive contraries be-
15   cause it itself receives contraries. For it receives sickness and health, and paleness and darkness; and because it itself receives the various things of this kind it is said to be able to receive contraries. It is, therefore, distinctive of substance that what is numerically one and the same is able to receive contraries. This brings to an end our discussion of substance.

POSTERIOR ANALYTICS (in part)

BOOK I

1. All teaching and all intellectual learning come about from already existing knowl-   71ᵃ
edge. This is evident if we consider it in every case; for the mathematical sciences
are acquired in this fashion, and so is each of the other arts. And similarly too with   5
arguments—both deductive and inductive arguments proceed in this way; for both
produce their teaching through what we are already aware of, the former getting
their premises as from men who grasp them, the latter proving the universal through
the particular's being clear. (And rhetorical arguments too persuade in the same way;   10
for they do so either through examples, which is induction, or through enthymemes,
which is deduction.)

It is necessary to be already aware of things in two ways: of some things it is necessary to believe already that they are, of some one must grasp what the thing said is,
and of others both—e.g. of the fact that everything is either affirmed or denied truly,
one must believe that it is; of the triangle, that it signifies this; and of the unit both (both   15
what it signifies and that it is). For each of these is not equally clear to us.

But you can become familiar by being familiar earlier with some things but getting knowledge of the others at the very same time—i.e. of whatever happens to be
under the universal of which you have knowledge. For that every triangle has angles
equal to two right angles was already known; but that there is a triangle in the semi-   20
circle here became familiar at the same time as the induction. (For in some cases
learning occurs in this way, and the last term does not become familiar through the
middle—in cases dealing with what are in fact particulars and not said of any underlying subject.)

Before the induction, or before getting a deduction, you should perhaps be said to   25
understand in a way—but in another way not. For if you did not know if it is *simpliciter*
[without qualification], how did you know that it has two right angles *simpliciter?* But
it is clear that you understand it in this sense—that you understand it universally—but
you do not understand it *simpliciter*. (Otherwise the puzzle in the *Meno* [80d] will re-   30
sult; for you will learn either nothing or what you know.)

For one should not argue in the way in which some people attempt to solve it: Do
you or don't you know of every pair that it is even? And when you said Yes, they
brought forward some pair of which you did not think that it was, nor therefore that it
was even. For they solve it by denying that people know of every pair that it is even, but
only of anything of which they know that it is a pair.—Yet they know it of that which
they have the demonstration about and which they got their premises about; and they   71ᵇ
got them not about everything of which they know that it is a triangle or that it is a
number, but of every number and triangle *simpliciter*. For no proposition of such a
type is assumed (that *what you know to be a number* . . . or *what you know to be
rectilineal* . . .), but they are assumed as holding of every case.   5

But nothing, I think, prevents one from in a sense understanding and in a sense
being ignorant of what one is learning; for what is absurd is not that you should know in

Aristotle, *Posterior Analytics*, Book I, 1–3, 8–10, 31; II, 1–2, 19, translated by Jonathan Barnes from *Complete Works of Aristotle*, edited by Jonathan Barnes (Princeton: Princeton University Press, 1984). Copyright © 1984 by PUP. Reprinted by permission.

some sense what you are learning, but that you should know it in this sense, i.e. in the way and sense in which you are learning it.

2. We think we understand a thing *simpliciter* (and not in the sophistic fashion accidentally) whenever we think we are aware both that the explanation because of which the object is is its explanation, and that it is not possible for this to be otherwise. It is clear, then, that to understand is something of this sort; for both those who do not understand and those who do understand—the former think they are themselves in such a state, and those who do understand actually are. Hence that of which there is understanding *simpliciter* cannot be otherwise.

Now whether there is also another type of understanding we shall say later; but we say now that we do know through demonstration. By demonstration I mean a scientific deduction; and by scientific I mean one in virtue of which, by having it, we understand something.

If, then, understanding is as we posited, it is necessary for demonstrative understanding in particular to depend on things which are true and primitive and immediate and more familiar than and prior to and explanatory of the conclusion (for in this way the principles will also be appropriate to what is being proved). For there will be deduction even without these conditions, but there will not be demonstration; for it will not produce understanding.

Now they must be true because one cannot understand what is not the case—e.g. that the diagonal is commensurate. And they must depend on what is primitive and non-demonstrable because otherwise you will not understand if you do not have a demonstration of them; for to understand that of which there is a demonstration non-accidentally is to have a demonstration. They must be both explanatory and more familiar and prior explanatory because we only understand when we know the explanation; and prior, if they are explanatory, and we are already aware of them not only in the sense of grasping them but also of knowing that they are.

Things are prior and more familiar in two ways; for it is not the same to be prior by nature and prior in relation to us, nor to be more familiar and more familiar to us. I call prior and more familiar in relation to us what is nearer to perception, prior and more familiar *simpliciter* what is further away. What is most universal is furthest away, and the particulars are nearest; and these are opposite to each other.

Depending on things that are primitive is depending on appropriate principles; for I call the same thing primitive and a principle. A principle of a demonstration is an immediate proposition, and an immediate proposition is one to which there is no other prior. A proposition is the one part of a contradiction, one thing said of one; it is dialectical if it assumes indifferently either part, demonstrative if it determinately assumes the one that is true. [A statement is either part of a contradiction.] A contradiction is an opposition of which of itself excludes any intermediate; and the part of a contradiction saying something *of* something is an affirmation, the one saying something *from* something is a denial.

An immediate deductive principle I call a posit if one cannot prove it but it is not necessary for anyone who is to learn anything to grasp it; and one which it is necessary for anyone who is going to learn anything whatever to grasp, I call an axiom (for there are some such things); for we are accustomed to use this name especially of such things.

A posit which assumes either of the parts of a contradiction—i.e., I mean, that something is or that something is not—I call a supposition; one without this, a definition. For a definition is a posit (for the arithmetician posits that a unit is what is quantitatively indivisible) but not a supposition (for what a unit is and that a unit is are not the same).

Since one should both be convinced of and know the object by having a deduction   25
of the sort we call a demonstration, and since this is the case when these things on
which the deduction depends are the case, it is necessary not only to be already aware of
the primitives (either all or some of them) but actually to be better aware of them. For a
thing always belongs better to that thing because of which it belongs—e.g. that because   30
of which we love is better loved. Hence if we know and are convinced because of the
primitives, we both know and are convinced of them better, since it is because of them
that we know and are convinced of what is posterior.

It is not possible to be better convinced than one is of what one knows, of what
one in fact neither knows nor is more happily disposed toward than if one in fact knew.
But this will result if someone who is convinced because of a demonstration is not already aware of the primitives, for it is necessary to be better convinced of the principles   35
(either all or some of them) than of the conclusion.

Anyone who is going to have understanding through demonstration must not only
be familiar with the principles and better convinced of them than of what is being
proved, but also there must be no other thing more convincing to him or more familiar   72ᵇ
among the opposites of the principles on which a deduction of the contrary error may
depend—if anyone who understands *simpliciter* must be unpersuadable.

3. Now some think that because one must understand the primitives there is no   5
understanding at all; others that there is, but that there are demonstrations of everything.
Neither of these views is either true or necessary.

For the one party, supposing that one cannot understand in another way, claim
that we are led back *ad infinitum* on the grounds that we would not understand what is
posterior because of what is prior if there are no primitives; and they argue correctly, for
it is impossible to go through infinitely many things. And if it comes to a stop and there   10
are principles, they say that these are unknowable since there is no *demonstration* of
them, which alone they say is understanding; but if one cannot know the primitives, neither can what depends on them be understood *simpliciter* or properly, but only on the
supposition that they are the case.

The other party agrees about understanding; for it, they say, occurs only through   15
demonstration. But they argue that nothing prevents there being demonstration of everything; for it is possible for the demonstration to come about in a circle and reciprocally.

But we say that neither is all understanding demonstrative, but in the case of the
immediates it is non-demonstrable—and that this is necessary is evident; for if it is necessary to understand the things which are prior and on which the demonstration de-   20
pends, and it comes to a stop at some time, it is necessary for these immediates to be
non-demonstrable. So as to that we argue thus; and we also say that there is not only understanding but also some principle of understanding by which we become familiar
with the definitions.

And that it is impossible to demonstrate *simpliciter* in a circle is clear, if demon-   25
stration must depend on what is prior and more familiar; for it is impossible for the
same things at the same time to be prior and posterior to the same things—unless one is
so in another way (i.e. one in relation to us, the other *simpliciter*), which induction
makes familiar. But if so, knowing *simpliciter* will not have been properly defined, but   30
will be twofold. Or is the other demonstration not demonstration *simpliciter* in that it
comes from about what is more familiar to *us?*

There results for those who say that demonstration is circular not only what has
just been described, but also that they say nothing other than that this is the case if this

35   is the case—and it is easy to prove everything in this way. It is clear that this results if we posit three terms. (For it makes no difference to say that it bends back through many terms or through few, or through few or two.) For whenever if A is the case, of necessity B is, and if this then C, then if A is the case C will be the case. Thus given that if A is the case it is necessary that B is, and if this is that A is (for that is what being circular

73ᵃ   is)—let A be C: so to say that if B is the case A is, is to say that C is, and this implies that if A is the case C is. But C is the same as A. Hence it results that those who assert that demonstration is circular say nothing but that if A is the case A is the case. And it is easy

5   to prove everything in this way.

Moreover, not even this is possible except in the case of things which follow one another, as properties do. Now if a single thing is laid down, it has been proved that it is never necessary that anything else should be the case (by a single thing I

10   mean that neither if one term nor if one posit is posited . . .), but two posits are the first and fewest from which it is possible, if at all, actually to deduce something. Now if A follows B and C, and these follow one another and A, in this way it is possible to prove all the postulates reciprocally in the first figure, as was proved in the

15   account of deduction. (And it was also proved that in the other figures either no deduction comes about or none about what was assumed.) But one cannot in any way prove circularly things which are not counterpredicated; hence, since there are few such things in demonstrations, it is evident that it is both empty and impossible to

20   say that demonstration is reciprocal and that because of this there can be demonstration of everything.

* * *

75ᵇ   8. It is evident too that, if the propositions on which the deduction depends are universal, it is necessary for the conclusion of such a demonstration and of a demonstration *simpliciter* to be eternal too. There is therefore no demonstration of perishable things,

25   nor understanding of them *simpliciter* but only accidentally, because it does not hold of it universally, but at some time and in some way.

And when there is such a demonstration it is necessary for the one proposition to be non-universal and perishable—perishable because when it is the case the conclusion too will be the case, and non-universal because its subjects will sometimes be and

30   sometimes not be—so that one cannot deduce universally, but only that it holds now.

The same goes for definitions too, since a definition is either a principle of demonstration or a demonstration differing in position or a sort of conclusion of a demonstration.

Demonstrations and sciences of things that come about often—e.g. eclipses of the moon—clearly hold always in so far as they are of such-and-such a thing, but are par-

35   ticular in so far as they do not hold always. As with the eclipse, so in the other cases.

9. Since it is evident that one cannot demonstrate anything except from its own principles if what is being proved belongs to it as that thing, understanding is not this— if a thing is proved from what is true and non-demonstrable and immediate. (For one

40   can conduct a proof in this way—as Bryson proved the squaring of the circle.) For such arguments prove in virtue of a common feature which will also belong to something

76ᵃ   else; that is why the arguments also apply to other things not of the same kind. So you do not understand it as that thing but accidentally; for otherwise the demonstration would not apply to another genus too.

We understand a thing non-accidentally when we know it in virtue of that in virtue of which it belongs, from the principles of that thing as that thing—e.g. we understand having angles equal to two right angles when we know it in virtue of that to which what has been said belongs in itself, from the principles of that thing. Hence if that too belongs in itself to what it belongs to, it is necessary for the middle to be in the same genus.

If this is not so, then the theorems are proved as harmonical theorems are proved through arithmetic. Such things are proved in the same way, but they differ; for the fact falls under a different science (for the underlying genus is different), but the reason under the higher science under which fall the attributes that belong in themselves. Hence from this too it is evident that one cannot demonstrate anything *simpliciter* except from its own principles. But the principles of these sciences have the common feature.

If this is evident, it is evident too that one cannot demonstrate the proper principles of anything; for those will be principles of everything, and understanding of them will be sovereign over everything. For you understand better if you know from the higher explanations; for you know from what is prior when you know from unexplainable explanations. Hence if you know better and best, that understanding too will be better and best. But demonstration does not apply to another genus—except, as has been said, geometrical demonstrations apply to mechanical or optical demonstrations, and arithmetical to harmonical.

It is difficult to be aware of whether one knows or not. For it is difficult to be aware of whether we know from the principles of a thing or not—and that is what knowing is. We think we understand if we have a deduction from some true and primitive propositions. But that is not so, but it must be of the same genus as the primitives.

10. I call principles in each genus those which it is not possible to prove to be. Now both what the primitives and what the things dependent on them signify is assumed; but that they are must be assumed for the principles and proved for the rest— e.g. we must assume what a unit or what straight and triangle signify, and that the unit and magnitude are; but we must prove that the others are.

Of the things they use in the demonstrative sciences some are proper to each science and others common—but common by analogy, since things are *useful* in so far as they bear on the genus under the science. Proper: e.g. that a line is *such and such,* and straight so and so; common: e.g. that if equals are taken from equals, the remainders are equal. But each of these is sufficient in so far as it bears on the genus; for it will produce the same result even if it is not assumed as holding of everything but only for the case of magnitudes—or, for the arithmetician, for numbers.

Proper too are the things which are assumed to be, about which the science considers what belongs to them in themselves—as e.g. arithmetic is about units, and geometry is about points and lines. For they assume these to be and to be this. As to what are attributes of these in themselves, they assume what each signifies—e.g. arithmetic assumes what odd or even or quadrangle or cube signifies, and geometry what irrational or inflection or verging signifies and they prove that they are, through the common items and from what has been demonstrated. And astronomy proceeds in the same way.

For every demonstrative science has to do with three things: what it posits to be (these form the genus of what it considers the attributes that belong to it in itself); and what are called the common axioms, the primitives from which it demonstrates. and thirdly the attributes, of which it assumes what each signifies. Nothing, however, prevents some sciences from overlooking some of these—e.g. from not supposing that its genus is, if it is evident that it is (for it is not equally clear that number is and that hot

and cold are), and from not assuming what the attributes signify, if they are clear—just
as in the case of the common items it does not assume what to take equals from equals
signifies, because it is familiar. But none the less there are by nature these three things,
that about which the science proves, what it proves, and the things from which it proves.

What necessarily is the case because of itself and necessarily seems to be the case
is not a supposition or a postulate. For demonstration is not addressed to external argument—but to argument in the soul—since deduction is not either. For one can always
object to external argument, but not always to internal argument.

Whatever a man assumes without proving it himself although it is provable—if he
assumes something that seems to be the case to the learner, he supposes it (and it is a
supposition not *simpliciter* but only in relation to the learner); but if he assumes the
same thing when there is either no opinion present in the learner or actually a contrary
one present, he postulates it. And it is in this that suppositions and postulates differ; for
a postulate is what is contrary to the opinion of the learner, which though it is demonstrable is assumed and used without being proved.

Now terms are not suppositions (for they are not said to be or not be anything),
but suppositions are among the propositions, whereas one need only grasp the terms;
and suppositions are not that (unless someone will say that hearing is a supposition), but
rather propositions such that, if they are the case, then by their being the case the conclusion comes about.

Nor does the geometer suppose falsehoods, as some have said, stating that one
should not use a falsehood but that the geometer speaks falsely when he says that the
line which is not a foot long is a foot long or that the drawn line which is not straight is
straight. But the geometer does not conclude anything from there being this line which
he himself has described, but from what is made clear through them.

Again, every postulate and supposition is either universal or particular; but terms
are neither of these.

* * *

87ᵇ 31. Nor can one understand through perception. For even if perception is of what is
30 such and such, and not of individuals, still one necessarily perceives an individual and
at a place and at a time, and it is impossible to perceive what is universal and holds in
every case; for that is not an individual not at a time; for then it would not be universal—for it is what is always and everywhere that we call universal.

So, since demonstrations are universal, and it is not possible to perceive these, it
is evident that it is not possible to understand through perception either; but it is clear
that even if one could perceive of the triangle that it has its angles equal to two right angles, we would seek a demonstration and would not, as some say, understand it; for one
necessarily perceives particulars, whereas understanding comes by becoming familiar
with the universal.

That is why if we were on the moon and saw the earth screening it we would not
88ᵃ know the explanation of the eclipse. For we would perceive that it is eclipsed and not
why at all; for there turned out to be no perception of the universal. Nevertheless, if,
from considering this often happening, we hunted the universal, we would have a
demonstration; for from several particulars the universal is clear.

The universal is valuable because it makes clear the explanation; hence universal
demonstration is more valuable than perception and comprehension—with regard to
those things whose explanation is something different; but for the primitives there is a
different account.

So it is evident that it is impossible by perceiving to understand anything demonstrable—unless someone calls this perceiving: having understanding through demonstration.   10

Yet some of our problems are referred to want of perception; for in some cases if we saw we should not seek—not on the grounds that we knew by seeing, but that we grasped the universal from seeing. E.g. if we saw the glass to be perforated and the light coming through it, it would also be clear why it does, even if seeing occurs separately   15 for each piece of glass while comprehending grasps at one time that it is thus in every case.

* * *

BOOK II

1. The things we seek are equal in number to those we understand. We seek four   89b
things: the fact, the reason why, if it is, what it is.

For when we seek whether it is this or this, putting it into a number (e.g. whether the sun is eclipsed or not), we seek the fact. Evidence for this: on finding that it is   25 eclipsed we stop; and if from the start we know that it is eclipsed, we do not seek whether it is. When we know the fact we seek the reason why (e.g. knowing that it is eclipsed and that the earth moves, we seek the reason why it is eclipsed or why it moves).   30

Now while we seek these things in this way, we seek some things in another fashion—e.g. if a centaur or a god is or is not (I mean if one is or not *simpliciter* and not if one is white or not). And knowing that it is, we seek what it is (e.g. so what is a god? or what is a man?).   35

2. Now what we seek and what on finding we know are these and thus many. We seek, whenever we seek the fact or if it is *simpliciter,* whether there is or is not a middle term for it; and whenever we become aware of either the fact or if it is—either   90a
partially or *simpliciter*—and again seek the reason why or what it is, then we seek what the middle term is. (I mean by the fact that it is partially and *simpliciter*—partially: Is the moon eclipsed? or is it increasing? (for in such cases we seek if it is something or is not something); *simpliciter:* if the moon or night is or is not.) It results, therefore, that in all our searches we seek either if there is a middle term or what   5 the middle term is.

For the middle term is the explanation, and in all cases that is sought. Is it eclipsed?—Is there some explanation or not? After that, aware that there is one, we seek what this is. For the explanation of a substance being not this or that but *simpliciter,* or   10 of its being not *simpliciter* but one of the things which belong to it in itself or accidentally—that is the middle term. I mean by *simpliciter* the underlying subject (e.g. moon or earth or sun or triangle) and by one of the things eclipse, equality, inequality, whether it is in the middle or not.

For in all these cases it is evident that what it is and why it is are the same. What is an eclipse? Privation of light from the moon by the earth's screening. Why is there an   15 eclipse? or Why is the moon eclipsed? Because the light leaves it when the earth screens it. What is a harmony? An arithmetical ratio between high and low. Why does the high harmonize with the low? Because an arithmetical ratio holds between the high   20 and the low. Can the high and the low harmonize?—Is there an arithmetical ratio be-tween them? Assuming that there is, what then is the ratio?

25   That the search is for the middle term is made clear by the cases in which the mid-dle is perceptible. For if we have not perceived it, we seek, e.g. for the eclipse, if there is one or not. But if we were on the moon we would seek neither if it comes about nor why, but it would be clear at the same time. For from perceiving, it would come about

30   that we knew the universal too. For perception tells us that it is now screening it (for it is clear that it is now eclipsed); and from this the universal would come about.

So, as we say, to know what it is is the same as to know why it is—and that either *simpliciter* and not one of the things that belong to it, or one of the things that belong to it, e.g. that it has two right angles, or that it is greater or less.

* * *

99ᵇ   19. Now as for deduction and demonstration, it is evident both what each is and how it
15   comes about—and at the same time this goes for demonstrative understanding too (for that is the same thing). But as for the principles—how they become familiar and what is the state that becomes familiar with them—that will be clear from what follows, when we have first set down the puzzles.

20   Now, we have said earlier that it is not possible to understand through demonstra-tion if we are not aware of the primitive, immediate, principles. But as to knowledge of the immediates, one might puzzle both whether it is the same or not the same—whether there is understanding of each, or rather understanding of the one and some other kind of thing of the other—and also whether the states are not present in us but come about

25   in us, or whether they are present in us but escape notice.

Well, if we have them, it is absurd; for it results that we have pieces of knowledge more precise than demonstration and yet this escapes notice. But if we get them without having them earlier, how might we become familiar with them and learn them from no pre-existing knowledge? For that is impossible, as we said in the case of demonstration

30   too. It is evidently impossible, then, both for us to have them and for them to come about in us when we are ignorant and have no such state at all. Necessarily, therefore, we have some capacity, but do not have one of a type which will be more valuable than these in respect of precision.

And *this* evidently belongs to all animals; for they have a connate discriminatory
35   capacity, which is called perception. And if perception is present in them, in some ani-mals retention of the percept comes about, but in others it does not come about. Now for those in which it does not come about, there is no knowledge outside perceiving (either none at all, or none with regard to that of which there is no retention); but for some per-

100ª   ceivers, it is possible to grasp it in their minds. And when many such things come about, then a difference comes about, so that some come to have an account from the retention of such things, and others do not.

So from perception there comes memory, as we call it, and from memory (when it occurs often in connection with the same thing), experience; for memories that are
5   many in number form a single experience. And from experience, or from the whole uni-versal that has come to rest in the soul (the one apart from the many, whatever is one and the same in all those things), there comes a principle of skill and of understanding—of skill if it deals with how things come about, of understanding if it deals with what is the case.

10   Thus the states neither belong in us in a determinate form, nor come about from other states that are more cognitive; but they come about from perception—as in a bat-

tle when a rout occurs, if one man makes a stand another does and then another, until a position of strength is reached. And the soul is such as to be capable of undergoing this.

What we have just said but not said clearly, let us say again: when one of the un-   15
differentiated things makes a stand, there is a primitive universal in the mind (for though one perceives the particular, perception is of the universal—e.g. of man but not of Callias the man); again a stand is made in these, until what has no parts and is universal   100b
stands—e.g. *such and such* an animal stands, until animal does, and in this a stand is made in the same way. Thus it is clear that it is necessary for us to become familiar with the primitives by induction; for perception too instils the universal in this way.   5

Since of the intellectual states by which we grasp truth some are always true and some admit falsehood (e.g. opinion and reasoning—whereas understanding and comprehension are always true), and no kind other than comprehension is more precise than understanding, and the principles of demonstrations are more familiar, and all understanding involves an account—there will not be understanding of the principles; and   10
since it is not possible for anything to be truer than understanding, except comprehension, there will be comprehension of the principles—both if we inquire from these facts and because demonstration is not a principle of demonstration so that understanding is not a principle of understanding either—so if we have no other true kind apart from understanding, comprehension will be the principle of understanding. And the principle   15
will be of the principle, and understanding as a whole will be similarly related to the whole object.

PHYSICS (in part)

BOOK I

1. When the objects of an inquiry, in any department, have principles, causes, or ele-   184a
ments, it is through acquaintance with these that knowledge and understanding is attained. For we do not think that we know a thing until we are acquainted with its primary causes or first principles, and have carried our analysis as far as its elements.   15
Plainly, therefore, in the science of nature too our first task will be to try to determine what relates to its principles.

The natural way of doing this is to start from the things which are more knowable and clear to us and proceed towards those which are clearer and more knowable by nature; for the same things are not knowable relatively to us and knowable without qualification. So we must follow this method and advance from what is more obscure by nature, but clearer to us, towards what is more clear and more knowable by nature.   20

Now what is to us plain and clear at first is rather confused masses, the elements and principles ofwhich become known to us later by analysis. Thus we must advance from universals to particulars; for it is a whole that is more knowable to sense-perception, and a universal is a kind of whole, comprehending many things within   25

184ᵇ   it, like parts. Much the same thing happens in the relation of the name to the formula. A name, e.g. "circle," means vaguely a sort of whole: its definition analyses this into particulars. Similarly a child begins by calling all men father, and all women mother, but later on distinguishes each of them.

15   2. The principles in question must be either one or more than one. If one, it must be either motionless, as Parmenides and Melissus assert, or in motion, as the physicists hold, some declaring air to be the first principle, others water. If more than one, then either a finite or an infinite plurality. If finite (but more than one), then either two or three or four or some other number. If infinite, then either as Democritus believed one in kind, but differing in shape; or different in kind and even contrary.

        A similar inquiry is made by those who inquire into the number of existents; for they inquire whether the ultimate constituents of existing things are one or many, and if 25   many, whether a finite or an infinite plurality. So they are inquiring whether the principle or element is one or many.

        Now to investigate whether what exists is one and motionless is not a contribution 185ᵃ   to the science of nature. For just as the geometer has nothing more to say to one who denies the principles of his science—this being a question for a different science or for one common to all—so a man investigating *principles* cannot argue with one who denies their existence. For if what exists is just one, and one in the way mentioned, there is a principle no longer, since a principle must be the principle of some thing or things.

5   To inquire therefore whether what exists is one in this sense would be like arguing against any other position maintained for the sake of argument (such as the Heraclitean thesis, or such a thesis as that what exists is one man) or like refuting a merely contentious argument—a description which applies to the arguments both of Melissus and of Parmenides: their premises are false and their conclusions do not follow. Or 10   rather the argument of Melissus is gross and offers no difficulty at all: accept one ridiculous proposition and the rest follows—a simple enough proceeding.

        We, on the other hand, must take for granted that the things that exist by nature are, either all or some of them, in motion—which is indeed made plain by induction. Moreover, no one is bound to solve every kind of difficulty that may be raised, but only 15   as many as are drawn falsely from the principles of the science: it is not our business to refute those that do not arise in this way; just as it is the duty of the geometer to refute the squaring of the circle by means of segments, but it is not his duty to refute Antiphon's proof. At the same time the holders of the theory of which we are speaking do incidentally raise physical questions, though nature is not their subject; so it will perhaps be as well to spend a few words on them, especially as the inquiry is not without 20   scientific interest.

        The most pertinent question with which to begin will be this: In what sense is it asserted that all things *are* one? For "is" is used in many ways. Do they mean that all things are substance or quantities or qualities? And, further, are all things *one* substance one man, one horse, or one soul or quality and that one and the same—white or 25   hot or something of the kind? These are all very different doctrines and all impossible to maintain.

        For if *both* substance and quantity and quality are, then, whether these exist independently of each other or not, what exists will be many.

        If on the other hand it is asserted that all things are quality or quantity, then, 30   whether substance exists or not, an absurdity results, if indeed the impossible can properly be called absurd. For none of the others can exist independently except substance; for everything is predicated of substance as subject. Now Melissus says that what exists is infinite. It is then a quantity. For the infinite is in the category of quantity, whereas substance or quality or affection cannot be infinite except accidentally, that is, if at the same time they are also quantities. For to define the infinite you must use quantity in your formula, but not substance or quality. If then what exists is both substance and quantity, it is two, not one; if only substance, it is not infinite and has no magnitude; for to have that it will have to be a quantity.

Again, "one" itself, no less than "is," is used in many ways, so we must consider in what way the word is used when it is said that the universe is one.

Now we say that the continuous is one or that the indivisible is one, or things are said to be one, when the account of their essence is one and the same, as liquor and drink.

If their One is one in the sense of continuous, it is many; for the continuous is divisible *ad infinitum*.

There is, indeed, a difficulty about part and whole, perhaps not relevant to the present argument, yet deserving consideration on its own account—namely, whether the part and the whole are one or more than one, and in what way they can be one or many, and, if they are more than one, in what way they are more than one. (Similarly with the parts of wholes which are not continuous.) Further, if each of the two parts is indivisibly one with the whole, the difficulty arises that they will be indivisibly one with each other also.

But to proceed: If their One is one as indivisible, nothing will have quantity or quality, and so what exists will not be infinite, as Melissus says—nor, indeed, limited, as Parmenides says; for though the limit is indivisible, the limited is not.

But if all things are one in the sense of having the same definition, like raiment and dress, then it turns out that they are maintaining the Heraclitean doctrine, for it will be the same thing to be good and to be bad, and to be good and to be not good, and so the same thing will be good and not good, and man and horse; in fact, their view will be, not that all things are one, but that they are nothing; and that to be of such-and-such a quality is the same as to be of such-and-such a quantity.

Even the more recent of the ancient thinkers were in a pother lest the same thing should turn out in their hands both one and many. So some, like Lycophron, were led to omit "is," others to change the mode of expression and say "the man has been whitened" instead of "is white," and "walks" instead of "is walking," for fear that if they added the word "is" they should be making the one to *be* many—as if "one" and "is" were always used in one and the same way. What is may be many either in definition (for example to be white is one thing, to be musical another, yet the same thing may be both, so the one is many) or by division, as the whole and its parts. On this point, indeed, they were already getting into difficulties and admitted that the one was many—as if there was any difficulty about the same thing being both one and many, provided that these are not opposites; for what is one may be either potentially one or actually one.

3. If, then, we approach the thesis in this way it seems impossible for all things to be one. Further, the arguments they use to prove their position are not difficult to expose. For both of them reason contentiously—I mean both Melissus and Parmenides. [Their premises are false and their conclusions do not follow. Or rather the argument of Melissus is gross and offers no difficulty at all: admit one ridiculous proposition and the rest follows—a simple enough proceeding.]

The fallacy of Melissus is obvious. For he supposes that the assumption "what has come into being always has a beginning" justifies the assumption "what has not

come into being has no beginning." Then this also is absurd, that in every case there should be a beginning of the *thing*—not of the time and not only in the case of coming
15 to be *simpliciter* but also in the case of qualitative change—as if change never took place all at once. Again, does it follow that what is, if one, is motionless? Why should it not move, the whole of it within itself, as parts of it do which are unities, e.g. this water? Again, why is qualitative change impossible? But, further, what is cannot be one in form, though it may be in what it is made of. (Even some of the physicists hold it to be
20 one in the latter way, though not in the former.) Man obviously differs from horse in form, and contraries from each other.

The same kind of argument holds good against Parmenides also, besides any that may apply specially to his view: the answer to him being that this is not true and *that* does not follow. His assumption that "is" is used in a single way only is false, because
25 it is used in several. His conclusion does not follow, because if we take only white things, and if "white" has a single meaning, none the less what is white will be many and not one. For what is white will not be one either in the sense that it is continuous or in the sense that it must be defined in only one way. Whiteness will be different from what has whiteness. Nor does this mean that there is anything that can exist separately,
30 over and above what is white. For whiteness and that which is white differ in definition, not in the sense that they are things which can exist apart from each other. But Parmenides had not come in sight of this distinction.

It is necessary for him, then, to assume not only that "is" has the same meaning, of whatever it is predicated, but further that it means what *just is* and what is *just one*. For an attribute is predicated of some subject, so that the subject to which "is" is attributed will not be, as it is something different from being. Something, therefore,
186ᵇ which is not will be. Hence what just is will not belong to anything else. For the subject cannot be a *being,* unless "is" means several things, in such a way that each is something. But *ex hypothesi* "is" means only one thing.

If, then, what just is is not attributed to anything, but other things are attributed to
5 it, how does what just is mean what is rather than what is not? For suppose that what just is is also white, and that being white is not what just is (for being cannot even be attributed to white, since nothing is which is not what just is), it follows that what is white
10 is not—and that not in the sense of not being something or other, but in the sense that it is not at all. Hence what just is is not; for it is true to say that it is white, and we found this to mean what is not. So "white" must also mean what just is; and then "is" has more than one meaning.

In particular, then, what is will not have magnitude, if it is what just is. For each of the two parts must *be* in a different way.

What just is is plainly divisible into other things which just are, if we consider the
15 mere nature of a definition. For instance, if man is, what just is, animal and biped must also be what just is. For if not, they must be attributes—and if attributes, attributes either of man or of some other subject. But neither is possible.

For an attribute is either that which may or may not belong to the subject or that
20 in whose definition the subject of which it is an attribute is involved. Thus sitting is an example of a separable attribute, while snubness contains the definition of nose, to which we attribute snubness. Further, the definition of the whole is not contained in the definitions of the contents or elements of the definitory formula; that of man for instance in biped, or that of white man in white. If then this is so, and if biped is supposed
25 to be an attribute of man, it must be either separable, so that man might possibly not be biped, or the definition of man must come into the definition of biped—which is impos-
30 sible, as the converse is the case.

If, on the other hand, we suppose that biped and animal are attributes not of man but of something else, and are not each of them what just is, then man too will be an attribute of something else. But we must assume that what just is is *not* the attribute of anything, and that the subject of which both biped and animal are predicated is the subject also of the complex. Are we then to say that the universe is composed of indivisibles?

Some thinkers did, in point of fact, give way to both arguments. To the argument   187ᵃ that all things are one if being means one thing, they conceded that what is not is; to that from bisection, they yielded by positing atomic magnitudes. But obviously it is not true that if being means one thing, and nothing can at the same time both be and not be, there will be nothing which is not; for even if what is not cannot be without qualification, there is no reason why it should not be something or other. To say that all things will be   5 one, if there is nothing besides what is itself, is absurd. For who understands "what is itself" to be anything but some particular thing? But if this is so, there is still nothing to   10 prevent there being many beings, as has been said.

It is, then, clearly impossible for what is to be one in this sense.

4. The physicists on the other hand have two modes of explanation.

The first set make the underlying body one—either one of the three or something else which is denser than fire and rarer than air—then generate everything else from this, and obtain multiplicity by condensation and rarefaction. (Now these are contraries,   15 which may be generalized into excess and defect. Compare Plato's "Great and Small"—except that he makes these his matter, the one his form, while the others treat the one which underlies as matter and the contraries as differentiae, i.e. forms.)

The second set assert that the contrarieties are contained in the one and emerge   20 from it by segregation, for example Anaximander and also all those who assert that what is is one and many, like Empedocles and Anaxagoras; for they too produce other things from their mixture by segregation. These differ, however, from each other in that the former imagines a cycle of such changes, the latter a single series. Anaxagoras again   25 made both his homogeneous substances and his contraries infinite, whereas Empedocles posits only the so-called elements.

The theory of Anaxagoras that the principles are infinite was probably due to his acceptance of the common opinion of the physicists that nothing comes into being from what is not. (For this is the reason why they use the phrase "all things were together" and the coming into being of such and such a kind of thing is reduced to change of qual-   30 ity, while some spoke of combination and separation.) Moreover, the fact that the contraries come into being from each other led them to the conclusion. The one, they reasoned, must have already existed in the other; for since everything that comes into being must arise either from what is or from what is not, and it is impossible for it to arise   35 from what is not (on this point all the physicists agree), they thought that the truth of the alternative necessarily followed, namely that things come into being out of existent things, i.e. out of things already present, but imperceptible to our senses because of the smallness of their bulk. So they assert that everything has been mixed in everything, be-   187ᵇ cause they saw everything arising out of everything. But things, as they say, appear different from one another and receive different names according to what is numerically predominant among the innumerable constituents of the mixture. For nothing, they say, is purely and entirely white or black or sweet, or bone or flesh, but the nature of a thing   5 is held to be that of which it contains the most.

Now the infinite *qua* infinite is unknowable, so that what is infinite in multitude or size is unknowable in quantity, and what is infinite in variety of kind is unknowable in   10 quality. But the principles in question are infinite both in multitude and in kind. Therefore it is impossible to know things which are composed of them; for it is when we know the nature and quantity of its components that we suppose we know a complex.

15   Further, if the parts of a whole may be indefinitely big or small (by parts I mean components into which a whole can be divided and which are actually present in it), it is necessary that the whole thing itself may also be of any size. Clearly, therefore, if it is impossible for an animal or plant to be indefinitely big or small, neither can its parts be such, or the whole will be the same. But flesh, bone, and the like are the parts of ani-

20   mals, and the fruits are the parts of plants. Hence it is obvious that neither flesh, bone, nor any such thing can be of indefinite size in the direction either of the greater or of the less.

Again, according to the theory all such things are already present in one another and do not come into being but are constituents which are separated out, and a thing receives its designation from its chief constituent. Further, anything may come out of

25   anything—water by segregation from flesh and flesh from water. Hence, since every finite body is exhausted by the repeated abstraction of a finite body, it is evident that everything cannot subsist in everything else. For let flesh be extracted from water and again more flesh be produced from the remainder by repeating the process of separa-

30   tion; then, even though the quantity separated out will continually decrease, still it will not fall below a certain magnitude. If, therefore, the process comes to an end, everything will not be in everything else (for there will be no flesh in the remaining water); if on the other hand it does not, and further extraction is always possible, there will be

35   an infinite multitude of finite equal parts in a finite quantity—which is impossible. Another proof may be added: since every body must diminish in size when something is taken from it, and flesh is quantitatively definite in respect both of greatness and

188ᵃ   smallness, it is clear that from the minimum quantity of flesh no body can be separated out; for the flesh left would be less than the minimum of flesh.

Again, in each of his infinite bodies there would be already present infinite flesh and blood and brain—having a distinct existence, however, from one another, and no less real than the infinite bodies, and each infinite: which is contrary to reason.

5   The statement that complete separation never will take place is correct enough, though Anaxagoras is not fully aware of what it means. For affections are indeed inseparable. If then colours and states had entered into the mixture, and if separation took place, there would be something white or healthy which was nothing *but* white or healthy, i.e. was not the predicate of a subject. So his Mind absurdly aims at the impos-

10   sible, if it is supposed to wish to separate them, and it is impossible to do so, both in respect of quantity and of quality—of quantity, because there is no minimum magnitude, and of quality, because affections are inseparable.

Nor is Anaxagoras right about the coming to be of homogeneous bodies. It is true there is a sense in which clay is divided into pieces of clay, but there is another in which

15   it is not. Water and air are, and are generated, from each other, but not in the way in which bricks come from a house and again a house from bricks. And it is better to assume a smaller and finite number of principles, as Empedocles does.

5. All thinkers then agree in making the contraries principles, both those who de-

20   scribe the universe as one and unmoved (for even Parmenides treats hot and cold as principles under the names of fire and earth) and those too who use the rare and the dense. The same is true of Democritus also, with his plenum and void, both of which exist, he says, the one as being, the other as not being. Again he speaks of differences in position, shape, and order, and these are genera of which the species are contraries,

namely, of position, above and below, before and behind; of shape, angular and angle- 25
less, straight and round.

It is plain then that they all in one way or another identify the contraries with the
principles. And with good reason. For first principles must not be derived from one another nor from anything else, while everything has to be derived from them. But these
conditions are fulfilled by the primary contraries, which are not derived from anything
else because they are primary, nor from each other because they are contraries. 30

But we must see how this can be arrived at as a reasoned result. Our first presup-
position must be that in nature nothing acts on, or is acted on by, any other thing at random, nor may anything come from anything else, unless we mean that it does so accidentally. For how could white come from musical, unless musical happened to be an at- 35
tribute of the not-white or of the black? No, white comes from not-white—and not from
any not-white, but from black or some intermediate. Similarly, musical comes to be 188ᵇ
from non-musical, but not from *any* thing other than musical, but from unmusical or
any intermediate state there may be.

Nor again do things pass away into the first chance thing; white does not pass
into musical (except, it may be, accidentally), but into not-white—and not into any 5
chance thing which is not white, but into black or an intermediate; musical passes into
not-musical—and not into any chance thing other than musical, but into unmusical or
any intermediate state there may be.

The same holds of other things also: even things which are not simple but complex follow the same principle, but the opposite state has not received a name, so we fail 10
to notice the fact. For what is in tune must come from what is not in tune, and *vice
versa;* the tuned passes into untunedness—and not into *any* untunedness, but into the
corresponding opposite. It does not matter whether we take attunement, order, or com- 15
position for our illustration; the principle is obviously the same in all, and in fact applies
equally to the production of a house, a statue, or anything else. A house comes from certain things in a certain state of separation instead of conjunction, a statue (or any other
thing that has been shaped) from shapelessness—each of these objects being partly or- 20
der and partly composition.

If then this is true, everything that comes to be or passes away comes from, or
passes into, its contrary or an intermediate state. But the intermediates are derived from
the contraries—colours, for instance, from black and white. Everything, therefore, that
comes to be by a natural process is either a contrary or a product of contraries. 25

Up to this point we have practically had most of the other writers on the subject
with us, as I have said already; for all of them identify their elements, and what they call
their principles, with the contraries, giving no reason indeed for the theory, but constrained as it were by the truth itself. They differ, however, from one another in that 30
some assume contraries which are prior, others contraries which are posterior; some
those more knowable in the order of explanation, others those more familiar to sense.
For some make hot and cold, or again moist and dry, the causes of becoming; while others make odd and even, or again Love and Strife; and these differ from each other in the 35
way mentioned.

Hence their principles are in one sense the same, in another different; different
certainly, as indeed most people think, but the same inasmuch as they are analogous; for
all are taken from the same table of columns, some of the pairs being wider, others nar- 189ᵃ
rower in extent. In this way then their theories are both the same and different, some
better, some worse; some, as I have said, take as their contraries what is more knowable
in the order of explanation, others what is more familiar to sense. (The universal is
knowable in the order of explanation, the particular in the order of sense; for explana- 5

tion has to do with the universal, sense with the particular.) The great and the small, for example, belong to the former class, the dense and the rare to the latter.

10   It is clear then that our principles must be contraries.

6. The next question is whether the principles are two or three or more in number.

One they cannot be; for there cannot be one contrary. Nor can they be innumerable, because, if so, what is will not be knowable; and in any one genus there is only one contrariety, and substance is one genus; also a finite number is sufficient, and a finite
15   number, such as the principles of Empedocles, is better than an infinite multitude; for Empedocles professes to obtain all that Anaxagoras obtains from his innumerable principles. Again, some contraries are prior to others, and some arise from others—for example sweet and bitter, white and black—whereas the principles must always remain principles.

20   This will suffice to show that the principles are neither one nor innumerable.

Granted, then, that they are a limited number, it is plausible to suppose them more than two. For it is difficult to see how either density should be of such a nature as to act in any way on rarity or rarity on density. The same is true of any other pair of contraries; for Love does not gather Strife together and make things out of it, nor does Strife make
25   anything out of Love, but both act on a third thing different from both. Some indeed assume more than one such thing from which they construct the world of nature.

Other objections to the view that it is not necessary to posit some other nature under the contraries may be added. We do not find that the contraries constitute the sub-
30   stance of any thing. But what is a first principle ought not to be predicated of any subject. If it were, there would be a principle of the supposed principle; for the subject is a principle, and prior presumably to what is predicated of it. Again, we hold that a substance is not contrary to another substance. How then can substance be derived from what are not substances? Or how can non-substance be prior to substance?

If then we accept both the former argument and this one, we must, to preserve
189ᵇ   both, posit some third thing, such as is spoken of by those who describe the universe as one nature—water or fire or what is intermediate between them. What is intermediate seems preferable; for fire, earth, air, and water are already involved with pairs of con-
5   traries. There is, therefore, much to be said for those who make the underlying substance different from these four; of the rest, the next best choice is air, as presenting sensible differences in a less degree than the others; and after air, water. All, however, agree in this, that they differentiate their One by means of the contraries, such as density and rarity and more and less, which may of course be generalized, as has already been
10   said, into excess and defect. Indeed this doctrine too (that the One and excess and defect are the principles of things) would appear to be of old standing, though in different forms; for the early thinkers made the two the active and the one the passive principle,
15   whereas some of the more recent maintain the reverse.

To suppose then that the elements are three in number would seem, from these and similar considerations, a plausible view, as I said before. On the other hand, the view that they are more than three in number would seem to be untenable.

For one thing is sufficient to be acted on; but if we have four contraries, there will
20   be two contrarieties, and we shall have to suppose an intermediate nature for each pair separately. If, on the other hand, the contrarieties, being two, can generate from each other, the second contrariety will be superfluous. Moreover, it is impossible that there
25   should be more than one *primary* contrariety. For substance is a single genus of being, so that the principles can differ only as prior and posterior, *not* in genus; for in a single

genus there is always a single contrariety, all the other contrarieties in it being held to be reducible to one.

It is clear then that the number of elements is neither one nor more than two or three; but whether two or three is, as I said, a question of considerable difficulty.

7. We will now give our own account, approaching the question first with reference to becoming in its widest sense; for we shall be following the natural order of inquiry if we speak first of common characteristics, and then investigate the characteristics of special cases.

We say that one thing comes to be from another thing, and something from something different, in the case both of simple and of complex things. I mean the following. We can say the man becomes musical, or what is not-musical becomes musical, or the not-musical man becomes a musical man. Now what becomes in the first two cases—man and not-musical—I call *simple,* and what each becomes—musical—simple also. But when we say the not-musical man becomes a musical man, both what becomes and what it becomes are *complex.*

In some cases, we say not only this becomes so-and-so, but also from being this, it comes to be so-and-so (e.g.: from being not-musical he comes to be musical); but we do not say this in all cases, as we do not say from being a man he came to be musical but only the man became musical.

When a simple thing is said to become something, in one case it survives through the process, in the other it does not. For the man remains a man and is such even when he becomes musical, whereas what is not musical or is unmusical does not survive, either simply or combined with the subject.

These distinctions drawn, one can gather from surveying the various cases of becoming in the way we are describing that there must always be an underlying something, namely that which becomes, and that this, though always one numerically, in form at least is not one. (By "in form" I mean the same as "in account.") For to be a man is not the same as to be unmusical. One part survives, the other does not: what is not an opposite survives (for the man survives), but not-musical or unmusical does not survive, nor does the compound of the two, namely the unmusical man.

We speak of "becoming that from this" instead of "this becoming that" more in the case of what does not survive the change—"becoming musical from unmusical," not "from man"—but we sometimes use the latter form of expression even of what survives; we speak of a statue coming to be from bronze, not of the bronze becoming a statue. The change, however, from an opposite which does not survive is described in both ways, "becoming that from this" or "this becoming that." We say both that the unmusical becomes musical, and that from unmusical he becomes musical. And so both forms are used of the complex, "becoming a musical from an unmusical man," and "an unmusical man becoming musical."

Things are said to come to be in different ways. In some cases we do not use the expression "come to be," but "come to be so-and-so." Only substances are said to come to be without qualification.

Now in all cases other than substance it is plain that there must be something underlying, namely, that which becomes. For when a thing comes to be of such a quantity or quality or in such a relation, time, or place, a subject is always presupposed, since substance alone is not predicated of another subject, but everything else of substance.

But that substances too, and anything that can be said to be without qualification, come to be from some underlying thing, will appear on examination. For we find in every case something that underlies from which proceeds that which comes to be; for instance, animals and plants from seed.

5   Things which come to be without qualification, come to be in different ways: by change of shape, as a statue; by addition, as things which grow; by taking away, as the Hermes from the stone; by putting together, as a house; by alteration, as things which turn in respect of their matter.

10   It is plain that these are all cases of coming to be from some underlying thing.

Thus, from what has been said, whatever comes to be is always complex. There is, on the one hand, something which comes to be, and again something which becomes that—the latter in two senses, either the subject or the opposite. By the opposite I mean the unmusical, by the subject, man; and similarly I call the absence of shape or form or
15   order the opposite, and the bronze or stone or gold the subject.

Plainly then, if there are causes and principles which constitute natural objects and from which they primarily are or have come to be—have come to be, I mean, what each is said to be in its substance, not what each is accidentally—plainly, I say, every-
20   thing comes to be from both subject and form. For the musical man is composed in a way of man and musical: you can analyse it into the definitions of its elements. It is clear then that what comes to be will come to be from these elements.

Now the subject is one numerically, though it is two in form. (For there is the
25   man, the gold—in general, the countable matter; for it is more of the nature of a "this," and what comes to be does not come from it accidentally; the privation, on the other hand, and the contrariety *are* accidental.) And the form is one—the order, the art of music, or any similar predicate.

There is a sense, therefore, in which we must declare the principles to be two, and a sense in which they are three; a sense in which the contraries are the principles—say
30   for example the musical and the unmusical, the hot and the cold, the tuned and the untuned—and a sense in which they are not, since it is impossible for the contraries to be acted on by each other. But this difficulty also is solved by the fact that what underlies
35   is different from the contraries; for it is itself not a contrary. The principles therefore are, in a way, not more in number than the contraries, but as it were two; nor yet pre-
191a   cisely two, since there is a difference of being, but three. For to be man is different from to be unmusical, and to be unformed from to be bronze.

We have now stated the number of the principles of natural objects which are subject to generation, and how the number is reached; and it is clear that there must be
5   something underlying the contraries, and that the contraries must be two. (Yet in another way of putting it this is not necessary, as one of the contraries will serve to effect the change by its absence and presence.)

The underlying nature can be known by analogy. For as the bronze is to the
10   statue, the wood to the bed, or the matter and the formless before receiving form to any thing which has form, so is the underlying nature to substance, i.e. the "this" or existent.

This then is one principle (though not one or existent in the same sense as the "this"); one is the form or definition; then further there is its contrary, the privation. In
15   what sense these are two, and in what sense more, has been stated above. We explained first that only the contraries were principles, and later that something else underlay them, and that the principles were three; our last statement has elucidated the difference between the contraries, the mutual relation of the principles, and the nature of what underlies. Whether the form or what underlies is the substance is not yet clear.
20   But that the principles are three, and in what sense, and the way in which each is a principle, is clear.

So much then for the question of the number and the nature of the principles.

8. We will now proceed to show that the difficulty of the early thinkers, as well as our own, is solved in this way alone.

The first of those who studied philosophy were misled in their search for truth and the nature of things by their inexperience, which as it were thrust them into another path. So they say that none of the things that are either comes to be or passes out of existence, because what comes to be must do so either from what is or from what is not, both of which are impossible. For what is cannot come to be (because it *is* already), and from what is not nothing could have come to be (because something must be underlying). So too they exaggerated the consequence of this, and went so far as to deny even the *existence* of a plurality of things maintaining that only what is itself is. Such then was their opinion, and such the reason for its adoption.

Our explanation on the other hand is that for something to come to be from what is or from what is not, or what is not or what is to do something or have something done to it or become some particular thing, are in one way no different from a doctor doing something or having something done to him, or being or becoming something from being a doctor. These expressions may be taken in two ways, and so too, clearly, may "from what is," and "what is acts or is acted on." A doctor builds a house, not *qua* doctor, but *qua* housebuilder, and turns gray, not *qua* doctor, but *qua* dark-haired. On the other hand he doctors or fails to doctor *qua* doctor. But we are using words most appropriately when we say that a doctor does something or undergoes something, or becomes something from being a doctor, if he does, undergoes, or becomes *qua* doctor. Clearly then also to come to be so-and-so from what is not means "*qua* what is not."

It was through failure to make this distinction that those thinkers gave the matter up, and through this error that they went so much farther astray as to suppose that nothing else comes to be or exists apart from what is itself, thus doing away with all becoming.

We ourselves are in agreement with them in holding that nothing can be said without qualification to come from what is not. But nevertheless we maintain that a thing may come to be from what is not in a qualified sense, i.e. accidentally. For a thing comes to be from the privation, which in its own nature is something which is not—this not surviving as a constituent of the result. Yet this causes surprise, and it is thought impossible that something should come to be in the way described from what is not.

In the same way we maintain that nothing comes to be from what is, and that what is does not come to be except accidentally. In that way, however, it does, just as animal might come to be from animal, and an animal of a certain kind from an animal of a certain kind. Thus, suppose a dog to come to be from a dog, or a horse from a horse. The dog would then, it is true, come to be from animal (as well as from an animal of a certain kind) but not as *animal,* for that is already there. But if anything is to become an animal, *not* accidentally, it will not be from animal; and if what is, not from what is—nor from what is not either, for it has been explained that by "from what is not" we mean *qua* what is not.

Note further that we do not subvert the principle that everything either is or is not.

This then is one way of solving the difficulty. Another consists in pointing out that the same things can be spoken of in terms of potentiality and actuality. But this has been done with greater precision elsewhere.

So, as we said, the difficulties which constrain people to deny the existence of some of the things we mentioned are now solved. For it was this reason which also caused some of the earlier thinkers to turn so far aside from the road which leads to coming to be and passing away and change generally. If they had come in sight of this nature, all their ignorance would have been dispelled.

35   9. Others, indeed, have apprehended the nature in question, but not adequately.

In the first place they allow that a thing may come to be without qualification
192ᵃ   from what is not, accepting on this point the statement of Parmenides. Secondly, they
think that if it is one numerically, it must have also only a single potentiality which is a
very different thing.

Now we distinguish matter and privation, and hold that one of these, namely the
matter, accidentally is not, while the privation in its own nature is not; and that the mat-
5   ter is nearly, in a sense *is,* substance, while the privation in no sense is. They, on the
other hand, identify their Great and Small alike with what is not, and that whether they
10   are taken together as one or separately. Their triad is therefore of quite a different kind
from ours. For they got so far as to see that there must be some underlying nature, but
they make it one—for even if one philosopher [Plato] makes a dyad of it, which he calls
Great and Small, the effect is the same; for he overlooked the other nature. For the one
which persists is a joint cause, with the form, of what comes to be—a mother, as it were.
15   But the other part of the contrariety may often seem, if you concentrate your attention
on it as an evil agent, not to exist at all.

For admitting that there is something divine, good, and desirable, we hold that
there are two other principles, the one contrary to it, the other such as of its own nature
to desire and yearn for it. But the consequence of their view is that the contrary desires
20   its own extinction. Yet the form cannot desire itself, for it is not defective; nor can the
contrary desire it, for contraries are mutually destructive. The truth is that what desires
the form is matter, as the female desires the male and the ugly the beautiful—only the
ugly or the female not in itself but accidentally.

25   The matter comes to be and ceases to be in one sense, while in another it does not.
As that which contains the privation, it ceases to be in its own nature; for what ceases to
be—the privation—is contained within it. But as potentiality it does not cease to be in
its own nature, but is necessarily outside the sphere of becoming and ceasing to be. For
30   if it came to be, something must have existed as a primary substratum from which it
should come and which should persist in it; but this is its own very nature, so that it will
be before coming to be. (For my definition of matter is just this—the primary substratum of each thing, from which it comes to be, and which persists in the result, not accidentally.) And if it ceases to be it will pass into that at the last, so it will have ceased to
be before ceasing to be.

The accurate determination of the first principle in respect of form, whether it is
35   one or many and what it is or what they are, is the province of first philosophy; so these
192ᵇ   questions may stand over till then. But of the natural, i.e. perishable, forms we shall
speak in the expositions which follow.

The above, then, may be taken as sufficient to establish that there are principles
and what they are and how many there are. Now let us make a fresh start and proceed.

BOOK II

1. Of things that exist, some exist by nature, some from other causes. By nature the an-
10   imals and their parts exist, and the plants and the simple bodies (earth, fire, air, water)—
for we say that these and the like exist by nature.

All the things mentioned plainly differ from things which are *not* constituted by
nature. For each of them has within itself a principle of motion and of stationariness (in
15   respect of place, or of growth and decrease, or by way of alteration). On the other hand,

a bed and a coat and anything else of that sort, *qua* receiving these designations—i.e. in so far as they are products of art—have no innate impulse to change. But in so far as they happen to be composed of stone or of earth or of a mixture of the two, they *do* have   20 such an impulse, and just to that extent which seems to indicate that nature is a principle or cause of being moved and of being at rest in that to which it belongs primarily, in virtue of itself and not accidentally.

I say "not accidentally," because (for instance) a man who is a doctor might himself be a cause of health to himself. Nevertheless it is not in so far as he is a patient that   25 he possesses the art of medicine: it merely has happened that the same man is doctor and patient—and that is why these attributes are not always found together. So it is with all other artificial products. None of them has in itself the principle of its own production. But while in some cases (for instance houses and the other products of manual   30 labour) that principle is in something else external to the thing, in others—those which may cause a change in themselves accidentally—it lies in the things themselves (but not in virtue of what they are).

Nature then is what has been stated. Things have a nature which have a principle of this kind. Each of them is a substance; for it is a subject, and nature is always in a subject.

The term "according to nature" is applied to all these things and also to the at-   35 tributes which belong to them in virtue of what they are, for instance the property of fire to be carried upwards—which is not a nature nor has a nature but is by nature or ac-   193a cording to nature.

What nature is, then, and the meaning of the terms "by nature" and "according to nature," has been stated. *That* nature exists, it would be absurd to try to prove; for it is obvious that there are many things of this kind, and to prove what is obvious by what is not is the mark of a man who is unable to distinguish what is self-evident from what is   5 not. (This state of mind is clearly possible. A man blind from birth might reason about colours.) Presumably therefore such persons must be talking about words without any thought to correspond.

Some identify the nature or substance of a natural object with that immediate con-   10 stituent of it which taken by itself is without arrangement, e.g. the wood is the nature of the bed, and the bronze the nature of the statue.

As an indication of this Antiphon points out that if you planted a bed and the rotting wood acquired the power of sending up a shoot, it would not be a bed that would come up, but *wood* which shows that the arrangement in accordance with the rules of   15 the art is merely an accidental attribute, whereas the substance is the other, which, further, persists continuously through the process.

But if the material of each of these objects has itself the same relation to something else, say bronze (or gold) to water, bones (or wood) to earth and so on, *that* (they   20 say) would be their nature and substance. Consequently some assert earth, others fire or air or water or some or all of these, to be the nature of the things that are. For whatever any one of them supposed to have this character—whether one thing or more than one thing—this or these he declared to be the whole of substance, all else being its affec-   25 tions, states, or dispositions. Every such thing they held to be eternal (for it could not pass into anything else), but other things to come into being and cease to be times without number.

This then is one account of nature, namely that it is the primary underlying matter of things which have in themselves a principle of motion or change.

Another account is that nature is the shape or form which is specified in the defi-   30 nition of the thing.

For the word "nature" is applied to what is according to nature and the natural in the same way as "art" is applied to what is artistic or a work of art. We should not say in the latter case that there is anything artistic about a thing, if it is a bed only poten-
35   tially, not yet having the form of a bed; nor should we call it a work of art. The same is true of natural compounds. What is potentially flesh or bone has not yet its own nature,
193ᵇ   and does not exist by nature, until it receives the form specified in the definition, which we name in defining what flesh or bone is. Thus on the second account of nature, it
5   would be the shape or form (not separable except in statement) of things which have in themselves a principle of motion. (The combination of the two, e.g. man, is not nature but by nature.)

The form indeed is nature rather than the matter; for a thing is more properly said to be what it is when it exists in actuality than when it exists potentially. Again man is born from man but not bed from bed. That is why people say that the shape is not the na-
10   ture of a bed, but the wood is—if the bed sprouted, not a bed but wood would come up. But even if the shape *is* art, then on the same principle the shape of man is his nature. For man is born from man.

Again, nature in the sense of a coming-to-be proceeds towards nature. For it is
15   not like doctoring, which leads not to the art of doctoring but to health. Doctoring must start from the art, not lead to it. But it is not in this way that nature is related to nature. What grows *qua* growing grows from something into something. Into what then does it grow? Not into that from which it arose but into that to which it tends. The shape then is nature.

Shape and nature are used in two ways. For the privation too is in a way form. But
20   whether in unqualified coming to be there is privation, i.e. a contrary, we must consider later.

2. We have distinguished, then, the different ways in which the term "nature" is used.

The next point to consider is how the mathematician differs from the student of nature; for natural bodies contain surfaces and volumes, lines and points, and these are
25   the subject-matter of mathematics.

Further, is astronomy different from natural science or a department of it? It seems absurd that the student of nature should be supposed to know the nature of sun or moon, but not to know any of their essential attributes, particularly as the writers on na-
30   ture obviously do discuss their shape and whether the earth and the world are spherical or not.

Now the mathematician, though he too treats of these things, nevertheless does not treat of them as the limits of a natural body; nor does he consider the attributes indicated as the attributes of such bodies. That is why he separates them, for in thought they are separable from motion, and it makes no difference, nor does any falsity result, if
35   they are separated. The holders of the theory of Forms do the same, though they are not aware of it; for they separate the objects of natural science, which are less separable
194ᵃ   than those of mathematics. This becomes plain if one tries to state in each of the two cases the definitions of the things and of their attributes. Odd and even, straight and curved, and likewise number, line, and figure, do not involve motion; not so flesh and
5   bone and man—*these* are defined like snub nose, not like curved.

Similar evidence is supplied by the more natural of the branches of mathematics, such as optics, harmonics, and astronomy. These are in a way the converse of geometry.
10   While geometry investigates natural lines but not *qua* natural, optics investigates mathematical lines, but *qua* natural, not *qua* mathematical.

Since two sorts of thing are called nature, the form and the matter, we must investigate its objects as we would the essence of snubness, that is neither independently of matter nor in terms of matter only. Here too indeed one might raise a difficulty. 15 Since there are two natures, with which is the student of nature concerned? Or should he investigate the combination of the two? But if the combination of the two, then also each severally. Does it belong then to the same or to different sciences to know each severally?

If we look at the ancients, natural science would seem to be concerned with the *matter*. (It was only very slightly that Empedocles and Democritus touched on form and 20 essence.)

But if on the other hand art imitates nature, and it is the part of the same discipline to know the form and the matter up to a point (e.g. the doctor has a knowledge of health and also of bile and phlegm, in which health is realized and the builder both of the form of the house and of the matter, namely that it is bricks and beams, and so 25 forth): if this is so, it would be the part of natural science also to know nature in both its senses.

Again, that for the sake of which, or the end, belongs to the same department of knowledge as the means. But the nature is the end or that for the sake of which. For if a thing undergoes a continuous change toward some end, that last stage is actually that for 30 the sake of which. (That is why the poet was carried away into making an absurd statement when he said "he has the end for the sake of which he was born." For not every stage that is last claims to be an end, but only that which is best.)

For the arts make their material (some simply make it, others make it serviceable), and we use everything as if it was there for our sake. (We also are in a sense an 35 end. "That for the sake of which" may be taken in two ways, as we said in our work *On Philosophy*.) The arts, therefore, which govern the matter and have knowledge are two, 194ᵇ namely the art which uses the product and the art which directs the production of it. That is why the using art also is in a sense directive; but it differs in that it knows the form, whereas the art which is directive as being concerned with production knows the matter. For the helmsman knows and prescribes what sort of form a helm should have, 5 the other from what wood it should be made and by means of what operations. In the products of art, however, we make the material with a view to the function, whereas in the products of nature the matter is there all along.

Again, matter is a relative thing—for different forms there is different matter.

How far then must the student of nature know the form or essence? Up to a point, 10 perhaps, as the doctor must know sinew or the smith bronze (i.e. until he understands the purpose of each); and the student of nature is concerned only with things whose forms are separable indeed, but do not exist apart from matter. Man is begotten by man and by the sun as well. The mode of existence and essence of the separable it is the busi- 15 ness of first philosophy to define.

3. Now that we have established these distinctions, we must proceed to consider causes, their character and number. Knowledge is the object of our inquiry, and men do not think they know a thing till they have grasped the "why" of it (which is to grasp its 20 primary cause). So clearly we too must do this as regards both coming to be and passing away and every kind of natural change, in order that, knowing their principles, we may try to refer to these principles each of our problems.

In one way, then, that out of which a thing comes to be and which persists, is called a cause, e.g. the bronze of the statue, the silver of the bowl, and the genera of 25 which the bronze and the silver are species.

In another way, the form or the archetype, i.e. the definition of the essence, and its genera, are called causes (e.g. of the octave the relation of 2:1, and generally number), and the parts in the definition.

30   Again, the primary source of the change or rest; e.g. the man who deliberated is a cause, the father is cause of the child, and generally what makes of what is made and what changes of what is changed.

Again, in the sense of end or that for the sake of which a thing is done, e.g. health is the cause of walking about. ("Why is he walking about?" We say: "To be healthy,"

35   and, having said that, we think we have assigned the cause.) The same is true also of all the intermediate steps which are brought about through the action of something else as means towards the end, e.g. reduction of flesh, purging, drugs, or surgical instruments

195ᵃ   are means towards health. All these things are for the sake of the end, though they differ from one another in that some are activities, others instruments.

This then perhaps exhausts the number of ways in which the term "cause" is used.

As things are called causes in many ways, it follows that there are several causes

5   of the same thing (not merely accidentally), e.g. both the art of the sculptor and the bronze are causes of the statue. These are causes of the statue *qua* statue, not in virtue of anything else that it may be—only not in the same way, the one being the material cause, the other the cause whence the motion comes. Some things cause each other reciprocally, e.g. hard work causes fitness and *vice versa,* but again not in the same way,

10   but the one as end, the other as the principle of motion. Further the same thing is the cause of contrary results. For that which by its presence brings about one result is sometimes blamed for bringing about the contrary by its absence. Thus we ascribe the wreck of a ship to the absence of the pilot whose presence was the cause of its safety.

All the causes now mentioned fall into four familiar divisions. The letters are the

15   causes of syllables, the material of artificial products, fire and the like of bodies, the parts of the whole, and the premises of the conclusion, in the sense of "that from which." Of these pairs the one set are causes in the sense of what underlies, e.g. the parts, the other set in the sense of essence—the whole and the combination and the

20   form. But the seed and the doctor and the deliberator, and generally the maker, are all sources whence the change or stationariness originates, which the others are causes in the sense of the end or the good of the rest; for that for the sake of which tends to be

25   what is best and the end of the things that lead up to it. (Whether we call it good or apparently good makes no difference.)

Such then is the number and nature of the kinds of cause.

Now the modes of causation are many, though when brought under heads they too can be reduced in number. For things are called causes in many ways and even

30   within the same kind one may be prior to another: e.g. the doctor and the expert are causes of health, the relation 2:1 and number of the octave, and always what is inclusive to what is particular. Another mode of causation is the accidental and its genera, e.g. in one way Polyclitus, in another a sculptor is the cause of a statue, because being Polycli-

35   tus and a sculptor are accidentally conjoined. Also the classes in which the accidental attribute is included; thus a man could be said to be the cause of a statue or, generally, a

195ᵇ   living creature. An accidental attribute too may be more or less remote, e.g. suppose that a pale man or a musical man were said to be the cause of the statue.

All causes, both proper and accidental, may be spoken of either as potential or as actual; e.g. the cause of a house being built is either a house-builder or a house-builder

5   building.

Similar distinctions can be made in the things of which the causes are causes, e.g. of this statue or of a statue or of an image generally, of this bronze or of bronze or of

material generally. So too with the accidental attributes. Again we may use a complex   10
expression for either and say, e.g., neither "Polyclitus" nor a "sculptor" but "Polyclitus,
the sculptor."

All these various uses, however, come to six in number, under each of which
again the usage is twofold. It is either what is particular or a genus, or an accidental
attribute or a genus of that, and these either as a complex or each by itself; and all ei-   15
ther as actual or as potential. The difference is this much, that causes which are actually at work and particular exist and cease to exist simultaneously with their effect,
e.g. this healing person with this being-healed person and that housebuilding man with
that being-built house; but this is not always true of potential causes—the house and   20
the housebuilder do not pass away simultaneously.

In investigating the cause of each thing it is always necessary to seek what is most
precise (as also in other things): thus a man builds because he is a builder, and a builder
builds in virtue of his art of building. This last cause then is prior; and so generally.   25

Further, generic effects should be assigned to generic causes, particular effects to
particular causes, e.g. statue to sculptor, this statue to this sculptor; and powers are relative to possible effects, actually operating causes to things which are actually being effected.

This must suffice for our account of the number of causes and the modes of   30
causation.

4. But chance and spontaneity are also reckoned among causes: many things are
said both to be and to come to be as a result of chance and spontaneity. We must inquire
therefore in what manner chance and spontaneity are present among the causes enu-   35
merated, and whether they are the same or different, and generally what chance and
spontaneity are.

Some people even question whether there are such things or not. They say that
nothing happens by chance, but that everything which we ascribe to chance or spon-   196ᵃ
taneity has some definite cause, e.g. coming by chance into the market and finding there
a man whom one wanted but did not expect to meet is due to one's wish to go and buy
in the market. Similarly, in other so-called cases of chance it is always possible, they   5
maintain, to find something which is the cause; but not chance, for if chance were real,
it would seem strange indeed, and the question might be raised, why on earth none of
the wise men of old in speaking of the causes of generation and decay took account of   10
chance; whence it would seem that they too did not believe that anything is by chance.
But there is a further circumstance that is surprising. Many things both come to be and
are by chance and spontaneity, and although all know that each of them can be ascribed
to some cause (as the old argument said which denied chance), nevertheless they all   15
speak of some of these things as happening by chance and others not. For this reason
they ought to have at least referred to the matter in some way or other.

Certainly the early physicists found no place for chance among the causes which
they recognized—love, strife, mind, fire, or the like. This is strange, whether they supposed that there is no such thing as chance or whether they thought there is but omitted
to mention it—and that too when they sometimes used it, as Empedocles does when he   20
says that the air is not always separated into the highest region, but as it may chance. At
any rate he says in his cosmogony that "it happened to run that way at that time, but it
often ran otherwise." He tells us also that most of the parts of animals came to be by
chance.

There are some who actually ascribe this heavenly sphere and all the worlds to   25
spontaneity. They say that the vortex arose spontaneously, i.e. the motion that separated

and arranged the universe in its present order. This statement might well cause surprise.
For they are asserting that chance is not responsible for the existence or generation of
30   animals and plants, nature or mind or something of the kind being the cause of them (for
it is not any chance thing that comes from a given seed but an olive from one kind and
a man from another); and yet at the same time they assert that the heavenly sphere and
the divinest of visible things arose spontaneously, having no such cause as is assigned
35   to animals and plants. Yet if this is so, it is a fact which deserves to be dwelt upon, and
something might well have been said about it. For besides the other absurdities of the
196ᵇ   statement, it is the more absurd that people should make it when they see nothing coming to be spontaneously in the heavens, but much happening by chance among the
things which as they say are not due to chance; whereas we should have expected exactly the opposite.
5   Others there are who believe that chance is a cause, but that it is inscrutable to human intelligence, as being a divine thing and full of mystery.
        Thus we must inquire what chance and spontaneity are, whether they are the same
or different, and how they fit into our division of causes.

10   5. First then we observe that some things always come to pass in the same way,
and others for the most part. It is clearly of neither of these that chance, or the result of
chance, is said to be the cause—neither of that which is by necessity and always, nor of
that which is for the most part. But as there is a third class of events besides these two—
15   events which all say are by chance—it is plain that there is such a thing as chance and
spontaneity; for we know that things of this kind are due to chance and that things due
to chance are of this kind.
        Of things that come to be, some come to be for the sake of something, others not.
Again, some of the former class are in accordance with intention, others not, but both
are in the class of things which are for the sake of something. Hence it is clear that even
20   among the things which are outside what is necessary and what is for the most part,
there are some in connexion with which the phrase "for the sake of something" is applicable. (Things that are for the sake of something include whatever may be done as a result of thought or of nature.) Things of this kind, then, when they come to pass acciden-
25   tally are said to be by chance. For just as a thing is something either in virtue of itself or
accidentally, so may it be a cause. For instance, the housebuilding faculty is in virtue of
itself a cause of a house, whereas the pale or the musical is an accidental cause. That
which is *per se* cause is determinate, but the accidental cause is indeterminable; for the
possible attributes of an individual are innumerable. As we said, then, when a thing of
30   this kind comes to pass among events which are for the sake of something, it is said to
be spontaneous or by chance. (The distinction between the two must be made later—for
the present it is sufficient if it is plain that both are in the sphere of things done for the
sake of something.)
        Example: A man is engaged in collecting subscriptions for a feast. He would
35   have gone to such and such a place for the purpose of getting the money, if he had
known. He actually went there for another purpose, and it was only accidentally that
he got his money by going there; and this was not due to the fact that he went there as
197ᵃ   a rule or necessarily, nor is the end effected (getting the money) a cause present in
himself—it belongs to the class of things that are objects of choice and the result of
thought. It is when these conditions are satisfied that the man is said to have gone by
chance. If he had chosen and gone for the sake of this—if he always or normally went
5   there when he was collecting payments—he would not be said to have gone by
chance.

It is clear then that chance is an accidental cause in the sphere of those actions for the sake of something which involves choice. Thought, then, and chance are in the same sphere, for choice implies thought.

It is necessary, no doubt, that the causes of what comes to pass by chance be indefinite; and that is why chance is supposed to belong to the class of the indefinite and 10 to be inscrutable to man, and why it might be thought that, in a way, nothing occurs by chance. For all these statements are correct, as might be expected. Things *do,* in a way, occur by chance, for they occur accidentally and chance is an accidental cause. But it is not the cause without qualification of anything; for instance, a housebuilder is the cause 15 of a house; accidentally, a fluteplayer may be so.

And the causes of the man's coming and getting the money (when he did not come for the sake of that) are innumerable. He may have wished to see somebody or been following somebody or avoiding somebody, or may have gone to see a spectacle. Thus to say that chance is unaccountable is correct. For an account is of what holds always or for the most part, whereas chance belongs to a third type of event. Hence, 20 since causes of this kind are indefinite, chance too is indefinite. (Yet in some cases one might raise the question whether *any* chance fact might be the cause of the chance occurrence, e.g. of health the fresh air or the sun's heat may be the cause, but having had one's hair cut *cannot;* for some accidental causes are more relevant to the effect than others.)

Chance is called good when the result is good, evil when it is evil. The terms 25 "good fortune" and "ill fortune" are used when either result is of considerable magnitude. Thus one who comes within an ace of some great evil or great good is said to be fortunate or unfortunate. The mind affirms the presence of the attribute, ignoring the hair's breadth of difference. Further, it is with reason that good fortune is regarded as unstable; for chance is unstable, as none of the things which result from it can hold al- 30 ways or for the most part.

Both are then, as I have said, accidental causes—both chance and spontaneity— in the sphere of things which are capable of coming to pass not simply, nor for the most part and with reference to such of these as might come to pass for the sake of 35 something.

6. They differ in that spontaneity is the wider. Every result of chance is from what is spontaneous, but not everything that is from what is spontaneous is from chance.

Chance and what results from chance are appropriate to agents that are capable 197^b of good fortune and of action generally. Therefore necessarily chance is in the sphere of actions. This is indicated by the fact that good fortune is thought to be the same, or nearly the same, as happiness, and happiness to be a kind of action, since it 5 is well-doing. Hence what is not capable of action cannot do anything by chance. Thus an inanimate thing or a beast or a child cannot do anything by chance, because it is incapable of choice; nor can good fortune or ill fortune be ascribed to them, except metaphorically, as Protarchus, for example, said that the stones of which altars 10 are made are fortunate because they are held in honour, while their fellows are trodden under foot. Even these things, however, can in a way be affected by chance, when one who is dealing with them does something to them by chance, but not otherwise.

The spontaneous on the other hand is found both in the beasts and in many inanimate objects. We say, for example, that the horse came spontaneously, because, though 15 his coming saved him, he did not come for the sake of safety. Again, the tripod fell spontaneously, because, though it stood on its feet so as to serve for a seat, it did not fall so as to serve for a seat.

Hence it is clear that events which belong to the general class of things that may come to pass for the sake of something, when they come to pass not for the sake of what

20   actually results, and have an external cause, may be described by the phrase "from spontaneity." These spontaneous events are said to be from chance if they have the further characteristics of being the objects of choice and happening to agents capable of choice. This is indicated by the phrase "in vain," which is used when one thing which is for the sake of another, does not result in it. For instance, taking a walk is for the sake of evacuation of the bowels; if this does not follow after walking, we say that we have walked in vain and that the walking was vain. This implies that what is naturally for the

25   sake of an end is in vain, when it does not effect the end for the sake of which it was the natural means—for it would be absurd for a man to say that he had bathed in vain because the sun was not eclipsed, since the one was not done for the sake of the other. Thus the spontaneous is even according to its derivation the case in which the thing itself happens in vain. The stone that struck the man did not fall for the sake of striking

30   him; therefore it fell spontaneously, because it might have fallen by the action of an agent and for the sake of striking. The difference between spontaneity and what results by chance is greatest in things that come to be by nature; for when anything comes to be contrary to nature, we do not say that it came to be by chance, but by spontaneity. Yet

35   strictly this too is different from the spontaneous proper; for the cause of the latter is external, that of the former internal.

198ª   We have now explained what chance is and what spontaneity is, and in what they differ from each other. Both belong to the mode of causation "source of change," for either some natural or some intelligent agent is always the cause; but in this sort of causation the number of possible causes is infinite.

5   Spontaneity and chance are causes of effects which, though they might result from intelligence or nature, have in fact been caused by something accidentally. Now since nothing which is accidental is prior to what is *per se*, it is clear that no accidental

10   cause can be prior to a cause *per se*. Spontaneity and chance, therefore, are posterior to intelligence and nature. Hence, however true it may be that the heavens are due to spontaneity, it will still be true that intelligence and nature will be prior causes of this universe and of many things in it besides.

7. It is clear then that there are causes, and that the number of them is what we

15   have stated. The number is the same as that of the things comprehended under the question "why." The "why" is referred ultimately either, in things which do not involve motion, e.g. in mathematics, to the "what" (to the definition of straight line or commensurable or the like); or to what initiated a motion, e.g. "why did they go to war?—because there had been a raid"; or we are inquiring "for the sake of what?"—"that they may

20   rule"; or in the case of things that come into being, we are looking for the matter. The causes, therefore, are these and so many in number.

Now, the causes being four, it is the business of the student of nature to know about them all, and if he refers his problems back to all of them, he will assign the

25   "why" in the way proper to his science—the matter, the form, the mover, that for the sake of which. The last three often coincide; for the what and that for the sake of which are one, while the primary source of motion is the same in species as these. For man generates man—and so too, in general, with all things which cause movement by being themselves moved; and such as are not of this kind are no longer inside the province of natural science, for they cause motion not by possessing motion

or a source of motion in themselves, but being themselves incapable of motion. Hence there are three branches of study, one of things which are incapable of mo-   30
tion, the second of things in motion, but indestructible, the third of destructible things.

The question "why," then, is answered by reference to the matter, to the form, and to the primary moving cause. For in respect of coming to be it is mostly in this last way that causes are investigated—"what comes to be after what? what was the primary agent or patient?" and so at each step of the series.   35

Now the principles which cause motion in a natural way are two, of which one is not natural, as it has no principle of motion in itself. Of this kind is whatever causes   198^b
movement, not being itself moved, such as that which is completely unchangeable, the primary reality, and the essence of a thing, i.e. the form; for this is the end or that for the sake of which. Hence since nature is for the sake of something, we must know this cause also. We must explain the "why" in all the senses of the term, namely, that from   5
this that will necessarily result ("from this" either without qualification or for the most part); that this must be so if that is to be so (as the conclusion presupposes the premises); that this was the essence of the thing; and because it is better thus (not without qualification, but with reference to the substance in each case).

8. We must explain then first why nature belongs to the class of causes which act   10
for the sake of something; and then about the necessary and its place in nature, for all writers ascribe things to this cause, arguing that since the hot and the cold and the like are of such and such a kind, therefore certain things *necessarily* are and come to be—
and if they mention any other cause (one friendship and strife, another mind), it is only   15
to touch on it, and then good-bye to it.

A difficulty presents itself: why should not nature work, not for the sake of something, nor because it is better so, but just as the sky rains, not in order to make the corn grow, but of necessity? (What is drawn up must cool, and what has been cooled must become water and descend, the result of this being that the corn grows.) Similarly if a   20
man's crop is spoiled on the threshing-floor, the rain did not fall for the sake of this—in order that the crop might be spoiled—but that result just followed. Why then should it not be the same with the parts in nature, e.g. that our teeth should come up of necessity—the front teeth sharp, fitted for tearing, the molars broad and useful for grinding   25
down the food—since they did not arise for this end, but it was merely a coincident result; and so with all other parts in which we suppose that there is purpose? Wherever then all the parts came about just what they would have been if they had come to be for an end, such things survived, being organized spontaneously in a fitting way; whereas   30
those which grew otherwise perished and continue to perish, as Empedocles says his "man-faced ox-progeny" did.

Such are the arguments (and others of the kind) which may cause difficulty on this point. Yet it is impossible that this should be the true view. For teeth and all other natural things either invariably or for the most part come about in a given way; but of   35
not one of the results of chance or spontaneity is this true. We do not ascribe to chance or mere coincidence the frequency of rain in winter, but frequent rain in summer we do;   199^a
nor heat in summer but only if we have it in winter. If then, it is agreed that things are either the result of coincidence or for the sake of something, and these cannot be the result of coincidence or spontaneity, it follows that they must be for the sake of some-   5
thing; and that such things are all due to nature even the champions of the theory which is before us would agree. Therefore action for an end is present in things which come to be and are by nature.

10   Further, where there is an end, all the preceding steps are for the sake of that. Now surely as in action, so in nature; and as in nature, so it is in each action, if nothing interferes. Now action is for the sake of an end; therefore the nature of things also is so. Thus if a house, e.g., had been a thing made by nature, it would have been made in the same way as it is now by art; and if things made by nature were made not only by nature but

15   also by art, they would come to be in the same way as by nature. The one, then, is for the sake of the other; and generally art in some cases completes what nature cannot bring to a finish, and in others imitates nature. If, therefore, artificial products are for the sake of an end, so clearly also are natural products. The relation of the later to the earlier items is the same in both.

20   This is most obvious in the animals other than man: they make things neither by art nor after inquiry or deliberation. That is why people wonder whether it is by intelligence or by some other faculty that these creatures work,—spiders, ants, and the like. By gradual advance in this direction we come to see clearly that in plants too that is pro-

25   duced which is conducive to the end—leaves, e.g. grow to provide shade for the fruit. If then it is both by nature and for an end that the swallow makes its nest and the spider its web, and plants grow leaves for the sake of the fruit and send their roots down (not up)

30   for the sake of nourishment, it is plain that this kind of cause is operative in things which come to be and are by nature. And since nature is twofold, the matter and the form, of which the latter is the end, and since all the rest is for the sake of the end, the form must be the cause in the sense of that for the sake of which.

Now mistakes occur even in the operations of art: the literate man makes a mis-

199ᵇ   take in writing and the doctor pours out the wrong dose. Hence clearly mistakes are possible in the operations of nature also. If then in art there are cases in which what is rightly produced serves a purpose, and if where mistakes occur there was a purpose in what was attempted, only it was not attained, so must it be also in natural products,

5   and monstrosities will be failures in the purposive effort. Thus in the original combinations the "ox-progeny," if they failed to reach a determinate end must have arisen through the corruption of some principle, as happens now when the seed is defective.

Further, seed must have come into being first, and not straightway the animals: what was "undifferentiated first" was seed.

10   Again, in plants too we find that for the sake of which, though the degree of organization is less. Were there then in plants also olive-headed vine-progeny, like the "man-headed ox-progeny," or not? An absurd suggestion; yet there must have been, if there were such things among animals.

Moreover, among the seeds anything must come to be at random. But the person

15   who asserts this entirely does away with nature and what exists by nature. For those things are natural which, by a continuous movement originated from an internal principle, arrive at some end: the same end is not reached from every principle; nor any chance end, but always the tendency in each is towards the same end, if there is no impediment.

The end and the means towards it may come about by chance. We say, for in-

20   stance, that a stranger has come by chance, paid the ransom, and gone away, when he does so as if he had come for that purpose, though it was not for that that he came. This is accidental, for chance is an accidental cause, as I remarked before. But when an event

25   takes place always or for the most part, it is not accidental or by chance. In natural products the sequence is invariable, if there is no impediment.

It is absurd to suppose that purpose is not present because we do not observe the agent deliberating. Art does not deliberate. If the ship-building art were in the wood, it

would produce the same results by nature. If, therefore, purpose is present in art, it is   30
present also in nature. The best illustration is a doctor doctoring himself: nature is like
that.

It is plain then that nature is a cause, a cause that operates for a purpose.

9. As regards what is of necessity, we must ask whether the necessity is hypo-   35
thetical, or simple as well. The current view places what is of necessity in the process
of production, just as if one were to suppose that the wall of a house necessarily   200ᵃ
comes to be because what is heavy is naturally carried downwards and what is light to
the top, so that the stones and foundations take the lowest place, with earth above because it is lighter, and wood at the top of all as being the lightest. Whereas, though the
wall does not come to be *without* these, it is not *due* to these, except as its material   5
cause: it comes to be for the sake of sheltering and guarding certain things. Similarly
in all other things which involve that for the sake of which: the product cannot come
to be without things which have a necessary nature, but it is not due to these (except
as its material); it comes to be for an end. For instance, why is a saw such as it is? To
effect so-and-so and for the sake of so-and-so. This end, however, cannot be realized   10
unless the saw is made of iron. It is, therefore, necessary for it to be of iron, if we are
to have a saw and perform the operation of sawing. What is necessary then, is necessary on a hypothesis, not as an end. Necessity is in the matter, while that for the sake
of which is in the definition.

Necessity in mathematics is in a way similar to necessity in things which   15
come to be through the operation of nature. Since a straight line is what it is, it is
necessary that the angles of a triangle should equal two right angles. But not conversely; though if the angles are *not* equal to two right angles, then the straight
line is not what it is either. But in things which come to be for an end, the reverse   20
is true. If the end is to exist or does exist, that also which precedes it will exist or
does exist; otherwise just as there, if the conclusion is not true, the principle will
not be true, so here the end or that for the sake of which will not exist. For this
too is itself a principle, but of the reasoning, not of the action. (In mathematics the
principle is the principle of the reasoning only, as there is no action.) If then there   25
is to be a house, such-and-such things must be made or be there already or exist,
or generally the matter relative to the end, bricks and stones if it is a house. But
the end is not due to these except as the matter, nor will it come to exist because
of them. Yet if they do not exist at all, neither will the house, or the saw—the former in the absence of stones, the latter in the absence of iron—just as in the other
case the principles will not be true, if the angles of the triangle are not equal to   30
two right angles.

The necessary in nature, then, is plainly what we call by the name of matter, and
the changes in it. Both causes must be stated by the student of nature, but especially the
end; for that is the cause of the matter, not *vice versa;* and the end is that for the sake of
which, and the principle starts from the definition or essence: as in artificial products,   200ᵇ
since a house is of such-and-such a kind, certain things must *necessarily* come to be or
be there already, or since health is this, these things must necessarily come to be or be
there already, so too if man is this, then these; if these, then those. Perhaps the necessary
is present also in the definition. For if one defines the operation of sawing as being a   5
certain kind of dividing, then this cannot come about unless the saw has teeth of a certain kind; and these cannot be unless it is of iron. For in the definition too there are some
parts that stand as matter.

METAPHYSICS (in part)

BOOK I

980ª   1. All men by nature desire to know. An indication of this is the delight we take in our senses; for even apart from their usefulness they are loved for themselves; and above all

25   others the sense of sight. For not only with a view to action, but even when we are not going to do anything, we prefer sight to almost everything else. The reason is that this, most of all the senses, makes us know and brings to light many differences between things.

By nature animals are born with the faculty of sensation, and from sensation

980ᵇ   memory is produced in some of them, though not in others. And therefore the former are more intelligent and apt at learning than those which cannot remember; those which are incapable of hearing sounds are intelligent though they cannot be taught, e.g. the bee, and any other race of animals that may be like it; and those which besides memory

25   have this sense of hearing, can be taught.

The animals other than man live by appearances and memories, and have but little of connected experience; but the human race lives also by art and reasonings. And from memory experience is produced in men; for many memories of the same thing

981ª   produce finally the capacity for a single experience. Experience seems to be very similar to science and art, but really science and art come to men *through* experience; for

5   "experience made art," as Polus says, "but inexperience luck." And art arises, when from many notions gained by experience one universal judgement about similar objects is produced. For to have a judgement that when Callias was ill of this disease this did him good, and similarly in the case of Socrates and in many individual cases, is a mat-

10   ter of experience; but to judge that it has done good to all persons of a certain constitution, marked off in one class, when they were ill of this disease, e.g. to phlegmatic or bilious people when burning with fever,—this is a matter of art.

With a view to action experience seems in no respect inferior to art, and we even see men of experience succeeding more than those who have theory without experi-

15   ence. The reason is that experience is knowledge of individuals, art of universals, and actions and productions are all concerned with the individual; for the physician does not cure a man, except in an incidental way, but Callias or Socrates or some other called by

20   some such individual name, who happens to be a man. If, then, a man has theory without experience, and knows the universal but does not know the individual included in this, he will often fail to cure; for it is the individual that is to be cured. But yet we think

25   that *knowledge* and *understanding* belong to art rather than to experience, and we suppose artists to be wiser than men of experience (which implies that wisdom depends in all cases rather on knowledge); and this because the former know the cause, but the latter do not. For men of experience know that the thing is so, but do not know why, while

30   the others know the "why" and the cause. Hence we think that the master-workers in each craft are more honourable and know in a truer sense and are wiser than the manual

981ᵇ   workers, because they know the causes of the things that are done (we think the manual workers are like certain lifeless things which act indeed, but act without knowing what they do, as fire burns,—but while the lifeless things perform each of their functions by

Aristotle, *Metaphysics,* Books I and XII, translated by W.D. Ross from *The Works of Aristotle,* translated into English under the editorship of W.D. Ross (Oxford: Clarendon Press, 1908–1952). Reprinted by permission of Oxford University Press.

a natural tendency, the labourers perform them through habit); thus we view them as be-   5
ing wiser not in virtue of being able to act, but of having the theory for themselves and
knowing the causes. And in general it is a sign of the man who knows, that he can teach,
and therefore we think art more truly knowledge than experience is; for artists can
teach, and men of mere experience cannot.

Again, we do not regard any of the senses as wisdom; yet surely these give the   10
most authoritative knowledge of particulars. But they do not tell us the "why" of anything—e.g. why fire is hot; they only say that it is hot.

At first he who invented any art that went beyond the common perceptions of man
was naturally admired by men, not only because there was something useful in the in-   15
ventions, but because he was thought wise and superior to the rest. But as more arts
were invented, and some were directed to the necessities of life, others to its recreation,
the inventors of the latter were always regarded as wiser than the inventors of the former, because their branches of knowledge did not aim at utility. Hence when all such   20
inventions were already established, the sciences which do not aim at giving pleasure or
at the necessities of life were discovered, and first in the places where men first began to
have leisure. This is why the mathematical arts were founded in Egypt; for there the
priestly caste was allowed to be at leisure.

We have said in the *Ethics* what the difference is between art and science and the   25
other kindred faculties; but the point of our present discussion is this, that all men suppose what is called wisdom to deal with the first causes and the principles of things.
This is why, as has been said before, the man of experience is thought to be wiser than   30
the possessors of any perception whatever, the artist wiser than the men of experience,
the master-worker than the mechanic, and the theoretical kinds of knowledge to be
more of the nature of wisdom than the productive. Clearly then wisdom is knowledge   982a
about certain causes and principles.

2. Since we are seeking this knowledge, we must inquire of what kind are the   5
causes and the principles, the knowledge of which is wisdom. If we were to take the notions we have about the wise man, this might perhaps make the answer more evident.
We suppose first, then, that the wise man knows all things, as far as possible, although
he has not knowledge of each of them individually; secondly, that he who can learn   10
things that are difficult, and not easy for man to know, is wise (sense-perception is common to all, and therefore easy and no mark of wisdom); again, he who is more exact and
more capable of teaching the causes is wiser, in every branch of knowledge; and of the
sciences, also, that which is desirable on its own account and for the sake of knowing it   15
is more of the nature of wisdom than that which is desirable on account of its results,
and the superior science is more of the nature of wisdom than the ancillary; for the wise
man must not be ordered but must order, and he must not obey another, but the less wise
must obey *him*.

Such and so many are the notions, then, which we have about wisdom and the   20
wise. Now of these characteristics that of knowing all things must belong to him who
has in the highest degree universal knowledge; for he knows in a sense all the subordinate objects. And these things, the most universal, are on the whole the hardest for
men to know; for they are furthest from the senses. And the most exact of the sciences   25
are those which deal most with first principles; for those which involve fewer principles are more exact than those which involve additional principles, e.g. arithmetic
than geometry. But the science which investigates causes is also more capable of
reaching, for the people who teach are those who tell the causes of each thing. And   30
understanding and knowledge pursued for their own sake are found most in the

knowledge of that which is most knowable; for he who chooses to know for the sake
982ᵇ of knowing will choose most readily that which is most truly knowledge, and such is
the knowledge of that which is most knowable; and the first principles and the causes
are most knowable; for by reason of these, and from these, all other things are known,
but these are not known by means of the things subordinate to them. And the science
which knows to what end each thing must be done is the most authoritative of the sci-
5 ences, and more authoritative than any ancillary science; and this end is the good in
each class, and in general the supreme good in the whole of nature. Judged by all the
tests we have mentioned, then, the name in question falls to the same science; this
must be a science that investigates the first principles and causes; for the good, i.e.
10 that for the sake of which, is one of the causes.

That it is not a science of production is clear even from the history of the earliest
philosophers. For it is owing to their wonder that men both now begin and at first began
to philosophize; they wondered originally at the obvious difficulties, then advanced little by little and stated difficulties about the greater matters, e.g. about the phenomena of
15 the moon and those of the sun and the stars, and about the genesis of the universe. And
a man who is puzzled and wonders thinks himself ignorant (whence even the lover of
20 myth is in a sense a lover of wisdom, for myth is composed of wonders); therefore since
they philosophized in order to escape from ignorance, evidently they were pursuing science in order to know, and not for any utilitarian end. And this is confirmed by the facts;
for it was when almost all the necessities of life and the things that make for comfort
and recreation were present, that such knowledge began to be sought. Evidently then we
25 do not seek it for the sake of any other advantage; but as the man is free, we say, who
exists for himself and not for another, so we pursue this as the only free science, for it
alone exists for itself.

Hence the possession of it might be justly regarded as beyond human power; for
in many ways human nature is in bondage, so that according to Simonides "God alone
30 can have this privilege," and it is unfitting that man should not be content to seek the
knowledge that is suited to him. If, then, there is something in what the poets say, and
jealousy is natural to the divine power, it would probably occur in this case above all,
983ᵃ and all who excelled in this knowledge would be unfortunate. But the divine power cannot be jealous (indeed, according to the proverb, "bards tell many a lie"), nor should any
5 science be thought more honourable than one of this sort. For the most divine science is
also most honourable; and this science alone is, in two ways, most divine. For the science which it would be most meet for God to have is a divine science, and so is any science that deals with divine objects; and this science alone has both these qualities; for
God is thought to be among the causes of all things and to be a first principle, and such
10 a science either God alone can have, or God above all others. All the sciences, indeed,
are more necessary than this, but none is better.

Yet the acquisition of it must in a sense end in something which is the opposite
of our original inquiries. For all men begin, as we said, by wondering that the matter
15 is so (as in the case of automatic marionettes or the solstices or the incommensurability of the diagonal of a square with the side; for it seems wonderful to all men who
have not yet perceived the explanation that there is a thing which cannot be measured
even by the smallest unit). But we must end in the contrary and, according to the
proverb, the better state, as is the case in these instances when men learn the cause;
20 for there is nothing which would surprise a geometer so much as if the diagonal
turned out to be commensurable.

We have stated, then, what is the nature of the science we are searching for, and
what is the mark which our search and our whole investigation must reach.

3. Evidently we have to acquire knowledge of the original causes (for we say we know each thing only when we think we recognize its first cause), and causes are spo- 25 ken of in four senses. In one of these we mean the substance, i.e. the essence (for the "why" is referred finally to the formula, and the ultimate "why" is a cause and principle); in another the matter or substratum, in a third the source of the change, and in a 30 fourth the cause opposed to this, that for the sake of which and the good (for this is the end of all generation and change). We have studied these causes sufficiently in our work on nature, but yet let us call to our aid those who have attacked the investigation of be- 983b ing and philosophized about reality before us. For obviously they too speak of certain principles and causes; to go over their views, then, will be of profit to the present inquiry, for we shall either find another kind of cause, or be more convinced of the cor- 5 rectness of those which we now maintain.

Of the first philosophers, most thought the principles which were of the nature of matter were the only principles of all things; that of which all things that are consist, and from which they first come to be, and into which they are finally resolved (the substance remaining, but changing in its modifications), this they say is the element and the prin- 10 ciple of things, and therefore they think nothing is either generated or destroyed, since this sort of entity is always conserved, as we say Socrates neither comes to be absolutely when he comes to be beautiful or musical, nor ceases to be when he loses these characteristics, because the substratum, Socrates himself, remains. So they say nothing 15 else comes to be or ceases to be; for there must be some entity—either one or more than one—from which all other things come to be, it being conserved.

Yet they do not all agree as to the number and the nature of these principles. 20 Thales, the founder of this school of philosophy, says the principle is water (for which reason he declared that the earth rests on water), getting the notion perhaps from seeing that the nutriment of all things is moist, and that heat itself is generated from the moist and kept alive by it (and that from which they come to be is a principle of all things). He 25 got his notion from this fact, and from the fact that the seeds of all things have a moist nature, and that water is the origin of the nature of moist things.

Some think that the ancients who lived long before the present generation, and first framed accounts of the gods, had a similar view of nature; for they made Ocean and 30 Tethys the parents of creation, and described the oath of the gods as being by water, which they themselves call Styx; for what is oldest is most honourable, and the most honourable thing is that by which one swears. It may perhaps be uncertain whether this 984a opinion about nature is primitive and ancient, but Thales at any rate is said to have declared himself thus about the first cause. Hippo no one would think fit to include among these thinkers, because of the paltriness of his thought.

Anaximenes and Diogenes make air prior to water, and the most primary of the 5 simple bodies, while Hippasus of Metapontium and Heraclitus of Ephesus say this of fire, and Empedocles says it of the four elements, adding a fourth—earth—to those which have been named; for these, he says, always remain and do not come to be, except that they come to be more or fewer, being aggregated into one and segregated out 10 of one.

Anaxagoras of Clazomenae, who, though older than Empedocles, was later in his philosophical activity, says the principles are infinite in number; for he says almost all the things that are homogeneous are generated and destroyed (as water or fire is) only by aggregation and segregation, and are not in any other sense generated or destroyed, 15 but remain eternally.

From these facts one might think that the only cause is the so-called material cause; but as men thus advanced, the very facts showed them the way and joined in forcing them to investigate the subject. However true it may be that all generation and destruction proceed from some one or more elements, why does this happen and what is the cause? For at least the substratum itself does not make itself change; e.g. neither the wood nor the bronze causes the change of either of them, nor does the wood manufacture a bed and the bronze a statue, but something else is the cause of the change. And to seek this is to seek the second cause, as *we* should say,—that from which comes the beginning of movement. Now those who at the very beginning set themselves to this kind of inquiry, and said the substratum was one, were not at all dissatisfied with themselves; but some at least of those who maintain it to be one—as though defeated by this search for the second cause—say the one and nature as a whole is unchangeable not only in respect of generation and destruction (for this is an ancient belief, and all agreed in it), but also of all other change; and this view is peculiar to them. Of those who said the universe was one, none succeeded in discovering a cause of this sort, except perhaps Parmenides, and he only insomuch that he supposes that there is not only one but in some sense two causes. But for those who make more elements it is more possible to state the second cause, e.g. for those who make hot and cold, or fire and earth, the elements; for they treat fire as having a nature which fits it to move things, and water and earth and such things they treat in the contrary way.

When these men and the principles of this kind had had their day, as the latter were found inadequate to generate the nature of things, men were again forced by the truth itself, as we said, to inquire into the next kind of cause. For surely it is not likely either that fire or earth or any such element should be the reason why things manifest goodness and beauty both in their being and in their coming to be, or that those thinkers should have supposed it was; nor again could it be right to ascribe so great a matter to spontaneity and luck. When one man said, then, that reason was present—as in animals, so throughout nature—as the cause of the world and of all its order, he seemed like a sober man in contrast with the random talk of his predecessors. We know that Anaxagoras certainly adopted these views, but Hermotimus of Clazomenae is credited with expressing them earlier. Those who thought thus stated that there is a principle of things which is at the same time the cause of beauty, and that sort of cause from which things acquire movement.

4. One might suspect that Hesiod was the first to look for such a thing or some one else who put love or desire among existing things as a principle, as Parmenides does; for he, in constructing the genesis of the universe, says:—

Love first of all the Gods she planned.

And Hesiod says:—

First of all things was chaos made, and then
Broad-breasted earth, and love that foremost is
Among all the immortals,

which implies that among existing things there must be a cause which will move things and bring them together. How these thinkers should be arranged with regard to priority of discovery let us be allowed to decide later; but since the contraries of the various forms of good were also perceived to be present in nature—not only order and the beautiful, but also disorder and the ugly, and bad things in greater number than good, and ignoble things than beautiful, therefore another thinker introduced friendship and strife, each of the two the cause of one of these two sets of qualities. For if we were to follow out the view of Empedocles, and interpret it according to its meaning and not to its lisping expression, we should find that friendship is the cause of good things, and strife of bad. Therefore, if we said that Empedocles in a sense both mentions, and is the first to mention, the bad and the good as principles, we should perhaps be right, since the cause of all goods is the good itself.

These thinkers, as we say, evidently got hold up to a certain point of two of the causes which we distinguished in our work on nature—the matter and the source of the movement,—vaguely, however, and with no clearness, but as untrained men behave in fights; for they go round their opponents and often strike fine blows, but they do not fight on scientific principles, and so these thinkers do not seem to know what they say; for it is evident that, as a rule, they make no use of their causes except to a small extent. For Anaxagoras uses reason as a *deus ex machina* for the making of the world, and when he is at a loss to tell for what cause something necessarily is, then he drags reason in, but in all other cases ascribes events to anything rather than to reason. And Empedocles, though he uses the causes to a greater extent than this, neither does so sufficiently nor attains consistency in their use. At least, in many cases he makes friendship segregate things, and strife aggregate them. For when the universe is dissolved into its elements by strife, fire is aggregated into one, and so is each of the other elements; but when again under the influence of friendship they come together into one, the parts must again be segregated out of each element.

Empedocles, then, in contrast with his predecessors, was the first to introduce this cause in a divided form, not positing one source of movement, but different and contrary sources. Again, he was the first to speak of four material elements; yet he does not *use* four, but treats them as two only; he treats fire by itself, and its opposites—earth, air, and water—as one kind of thing. We may learn this by study of his verses.

This philosopher then, as we say, spoke of the principles in this way, and made them of this number. Leucippus and his associate Democritus say that the full and the empty are the elements, calling the one being and the other non-being—the full and solid being, the empty non-being (that is why they say that what is is no more than what is not, because body no more is than the void); and they make these the material causes of things. And as those who make the underlying substance one generate all other things by its modifications, supposing the rare and the dense to be the sources of the modifications, in the same way these philosophers say the differences in the elements are the causes of all other qualities. These differences, they say, are three—shape and order and position. For they say that what is is differentiated only by "rhythm" and "inter-contact" and "turning"; and of these rhythm is shape, inter-contact is order, and turning is position; for A differs from N in shape, AN from NA in order, Ⅱ from H in position. The question of movement—whence or how it belongs to things—these thinkers, like the others, lazily neglected.

Regarding the two causes, then, as we say, the inquiry seems to have been pushed thus far by the early philosophers.

5. Contemporaneously with these philosophers and before them, the Pythagoreans, as they are called, devoted themselves to mathematics; they were the first to advance this study, and having been brought up in it they thought its principles were the principles of all things. Since of these principles numbers are by nature the first, and in numbers they seemed to see many resemblances to the things that exist and come into being—more than in fire and earth and water (such and such a modification of numbers being justice, another being soul and reason, another being opportunity—and similarly

almost all other things being numerically expressible); since, again, they saw that the attributes and the ratios of the musical scales were expressible in numbers; since, then, all
986ᵃ   other things seemed in their whole nature to be modelled after numbers, and numbers
seemed to be the first things in the whole of nature, they supposed the elements of numbers to be the elements of all things, and the whole heaven to be a musical scale and a
number. And all the properties of numbers and scales which they could show to agree
5   with the attributes and parts and the whole arrangement of the heavens, they collected
and fitted into their scheme; and if there was a gap anywhere, they readily made additions so as to make their whole theory coherent. E.g. as the number 10 is thought to be
10   perfect and to comprise the whole nature of numbers, they say that the bodies which
move through the heavens are ten, but as the visible bodies are only nine, to meet this
they invent a tenth—the "counter-earth." We have discussed these matters more exactly
elsewhere.

But the object of our discussion is that we may learn from these philosophers also
what they suppose to be the principles and how these fall under the causes we have
15   named. Evidently, then, these thinkers also consider that number is the principle both as
matter for things and as forming their modifications and states, and hold that the elements of number are the even and the odd, and of these the former is unlimited, and the
20   latter limited; and the 1 proceeds from both of these (for it is both even and odd), and
number from the 1; and the whole heaven, as has been said, is numbers.

Other members of this same school say there are ten principles, which they arrange in two columns of cognates—limit and unlimited, odd and even, one and plu-
25   rality, right and left, male and female, resting and moving, straight and curved, light
and darkness, good and bad, square and oblong. In this way Alcmaeon of Croton
30   seems also to have conceived the matter, and either he got this view from them or
they got it from him; for he expressed himself similarly to them. For he says most
human affairs go in pairs, meaning not definite contrarieties such as the Pythagoreans speak of, but any chance contrarieties, e.g. white and black, sweet and bitter,
good and bad, great and small. He threw out indefinite suggestions about the other
986ᵇ   contrarieties, but the Pythagoreans declared both how many and which their contrarieties are.

From both these schools, then, we can learn this much, that the contraries are the
principles of things; and how many these principles are and which they are, we can
5   learn from one of the two schools. But how these principles can be brought together under the causes we have named has not been clearly and articulately stated by them; they
seem, however, to range the elements under the head of matter; for out of these as im-
manent parts they say substance is composed and moulded.

From these facts we may sufficiently perceive the meaning of the ancients who
said the elements of nature were more than one; but there are some who spoke of the
10   universe as if it were one entity, though they were not all alike either in the excellence
of their statement or in regard to the nature of the entity. The discussion of them is in no
way appropriate to our present investigation of causes, for they do not, like some of the
15   natural philosophers, assume what exists to be one and yet generate it out of the one as
out of matter, but they speak in another way; those others add change, since they generate the universe, but these thinkers say the universe is unchangeable. Yet this much is
appropriate to the present inquiry: Parmenides seems to fasten on that which is one in
20   formula, Melissus on that which is one in matter, for which reason the former says that
it is limited, the latter that it is unlimited; while Xenophanes, the first of this school of
monists (for Parmenides is said to have been his pupil), gave no clear statement, nor
does he seem to have grasped either of these two kinds of unity, but he contemplates the

whole heaven and says the One is God. Now these thinkers, as we said, must be ne-   25
glected for the purposes of the present inquiry—two of them entirely, as being a little
too naive, viz. Xenophanes and Melissus; but Parmenides seems to speak with somewhat more insight. For, claiming that, besides the existent, nothing non-existent exists,
he thinks that the existent is of necessity one and that nothing else exists (on this we   30
have spoken more clearly in our work on nature), but being forced to follow the
phenomena, and supposing that what is is one in formula but many according to perception, he now posits two causes and two principles, calling them hot and cold, i.e.
fire and earth; and of these he ranges the hot with the existent, and the other with   987a
the non-existent.

From what has been said, then, and from the wise men who have now sat in council with us, we have got this much both from the earliest philosophers, who regard the
first principle as corporeal (for water and fire and such things are bodies), and of whom   5
some suppose that there is one corporeal principle, others that there are more than one,
but both put these under the head of matter; and from some others who posit both this
cause and besides this the source of movement, which is stated by some as one and by
others as two.

Down to the Italian school, then, and apart from it, philosophers have treated   10
these subjects rather obscurely, except that, as we said, they have used two kinds of
cause, and one of these—the source of movement—some treat as one and others as two.
But the Pythagoreans have said in the same way that there are two principles, but added
this much, which is peculiar to them, that they thought finitude and infinity were not at-   15
tributes of certain other things, e.g. of fire or earth or anything else of this kind, but that
infinity itself and unity itself were the substance of the things of which they are predicated. This is why number was the substance of all things. On this subject, then, they
expressed themselves thus; and regarding the question of essence they began to make   20
statements and definitions, but treated the matter too simply. For they both defined su-
perficially and thought that the first subject of which a given term would be predicable,
was the substance of the thing, as if one supposed that double and 2 were the same, because 2 is the first thing of which double is predicable. But surely to be double and to be   25
2 are not the same; if they are, one thing will be many—a consequence which they actually drew. From the earlier philosophers, then, and from their successors we can learn
this much.

6. After the systems we have named came the philosophy of Plato, which in most   30
respects followed these thinkers, but had peculiarities that distinguished it from the philosophy of the Italians. For, having in his youth first become familiar with Cratylus and
with the Heraclitean doctrines (that all sensible things are ever in a state of flux and
there is no knowledge about them), these views he held even in later years. Socrates,
however, was busying himself about ethical matters and neglecting the world of nature   987b
as a whole but seeking the universal in these ethical matters, and fixed thought for the
first time on definitions; Plato accepted his teaching, but held that the problem applied   5
not to any sensible thing but to entities of another kind—for this reason, that the common definition could not be a definition of any sensible thing, as they were always
changing. Things of this other sort, then, he called Ideas, and sensible things, he said,
were apart from these, and were all called after these; for the multitude of things which
have the same name as the Form exist by participation in it. Only the name "participa-   10
tion" was new; for the Pythagoreans say that things exist by imitation of numbers, and
Plato says they exist by participation, changing the name. But what the participation or
the imitation of the Forms could be they left an open question.

15   Further, besides sensible things and Forms he says there are the objects of mathematics, which occupy an intermediate position, differing from sensible things in being eternal and unchangeable, from Forms in that there are many alike, while the Form itself is in each case unique.

20   Since the Forms are the causes of all other things, he thought their elements were the elements of all things. As matter, the great and the small were principles; as substance, the One; for from the great and the small, by participation in the One, come the numbers.

But he agreed with the Pythagoreans in saying that the One is substance and not a
25   predicate of something else; and in saying that the numbers are the causes of the substance of other things, he also agreed with them; but positing a dyad and constructing the infinite out of great and small, instead of treating the infinite as one, is peculiar to him; and so is his view that the numbers exist apart from sensible things, while *they* say that the things themselves are numbers, and do not place the objects of mathematics be-
30   tween Forms and sensible things. His divergence from the Pythagoreans in making the One and the numbers separate from things, and his introduction of the Forms, were due to his inquiries in the region of definitory formulae (for the earlier thinkers had no tincture of dialectic), and his making the other entity besides the One a dyad was due to the belief that the numbers, except those which were prime, could be neatly produced out of the dyad as out of a plastic material.

988a   Yet what happens is the contrary; the theory is not a reasonable one. For they make many things out of the matter, and the form generates only once, but what we observe is that one table is made from one matter, while the man who applies the form,
5   though he is one, makes many tables. And the relation of the male to the female is similar; for the latter is impregnated by one copulation, but the male impregnates many females; yet these are imitations of those first principles.

Plato, then, declared himself thus on the points in question; it is evident from what has been said that he has used only two causes, that of the essence and the mate-
10   rial cause (for the Forms are the cause of the essence of all other things, and the One is the cause of the essence of the Forms); and it is evident what the underlying matter is, of which the Forms are predicated in the case of sensible things, and the One in the case of Forms, viz. that this is a dyad, the great and the small. Further, he has assigned the
15   cause of good and that of evil to the elements, one to each of the two, as we say some of his predecessors sought to do, e.g. Empedocles and Anaxagoras.

7. Our account of those who have spoken about first principles and reality and of
20   the way in which they have spoken, has been concise and summary; but yet we have learnt this much from them, that of those who speak about principle and cause no one has mentioned any principle except those which have been distinguished in our work on nature, but all evidently have some inkling of *them,* though only vaguely. For some
25   speak of the first principle as matter, whether they suppose one or more first principles, and whether they suppose this to be a body or to be incorporeal; e.g. Plato spoke of the great and the small, the Italians of the infinite, Empedocles of fire, earth, water, and air, Anaxagoras of the infinity of homogeneous things. These, then, have all had a notion of this kind of cause, and so have all who speak of air or fire or water, or something denser
30   than fire and rarer than air; for some have said the prime element is of this kind. These thinkers grasped this cause only; but certain others have mentioned the source of movement, e.g. those who make friendship and strife, or reason, or love, a principle.
35   The essence, i.e. the substance of things, no one has expressed distinctly. It is mentioned chiefly by those who believe in the Forms; for they do not suppose either

that the Forms are the matter of sensible things, and the One the matter of the Forms, or   988ᵇ
that they are the source of movement (for they say these are causes rather of immobility
and of being at rest), but they furnish the Forms as the essence of every other thing, and   5
the One as the essence of the Forms.

That for the sake of which actions and changes and movements take place, they
assert to be a cause in a way, but not in this way, i.e. not in the way in which it is its *na-*
ture to be a cause. For those who speak of reason or friendship class these causes as
goods; they do not speak, however, as if anything that exists either existed or came into
being for the sake of these, but as if movements started from these. In the same way   10
those who say the One or the existent is the good, say that it is the cause of substance,
but not that substance either is or comes to be for the sake of this. Therefore it turns out
that in a sense they both say and do not say the good is a cause; for they do not call it a   15
cause *qua* good but only incidentally.

All these thinkers, then, as they cannot pitch on another cause, seem to testify that
we have determined rightly both how many and of what sort the causes are. Besides this
it is plain that when the causes are being looked for, either all four must be sought thus
or they must be sought in one of these four ways. Let us next discuss the possible diffi-   20
culties with regard to the way in which each of these thinkers has spoken, and with regard to his views about the first principles.

8. Those, then, who say the universe is one and posit one kind of thing as matter,
and as corporeal matter which has spatial magnitude, evidently go astray in many ways.
For they posit the elements of bodies only, not of incorporeal things, though there are   25
incorporeal things. And in trying to state the causes of generation and destruction, and
in giving an account of the nature of all things, they do away with the cause of movement. Further, they err in not positing the substance, i.e. the essence, as the cause of
anything, and besides this in lightly calling any of the simple bodies except earth the
first principle, without inquiring how they are produced out of one another,—I mean   30
fire, water, earth, and air. For some things are produced out of others by combination,
others by separation, and this makes the greatest difference to their priority and posteriority. For in a way the property of being most elementary of all would seem to belong   35
to the first thing from which they are produced by combination, and *this* property would   989ᵃ
belong to the most fine-grained and subtle of bodies. Therefore those who make fire the
principle would be most in agreement with this argument. But each of the other thinkers
agrees that the element of corporeal things is of this sort. At least none of the later   5
philosophers who said the world was one claimed that earth was the element, evidently
because of the coarseness of its grain. (Of the other three elements each has found some
judge on its side; for some maintain that fire, others that water, others that air is the element. Yet why, after all, do they not name earth also, as most men do—for people say
all things are earth. And Hesiod says earth was produced first of corporeal things; so an-   10
cient and popular has the opinion been.) According to this argument, then, no one
would be right who either says the first principle is any of the elements other than fire,
or supposes it to be denser than air but rarer than water. But if that which is later in gen-   15
eration is prior in nature, and that which is concocted and compounded is later in generation, the contrary of what we have been saying must be true,—water must be prior to
air, and earth to water.

Let this suffice, then, as our statement about those who posit one cause such as we
mentioned; but the same is true if we suppose more of these, as Empedocles says the
matter of things is four bodies. For he too is confronted by consequences some of which   20
are the same as have been mentioned, while others are peculiar to him. For we see these

bodies produced from one another, which implies that the same body does not always
remain fire or earth (we have spoken about this in our works on nature); and regarding
the moving cause and the question whether we must suppose one or two, he must be
thought to have spoken neither correctly nor altogether plausibly. And in general those
who speak in this way must do away with change of quality, for on their view cold will
not come from hot nor hot from cold. For if it did there would be something that accepted those very contraries, and there would be some one entity that became fire and
water, which Empedocles denies.

As regards Anaxagoras, if one were to suppose that he said there were two elements, the supposition would accord thoroughly with a view which Anaxagoras himself
did not state articulately, but which he must have accepted if any one had developed his
view. True, to say that in the beginning all things were mixed is absurd both on other
grounds and because it follows that they must have existed before in an unmixed form,
and because nature does not allow any chance thing to be mixed with any chance thing,
and also because on this view modifications and accidents could be separated from substances (for the same things which are mixed can be separated); yet if one were to follow him up, piecing together what he means, he would perhaps be seen to be somewhat
modern in his views. For when nothing was separated out, evidently nothing could be
truly asserted of the substance that then existed. I mean, e.g. that it was neither white
nor black, nor grey nor any other colour, but of necessity colourless; for if it had been
coloured, it would have had one of these colours. And similarly, by this same argument,
it was flavourless, nor had it any similar attribute; for it could not be either of any quality or of any size, nor could it be any definite kind of thing. For if it were, one of the particular forms would have belonged to it, and this is impossible, since all were mixed together; for the particular form would necessarily have been already separated out, but
he says all were mixed except reason, and this alone was unmixed and pure. From this
it follows, then, that he must say the principles are the One (for this is simple and unmixed) and the Other, which is of such a nature as we suppose the indefinite to be before it is defined and partakes of some form. Therefore, while expressing himself neither rightly nor clearly, he means something like what the later thinkers say and what is
now more clearly seen to be the case.

But these thinkers are, after all, at home only in arguments about generation and
destruction and movement; for it is practically only of this sort of substance that they
seek the principles and the causes. But those who extend their vision to all things that
exist, and of existing things suppose some to be perceptible and others not perceptible,
evidently study both classes, which is all the more reason why one should devote some
time to seeing what is good in their views and what bad from the stand-point of the inquiry we have now before us.

The "Pythagoreans" use stranger principles and elements than the natural
philosophers (the reason is that they got the principles from non-sensible things, for the
objects of mathematics, except those of astronomy, are of the class of things without
movement); yet their discussions and investigations are all about nature; for they generate the heavens, and with regard to their parts and attributes and functions they observe
the phenomena, and use up the principles and the causes in explaining these, which implies that they agree with the others, the natural philosophers, that what exists is just all
that which is perceptible and contained by the so-called heavens. But the causes and the
principles which they mention are, as we said, sufficient to act as steps even up to the
higher realms of reality, and are more suited to these than to theories about nature. They
do not tell us at all, however, how there can be movement if limit and unlimited and odd
and even are the only things assumed, or how without process and change there can be

generation and destruction, or how the bodies that move through the heavens can do what they do. Further, if we either granted them that spatial magnitude consists of these elements, or this were proved still how would some bodies be light and others have weight? To judge from what they assume and maintain, they speak no more of mathematical bodies than of perceptible; hence they have said nothing whatever about fire or earth or the other bodies of this sort, I suppose because they have nothing to say which applies *peculiarly* to perceptible things.

Further, how are we to combine the beliefs that the modifications of number, and number itself, are causes of what exists and happens in the heavens both from the beginning and now, and that there is no other number than this number out of which the world is composed? When in one particular region they place opinion and opportunity, and, a little above or below, injustice and sifting or mixture, and allege as proof of this that each one of these is a number, but when there happens to be already in each place a plurality of the extended bodies composed of numbers, because these modifications of number attach to the various groups of places,—this being so, is this number, which we must suppose each of these abstractions to be, the same number which is exhibited in the material universe, or is it another than this? Plato says it is different; yet even he thinks that both these bodies and their causes are numbers, but that the *intelligible* numbers are causes, while the others are *sensible*.

9. Let us leave the Pythagoreans for the present; for it is enough to have touched on them as much as we have done. But as for those who posit the Ideas as causes, firstly, in seeking to grasp the causes of the things around us, they introduced others equal in number to these, as if a man who wanted to count things thought he could not do it while they were few, but tried to count them when he had added to their number. For the Forms are practically equal to or not fewer than the things, in trying to explain which these thinkers proceeded from them to the Forms. For to each set of substances there answers a Form which has the same name and exists apart from the substances, and so also in the case of all other groups in which there is one character common to many things, whether the things are in this changeable world or are eternal.

Further, of the ways in which we prove that the Forms exist, none is convincing; for from some no inference necessarily follows, and from some it follows that there are Forms of things of which we think there are no Forms.

For according to the arguments from the existence of the sciences there will be Forms of all things of which there are sciences, and according to the argument that there is one attribute common to many things there will be Forms even of negations, and according to the argument that there is an object for thought even when the thing has perished, there will be Forms of perishable things; for we can have an image of these.

Further, of the more accurate arguments, some lead to Ideas of relations, of which we say there is no independent class, and others involve the difficulty of the "third man."

And in general the arguments for the Forms destroy the things for whose existence we are more anxious than for the existence of the Ideas; for it follows that not the dyad but number is first, i.e. that the relative is prior to the absolute—besides all the other points on which certain people by following out the opinions held about the Ideas have come into conflict with the principles of the theory.

Further, according to the assumption on which our belief in the Ideas rests, there will be Forms not only of substances but also of many other things (for the concept is single not only in the case of substances but also in the other cases, and there are sciences not only of substance but also of other things, and a thousand other such conclu-

sions also follow). But according to the necessities of the case and the opinions held
about the Forms, if they can be shared there must be Ideas of substances only. For they
are not shared incidentally, but a thing must share in its Form as in something not predicated of a subject (e.g. if a thing shares in double itself, it shares also in eternal, but incidentally; for eternal happens to be predicable of the double). Therefore the Forms will
be substance; and the same terms indicate substance in this and in the ideal world (or
what will be the meaning of saying that there is something apart from the particulars—
the one over many?). And if the Ideas and the particulars that share them have the same
Form, there will be something common to these; for why should 2 be one and the same
in the perishable 2's or in those which are many but eternal, and not the same in the 2 itself as in the particular 2? But if they have not the same Form, they must have only the
name in common, and it is as if one were to call both Callias and a wooden image a
man, without observing any community between them.

Above all one might discuss the question what on earth the Forms contribute to
sensible things, either to those that are eternal or to those that come into being and cease
to be. For they cause neither movement nor any change in them. But again they help in
no way towards the *knowledge* of the other things (for they are not even the substance
of these, else they would have been in them), nor towards their being, if they are not *in*
the particulars which share in them; though if they were, they might be thought to be
causes, as white causes whiteness in that with which it is mixed. But this argument,
which first Anaxagoras and later Eudoxus and certain others used, is too easily upset;
for it is not difficult to collect many insuperable objections to such a view.

But further all other things cannot come from the Forms in any of the usual senses
of "from." And to say that they are patterns and the other things share them is to use
empty words and poetical metaphors. For what is it that works, looking to the Ideas?
Anything can either be, or become, like another without being copied from it, so that
whether Socrates exists or not a man might come to be like Socrates; and evidently this
might be so even if Socrates were eternal. And there will be several patterns of the same
thing, and therefore several Forms, e.g. animal and two-footed and also man himself
will be Forms of man. Again, the Forms are patterns not only of sensible things, but of
themselves too, e.g. the Form of genus will be a genus of Forms; therefore the same
thing will be pattern and copy.

Again it must be held to be impossible that the substance and that of which it is
the substance should exist apart; how, therefore, can the Ideas, being the substances of
things, exist apart?

In the *Phaedo* the case is stated in this way—that the Forms are causes both of being and of becoming; yet when the Forms exist, still the things that share in them do not
come into being, unless there is some efficient cause; and many other things come into
being (e.g. a house or a ring), of which we say there are no Forms. Clearly, therefore,
even the other things can both be and come into being owing to such causes as produce
the things just mentioned.

Again, if the forms are numbers, how can they be causes? Is it because existing
things are other numbers, e.g. one number is man, another is Socrates, another Callias?
Why then are the one set of numbers causes of the other set? It will not make any difference even if the former are eternal and the latter are not. But if it is because things in
this sensible world (e.g. harmony) are ratios of numbers, evidently there is some one
class of things of which they are ratios. If, then, this—the matter—is some definite
thing, evidently the numbers themselves too will be ratios of something to something
else. E.g. if Callias is a numerical ratio between fire and earth and water and air, his Idea
also will be a number of certain other underlying things; and the Idea of man, whether

it is a number in a sense or not, will still be a numerical ratio of certain things and not a number proper, nor will it be a number merely because it is a numerical ratio.   20

Again, from many numbers one number is produced, but how can one Form come from many Forms? And if the number comes not from the many numbers themselves but from the units in them, e.g. in 10,000, how is it with the units? If they are specifically alike, numerous absurdities will follow, and also if they are not alike (neither the   25
units in the same number being like one another nor those in different numbers being all like to all); for in what will they differ, as they are without quality? This is not a plausible view, nor can it be consistently thought out. Further, they must set up a second kind of number (with which arithmetic deals), and all the objects which are called intermedi-   30
ate by some thinkers; and how do these exist or from what principles do they proceed? Or why must they be intermediate between the things in this sensible world and the things-in-themselves? Further, the units in 2 must each come from a prior 2; but this is impossible. Further, why is a number, when taken all together, one? Again, besides   992a
what has been said, if the units are *diverse* they should have spoken like those who say there are four, or two, elements; for each of these thinkers gives the name of element not to that which is common, e.g. to body, but to fire and earth, whether there is something   5
common to them, viz. body, or not. But in fact they speak as if the One were homogeneous like fire or water; and if this is so, the numbers will not be substances. Evidently, if there is a One-in-itself and this is a first principle, "one" is being used in more than one sense; for otherwise the theory is impossible.

When we wish to refer substances to their principles, we state that lines come   10
from the short and long (i.e. from a kind of small and great), and the plane from the broad and narrow, and the solid from the deep and shallow. Yet how then can the plane contain a line, or the solid a line or a plane? For the broad and narrow is a different class of things from the deep and shallow. Therefore, just as number is not present in these,   15
because the many and few are different from these, evidently no other of the higher classes will be present in the lower. But again the broad is not a genus which includes the deep, for then the solid would have been a species of plane. Further, from what principle will the presence of the points in the line be derived? Plato even used to object to this class of things as being a geometrical fiction. He called the indivisible lines the   20
principle of lines—and he used to lay this down often. Yet these must have a limit; therefore the argument from which the existence of the line follows proves also the existence of the point.

In general, though philosophy seeks the cause of perceptible things, we have   25
given this up (for we say nothing of the cause from which change takes its start), but while we fancy we are stating the substance of perceptible things, we assert the existence of a second class of substances, while our account of the way in which they are the substances of perceptible things is empty talk; for sharing, as we said before, means nothing. Nor have the Forms any connexion with that which we see to be the   30
cause in the case of the sciences, and for whose sake mind and nature produce all that they do produce,—with this cause we assert to be one of the first principles; but mathematics has come to be the whole of philosophy for modern thinkers, though they say that it should be studied for the sake of other things. Further, one might suppose that   992b
the substance which according to them underlies as matter is too mathematical, and is a predicate and differentia of the substance, i.e. of the matter, rather than the matter itself; i.e. the great and the small are like the rare and the dense which the natural philosophers speak of, calling these the primary differentiae of the substratum; for   5
these are a kind of excess and defect. And regarding movement, if the great and the small are to *be* movement, evidently the Forms will be moved; but if they are not,

whence did movement come? If we cannot answer this the whole study of nature has been annihilated.

10   And what is thought to be easy—to show that all things are one—is not done; for by "exposition" all things do not come to be one but there comes to be a One-in-itself, if we grant all the assumptions. And not even this follows, if we do not grant that the universal is a class; and this in some cases it cannot be.

15   Nor can it be explained either how the lines and planes and solids that come after the numbers exist or can exist, or what meaning they have; for these can neither be Forms (for they are not numbers), nor the intermediates (for those are the objects of mathematics), nor the perishable things. This is evidently a distinct fourth class.

In general, if we search for the elements of existing things without distinguish-
20   ing the many senses in which things are said to exist, we cannot succeed, especially if the search for the elements of which things are made is conducted in this manner. For it is surely impossible to discover what acting or being acted on, or the straight, is made of, but if elements can be discovered at all, it is only the elements of substances; therefore to seek the elements of all existing things or to think one has them
25   is incorrect. And how could we *learn* the elements of all things? Evidently we cannot start by knowing something before. For as he who is learning geometry, though he may know other things before, knows none of the things with which the science deals and about which he is to learn, so is it in all other cases. Therefore if there is
30   a science of all things, as some maintain, he who is learning this will know nothing before. Yet all learning is by means of premises which are (either all or some of them) known before,—whether the learning be by demonstration or by definitions; for the elements of the definition must be known before and be familiar; and learn-
993ª   ing by induction proceeds similarly. But again, if the science is innate, it is wonderful that we are unaware of our possession of the greatest of sciences. Again, how is one to *know* what all things are made of, and how is this to be made *evident?* This also affords a difficulty; for there might be a conflict of opinion, as there is about
5   certain syllables; some say *za* is made out of *s* and *d* and *a,* while others say it is a distinct sound and none of those that are familiar. Further, how could we know the objects of sense without having the sense in question? Yet we should, if the ele-
10   ments of which all things consist, as complex sounds consist of their proper elements, are the same.

10. It is evident, then, even from what we have said before, that all men seem to seek the causes named in the *Physics,* and that we cannot name any beyond these; but they seek these vaguely; and though in a sense they have all been described before, in a sense they have not been described at all. For the earliest philosophy is, on all subjects,
15   like one who lisps, since in its beginnings it is but a child. For even Empedocles says bone exists by virtue of the ratio in it. Now this is the essence and the substance of the
20   thing. But it is similarly necessary that the ratio should be the substance of flesh and of everything else, or of none; there it is on account of this that flesh and bone and everything else will exist, and not on account of the matter, which *he* names,—fire and earth and water and air. But while he would necessarily have agreed if another had said this, he has not said it clearly.
25   On such questions our views have been expressed before; but let us return to enumerate the difficulties that might be raised on these same points; for perhaps we may get some help towards our later difficulties.

BOOK XII

1. Substance is the subject of our inquiry; for the principles and the causes we are seek-   1069a
ing are those of substances. For if the universe is of the nature of a whole, substance is
its first part; and if it coheres by virtue of succession, on this view also substance is first,   20
and is succeeded by quality, and then by quantity. At the same time these latter are not
even beings in the unqualified sense, but are quantities and movements or else even the
not-white and the not-straight would be; at least we say even these *are,* e.g. "there is a
not-white." Further, none of the others can exist apart. And the old philosophers also in   25
effect testify to this; for it was of substance that they sought the principles and elements
and causes. The thinkers of the present day tend to rank universals as substances (for
genera are universals, and these they tend to describe as principles and substances, owing to the abstract nature of their inquiry); but the old thinkers ranked particular things
as substances, e.g. fire and earth, but not what is common to both, body.

There are three kinds of substance—one that is sensible (of which one subdivi-   30
sion is eternal and another is perishable, and which all recognize, as comprising e.g.
plants and animals),—of this we must grasp the elements, whether one or many; and another that is immovable, and this certain thinkers assert to be capable of existing apart,
some dividing it into two, others combining the Forms and the objects of mathematics   35
into one class, and others believing only in the mathematical part of this class. The former two kinds of substance are the subject of natural science (for they imply movement); but the third kind belongs to another science, if there is no principle common to   1069b
it and to the other kinds.

Sensible substance is changeable. Now if change proceeds from opposites or
from intermediate points, and not from all opposites (for the voice is not-white) but   5
from the contrary, there must be something underlying which changes into the contrary
state; for the contraries do not change.

2. Further, something persists, but the contrary does not persist; there is, then,
some third thing besides the contraries, viz. the matter. Now since changes are of four
kinds—either in respect of the essence or of the quality or of the quantity or of the
place, and change in respect of the "this" is simple generation and destruction, and   10
change in quantity is increase and diminution, and change in respect of an affection is
alteration, and change in place is motion, changes will be from given states into those
contrary to them in these several respects. The matter, then, which changes must be ca-   15
pable of both states. And since things are said to be in two ways, everything changes
from that which is potentially to that which is actually, e.g. from the potentially white to
the actually white, and similarly in the case of increase and diminution. Therefore not
only can a thing come to be, incidentally, out of that which is not, but also all things
come to be out of that which is, but is potentially, and is not actually. And this is the   20
"One" of Anaxagoras; for instead of "all things were together" and the "Mixture" of
Empedocles and Anaximander and the account given by Democritus, it is better to say
all things were together potentially but not actually. Therefore these thinkers seem to
have had some notion of matter.

Now all things that change have matter, but different matter; and of eternal things   25
those which are not generable but are movable in space have matter—not matter for
generation, however, but for motion from one place to another.

(One might raise the question from what sort of non-being generation proceeds;
for things are said not to be in three ways.)

       If, then, a thing exists potentially, still it is not potentially any and every thing, but
30   different things come from different things; nor is it satisfactory to say that all things
were together; for they differ in their matter, since otherwise why did an infinity of
things come to be, and not one thing? For Reason is one, so that if matter also is one,
that must have come to be in actuality what the matter was in potentiality. The causes
and the principles, then, are three, two being the pair of contraries of which one is formula and form and the other is privation, and the third being the matter.

35   3. Next we must observe that neither the matter nor the form comes to be—i.e.
the proximate matter and form. For everything that changes is something and is
1070ᵃ   changed by something and into something. That by which it is changed is the primary
mover; that which is changed, the matter; that into which it is changed, the form. The
process, then, will go on to infinity, if not only the bronze comes to be round but also
the round or the bronze comes to be; therefore there must be a stop at some point.

5   Next we must observe that each substance comes into being out of something
synonymous. (Natural objects and other things are substances.) For things come into
being either by art or by nature or by chance or by spontaneity. Now art is a principle of
movement in something other than the thing moved, nature is a principle in the thing itself (for man begets man), and the other causes are privations of these two.

10   There are three kinds of substance—the matter, which is a "this" by being perceived (for all things that are characterized by contact and not by organic unity are matter and substratum); the nature, a "this" and a state that it moves towards; and again,
thirdly, the particular substance which is composed of these two, e.g. Socrates or Callias. Now in some cases the "this" does not exist apart from the composite substance,
15   e.g. the form of house does not so exist, unless the art of building exists apart (nor is
there generation and destruction of these forms, but it is in another way that the house
apart from its matter, and health, and all things of art, exist and do not exist); but if it
does it is only in the case of natural objects. And so Plato was not far wrong when he
said that there are as many Forms as there are kinds of natural things (if there are Forms
20   at all),—though not of such things as fire, flesh, head; for all these are matter, and the
last matter is the matter of that which is in the fullest sense substance. The moving
causes exist as things preceding the effects, but causes in the sense of formulae are simultaneous with their effects. For when a man is healthy, then health also exists; and
the shape of a bronze sphere exists at the same time as the bronze sphere. But we must
25   examine whether any form also survives afterwards. For in some cases this may be so,
e.g. the soul may be of this sort—not all soul but the reason; for doubtless it is impossible that *all* soul should survive. Evidently then there is no necessity, on this ground at
least, for the existence of the Ideas. For man is begotten by man, each individual by an
30   individual; and similarly in the arts; for the medical art is the formula of health.

       4. The causes and the principles of different things are in a sense different, but in
a sense, if one speaks universally and analogically, they are the same for all. For we
might raise the question whether the principles and elements are different or the same
for substances and for relatives, and similarly in the case of each of the categories. But
35   it is paradoxical that they should be the same for all. For then from the same elements
1070ᵇ   will proceed relatives and substances. What then will this common element be? For
there is nothing common to and distinct from substance and the other things which are
predicated; but the element is prior to the things of which it is an element. But again
substance is not an element of relatives, nor is any of these an element of substance.
5   Further, how can all things have the same elements? For none of the elements can be the

same as that which is composed of the elements, e.g. *b* or *a* cannot be the same as *ba*. (None, therefore, of the intelligibles, e.g. unity or being, is an element; for these are predicable of each of the compounds as well.) None of the elements then would be either a substance or a relative; but it must be one or other. All things then have not the same elements.

Or, as we put it, in a sense they have and in a sense they have not; e.g. perhaps the   10
elements of perceptible bodies are, as *form,* the hot, and in another sense the cold, which is the *privation;* and, as *matter,* that which directly and of itself is potentially these; and both these are substances and also the things composed of these, of which these are the principles (i.e. any unity which is produced out of the hot and the cold, e.g. flesh or bone); for the product must be different from the elements. These things then   15
have the same elements and principles, but different things have different elements; and if we put the matter thus, all things have not the same elements, but analogically they have; i.e. one might say that there are three principles—the form, the privation, and the matter. But each of these is different for each class, e.g. in colour they are white, black,   20
and surface. Again, there is light, darkness, and air; and out of these are produced day and night.

Since not only the elements present in a thing are causes, but also something external, i.e. the moving cause, clearly while principle and element are different both are causes, and principle is divided into these two kinds; and that which moves a thing or makes it rest is a principle and a substance. Therefore analogically there are three ele-   25
ments, and four causes and principles; but the elements are different in different things, and the primary moving cause is different for different things. Health, disease, body; the moving cause is the medical art. Form, disorder of a particular kind, bricks; the moving cause is the building art. And since the moving cause in the case of natural things is, for   30
instance man, and in the products of thought it is the form or its contrary, there are in a sense three causes, while in a sense there are four. For the medical art is in some sense health, and the building art is the form of the house, and man begets man; further, besides these there is that which as first of all things moves all things.   35

5. Some things can exist apart and some cannot, and it is the former that are sub-   1071ª
stances. And therefore all things have the same causes, because, without substances, affections and movements do not exist. Further, these causes will probably be soul and body, or reason and desire and body.

And in yet another way, analogically identical things are principles, i.e., actuality   5
and potency; but these also are not only different for different things but also apply in different senses to them. For in some cases the same thing exists at one time actually and at another potentially, e.g. wine or flesh or man does so. (And these too fall under the above-named causes. For the form exists actually, if it can exist apart, and so does the complex of form and matter, and the privation, e.g. darkness or the diseased. But the   10
matter exists potentially; for this is that which can become both the actual things.) But the distinction of actuality and potentiality applies differently to cases where the matter is not the same, in which cases the form also is not the same but different; e.g. the cause of man is the elements in man (viz. fire and earth as matter, and the peculiar form), and the external cause, whatever it is, e.g. the father, and besides these the sun and its oblique course, which are neither matter nor form nor privation nor of the same species   15
with man, but moving causes.

Further, one must observe that some causes can be expressed in universal terms, and some cannot. The primary principles of all things are the actual primary "this" and another thing which exists potentially. The universal causes, then, of which we spoke   20 do not *exist.* For the *individual* is the source of the individuals. For while man is the cause of man universally, there *is* no universal man; but Peleus is the cause of Achilles, and your father of you, and this particular *b* of this particular *ba,* though *b* in general is the cause of *ba* taken without qualification.

25

30

35

Again, if the causes of substances are causes of everything, still different things have different causes and elements, as was said; the causes of things that are not in the same class, e.g. of colours, sounds, substances, and quantities, are different except in an analogical sense; and those of things in the same species are different, not in species, but in the sense that the causes of different individuals are different, your matter and form and moving cause being different from mine, while in their universal formula they are the same. And if we inquire what are the principles or elements of substances and relations and qualities—whether they are the same or different, clearly when the terms "principle" and "element" are used in several senses the principles and elements of all are the same, but when the senses are distinguished the causes are not the same but different, except that in a special sense the causes of all are the same. They are in a special sense the same, i.e. by analogy, because matter, form, privation, and the moving cause are common to all things; and the causes of substances may be treated as causes of all things in this sense, that when they are removed all things are removed; further, that which is first in respect of fulfillment is the cause of all things. But in another sense there are different first causes, viz. all the contraries which are neither stated as classes nor spoken of in several ways; and, further, the matters of different things are different.

1071ᵇ   We have stated, then, what are the principles of sensible things and how many they are, and in what sense they are the same and in what sense different.

6. Since there were three kinds of substance, two of them natural and one unmovable, regarding the latter we must assert that it is necessary that there should be an eternal unmovable substance. For substances are the first of existing things, and if they are all destructible, all things are destructible. But it is impossible that movement should either come into being or cease to be; for it must always have existed. Nor can time come into being or cease to be; for there could not be a before and an after if time did not exist. Movement also is continuous, then, in the sense in which time is; for time is either the same thing as movement or an attribute of movement. And there is no continuous movement except movement in place, and of this only that which is circular is continuous.

5

10

But if there is something which is capable of moving things or acting on them, but is not actually doing so, there will not be movement; for that which has a capacity need not exercise it. Nothing, then, is gained even if we suppose eternal substances, as the believers in the Forms do, unless there is to be in them some principle which can cause movement; and even this is not enough, nor is another substance besides the Forms enough; for if it does not *act,* there will be no movement. Further, even if it acts, this will not be enough, if its substance is potentiality; for there will not be *eternal* movement; for that which is potentially may possibly not be. There must, then, be such a principle, whose very substance is actuality. Further, then, these substances must be without matter; for they must be eternal, at least if anything else is eternal. Therefore they must be actuality.

15

20

Yet there is a difficulty; for it is thought that everything that acts is able to act, but that not everything that is able to act acts, so that the potentiality is prior. But if this is so, nothing at all will exist; for it is possible for things to be capable of existing but not yet to exist. Yet if we follow the mythologists who generate the world from night, or the natural philosophers who say that all things were together, the same impossible result

25

ensues. For how will there be movement, if there is no actual cause? Matter will surely not move itself—the carpenter's art must act on it; nor will the menstrual fluids nor the earth set themselves in motion, but the seeds and the semen must act on them.   30

This is why some suppose eternal actuality—e.g. Leucippus and Plato; for they say there is always movement. But why and what this movement is they do not say, nor, if the world moves in this way or that, do they tell us the cause of its doing so. Now nothing is moved at random, but there must always be something present, e.g. as a matter of fact a thing moves in one way by nature, and in another by force or through the in-   35
fluence of thought or something else. Further, what sort of movement is primary? This makes a vast difference. But again Plato, at least, cannot even say what it is that he sometimes supposes to be the source of movement—that which moves itself; for the   1072ª
soul is later, and simultaneous with the heavens, according to his account. To suppose potentiality prior to actuality, then, is in a sense right, and in a sense not; and we have specified these senses.

That actuality is prior is testified by Anaxagoras (for his thought is actuality) and   5
by Empedocles in his doctrine of love and strife, and by those who say that there is always movement, e.g. Leucippus.

Therefore chaos or night did not exist for any infinite time, but the same things have always existed (either passing through a cycle of changes or in some other way), since actuality is prior to potentiality. If, then, there is a constant cycle, something must always remain, acting in the same way. And if there is to be generation and destruction,   10
there must be something else which is always acting in different ways. This must, then, act in one way in virtue of itself, and in another in virtue of something else—either of a third agent, therefore, or of the first. But it must be in virtue of the first. For otherwise this again causes the motion both of the third agent and of the second. Therefore it is better to say the first. For it was the cause of eternal movement; and something else is   15
the cause of variety, and evidently both together are the cause of eternal variety. This, accordingly, is the character which the motions actually exhibit. What need then is there to seek for other principles?

7. Since this is a possible account of the matter, and if it were not true, the world would have proceeded out of night and "all things together" and out of non-being, these   20
difficulties may be taken as solved. There is, then, something which is always moved with an unceasing motion, which is motion in a circle; and this is plain not in theory only but in fact. Therefore the first heavens must be eternal. There is therefore also something which moves them. And since that which is moved and moves is intermediate, there is a mover which moves without being moved, being eternal, substance, and   25
actuality. And the object of desire and the object of thought move in this way; they move without being moved. The primary objects of desire and of thought are the same. For the apparent good is the object of appetite, and the real good is the primary object of wish. But desire is consequent on opinion rather than opinion on desire; for the thinking is the starting-point. And thought is moved by the object of thought, and one side of   30
the list of opposites is in itself the object of thought; and in this, substance is first, and in substance, that which is simple and exists actually. (The one and the simple are not the same; for "one" means a measure, but "simple" means that the thing itself has a certain nature.) But the good, also, and that which is in itself desirable are on this same side of   35
the list; and the first in any class is always best, or analogous to the best.

That that for the sake of which is found among the unmovables is shown by mak-   1072ᵇ
ing a distinction; for that for the sake of which is both that *for* which and that *towards* which, and of these the one is unmovable and the other is not. Thus it produces motion

by being loved, and it moves the other moving things. Now if something is moved it is
5   capable of being otherwise than as it is. Therefore if the actuality of the heavens is primary motion, then in so far as they are in motion, in *this* respect they are capable of being otherwise,—in place, even if not in substance. But since there is something which
moves while itself unmoved, existing actually, this can in no way be otherwise than as
it is. For motion in space is the first of the kinds of change, and motion in a circle the
10 first kind of spatial motion; and this the first mover *produces*. The first mover, then, of
necessity exists; and in so far as it is necessary, it is good, and in this sense a first principle. For the necessary has all these senses—that which is necessary perforce because
it is contrary to impulse, that without which the good is impossible, and that which cannot be otherwise but is *absolutely* necessary.

On such a principle, then, depend the heavens and the world of nature. And its life
is such as the best which we enjoy, and enjoy for but a short time. For it is ever in this
15 state (which we cannot be), since its actuality is also pleasure. (And therefore waking,
perception, and thinking are most pleasant, and hopes and memories are so because of
their reference to these.) And thought in itself deals with that which is best in itself, and
that which is thought in the fullest sense with that which is best in the fullest sense. And
20 thought thinks itself because it shares the nature of the object of thought; for it becomes
an object of thought in coming into contact with and thinking its objects, so that thought
and object of thought are the same. For that which is *capable* of receiving the object of
thought, i.e. the substance, is thought. And it is active when it *possesses* this object.
Therefore the latter rather than the former is the divine element which thought seems to
contain, and the act of contemplation is what is most pleasant and best. If, then, God is
25 always in that good state in which we sometimes are, this compels our wonder; and if in
a better this compels it yet more. And God *is* in a better state. And life also belongs to
God; for the actuality of thought is life, and God is that actuality; and God's essential
actuality is life most good and eternal. We say therefore that God is a living being, eternal, most good, so that life and duration continuous and eternal belong to God; for this
is God.

30   Those who suppose, as the Pythagoreans and Speusippus do, that supreme beauty
and goodness are not present in the beginning, because the beginnings both of plants
35 and of animals are *causes,* but beauty and completeness are in the *effects* of these, are
wrong in their opinion. For the seed comes from other individuals which are prior and
1073ᵃ complete, and the first thing is not seed but the complete being, e.g. we must say that before the seed there is a man,—not the man produced from the seed, but another from
whom the seed comes.

It is clear then from what has been said that there is a substance which is eternal
and unmovable and separate from sensible things. It has been shown also that this sub-
5   stance cannot have any magnitude, but is without parts and indivisible. For it produces
movement through infinite time, but nothing finite has infinite power. And, while every
magnitude is either infinite or finite, it cannot, for the above reason, have finite magni-
10 tude, and it cannot have infinite magnitude because there is no infinite magnitude at all.
But it is also clear that it is impassive and unalterable; for all the other changes are posterior to change of place. It is clear, then, why the first mover has these attributes.

8. We must not ignore the question whether we have to suppose one such substance or more than one, and if the latter, how many; we must also mention, regarding
15 the opinions expressed by others, that they have said nothing that can even be clearly
stated about the number of the substances. For the theory of Ideas has no special dis-

cussion of the subject; for those who believe in Ideas say the Ideas are numbers, and they speak of numbers now as unlimited, now as limited by the number 10; but as for the reason why there should be just so many numbers, nothing is said with any demonstrative exactness.

20

We however must discuss the subject, starting from the presuppositions and distinctions we have mentioned. The first principle or primary being is not movable either in itself or accidentally, but produces the primary eternal and single movement. And since that which is moved must be moved by something, and the first mover must be in itself unmovable, and eternal movement must be produced by something eternal and a single movement by a single thing, and since we see that besides the simple spatial movement of the universe, which we say the first and unmovable substance produces, there are other spatial movements—those of the planets—which are eternal (for the body which moves in a circle is eternal and unresting; we have proved these points in the *Physics*), each of these movements also must be caused by a substance unmovable in itself and eternal. For the nature of the stars is eternal, being a kind of substance, and the mover is eternal and prior to the moved, and that which is prior to a substance must be a substance. Evidently, then, there must be substances which are of the same number as the movements of the stars, and in their nature eternal, and in themselves unmovable, and without magnitude, for the reason before mentioned.

25

30

35

That the movers are substances, then, and that one of these is first and another second according to the same order as the movements of the stars, is evident. But in the number of movements we reach a problem which must be treated from the standpoint of that one of the mathematical sciences which is most akin to philosophy—viz. of astronomy; for this science speculates about substance which is perceptible but eternal, but the other mathematical sciences, i.e. arithmetic and geometry, treat of no substance. That the movements are more numerous than the bodies that are moved, is evident to those who have given even moderate attention to the matter; for each of the planets has more than one movement. But as to the actual number of these movements, we now—to give some notion of the subject—quote what some of the mathematicians say, that our thought may have some definite number to grasp; but, for the rest, we must partly investigate for ourselves, partly learn from other investigators, and if those who study this subject form an opinion contrary to what we have now stated, we must esteem both parties indeed, but follow the more accurate.

1073b

5

10

15

Eudoxus supposed that the motion of the sun or of the moon involves, in either case, three spheres, of which the first is the sphere of the fixed stars, and the second moves in the circle which runs along the middle of the zodiac, and the third in the circle which is inclined across the breadth of the zodiac; but the circle in which the moon moves is inclined at a greater angle than that in which the sun moves. And the motion of the planets involves, in each case, four spheres, and of these also the first and second are the same as the first two mentioned above (for the sphere of the fixed stars is that which moves all the other spheres, and that which is placed beneath this and has its movement in the circle which bisects the zodiac is common to all), but the *poles* of the third sphere of each planet are in the circle which bisects the zodiac, and the motion of the fourth sphere is in the circle which is inclined at an angle to the equator of the third sphere; and the poles of the third spheres are different for the other planets, but those of Venus and Mercury are the same.

20

25

30

Callippus made the position of the spheres the same as Eudoxus did, but while he assigned the same number as Eudoxus did to Jupiter and to Saturn, he thought two more spheres should be added to the sun and two to the moon, if we were to explain the phenomena, and one more to each of the other planets.

35

1074ª   But it is necessary, if all the spheres combined are to explain the phenomena, that
for each of the planets there should be other spheres (one fewer than those hitherto assigned) which counteract those already mentioned and bring back to the same position
5   the first sphere of the star which in each case is situated below the star in question; for
only thus can all the forces at work produce the motion of the planets. Since, then, the
spheres by which the planets themselves are moved are eight and twenty-five, and of
these only those by which the lowest-situated planet is moved need not be counteracted,
the spheres which counteract those of the first two planets will be six in number, and the
10   spheres which counteract those of the next four planets will be sixteen, and the number
of all the spheres—those which move the planets and those which counteract these—
will be fifty-five. And if one were not to add to the moon and to the sun the movements
we mentioned, all the spheres will be forty-nine in number.
15   Let this then be taken as the number of the spheres, so that the unmovable substances and principles may reasonably be taken as just so many; the assertion of *necessity* must be left to more powerful thinkers.
        If there can be no spatial movement which does not conduce to the moving of a
star, and if further every being and every substance which is immune from change and
in virtue of itself has attained to the best must be considered an end, there can be no
20   other being apart from these we have named, but this must be the number of the substances. For if there are others, they will cause change as being an end of movement; but
there *cannot* be other movements besides those mentioned. And it is reasonable to infer
25   this from a consideration of the bodies that are moved; for if everything that moves is
for the sake of that which is moved, and every movement belongs to something that is
moved, no movement can be for the sake of itself or of another movement, but all
movements must be for the sake of the stars. For if a movement is to be for the sake of
a movement, this latter also will have to be for the sake of something else; so that since
30   there cannot be an infinite regress, the end of every movement will be one of the divine
bodies which move through the heaven.
        Evidently there is but one heaven. For if there are many heavens as there are
many men, the moving principles, of which each heaven will have one, will be one in
form but in number many. But all things that are many in number have matter. (For one
and the same formula applies to *many* things, e.g. the formula of man; but Socrates is
35   *one*.) But the primary essence has not matter; for it is fulfillment. So the unmovable first
mover is one both in formula and in number; therefore also that which is moved always
and continuously is one alone; therefore there is one heaven alone.
1074ᵇ   Our forefathers in the most remote ages have handed down to us their posterity a
tradition, in the form of a myth, that these substances are gods and that the divine encloses the whole of nature. The rest of the tradition has been added later in mythical
5   form with a view to the persuasion of the multitude and to its legal and utilitarian expe-
diency; they say these gods are in the form of men or like some of the other animals, and
they say other things consequent on and similar to these which we have mentioned. But
if we were to separate the first point from these additions and take it alone—that they
10   thought the first substances to be gods—we must regard this as an inspired utterance,
and reflect that, while probably each art and science has often been developed as far as
possible and has again perished, these opinions have been preserved like relics until the
present. Only thus far, then, is the opinion of our ancestors and our earliest predecessors
clear to us.

15   9. The nature of the divine thought involves certain problems; for while thought
is held to be the most divine of phenomena, the question what it must be in order to have

that character involves difficulties. For if it thinks nothing, what is there here of dignity? It is just like one who sleeps. And if it thinks, but this depends on something else, then (as that which is its substance is not the act of thinking, but a capacity) it cannot be the best substance; for it is through thinking that its value belongs to it. Further, whether its   20 substance is the faculty of thought or the act of thinking, what does it think? Either itself or something else; and if something else, either the same always or something different. Does it matter, then, or not, whether it thinks the good or any chance thing? Are there not some things about which it is incredible that it should think? Evidently, then, it   25 thinks that which is most divine and precious, and it does not change; for change would be change for the worse, and this would be already a movement. First, then, if it is not the act of thinking but a capacity, it would be reasonable to suppose that the continuity of its thinking is wearisome to it. Secondly, there would evidently be something else more precious than thought, viz. that which is thought. For both thinking and the act of   30 thought will belong even to one who has the worst of thoughts. Therefore if this ought to be avoided (and it ought, for there are even some things which it is better not to see than to see), the act of thinking cannot be the best of things. Therefore it must be itself that thought thinks (since it is the most excellent of things), and its thinking is a thinking on thinking.

But evidently knowledge and perception and opinion and understanding have al-   35 ways something else as their object, and themselves only by the way. Further, if thinking and being thought are different, in respect of which does goodness belong to thought? For being an act of thinking and being an object of thought are not the same. We answer that in some cases the knowledge is the object. In the productive sciences (if   1075ᵃ we abstract from the matter) the substance in the sense of essence, and in the theoretical sciences the formula or the act of thinking, is the object. As, then, thought and the object of thought are not different in the case of things that have not matter, they will be the same, i.e. the thinking will be one with the object of its thought.

A further question is left—whether the object of the thought is composite; for if it   5 were, thought would change in passing from part to part of the whole. We answer that everything which has not matter is indivisible. As human thought, or rather the thought of composite objects, is in a certain period of time (for it does not possess the good at this moment or at that, but its best, being something different from it, is attained only in   10 a whole period of time), so throughout eternity is the thought which has *itself* for its object.

10. We must consider also in which of two ways the nature of the universe contains the good or the highest good, whether as something separate and by itself, or as the order of the parts. Probably in both ways, as an army does. For the good is found both in the order and in the leader, and more in the latter; for he does not depend on the order   15 but it depends on him. And all things are ordered together somehow, but not all alike,— both fishes and fowls and plants; and the world is not such that one thing has nothing to do with another, but they are connected. For all are ordered together to one end. (But it is as in a house, where the freemen are least at liberty to act as they will, but all things   20 or most things are already ordained for them, while the slaves and the beasts do little for the common good, and for the most part live at random; for this is the sort of principle that constitutes the nature of each.) I mean, for instance, that all must at least come to be dissolved into their elements, and there are other functions similarly in which all share for the good of the whole.

We must not fail to observe how many impossible or paradoxical results confront   25 those who hold different views from our own, and what are the views of the subtler thinkers, and which views are attended by fewest difficulties. All make all things out of contraries. But neither "all things" nor "out of contraries" is right; nor do they tell us how the things in which the contraries are present can be made out of the contraries; for contraries are not affected by one another. Now for us this difficulty is solved naturally by the fact that there is a third factor. These thinkers however make one of the two contraries matter; this is done for instance by those who make the unequal matter for the equal, or the many matter for the one. But this also is refuted in the same way; for the matter which is one is contrary to nothing. Further, all things, except the one, will, on the view we are criticizing, partake of evil; for the bad is itself one of the two elements. But the other school does not treat the good and the bad even as principles; yet in all things the good is in the highest degree a principle. The school we first mentioned is right in saying that it is a principle, but how the good is a principle they do not say—whether as end or as mover or as form.

1075ᵇ   Empedocles also has a paradoxical view; for he identifies the good with love. But this is a principle both as mover (for it brings things together) and as matter (for it is part of the mixture). Now even if it happens that the same thing is a principle both as matter and as mover, still *being* them is not the same. In which respect then is love a principle? It is paradoxical also that strife should be imperishable; strife is for him the nature of the bad.

Anaxagoras makes the good a motive principle; for thought moves things, but moves them for the sake of something, which must be something other than it, except according to *our* way of stating the case; for the medical art is in a sense health. It is paradoxical also not to suppose a contrary to the good, i.e. to thought. But all who speak of the contraries make no use of the contraries, unless we bring their views into shape. And why some things are perishable and others imperishable, no one tells us; for they make all existing things out of the same principles. Further, some make existing things out of the non-existent; and others to avoid the necessity of this make all things one.

Further, why should there always be becoming, and what is the cause of becoming?—this no one tells us. And those who suppose two principles must suppose another, a superior principle, and so must those who believe in the Forms; for why did things come to participate, or why do they participate, in the Forms? And all other thinkers are confronted by the necessary consequence that there is something contrary to Wisdom, i.e. to the highest knowledge; but we are not. For there is nothing contrary to that which is primary (for all contraries have matter and are potentially); and the ignorance which is contrary would lead us to a contrary object; but what is primary has no contrary.

Again, if besides sensible things no others exist, there will be no first principle, no order, no becoming, no heavenly bodies, but each principle will have a principle before it, as in the accounts of the mythologists and all the natural philosophers. But if the Forms or the numbers are to exist, they will be causes of nothing; or if not that, at least not of movement.

Further, how is extension, i.e. a *continuum,* to be produced out of unextended parts? For number will not, either as mover or as form, produce a *continuum.* But again there cannot be any contrary that is also a productive or moving principle; for it would be possible for it not to be. Or at least its action would be posterior to its capacity. The world then would not be eternal. But it is; one of these premises, then, must be denied. And we have said how this must be done. Further, in virtue of what the numbers, or the soul and the body, or in general the form and the thing, are one of this no one tells us anything; nor can any one tell, unless he says, as we do, that the mover makes them one. And those who say mathematical number is first and go on to generate one kind of substance after another and give different principles for each, make the substance of the universe a series of episodes (for one substance has no influence on another by its existence or non-existence), and they give us many principles; but the world must not be governed badly.

"The rule of many is not good; let there be one ruler."

ON THE SOUL (in part)

BOOK II

1. Let the foregoing suffice as our account of the views concerning the soul which have   412ᵃ
been handed on by our predecessors; let us now make as it were a completely fresh
start, endeavouring to answer the question, What is soul? i.e. to formulate the most gen-   5
eral possible account of it.

We say that substance is one kind of what is, and that in several senses: in the
sense of matter or that which in itself is not a this, and in the sense of form or essence,
which is that precisely in virtue of which a thing is called a this, and thirdly in the sense
of that which is compounded of both. Now matter is potentiality, form actuality; and ac-   10
tuality is of two kinds, one as e.g. knowledge, the other as e.g. reflecting.

Among substances are by general consent reckoned bodies and especially natural
bodies; for they are the principles of all other bodies. Of natural bodies some have life
in them, others not; by life we mean self-nutrition and growth and decay. It follows that   15
every natural body which has life in it is a substance in the sense of a composite.

Now given that there are bodies of such and such a kind, viz. having life, the soul
cannot be a body; for the body is the subject or matter, not what is attributed to it. Hence
the soul must be a substance in the sense of the form of a natural body having life po-   20
tentially within it. But substance is actuality, and thus soul is the actuality of a body as
above characterized. Now there are two kinds of actuality corresponding to knowledge
and to reflecting. It is obvious that the soul is an actuality like knowledge; for both
sleeping and waking presuppose the existence of soul, and of these waking corresponds   25
to reflecting, sleeping to knowledge possessed but not employed, and knowledge of
something is temporally prior.

That is why the soul is an actuality of the first kind of a natural body having life
potentially in it. The body so described is a body which is organized. The parts of   412ᵇ
plants in spite of their extreme simplicity are organs; e.g. the leaf serves to shelter the
pericarp, the pericarp to shelter the fruit, while the roots of plants are analogous to the
mouth of animals, both serving for the absorption of food. If, then, we have to give a
general formula applicable to all kinds of soul, we must describe it as an actuality of   5
the first kind of a natural organized body. That is why we can dismiss as unnecessary
the question whether the soul and the body are one: it is as though we were to ask
whether the wax and its shape are one, or generally the matter of a thing and that of
which it is the matter. Unity has many senses (as many as "is" has), but the proper one
is that of actuality.

Reprinted by permission of the publishers and the Loeb Classical Library from Aristotle, *On the Soul,* Book
II, 1–3; III, 4–5, translated by J.A. Smith from *Complete Works of Aristotle,* edited by Jonathan Barnes. Cambridge, MA: Harvard University Press, 1984. Copyright © 1984 by Harvard University Press.

10   We have now given a general answer to the question, What is soul? It is substance in the sense which corresponds to the account of a thing. That means that it is what it is to be for a body of the character just assigned. Suppose that a tool, e.g. an axe, were a *natural* body, then being an axe would have been its essence, and so its soul; if this dis-

15   appeared from it, it would have ceased to be an axe, except in name. As it is, it is an axe; for it is not of a body of that sort that what it is to be, i.e. its account, is a soul, but of a natural body of a particular kind, viz. one having in itself the power of setting itself in movement and arresting itself. Next, apply this doctrine in the case of the parts of the living body. Suppose that the eye were an animal—sight would have been its soul, for

20   sight is the substance of the eye which corresponds to the account, the eye being merely the matter of seeing; when seeing is removed the eye is no longer an eye, except in name—no more than the eye of a statue or of a painted figure. We must now extend our consideration from the parts to the whole living body; for what the part is to the part, that the whole faculty of sense is to the whole sensitive body as such.

25   We must not understand by that which is potentially capable of living what has lost the soul it had, but only what still retains it; but seeds and fruits are bodies which are potentially of that sort. Consequently, while waking is actuality in a sense corre- sponding to the cutting and the seeing, the soul is actuality in the sense corresponding to

413ᵃ   sight and the power in the tool; the body corresponds to what is in potentiality; as the pupil *plus* the power of sight constitutes the eye, so the soul *plus* the body constitutes the animal.

From this it is clear that the soul is inseparable from its body, or at any rate that

5   certain parts of it are (if it has parts)—for the actuality of some of them is the actual- ity of the parts themselves. Yet some may be separable because they are not the actu- alities of any body at all. Further, we have no light on the problem whether the soul may not be the actuality of its body in the sense in which the sailor is the actuality of the ship.

10   This must suffice as our sketch or outline of the nature of soul.

2. Since what is clear and more familiar in account emerges from what in itself is confused but more observable by us, we must reconsider our results from this point of view. For it is not enough for a definitional account to express as most now do the mere

15   fact; it must include and exhibit the cause also. At present definitions are given in a form analogous to the conclusion of an argument; e.g. What is squaring? The construc- tion of an equilateral rectangle equal to a given oblong rectangle. Such a definition is in form equivalent to a conclusion. One that tells us that squaring is the discovery of a mean proportional discloses the cause of what is defined.

We resume our inquiry from a fresh starting-point by calling attention to the fact

20   that what has soul in it differs from what has not in that the former displays life. Now this word has more than one sense, and provided any one alone of these is found in a thing we say that thing is living—viz. thinking or perception or local movement and rest, or movement in the sense of nutrition, decay and growth. Hence we think of plants

25   also as living, for they are observed to possess in themselves an originative power through which they increase or decrease in all spatial directions; they do not grow up but not down—they grow alike in both, indeed in all, directions; and that holds for ev- erything which is constantly nourished and continues to live, so long as it can absorb

30   nutriment.

This power of self-nutrition can be separated from the other powers mentioned, but not they from it—in mortal beings at least. The fact is obvious in plants; for it is the only psychic power they possess.

This is the originative power the possession of which leads us to speak of things   413ᵇ
as *living* at all, but it is the possession of sensation that leads us for the first time to
speak of living things as *animals;* for even those beings which possess no power of local movement but do possess the power of sensation we call animals and not merely living things.

The primary form of sense is touch, which belongs to all animals. Just as the   5
power of self-nutrition can be separated from touch and sensation generally, so touch
can be separated from all other forms of sense. (By the power of self-nutrition we mean
that part of the soul which is common to plants and animals: all animals whatsoever are
observed to have the sense of touch.) What the explanation of these two facts is, we
must discuss later. At present we must confine ourselves to saying that soul is the source   10
of these phenomena and is characterized by them, viz. by the powers of self-nutrition,
sensation, thinking, and movement.

Is each of these a soul or a part of a soul? And if a part, a part merely distinguishable by definition or a part distinct in local situation as well? In the case of certain of   15
these powers, the answers to these questions are easy, in the case of others we are puzzled what to say. Just as in the case of plants which when divided are observed to continue to live though separated from one another (thus showing that in *their* case the soul
of each individual plant was actually one, potentially many), so we notice a similar result in other varieties of soul, i.e. in insects which have been cut in two; each of the seg-   20
ments possesses both sensation and local movement; and if sensation, necessarily also
imagination and appetition; for, where there is sensation, there is also pleasure and pain,
and, where these, necessarily also desire.

We have no evidence as yet about thought or the power of reflexion; it seems to   25
be a different kind of soul, differing as what is eternal from what is perishable; it alone
is capable of being separated. All the other parts of soul, it is evident from what we have
said, are, in spite of certain statements to the contrary, incapable of separate existence
though, of course, distinguishable by definition. If opining is distinct from perceiving,   30
to be capable of opining and to be capable of perceiving must be distinct, and so with all
the other forms of living above enumerated. Further, some animals possess all these
parts of soul, some certain of them only, others one only (this is what enables us to classify animals); the cause must be considered later. A similar arrangement is found also   414ᵃ
within the field of the senses; some classes of animals have all the senses, some only
certain of them, others only one, the most indispensable, touch.

Since the expression "that whereby we live and perceive" has two meanings,   5
just like the expression "that whereby we know"—that may mean either knowledge or
the soul, for we can speak of knowing *by* either, and similarly that whereby we are in
health may be either health or the body or some part of the body; and since of these
knowledge or health is a form, essence, or account, or if we so express it an activity
of a recipient matter—knowledge of what is capable of knowing, health of what is ca-   10
pable of being made healthy (for the activity of that which is capable of originating
change seems to take place in what is changed or altered); further, since it is the soul
by which primarily we live, perceive, and think:—it follows that the soul must be an
account and essence, not matter or a subject. For, as we said, the word substance has
three meanings—form, matter, and the complex of both—and of these matter is po-   15
tentiality, form actuality. Since then the complex here is the living thing, the body
cannot be the actuality of the soul; it is the soul which is the actuality of a certain kind
of body. Hence the rightness of the view that the soul cannot *be* without a body, while   20
it cannot be a body; it is not a body but something relative to a body. That is why it is
in a body, and a body of a definite kind. It was a mistake, therefore, to do as former

25 thinkers did, merely to fit it into a body without adding a definite specification of the kind or character of that body, although evidently one chance thing will not receive another. It comes about as reason requires: the actuality of any given thing can only be realized in what is already potentially that thing, i.e. in a matter of its own appropriate to it. From all this it is plain that soul is an actuality or account of something that possesses a potentiality of being such.

3. Of the psychic powers above enumerated some kinds of living things, as we
30 have said, possess all, some less than all, others one only. Those we have mentioned are the nutritive, the appetitive, the sensory, the locomotive, and the power of think-
414ᵇ ing. Plants have none but the first, the nutritive, while another order of living things has this *plus* the sensory. If any order of living things has the sensory, it must also have the appetitive; for appetite is the genus of which desire, passion, and wish are the species; now all animals have one sense at least, viz. touch, and whatever has a sense has the capacity for pleasure and pain and therefore has pleasant and painful
5 objects present to it, and wherever these are present, there is desire, for desire is appetition of what is pleasant. Further, all animals have the sense for food (for touch is the sense for food); the food of all living things consists of what is dry, moist, hot,
10 cold, and these are the qualities apprehended by touch; all other sensible qualities are apprehended by touch only indirectly. Sounds, colours, and odours contribute nothing to nutriment; flavours fall within the field of tangible qualities. Hunger and thirst are forms of desire, hunger a desire for what is dry and hot, thirst a desire for
15 what is cold and moist; flavour is a sort of seasoning added to both. We must later clear up these points, but at present it may be enough to say that all animals that possess the sense of touch have also appetition. The case of imagination is obscure; we must examine it later. Certain kinds of animals possess in addition the power of locomotion, and still others, i.e. man and possibly another order like man or superior
20 to him, the power of thinking and thought. It is now evident that a single definition can be given of soul only in the same sense as one can be given of figure. For, as in that case there is no figure apart from triangle and those that follow in order, so here there is no soul apart from the forms of soul just enumerated. It is true that a common definition can be given for figure which will fit all figures without expressing the peculiar nature of any figure. So here in the case of soul and its specific forms.
25 Hence it is absurd in this and similar cases to look for a common definition which will not express the peculiar nature of anything that is and will not apply to the appropriate indivisible species, while at the same time omitting to look for an account which will. The cases of figure and soul are exactly parallel; for the particulars sub-
30 sumed under the common name in both cases—figures and living beings—constitute a series, each successive term of which potentially contains its predecessor, e.g. the square the triangle, the sensory power the self-nutritive. Hence we must ask in the case of each order of living things, What is its soul, i.e. What is the soul of plant, man, beast? Why the terms are related in this serial way must form the subject of
415ᵃ examination. For the power of perception is never found apart from the power of self-nutrition, while—in plants—the latter is found isolated from the former. Again,
5 no sense is found apart from that of touch, while touch *is* found by itself; many animals have neither sight, hearing, nor smell. Again, among living things that possess sense some have the power of locomotion, some not. Lastly, certain living beings— a small minority—possess calculation and thought, for (among mortal beings) those
10 which possess calculation have all the other powers above mentioned, while the con-

verse does not hold—indeed some live by imagination alone, while others have not even imagination. Reflective thought presents a different problem.

It is evident that the way to give the most adequate definition of soul is to seek in the case of *each* of its forms for the most appropriate definition.

*   *   *

BOOK III

*   *   *

4. Turning now to the part of the soul with which the soul knows and (whether this is separable from the others in definition only, or spatially as well) we have to inquire what differentiates this part, and how thinking can take place.   429ᵃ 10

If thinking is like perceiving, it must be either a process in which the soul is acted upon by what is capable of being thought, or a process different from but analogous to that. The thinking part of the soul must therefore be, while impassible, capable of receiving the form of an object; that is, must be potentially identical in character with its object without being the object. Thought must be related to what is thinkable, as sense is to what is sensible.   15

Therefore, since everything is a possible object of thought, mind in order, as Anaxagoras says, to dominate, that is, to know, must be pure from all admixture; for the co-presence of what is alien to its nature is a hindrance and a block: it follows that it can have no nature of its own, other than that of having a certain capacity. Thus that in the soul which is called thought (by thought I mean that whereby the soul thinks and judges) is, before it thinks, not actually any real thing. For this reason it cannot reasonably be regarded as blended with the body: if so, it would acquire some quality, e.g. warmth or cold, or even have an organ like the sensitive faculty: as it is, it has none. It was a good idea to call the soul "the place of forms," though this description holds only of the thinking soul, and even this is the forms only potentially, not actually.   20   25

Observation of the sense-organs and their employment reveals a distinction between the impassibility of the sensitive faculty and that of the faculty of thought. After strong stimulation of a sense we are less able to exercise it than before, as e.g. in the case of a loud sound we cannot hear easily immediately after, or in the case of a bright colour or a powerful odour we cannot see or smell, but in the case of thought thinking about an object that is highly thinkable renders it more and not less able afterwards to think of objects that are less thinkable: the reason is that while the faculty of sensation is dependent upon the body, thought is separable from it.   30   429ᵇ

When thought has become each thing in the way in which a man who actually knows is said to do so (this happens when he is now able to exercise the power on his own initiative), its condition is still one of potentiality, but in a different sense from the potentiality which preceded the acquisition of knowledge by learning or discovery; and thought is then able to think of itself.   5

Since we can distinguish between a magnitude and what it is to be a magnitude, and between water and what it is to be water, and so in many other cases (though not in all; for in certain cases the thing and its form are identical), flesh and what it is to be flesh are discriminated either by different faculties, or by the same faculty in two differ-   10

ent states; for flesh necessarily involves matter and is like what is snub-nosed, a *this* in a *this*. Now it is by means of the sensitive faculty that we discriminate the hot and the
15   cold, i.e. the factors which combined in a certain ratio constitute flesh: the essential character of flesh is apprehended by something different either wholly separate from the sensitive faculty or related to it as a bent line to the same line when it has been straightened out.

Again in the case of abstract objects what is straight is analogous to what is snubnosed; for it necessarily implies a continuum: its constitutive essence is different, if we may distinguish between straightness and what is straight: let us take it to be two-ness.
20   It must be apprehended, therefore, by a different power or by the same power in a different state. To sum up, in so far as the realities it knows are capable of being separated from their matter, so it is also with the powers of thought.

The problem might be suggested: if thinking is a passive affection, then if thought
25   is simple and impassible and has nothing in common with anything else, as Anaxagoras says, how can it come to think at all? For interaction between two factors is held to require a precedent community of nature between the factors. Again it might be asked, is thought a possible object of thought to itself? For if thought is thinkable *per se* and what is thinkable is in kind one and the same, then either thought will belong to everything,
30   or it will contain some element common to it with all other realities which makes them all thinkable.

Have not we already disposed of the difficulty about interaction involving a common element, when we said that thought is in a sense potentially whatever is thinkable, though actually it is nothing until it has thought? What it thinks must be in it just as
430ª   characters may be said to be on a writing-table on which as yet nothing actually stands written: this is exactly what happens with thought.

Thought is itself thinkable in exactly the same way as its objects are. For in the case of objects which involve no matter, what thinks and what is thought are identical; for speculative knowledge and its object are identical. (Why thought is not always
5   thinking we must consider later.) In the case of those which contain matter each of the objects of thought is only potentially present. It follows that while they will not have thought in them (for thought is a potentiality of them only in so far as they are capable of being disengaged from matter) thought may yet be thinkable.

10   5. Since in every class of things, as in nature as a whole, we find two factors involved, a matter which is potentially all the particulars included in the class, a cause which is productive in the sense that it makes them all (the latter standing to the former, as e.g. an art to its material), these distinct elements must likewise be found within the soul.

And in fact thought, as we have described it, is what it is by virtue of becoming all
15   things, while there is another which is what it is by virtue of making all things: this is a sort of positive state like light; for in a sense light makes potential colours into actual colours.

Thought in this sense of it is separable, impassible, unmixed, since it is in its essential nature activity (for always the active is superior to the passive factor, the originating force to the matter).
20   Actual knowledge is identical with its object: in the individual, potential knowledge is in time prior to actual knowledge, but absolutely it is not prior even in time. It does not sometimes think and sometimes not think. When separated it is alone just what it is, and this above is immortal and eternal (we do not remember because, while this is
25   impossible, passive thought is perishable); and without this nothing thinks.

NICHOMACHEAN ETHICS (in part)

BOOK I

1. Every art and every inquiry, and similarly every action and choice, is thought to aim   1094ᵃ
at some good; and for this reason the good has rightly been declared to be that at which
all things aim. But a certain difference is found among ends; some are activities, others
are products apart from the activities that produce them. Where there are ends apart
from the actions, it is the nature of the products to be better than the activities. Now, as   5
there are many actions, arts, and sciences, their ends also are many; the end of the medical art is health, that of shipbuilding a vessel, that of strategy victory, that of economics
wealth. But where such arts fall under a single capacity—as bridle-making and the other   10
arts concerned with the equipment of horses fall under the art of riding, and this and every military action under strategy, in the same way other arts fall under yet others—in
all of these the ends of the master arts are to be preferred to all the subordinate ends; for   15
it is for the sake of the former that the latter are pursued. It makes no difference whether
the activities themselves are the ends of the actions, or something else apart from the activities, as in the case of the sciences just mentioned.

    2. If, then, there is some end of the things we do, which we desire for its own
sake (everything else being desired for the sake of this), and if we do not choose everything for the sake of something else (for at that rate the process would go on to infinity,   20
so that our desire would be empty and vain), clearly this must be the good and the chief
good. Will not the knowledge of it, then, have a great influence on life? Shall we not,
like archers who have a mark to aim at, be more likely to hit upon what we should? If
so, we must try, in outline at least, to determine what it is, and of which of the sciences   25
or capacities it is the object. It would seem to belong to the most authoritative art and
that which is most truly the master art. And politics appears to be of this nature; for it is
this that ordains which of the sciences should be studied in a state, and which each class
of citizens should learn and up to what point they should learn them; and we see even   1094ᵇ
the most highly esteemed of capacities to fall under this, e.g. strategy, economics,
rhetoric; now, since politics uses the rest of the sciences, and since, again, it legislates   5
as to what we are to do and what we are to abstain from, the end of this science must include those of the others, so that this end must be the good for man. For even if the end
is the same for a single man and for a state, that of the state seems at all events something greater and more complete both to attain and to preserve; for though it is worthwhile to attain the end merely for one man, it is finer and more godlike to attain it for a   10
nation or for city-states. These, then, are the ends at which our inquiry, being concerned
with politics, aims.

    3. Our discussion will be adequate if it has as much clearness as the subject mat-
ter admits of; for precision is not to be sought for alike in all discussions, any more than
in all the products of the crafts. Now fine and just actions, which political science investigates, exhibit much variety and fluctuation, so that they may be thought to exist
only by convention, and not by nature. And goods also exhibit a similar fluctuation be-   15

Aristotle, *The Nichomachean Ethics,* Book I–II; III, 1–5; IV, 3; VI–VII; X, 6–8, translated by David Ross, revised by J.O. Urmson (Oxford: Oxford University Press, 1980). Reprinted by permission of Oxford University Press.

cause they bring harm to many people; for before now men have been undone by reason of their wealth, and others by reason of their courage. We must be content, then, in speaking of such subjects and with such premises to indicate the truth roughly and in outline, and in speaking about things which are only for the most part true and with premises of the same kind to reach conclusions that are no better. In the same spirit, therefore, should each of our statements be *received;* for it is the mark of an educated man to look for precision in each class of things just so far as the nature of the subject admits: it is evidently equally foolish to accept probable reasoning from a mathematician and to demand from a rhetorician demonstrative proofs.

Now each man judges well the things he knows, and of these he is a good judge. And so the man who has been educated in a subject is a good judge of that subject, and the man who has received an all-round education is a good judge in general. Hence a young man is not a proper hearer of lectures on political science; for he is inexperienced in the actions that occur in life, but its discussions start from these and are about these; and, further, since he tends to follow his passions, his study will be vain and unprofitable, because the end aimed at is not knowledge but action. And it makes no difference whether he is young in years or youthful in character; the defect does not depend on time, but on his living and pursuing each successive object as passion directs. For to such persons, as to the incontinent, knowledge brings no profit; but to those who desire and act in accordance with a rational principle knowledge about such matters will be of great benefit.

These remarks about the student, the way in which our statements should be received, and the purpose of the inquiry, may be taken as our preface.

4. Let us resume our inquiry and state, in view of the fact that all knowledge and choice aims at some good, what it is that we say political science aims at and what is the highest of all goods achievable by action. Verbally there is very general agreement; for both the general run of men and people of superior refinement say that it is happiness, and identify living well and faring well with being happy; but with regard to what happiness is they differ, and the many do not give the same account as the wise. For the former think it is some plain and obvious thing, like pleasure, wealth, or honour; they differ, however, from one another—and often even the same man identifies it with different things, with health when he is ill, with wealth when he is poor; but, conscious of their ignorance, they admire those who proclaim some great thing that is above their comprehension. Now some thought that apart from these many goods there is another which is good in itself and causes the goodness of all these as well. To examine all the opinions that have been held would no doubt be somewhat fruitless: it is enough to examine those that are most prevalent or that seem to have some reason in their favour.

Let us not fail to notice, however, that there is a difference between arguments from and those to the first principles. For Plato, too, was right in raising this question and asking, as he used to do, "are we on the way from or to the first principles?" There is a difference, as there is in a race-course between the course from the judges to the turning-point and the way back. For, while we must begin with what is familiar, things are so in two ways—some to us, some without qualification. Presumably, then, we must begin with things familiar to us. Hence any one who is to listen intelligently to lectures about what is noble and just and, generally, about the subjects of political science must have been brought up in good habits. For the facts are the starting-point, and if they are sufficiently plain to him, he will not need the reason as well; and the man who has been well brought up has or can easily get starting-points. And as for him who neither has nor can get them, let him hear the words of Hesiod:

Far best is he who knows all things himself;   10
Good, he that hearkens when men counsel right;
But he who neither knows, nor lays to heart
Another's wisdom, is a useless wight.

5. Let us, however, resume our discussion from the point at which we digressed.
To judge from the lives that men lead, most men, and men of the most vulgar type, seem
(not without some reason) to identify the good, or happiness, with pleasure; which is the   15
reason why they love the life of enjoyment. For there are, we may say, three prominent
types of life—that just mentioned, the political, and thirdly the contemplative life. Now
the mass of mankind are evidently quite slavish in their tastes, preferring a life suitable
to beasts, but they get some reason for their view from the fact that many of those in   20
high places share the tastes of Sardanapallus. But people of superior refinement and of
active disposition identify happiness with honour; for this is, roughly speaking, the end
of the political life. But it seems too superficial to be what we are looking for, since it is
thought to depend on those who bestow honour rather than on him who receives it, but   25
the good we divine to be something of one's own and not easily taken from one. Further, men seem to pursue honour in order that they may be assured of their merit; at
least it is by men of practical wisdom that they seek to be honoured, and among those
who know them, and on the ground of their excellence; clearly, then, according to them,
at any rate, excellence is better. And perhaps one might even suppose this to be, rather   30
than honour, the end of the political life. But even this appears somewhat incomplete;
for possession of excellence seems actually compatible with being asleep, or with life-
long inactivity, and, further, with the greatest sufferings and misfortunes; but a man
who was living so no one would call happy, unless he were maintaining a thesis at all   1096a
costs. But enough of this; for the subject has been sufficiently treated even in ordinary
discussions. Third comes the contemplative life, which we shall consider later.   5
The life of money-making is one undertaken under compulsion, and wealth is evidently not the good we are seeking; for it is merely useful and for the sake of something
else. And so one might rather take the aforenamed objects to be ends; for they are loved
for themselves. But it is evident that not even these are ends although many arguments   10
have been thrown away in support of them. Let us then dismiss them.

6. We had perhaps better consider the universal good and discuss thoroughly
what is meant by it, although such an inquiry is made an uphill one by the fact that the
Forms have been introduced by friends of our own. Yet it would perhaps be thought to
be better, indeed to be our duty, for the sake of maintaining the truth even to destroy
what touches us closely, especially as we are philosophers; for, while both are dear,   15
piety requires us to honour truth above our friends.
The men who introduced this doctrine did not posit Ideas of classes within which
they recognized priority and posteriority (which is the reason why they did not maintain
the existence of an Idea embracing all numbers); but things are called good both in the   20
category of substance and in that of quality and in that of relation, and that which is *per
se,* i.e. substance, is prior in nature to the relative (for the latter is like an offshoot and
accident of what is); so that there could not be a common Idea set over all these goods.
Further, since things are said to be good in as many ways as they are said to be (for   25
things are called good both in the category of substance, as God and reason, and in quality, e.g. the virtues, and in quantity, e.g. that which is moderate, and in relation, e.g. the
useful, and in time, e.g. the right opportunity, and in place, e.g. the right locality and the
like), clearly the good cannot be something universally present in all cases and single;

for then it would not have been predicated in all the categories but in one only. Further,
since of the things answering to one Idea there is one science, there would have been
one science of all the goods; but as it is there are many sciences even of the things that
fall under one category, e.g. of opportunity (for opportunity in war is studied by strategy
and in disease by medicine), and the moderate in food is studied by medicine and in exercise by the science of gymnastics. And one might ask the question, what in the world
they *mean* by "a thing itself," if in man himself and in a particular man the account of
man is one and the same. For in so far as they are men, they will in no respect differ; and
if this is so, neither will there be a difference in so far as they are good. But again it will
not be good any the more for being eternal, since that which lasts long is no whiter than
that which perishes in a day. The Pythagoreans seem to give a more plausible account
of the good, when they place the one in the column of goods; and it is they that Speusippus seems to have followed.

But let us discuss these matters elsewhere; an objection to what we have said,
however, may be discerned in the fact that the Platonists have not been speaking about
all goods, and that the goods that are pursued and loved for themselves are called good
by reference to a single Form, while those which tend to produce or to preserve these
somehow or to prevent their contraries are called so by reference to these, and in a different sense. Clearly, then, goods must be spoken of in two ways, and some must be
good in themselves, the others by reason of these. Let us separate, then, things good in
themselves from things useful, and consider whether the former are called good by reference to a single Idea. What sort of goods would one call good in themselves? Is it
those that are pursued even when isolated from others, such as intelligence, sight, and
certain pleasures and honours? Certainly, if we pursue these also for the sake of something else, yet one would place them among things good in themselves. Or is nothing
other than the Idea good in itself? In that case the Form will be empty. But if the things
we have named are also things good in themselves, the account of the good will have to
appear as something identical in them all, as that of whiteness is identical in snow and
in white lead. But of honour, wisdom, and pleasure, just in respect of their goodness, the
accounts are distinct and diverse. The good, therefore, is not something common answering to one Idea.

But then in what way are things called good? They do not seem to be like the
things that only chance to have the same name. Are goods one, then, by being derived
from one good or by all contributing to one good, or are they rather one by analogy?
Certainly as sight is in the body, so is reason in the soul, and so on in other cases. But
perhaps these subjects had better be dismissed for the present; for perfect precision
about them would be more appropriate to another branch of philosophy. And similarly
with regard to the Idea; even if there is some one good which is universally predicable
of goods or is capable of separate and independent existence, clearly it could not be
achieved or attained by man; but we are now seeking something attainable. Perhaps,
however, some one might think it worthwhile to have knowledge of it with a view to the
goods that are attainable and achievable; for having this as a sort of pattern we shall
know better the goods that are good for us, and if we know them shall attain them. This
argument has some plausibility, but seems to clash with the procedure of the sciences;
for all of these, though they aim at some good and seek to supply the deficiency of it,
leave on one side the knowledge of the good. Yet that all the exponents of the arts
should be ignorant of, and should not even seek, so great an aid is not probable. It is
hard, too, to see how a weaver or a carpenter will be benefited in regard to his own craft
by knowing this "good itself," or how the man who has viewed the Idea itself will be a
better doctor or general thereby. For a doctor seems not even to study health in this way,

but the health of man, or perhaps rather the health of a particular man; for it is individuals that he is healing. But enough of these topics.

    7. Let us again return to the good we are seeking, and ask what it can be. It seems   15
different in different actions and arts; it is different in medicine, in strategy, and in the
other arts likewise. What then is the good of each? Surely that for whose sake everything else is done. In medicine this is health, in strategy victory, in architecture a house,
in any other sphere something else, and in every action and choice the end; for it is for   20
the sake of this that all men do whatever else they do. Therefore, if there is an end for
all that we do, this will be the good achievable by action, and if there are more than one,
these will be the goods achievable by action.
    So the argument has by a different course reached the same point; but we must try
to state this even more clearly. Since there are evidently more than one end, and we
choose some of these (e.g. wealth, flutes, and in general instruments) for the sake of   25
something else, clearly not all ends are complete ends; but the chief good is evidently
something complete. Therefore, if there is only one complete end, this will be what we
are seeking, and if there are more than one, the most complete of these will be what we
are seeking. Now we call that which is in itself worthy of pursuit more complete than   30
that which is worthy of pursuit for the sake of something else, and that which is never
desirable for the sake of something else more complete than the things that are desirable
both in themselves and for the sake of that other thing, and therefore we call complete
without qualification that which is always desirable in itself and never for the sake of
something else.
    Now such a thing happiness, above all else, is held to be; for this we choose always for itself and never for the sake of something else, but honour, pleasure, reason,   1097b
and every excellence we choose indeed for themselves (for if nothing resulted from
them we should still choose each of them), but we choose them also for the sake of happiness, judging that through them we shall be happy. Happiness, on the other hand, no   5
one chooses for the sake of these, nor, in general, for anything other than itself.
    From the point of view of self-sufficiency the same result seems to follow; for the
complete good is thought to be self-sufficient. Now by self-sufficient we do not mean
that which is sufficient for a man by himself, for one who lives a solitary life, but also
for parents, children, wife, and in general for his friends and fellow citizens, since man   10
is sociable by nature. But some limit must be set to this; for if we extend our requirement to ancestors and descendants and friends' friends we are in for an infinite series.
Let us examine this question, however, on another occasion; the self-sufficient we now   15
define as that which when isolated makes life desirable and lacking in nothing; and such
we think happiness to be; and further we think it most desirable of all things, without
being counted as one good thing among others—if it were so counted it would clearly
be made more desirable by the addition of even the least of goods; for that which is
added becomes an excess of goods, and of goods the greater is always more desirable.   20
Happiness, then, is something complete and self-sufficient, and is the end of action.
    Presumably, however, to say that happiness is the chief good seems a platitude,
and a clearer account of what it is is still desired. This might perhaps be given, if we
could first ascertain the function of man. For just as for a flute-player, a sculptor, or any   25
artist, and, in general, for all things that have a function or activity, the good and the
"well" is thought to reside in the function, so would it seem to be for man, if he has a
function. Have the carpenter, then, and the tanner certain functions or activities, and has
man none? Is he naturally functionless? Or as eye, hand, foot, and in general each of the   30
parts evidently has a function, may one lay it down that man similarly has a function

apart from all these? What then can this be? Life seems to be common even to plants, but we are seeking what is peculiar to man. Let us exclude, therefore, the life of nutrition and growth. Next there would be a life of perception, but *it* also seems to be common even to the horse, the ox, and every animal. There remains, then, an active life of the element that has a rational principle (of this, one part has such a principle in the sense of being obedient to one, the other in the sense of possessing one and exercising thought); and as this too can be taken in two ways, we must state that life in the sense of activity is what we mean; for this seems to be the more proper sense of the term. Now if the function of man is an activity of soul in accordance with, or not without, rational

Lapith and Centaur, Metope from Parthenon, 477–438 B.C. According to a Greek myth, the Lapiths invited the Centaurs to the wedding feast of their king, Peirthon, as a gesture of good will. Upon seeing the beauty of the Lapiety bride, the Centaurs succumbed to their animal instincts of lust and drunkenness and turned the feast into an abduction attempt and brawl. The Lapith warriors, under the cool wisdom of Apollo, brought a sense of calm to the chaos. The image is a symbolic lesson in its appeal for human reason and order over the lower animal instinct of passion—a lesson also taught by Aristotle in the Nichomachean Ethics. (©Archivi Alinari, 1989/Art Resource)

principle, and if we say a so-and-so and a good so-and-so have a function which is the same in kind, e.g. a lyre-player and a good lyre-player, and so without qualification in all cases, eminence in respect of excellence being added to the function (for the function of a lyre-player is to play the lyre, and that of a good lyre-player is to do so well): if this is the case, [and we state the function of man to be a certain kind of life, and this to be an activity or actions of the soul implying a rational principle, and the function of a good man to be the good and noble performance of these, and if any action is well performed when it is performed in accordance with the appropriate excellence: if this is the case,] human good turns out to be activity of soul in conformity with excellence, and if there are more than one excellence, in conformity with the best and most complete.

But we must add "in a complete life." For one swallow does not make a summer, nor does one day; and so too one day, or a short time, does not make a man blessed and happy.

Let this serve as an outline of the good; for we must presumably first sketch it roughly, and then later fill in the details. But it would seem that any one is capable of carrying on and articulating what has once been well outlined, and that time is a good discoverer or partner in such a work; to which facts the advances of the arts are due; for any one can add what is lacking. And we must also remember what has been said before, and not look for precision in all things alike, but in each class of things such precision as accords with the subject-matter, and so much as is appropriate to the inquiry. For a carpenter and a geometer look for right angles in different ways; the former does so in so far as the right angle is useful for his work, while the latter inquires what it is or what sort of thing it is; for he is a spectator of the truth. We must act in the same way, then, in all other matters as well, that our main task may not be subordinated to minor questions. Nor must we demand the cause in all matters alike; it is enough in some cases that the *fact* be well established, as in the case of the first principles; the fact is a primary thing or first principle. Now of first principles we see some by induction, some by perception, some by a certain habituation, and others too in other ways. But each set of principles we must try to investigate in the natural way, and we must take pains to determine them correctly, since they have a great influence on what follows. For the beginning is thought to be more than half of the whole, and many of the questions we ask are cleared up by it.

8. We must consider it, however, in the light not only of our conclusion and our premises, but also of what is commonly said about it; for with a true view all the facts harmonize, but with a false one they soon clash. Now goods have been divided into three classes, and some are described as external, others as relating to soul or to body; and we call those that relate to soul most properly and truly goods. But we are positing actions and activities relating to soul. Therefore our account must be sound, at least according to this view, which is an old one and agreed on by philosophers. It is correct also in that we identify the end with certain actions and activities; for thus it falls among goods of the soul and not among external goods. Another belief which harmonizes with our account is that the happy man lives well and fares well; for we have practically defined happiness as a sort of living and faring well. The characteristics that are looked for in happiness seem also, all of excellence, some with practical wisdom, others with a kind of philosophic wisdom, others with these, or one of these, accompanied by pleasure or not without pleasure; while others include also external prosperity. Now some of these views have been held by many men and men of old, others by a few persons; and it is not probable that either of these should be entirely mistaken, but rather that they should be right in at least some one respect or even in most respects.

30   With those who identify happiness with excellence or some one excellence our account is in harmony; for to excellence belongs activity in accordance with excellence. But it makes, perhaps, no small difference whether we place the chief good in possession or in use, in state or in activity. For the state may exist without producing any good

1099ᵃ   result, as in a man who is asleep or in some other way quite inactive, but the activity cannot; for one who has the activity will of necessity be acting, and acting well. And as in the Olympic Games it is not the most beautiful and the strongest that are crowned but

5   those who compete (for it is some of these that are victorious), so those who act rightly win the noble and good things in life.

Their life is also in itself pleasant. For pleasure is a state of soul, and to each man that which he is said to be a lover of is pleasant; e.g. not only is a horse pleasant

10   to the lover of horses, and a spectacle to the lover of sights, but also in the same way just acts are pleasant to the lover of justice and in general excellent acts to the lover of excellence. Now for most men their pleasures are in conflict with one another because these are not by nature pleasant, but the lovers of what is noble find pleasant the things that are by nature pleasant; and excellent actions are such, so that these are pleasant for such men as well as in their own nature. Their life, therefore, has no fur-

15   ther need of pleasure as a sort of adventitious charm, but has its pleasure in itself. For, besides what we have said, the man who does not rejoice in noble actions is not even good; since no one would call a man just who did not enjoy acting justly, nor any man

20   liberal who did not enjoy liberal actions; and similarly in all other cases. If this is so, excellent actions must be in themselves pleasant. But they are also *good* and *noble*, and have each of these attributes in the highest degree, since the good man judges well about these attributes and he judges in the way we have described. Happiness

25   then is the best, noblest, and most pleasant thing, and these attributes are not severed as in the inscription at Delos—

Most noble is that which is justest, and best is health;
But pleasantest is it to win what we love.

30   For all these properties belong to the best activities; and these, or one—the best of these, we identify with happiness.

Yet evidently, as we said, it needs the external goods as well; for it is impossible,

1099ᵇ   or not easy, to do noble acts without the proper equipment. In many actions we use friends and riches and political power as instruments; and there are some things the lack of which takes the lustre from blessedness, as good birth, satisfactory children, beauty; for the man who is very ugly in appearance or ill-born or solitary and childless is hardly happy, and perhaps a man would be still less so if he had thoroughly bad children or

5   friends or had lost good children or friends by death. As we said, then, happiness seems to need this sort of prosperity in addition; for which reason some identify happiness with good fortune, though others identify it with excellence.

9. For this reason also the question is asked, whether happiness is to be acquired

10   by learning or by habituation or some other sort of training, or comes in virtue of some divine providence or again by chance. Now if there is *any* gift of the gods to men, it is reasonable that happiness should be god-given, and most surely god-given of all human things inasmuch as it is the best. But this question would perhaps be more appropriate to another inquiry; happiness seems, however, even if it is not god-sent but comes as a

15   result of excellence and some process of learning or training, to be among the most god-like things; for that which is the prize and end of excellence seems to be the best thing and something godlike and blessed.

It will also on this view be very generally shared; for all who are not maimed as regards excellence may win it by a certain kind of study and care. But if it is better to be happy thus than by chance, it is reasonable that the facts should be so, since everything   20
that depends on the action of nature is by nature as good as it can be, and similarly everything that depends on art or any cause, and especially if it depends on the best of all causes. To entrust to chance what is greatest and most noble would be a very defective arrangement.

The answer to the question we are asking is plain also from the definition; for it   25
has been said to be a certain kind of activity of soul. Of the remaining goods, some are necessary and others are naturally co-operative and useful as instruments. And this will be found to agree with what we said at the outset; for we stated the end of political science to be the best end, and political science spends most of its pains on making the cit-   30
izens to be of a certain character, viz. good and capable of noble acts.

It is natural, then, that we call neither ox nor horse nor any other of the animals happy; for none of them is capable of sharing in such activity. For this reason also a boy   1100a
is not happy; for he is not yet capable of such acts, owing to his age; and boys who are called happy are being congratulated by reason of the hopes we have for them. For there is required, as we said, not only complete excellence but also a complete life, since   5
many changes occur in life, and all manner of chances, and the most prosperous may fall into great misfortunes in old age, as is told of Priam in the Trojan Cycle; and one who has experienced such chances and has ended wretchedly no one calls happy.

10. Must no one at all, then, be called happy while he lives; must we, as Solon   10
says, see the end? Even if we are to lay down this doctrine, is it also the case that a man is happy when he is *dead?* Or is not this quite absurd, especially for us who say that happiness is an activity? But if we do not call the dead man happy, and if   15
Solon does not mean this, but that one can then safely *call* a man blessed as being at last beyond evils and misfortunes, this also affords matter for discussion; for both evil and good are thought to exist for a dead man, as much as for one who is alive but not aware of them; e.g. honours and dishonours and the good or bad fortunes of   20
children and in general of descendants. And this also presents a problem; for though a man has lived blessedly up to old age and has had a death worthy of his life, many reverses may befall his descendants—some of them may be good and attain   25
the life they deserve, while with others the opposite may be the case; and clearly too the degrees of relationship between them and their ancestors may vary indefinitely. It would be odd, then, if the dead man were to share in these changes and become at one time happy, at another wretched; while it would also be odd if the   30
fortunes of the descendants did not for *some* time have *some* effect on the happiness of their ancestors.

But we must return to our first difficulty; for perhaps by a consideration of it our present problem might be solved. Now if we must see the end and only then call a man blessed, not as being blessed but as having been so before, surely it is odd that when he is happy the attribute that belongs to him is not to be truly predicated of him because we do not wish to call living men happy, on account of the changes that may befall them,   1100b
and because we have assumed happiness to be something permanent and by no means easily changed, while a single man may suffer many turns of fortune's wheel. For clearly if we were to follow his fortunes, we should often call the same man happy and   5
again wretched, making the happy man out to be a "chameleon and insecurely based." Or is this following his fortunes quite wrong? Success or failure in life does not depend on these, but human life, as we said, needs these as well, while excellent activities or   10
their opposites are what determine happiness or the reverse.

The question we have now discussed confirms our definition. For no function of man has so much permanence as excellent activities (these are thought to be more durable even than knowledge), and of these themselves the most valuable are more durable because those who are blessed spend their life most readily and most continuously in these; for this seems to be the reason why we do not forget them. The attribute in question, then, will belong to the happy man, and he will be happy throughout his life; for always, or by preference to everything else, he will do and contemplate what is excellent, and he will bear the chances of life most nobly and altogether decorously, if he is "truly good" and "foursquare beyond reproach."

Now many events happen by chance, and events differing in importance; small pieces of good fortune or of its opposite clearly do not weigh down the scales of life one way or the other, but a multitude of great events if they turn out well will make life more blessed (for not only are they themselves such as to add beauty to life, but the way a man deals with them may be noble and good), while if they turn out ill they crush and maim blessedness; for they both bring pain with them and hinder many activities. Yet even in these nobility shines through, when a man bears with resignation many great misfortunes, not through insensibility to pain but through nobility and greatness of soul.

If activities are, as we said, what determines the character of life, no blessed man can become miserable; for he will never do the acts that are hateful and mean. For the man who is truly good and wise, we think, bears all the chances of life becomingly and always makes the best of circumstances, as a good general makes the best military use of the army at his command and a shoemaker makes the best shoes out of the hides that are given him; and so with all other craftsmen. And if this is the case, the happy man can never become miserable—though he will not reach *blessedness,* if he meet with fortunes like those of Priam.

Nor, again, is he many-coloured and changeable; for neither will he be moved from his happy state easily or by any ordinary misadventures, but only by many great ones, nor, if he has had many great misadventures, will he recover his happiness in a short time, but if at all, only in a long and complete one in which he has attained many splendid successes.

Why then should we not say that he is happy who is active in conformity with complete excellence and is sufficiently equipped with external goods, not for some chance period but throughout a complete life? Or must we add "and who is destined to live thus and die as befits his life"? Certainly the future is obscure to us, while happiness, we claim, is an end and something in every way final. If so, we shall call blessed those among living men in whom these conditions are, and are to be, fulfilled—but blessed *men.* So much for these questions.

11. That the fortunes of descendants and of all a man's friends should not affect his happiness at all seems a very unfriendly doctrine, and one opposed to the opinions men hold; but since the events that happen are numerous and admit of all sorts of difference, and some come more near to us and others less so, it seems a long—indeed an endless—task to discuss each in detail; a general outline will perhaps suffice. If, then, as some of a man's own misadventures have a certain weight and influence on life while others are, as it were, lighter, so too there are differences among the misadventures of all our friends, and it makes a difference whether the various sufferings befall the living or the dead (much more even than whether lawless and terrible deeds are presupposed in a tragedy or done on the stage), this difference also must be taken into account; or rather, perhaps, the fact that doubt is felt whether the dead share in any good or evil. For it seems, from these considerations, that even if anything whether good or evil pene-

trates to them, it must be something weak and negligible, either in itself or for them, or if not, at least it must be such in degree and kind as not to make happy those who are not happy nor to take away their blessedness from those who are. The good or bad fortunes of friends, then, seem to have some effects on the dead, but effects of such a kind and degree as neither to make the happy unhappy nor to produce any other change of the kind.

12. These questions having been answered, let us consider whether happiness is among the things that are praised or rather among the things that are prized; for clearly it is not to be placed among *potentialities*. Everything that is praised seems to be praised because it is of a certain kind and is related somehow to something else; for we praise the just or brave man and in general both the good man and excellence itself because of the actions and functions involved, and we praise the strong man, the good runner, and so on, because he is of a certain kind and is related in a certain way to something good and important. This is clear also from the praises of the gods; for it seems absurd that the gods should be referred to our standard, but this is done because praise involves a reference, as we said, to something else. But if praise is for things such as we have de-scribed, clearly what applies to the best things is not praise, but something greater and better, as is indeed obvious; for what we do to the gods and the most godlike of men is to call them blessed and happy. And so too with good things; no one praises happiness as he does justice, but rather calls it blessed, as being something more divine and better.

Eudoxus also seems to have been right in his method of advocating the supremacy of pleasure; he thought that the fact that, though a good, it is not praised in-dicated it to be better than the things that are praised, and that this is what God and the good are; for by reference to these all other things are judged. Praise is appropriate to excellence; for as a result of excellence men tend to do noble deeds (*encomia* are be-stowed on acts, whether of the body or of the soul—but perhaps nicety in these matters is more proper to those who have made a study of encomia); but to us it is clear from what has been said that happiness is among the things that are prized and complete. It seems to be so also from the fact that it is a first principle; for it is for the sake of this that we all do everything else, and the first principle and cause of goods is, we claim, something prized and divine.

13. Since happiness is an activity of soul in accordance with complete excel-lence, we must consider the nature of excellence; for perhaps we shall thus see better the nature of happiness. The true student of politics, too, is thought to have studied this above all things; for he wishes to make his fellow citizens good and obedient to the laws. As an example of this we have the lawgivers of the Cretans and the Spartans, and any others of the kind that there may have been. And if this inquiry belongs to political science, clearly the pursuit of it will be in accordance with our original plan. But clearly the excellence we must study is human excellence; for the good we were seeking was human good and the happiness human happiness. By human excellence we mean not that of the body but that of the soul; and happiness also we call an activity of soul. But if this is so, clearly the student of politics must know somehow the facts about soul, as the man who is to heal the eyes must know about the whole body also; and all the more since politics is more prized and better than medicine; but even among doctors the best educated spend much labour on acquiring knowledge of the body. The student of poli-tics, then, must study the soul, and must study it with these objects in view, and do so just to the extent which is sufficient for the questions we are discussing; for further pre-cision is perhaps something more laborious than our purposes require.

Some things are said about it, adequately enough, even in the discussions outside our school, and we must use these; e.g. that one element in the soul is irrational and one has a rational principle. Whether these are separated as the parts of the body
30   or of anything divisible are, or are distinct by definition but by nature inseparable, like convex and concave in the circumference of a circle, does not affect the present question.

Of the irrational element one division seems to be widely distributed, and vegetative in its nature, I mean that which causes nutrition and growth; for it is this kind
1102ᵇ   of power of the soul that one must assign to all nurslings and to embryos, and this same power to full-grown creatures; this is more reasonable than to assign some different power to them. Now the excellence of this seems to be common to all and not specifically human; for this part or faculty seems to function most in sleep, while good-
5   ness and badness are least manifest in sleep (whence comes the saying that the happy are not better off than the wretched for half their lives; and this happens naturally enough, since sleep is an inactivity of the soul in that respect in which it is called good
10   or bad), unless perhaps to a small extent some of the movements actually penetrate, and in this respect the dreams of good men are better than those of ordinary people. Enough of this subject, however; let us leave the nutritive faculty alone, since it has by its nature no share in human excellence.

There seems to be also another irrational element in the soul—one which in a sense, however, shares in a rational principle. For we praise the reason of the conti-
15   nent man and of the incontinent, and the part of their soul that has reason, since it urges them aright and towards the best objects; but there is found in them also another natural element beside reason, which fights against and resists it. For exactly as paralysed limbs when we choose to move them to the right turn on the contrary to the left, so is it with the soul; the impulses of incontinent people move in contrary directions.
20   But while in the body we see that which moves astray, in the soul we do not. No doubt, however, we must none the less suppose that in the soul too there is something beside reason, resisting and opposing it. In what sense it is distinct from the other el-
25   ements does not concern us. Now even this seems to have a share in reason, as we said; at any rate in the continent man it obeys reason—and presumably in the temperate and brave man it is still more obedient; for in them it speaks, on all matters, with the same voice as reason.

30   Therefore the irrational element also appears to be twofold. For the vegetative element in no way shares in reason, but the appetitive and in general the desiring element in a sense shares in it, in so far as it listens to and obeys it; this is the sense in which we speak of paying heed to one's father or one's friends, not that in which we speak of "the rational" in mathematics. That the irrational element is in some sense persuaded by reason is indicated also by the giving of advice and by all reproof and exhortation. And if
1103ᵃ   this element also must be said to have reason, that which has reason also will be twofold, one subdivision having it in the strict sense and in itself, and the other having a tendency to obey as one does one's father.

Excellence too is distinguished into kinds in accordance with this difference;
5   for we say that some excellences are intellectual and others moral, philosophic wisdom and understanding and practical wisdom being intellectual, liberality and temperance moral. For in speaking about a man's character we do not say that he is wise or has understanding but that he is good-tempered or temperate; yet we praise
10   the wise man also with respect to his state; and of states we call those which merit praise excellences.

BOOK II

1. Excellence, then, being of two kinds, intellectual and moral, intellectual excellence in the main owes both its birth and its growth to teaching (for which reason it requires   15
experience and time), while moral excellence comes about as a result of habit, whence also its name is one that is formed by a slight variation from the word for "habit." From this it is also plain that none of the moral excellences arises in us by nature; for nothing that exists by nature can form a habit contrary to its nature. For instance the stone which   20
by nature moves downwards cannot be habituated to move upwards, not even if one tries to train it by throwing it up ten thousand times; nor can fire be habituated to move downwards, nor can anything else that by nature behaves in one way be trained to be-have in another. Neither by nature, then, nor contrary to nature do excellences arise in us; rather we are adapted by nature to receive them, and are made perfect by habit.   25

Again, of all the things that come to us by nature we first acquire the potentiality and later exhibit the activity (this is plain in the case of the senses; for it was not by of-ten seeing or often hearing that we got these senses, but on the contrary we had them be-fore we used them, and did not come to have them by using them); but excellences we   30
get by first exercising them, as also happens in the case of the arts as well. For the things we have to learn before we can do, we learn by doing, e.g. men become builders by building and lyre-players by playing the lyre; so too we become just by doing just acts, temperate by doing temperate acts, brave by doing brave acts.   1103ᵇ

This is confirmed by what happens in states; for legislators make the citizens good by forming habits in them, and this is the wish of every legislator; and those who do not effect it miss their mark, and it is in this that a good constitution differs from a   5
bad one.

Again, it is from the same causes and by the same means that every excellence is both produced and destroyed, and similarly every art; for it is from playing the lyre that both good and bad lyre-players are produced. And the corresponding statement is true of builders and of all the rest; men will be good or bad builders as a result of building   10
well or badly. For if this were not so, there would have been no need of a teacher, but all men would have been born good or bad at their craft. This, then, is the case with the excellences also; by doing the acts that we do in our transactions with other men we become just or unjust, and by doing the acts that we do in the presence of danger,   15
and being habituated to feel fear or confidence, we become brave or cowardly. The same is true of appetites and feelings of anger; some men become temperate and good-tempered, others self-indulgent and irascible, by behaving in one way or the   20
other in the appropriate circumstances. Thus, in one word, states arise out of like ac-tivities. This is why the activities we exhibit must be of a certain kind; it is because the states correspond to the differences between these. It makes no small difference, then, whether we form habits of one kind or of another from our very youth; it makes   25
a very great difference, or rather all the difference.

2. Since, then, the present inquiry does not aim at theoretical knowledge like the others (for we are inquiring not in order to know what excellence is, but in order to be-come good, since otherwise our inquiry would have been of no use), we must examine the nature of actions, namely how we ought to do them; for these determine also the na-   30
ture of the states that are produced, as we have said. Now, that we must act according to right reason is a common principle and must be assumed—it will be discussed later, i.e. both what it is, and how it is related to the other excellences. But this must be agreed   1104ᵃ

upon beforehand, that the whole account of matters of conduct must be given in outline and not precisely, as we said at the very beginning that the accounts we demand must be in accordance with the subject-matter; matters concerned with conduct and questions of

5   what is good for us have no fixity, any more than matters of health. The general account being of this nature, the account of particular cases is yet more lacking in exactness; for they do not fall under any art or set of precepts, but the agents themselves must in each case consider what is appropriate to the occasion, as happens also in the art of medicine or of navigation.

10   But though our present account is of this nature we must give what help we can. First, then, let us consider this, that it is the nature of such things to be destroyed by defect and excess, as we see in the case of strength and of health (for to gain light on things imperceptible we must use the evidence of sensible things); both excessive and

15   defective exercise destroys the strength, and similarly drink or food which is above or below a certain amount destroys the health, while that which is proportionate both produces and increases and preserves it. So too is it, then, in the case of temperance and

20   courage and the other excellences. For the man who flies from and fears everything and does not stand his ground against anything becomes a coward, and the man who fears nothing at all but goes to meet every danger becomes rash; and similarly the man who indulges in every pleasure and abstains from none becomes self-indulgent, while the

25   man who shuns every pleasure, as boors do, becomes in a way insensible; temperance and courage, then, are destroyed by excess and defect, and preserved by the mean.

But not only are the sources and causes of their origination and growth the same as those of their destruction, but also the sphere of their activity will be the same; for

30   this is also true of the things which are more evident to sense, e.g. of strength; it is produced by taking much food and undergoing much exertion, and it is the strong man that will be most able to do these things. So too is it with the excellences; by abstaining from pleasures we become temperate, and it is when we have become so that we are most

1104ᵇ   able to abstain from them; and similarly too in the case of courage; for by being habituated to despise things that are terrible and to stand our ground against them we become brave, and it is when we have become so that we shall be most able to stand our ground against them.

5   3. We must take as a sign of states the pleasure or pain that supervenes on acts; for the man who abstains from bodily pleasures and delights in this very fact is temperate, while the man who is annoyed at it is self-indulgent, and he who stands his ground against things that are terrible and delights in this or at least is not pained is brave, while the man who is pained is a coward. For moral excellence is concerned with pleasures

10   and pains; it is on account of pleasure that we do bad things, and on account of pain that we abstain from noble ones. Hence we ought to have been brought up in a particular way from our very youth, as Plato says, so as both to delight in and to be pained by the things that we ought; for this is the right education.

Again, if the excellences are concerned with actions and passions, and every passion and every action is accompanied by pleasure and pain, for this reason also excel-

15   lence will be concerned with pleasures and pains. This is indicated also by the fact that punishment is inflicted by these means; for it is a kind of cure, and it is the nature of cures to be effected by contraries.

Again, as we said but lately, every state of soul has a nature relative to and con-

20   cerned with the kind of things by which it tends to be made worse or better; but it is by reason of pleasures and pains that men become bad, by pursuing and avoiding these— either the pleasures and pains they ought not or when they ought not or as they ought

not, or by going wrong in one of the other similar ways that reason can distinguish. Hence men even define the excellences as certain states of impassivity and rest; not well, however, because they speak absolutely, and do not say "as one ought" and "as one ought not" and "when one ought or ought not," and the other things that may be added. We assume, then, that this kind of excellence tends to do what is best with regard to pleasures and pains, and badness does the contrary.

The following facts also may show us that they are concerned with these same things. There being three objects of choice and three of avoidance, the noble, the advantageous, the pleasant, and their contraries, the base, the injurious, the painful, about all of these the good man tends to go right and the bad man to go wrong, and especially about pleasure; for this is common to the animals, and also it accompanies all objects of choice; for even the noble and the advantageous appear pleasant.

Again, it has grown up with us all from our infancy; this is why it is difficult to rub off this passion, engrained as it is in our life. And we measure even our actions, some of us more and others less, by pleasure and pain. For this reason, then, our whole inquiry must be about these; for to feel delight and pain rightly or wrongly has no small effect on our actions.

Again, it is harder to fight with pleasure than with anger, to use Heraclitus' phrase, but both art and excellence are always concerned with what is harder; for even the good is better when it is harder. Therefore for this reason also the whole concern both of excellence and of political science is with pleasures and pains; for the man who uses these well will be good, he who uses them badly bad.

That excellence, then, is concerned with pleasures and pains, and that by the acts from which it arises it is both increased and, if they are done differently, destroyed, and that the acts from which it arose are those in which it actualizes itself—let this be taken as said.

4. The question might be asked, what we mean by saying that we must become just by doing just acts, and temperate by doing temperate acts; for if men do just and temperate acts, they are already just and temperate, exactly as, if they do what is grammatical or musical they are proficient in grammar and music.

Or is this not true even of the arts? It is possible to do something grammatical either by chance or under the guidance of another. A man will be proficient in grammar, then, only when he has both done something grammatical and done it grammatically; and this means doing it in accordance with the grammatical knowledge in himself.

Again, the case of the arts and that of the excellences are not similar; for the products of the arts have their goodness in themselves, so that it is enough that they should have a certain character, but if the acts that are in accordance with the excellences have themselves a certain character it does not follow that they are done justly or temperately. The agent also must be in a certain condition when he does them; in the first place he must have knowledge, secondly he must choose the acts, and choose them for their own sakes, and thirdly his action must proceed from a firm and unchangeable character. These are not reckoned in as conditions of the possession of the arts, except the bare knowledge; but as a condition of the possession of the excellences, knowledge has little or no weight, while the other conditions count not for a little but for everything, i.e. the very conditions which result from often doing just and temperate acts.

Actions, then, are called just and temperate when they are such as the just or the temperate man would do; but it is not the man who does these that is just and temperate, but the man who also does them as just and temperate men do them. It is well said, then, that it is by doing just acts that the just man is produced, and by doing temperate acts the

10   temperate man; without doing these no one would have even a prospect of becoming good.

But most people do not do these, but take refuge in theory and think they are being philosophers and will become good in this way, behaving somewhat like patients
15   who listen attentively to their doctors, but do none of the things they are ordered to do. As the latter will not be made well in body by such a course of treatment, the former will not be made well in soul by such a course of philosophy.

5. Next we must consider what excellence is. Since things that are found in the
20   soul are of three kinds—passions, faculties, states—excellence must be one of these. By passions I mean appetite, anger, fear, confidence, envy, joy, love, hatred, longing, emulation, pity, and in general the feelings that are accompanied by pleasure or pain; by faculties the things in virtue of which we are said to be capable of feeling these, e.g. of be-
25   coming angry or being pained or feeling pity; by states the things in virtue of which we stand well or badly with reference to the passions, e.g. with reference to anger we stand badly if we feel it violently or too weakly, and well if we feel it moderately; and similarly with reference to the other passions.

30   Now neither the excellences nor the vices are *passions,* because we are not called good or bad on the ground of our passions, but are so called on the ground of our excellences and our vices, and because we are neither praised nor blamed for our passions (for the man who feels fear or anger is not praised, nor is the man who simply feels
1106ᵃ   anger blamed, but the man who feels it in a certain way), but for our excellences and our vices we *are* praised or blamed.

Again, we feel anger and fear without choice, but the excellences are choices or
5   involve choice. Further, in respect of the passions we are said to be moved, but in respect of the excellences and the vices we are said not to be moved but to be disposed in a particular way.

For these reasons also they are not *faculties;* for we are neither called good nor bad, nor praised nor blamed, for the simple capacity of feeling the passions; again, we have the faculties by nature, but we are not made good or bad by nature; we have spo-
10   ken of this before.

If, then, the excellences are neither passions nor faculties, all that remains is that they should be *states.*

Thus we have stated what excellence is in respect of its genus.

6. We must, however, not only describe it as a state, but also say what sort of
15   state it is. We may remark, then, that every excellence both brings into good condition the thing of which it is the excellence and makes the work of that thing be done well; e.g. the excellence of the eye makes both the eye and its work good; for it is by the excellence of the eye that we see well. Similarly the excellence of the horse makes a horse
20   both good in itself and good at running and at carrying its rider and at awaiting the attack of the enemy. Therefore, if this is true in every case, the excellence of man also will be the state which makes a man good and which makes him do his own work well.

How this is to happen we have stated already, but it will be made plain also by the
25   following consideration of the nature of excellence. In everything that is continuous and divisible it is possible to take more, less, or an equal amount, and that either in terms of the thing itself or relatively to us; and the equal is an intermediate between excess and
30   defect. By the intermediate in the object I mean that which is equidistant from each of the extremes, which is one and the same for all men; by the intermediate relatively to us that which is neither too much nor too little and this is not one, nor the same for all. For

instance, if ten is many and two is few, six is intermediate, taken in terms of the object; for it exceeds and is exceeded by an equal amount; this is intermediate according to arithmetical proportion. But the intermediate relatively to us is not to be taken so; if ten pounds are too much for a particular person to eat and two too little, it does not follow that the trainer will order six pounds; for this also is perhaps too much for the person who is to take it, or too little—too little for Milo, too much for the beginner in athletic exercises. The same is true of running and wrestling. Thus a master of any art avoids excess and defect, but seeks the intermediate and chooses this—the intermediate not in the object but relatively to us.

If it is thus, then, that every art does its work well—by looking to the intermediate and judging its works by this standard (so that we often say of good works of the art that it is not possible either to take away or to add anything, implying that excess and defect destroy the goodness of works of art, while the mean preserves it; and good artists, as we say, look to this in their work), and if, further, excellence is more exact and better than any art, as nature also is, then it must have the quality of aiming at the intermediate. I mean moral excellence; for it is this that is concerned with passions and actions, and in these there is excess, defect, and the intermediate. For instance, both fear and confidence and appetite and anger and pity and in general pleasure and pain may be felt both too much and too little, and in both cases not well; but to feel them at the right times, with reference to the right objects, towards the right people, with the right aim, and in the right way, is what is both intermediate and best, and this is characteristic of excellence. Similarly with regard to actions also there is excess, defect, and the intermediate. Now excellence is concerned with passions and actions, in which excess is a form of failure, and so is defect, while the intermediate is praised and is a form of success; and both these things are characteristics of excellence. Therefore excellence is a kind of mean, since it aims at what is intermediate.

Again, it is possible to fail in many ways (for evil belongs to the class of the unlimited, as the Pythagoreans conjectured, and good to that of the limited), while to succeed is possible only in one way (for which reason one is easy and the other difficult—to miss the mark easy, to hit it difficult); for these reasons also, then, excess and defect are characteristic of vice, and the mean of excellence.

For men are good in but one way, but bad in many.

Excellence, then, is a state concerned with choice, lying in a mean relative to us, this being determined by reason and in the way in which the man of practical wisdom would determine it. Now it is a mean between two vices, that which depends on excess and that which depends on defect; and again it is a mean because the vices respectively fall short of or exceed what is right in both passions and actions, while excellence both finds and chooses that which is intermediate. Hence in respect of its substance and the account which states its essence virtue is a mean, with regard to what is best and right it is an extreme.

But not every action nor every passion admits of a mean; for some have names that already imply badness, e.g. spite, shamelessness, envy, and in the case of actions adultery, theft, murder; for all of these and suchlike things imply by their names that they are themselves bad, and not the excesses or deficiencies of them. It is not possible, then, ever to be right with regard to them; one must always be wrong. Nor does goodness or badness with regard to such things depend on committing adultery with the right woman, at the right time, and in the right way, but simply to do any of them is to go wrong. It would be equally absurd, then, to expect that in unjust, cowardly, and self-indulgent action there should be a mean, an excess, and a deficiency; for at that rate there would be a mean of excess and of deficiency, an excess of excess, and a deficiency

of deficiency. But as there is no excess and deficiency of temperance and courage because what is intermediate is in a sense an extreme, so too of the actions we have mentioned there is no mean nor any excess and deficiency, but however they are done they
25   are wrong; for in general there is neither a mean of excess and deficiency, nor excess and deficiency of a mean.

7. We must, however, not only make this general statement, but also apply it to the individual facts. For among statements about conduct those which are general apply
30   more widely, but those which are particular are more true, since conduct has to do with individual cases, and our statements must harmonize with the facts in these cases. We may take these cases from our table. With regard to feelings of fear and confidence
1107ᵇ   courage is the mean; of the people who exceed, he who exceeds in fearlessness has no name (many of the states have no name), while the man who exceeds in confidence is rash, and he who exceeds in fear and falls short in confidence is a coward. With regard
5   to pleasures and pains—not all of them, and not so much with regard to the pains—the mean is temperance, the excess self-indulgence. Persons deficient with regard to the pleasures are not often found; hence such persons also have received no name. But let us call them "insensible."
With regard to giving and taking of money the mean is liberality, the excess and
10   the defect prodigality and meanness. They exceed and fall short in contrary ways to one another: the prodigal exceeds in spending and falls short in taking, while the mean man exceeds in taking and falls short in spending. (At present we are giving a mere outline
15   or summary, and are satisfied with this; later these states will be more exactly determined.) With regard to money there are also other dispositions—a mean, magnificence (for the magnificent man differs from the liberal man; the former deals with large sums,
20   the latter with small ones), an excess, tastelessness and vulgarity, and a deficiency, niggardliness; these differ from the states opposed to liberality, and the mode of their difference will be stated later.
With regard to honour and dishonour the mean is proper pride, the excess is known as a sort of empty vanity, and the deficiency is undue humility; and as we said
25   liberality was related to magnificence, differing from it by dealing with small sums, so there is a state similarly related to proper pride, being concerned with small honours while that is concerned with great. For it is possible to desire small honours as one ought, and more than one ought, and less, and the man who exceeds in his desires is called ambitious, the man who falls short unambitious, while the intermediate person
30   has no name. The dispositions also are nameless, except that that of the ambitious man is called ambition. Hence the people who are at the extremes lay claim to the middle place; and we ourselves sometimes call the intermediate person ambitious and sometimes unambitious, and sometimes praise the ambitious man and sometimes the unam-
1108ᵃ   bitious. The reason of our doing this will be stated in what follows; but now let us speak of the remaining states according to the method which has been indicated.
With regard to anger also there is an excess, a deficiency, and a mean. Although
5   they can scarcely be said to have names, yet since we call the intermediate person good-tempered let us call the mean good temper; of the persons at the extremes let the one who exceeds be called irascible, and his vice irascibility, and the man who falls short an inirascible sort of person, and the deficiency inirascibility.
10   There are also three other means, which have a certain likeness to one another, but differ from one another: for they are all concerned with intercourse in words and actions, but differ in that one is concerned with truth in this sphere, the other two with pleasantness; and of this one kind is exhibited in giving amusement, the other in all the circumstances of life. We must therefore speak of these too, that we may the better see

that in all things the mean is praiseworthy, and the extremes neither praiseworthy nor   15
right, but worthy of blame. Now most of these states also have no names, but we must
try, as in the other cases, to invent names ourselves so that we may be clear and easy to
follow. With regard to truth, then, the intermediate is a truthful sort of person and the
mean may be called truthfulness, while the pretence which exaggerates is boastfulness   20
and the person characterized by it a boaster, and that which understates is mock modesty and the person characterized by it mock-modest. With regard to pleasantness in the
giving of amusement the intermediate person is ready-witted and the disposition ready
wit, the excess is buffoonery and the person characterized by it a buffoon, while the   25
man who falls short is a sort of boor and his state is boorishness. With regard to the remaining kind of pleasantness, that which is exhibited in life in general, the man who is
pleasant in the right way is friendly and the mean is friendliness, while the man who exceeds is an obsequious person if he has no end in view, a flatterer if he is aiming at his
own advantage, and the man who falls short and is unpleasant in all circumstances is a
quarrelsome and surly sort of person.   30

There are also means in the passions and concerned with the passions; since
shame is not an excellence, and yet praise is extended to the modest man. For even in
these matters one man is said to be intermediate, and another to exceed, as for instance the bashful man who is ashamed of everything; while he who falls short or is
not ashamed of anything at all is shameless, and the intermediate person is modest.
Righteous indignation is a mean between envy and spite, and these states are con-   1108^b
cerned with the pain and pleasure that are felt at the fortunes of our neighbours; the
man who is characterized by righteous indignation is pained at undeserved good fortune, the envious man, going beyond him, is pained at all good fortune, and the spite-   5
ful man falls so far short of being pained that he even rejoices. But these states there
will be an opportunity of describing elsewhere; with regard to justice, since it has not
one simple meaning, we shall, after describing the other states, distinguish its two
kinds and say how each of them is a mean; and similarly we shall treat also of the ra-   10
tional excellences.

8. There are three kinds of disposition, then, two of them vices, involving excess and deficiency and one an excellence, viz. the mean, and all are in a sense opposed to all; for the extreme states are contrary both to the intermediate state and to
each other, and the intermediate to the extremes; as the equal is greater relatively to   15
the less, less relatively to the greater, so the middle states are excessive relatively
to the deficiencies, deficient relatively to the excesses, both in passions and in actions.
For the brave man appears rash relatively to the coward, and cowardly relatively to   20
the rash man; and similarly the temperate man appears self-indulgent relatively to the
insensible man, insensible relatively to the self-indulgent, and the liberal man prodigal
relatively to the mean man, mean relatively to the prodigal. Hence also the people at
the extremes push the intermediate man each over to the other, and the brave man is   25
called rash by the coward, cowardly by the rash man, and correspondingly in the other
cases.

These states being thus opposed to one another, the greatest contrariety is that of
the extremes to each other, rather than to the intermediate; for these are further from
each other than from the intermediate, as the great is further from the small and the
small from the great than both are from the equal. Again, to the intermediate some ex-   30
tremes show a certain likeness, as that of rashness to courage and that of prodigality to
liberality; but the extremes show the greatest unlikeness to each other; now contraries
are defined as the things that are furthest from each other, so that things that are further
apart are more contrary.

1109ª   To the mean in some cases the deficiency, in some the excess is more opposed; e.g. it is not rashness, which is an excess, but cowardice, which is a deficiency, that is more opposed to courage, and not insensibility, which is a deficiency,
but self-indulgence, which is an excess, that is more opposed to temperance. This
5   happens from two reasons, one being drawn from the thing itself; for because one
extreme is nearer and liker to the intermediate, we oppose not this but rather its contrary to the intermediate. E.g., since rashness is thought liker and nearer to courage,
10   and cowardice more unlike, we oppose rather the latter to courage; for things that
are further from the intermediate are thought more contrary to it. This, then, is one
cause, drawn from the thing itself; another is drawn from ourselves; for the things to
15   which we ourselves more naturally tend seem more contrary to the intermediate. For
instance, we ourselves tend more naturally to pleasures, and hence are more easily
carried away towards self-indulgence than towards propriety. We describe as contrary to the mean, then, the states into which we are more inclined to lapse; and
therefore self-indulgence, which is an excess, is the more contrary to temperance.

20   9. That moral excellence is a mean, then, and in what sense it is so, and that it is
a mean between two vices, the one involving excess, the other deficiency, and that it is
such because its character is to aim at what is intermediate in passions and in actions,
has been sufficiently stated. Hence also it is no easy task to be good. For in everything
25   it is no easy task to find the middle, e.g. to find the middle of a circle is not for everyone
but for him who knows; so, too, anyone can get angry—that is easy—or give or spend
money; but to do this to the right person, to the right extent, at the right time, with the
right aim, and in the right way, *that* is not for everyone, nor is it easy; that is why goodness is both rare and laudable and noble.
         Hence he who aims at the intermediate must first depart from what is the more
30   contrary to it, as Calypso advises—

     Hold the ship out beyond that surf and spray.

For of the extremes one is more erroneous, one less so; therefore, since to hit the mean
is hard in the extreme, we must as a second best, as people say, take the least of the
1109ᵇ   evils; and this be done best in the way we describe.
         But we must consider the things towards which we ourselves also are easily car-
ried away; for some of us tend to one thing, some to another; and this will be recognizable from the pleasure and the pain we feel. We must drag ourselves away to the con-
5   trary extreme; for we shall get into the intermediate state by drawing well away from error, as people do in straightening sticks that are bent.
         Now in everything the pleasant or pleasure is most to be guarded against; for we
do not judge it impartially. We ought, then, to feel towards pleasure as the elders of the
10   people felt towards Helen, and in all circumstances repeat their saying; for if we dismiss
pleasure thus we are less likely to go astray. It is by doing this, then, (to sum the matter
up) that we shall best be able to hit the mean.
         But this is no doubt difficult, and especially in individual cases; for it is not easy
15   to determine both how and with whom and on what provocation and how long one
should be angry; for we too sometimes praise those who fall short and call them good-
tempered, but sometimes we praise those who get angry and call them manly. The man,
however who deviates little from goodness is not blamed, whether he do so in the direction of the more or of the less, but only the man who deviates more widely; for *he*
20   does not fail to be noticed. But up to what point and to what extent a man must deviate

before he becomes blameworthy it is not easy to determine by reasoning, any more than anything else that is perceived by the senses; such things depend on particular facts, and the decision rests with perception. So much, then, makes it plain that the intermediate state is in all things to be praised, but that we must incline sometimes towards the excess, sometimes towards the deficiency; for so shall we most easily hit the mean and 25 what is right.

BOOK III

1. Since excellence is concerned with passions and actions, and on voluntary passions 30 and actions praise and blame are bestowed, on those that are involuntary forgiveness, and sometimes also pity, to distinguish the voluntary and the involuntary is presumably necessary for those who are studying excellence and useful also for legislators with a view to the assigning both of honours and of punishments.

Those things, then, are thought involuntary, which take place under compulsion or owing to ignorance; and that is compulsory of which the moving principle is outside, 1110ᵃ being a principle in which nothing is contributed by the person who acts or is acted upon, e.g. if he were to be carried somewhere by a wind, or by men who had him in their power.

But with regard to the things that are done from fear of greater evils or for some noble object (e.g. if a tyrant were to order one to do something base, having one's parents and children in his power, and if one did the action they were to be saved, but oth- 5 erwise would be put to death), it may be debated whether such actions are involuntary or voluntary. Something of the sort happens also with regard to the throwing of goods overboard in a storm; for in the abstract no one throws goods away voluntarily, but on 10 condition of its securing the safety of himself and his crew any sensible man does so. Such actions, then, are mixed, but are more like voluntary actions; for they are worthy of choice at the time when they are done, and the end of an action is relative to the occasion. Both the terms, then, "voluntary" and "involuntary," must be used with reference to the moment of action. Now the man acts voluntarily; for the principle that moves the instrumental parts of the body in such actions is in him, and the things of 15 which the moving principle is in a man himself are in his power to do or not to do. Such actions, therefore, are voluntary, but in the abstract perhaps involuntary; for no one would choose any such act in itself.

For such actions men are sometimes even praised, when they endure something 20 base or painful in return for great and noble objects gained; in the opposite case they are blamed, since to endure the greatest indignities for no noble end or for a trifling end is the mark of an inferior person. On some actions praise indeed is not bestowed, but forgiveness is, when one does what he ought not under pressure which overstrains human nature and which no one could withstand. But some acts, perhaps, we cannot be forced 25 to do, but ought rather to face death after the most fearful sufferings; for the things that forced Euripides' Alcmaeon to slay his mother seem absurd. It is difficult sometimes to determine what should be chosen at what cost, and what should be endured in return for what gain, and yet more difficult to abide by our decisions; for as a rule what is ex- 30 pected is painful, and what we are forced to do is base, whence praise and blame are bestowed on those who have been compelled or have not.

What sort of acts, then, should be called compulsory? We answer that without 1110ᵇ qualification actions are so when the cause is in the external circumstances and the

5   agent contributes nothing. But the things that in themselves are involuntary, but now and in return for these gains are worthy of choice, and whose moving principle is in the agent, are in themselves involuntary, but now and in return for these gains voluntary. They are more like voluntary acts; for actions are in the class of particulars, and the particular acts here are voluntary. What sort of things are to be chosen in return for what it is not easy to state; for there are many differences in the particular cases.

10   But if someone were to say that pleasant and noble objects have a compelling power, forcing us from without, all acts would be for him compulsory; for it is for these objects that all men do everything they do. And those who act under compulsion and unwillingly act with pain, but those who do acts for their pleasantness and nobility do them with pleasure; it is absurd to make external circumstances responsible, and not oneself, as being easily caught by such attractions, and to make oneself responsible for noble acts but the pleasant objects responsible for base acts. The compulsory, then,

15   seems to be that whose moving principle is outside, the person compelled contributing nothing.

Everything that is done by reason of ignorance is *non*-voluntary; it is only what produces pain and regret that is *in*voluntary. For the man who has done something ow-

20   ing to ignorance, and feels not the least vexation at his action, has not acted voluntarily, since he did not know what he was doing, nor yet involuntarily, since he is not pained. Of people, then, who act by reason of ignorance he who regrets is thought an involuntary agent, and the man who does not regret may, since he is different, be called a non-voluntary agent; for, since he differs from the other, it is better that he should have a name of his own.

25   Acting by reason of ignorance seems also to be different from acting *in* ignorance; for the man who is drunk or in a rage is thought to act as a result not of ignorance but of one of the causes mentioned, yet not knowingly but in ignorance.

Now every wicked man is ignorant of what he ought to do and what he ought to abstain from, and error of this kind makes men unjust and in general bad; but the term

30   "involuntary" tends to be used not if a man is ignorant of what is to his advantage—for it is not ignorance in choice that makes action involuntary (it makes men wicked), nor ignorance of the universal (for *that* men are *blamed*), but ignorance of particular circumstances of the action and the objects with which it is concerned. For it is on these

1111ᵃ   that both pity and forgiveness depend, since the person who is ignorant of any of these acts involuntarily.

Perhaps it is just as well, therefore, to determine their nature and number. A man may be ignorant, then, of who he is, what he is doing, what or whom he is acting on, and sometimes also what (e.g. what instrument) he is doing it with, and to what end (e.g. for

5   safety), and how he is doing it (e.g. whether gently or violently). Now of all of these no one could be ignorant unless he were mad, and evidently also he could not be ignorant of the agent; for how could he not know himself? But of what he is doing a man might be ignorant, as for instance people say "it slipped out of their mouths as they were speaking," or "they did not know it was a secret," as Aeschylus said of the mysteries, or

10   a man might say he "let it go off when he merely wanted to show it's working," as the man did with the catapult. Again, one might think one's son was an enemy, as Merope did, or that a pointed spear had a button on it, or that a stone was pumice-stone; or one might give a man a draught to save him, and really kill him; or one might want to touch a man, as people do in sparring, and really strike him. The ignorance may relate, then,

15   to any of these things, i.e. of the circumstances of the action, and the man who was ignorant of any of these is thought to have acted involuntarily, and especially if he was ignorant on the most important points; and these are thought to be what he is doing and

with what aim. Further, the doing of an act that is called involuntary in virtue of igno- 20
rance of this sort must be painful and involve regret.

Since that which is done under compulsion or by reason of ignorance is involuntary, the voluntary would seem to be that of which the moving principle is in the
agent himself, he being aware of the particular circumstances of the action. Presumably acts done by reason of anger or appetite are not rightly called involuntary. For in 25
the first place, on that showing none of the other animals will act voluntarily, nor will
children; and secondly, is it meant that we do not do voluntarily any of the acts that
are due to appetite or anger, or that we do the noble acts voluntarily and the base acts
involuntarily? Is not this absurd, when one and the same thing is the cause? But it
would surely be odd to describe as involuntary the things one ought to desire; and we
ought both to be angry at certain things and to have an appetite for certain things, e.g. 30
for health and for learning. Also what is involuntary is thought to be painful, but what
is in accordance with appetite is thought to be pleasant. Again, what is the difference
in respect of involuntariness between errors committed upon calculation and those
committed in anger? Both are to be avoided, but the irrational passions are thought not 1111b
less human than reason is, and therefore also the actions which proceed from anger or
appetite are the man's actions. It would be odd, then, to treat them as involuntary.

2. Both the voluntary and the involuntary having been delimited, we must next
discuss choice; for it is thought to be most closely bound up with excellence and to dis- 5
criminate characters better than actions do.

Choice, then, seems to be voluntary, but not the same thing as the voluntary; the
latter extends more widely. For both children and the other animals share in voluntary
action, but not in choice, and acts done on the spur of the moment we describe as voluntary, but not as chosen. 10

Those who say it is appetite or anger or wish or a kind of opinion do not seem to
be right. For choice is not common to irrational creatures as well, but appetite and anger
are. Again, the incontinent man acts with appetite, but not with choice; while the continent man on the contrary acts with choice, but not with appetite. Again, appetite is con- 15
trary to choice, but not appetite to appetite. Again, appetite relates to the pleasant and
the painful, choice neither to the painful nor to the pleasant.

Still less is it anger; for acts due to anger are thought to be less than any other objects of choice.

But neither is it wish, though it seems near to it; for choice cannot relate to im- 20
possibles, and if any one said he chose them he would be thought silly; but there may be
a wish even for impossibles, e.g. for immortality. And wish may relate to things that
could in no way be brought about by one's own efforts, e.g. that a particular actor or
athlete should win in a competition; but no one chooses such things, but only the things 25
that he thinks could be brought about by his own efforts. Again, wish relates rather to
the end, choice to what contributes to the end; for instance, we wish to be healthy, but
we choose the acts which will make us healthy, and we wish to be happy and say we do,
but we cannot well say we choose to be so; for, in general, choice seems to relate to the
things that are in our own power. 30

For this reason, too, it cannot be opinion; for opinion is thought to relate to all
kinds of things, no less to eternal things and impossible things than to things in our own
power; and it is distinguished by its falsity or truth, not by its badness or goodness,
while choice is distinguished rather by these.

Now with opinion in general perhaps no one really says it is identical. But it is not 1112a
identical even with any kind of opinion; for by choosing what is good or bad we are

men of a certain character, which we are not by holding certain opinions. And we choose to get or avoid something good or bad, but we have opinions about what a thing is or whom it is good for or how it is good for him; we can hardly be said to opine to get or avoid anything. And choice is praised for being related to the right object rather than for being rightly related to it, opinion for being truly related to its object. And we choose what we best know to be good, but we opine what we do not know at all; and it is not the same people that are thought to make the best choices and to have the best opinions, but some are thought to have fairly good opinions, but by reason of vice to choose what they should not. If opinion precedes choice or accompanies it, that makes no difference; for it is not this that we are considering, but whether it is *identical* with some kind of opinion.

What, then, or what kind of thing is it, since it is none of the things we have mentioned? It seems to be voluntary, but not all that is voluntary to be an object of choice. Is it, then, what has been decided on by previous deliberation? For choice involves reason and thought. Even the name seems to suggest that it is what is chosen before other things.

3. Do we deliberate about everything, and is everything a possible subject of deliberation, or is deliberation impossible about some things? We ought presumably to call not what a fool or a madman would deliberate about, but what a sensible man would deliberate about, a subject of deliberation. Now about eternal things no one deliberates, e.g. about the universe or the incommensurability of the diagonal and the side of a square. But no more do we deliberate about the things that involve movement but always happen in the same way, whether of necessity or by nature or from any other cause, e.g. the solstices and the risings of the stars; nor about things that happen now in one way, now in another, e.g. droughts and rains; nor about chance events, like the finding of treasure. But we do not deliberate even about all human affairs; for instance, no Spartan deliberates about the best constitution for the Scythians. For none of these things can be brought about by our own efforts.

We deliberate about things that are in our power and can be done; and these are in fact what is left. For nature, necessity, and chance are thought to be causes, and also thought and everything that depends on man. Now every class of men deliberates about the things that can be done by their own efforts. And in the case of exact and self-contained sciences there is no deliberation, e.g. about the letters of the alphabet (for we have no doubt how they should be written); but the things that are brought about by our own efforts, but not always in the same way, are the things about which we deliberate, e.g. questions of medical treatment or of money-making. And we do so more in the case of the art of navigation than in that of gymnastics, inasmuch as it has been less exactly worked out, and again about other things in the same ratio, and more also in the case of the arts than in that of the sciences; for we have more doubt about the former. Deliberation is concerned with things that happen in a certain way for the most part, but in which the event is obscure, and with things in which it is indeterminate. We call in others to aid us in deliberation on important questions, distrusting ourselves as not being equal to deciding.

We deliberate not about ends but about what contributes to ends. For a doctor does not deliberate whether he shall heal, nor an orator whether he shall convince, nor a statesman whether he shall produce law and order, nor does any one else deliberate about his end. Having set the end they consider how and by what means it is to be attained; and if it seems to be produced by several means they consider by which it is most easily and best produced, while if it is achieved by one only they consider how it will be achieved by this and by what means *this* will be achieved, till they come to the first cause, which in the order of discovery is last. For the person who deliberates seems   20 to inquire and analyse in the way described as though he were analysing a geometrical construction (not all inquiry appears to be deliberation—for instance mathematical inquiries—but all deliberation is inquiry), and what is last in the order of analysis seems to be first in the order of becoming. And if we come on an impossibility, we give up the   25 search, e.g. if we need money and this cannot be got; but if a thing appears possible we try to do it. By "possible" things I mean things that might be brought about by our own efforts; and these in a sense include things that can be brought about by the efforts of our friends, since the moving principle is in ourselves. The subject of investigation is sometimes the instruments, sometimes the use of them; and similarly in the other cases—sometimes the means, sometimes the mode of using it or the means of bringing   30 it about. It seems, then, as has been said, that man is a moving principle of actions; now deliberation is about the things to be done by the agent himself, and actions are for the sake of things other than themselves. For the end cannot be a subject of deliberation, but only what contributes to the ends; nor indeed can the particular facts be a subject of it, as whether this is bread or has been baked as it should; for these are matters of percep-   1113a tion. If we are to be always deliberating, we shall have to go on to infinity.

The same thing is deliberated upon and is chosen, except that the object of choice is already determinate, since it is that which has been decided upon as a result of delib-   5 eration that is the object of choice. For everyone ceases to inquire how he is to act when he has brought the moving principle back to himself and to the ruling part of himself; for this is what chooses. This is plain also from the ancient constitutions, which Homer represented; for the kings announced their choices to the people. The object of choice being one of the things in our own power which is desired after deliberation, choice will   10 be deliberate desire of things in our own power; for when we have decided as a result of deliberation, we desire in accordance with our deliberation.

We may take it, then, that we have described choice in outline, and stated the nature of its objects and the fact that it is concerned with what contributes to the ends.

4. That *wish* is for the end has already been stated; some think it is for the good,   15 others for the apparent good. Now those who say that the good is the object of wish must admit in consequence that that which the man who does not choose aright wishes for is not an object of wish (for if it is to be so, it must also be good; but it was, if it so happened, bad); while those who say the apparent good is the object of wish must   20 admit that there is no natural object of wish, but only what seems so to each man. Now different things appear so to different people, and, if it so happens, even contrary things.

If these consequences are unpleasing, are we to say that absolutely and in truth the good is the object of wish, but for each person the apparent good; that that which is in truth an object of wish is an object of wish to the good man, while any chance thing may   25 be so to the bad man, as in the case of bodies also the things that are in truth wholesome are wholesome for bodies which are in good condition, while for those that are diseased other things are wholesome or bitter or sweet or hot or heavy, and so on; since the good   30 man judges each class of things rightly, and in each the truth appears to him? For each state of character has its own ideas of the noble and the pleasant, and perhaps the good man differs from others most by seeing the truth in each class of things, being as it were the norm and measure of them. In most things the error seems to be due to pleasure; for it appears a good when it is not. We therefore choose the pleasant as a good, and avoid   1113b pain as an evil.

5. The end, then, being what we wish for, the things contributing to the end what we deliberate about and choose, actions concerning the latter must be according to choice and voluntary. Now the exercise of the excellences is concerned with these. Therefore excellence also is in our own power, and so too vice. For where it is in our power to act it is also in our power not to act, and *vice versa;* so that, if to act, where this is noble, is in our power, not to act, which will be base, will also be in our power, and if not to act, where this is noble, is in our power, to act, which will be base, will also be in our power. Now if it is in our power to do noble or base acts, and likewise in our power not to do them, and this was what being good or bad meant, then it is in our power to be virtuous or vicious.

The saying that "no one is voluntarily wicked nor involuntarily blessed" seems to be partly false and partly true; for no one is involuntarily blessed, but wickedness *is* voluntary. Or else we shall have to dispute what has just been said, at any rate, and deny that man is a moving principle or begetter of his actions as of children. But if these facts are evident and we cannot refer actions to moving principles other than those in ourselves, the acts whose moving principles are in us must themselves also be in our power and voluntary.

Witness seems to be borne to this both by individuals in their private capacity and by legislators themselves; for these punish and take vengeance on those who do wicked acts (unless they have acted under compulsion or as a result of ignorance for which they are not themselves responsible), while they honour those who do noble acts, as though they meant to encourage the latter and deter the former. But no one is encouraged to do the things that are neither in our power nor voluntary; it is assumed that there is no gain in being persuaded not to be hot or in pain or hungry or the like, since we shall experience these feelings none the less. Indeed, we punish a man for his very ignorance, if he is thought responsible for the ignorance, as when penalties are doubled in the case of drunkenness; for the moving principle is in the man himself, since he had the power of not getting drunk and his getting drunk was the cause of his ignorance. And we punish those who are ignorant of anything in the laws that they ought to know and that is not difficult, and so too in the case of anything else that they are thought to be ignorant of through carelessness; we assume that it is in their power not to be ignorant, since they have the power of taking care.

But perhaps a man is the kind of man not to take care. Still they are themselves by their slack lives responsible for becoming men of that kind, and men are themselves responsible for being unjust or self-indulgent, in that they cheat or spend their time in drinking bouts and the like; for it is activities exercised on particular objects that make the corresponding character. This is plain from the case of people training for any contest or action; they practise the activity the whole time. Now not to know that it is from the exercise of activities on particular objects that states of character are produced is the mark of a thoroughly senseless person. Again, it is irrational to suppose that a man who acts unjustly does not wish to be unjust or a man who acts self-indulgently to be self-indulgent. But if without being ignorant a man does the things which will make him unjust, he will be unjust voluntarily. Yet it does not follow that if he wishes he will cease to be unjust and will be just. For neither does the man who is ill become well on those terms—although he may, perhaps, be ill voluntarily, through living incontinently and disobeying his doctors. In that case it was *then* open to him not to be ill, but not now, when he has thrown away his chance, just as when you have let a stone go it is too late to recover it; but yet it was in your power to throw it, since the moving principle was in you. So, too, to the unjust and to the self-indulgent man it was open at the beginning not to become men of this kind, and so they are such voluntarily; but now that they have become so it is not possible for them not to be so.

But not only are the vices of the soul voluntary, but those of the body also for some men, whom we accordingly blame; while no one blames those who are ugly by nature, we blame those who are so owing to want of exercise and care. So it is, too, with respect to weakness and infirmity; no one would reproach a man blind from birth or by disease or from a blow, but rather pity him, while everyone would blame a man who was blind from alcoholism or some other form of self-indulgence. Of vices of the body, then, those in our own power are blamed, those not in our power are not. And if this be so, in the other cases also the vices that are blamed must be in our own power. 25

30

Now someone may say that all men aim at the apparent good, but have no control over how things appear to him; but the end appears to each man in a form answering to his character. We reply that if each man is somehow responsible for the state he is in, he will also be himself somehow responsible for how things appear; but if not, no one is responsible for his own evildoing, but everyone does evil acts through ignorance of the end, thinking that by these he will get what is best, and the aiming at the end is not self-chosen but one must be born with an eye, as it were, by which to judge rightly and choose what is truly good, and he is well endowed by nature who is well endowed with this. For it is what is greatest and most noble, and what we cannot get or learn from another, but must have just such as it was when given us at birth, and to be well and nobly endowed with this will be complete and true natural endowment. If this is true, then, how will excellence be more voluntary than vice? To both men alike, the good and the bad, the end appears and is fixed by nature or however it may be, and it is by referring everything else to this that men do whatever they do. 1114[b]

5

10

15

Whether, then, it is not by nature that the end appears to each man such as it does appear, but something also depends on him, or the end is natural but because the good man does the rest voluntarily excellence is voluntary, vice also will be none the less voluntary; for in the case of the bad man there is equally present that which depends on himself in his actions even if not in his end. If, then, as is asserted, the excellences are voluntary (for we are ourselves somehow part-causes of our states of character, and it is by being persons of a certain kind that we assume the end to be so and so), the vices also will be voluntary; for the same is true of them. 20

25

With regard to the excellences in *general* we have stated their genus in outline, viz. that they are means and that they are states, and that they tend by their own nature to the doing of the acts by which they are produced, and that they are in our power and voluntary, and act as right reason prescribes. But actions and states are not voluntary in the same way; for we are masters of our actions from the beginning right to the end, if we know the particular facts, but though we control the beginning of our states the gradual progress is not obvious, any more than it is in illnesses; because it was in our power, however, to act in this way or not in this way, therefore the states are voluntary. 30

1115[a]

* * *

BOOK IV

* * *

3. Pride seems even from its name to be concerned with great things; what sort of great things, is the first question we must try to answer. It makes no difference whether we consider the state or the man characterized by it. Now the man is thought to be proud 1123[a]

35

1123[b]

who thinks himself worthy of great things, being worthy of them; for he who does so beyond his deserts is a fool, but no excellent man is foolish or silly. The proud man, then, is the man we have described. For he who is worthy of little and thinks himself
5   worthy of little is temperate, but not proud; for pride implies greatness, as beauty implies a good-sized body, and little people may be neat and well-proportioned but cannot be beautiful. On the other hand, he who thinks himself worthy of great things, being unworthy of them, is vain; though not everyone who thinks himself worthy of more than he really is worthy of is vain. The man who thinks himself worthy of less than he is re-
10   ally worthy of is unduly humble, whether his deserts be great or moderate, or his deserts be small but his claims yet smaller. And the man whose deserts are great would seem *most* unduly humble; for what would he have done if they had been less? The proud man, then, is an extreme in respect of the greatness of his claims, but a man in respect of the rightness of them; for he claims what is in accordance with his merits, while the
15   others go to excess or fall short.

If, then, he deserves and claims great things, and above all the greatest things, he will be concerned with one thing in particular. Desert is relative to external goods; and the greatest of these, we should say, is that which we render to the gods, and which peo-
20   ple of position most aim at, and which is the prize appointed for the noblest deeds; and this is honour; that is surely the greatest of external goods. Honours and dishonours, therefore, are the objects with respect to which the proud man is as he should be. And even apart from argument it is with honour that proud men appear to be concerned; for it is honour that they chiefly claim, but in accordance with their deserts. The unduly humble man falls short both in comparison with his own merits and in comparison with the proud man's claims. The vain man goes to excess in comparison with his own mer-
25   its, but does not exceed the proud man's claims.

Now the proud man, since he deserves most, must be good in the highest degree; for the better man always deserves more, and the best man most. Therefore the truly
30   proud man must be good. And greatness in every excellence would seem to be characteristic of a proud man. And it would be most unbecoming for a proud man to run from danger, swinging his arms by his sides, or to wrong another; for to what end should he do disgraceful acts, he to whom nothing is great? If we consider him point by point we shall see the utter absurdity of a proud man who is not good. Nor, again, would he be worthy of honour if he were bad; for honour is the prize of excellence and it is to the
1124ᵃ   good that it is rendered. Pride, then, seems to be a sort of crown of the excellences; for it makes them greater, and it is not found without them. Therefore it is hard to be truly proud; for it is impossible without nobility and goodness of character. It is chiefly with
5   honours and dishonours, then, that the proud man is concerned; and at honours that are great and conferred by good men he will be moderately pleased, thinking that he is coming by his own or even less than his own; for there can be no honour that is worthy of perfect excellence, yet he will at any rate accept it since they have nothing greater to
10   bestow on him; but honour from casual people and on trifling grounds he will utterly despise, since it is not this that he deserves, and dishonour too, since in his case it cannot be just. In the first place, then, as has been said, the proud man is concerned with honours; yet he will also bear himself with moderation towards wealth and power and
15   all good or evil fortune, whatever may befall him, and will be neither overjoyed by good fortune nor over-pained by evil. For not even about honour does he care much, although it is the greatest thing (for power and wealth are desirable for the sake of honour—at least those who have them wish to get honour by means of them); and for him
20   to whom even honour is a little thing the others must be so too. Hence proud men are thought to be disdainful.

The goods of fortune also are thought to contribute towards pride. For men who are well-born are thought worthy of honour, and so are those who enjoy power or wealth; for they are in a superior position, and everything that has a superiority in something good is held in greater honour. Hence even such things make men prouder; for they are honoured by some for having them; but in truth the good man alone is to be honoured; he, however, who has both advantages is thought the more worthy of honour. 25 But those who without excellence have such goods are neither justified in making great claims nor entitled to the name of "proud"; for these things imply perfect excellence. Disdainful and insolent, however, even those who have such goods become. For without excellence it is not easy to bear gracefully the goods of fortune; and, being unable to 1124b bear them, and thinking themselves superior to others, they despise others and themselves do what they please. They imitate the proud man without being like him, and this they do where they can; so they do not act excellently, but they do despise others. For 5 the proud man despises justly (since he thinks truly), but the many do so at random.

He does not run into trifling dangers, nor is he fond of danger, because he honours few things; but he will face great dangers, and when he is in danger he is unsparing of his life, knowing that there are conditions on which life is not worth having. And he is the sort of man to confer benefits, but he is ashamed of receiving them; for the one is the 10 mark of a superior, the other of an inferior. And he is apt to confer greater benefits in return; for thus the original benefactor besides being paid will incur a debt to him, and will be the gainer by the transaction. They seem also to remember any service they have done, but not those they have received (for he who receives a service is inferior to him who has done it, but the proud man wishes to be superior), and to hear of the former with pleasure, of the latter with displeasure; this, it seems, is why Thetis did not men- 15 tion to Zeus the services she had done him, and why the Spartans did not recount their services to the Athenians, but those they had received. It is a mark of the proud man also to ask for nothing or scarcely anything, but to give help readily, and to be dignified towards people who enjoy high position and good fortune, but unassuming towards those of the middle class; for it is a difficult and lofty thing to be superior to the former, but 20 easy to be so to the latter, and a lofty bearing over the former is no mark of ill-breeding, but among humble people it is as vulgar as a display of strength against the weak. Again, it is characteristic of the proud man not to aim at the things commonly held in honour, or the things in which others excel; to be sluggish and to hold back except where great honour as a great result is at stake, and to be a man of few deeds, but of 25 great and notable ones. He must also be open in his hate and in his love (for to conceal one's feelings is a mark of timidity), and must care more for truth than for what people will think, and must speak and act openly; for he is free of speech because he is contemptuous, and he is given to telling the truth, except when he speaks in irony to the 30 vulgar. He must be unable to make his life revolve round another, unless it be a friend; for this is slavish, and for this reason all flatterers are servile and people lacking in self-respect are flatterers. Nor is he given to admiration; for nothing to him is great. Nor is 1125a he mindful of wrongs; for it is not the part of a proud man to have a long memory, especially for wrongs, but rather to overlook them. Nor is he a gossip; for he will speak 5 neither about himself nor about another, since he cares not to be praised nor for others to be blamed; nor again is he given to praise; and for the same reason he is not an evil-speaker, even about his enemies, except from haughtiness. With regard to necessary or small matters he is least of all men given to lamentation or the asking of favours; for it 10 is the part of one who takes such matters seriously to behave so with respect to them. He is one who will possess beautiful and profitless things rather than profitable and useful ones; for this is more proper to a character that suffices to itself.

Further, a slow step is thought proper to the proud man, a deep voice, and a level utterance; for the man who takes few things seriously is not likely to be hurried, nor the
15   man who thinks nothing great to be excited, while a shrill voice and a rapid gait are the results of hurry and excitement.

Such, then, is the proud man; the man who falls short of him is unduly humble, and the man who goes beyond him is vain. Now these too are not thought to be bad (for they are not evil-doers), but only mistaken. For the unduly humble man, being worthy
20   of good things, robs himself of what he deserves, and seems to have something bad about him from the fact that he does not think himself worthy of good things, and seems also not to know himself; else he would have desired the things he was worthy of, since these were good. Yet such people are not thought to be fools, but rather unduly retiring. Such an estimate, however, seems actually to make them worse; for each class of peo-
25   ple aims at what corresponds to its worth, and these people stand back even from noble actions and undertakings, deeming themselves unworthy, and from external goods no less. Vain people, on the other hand, are fools and ignorant of themselves, and that man-ifestly; for, not being worthy of them, they attempt honourable undertakings, and then
30   are found out; and they adorn themselves with clothing and outward show and such things, and wish their strokes of good fortune to be made public, and speak about them as if they would be honoured for them. But undue humility is more opposed to pride than vanity is; for it is both commoner and worse.

Pride, then, is concerned with honour on the grand scale, as has been said.

* * *

BOOK VI

1138b   1. Since we have previously said that one ought to choose that which is intermediate, not the excess nor the defect, and that the intermediate is determined by the dictates of
20   reason, let us discuss this. In all the states we have mentioned, as in all other matters, there is a mark to which the man who possesses reason looks, and heightens or relaxes his activity accordingly, and there is a standard which determines the mean states which
25   we say are intermediate between excess and defect, being in accordance with right rea-son. But such a statement, though true, is by no means illuminating; for in all other pur-suits which are objects of knowledge it is indeed true to say that we must not exert our-selves nor relax our efforts too much nor too little, but to an intermediate extent and as right reason dictates; but if a man had only this knowledge he would be none the
30   wiser—e.g. we should not know what sort of medicines to apply to our body if some one were to say "all those which the medical art prescribes, and which agree with the practice of one who possesses the art." Hence it is necessary with regard to the states of the soul also not only that this true statement should be made, but also that it should be determined what right reason is and what is the standard that fixes it.

We divided the excellences of the soul and said that some are excellences of char-
1139a   acter and others of intellect. Now we have discussed the moral excellences; with regard to the others let us express our view as follows, beginning with some remarks about the
5   soul. We said before that there are two parts of the soul—that which possesses reason and that which is irrational; let us now draw a similar distinction within the part which possesses reason. And let it be assumed that there are two parts which possess reason— one by which we contemplate the kind of things whose principles cannot be otherwise,

and one by which we contemplate variable things; for where objects differ in kind the part of the soul answering to each of the two is different in kind, since it is in virtue of a   10
certain likeness and kinship with their objects that they have the knowledge they have. Let one of these parts be called the scientific and the other the calculative; for to deliberate and to calculate are the same thing, but no one deliberates about what cannot be otherwise. Therefore the calculative is one part of the faculty which possesses reason.   15
We must, then, learn what is the best state of each of these two parts; for this is the excellence of each.

2. The excellence of a thing is relative to its proper function. Now there are three things in the soul which control action and truth—sensation, thought, desire.

Of these sensation originates no action; this is plain from the fact that beasts have sensation but no share in action.   20

What affirmation and negation are in thinking, pursuit and avoidance are in desire; so that since moral excellence is a state concerned with choice, and choice is deliberate desire, therefore both the reasoning must be true and the desire right, if the choice is to be good, and the latter must pursue just what the former asserts. Now this   25
kind of intellect and of truth is practical; of the intellect which is contemplative, not practical nor productive, the good and the bad state are truth and falsity (for this is the function of everything intellectual); while of the part which is practical and intellectual   30
the good state is truth in agreement with right desire.

The origin of action—its efficient, not its final cause—is choice, and that of choice is desire and reasoning with a view to an end. This is why choice cannot exist either without thought and intellect or without a moral state; for good action and its opposite cannot exist without a combination of intellect and character. Intellect itself,   35
however, moves nothing, but only the intellect which aims at an end and is practical; for this rules the productive intellect as well, since everyone who makes makes for an end,   1139b
and that which is made is not an end in the unqualified sense (but only relative to something, i.e. of something)—only that which is *done* is that; for good action is an end, and desire aims at this. Hence choice is either desiderative thought or intellectual desire, and   5
such an origin of action is a man. (Nothing that is past is an object of choice, e.g. no one chooses to have sacked Troy; for no one *deliberates* about the past, but about what is future and contingent, while what is past is not capable of not having taken place; hence Agathon is right in saying

For this alone is lacking even to God,   10
To make undone things that have once been done.)

The function of both the intellectual parts, then, is truth. Therefore the states that are most strictly those in respect of which each of these parts will reach truth are the excellences of the two parts.

3. Let us begin, then, from the beginning, and discuss these states once more. Let it be assumed that the states by virtue of which the soul possesses truth by way of affir   15
mation or denial are five in number, i.e. art, knowledge, practical wisdom, philosophic wisdom, comprehension; for belief and opinion may be mistaken.

Now what *knowledge* is, if we are to speak exactly and not follow mere similarities, is plain from what follows. We all suppose that what we know is not capable of be   20
ing otherwise; of things capable of being otherwise we do not know, when they have passed outside our observation, whether they exist or not. Therefore the object of

knowledge is of necessity. Therefore it is eternal; for things that are of necessity in the unqualified sense are all eternal; and things that are eternal are ungenerated and imper-
25 ishable. Again, every science is thought to be capable of being taught, and its object of being learned. And all teaching starts from what is already known, as we maintain in the *Analytics* [*Posterior Analytics*, I, 1] also; for it proceeds sometimes through induction and sometimes by deduction. Now induction is of first principles and of the universal and deduction proceeds from universals. There are therefore principles from which de-
30 duction proceeds, which are not reached by deduction; it is therefore by induction that they are acquired. Knowledge, then, is a state of capacity to demonstrate, and has the other limiting characteristics which we specify in the *Analytics;* for it is when a man be-
35 lieves in a certain way and the principles are known to him that he has knowledge, since if they are not better known to him than the conclusion, he will have his knowledge only incidentally.

Let this, then, be taken as our account of knowledge.

1140ª 4. Among things that can be otherwise are included both things made and things done; making and acting are different (for their nature we treat even the discussions out-side our school as reliable); so that the reasoned state of capacity to act is different from
5 the reasoned state of capacity to make. Nor are they included one in the other; for nei-ther is acting making nor is making acting. Now since building is an art and is essen-tially a reasoned state of capacity to make, and there is neither any art that is not such a
10 state nor any such state that is not an art, art is identical with a state of capacity to make, involving a true course of reasoning. All art is concerned with coming into being, i.e. with contriving and considering how something may come into being which is capable of either being or not being, and whose origin is in the maker and not in the thing made; for art is concerned neither with things that are, or come into being, by necessity, nor with things that do so in accordance with nature (since these have their origin in them-
15 selves). Making and acting being different, art must be a matter of making, not of act-ing. And in a sense chance and art are concerned with the same objects; as Agathon
20 says, "art loves chance and chance loves art." Art, then, as has been said, is a state con-cerned with making, involving a true course of reasoning, and lack of art on the con-trary is a state concerned with making, involving a false course of reasoning; both are concerned with what can be otherwise.

5. Regarding *practical wisdom* we shall get at the truth by considering who are
25 the persons we credit with it. Now it is thought to be a mark of a man of practical wis-dom to be able to deliberate well about what is good and expedient for himself, not in some particular respect, e.g. about what sorts of thing conduce to health or to strength, but about what sorts of thing conduce to the good life in general. This is shown by the fact that we credit men with practical wisdom in some particular respect when they have calculated well with a view to some good end which is one of those that are not the
30 object of any art. Thus in general the man who is capable of deliberating has practical wisdom. Now no one deliberates about things that cannot be otherwise nor about things that it is impossible for him to do. Therefore, since knowledge involves demonstration, but there is no demonstration of things whose first principles can be otherwise (for all
1140ᵇ such things might actually be otherwise), and since it is impossible to deliberate about things that are of necessity, practical wisdom cannot be knowledge nor art; not knowl-edge because that which can be done is capable of being otherwise, not art because ac-tion and making are different kinds of thing. It remains, then, that it is a true and rea-
5 soned state of capacity to act with regard to the things that are good or bad for man. For

while making has an end other than itself, action cannot; for good action itself is its end. It is for this reason that we think Pericles and men like him have practical wisdom, viz. because they can see what is good for themselves and what is good for men in general; we consider that those can do this who are good at managing households or states. (This is why we call temperance by this name; we imply that it preserves one's practical wisdom. Now what it preserves is a belief of the kind we have described. For it is not any and every belief that pleasant and painful objects destroy and pervert, e.g. the belief that the triangle has or has not its angles equal to two right angles, but only beliefs about what is to be done. For the principles of the things that are done consist in that for the sake of which they are to be done; but the man who has been ruined by pleasure or pain forthwith fails to see any such principle—to see that for the sake of this or because of this he ought to choose and do whatever he chooses and does; for vice is destructive of the principle.)

Practical wisdom, then, must be a reasoned and true state of capacity to act with regard to human goods. But further, while there is such a thing as excellence in art, there is no such thing as excellence in practical wisdom; and in art he who errs willingly is preferable, but in practical wisdom, as in the excellences he is the reverse. Plainly, then, practical wisdom is an excellence and not an art. There being two parts of the soul that possess reason, it must be the excellence of one of the two, i.e. of that part which forms opinions; for opinion is about what can be otherwise, and so is practical wisdom. But yet it is not only a reasoned state; this is shown by the fact that a state of that sort may be forgotten but practical wisdom cannot.

6. Knowledge is belief about things that are universal and necessary, and there are principles of everything that is demonstrated and of all knowledge (for knowledge involves reasoning). This being so, the first principle of what is known cannot be an object of knowledge, of art, or of practical wisdom; for that which can be known can be demonstrated, and art and practical wisdom deal with things that can be otherwise. Nor are these first principles the objects of wisdom, for it is a mark of the wise man to have *demonstration* about some things. If, then, the states by which we have truth and are never deceived about things that cannot—or can—be otherwise are knowledge, practical wisdom, philosophic wisdom, and comprehension, and it cannot be any of the three (i.e. practical wisdom, scientific knowledge, or philosophic wisdom), the remaining alternative is that it is comprehension that grasps the first principles.

7. *Wisdom* in the arts we ascribe to their most finished exponents, e.g. to Phidias as a sculptor and to Polyclitus as a maker of statues, and here we mean nothing by wisdom except excellence in art; but we think that some people are wise in general, not in some particular field or in any other limited respect, as Homer says in the *Margites*,

Him did the gods make neither a digger nor yet a ploughman
Nor wise in anything else.

Therefore wisdom must plainly be the most finished of the forms of knowledge. It follows that the wise man must not only know what follows from the first principles, but must also possess truth about the first principles. Therefore wisdom must be comprehension combined with knowledge—knowledge of the highest objects which has received as it were its proper completion.

For it would be strange to think that the art of politics, or practical wisdom, is the best knowledge, since man is not the best thing in the world. Now if what is

healthy or good is different for men and for fishes, but what is white or straight is always the same, anyone would say that what is wise is the same but what is practically
25   wise is different; for it is to that which observes well the various matters concerning itself that one ascribes practical wisdom, and it is to this that one will entrust such matters. This is why we say that some even of the lower animals have practical wisdom, viz. those which are found to have a power of foresight with regard to their own
30   life. It is evident also that wisdom and the art of politics cannot be the same; for if the state of mind concerned with a man's own interests is to be called wisdom, there will be many wisdoms; there will not be one concerned with the good of all animals (any more than there is one art of medicine for all existing things), but a different wisdom about the good of each species.

But if the argument be that man is the best of the animals, this makes no difference; for there are other things much more divine in their nature even than man, e.g.
1141ᵇ   most conspicuously, the bodies of which the heavens are framed. From what has been said it is plain, then, that wisdom is knowledge, combined with comprehension, of the things that are highest by nature. This is why we say Anaxagoras, Thales, and men like
5   them have wisdom but not practical wisdom, when we see them ignorant of what is to their own advantage, and why we say that they know things that are remarkable, admirable, difficult, and divine, but useless; viz. because it is not human goods that they seek.

Practical wisdom on the other hand is concerned with things human and things about which it is possible to deliberate; for we say this is above all the work of the man
10   of practical wisdom, to deliberate well, but no one deliberates about things that cannot be otherwise, nor about things which have not an end, and that a good that can be brought about by action. The man who is without qualification good at deliberating is the man who is capable of aiming in accordance with calculation at the best for man of
15   things attainable by action. Nor is practical wisdom concerned with universals only—it must also recognize the particulars; for it is practical, and practice is concerned with particulars. This is why some who do not know, and especially those who have experience, are more practical than others who know; for if a man knew that light meats are digestible and wholesome, but did not know which sorts of meat are light, he would not produce health, but the man who knows that chicken is wholesome is more likely to
20   produce health.

Now practical wisdom is concerned with action; therefore one should have both forms of it, or the latter in preference to the former. Here, too, there must be a controlling kind.

8. Political wisdom and practical wisdom are the same state of mind, but to be them is not the same. Of the wisdom concerned with the city, the practical wisdom
25   which plays a controlling part is legislative wisdom, while that which is related to this as particulars to their universal is known by the general name "political wisdom"; this has to do with action and deliberation, for a decree is a thing to be carried out in the form of an individual act. This is why the exponents of this act are alone said to take part in politics; for these alone do things as manual labourers do things.
30   Practical wisdom also is identified especially with that form of it which is concerned with a man himself—with the individual; and this is known by the general name "practical wisdom"; of the other kinds one is called household management, another legislation, the third politics, and of the last one part is called deliberative and the other judicial. Now knowing what is good for oneself will be one kind of knowledge, but is very different from the other kinds; and the man who knows and concerns himself with

his own interests is thought to have practical wisdom, while politicians are thought to be   1142ᵃ
busybodies; hence the words of Euripides,

> But how could I be wise, who might at ease,
> Numbered among the army's multitude,
> Have had an equal share?. . .   5
> For those who aim too high and do too much. . . .

Those who think thus seek their own good, and consider that one ought to do so. From
this opinion, then, has come the view that such men have practical wisdom; yet perhaps one's own good cannot exist without household management, nor without a form
of government. Further, how one should order one's own affairs is not clear and needs   10
inquiry.

What has been said is confirmed by the fact that while young men become geo-
metricians and mathematicians and wise in matters like these, it is thought that a young
man of practical wisdom cannot be found. The cause is that such wisdom is concerned
not only with universals but with particulars, which become familiar from experience,
but a young man has no experience, for it is length of time that gives experience; indeed   15
one might ask this question too, why a boy may become a mathematician, but not a wise
man or a natural scientist. Is it because the objects of mathematics exist by abstraction,
while the first principles of these other subjects come from experience, and because
young men have no conviction about the latter but merely use the proper language,   20
while the essence of mathematical objects is plain enough to them?

Further, error in deliberation may be either about the universal or about the particular; we may fail to know either that all water that weighs heavy is bad, or that this
particular water weighs heavy.

That practical wisdom is not knowledge is evident; for it is, as has been said, concerned with the ultimate particular fact, since the thing to be done is of this nature. It is
opposed, then, to comprehension; for comprehension is of the definitions, for which no   25
reason can be given, while practical wisdom is concerned with the ultimate particular,
which is the object not of knowledge but of perception—not the perception of qualities
peculiar to one sense but a perception akin to that by which we perceive that the particular figure before us is a triangle; for in that direction too there will be a limit. But this
is rather perception than practical wisdom, though it is another kind of perception.   30

9. There is a difference between inquiry and deliberation; for deliberation is a
particular kind of inquiry. We must grasp the nature of excellence in deliberation as
well—whether it is a form of knowledge, or opinion, or skill in conjecture, or some
other kind of thing. It is not *knowledge;* for men do not inquire about the things they
know about, but good deliberation is a kind of deliberation, and he who deliberates in-   1142ᵇ
quires and calculates. Nor is it *skill in conjecture;* for this both involves no reasoning
and is something that is quick in its operation, while men deliberate a long time, and
they say that one should carry out quickly the conclusions of one's deliberation, but   5
should deliberate slowly. Again, *readiness of mind* is different from excellence in deliberation; it is a sort of skill in conjecture. Nor again is excellence in deliberation *opinion* of any sort. But since the man who deliberates badly makes a mistake, while he who
deliberates well does so correctly, excellence in deliberation is clearly a kind of correctness, but neither of knowledge nor of opinion; for there is no such thing as correctness of knowledge (since there is no such thing as error of knowledge), and correctness   10
of opinion is truth; and at the same time everything that is an object of opinion is al-

ready determined. But again excellence in deliberation involves reasoning. The remaining alternative, then, is that it is *correctness of thinking;* for this is not yet assertion, since, while opinion is not inquiry but already assertion, the man who is deliberating,
15   whether he does so well or ill, is searching for something and calculating.

But excellence in deliberation is a certain correctness of deliberation; hence we must first inquire what deliberation is and what it is about. And, there being more than one kind of correctness, plainly excellence in deliberation is not any and every kind; for the incontinent man and the bad man will reach as a result of his calculation what he sets himself to do, so that he will have deliberated correctly, but he will have got for
20   himself a great evil. Now to have deliberated well is thought to be a good thing; for it is this kind of correctness of deliberation that is excellence in deliberation, viz. that which tends to attain what is good. But it is possible to attain even good by a false deduction and to attain what one ought to do but not by the right means, the middle term being
25   false; so that this too is not yet excellence in deliberation—this state in virtue of which one attains what one ought but not by the right means. Again it is possible to attain it by long deliberation while another man attains it quickly. Therefore in the former case we have not yet got excellence in deliberation, which is rightness with regard to the expedient—rightness in respect both of the conclusion, the manner, and the time. Further it is possible to have deliberated well either in the unqualified sense or with reference to a
30   particular end. Excellence in deliberation in the unqualified sense, then, is that which succeeds with reference to what is the end in the unqualified sense, and excellence in deliberation in a particular sense is that which succeeds relatively to a particular end. If, then, it is characteristic of men of practical wisdom to have deliberated well, excellence in deliberation will be correctness with regard to what conduces to the end of which practical wisdom is the true apprehension.

10. Understanding, also, and goodness of understanding, in virtue of which men
1143ᵃ   are said to be men of understanding or of good understanding, are neither entirely the same as opinion or knowledge (for at that rate all men would have been men of understanding), nor are they one of the particular sciences, such as medicine, the science of things connected with health, or geometry, the science of spatial magnitudes. For understanding is neither about things that are always and are unchangeable, nor about any
5   and every one of the things that come into being, but about things which may become subjects of questioning and deliberation. Hence it is about the same objects as practical wisdom; but understanding and practical wisdom are not the same. For practical wisdom issues commands, since its end is what ought to be done or not to be done; but un-
10   derstanding only judges. (Understanding is identical with goodness of understanding, men of understanding with men of good understanding.) Now understanding is neither the having nor the acquiring of practical wisdom; but as learning is called understanding when it means the exercise of the faculty of knowledge, so "understanding" is ap-
15   plicable to the exercise of the faculty of opinion for the purpose of judging of what someone else says about matters with which practical wisdom is concerned—and of judging soundly; for "well" and "soundly" are the same thing. And from this has come the use of the name "understanding" in virtue of which men are said to be of good understanding, viz. from the application of the word to learning; for we often call learning understanding.

11. What is called judgement, in virtue of which men are said to be forgiving and
20   to have judgement, is the right discrimination of the equitable. This is shown by the fact that we say the equitable man is above all others a man of forgiveness and identify eq-

uity with forgiveness about certain facts. And forgiveness is judgement which discriminates what is equitable and does so correctly; and correct judgement is that which judges what is true.

Now all the states we have considered converge, as might be expected, on the   25
same point; for when we speak of judgement and understanding and practical wisdom and comprehension we credit the same people with possessing judgement and comprehension and with having practical wisdom and understanding. For all these faculties deal with ultimates, i.e. with particulars; and being a man of understanding and of good judgement or of forgiveness consists in being able to judge about the things with which   30
practical wisdom is concerned; for the equities are common to all good men in relation to other men. Now all things which have to be done are included among particulars or ultimates; for not only must the man of practical wisdom know particular facts, but understanding and judgement are also concerned with things to be done, and these are ul-   35
timates. And comprehension is concerned with the ultimates in both directions; for both the primary definitions and the ultimates are objects of comprehension and not of argu-   1143ᵇ
ment, and in demonstrations comprehension grasps the unchangeable and primary definitions, while in practical reasonings it grasps the last and contingent fact, i.e. the second proposition. For these are the starting-points of that for the sake of which, since the universals are reached from the particulars; of these therefore we must have perception,   5
and this is comprehension.

This is why these states are thought to be natural endowments—why, while no one is thought to be wise by nature, people are thought to have by nature judgement, understanding, and comprehension. This is shown by the fact that we think our powers correspond to our time of life, and that a particular age brings with it comprehension and judgement; this implies that nature is the cause. [Hence comprehension is both be-   10
ginning and end; for demonstrations are from these and about these.] Therefore we ought to attend to the undemonstrated sayings and opinions of experienced and older people or of people of practical wisdom not less than to demonstrations; for because experience has given them an eye they see aright.

We have stated, then, what practical wisdom and wisdom are, and with what each   15
of them is concerned, and we have said that each is the excellence of a different part of the soul.

12. Difficulties might be raised as to the utility of these qualities of mind. For wisdom will contemplate none of the things that will make a man happy (for it is not concerned with any coming into being), and though practical wisdom has this merit, for   20
what purpose do we need it? Practical wisdom is the quality of mind concerned with things just and noble and good for man, but these are the things which it is the mark of a *good* man to do, and we are none the more able to act for *knowing* them if the excel-   25
lences are states, just as we are none the better able to act for knowing the things that are healthy and sound, in the sense not of producing but of issuing from the state of health; for we are none the more able to act for having the art of medicine or of gymnastics. But if we are to say that it is useful not for the sake of this but for the sake of becoming good, practical wisdom will be of no use to those who are good; but again it is of no use   30
to those who are not; for it will make no difference whether they have practical wisdom themselves or obey others who have it, and it would be enough for us to do what we do in the case of health; though we wish to become healthy, yet we do not learn the art of medicine. Besides this, it would be thought strange if practical wisdom, being inferior to wisdom, is to be put in authority over it, as seems to be implied by the fact that the art which produces anything rules and issues commands about that thing.   35

These, then, are the questions we must discuss; so far we have only stated the difficulties.

1144ª   Now first let us say that in themselves these states must be worthy of choice because they are the excellences of the two parts of the soul respectively, even if neither of them produces anything.

Secondly, they do produce something, not as the art of medicine produces health, however, but as health produces health; so does wisdom produce happiness; for, being

5   a part of excellence entire, by being possessed and by actualizing itself it makes a man happy.

Again, the function of man is achieved only in accordance with practical wisdom as well as with moral excellence; for excellence makes the aim right, and practical wisdom the things leading to it. (Of the fourth part of the soul—the nutritive—there is no

10   such excellence; for there is nothing which it is in its power to do or not to do.)

With regard to our being none the more able to do because of our practical wisdom what is noble and just, let us begin a little further back, starting with the following principle. As we say that some people who do just acts are not necessarily just, i.e. those

15   who do the acts ordained by the laws either unwillingly or owing to ignorance or for some other reason and not for the sake of the acts themselves (though, to be sure, they do what they should and all the things that the good man ought), so is it, it seems, that in order to be good one must be in a certain state when one does the several acts, i.e. one must do them as a result of choice and for the sake of the acts themselves. Now excel-

20   lence makes the choice right, but the question of the things which should naturally be done to carry out our choice belongs not to excellence but to another faculty. We must devote our attention to these matters and give a clearer statement about them. There is a

25   faculty which is called cleverness; and this is such as to be able to do the things that tend towards the mark we have set before ourselves, and to hit it. Now if the mark be noble, the cleverness is laudable, but if the mark be bad, the cleverness is mere villainy; hence we call clever both men of practical wisdom and villains. Practical wisdom is not the faculty, but it does not exist without this faculty. And this eye of the soul acquires its

30   formed state not without the aid of excellence as has been said and is plain; for inferences which deal with acts to be done are things which involve a starting-point, viz. "since the end, i.e. what is best, is of such and such a nature," whatever it may be (let it for the sake of argument be what we please); and this is not evident except to the good

35   man; for wickedness perverts us and causes us to be deceived about the starting-points of action. Therefore it is evident that it is impossible to be practically wise without being good.

1144ᵇ   13. We must therefore consider excellence also once more; for virtue too is similarly related; as practical wisdom is to cleverness—not the same, but like it—so is natural excellence to excellence in the strict sense. For all men think that each type of character belongs to its possessors in some sense by nature; for from the very moment

5   of birth we are just or fitted for self-control or brave or have the other moral qualities; but yet we seek something else as that which is good in the strict sense—we seek for the presence of such qualities in another way. For both children and brutes have the

10   natural dispositions to these qualities, but without thought these are evidently hurtful. Only we seem to see this much, that, while one may be led astray by them, as a strong body which moves without sight may stumble badly because of its lack of sight, still, if a man once acquires thought that makes a difference in action; and his state, while still like what it was, will then be excellence in the strict sense. Therefore, as in the part of

15   us which forms opinions there are two types, cleverness and practical wisdom, so too in

the moral part there are two types, natural excellence and excellence in the strict sense, and of these the latter involves practical wisdom. This is why some say that all the excellences are forms of practical wisdom, and why Socrates in one respect was on the right track while in another he went astray; in thinking that all the excellences were forms of practical wisdom he was wrong, but in saying they implied practical wisdom 20 he was right. This is confirmed by the fact that even now all men, when they define excellence, after naming the state and its objects add "that (state) which is in accordance with the right reason"; now the right reason is that which is in accordance with practi- 25 cal wisdom. All men, then, seem somehow to divine that this kind of state is excellence, viz. that which is in accordance with practical wisdom. But we must go a little further. For it is not merely the state in accordance with right reason, but the state that implies the *presence* of right reason, that is excellence; and practical wisdom is right reason about such matters. Socrates, then, thought the excellences were forms of reason (for he thought they were, all of them, forms of knowledge), while we think they *involve* reason.

It is clear, then, from what has been said, that it is not possible to be good in the 30 strict sense without practical wisdom, nor practically wise without moral excellence. But in this way we may also refute the dialectical argument whereby it might be contended that the excellences exist in separation from each other; the same man, it might be said, is not best equipped by nature for all the excellences, so that he will have al- 35 ready acquired one when he has not yet acquired another. This is possible in respect of the natural excellences, but not in respect of those in respect of which a man is called without qualification good; for with the presence of the one quality, practical wisdom, 1145ᵃ will be given all the excellences. And it is plain that, even if it were of no practical value, we should have needed it because it is the excellence of the part of us in question; plain too that the choice will not be right without practical wisdom any more than with- 5 out excellence; for the one determines the end and the other makes us do the things that lead to the end.

But again it is not *supreme* over wisdom, i.e. over the superior part of us, any more than the art of medicine is over health; for it does not use it but provides for its coming into being; it issues orders, then, for its sake, but not to it. Further, to maintain 10 its supremacy would be like saying that the art of politics rules the gods because it issues orders about all the affairs of the state.

BOOK VII

1. Let us now make a fresh beginning and point out that of moral states to be avoided 15 there are three kinds—vice, incontinence, brutishness. The contraries of two of these are evident—one we call excellence, the other continence; to brutishness it would be most fitting to oppose superhuman excellence, something heroic and divine, as Homer has represented Priam saying of Hector that he was very good, 20

> For he seemed not, he,
> The child of a mortal man, but as one that of God's seed came.

Therefore if, as they say, men become gods by excess of excellence, of this kind must evidently be the state opposed to the brutish state; for as a brute has no vice or excel- 25 lence, so neither has a god; his state is higher than excellence, and that of a brute is a different kind of state from vice.

Now, since it is rarely that a godlike man is found—to use the epithet of the Spar-
30   tans, who when they admire anyone highly call him a "godlike man"—so too the
brutish type is rarely found among men, it is found chiefly among foreigners, but some
brutish qualities are also produced by disease or deformity; and we also call by this evil
name those who surpass ordinary men in vice. Of this kind of disposition, however, we
must later make some mention, while we have discussed vice before; we must now dis-
35   cuss incontinence and softness (or effeminacy), and continence and endurance; for we
must treat each of the two neither as identical with excellence or wickedness, nor as a
1145ᵇ   different genus. We must, as in all other cases, set the phenomena before us and, after
first discussing the difficulties, go on to prove, if possible, the truth of all the reputable
5   opinions about these affections or, failing this, of the greater number and the most authoritative; for if we both resolve the difficulties and leave the reputable opinions undis-
turbed, we shall have proved the case sufficiently.

Now both continence and endurance are thought to be included among things
good and praiseworthy, and both incontinence and softness among things bad and
10   blameworthy; and the same man is thought to be continent and ready to abide by the result of his calculations, or incontinent and ready to abandon them. And the incontinent
man, knowing that what he does is bad, does it as a result of passion, while the continent
man, knowing that his appetites are bad, does not follow them because of his reason.
The temperate man all men call continent and disposed to endurance, while the conti-
15   nent man some maintain to be always temperate but others do not; and some call the
self-indulgent man incontinent and the incontinent man self-indulgent indiscriminately,
while others distinguish them. The man of practical wisdom, they sometimes say, cannot be incontinent, while sometimes they say that some who are practically wise and
20   clever are incontinent. Again men are said to be incontinent with respect to anger, honour, and gain.—These, then, are the things that are said.

2. Now we may ask what kind of right belief is possessed by the man who behaves incontinently. That he should behave so when he has knowledge, some say is
impossible; for it would be strange—so Socrates thought—if when knowledge was
in a man something else could master it and drag it about like a slave. For *Socrates*
25   was entirely opposed to the view in question, holding that there is no such thing as
incontinence; no one, he said, acts against what he believes best—people act so only
by reason of ignorance. Now this view contradicts the plain phenomena, and we
must inquire about what happens to such a man; if he acts by reason of ignorance,
30   what is the manner of his ignorance? For that the man who behaves incontinently
does not, before he gets into this state, *think* he ought to act so, is evident. But there
are some who concede certain of Socrates' contentions but not others; that nothing is
stronger than knowledge they admit, but not that no one acts contrary to what has
35   seemed to him the better course, and therefore they say that the incontinent man has
not knowledge when he is mastered by his pleasures, but opinion. But *if* it is opinion and not knowledge, if it is not a strong belief that resists but a weak one, as in
1146ᵃ   men who hesitate, we forgive their failure to stand by such convictions against
strong appetites; but we do not forgive wickedness, nor any of the other blameworthy states. It is then *practical wisdom* whose resistance is mastered? That is the
5   strongest of all states. But this is absurd; the same man will be at once practically
wise and incontinent, but *no one* would say that it is the part of a practically wise
man to do willingly the basest acts. Besides, it has been shown before that the man
of practical wisdom is one who will *act* (for he is a man concerned with the individual facts) and who has the other excellences.

Further, if continence involves having strong and bad appetites, the temperate   10
man will not be continent nor the continent man temperate; for a temperate man will
have neither excessive nor bad appetites. But the continent man *must;* for if the appetites
are good, the state that restrains us from following them is bad, so that not all continence
will be good; while if they are weak and not bad, there is nothing admirable in resisting   15
them, and if they are weak and bad, there is nothing great in resisting these either.

Further, if continence makes a man ready to stand by any and every opinion, it is
bad, i.e. if it makes him stand even by a false opinion; and if incontinence makes a man
apt to abandon any and every opinion, there will be a good incontinence, of which
Sophocles' Neoptolemus in the *Philoctetes* will be an instance; for he is to be praised   20
for not standing by what Odysseus persuaded him to do, because he is pained at telling
a lie.

Further, the sophistic argument presents a difficulty; for, because they want to
produce paradoxical results to show how clever they are, when they succeed the resulting inference presents a difficulty (for thought is bound fast when it will not rest because the conclusion does not satisfy it, and cannot advance because it cannot refute the   25
argument). There is an argument from which it follows that folly coupled with incontinence is excellence; for a man does the opposite of what he believes owing to incontinence, but believes what is good to be evil and something that he should not do, and in   30
consequence he will do what is good and not what is evil.

Further, he who on conviction does and pursues and chooses what is pleasant
would be thought to be better than one who does so as a result not of calculation but of
incontinence; for he is easier to cure since he may be persuaded to change his mind. But
to the incontinent man may be applied the proverb "when water chokes, what is one to
wash it down with?" If he had been persuaded of the rightness of what he does, he
would have desisted when he was persuaded to change his mind; but now he acts in   1146^b
spite of his being persuaded of something quite different.

Further, if incontinence and continence are concerned with any and every kind of
object, who is it that is incontinent in the unqualified sense? No one has all the forms of
incontinence, but we say some people are incontinent without qualification.   5

3. Of some such kind are the difficulties that arise; some of these points must be
refuted and the others left in possession of the field; for the solution of the difficulty is
the discovery of the truth. We must consider first, then, whether incontinent people act
knowingly or not, and in what sense knowingly; then with what sorts of object the incontinent and the continent man may be said to be concerned (i.e. whether with any and   10
every pleasure and pain or with certain determinate kinds), and whether the continent
man and the man of endurance are the same or different; and similarly with regard to the
other matters germane to this inquiry. The starting-point of our investigation is the
question whether the continent man and the incontinent are differentiated by their ob-   15
jects or by their attitude, i.e. whether the incontinent man is incontinent simply by being
concerned with such and such objects, or, instead, by his attitude, or, instead of that, by
both these things; the second question is whether incontinence and continence are concerned with any and every object or not. The man who is incontinent in the unqualified
sense is neither concerned with any and every object, but with precisely those with
which the self-indulgent man is concerned, nor is he characterized by being simply re-   20
lated to these (for then his state would be the same as self-indulgence), but by being related to them in a certain way. For the one is led on in accordance with his own choice,
thinking that he ought always to pursue the present pleasure; while the other does not
think so, but yet pursues it.

As for the suggestion that it is true opinion and not knowledge against which we
act incontinently, that makes no difference to the argument; for some people when in a
state of opinion do not hesitate, but think they know exactly. If, then, it is owing to their
weak conviction those who have opinion are more likely to act against their belief than
those who know, there will be no difference between knowledge and opinion; for some
men are no less convinced of what they think than others of what they know; as is
shown by the case of Heraclitus. But since we use the word "know" in two senses (for
both the man who has knowledge but is not using it and he who is using it are said to
know), it *will* make a difference whether, when a man does what he should not, he has
the knowledge but is not exercising it, or *is* exercising it; for the latter seems strange,
but not the former.

Further, since there are two kinds of propositions, there is nothing to prevent a
man's having both and acting against his knowledge, provided that he is using only the
universal and not the particular; for it is particular acts that have to be done. And there
are also two kinds of universal; one is predicable of the agent, the other of the object;
e.g. "dry food is good for every man," and "I am a man," or "such and such food is dry";
but whether this food is such and such, of this the incontinent man either has not or is
not exercising the knowledge. There will, then, be, firstly, an enormous difference between these manners of knowing, so that to know in one way would not seem anything
strange, while to know in the other way would be extraordinary.

And further the possession of knowledge in another sense than those just named
is something that happens to men; for within the case of having knowledge but not using it we see a difference of state, admitting of the possibility of having knowledge in a
sense and yet not having it, as in the instance of a man asleep, mad, or drunk. But now
this is just the condition of men under the influence of passions; for outbursts of anger
and sexual appetites and some other such passions, it is evident, actually alter our bodily condition, and in some men even produce fits of madness. It is plain, then, that incontinent people must be said to be in a similar condition to these. The fact that men use
the language that flows from knowledge proves nothing; for even men under the influence of these passions utter scientific proofs and verses of Empedocles, and those who
have just begun to learn can string together words, but do not yet know; for it has to become part of themselves, and that takes time; so that we must suppose that the use of
language by men in an incontinent state means no more than its utterance by actors on
the stage.

Again, we may also view the cause as follows with reference to the facts of nature. The one opinion is universal, the other is concerned with the particular facts, and
here we come to something within the sphere of perception; when a single opinion results from the two, the soul must in one type of case affirm the conclusion, while in the
case of opinions concerned with production it must immediately act (e.g. if everything
sweet ought to be tasted, and this is sweet, in the sense of being one of the particular
sweet things, the man who can act and is not restrained must at the same time actually
act accordingly). When, then, the universal opinion is present in us restraining us from
tasting, and there is also the opinion that everything sweet is pleasant, and that this is
sweet (now this is the opinion that is active), and when appetite happens to be present in
us, the one opinion bids us avoid the object, but appetite leads us towards it (for it can
move each of our bodily parts); so that it turns out that a man behaves incontinently under the influence (in a sense) of reason and opinion, and of opinion not contrary in itself,
but only incidentally—for the appetite is contrary not the opinion—to right reason. It
also follows that this is the reason why the lower animals are not incontinent, viz. because they have no universal beliefs but only imagination and memory of particulars.

The explanation of how the ignorance is dissolved and the incontinent man re-gains his knowledge, is the same as in the case of the man drunk or asleep and is not pe-culiar to this condition; we must go to the students of natural science for it. Now, the last proposition both being an opinion about a perceptible object, and being what deter-mines our actions, this a man either has not when he is in the state of passion, or has it   10
in the sense in which having knowledge did not mean knowing but only talking, as a drunken man may utter the verses of Empedocles. And because the last term is not uni-versal nor equally an object of knowledge with the universal term, the position that Socrates sought to establish actually seems to result; for it is not what is thought to be   15
knowledge proper that the passion overcomes (nor is it this that is dragged about as a re-sult of the passion), but perceptual knowledge.

This must suffice as our answer to the question of whether men can act inconti-nently when they know or not, and in what sense they know.

4. We must next discuss whether there is any one who is incontinent without   20
qualification, or all men who are incontinent are so in a particular sense, and if so, with what sort of objects. That both continent persons and persons of endurance, and incon-tinent and soft persons, are concerned with pleasures and pains, is evident.

Now of the things that produce pleasure some are necessary, while others are worthy of choice in themselves but admit of excess, the bodily causes of pleasure being   25
necessary (by such I mean both those concerned with food and those concerned with sexual intercourse, i.e. the bodily matters with which we defined self-indulgence and temperance as being concerned), while the others are not necessary but worthy of choice in themselves (e.g. victory, honour, wealth, and good and pleasant things of this   30
sort). This being so, those who go to excess with reference to the latter, contrary to the right reason which is in themselves, are not called incontinent simply, but incontinent with the qualification "in respect of money, gain, honour, or anger,"—not simply in-continent, on the ground that they are different from incontinent people and are called incontinent by reason of a resemblance. (Compare the case of Man, who won a contest at the Olympic games; in his case the general formula of man differed little from the one peculiar to *him,* but yet it was different.) This is shown by the fact that incontinence ei-   1148ᵃ
ther without qualification or in some particular respect is blamed not only as a fault but as a kind of vice, while none of the others is so blamed.

But of the people who are incontinent with respect to bodily enjoyments, with   5
which we say the temperate and the self-indulgent man are concerned, he who pursues the excesses of things pleasant—and shuns those of things painful, of hunger and thirst and heat and cold and all the objects of touch and taste—not by choice but contrary to his choice and his judgement, is called incontinent, not with the qualification "in respect   10
of this or that," e.g. of anger, but without qualification. This is confirmed by the fact that men are called soft with regard to these pleasures, but not with regard to any of the oth-ers. And for this reason we group together the incontinent and the self-indulgent, the continent and the temperate man—but not any of these other types—because they are   15
concerned somehow with the same pleasures and pains; but although these are con-cerned with the same objects, they are not similarly related to them, but some of them choose them while the others do not choose them.

This is why we should describe as self-indulgent rather the man who without appetite or with but a slight appetite pursues the excesses and avoids moderate pains, than the man who does so because of his strong appetites; for what would the former   20
do, if he had in addition a vigorous appetite, and a violent pain at the lack of the nec-essary objects?

Now of appetites and pleasures some belong to the class of things generically noble and good—for some pleasant things are by nature worthy of choice—while others
25   are contrary to these, and others are intermediate, to adopt our previous distinction, e.g. wealth, gain, victory, honour. And with reference to all objects whether of this or of the intermediate kind men are not blamed for being affected by them, for desiring and loving them, but for doing so in a certain way, i.e. for going to excess. (This is why all those who contrary to reason either are mastered by or pursue one of the objects which
30   are naturally noble and good, e.g. those who busy themselves more than they ought about honour or about children and parents—for these too are goods, and those who busy themselves about them are praised; but yet there is an excess even in them—if like Niobe one were to fight even against the gods, or were to be as much devoted to one's
1148ᵇ   father as Satyrus nicknamed "the filial," who was thought to be very silly on this point.) There is no wickedness, then, with regard to these objects, for the reason named, viz. because each of them is by nature a thing worthy of choice for its own sake; yet excesses in respect of them are bad and to be avoided. Similarly there is no incontinence
5   with regard to them; for incontinence is not only to be avoided but is also a thing worthy of blame; but owing to a similarity in the passion people apply the name incontinence, adding in each case what it is in respect of, as we may describe as a bad doctor or a bad actor one whom we should not call bad, simply. As, then, is the case we do not
10   apply the term without qualification because each of these conditions is not badness but only analogous to it, so it is clear that in the other case also that alone must be taken to be incontinence and continence which is concerned with the same objects as temperance and self-indulgence, but we apply the term to anger by virtue of a resemblance; and this is why we say with a qualification "incontinent in respect of anger" as we say "incontinent in respect of honour, or of gain."

15   5. Some things are pleasant by nature, and of these some are so without qualification, and others are so with reference to particular classes either of animals or of men; while others are not pleasant by nature, but some of them become so by reason of deformities, and others by reason of habits, and others by reason of bad natures. This being so it is possible with regard to each of the latter kinds to discover similar
20   states; I mean the brutish states, as in the case of the female who, they say, rips open pregnant women and devours the infants, or of the things in which some of the tribes about the Black Sea that have gone savage are said to delight—in raw meat or in human flesh, or in lending their children to one another to feast upon—or of the story of Phalaris.
25   These states are brutish, but others arise as a result of disease (or, in some cases, of madness, as with the man who sacrificed and ate his mother, or with the slave who ate the liver of his fellow), and others are morbid states resulting from custom, e.g. the habit of plucking out the hair or of gnawing the nails, or even coals or earth, and in addition to these paederasty; for these arise in some by nature and in others, as in those
30   who have been the victims of lust from childhood, from habit.
Now those in whom nature is the cause of such a state no one would call incontinent, any more than one would apply the epithet to women because of the passive part they play in copulation; nor would one apply it to those who are in a morbid condition as a result of habit. To have these various types of habit is beyond the limits of
1149ᵃ   vice, as brutishness is too; for a man who has them to master or be mastered by them is not simple incontinence but that which is so by analogy, as the man who is in this condition in respect of fits of anger is to be called incontinent in respect of that feeling, but not incontinent.

For every excessive state whether of folly, of cowardice, of self-indulgence, or of   5
bad temper, is either brutish or morbid; the man who is by nature apt to fear everything,
even the squeak of a mouse, is cowardly with a brutish cowardice, while the man who
feared a weasel did so in consequence of disease; and of foolish people those who by
nature are thoughtless and live by their senses alone are brutish, like some races of the   10
distant foreigners, while those who are so as a result of disease (e.g. of epilepsy) or of
madness are morbid. Of these characteristics it is possible to have some only at times,
and not to be mastered by them, e.g. Phalaris may have restrained a desire to eat the
flesh of a child or an appetite for unnatural sexual pleasure; but it is also possible to be
mastered, not merely to have the feelings. Thus, as the wickedness which is on the hu-   15
man level is called wickedness simply, while that which is not is called wickedness not
simply but with the qualification "brutish" or "morbid," in the same way it is plain that
some incontinence is brutish and some morbid, while only that which corresponds to
human self-indulgence is incontinence simply.   20

That incontinence and continence, then, are concerned only with the same objects
as self-indulgence and temperance and that what is concerned with other objects is a
type distinct from incontinence, and called incontinence by a metaphor and not simply,
is plain.

6. That incontinence in respect of anger is less disgraceful than that in respect of
the appetites is what we will now proceed to see. Anger seems to listen to reason to   25
some extent, but to mishear it, as do hasty servants who run out before they have heard
the whole of what one says, and then muddle the order, or as dogs bark if there is but a
knock at the door, before looking to see if it is a friend; so anger by reason of the
warmth and hastiness of its nature, though it hears, does not hear an order, and springs   30
to take revenge. For reason or imagination informs us that we have been insulted or
slighted, and anger, reasoning as it were that anything like this must be fought against,
boils up straightway; while appetite, if reason or perception merely says that an object   35
is pleasant, springs to the enjoyment of it. Therefore anger obeys reason in a sense, but
appetite does not. It is therefore more disgraceful; for the man who is incontinent in re-   1149b
spect of anger is in a sense conquered by reason, while the other is conquered by appetite and not by reason.

Further, we forgive people more easily for following natural desires, since we for-   5
give them more easily for following such appetites as are common to all men, and in so
far as they are common; now anger and bad temper are more natural than the appetites
for excess, i.e. for unnecessary objects. Take for instance the man who defended himself on the charge of striking his father by saying "yes, but *he* struck *his* father, and *he*
struck *his,* and" (pointing to his child) "this boy will strike *me* when he is a man; it runs   10
in the family"; of the man who when he was being dragged along by his son bade him
stop at the doorway, since he himself had dragged his father only as far as that.

Further, those who are more given to plotting against others are more unjust. Now
a passionate man is not given to plotting, nor is anger itself—it is open; but the nature
of appetite is illustrated by what the poets call Aphrodite, "guile-weaving daughter of   15
Cyprus," and by Homer's words about her "embroidered girdle":

And the whisper of wooing is there,
Whose subtlety stealeth the wits of the wise, how prudent soe'er.

Therefore if this form of incontinence is more unjust and disgraceful than that in respect
of anger, it is both incontinence without qualification and in a sense vice.

20   Further, no one commits wanton outrage with a feeling of pain, but every one who acts in anger acts with pain, while the man who commits outrage acts with pleasure. If, then, those acts at which it is most just to be angry are more unjust, the incontinence which is due to appetite is the more unjust; for there is no wanton outrage involved in anger.

Plainly, then, the incontinence concerned with appetite is more disgraceful than 25   that concerned with anger, and continence and incontinence are concerned with bodily appetites and pleasures; but we must grasp the differences among the latter themselves. For, as has been said at the beginning, some are human and natural both in kind and in 30   magnitude, others are brutish, and others are due to deformities and diseases. Only with the first of these are temperance and self-indulgence concerned; this is why we call the lower animals neither temperate nor self-indulgent except by a metaphor, and only if some one kind of animals exceeds another as a whole in wantonness, destructiveness, and omnivorous greed; these have no power of choice or calculation, but they are de-

1150ᵃ   partures from what is natural as, among men, madmen are. Now brutishness is less evil than vice, though more alarming; for it is not that the better part has been perverted, as in man,—they *have* no better part. Thus it is like comparing a lifeless thing with a liv-5   ing in respect of badness; for the badness of that which has no source of movement is always less hurtful, and thought is a source. Thus it is like comparing injustice with an unjust man. Each is in some sense worse; for a bad man will do ten thousand times as much evil as a brute.

7. With regard to the pleasures and pains and appetites and aversions arising through touch and taste, to which both self-indulgence and temperance were formerly 10   narrowed down, it is possible to be in such a state as to be defeated even by those of them which most people master, or to master even those by which most people are defeated; among these possibilities, those relating to pleasures are incontinence and continence, those relating to pains softness and endurance. The state of most people is inter-15   mediate, even if they lean more towards the worse states.

Now, since some pleasures are necessary while others are not, and are necessary up to a point while the excesses of them are not, nor the deficiencies, and this is equally true of appetites and pains, the man who pursues the excesses of things pleasant, or pursues to excess necessary objects, and does so by choice, for their own sake and not at all 20   for the sake of any result distinct from them, is self-indulgent; for such a man is of necessity without regrets, and therefore incurable, since a man without regrets cannot be cured. The man who is deficient is the opposite; the man who is intermediate is temperate. Similarly, there is the man who avoids bodily pains not because he is defeated by 25   them but by choice. (Of those who do not *choose* such acts, one kind of man is led to them as a result of the pleasure involved, another because he avoids the pain arising from the appetite, so that these types differ from one another. Now any one would think worse of a man if with no appetite or with weak appetite he were to do something disgraceful, than if he did it under the influence of powerful appetite, and worse of him if 30   he struck a blow not in anger than if he did it in anger; for what would he have done if he had been strongly affected? This is why the self-indulgent man is worse than the incontinent.) Of the states named, then, the latter is rather a kind of softness; the former is self-indulgence. While to the incontinent man is opposed the continent, to the soft is opposed the man of endurance; for endurance consists in resisting, while continence con-35   sists in conquering, and resisting and conquering are different, as not being beaten is different from winning; this is why continence is also more worthy of choice than en-

1150ᵇ   durance. Now the man who is defective in respect of resistance to the things which most

men both resist and resist successfully is soft and effeminate; for effeminacy too is a kind of softness; such a man trails his cloak to avoid the pain of lifting it, and plays the invalid without thinking himself wretched, though the man he imitates is a wretched   5
man.

The case is similar with regard to continence and incontinence. For if a man is defeated by violent and excessive pleasures or pains, there is nothing wonderful in that; indeed we are ready to forgive him if he has resisted, as Theodectes' Philoctetes does when bitten by the snake, or Carcinus' Cercyon in the *Alope,* and as people who try to   10
restrain their laughter burst out in a guffaw, as happened to Xenophantus. But it is surprising if a man is defeated by and cannot resist pleasures or pains which most men can hold out against, when this is not due to heredity or disease, like the softness that is   15
hereditary with the kings of the Scythians, or that which distinguishes the female sex from the male.

The lover of amusement, too, is thought to be self-indulgent, but is really soft. For amusement is a relaxation, since it is a rest; and the lover of amusement is one of the people who go to excess in this.

Of incontinence one kind is impetuosity, another weakness. For some men after deliberating fail, owing to their passion, to stand by the conclusions of their deliberation, others because they have not deliberated are led by their passion; since some men   20
(just as people who first tickle others are not tickled themselves), if they have first perceived and seen what is coming and have first roused themselves and their calculative faculty, are not defeated by their passion, whether it be pleasant or painful. It is keen and excitable people that suffer especially from the impetuous form of incontinence; for   25
the former because of their quickness and the latter because of the violence of their passions do not wait on reason, because they are apt to follow their imagination.

8. The self-indulgent man, as was said, has no regrets; for he stands by his choice; but any incontinent man is subject to regrets. This is why the position is not as   30
it was expressed in the formulation of the problem, but the self-indulgent man is incurable and the incontinent man curable; for wickedness is like a disease such as dropsy or consumption, while incontinence is like epilepsy; the former is a permanent, the latter an intermittent badness. And generally incontinence and vice are different in kind; vice   35
is unconscious of itself, incontinence is not (of incontinent men themselves, those who become beside themselves are better than those who possess reason but do not abide by   1151a
it, since the latter are defeated by a weaker passion, and do not act without previous deliberation like the others); for the incontinent man is like the people who get drunk quickly and on little wine, i.e. on less than most people.   5

Evidently, then, incontinence is not vice (though perhaps it is so in a qualified sense); for incontinence is contrary to choice while vice is in accordance with choice; not but what they are similar in respect of the actions they lead to; as in the saying of Demodocus about the Milesians, "the Milesians are not without sense, but they do the things that senseless people do," so too incontinent people are not unjust but they will   10
do unjust acts.

Now, since the incontinent man is apt to pursue, not on conviction, bodily pleasures that are excessive and contrary to right reason, while the self-indulgent man is convinced because he is the sort of man to pursue them, it is on the contrary the former that is easily persuaded to change his mind, while the latter is not. For excellence and vice respectively preserve and destroy the first principle, and in actions that for the sake   15
of which is the first principle, as the hypotheses are in mathematics; neither in that case is it reason that teaches the first principles, nor is it so here—excellence either natural

or produced by habituation is what teaches right opinion about the first principle. Such a man as this, then, is temperate; his contrary is the self-indulgent.

20   But there is a sort of man who is carried away as a result of passion and contrary to right reason—a man whom passion masters so that he does not act according to right reason, but does not master to the extent of making him ready to believe that he ought to pursue such pleasures without reserve; this is the incontinent man, who is better than the self-indulgent man, and not bad without qualification; for the best thing in him, the

25   first principle, is preserved. And contrary to him is another kind of man, he who abides by his convictions and is not carried away, at least as a result of passion. It is evident from these considerations that the latter is a good state and the former a bad one.

      9. Is the man continent who abides by any and every reasoning and any and ev-
30   ery choice, or the man who abides by the right choice, and is he incontinent who abandons any and every choice and any and every reasoning, or he who abandons the reasoning that is not false and the choice that is right? This is how we put it before our statement of the problem. Or is it incidentally any and every choice but *per se* the true reasoning and the right choice by which the one abides and the other does not? If any-
1151ᵇ   one chooses or pursues this for the sake of that, *per se* he pursues and chooses the latter, but incidentally the former. But when we speak without qualification we mean what is per se. Therefore in a sense the one abides by, and the other abandons, any and every opinion; but without qualification, the true opinion.

5   There are some who are apt to abide by their opinion, who are called strong-headed, viz. those who are hard to persuade and are not easily persuaded to change; these have in them something like the continent man, as the prodigal is in a way like the liberal man and the rash man like the confident man; but they are different in many respects. For it is to passion and appetite that the one will not yield, since on occasion the
10   continent man *will* be easy to persuade; but it is to reason that the others refuse to yield, for they do form appetites and many of them are led by their pleasures. Now the people who are strong-headed are the opinionated, the ignorant, and the boorish—the opinionated being influenced by pleasure and pain; for they delight in the victory they gain if they are not persuaded to change, and are pained if their decisions become null and void
15   as decrees sometimes do; so that they are more like the incontinent than the continent man.

      But there are some who fail to abide by their resolutions, not as a result of incontinence, e.g. Neoptolemus in Sophocles' *Philoctetes;* yet it was for the sake of pleasure that he did not stand fast—but a noble pleasure; for telling the truth was noble to him,
20   but he had been persuaded by Odysseus to tell the lie. For not every one who does anything for the sake of pleasure is either self-indulgent or bad or incontinent, but he who does it for a disgraceful pleasure.

      Since there is also a sort of man who takes less delight than he should in bodily things, and does not abide by reason, he who is intermediate between him and the in-
25   continent man is the continent man; for the incontinent man fails to abide by reason because he delights too much in them, and this man because he delights in them too little; while the continent man abides by it and does not change on either account. Now if continence is good, both the contrary states must be bad, as they actually appear to be; but
30   because the other extreme is seen in few people and seldom, as temperance is thought to be contrary only to self-indulgence, so is continence to incontinence.

      Since many names are applied analogically, it is by analogy that we have come to speak of the continence of the temperate man; for both the continent man and the temperate man are such as to do nothing contrary to reason for the sake of the bodily plea-

sures, but the former has and the latter has not bad appetites, and the latter is such as not   1152ᵃ
to feel pleasure contrary to reason, while the former is such as to feel pleasure but not to
be led by it. And the incontinent and the self-indulgent man are also like one another;
they are different, but both pursue bodily pleasures—the latter, however, also thinking   5
that he ought to do so, while the former does not think this.

10. Nor can the same man have practical wisdom and be incontinent; for it has
been shown that a man is at the same time practically wise, and good in respect of character. Further, a man has practical wisdom not by knowing only but by acting; but the
incontinent man is unable to act—there is, however, nothing to prevent a clever man   10
from being incontinent; this is why it is sometimes actually thought that some people
have practical wisdom but are incontinent, viz. because cleverness and practical wisdom differ in the way we have described in our first discussions, and are near together
in respect of their reasoning, but differ in respect of their choice—nor yet is the incontinent man like the man who knows and is contemplating a truth, but like the man who   15
is asleep or drunk. And he acts voluntarily (for he acts in a sense with knowledge both
of what he does and of that for the sake of which he does it), but is not wicked since his
choice is good; so that he is half-wicked. And he is not unjust; for he does not act of
malice aforethought; of the two types of incontinent man the one does not abide by the
conclusions of his deliberation, while the excitable man does not deliberate at all. And
thus the incontinent man is like a city which passes all the right decrees and has good   20
laws, but makes no use of them, as in Anaxandrides' jesting remark,

"The city willed it, that cares nought for laws";

but the wicked man is like a city that uses its laws, but has wicked laws to use.

Now incontinence and continence are concerned with that which is in excess of   25
the state characteristic of most men; for the continent man abides by his resolutions
more and the incontinent man less than most men can.

Of the forms of incontinence, that of excitable people is more curable than that of
those who deliberate but do not abide by their decisions, and those who are incontinent
through habituation are more curable than those in whom incontinence is innate; for it
is easier to change a habit than to change one's nature; even habit is hard to change just   30
because it is like nature, as Evenus says:

I say that habit's but long practice, friend,
And this becomes men's nature in the end.

We have now stated what continence, incontinence, endurance, and softness are, and
how these states are related to each other.

11. The study of pleasure and pain belongs to the province of the political   1152ᵇ
philosopher; for he is the architect of the end, with a view to which we call one thing
bad and another good without qualification. Further, it is one of our necessary tasks to
consider them; for not only did we lay it down that moral excellence and vice are con-   5
cerned with pains and pleasures, but most people say that happiness involves pleasure;
this is why the blessed man is called by a name derived from a word meaning enjoyment.

Now some people think that no pleasure is a good, either in itself or incidentally,
since the good and pleasure are not the same; others think that some pleasures are good   10

but that most are bad. Again there is a third view, that even if all pleasures are goods, yet the best thing cannot be pleasure. The reasons given for the view that pleasure is not a good at all are *(a)* that every pleasure is a perceptible process to a natural state, and that no process is of the same kind as its end, e.g. no process of building of the same
15   kind as a house. *(b)* A temperate man avoids pleasures. *(c)* A man of practical wisdom pursues what is free from pain, not what is pleasant. *(d)* The pleasures are a hindrance to thought, and the more so the more one delights in them, e.g. in sexual pleasure; for no one could think of anything while absorbed in this. *(e)* There is no art of pleasure; but
20   every good is the product of some art. *(f)* Children and the brutes pursue pleasures. The reasons for the view that not all pleasures are good are that *(a)* there are pleasures that are actually base and objects of reproach, and *(b)* there are harmful pleasures; for some pleasant things are unhealthy. The reason for the view that the best thing is not pleasure is that pleasure is not an end but a process.

12. These are pretty much the things that are said. That it does not follow from
25   these grounds that pleasure is not a good, or even the chief good, is plain from the following considerations. First, since that which is good may be so in either of two senses (one thing good simply and another good for a particular person), natural constitutions and states, and therefore also movements and processes, will be correspondingly divisible. Of those which are thought to be bad some will be bad without qualification but not bad for a particular person, but worthy of his choice, and some will not be worthy of
30   choice even for a particular person, but only at a particular time and for a short period, though not without qualification; while others are not even pleasures, but seem to be so, viz. all those which involve pain and whose end is curative, e.g. the processes that go on in sick persons.
Further, one kind of good being activity and another being state, the processes
35   that restore us to our natural state are only incidentally pleasant; for that matter the activity at work in the appetites for them is the activity of so much of our state and nature as has remained unimpaired; for there are actually pleasures that involve *no* pain
1153ᵃ   or appetite (e.g. those of contemplation), the nature in such a case not being defective at all. That the others are incidental is indicated by the fact that men do not enjoy the same things when their nature is in its settled state as they do when it is being replenished, but in the former case they enjoy the things that are pleasant without qualifica-
5   tion, in the latter the contraries of these as well; for then they enjoy even sharp and bitter things, none of which is pleasant either by nature or without qualification. Nor, then, are the pleasures; for as pleasant things differ, so do the pleasures arising from them.
Again, it is not necessary that there should be something else better than pleasure, as some say the end is better than the process; for pleasures are not processes nor do
10   they all involve process—they are activities and ends; nor do they arise when we are becoming something, but when we are exercising some faculty; and not all pleasures have an end different from themselves, but only the pleasures of persons who are being led to the completing of their nature. This is why it is not right to say that pleasure is a perceptible process, but it should rather be called activity of the natural state, and instead of
15   "perceptible" "unimpeded." It is thought to be a process just because they think it is in the strict sense *good;* for they think that activity is a process which it is not.
The view that pleasures are bad because some pleasant things are unhealthy is like saying that healthy things are bad because some healthy things are bad for the pocket; both are bad in the respect mentioned, but they are not *bad* for *that* reason—
20   indeed, contemplation itself is sometimes injurious to health.

Neither practical wisdom or any state is impeded by the pleasure arising from it; it is foreign pleasures that impede, for the pleasures arising from contemplation and learning will make us contemplate and learn all the more.

The fact that no pleasure is the product of any art arises naturally enough; there is no art of any other activity either, but only of the capacity; though for that matter the arts of the perfumer and the cook *are* thought to be arts of pleasure.   25

The arguments that the temperate man avoids pleasure and that the man of practical wisdom pursues the painless life, and that children and the brutes pursue pleasure, are all refuted by the same consideration. We have pointed out in what sense pleasures are good without qualification and in what sense some are not good; now both the   30
brutes and children pursue pleasures of the latter kind (and the man of practical wisdom pursues tranquil freedom from that kind), viz. those which imply appetite and pain, i.e. the bodily pleasures (for it is these that are of this nature) and the excesses of them, in respect of which the self-indulgent man is self-indulgent. This is why the temperate   35
man avoids these pleasures; for even he has pleasures of his own.

13. But further it is agreed that pain is bad and to be avoided; for some pain is   1153ᵇ
without qualification bad, and other pain is bad because it is in some respect an impediment to us. Now the contrary of that which is to be avoided, *qua* something to be avoided and bad, is good. Pleasure, then, is necessarily a good. For the answer of Speusippus, that it is just as the greater is contrary both to the less and to the equal, is   5
not successful; since he would not say that pleasure is essentially a species of evil.

And if certain pleasures are bad, that does not prevent the best thing from being some pleasure—just as knowledge might be, though certain kinds of knowledge are bad. Perhaps it is even necessary, if each state has unimpeded activities, that whether   10
the activity (if unimpeded) of all our states or that of some one of them is happiness, this should be the thing most worthy of our choice; and this activity is a pleasure. Thus the chief good would be some pleasure, though most pleasures might perhaps be bad without qualification. And for this reason all men think that the happy life is pleasant and weave pleasure into happiness—and reasonably too; for no activity is complete when it   15
is impeded, and happiness is a complete thing; this is why the happy man needs the goods of the body and external goods, i.e. those of fortune, viz. in order that he may not be impeded in these ways. Those who say that the victim on the rack or the man who falls into great misfortunes is happy if he is good, are, whether they mean to or not, talk-   20
ing nonsense. Now because we need fortune as well as other things, some people think good fortune the same thing as happiness; but it is not that, for even good fortune itself when in excess is an impediment, and perhaps should then be no longer called good fortune; for its limit is fixed by reference to happiness.

And indeed the fact that all things, both brutes and men, pursue pleasure is an in-   25
dication of its being somehow the chief good:

No voice is wholly lost that many peoples. . . .

But since no one nature or state either is or is thought the best for all, neither do all pursue the same pleasure; yet all pursue pleasure. And perhaps they actually pursue not the   30
pleasure they think they pursue nor that which they would say they pursue, but the same pleasure; for all things have by nature something divine in them. But the bodily pleasures have appropriated the name both because we oftenest steer our course for them   35
and because all men share in them; thus because they alone are familiar, men think there are no others.

1154ᵃ   It is evident also that if pleasure and activity is not a good, it will not be the case
that the happy man lives a pleasant life; for to what end should he need pleasure, if it is

5   not a good but the happy man may even live a painful life? For pain is neither an evil
nor a good, if pleasure is not; why then should he avoid it?

Therefore, too, the life of the good man will not be pleasanter than that of anyone
else, if his activities are not more pleasant.

14. With regard to the bodily pleasures, those who say that some pleasures are
very much to be chosen, viz. the noble pleasures, but not the bodily pleasures, i. e. those

10   with which the self-indulgent man is concerned, must consider why, then, the contrary
pains are bad. For the contrary of bad is good. Are the necessary pleasures good in the
sense in which even that which is not bad is good? Or are they good up to a point? Is it
that where you have states and processes of which there cannot be too much, there cannot be too much of the corresponding pleasure, and that where there can be too much of
the one there can be too much of the other also? Now there can be too much of bodily

15   goods, and the bad man is bad by virtue of pursuing the excess, not by virtue of pursuing the necessary pleasures (for *all* men enjoy in some way or other both dainty foods
and wines and sexual intercourse, but not all men do so as they ought). The contrary is

20   the case with pain; for he does not avoid the excess of it, he avoids it altogether; for the
alternative to excess of pleasure is not pain, except to the man who pursues this excess.

Since we should state not only the truth, but also the cause of error—for this
contributes towards producing conviction, since when a reasonable explanation is

25   given of why the false view appears true, this tends to produce belief in the true
view—therefore we must state why the bodily pleasures appear the more worthy of
choice. Firstly, then, it is because they expel pain; owing to the excesses of pain men
pursue excessive and in general bodily pleasure as being a cure for the pain. Now cu-

30   rative agencies produce intense feeling—which is the reason why they are pursued—
because they show up against the contrary pain. (Indeed pleasure is thought not to be
good for these two reasons, as has been said, viz. that some of them are activities belonging to a bad nature—either congenital, as in the case of a brute, or due to habit,
i.e. those of bad men; while others are meant to cure a defective nature, and it is bet-

1154ᵇ   ter to be in a healthy state than to be getting into it, but these arise during the process
of being made complete and are therefore only incidentally good.) Further, they are
pursued because of their violence by those who cannot enjoy other pleasures. At all

5   events some people manufacture thirsts for themselves. When these are harmless, the
practice is irreproachable; when they are hurtful, it is bad. For they have nothing else
to enjoy, and, besides, a neutral state is painful to many people because of their nature. For animals are always toiling, as the students of natural science also testify, say-

10   ing that sight and hearing are painful; but we have become used to this, as they maintain. Similarly, while, in youth, people are, owing to the growth that is going on, in a
situation like that of drunken men, and youth is pleasant, on the other hand people of
excitable nature always need relief; for even their body is ever in torment owing to its
special composition, and they are always under the influence of violent desire; but
pain is driven out both by the contrary pleasure, and by any chance pleasure if it be

15   strong; and for these reasons they become self-indulgent and bad. But the pleasures
that do not involve pains do not admit of excess; and these are among the things
pleasant by nature and not incidentally. By things pleasant incidentally I mean those
that act as cures (for because as a result people are cured, through some action of the
part that remains healthy, for this reason the process is thought pleasant); things natu-

20   rally pleasant are those that stimulate the action of the healthy nature.

There is no one thing that is always pleasant, because our nature is not simple but there is another element in us as well, inasmuch as we are perishable creatures, so that if the one element does something, this is unnatural to the other nature, and when the two elements are evenly balanced, what is done seems neither painful nor pleasant; for if the nature of anything were simple, the same action would always be most pleasant to   25
it. This is why God always enjoys a single and simple pleasure; for there is not only an activity of movement but an activity of immobility, and pleasure is found more in rest than in movement. But "change in all things is sweet," as the poet says, because of some vice; for as it is the vicious man that is changeable, so the nature that needs change is vi-   30
cious; for it is not simple nor good.

We have now discussed continence and incontinence, and pleasure and pain, both what each is and in what sense some of them are good and others bad. . . .

* * *

BOOK X

* * *

6. Now that we have spoken of the excellences, the forms of friendship, and the vari-   1176ᵃ
eties of pleasure, what remains is to discuss in outline the nature of happiness, since this   30
is what we state the end of human nature to be. Our discussion will be the more concise if we first sum up what we have said already. We said, then, that it is not a state; for if it were it might belong to some one who was asleep throughout his life, living the life of a plant, or, again, to some one who was suffering the greatest misfortunes. If these im-   35
plications are unacceptable, and we must rather class happiness as an activity, as we   1176ᵇ
have said before, and if some activities are necessary and desirable for the sake of something else, while others are so in themselves, evidently happiness must be placed among those desirable in themselves, not among those desirable for the sake of something else; for happiness does not lack anything, but is self-sufficient. Now those activ-   5
ities are desirable in themselves from which nothing is sought beyond the activity. And of this nature excellent actions are thought to be; for to do noble and good deeds is a thing desirable for its own sake.

Pleasant amusements also are thought to be of this nature; we choose them not for the sake of other things; for we are injured rather than benefited by them, since we are led   10
to neglect our bodies and our property. But most of the people who are deemed happy take refuge in such pastimes, which is the reason why those who are ready-witted at them are highly esteemed at the courts of tyrants; they make themselves pleasant companions in the tyrant's favourite pursuits, and that is the sort of man they want. Now these things   15
are thought to be of the nature of happiness because people in despotic positions spend their leisure in them, but perhaps such people prove nothing; for excellence and thought, from which good activities flow, do not depend on despotic position; nor, if these people, who have never tasted pure and generous pleasure, take refuge in the bodily pleasures,   20
should these for that reason be thought more desirable; for boys, too, think the things that are valued among themselves are the best. It is to be expected, then, that, as different things seem valuable to boys and to men, so they should to bad men and to good. Now, as we have often maintained, those things are both valuable and pleasant which are such to   25
the good man; and to each man the activity in accordance with his own state is most de-

sirable, and, therefore, to the good man that which is in accordance with excellence. Happiness, therefore, does not lie in amusement; it would, indeed, be strange if the end were amusement, and one were to take trouble and suffer hardship all one's life in order to amuse oneself. For, in a word, everything that we choose we choose for the sake of something else—except happiness, which is an end. Now to exert oneself and work for the
30   sake of amusement seems silly and utterly childish. But to amuse oneself in order that one may exert oneself, as Anacharsis puts it, seems right; for amusement is a sort of relaxation, and we need relaxation because we cannot work continuously. Relaxation, then, is
1177ª   not an end; for it is taken for the sake of activity.

The happy life is thought to be one of excellence; now an excellent life requires exertion, and does not consist in amusement. And we say that serious things are better than laughable things and those connected with amusement, and that the activity of the
5   better of any two things—whether it be two parts or two men—is the better; but the activity of the better is *ipso facto* superior and more of the nature of happiness. And any chance person even a slave—can enjoy the bodily pleasures no less than the best man; but no one assigns to a slave a share in happiness—unless he assigns to him also a share in human life. For happiness does not lie in such occupations, but, as we have said be-
10   fore, in excellent activities.

7. If happiness is activity in accordance with excellence, it is reasonable that it should be in accordance with the highest excellence; and this will be that of the best thing in us. Whether it be intellect or something else that is this element which is
15   thought to be our natural ruler and guide and to take thought of things noble and divine, whether it be itself also divine or only the most divine element in us, the activity of this in accordance with its proper excellence will be complete happiness. That this activity is contemplative we have already said.

Now this would seem to be in agreement both with what we said before and with
20   the truth. For this activity is the best (since not only is intellect the best thing in us, but the objects of intellect are the best of knowable objects); and, secondly, it is the most continuous, since we can contemplate truth more continuously than we can *do* anything. And we think happiness has pleasure mingled with it, but the activity of wisdom is admittedly the pleasantest of excellent activities; at all events philosophy is thought to of-
25   fer pleasures marvellous for their purity and their enduringness, and it is to be expected that those who know will pass their time more pleasantly than those who inquire. And the self-sufficiency that is spoken of must belong most to the contemplative activity. For while a wise man, as well as a just man and the rest, needs the necessaries of life, when they are sufficiently equipped with things of that sort the just man needs people
30   towards whom and with whom he shall act justly, and the temperate man, the brave man, and each of the others is in the same case, but the wise man, even when by himself, can contemplate truth, and the better the wiser he is; he can perhaps do so better if
1177ᵇ   he has fellow-workers, but still he is the most self-sufficient. And this activity alone would seem to be loved for its own sake; for nothing arises from it apart from the contemplating, while from practical activities we gain more or less apart from the action.
5   And happiness is thought to depend on leisure; for we are busy that we may have leisure, and make war that we may live in peace. Now the activity of the practical excellences is exhibited in political or military affairs, but the actions concerned with these seem to be unleisurely. Warlike actions are completely so (for no one chooses to
10   be at war, or provokes war, for the sake of being at war; anyone would seem absolutely murderous if he were to make enemies of his friends in order to bring about battle and slaughter); but the action of the statesman is also unleisurely, and—apart from the po-

litical action itself—aims at despotic power and honours, or at all events happiness, for him and his fellow citizens—a happiness different from political action, and evidently sought as being different. So if among excellent actions political and military 15 actions are distinguished by nobility and greatness, and these are unleisurely and aim at an end and are not desirable for their own sake, but the activity of intellect, which is contemplative, seems both to be superior in worth and to aim at no end beyond itself, and to have its pleasure proper to itself (and this augments the activity), and the 20 self-sufficiency, leisureliness, unweariedness (so far as this is possible for man), and all the other attributes ascribed to the blessed man are evidently those connected with this activity, it follows that this will be the complete happiness of man, if it be allowed 25 a complete term of life (for none of the attributes of happiness is *in*complete).

But such a life would be too high for man; for it is not in so far as he is man that he will live so, but in so far as something divine is present in him; and by so much as this is superior to our composite nature is its activity superior to that which is the exercise of the other kind of excellence. If intellect is divine, then, in comparison with man, 30 the life according to it is divine in comparison with human life. But we must not follow those who advise us, being men, to think of human things, and, being mortal, of mortal things, but must, so far as we can, make ourselves immortal, and strain every nerve to live in accordance with the best thing in us; for even if it be small in bulk, much more 1178a does it in power and worth surpass everything. This would seem, too, to be each man himself, since it is the authoritative and better part of him. It would be strange, then, if he were to choose not the life of himself but that of something else. And what we said before will apply now; that which is proper to each thing is by nature best and most 5 pleasant for each thing; for man, therefore, the life according to intellect is best and pleasantest, since intellect more than anything else *is* man. This life therefore is also the happiest.

8. But in a secondary degree the life in accordance with the other kind of excellence is happy; for the activities in accordance with this befit our human estate. Just and 10 brave acts, and other excellent acts, we do in relation to each other, observing what is proper to each with regard to contracts and services and all manner of actions and with regard to passions; and all of these seem to be human. Some of them seem even to arise from the body, and excellence of character to be in many ways bound up with the passions. Practical wisdom, too, is linked to excellence of character, and this to practical 15 wisdom, since the principles of practical wisdom are in accordance with the moral excellences and rightness in the moral excellences is in accordance with practical wisdom. Being connected with the passions also, the moral excellences must belong to our composite nature; and the excellences of our composite nature are human; so, therefore, are 20 the life and the happiness which correspond to these. The excellence of the intellect is a thing apart; we must be content to say this much about it, for to describe it precisely is a task greater than our purpose requires. It would seem, however, also to need external equipment but little, or less than moral excellence does. Grant that both need the necessaries, and do so equally, even if the statesman's work is the more concerned with the body and things of that sort; for there will be little difference there; but in what they need for the exercise of their activities there will be much difference. The liberal man will need money for the doing of his liberal deeds, and the just man too will need it for the returning of services (for wishes are hard to discern, and even people who are not 30 just pretend to wish to act justly); and the brave man will need power if he is to accomplish any of the acts that correspond to his excellence, and the temperate man will need opportunity; for how else is either he or any of the others to be recognized? It is de-

bated, too, whether the choice or the deed is more essential to excellence, which is assumed to involve both; it is surely clear that its completion involves both; but for deeds many things are needed, and more, the greater and nobler the deeds are. But the man who is contemplating the truth needs no such thing, at least with a view to the exercise of his activity; indeed they are, one may say, even hindrances, at all events to his contemplation; but in so far as he is a man and lives with a number of people, he chooses to do excellent acts; he will therefore need such aids to living a human life.

But that complete happiness is a contemplative activity will appear from the following consideration as well. We assume the gods to be above all other beings blessed and happy; but what sort of actions must we assign to them? Acts of justice? Will not the gods seem absurd if they make contracts and return deposits, and so on? Acts of a brave man, then, confronting dangers and running risks because it is noble to do so? Or liberal acts? To whom will they give? It will be strange if they are really to have money or anything of the kind. And what would their temperate acts be? Is not such praise tasteless, since they have no bad appetites? If we were to run through them all, the circumstances of action would be found trivial and unworthy of gods. Still, everyone supposes that they *live* and therefore that they are active; we cannot suppose them to sleep like Endymion. Now if you take away from a living being action, and still more production, what is left but contemplation? Therefore the activity of God, which surpasses all others in blessedness, must be contemplative; and of human activities, therefore, that which is most akin to this must be most of the nature of happiness.

This is indicated, too, by the fact that the other animals have no share in happiness, being completely deprived of such activity. For while the whole life of the gods is blessed, and that of men too in so far as some likeness of such activity belongs to them, none of the other animals is happy, since they in no way share in contemplation. Happiness extends, then, just so far as contemplation does, and those to whom contemplation more fully belongs are more truly happy, not accidentally, but in virtue of the contemplation; for this is in itself precious. Happiness, therefore, must be some form of contemplation.

But, being a man, one will also need external prosperity; for our nature is not self-sufficient for the purpose of contemplation, but our body also must be healthy and must have food and other attention. Still, we must not think that the man who is to be happy will need many things or great things, merely because he cannot be blessed without external goods; for self-sufficiency and action do not depend on excess, and we can do noble acts without ruling earth and sea; for even with moderate advantages one can act excellently (this is manifest enough; for private persons are thought to do worthy acts no less than despots—indeed even more); and it is enough that we should have so much as that; for the life of the man who is active in accordance with excellence will be happy. Solon, too, was perhaps sketching well the happy man when he described him as moderately furnished with externals but as having done (as Solon thought) the noblest acts, and lived temperately; for one can with but moderate possessions do what one ought. Anaxagoras also seems to have supposed the happy man not to be rich nor a despot, when he said that he would not be surprised if the happy man were to seem to most people a strange person; for they judge by externals, since these are all they perceive. The opinions of the wise seem, then, to harmonize with our arguments. But while even such things carry some conviction, the truth in practical matters is discerned from the facts of life; for these are the decisive factor. We must therefore survey what we have already said, bringing it to the test of the facts of life, and if it harmonizes with the facts we must accept it, but if it clashes with them we must suppose it to be mere theory. Now he who exercises his intellect and cultivates it seems to be both in the best state and most dear to the gods. For if the gods have any care for human affairs, as they are thought to have, it would be reasonable both that they should delight in that which was best and most   25 akin to them (i.e. intellect) and that they should reward those who love and honour this most, as caring for the things that are dear to them and acting both rightly and nobly. And that all these attributes belong most of all to the wise man is manifest. He therefore   30 is the dearest to the gods. And he who is that will presumably be also the happiest; so that in this way too the wise man will more than any other be happy.

Hellenistic and Roman Philosophy

Following the death of Alexander the Great in 323 B.C., three of his generals, Ptolemy, Seleucus, and Antigonus, carved up the empire he had created. For the next three centuries the descendants of these three men ruled the eastern Mediterranean world. By 30 B.C., with the Roman Emperor Octavian's defeat of Anthony and Cleopatra and the annexation of Egypt, the period of Greek rule (known as the "Hellenistic" period from the word ⟨*hellen*⟩, or "Greek") was over. Real power in the area had shifted westward to emerging Rome.

This shift from Greek to Roman authority did not happen without social and political turmoil, and the philosophies that developed during this period reflect that turmoil. Gone were the complete systems of thought proposed by Plato and Aristotle, and in their place were theories focusing on the practical questions of the good life for individuals. In a world that seemed more and more chaotic and uncontrollable, philosophers began to seek personal salvation more than comprehensive theories. Even the Platonic Academy and the Aristotelian Lyceum, which continued for centuries, moved from the constructive doctrines of their founders to more narrowly defined critical issues.

Reprinted in this section are selections from the three major Hellenistic schools—the Stoic, the Epicurean, and the Skeptical. All three of these schools continued into the Roman period and were adapted and modified by their Roman adherents. In order to understand these Hellenistic schools, we must return to Socrates for all three schools had roots in his life and teaching.

The roots of the Stoic school can be traced back to Socrates' follower Antisthenes. Antisthenes, a rhetorician with an Athenian father and a Phrygian, non-Greek mother, had been a teacher before he met Socrates, who made a profound impression on him. It seems to have been Socrates' character—his self-control and self-sufficiency, his indifference to winter cold (see the *Symposium*) and the opinions of others (see the *Apology*), his serenely ironic superiority in every experience—that struck Antisthenes with the force of revelation. What he learned from Socrates was neither a metaphysic nor even a philosophic method but, as he put it, "to live with myself." When he disposed of his possessions, keeping only a ragged old coat, Socrates is said to have taunted him: "I see your vanity through the holes of your coat." Antisthenes founded a school whose members acquired the nickname of "Cynics" ⟨*kynikos*⟩, Greek for "doglike." The Cynics slept on the ground, neglected their clothes, let their beards grow to unusual lengths, and despised the conventions of society, insisting that virtue and happiness consist in self-control and independence. They believed that human dignity was independent of human laws and customs.

Of Antisthenes' Cynic disciples none was more famous than Diogenes, who went about carrying a lantern in daylight and, when asked why, would reply, "I am looking for an honest man." He made his home in a tub. His eccentric behavior attracted the attention of even Alexander the Great, who, on visiting him, asked whether there was anything at all that he could do to please him. Diogenes replied: "Yes, get out of my sunlight."

Emphasizing self-control and independence, and locating human dignity outside law and convention, the Cynicism of Antisthenes and Diogenes flowed like a tributary into Stoicism. Stoicism, in turn, became the dominant philosophy of the Roman Empire.

Another early Socratic school, the Cyrenaics, was founded by one of Socrates' associates and admirers, Aristippus of Cyrene, from Libya, North Africa. The Cyrenaics disparaged speculative philosophy and extolled the pleasure of the moment. But, following Aristippus, they maintained that the purest pleasure derives from self-mastery and the philosophic life. Only philosophy can protect human beings from passion, which inevitably brings suffering. While despising popular opinion, the Cyrenaics did believe that custom, law, and altruism contributed to long-range pleasure. The Cyrenaic philosophy, with its understanding of the good life as enjoyment of stable pleasures, led to the development of the Epicurean school.

A third Hellenistic school of philosophy, Skepticism, also had its roots in Socrates' teachings: specifically, in Socrates' repeated claim that he did not know anything. Based on the work of Pyrrho of Elis (ca. 360–270 B.C.), this movement stressed the contradictory nature of knowledge and advocated suspending judgment and achieving an attitude of detachment.

Reviewing the development of Greek philosophy from the Pre-Socratics to the Stoics, Epicureans, and Skeptics, one is struck by the overwhelming concern in the later schools with peace of mind. There is, as a consequence, one quality that preclassical and classical Greeks possessed preeminently and that Stoics, Epicureans, and Skeptics preeminently lacked: enthusiasm. But there was another movement developing in the ancient world—one that abounded in enthusiasm and changed the course of Western philosophy: Christianity. Though the

Laocoön, second century B.C., by Hagesandros, Polydoros, and Athenodoros, all of Rhodes. The Trojan prince Laocoön protested against bringing the Greeks' wooden horse into the city. According to one version of the legend, he was punished for his interference when Apollo sent two serpents to kill him and his sons. The Hellenistic philosophers sought relief from tortured emotions such as this work depicts. (Hirmer Fotoarchiv)

dates of this movement overlap the dates of the philosophers in this volume, I have chosen to save the Christian story for Volume II as an introduction to medieval philosophy.

The last great movement of Greek philosophy was Neoplatonism. The leader of this return to Platonic concepts, Plotinus (A.D. 204–270), did not lack enthusiasm, but he was, nevertheless, more remote from classical Greek attitudes than were the Hellenistic philosophers. He extolled the spirit to the point of saying he was ashamed to have a body; his fervor was entirely mystical, and he longed, to cite his famous words, to attain "the flight of the Alone to the Alone." Thus he perfected the less classical tendencies of Plato's thought, merging those tendencies with Neopythagoreanism and with Oriental notions such as the emanations from the One.

In A.D. 529, Plato's Academy was closed by Emperor Justinian, bringing to an end a millennium of Greek philosophy.

*   *   *

For clear, concise introductions to the Hellenistic and Roman philosophers, see Frederick Copleston, "Post-Aristotelian Philosophy," in his *A History of Philosophy: Volume I, Greece and Rome, Part II* (Garden City, NY: Image Books, 1962), and D.W. Hamlyn, "Greek Philosophy after Aristotle," in D.J. O'Connor, ed., *A Critical History of Western Philosophy* (New York: Free Press, 1964). Eduard Zeller, *The Stoics, Epicureans, and Sceptics,* translated by Oswald J. Reichel (New York: Russell & Russell, 1962); Émile Bréhier, *The Hellenistic and Roman Age,* translated by Wade Baskin (Chicago: University of Chicago Press, 1965); and A.A. Long, *Hellenistic Philosophy: Stoics, Epicureans, Scep-*

tics (New York: Scribners, 1974), are all solid histories of the period, while A.A. Long and D.N. Sedley, eds., *The Hellenistic Philosophers* (Cambridge: Cambridge University Press, 1987), provide source material. For primary sources and helpful introductions, see Whitney J. Oates, *The Stoic and Epicurean Philosophers: The Complete Extant Writings of Epicurus, Epictetus, Lucretius, Marcus Aurelius* (New York: Random House, 1940).

Epicurus
341–270 B.C.

Epicurus was born, like Pythagoras, on the Greek island of Samos, approximately seven years after Plato's death. At eighteen he went to Athens for a year, then joined his father in Colophon, the city where Xenophanes had been born. He studied the writings of Democritus and eventually set up his own school on the island of Lesbos. From there he moved to the Hellespont and, finally, to Athens in 307 B.C. As he moved from place to place, many of his students followed him. In Athens he established a community known as the "Garden" where he spent the rest of his life teaching and writing.

Epicurus' community welcomed people of all classes and of both sexes. The school required no fee from students, accepting what each individual was able and willing to pay. Epicurus himself was almost worshiped by his disciples, and members of his group had to swear an oath; "I will be faithful to Epicurus in accordance with whom I have made it my choice to live."* Among the later followers of Epicurus' thought, the Roman poet Lucretius (98–55 B.C.) considered him to be a god. Yet Epicurus was not overbearing or authoritarian. According to all accounts, he was kind and generous, treating his followers as friends, not subordinates. While dying in agony from a

*Reported in J.V. Luce, *Introduction to Greek Philosophy* (New York: Thames and Hudson, 1992), p. 140.

urinary obstruction, Epicurus wrote a letter that illustrates his gracious spirit. The extant portion includes these words to his friend Idomeneus: "I have a bulwark against all this pain from the joy in my soul at the memory of our conversations together."*

Epicurus wrote over three hundred volumes, but all that has survived are some fragments, three complete letters, and a short treatise summarizing his views. These surviving works provide an understanding of Epicurus' physics and his ethics and give some sense of his psychology and theory of knowledge. Epicurus' first letter, *To Herodotus,* explains his atomistic theory. Like Democritus, Epicurus asserts that reality is composed of atoms and the void. But unlike Democritus, whose atomism is deterministic, Epicurus broaches the notion that atoms sometimes inexplicably "swerve." As atoms "fell downward" through the void, some of them swerved from their paths and collided with other atoms, setting off a chain reaction that eventually led to the world as we know it. Epicurus goes on to explore the implications of this theory for perception and knowledge.

The second letter, *To Pythocles,* on astronomy and meteorology, is of questionable origin and adds little to our understanding of Epicurus' thought. But the third letter, *To Menoeceus,* together with the short work, *Principle Doctrines,* explains his central ethical theory. Epicurus declares that pleasure is the highest good, though some pleasures are unnatural and unnecessary. In contrast to the modern understanding of the word "epicurean," Epicurus opposed exotic meals and profuse consumption. Such indulgences never bring permanent pleasure and frequently lead to its opposite: pain. Instead Epicurus advocates enjoying only the "natural" pleasures—those most likely to lead to contentment and repose.

The surviving complete works were incorporated by Diogenes Laertius in his *Lives of Eminent Philosophers.* Using the Cyril Bailey translation, all but the second letter are given here.

*   *   *

The classic secondary work on Epicurus is Cyril Bailey, *The Greek Atomists and Epicurus* (Oxford: Clarendon Press, 1928). Norman Wentworth De Witt, *Epicurus and His Philosophy* (Minneapolis: University of Minnesota Press, 1954), provides an interesting interpretation—one which John M. Rist, *Epicurus: An Introduction* (Cambridge: Cambridge University Press, 1972), contests. A.E. Taylor, *Epicurus* (1911; reprinted New York: Books for Libraries Press, 1969); G.K. Stradach, *The Philosophy of Epicurus* (Evanston, IL: Northwestern University Press, 1963); and Diskin Clay, *Lucretius and Epicurus* (Ithaca, NY: Cornell University Press, 1983), give helpful overviews. A.J. Festugière, *Epicurus and His Gods,* translated by C.W. Chilton (1955; reprinted London: Russell, 1969), and James H. Nichols, Jr., *Epicurean Political Philosophy* (Ithaca, NY: Cornell University Press, 1976), deal with specific topics.

*Ibid.

EPICURUS TO HERODOTUS

For those who are unable, Herodotus, to work in detail through all that I have written about nature, or to peruse the larger books which I have composed, I have already prepared at sufficient length an epitome of the whole system, that they may keep adequately in mind at least the most general principles in each department, in order that as occasion arises they may be able to assist themselves on the most important points, in so far as they undertake the study of nature. But those also who have made considerable progress in the survey of the main principles ought to bear in mind the scheme of the whole system set forth in its essentials. For we have frequent need of the general view, but not so often of the detailed exposition. Indeed it is necessary to go back on the main principles, and constantly to fix in one's memory enough to give one the most essential comprehension of the truth. And in fact the accurate knowledge of details will be fully discovered, if the general principles in the various departments are thoroughly grasped and borne in mind; for even in the case of one fully initiated the most essential feature in all accurate knowledge is the capacity to make a rapid use of observation and mental apprehension, and this can be done if everything is summed up in elementary principles and formulae. For it is not possible for anyone to abbreviate the complete course through the whole system, if he cannot embrace in his own mind by means of short formulae all that might be set out with accuracy in detail. Wherefore since the method I have described is valuable to all those who are accustomed to the investigation of nature, I who urge upon others the constant occupation in the investigation of nature, and find my own peace chiefly in a life so occupied, have composed for you another epitome on these lines, summing up the first principles of the whole doctrine.

First of all, Herodotus, we must grasp the ideas attached to words, in order that we may be able to refer to them and so to judge the inferences of opinion or problems of investigation or reflection, so that we may not either leave everything uncertain and go on explaining to infinity or use words devoid of meaning. For this purpose it is essential that the first mental image associated with each word should be regarded, and that there should be no need of explanation, if we are really to have a standard to which to refer a problem of investigation or reflection or a mental inference. And besides we must keep all our investigations in accord with our sensations, and in particular with the immediate apprehensions whether of the mind or of any one of the instruments of judgement, and likewise in accord with the feelings existing in us, in order that we may have indications whereby we may judge both the problem of sense-perception and the unseen.

Having made these points clear, we must now consider things imperceptible to the senses. First of all, that nothing is created out of that which does not exist: for if it were, everything would be created out of everything with no need of seeds. And again, if that which disappears were destroyed into that which did not exist, all things would have perished, since that into which they were dissolved would not exist. Furthermore, the universe always was such as it is now, and always will be the same. For there is nothing into which it changes: for outside the universe there is nothing which could come into it and bring about the change.

Epicurus, *Letter to Herodotus,* from Epicurus, *The Extant Remains,* translated by Cyril Bailey (Oxford: The Clarendon Press, 1926). Reprinted by permission of Oxford University Press.

Moreover, the universe is bodies and space: for that bodies exist, sense itself witnesses in the experience of all men, and in accordance with the evidence of sense we must of necessity judge of the imperceptible by reasoning, as I have already said. And if there were not that which we term void and place and intangible existence, bodies would have nowhere to exist and nothing through which to move, as they are seen to move. And besides these two nothing can even be thought of either by conception or on the analogy of things conceivable such as could be grasped as whole existences and not spoken of as the accidents or properties of such existences. Furthermore, among bodies some are compounds, and others those of which compounds are formed. And these latter are indivisible and unalterable (if, that is, all things are not to be destroyed into the non-existent, but something permanent is to remain behind at the dissolution of compounds): they are completely solid in nature, and can by no means be dissolved in any part. So it must needs be that the first-beginnings are indivisible corporeal existences.

Moreover, the universe is boundless. For that which is bounded has an extreme point: and the extreme point is seen against something else. So that as it has no extreme point, it has no limit; and as it has no limit, it must be boundless and not bounded. Furthermore, the infinite is boundless both in the number of the bodies and in the extent of the void. For if on the one hand the void were boundless, and the bodies limited in number, the bodies could not stay anywhere, but would be carried about and scattered through the infinite void, not having other bodies to support them and keep them in place by means of collisions. But if, on the other hand, the void were limited, the infinite bodies would not have room wherein to take their place.

Besides this the indivisible and solid bodies, out of which too the compounds are created and into which they are dissolved, have an incomprehensible number of varieties in shape: for it is not possible that such great varieties of things should arise from the same atomic shapes, if they are limited in number. And so in each shape the atoms are quite infinite in number, but their differences of shape are not quite infinite, but only incomprehensible in number.

And the atoms move continuously for all time, some of them falling straight down, others swerving, and others recoiling from their collisions. And of the latter, some are borne on, separating to a long distance from one another, while others again recoil and recoil, whenever they chance to be checked by the interlacing with others, or else shut in by atoms interlaced around them. For on the one hand the nature of the void which separates each atom by itself brings this about, as it is not able to afford resistance, and on the other hand the hardness which belongs to the atoms makes them recoil after collision to as great a distance as the interlacing permits separation after the collision. And these motions have no beginning, since the atoms and the void are the cause.

These brief sayings, if all these points are borne in mind, afford a sufficient outline for our understanding of the nature of existing things.

Furthermore, there are infinite worlds both like and unlike this world of ours. For the atoms being infinite in number, as was proved already, are borne on far out into space. For those atoms, which are of such nature that a world could be created out of them or made by them, have not been used up either on one world or on a limited number of worlds, nor again on all the worlds which are alike, or on those which are different from these. So that there nowhere exists an obstacle to the infinite number of the worlds.

Moreover, there are images like in shape to the solid bodies, far surpassing perceptible things in their subtlety of texture. For it is not impossible that such emanations should be formed in that which surrounds the objects, nor that there should be opportunities for the formation of such hollow and thin frames, nor that there should be effluences which preserve the respective position and order which they had before in the solid bodies: these images we call idols.

Next, nothing among perceptible things contradicts the belief that the images have unsurpassable fineness of texture. And for this reason they have also unsurpassable speed of motion, since the movement of all their atoms is uniform, and besides nothing or very few things hinder their emission by collisions, whereas a body composed of many or infinite atoms is at once hindered by collisions. Besides this, nothing contradicts the belief that the creation of the idols takes place as quick as thought. For the flow of atoms from the surface of bodies is continuous, yet it cannot be detected by any lessening in the size of the object because of the constant filling up of what is lost. The flow of images preserves for a long time the position and order of the atoms in the solid body, though it is occasionally confused. Moreover, compound idols are quickly formed in the air around, because it is not necessary for their substance to be filled in deep inside: and besides there are certain other methods in which existences of this sort are produced. For not one of these beliefs is contradicted by our sensations, if one looks to see in what way sensation will bring us the clear visions from external objects, and in what way again the corresponding sequences of qualities and movements.

Now we must suppose too that it is when something enters us from external objects that we not only see but think of their shapes. For external objects could not make on us an impression of the nature of their own colour and shape by means of the air which lies between us and them, nor again by means of the rays or effluences of any sort which pass from us to them—nearly so well as if models, similar in colour and shape, leave the objects and enter according to their respective size either into our sight or into our mind; moving along swiftly, and so by this means reproducing the image of a single continuous thing and preserving the corresponding sequence of qualities and movements from the original object as the result of their uniform contact with us, kept up by the vibration of the atoms deep in the interior of the concrete body.

And every image which we obtain by an act of apprehension on the part of the mind or of the sense-organs, whether of shape or of properties, this image is the shape or the properties of the concrete object, and is produced by the constant repetition of the image or the impression it has left. Now falsehood and error always lie in the addition of opinion with regard to what is waiting to be confirmed or not contradicted, and then is not confirmed or is contradicted. For the similarity between the things which exist, which we call real and the images received as a likeness of things and produced either in sleep or through some other acts of apprehension on the part of the mind or the other instruments of judgement, could never be, unless there were some effluences of this nature actually brought into contact with our senses. And error would not exist unless another kind of movement too were produced inside ourselves, closely linked to the apprehension of images, but differing from it; and it is owing to this, supposing it is not confirmed, or is contradicted, that falsehood arises; but if it is confirmed or not contradicted, it is true. Therefore we must do our best to keep this doctrine in mind, in order that on the one hand the standards of judgement dependent on the clear visions may not be undermined, and on the other error may not be as firmly established as truth and so throw all into confusion.

Moreover, hearing, too, results when a current is carried off from the object speaking or sounding or making a noise, or causing in any other way a sensation of hearing. Now this current is split up into particles, each like the whole, which at the same time preserve a correspondence of qualities with one another and a unity of character which stretches right back to the object which emitted the sound: this unity it is which in most cases produces comprehension in the recipient, or, if not, merely makes manifest the presence of the external object. For without the transference from the object of some correspondence of qualities, comprehension of this nature could not result. We must not then suppose that the actual air is moulded into shape by the voice which is emitted or by other similar sounds—for it will be very far from being so acted upon by it—but that the blow which takes place inside us, when we emit our voice, causes at once a squeezing out of certain particles, which produce a stream of breath, of such a character as to afford us the sensation of hearing.

Furthermore, we must suppose that smell too, just like hearing, could never bring about any sensation, unless there were certain particles carried off from the object of suitable size to stir this sense-organ, some of them in a manner disorderly and alien to it, others in a regular manner and akin in nature.

Moreover, we must suppose that the atoms do not possess any of the qualities belonging to perceptible things, except shape, weight, and size, and all that necessarily goes with shape. For every quality changes; but the atoms do not change at all, since there must needs be something which remains solid and indissoluble at the dissolution of compounds, which can cause changes; not changes into the non-existent or from the non-existent, but changes effected by the shifting of position of some particles, and by the addition or departure of others. For this reason it is essential that the bodies which shift their position should be imperishable and should not possess the nature of what changes, but parts and configuration of their own. For thus much must needs remain constant. For even in things perceptible to us which change their shape by the withdrawal of matter it is seen that shape remains to them, whereas the qualities do not remain in the changing object, in the way in which shape is left behind, but are lost from the entire body. Now these particles which are left behind are sufficient to cause the differences in compound bodies, since it is essential that some things should be left behind and not be destroyed into the non-existent.

Moreover, we must not either suppose that every size exists among the atoms, in order that the evidence of phenomena may not contradict us, but we must suppose that there are some variations of size. For if this be the case, we can give a better account of what occurs in our feelings and sensations. But the existence of atoms of every size is not required to explain the differences of qualities in things, and at the same time some atoms would be bound to come within our ken and be visible; but this is never seen to be the case, nor is it possible to imagine how an atom could become visible.

Besides this we must not suppose that in a limited body there can be infinite parts or parts of every degree of smallness. Therefore, we must not only do away with division into smaller and smaller parts to infinity, in order that we may not make all things weak, and so in the composition of aggregate bodies be compelled to crush and squander the things that exist into the non-existent, but we must not either suppose that in limited bodies there is a possibility of continuing to infinity in passing even to smaller and smaller parts. For if once one says that there are infinite parts in a body or parts of any degree of smallness, it is not possible to conceive how this should be, and indeed how could the body any longer be limited in size? (For it is obvious that these infinite particles must be of some size or other; and however small they may be, the size of the body too would be infinite.) And again, since the limited body has an extreme point, which is distinguishable, even though not perceptible by itself, you cannot conceive that the succeeding point to it is not similar in character, or that if you go on in this way from one point to another, it should be possible for you to proceed to infinity marking such points in your mind. We must notice also that the least thing in sensation is neither exactly like that which admits of progression from one part to another, nor again is it in every respect wholly unlike it, but it has a certain affinity with such bodies, yet cannot be divided into parts. But when on the analogy of this resemblance we think to divide off parts of it, one on the one side and another on the other, it must needs be that another point like the first meets our view. And we look at these points in succession starting from the first, not within the limits of the same point nor in contact part with part, but yet by means of their own proper characteristics measuring the size of bodies, more in a greater body and fewer in a smaller. Now we must suppose that the least part in the atom too bears the same relation to the whole; for though in smallness it is obvious that it exceeds that which is seen by sensation, yet it has the same relations. For indeed we have already declared on the ground of its relation to sensible bodies that the atom has size, only we placed it far below them in smallness. Further, we must consider these least indivisible points as boundary-marks, providing in themselves as primary units the measure of size for the atoms, both for the smaller and the greater, in our contemplation of these unseen bodies by means of thought. For the affinity which the least parts of the atom have to the homogeneous parts of sensible things is sufficient to justify our conclusion to this extent: but that they should ever come together as bodies with motion is quite impossible.

[Furthermore, in the infinite we must not speak of "up" or "down," as though with reference to an absolute highest or lowest—and indeed we must say that, though it is possible to proceed to infinity in the direction above our heads from wherever we take our stand, the absolute highest point will never appear to us—nor yet can that which passes beneath the point thought of to infinity be at the same time both up and down in reference to the same thing: for it is impossible to think this. So that it is possible to consider as one single motion that which is thought of as the upward motion to infinity and as another the downward motion, even though that which passes from us into the regions above our heads arrives countless times at the feet of beings above and that which passes downwards from us at the head of beings below; for none the less the whole motions are thought of as opposed, the one to the other, to infinity.]

Moreover, the atoms must move with equal speed, when they are borne onwards through the void, nothing colliding with them. For neither will the heavy move more quickly than the small and light, when, that is, nothing meets them: nor again the small more quickly than the great, having their whole course uniform, when nothing collides with them either: nor is the motion upwards or sideways owing to blows quicker, nor again that downwards owing to their own weight. For as long as either of the two motions prevails, so long will it have a course as quick as thought, until something checks it either from outside or from its own weight counteracting the force of that which dealt the blow. Moreover, their passage through the void, when it takes place without meeting any bodies which might collide, accomplishes every comprehensible distance in an inconceivably short time. For it is collision and its absence which take the outward appearance of slowness and quickness. Moreover, it will be said that in compound bodies too one atom is faster than another, though as a matter of fact all are equal in speed: this will be said because even in the least period of continuous time all the atoms in aggregate bodies move towards one place, even though in moments of time perceptible only by thought they do not move towards one place but are constantly jostling one against another, until the continuity of their movement comes under the ken of sensation. For the addition of opinion with regard to the unseen, that the moments perceptible only by thought will also contain continuity of motion, is not true in such cases; for we must remember that it is what we observe with the senses or grasp with the mind by an apprehension that is true. Nor must it either be supposed that in moments perceptible only by thought the moving body too passes to the several places to which its component atoms move (for this too is unthinkable, and in that case, when it arrives all together in a sensible period of time from any point that may be in the infinite void, it would not be taking its departure from the place from which we apprehend its motion); for the motion of the whole body will be the outward expression of its internal collisions, even though up to the limits of perception we suppose the speed of its motion not to be retarded by collision. It is of advantage to grasp this first principle as well.

Next, referring always to the sensations and the feelings, for in this way you will obtain the most trustworthy ground of belief, you must consider that the soul is a body of fine particles distributed throughout the whole structure, and most resembling wind with a certain admixture of heat, and in some respects like to one of these and in some to the other. There is also the part which is many degrees more advanced even than these in fineness of composition, and for this reason is more capable of feeling in harmony with the rest of the structure as well. Now all this is made manifest by the activities of the soul and the feelings and the readiness of its movements and its processes of thought and by what we lose at the moment of death. Further, you must grasp that the soul possesses the chief cause of sensation: yet it could not have acquired sensation, unless it were in some way enclosed by the rest of the structure. And this in its turn having afforded the soul this cause of sensation acquires itself too a share in this contingent capacity from the soul. Yet it does not acquire all the capacities which the soul possesses: and therefore when the soul is released from the body, the body no longer has sensation. For it never possessed this power in itself, but used to afford opportunity for it to another existence, brought into being at the same time with itself: and this existence, owing to the power now consummated within itself as a result of motion, used spontaneously to produce for itself the capacity of sensation and then to communicate it to the body as well, in virtue of its contact and correspondence of movement, as I have already said. Therefore, so long as the soul remains in the body, even though some other part of the body be lost, it will never lose sensation; nay more, whatever portions of the soul may perish too, when that which enclosed it is removed either in whole or in part, if the soul continues to exist at all, it will retain sensation. On the other hand the rest of the structure, though it continues to exist either as a whole or in part, does not retain sensation, if it has once lost that sum of atoms, however small it be, which together goes to produce the nature of the soul. Moreover, if the whole structure is dissolved, the soul is dispersed and no longer has the same powers nor performs its movements, so that it does not possess sensation either. For it is impossible to imagine it with sensation, if it is not in this organism and cannot effect these movements, when what encloses and surrounds it is no longer the same as the surroundings in which it now exists and performs these movements. Furthermore, we must clearly comprehend as well, that the incorporeal in the general acceptation of the term is applied to that which could be thought of as such as an independent existence. Now it is impossible to conceive the incorporeal as a separate existence, except the void: and the void can neither act nor be acted upon, but only provides opportunity of motion through itself to bodies. So that those who say that the soul is incorporeal are talking idly. For it would not be able to act or be acted on in any respect, if it were of this nature. But as it is, both these occurrences are clearly distinguished in respect of the soul. Now if one refers all these reasonings about the soul to the standards of feeling and sensation and remembers what was said at the outset, he will see that they are sufficiently embraced in these general formulae to enable him to work out with certainty on this basis the details of the system as well.

Moreover, as regards shape and colour and size and weight and all other things that are predicated of body, as though they were concomitant properties either of all things or of things visible or recognizable through the sensation of these qualities, we must not suppose that they are either independent existences (for it is impossible to imagine that), nor that they absolutely do not exist, nor that they are some other kind of incorporeal existence accompanying body, nor that they are material parts of body:

rather we should suppose that the whole body in its totality owes its own permanent existence to all these, yet not in the sense that it is composed of properties brought together to form it (as when, for instance, a larger structure is put together out of the parts which compose it, whether the first units of size or other parts smaller than itself, whatever it is), but only, as I say, that it owes its own permanent existence to all of them. All these properties have their own peculiar means of being perceived and distinguished, provided always that the aggregate body goes along with them and is never wrested from them, but in virtue of its comprehension as an aggregate of qualities acquires the predicate of body.

Furthermore, there often happen to bodies and yet do not permanently accompany them accidents, of which we must suppose neither that they do not exist at all nor that they have the nature of a whole body, nor that they can be classed among unseen things nor as incorporeal. So that when according to the most general usage we employ this name, we make it clear that accidents have neither the nature of the whole, which we comprehend in its aggregate and call body, nor that of the qualities which permanently accompany it, without which a given body cannot be conceived. But as the result of certain acts of apprehension, provided the aggregate body goes along with them, they might each be given this name, but only on occasions when each one of them is seen to occur, since accidents are not permanent accompaniments. And we must not banish this clear vision from the realm of existence, because it does not possess the nature of the whole to which it is joined nor that of the permanent accompaniments, nor must we suppose that such contingencies exist independently (for this is inconceivable both with regard to them and to the permanent properties), but, just as it appears in sensation, we must think of them all as accidents occurring to bodies, and that not as permanent accompaniments, or again as having in themselves a place in the ranks of material existence; rather they are seen to be just what our actual sensation shows their proper character to be.

Moreover, you must firmly grasp this point as well; we must not look for time, as we do for all other things which we look for in an object, by referring them to the general conceptions which we perceive in our own minds, but we must take the direct intuition, in accordance with which we speak of "a long time" or "a short time," and examine it, applying our intuition to time as we do to other things. Neither must we search for expressions as likely to be better, but employ just those which are in common use about it. Nor again must we predicate of time anything else as having the same essential nature as this special perception, as some people do, but we must turn our thoughts particularly to that only with which we associate this peculiar perception and by which we measure it. For indeed this requires no demonstration, but only reflection, to show that it is with days and nights and their divisions that we associate it and likewise also with internal feelings or absence of feeling, and with movements and states of rest; in connexion with these last again we think of this very perception as a peculiar kind of accident, and in virtue of this we call it time.

And in addition to what we have already said we must believe that worlds, and indeed every limited compound body which continuously exhibits a similar appearance to the things we see, were created from the infinite, and that all such things, greater and less alike, were separated off from individual agglomerations of matter; and that all are again dissolved, some more quickly, some more slowly, some suffering from one set of causes, others from another. And further we must believe that these worlds were neither created all of necessity with one configuration nor yet with every kind of shape. Furthermore, we must believe that in all worlds there are living creatures and plants and other things we see in this world; for indeed no one could prove that in a world of one kind there might or might not have been included the kinds of seeds from which living things and plants and all the rest of the things we see are composed, and that in a world of another kind they could not have been.

Moreover, we must suppose that human nature too was taught and constrained to do many things of every kind merely by circumstances; and that later on reasoning elaborated what had been suggested by nature and made further inventions, in some matters quickly, in others slowly, at some epochs and times making great advances, and lesser again at others. And so names too were not at first deliberately given to things, but men's natures according to their different nationalities had their own peculiar feelings and received their peculiar impressions, and so each in their own way emitted air formed into shape by each of these feelings and impressions, according to the differences made in the different nations by the places of their abode as well. And then later on by common consent in each nationality special names were deliberately given in order to make their meanings less ambiguous to one another and more briefly demonstrated. And sometimes those who were acquainted with them brought in things hitherto unknown and introduced sounds for them, on some occasions being naturally constrained to utter them, and on others choosing them by reasoning in accordance with the prevailing mode of formation, and thus making their meaning clear.

Furthermore, the motions of the heavenly bodies and their turnings and eclipses and risings and settings, and kindred phenomena to these, must not be thought to be due to any being who controls and ordains or has ordained them and at the same time enjoys perfect bliss together with immortality (for trouble and care and anger and kindness are not consistent with a life of blessedness, but these things come to pass where there is weakness and fear and dependence on neighbours). Nor again must we believe that they, which are but fire agglomerated in a mass, possess blessedness, and voluntarily take upon themselves these movements. But we must preserve their full majestic significance in all expressions which we apply to such conceptions, in order that there may not arise out of them opinions contrary to this notion of majesty. Otherwise this very contradiction will cause the greatest disturbance in men's souls. Therefore we must believe that it is due to the original inclusion of matter in such agglomerations during the birth-process of the world that this law of regular succession is also brought about.

Furthermore, we must believe that to discover accurately the cause of the most essential facts is the function of the science of nature, and that blessedness for us in the knowledge of celestial phenomena lies in this and in the understanding of the nature of the existences seen in these celestial phenomena, and of all else that is akin to the exact knowledge requisite for our happiness: in knowing too that what occurs in several ways or is capable of being otherwise has no place here but that nothing which suggests doubt or alarm can be included at all in that which is naturally immortal and blessed. Now this we can ascertain by our mind is absolutely the case. But what falls within the investigation of risings and settings and turnings and eclipses, and all that is akin to this, is no longer of any value for the happiness which knowledge brings, but persons who have perceived all this, but yet do not know what are the natures of these things and what are the essential causes, are still in fear, just as if they did not know these things at all: indeed, their fear may be even greater, since the wonder which arises out of the observation of these things cannot discover any solution or realize the regulation of the essentials. And for this very reason, even if we discover several causes for turnings and settings and risings and eclipses and the like, as has been the case already in our investigation of detail, we must not suppose that our inquiry into these things has not reached sufficient accuracy to contribute to our peace of mind and happiness. So we must carefully consider in how many ways a similar phenomenon is produced on earth, when we reason about the causes of celestial phenomena and all that is imperceptible to the senses; and we must despise those persons who do not recognize either what exists or comes into being in one way only, or that which may occur in several ways in the case of things which can only be seen by us from a distance, and further are not aware under what conditions it is impossible to have peace of mind. If, therefore, we think that a phenomenon probably occurs in some such particular way, and that in circumstances under which it is equally possible for us to be at peace, when we realize that it may occur in several ways, we shall be just as little disturbed as if we know that it occurs in some particular way.

And besides all these matters in general we must grasp this point, that the principal disturbance in the minds of men arises because they think that these celestial bodies are blessed and immortal, and yet have wills and actions and motives inconsistent with these attributes; and because they are always expecting or imagining some everlasting misery, such as is depicted in legends, or even fear the loss of feeling in death as though it would concern them themselves; and, again, because they are brought to this pass not by reasoned opinion, but rather by some irrational presentiment, and therefore, as they do not know the limits of pain, they suffer a disturbance equally great or even more extensive than if they had reached this belief by opinion. But peace of mind is being delivered from all this, and having a constant memory of the general and most essential principles.

Wherefore we must pay attention to internal feelings and to external sensations in general and in particular, according as the subject is general or particular, and to every immediate intuition in accordance with each of the standards of judgement. For if we pay attention to these, we shall rightly trace the causes whence arose our mental disturbance and fear, and, by learning the true causes of celestial phenomena and all other occurrences that come to pass from time to time, we shall free ourselves from all which produces the utmost fear in other men.

Here, Herodotus, is my treatise on the chief points concerning the nature of the general principles, abridged so that my account would be easy to grasp with accuracy. I think that, even if one were unable to proceed to all the detailed particulars of the system, he would from this obtain an unrivalled strength compared with other men. For indeed he will clear up for himself many of the detailed points by reference to our general system, and these very principles, if he stores them in his mind, will constantly aid him. For such is their character that even those who are at present engaged in working out the details to a considerable degree, or even completely, will be able to carry out the greater part of their investigations into the nature of the whole by conducting their analysis in reference to such a survey as this. And as for all who are not fully among those on the way to being perfected, some of them can from this summary obtain a hasty view of the most important matters without oral instruction so as to secure peace of mind.

EPICURUS TO MENOECEUS

Let no one when young delay to study philosophy, nor when he is old grow weary of his study. For no one can come too early or too late to secure the health of his soul. And the man who says that the age for philosophy has either not yet come or has gone by is like

Epicurus, *Letter to Menoeceus,* from Epicurus, *The Extant Remains,* translated by Cyril Bailey (Oxford: The Clarendon Press, 1926). Reprinted by permission of Oxford University Press.

the man who says that the age for happiness is not yet come to him, or has passed away. Wherefore both when young and old a man must study philosophy, that as he grows old he may be young in blessings through the grateful recollection of what has been, and that in youth he may be old as well, since he will know no fear of what is to come. We must then meditate on the things that make our happiness, seeing that when that is with us we have all, but when it is absent we do all to win it.

The things which I used unceasingly to commend to you, these do and practise, considering them to be the first principles of the good life. First of all believe that god is a being immortal and blessed, even as the common idea of a god is engraved on men's minds, and do not assign to him anything alien to his immortality or ill-suited to his blessedness: but believe about him everything that can uphold his blessedness and immortality. For gods there are, since the knowledge of them is by clear vision. But they are not such as the many believe them to be: for indeed they do not consistently represent them as they believe them to be. And the impious man is not he who denies the gods of the many, but he who attaches to the gods the beliefs of the many. For the statements of the many about the gods are not conceptions derived from sensation, but false suppositions, according to which the greatest misfortunes befall the wicked and the greatest blessings the good by the gift of the gods. For men being accustomed always to their own virtues welcome those like themselves, but regard all that is not of their nature as alien.

Become accustomed to the belief that death is nothing to us. For all good and evil consists in sensation, but death is deprivation of sensation. And therefore a right understanding that death is nothing to us makes the mortality of life enjoyable, not because it adds to it an infinite span of time, but because it takes away the craving for immortality. For there is nothing terrible in life for the man who has truly comprehended that there is nothing terrible in not living. So that the man speaks but idly who says that he fears death not because it will be painful when it comes, but because it is painful in anticipation. For that which gives no trouble when it comes, is but an empty pain in anticipation. So death, the most terrifying of ills, is nothing to us, since so long as we exist, death is not with us; but when death comes, then we do not exist. It does not then concern either the living or the dead, since for the former it is not, and the latter are no more.

But the many at one moment shun death as the greatest of evils, at another yearn for it as a respite from the evils in life. But the wise man neither seeks to escape life nor fears the cessation of life, for neither does life offend him nor does the absence of life seem to be any evil. And just as with food he does not seek simply the larger share and nothing else, but rather the most pleasant, so he seeks to enjoy not the longest period of time, but the most pleasant.

And he who counsels the young man to live well, but the old man to make a good end, is foolish, not merely because of the desirability of life, but also because it is the same training which teaches to live well and to die well. Yet much worse still is the man who says it is good not to be born, but

"once born make haste to pass the gates of Death." [*Theognis, 427*]

For if he says this from conviction why does he not pass away out of life? For it is open to him to do so, if he had firmly made up his mind to this. But if he speaks in jest, his words are idle among men who cannot receive them.

We must then bear in mind that the future is neither ours, nor yet wholly not ours, so that we may not altogether expect it as sure to come, nor abandon hope of it, as if it will certainly not come.

We must consider that of desires some are natural, others vain, and of the natural some are necessary and others merely natural; and of the necessary some are necessary for happiness, others for the repose of the body, and others for very life. The right understanding of these facts enables us to refer all choice and avoidance to the health of the body and the soul's freedom from disturbance, since this is the aim of the life of blessedness. For it is to obtain this end that we always act, namely, to avoid pain and fear. And when this is once secured for us, all the tempest of the soul is dispersed, since the living creature has not to wander as though in search of something that is missing, and to look for some other thing by which he can fulfil the good of the soul and the good of the body. For it is then that we have need of pleasure, when we feel pain owing to the absence of pleasure; but when we do not feel pain, we no longer need pleasure. And for this cause we call pleasure the beginning and end of the blessed life. For we recognize pleasure as the first good innate in us, and from pleasure we begin every act of choice and avoidance, and to pleasure we return again, using the feeling as the standard by which we judge every good.

And since pleasure is the first good and natural to us, for this very reason we do not choose every pleasure, but sometimes we pass over many pleasures, when greater discomfort accrues to us as the result of them: and similarly we think many pains better than pleasures, since a greater pleasure comes to us when we have endured pains for a long time. Every pleasure then because of its natural kinship to us is good, yet not every pleasure is to be chosen: even as every pain also is an evil, yet not all are always of a nature to be avoided. Yet by a scale of comparison and by the consideration of advantages and disadvantages we must form our judgement on all these matters. For the good on certain occasions we treat as bad, and conversely the bad as good.

And again independence of desire we think a great good—not that we may at all times enjoy but a few things, but that, if we do not possess many, we may enjoy the few in the genuine persuasion that those have the sweetest pleasure in luxury who least need it, and that all that is natural is easy to be obtained, but that which is superfluous is hard. And so plain savours bring us a pleasure equal to a luxurious diet, when all the pain due to want is removed; and bread and water produce the highest pleasure, when one who needs them puts them to his lips. To grow accustomed therefore to simple and not luxurious diet gives us health to the full, and makes a man alert for the needful employments of life, and when after long intervals we approach luxuries, disposes us better towards them, and fits us to be fearless of fortune.

When, therefore, we maintain that pleasure is the end, we do not mean the pleasures of profligates and those that consist in sensuality, as is supposed by some who are either ignorant or disagree with us or do not understand, but freedom from pain in the body and from trouble in the mind. For it is not continuous drinkings and revellings, nor the satisfaction of lusts, nor the enjoyment of fish and other luxuries of the wealthy table, which produce a pleasant life, but sober reasoning, searching out the motives for all choice and avoidance, and banishing mere opinions, to which are due the greatest disturbance of the spirit.

Of all this the beginning and the greatest good is prudence. Wherefore prudence is a more precious thing even than philosophy: for from prudence are sprung all the other virtues, and it teaches us that it is not possible to live pleasantly without living prudently and honourably and justly, nor, again, to live a life of prudence, honour, and justice without living pleasantly. For the virtues are by nature bound up with the pleasant life, and the pleasant life is inseparable from them. For indeed who, think you, is a better man than he who holds reverent opinions concerning the gods, and is at all times free from fear of death, and has reasoned out the end ordained by nature? He understands that the limit of good things is easy to fulfil and easy to attain, whereas the course of ills is either short in time or slight in pain: he laughs at destiny, whom some have introduced as the mistress of all things. He thinks that with us lies the chief power in determining events, some of which happen by necessity and some by chance, and some are within our control; for while necessity cannot be called to account, he sees that chance is inconstant, but that which is in our control is subject to no master, and to it are naturally attached praise and blame. For, indeed, it were better to follow the myths about the gods than to become a slave to the destiny of the natural philosophers: for the former suggests a hope of placating the gods by worship, whereas the latter involves a necessity which knows no placation. As to chance, he does not regard it as a god as most men do (for in a god's acts there is no disorder), nor as an uncertain cause of all things: for he does not believe that good and evil are given by chance to man for the framing of a blessed life, but that opportunities for great good and great evil are afforded by it. He therefore thinks it better to be unfortunate in reasonable action than to prosper in unreason. For it is better in a man's actions that what is well chosen should fail, rather than that what is ill chosen should be successful owing to chance.

Meditate therefore on these things and things akin to them night and day by yourself, and with a companion like to yourself, and never shall you be disturbed waking or asleep, but you shall live like a god among men. For a man who lives among immortal blessings is not like to a mortal being.

PRINCIPLE DOCTRINES

I. The blessed and immortal nature knows no trouble itself nor causes trouble to any other, so that it is never constrained by anger or favour. For all such things exist only in the weak.

II. Death is nothing to us: for that which is dissolved is without sensation; and that which lacks sensation is nothing to us.

III. The limit of quantity in pleasures is the removal of all that is painful. Wherever pleasure is present, as long as it is there, there is neither pain of body nor of mind, nor of both at once.

IV. Pain does not last continuously in the flesh, but the acutest pain is there for a very short time, and even that which just exceeds the pleasure in the flesh does not continue for many days at once. But chronic illnesses permit a predominance of pleasure over pain in the flesh.

V. It is not possible to live pleasantly without living prudently and honourably and justly, nor again to live a life of prudence, honour, and justice without living pleasantly. And the man who does not possess the pleasant life, is not living prudently and honourably and justly, and the man who does not possess the virtuous life, cannot possibly live pleasantly.

VI. To secure protection from men anything is a natural good, by which you may be able to attain this end.

Epicurus, *Principle Doctrines,* from Epicurus, *The Extant Remains,* translated by Cyril Bailey (Oxford: The Clarendon Press, 1926). Reprinted by permission of Oxford University Press.

VII. Some men wished to become famous and conspicuous, thinking that they would thus win for themselves safety from other men. Wherefore if the life of such men is safe, they have obtained the good which nature craves; but if it is not safe, they do not possess that for which they strove at first by the instinct of nature.

VIII. No pleasure is a bad thing in itself: but the means which produce some pleasures bring with them disturbances many times greater than the pleasures.

IX. If every pleasure could be intensified so that it lasted and influenced the whole organism or the most essential parts of our nature, pleasures would never differ from one another.

X. If the things that produce the pleasures of profligates could dispel the fears of the mind about the phenomena of the sky and death and its pains, and also teach the limits of desires and of pains, we should never have cause to blame them: for they would be filling themselves full with pleasures from every source and never have pain of body or mind, which is the evil of life.

XI. If we were not troubled by our suspicions of the phenomena of the sky and about death, fearing that it concerns us, and also by our failure to grasp the limits of pains and desires, we should have no need of natural science.

XII. A man cannot dispel his fear about the most important matters if he does not know what is the nature of the universe but suspects the truth of some mythical story. So that without natural science it is not possible to attain our pleasures unalloyed.

XIII. There is no profit in securing protection in relation to men, if things above and things beneath the earth and indeed all in the boundless universe remain matters of suspicion.

XIV. The most unalloyed source of protection from men, which is secured to some extent by a certain force of expulsion, is in fact the immunity which results from a quiet life and the retirement from the world.

XV. The wealth demanded by nature is both limited and easily procured; that demanded by idle imaginings stretches on to infinity.

XVI. In but few things chance hinders a wise man, but the greatest and most important matters reason has ordained and throughout the whole period of life does and will ordain.

XVII. The just man is most free from trouble, the unjust most full of trouble.

XVIII. The pleasure in the flesh is not increased, when once the pain due to want is removed, but is only varied: and the limit as regards pleasure in the mind is begotten by the reasoned understanding of these very pleasures and of the emotions akin to them, which used to cause the greatest fear to the mind.

XIX. Infinite time contains no greater pleasure than limited time, if one measures by reason the limits of pleasure.

XX. The flesh perceives the limits of pleasure as unlimited and unlimited time is required to supply it. But the mind, having attained a reasoned understanding of the ultimate good of the flesh and its limits and having dissipated the fears concerning the time to come, supplies us with the complete life, and we have no further need of infinite time: but neither does the mind shun pleasure, nor, when circumstances begin to bring about the departure from life, does it approach its end as though it fell short in any way of the best life.

XXI. He who has learned the limits of life knows that that which removes the pain due to want and makes the whole of life complete is easy to obtain; so that there is no need of actions which involve competition.

XXII. We must consider both the real purpose and all the evidence of direct perception, to which we always refer the conclusions of opinion; otherwise, all will be full of doubt and confusion.

XXIII. If you fight against all sensations, you will have no standard by which to judge even those of them which you say are false.

XXIV. If you reject any single sensation and fail to distinguish between the conclusion of opinion as to the appearance awaiting confirmation and that which is actually given by the sensation or feeling, or each intuitive apprehension of the mind, you will confound all other sensations as well with the same groundless opinion, so that you will reject every standard of judgement. And if among the mental images created by your opinion you affirm both that which awaits confirmation and that which does not, you will not escape error, since you will have preserved the whole cause of doubt in every judgement between what is right and what is wrong.

XXV. If on each occasion instead of referring your actions to the end of nature, you turn to some other nearer standard when you are making a choice or an avoidance, your actions will not be consistent with your principles.

XXVI. Of desires, all that do not lead to a sense of pain, if they are not satisfied, are not necessary, but involve a craving which is easily dispelled, when the object is hard to procure or they seem likely to produce harm.

XXVII. Of all the things which wisdom acquires to produce the blessedness of the complete life, far the greatest is the possession of friendship.

XXVIII. The same conviction which has given us confidence that there is nothing terrible that lasts forever or even for long, has also seen the protection of friendship most fully completed in the limited evils of this life.

XXIX. Among desires some are natural and necessary, some natural but not necessary, and others neither natural nor necessary, but due to idle imagination.

XXX. Wherever in the case of desires which are physical, but do not lead to a sense of pain, if they are not fulfilled, the effort is intense, such pleasures are due to idle imagination, and it is not owing to their own nature that they fail to be dispelled, but owing to the empty imaginings of the man.

XXXI. The justice which arises from nature is a pledge of mutual advantage to restrain men from harming one another and save them from being harmed.

XXXII. For all living things which have not been able to make compacts not to harm one another or be harmed, nothing ever is either just or unjust; and likewise too for all tribes of men which have been unable or unwilling to make compacts not to harm or be harmed.

XXXIII. Justice never is anything in itself, but in the dealings of men with one another in any place whatever and at any time it is a kind of compact not to harm or be harmed.

XXXIV. Injustice is not an evil in itself, but only in consequence of the fear which attaches to the apprehension of being unable to escape those appointed to punish such actions.

XXXV. It is not possible for one who acts in secret contravention of the terms of the compact not to harm or be harmed, to be confident that he will escape detection, even if at present he escapes a thousand times. For up to the time of death it cannot be certain that he will indeed escape.

XXXVI. In its general aspect justice is the same for all, for it is a kind of mutual advantage in the dealings of men with one another: but with reference to the individual peculiarities of a country or any other circumstances the same thing does not turn out to be just for all.

XXXVII. Among actions which are sanctioned as just by law, that which is proved on examination to be of advantage in the requirements of men's dealings with one another, has the guarantee of justice, whether it is the same for all or not. But if a man makes a law and it does not turn out to lead to advantage in men's dealings with each other, then it no longer has the essential nature of justice. And even if the advantage in the matter of justice shifts from one side to the other, but for a while accords with the general concept, it is none the less just for that period in the eyes of those who do not confound themselves with empty sounds but look to the actual facts.

XXXVIII. Where, provided the circumstances have not been altered, actions which were considered just, have been shown not to accord with the general concept in actual practice, then they are not just. But where, when circumstances have changed, the same actions which were sanctioned as just no longer lead to advantage, there they were just at the time when they were of advantage for the dealings of fellow-citizens with one another; but subsequently they are no longer just, when no longer of advantage.

XXXIX. The man who has best ordered the element of disquiet arising from external circumstances has made those things that he could akin to himself and the rest at least not alien: but with all to which he could not do even this, he has refrained from mixing, and has expelled from his life all which it was of advantage to treat thus.

XL. As many as possess the power to procure complete immunity from their neighbours, these also live most pleasantly with one another, since they have the most certain pledge of security, and after they have enjoyed the fullest intimacy, they do not lament the previous departure of a dead friend, as though he were to be pitied.

The Early Stoa:
Zeno of Citium *ca. 336–ca. 265 B.C.*
and
Cleanthes *ca. 331–ca. 233 B.C.*

Zeno was born in the small town of Citium on the island of Cyprus. As a young man he moved to Athens, where, it is said, he discovered philosophy by reading Xenophon's description of Socrates, the *Memorabilia*. Socrates being long dead, Zeno attached himself for some time to the Cynics. Zeno agreed with the Cynics that self-control over emotions was essential to a virtuous life. Zeno was also attracted to the teachings of Heraclitus—particularly to the Heraclitean notion of an eternal fire or *logos* that controls the universe. Sometime around 300 B.C., Zeno set up a school of philosophy in the Painted Porch, ⟨*Stoa Poikile*⟩, a school that came to be known as "Stoic." His Stoic school may have been established specifically to counter the philosophy of Epicurus. At any rate, he argued that virtue, not pleasure, was the only good, and that natural law, not the random swerving of atoms, was the key principle of the universe. While teaching at his school, Zeno read widely and was greatly respected for his learning, his character, and the simplicity of his life. A severe and austere man, he was, like some of the Pre-Socratics, a sage as well as a philosopher. Zeno believed strongly in divine signs. He is said to have committed suicide after breaking his toe on a rock, believing the incident to be a sign of God's will.

Like Epicurus before him, Zeno divided philosophy into logic (including the theory of knowledge), physics, and ethics. In their discussions of logic, Zeno and his followers examined at great length the relationships among words, their meanings, and the objects to which they refer. They developed several subtle distinctions that are still examined and discussed today (see the suggested readings). They also developed an understanding of sensory knowledge based on impressions that was similar to the theories of Epicurus.

In physics, Zeno developed an elaborate cosmology that includes both a passive and an active principle. The passive principle is matter, while the active principle is the "fiery breath," ⟨*pneuma*⟩, known by such names as god, mind, fate, Zeus, and *logos*. This active principle is not separate from the world, but permeates it, molding passive matter into an ordered universe. Permeating everything, god/mind directs the course of affairs and connects all parts into one whole, like a giant organism. The key to ethics for Zeno and his disciples is to live in harmony with this active principle. This requires both the wisdom to know what part we are to play and the "apathy" ⟨*apatheia*⟩, or avoidance of strong emotions, to accept what we cannot change. Happiness, or more accurately, contentment, is possible in any condition. In fact, among prominent later Stoics, Epictetus was born a slave while Marcus Aurelius was a Roman emperor.

The selection here is from Diogenes Laertius' *Lives of Eminent Philosophers,* in which Laertius summarizes Stoic ethics and physics. It should be noted that Laertius refers not only to Zeno and Cleanthes, but also to Chrysippus, Cleanthes' successor at the Stoa, and to the later Stoics Archedemus and Posidonius. The translation is that of R.D. Hicks.

Cleanthes was born in Assos and raised in Athens. He too studied first with the Cynics before becoming a disciple of Zeno at the Stoa. Following Zeno's death, Cleanthes became head of the Stoic school. Unlike his master, Cleanthes was known as a gentle man with great patience. He was like his master in another respect, however—he too is reported to have killed himself. Cleanthes is best known for his "Hymn to Zeus," a strong tribute to nature's orderliness and benevolence. The translation is that of James Adam.

*   *   *

For general introductions to the Stoics, see E. Vernon Arnold, *Roman Stoicism* (1911; reprinted New York: Humanities Press, 1958); L. Edelstein, *The Meaning of Stoicism* (Cambridge, MA: Harvard University Press, 1966); John M. Rist, *Stoic Philosophy* (Cambridge: Cambridge University Press, 1969); and F.H. Sandbach, *The Stoics* (New York: Norton, 1975). For comparisons between Stoicism and other Hellenistic schools, see R.M. Wenley, *Stoicism and Its Influence* (1924; reprinted New York: Cooper Square, 1963); Edwin R. Bevan, *Stoics and Sceptics* (Oxford: Clarendon Press, 1913); and R.D. Hicks, *Stoic and Epicurean* (1910; reprinted New York: Russell & Russell, 1962). For collections of essays consult A.A. Long, ed., *Problems in Stoicism* (London: Athlone Press, 1971), and J.M. Rist, ed., *The Stoics* (Berkeley: University of California Press, 1978). For specialized studies, I suggest Benson Mates, *Stoic Logic* (Berkeley: University of California Press, 1953); Samuel Sambursky, *Physics of the Stoics* (London: Russell, 1959); and Gerard Watson, *The Stoic Theory of Knowledge* (Belfast: Queen's University, 1966).

ZENO OF CITIUM (Selections from Diogenes Laertius)

ETHICS

An animal's first impulse, say the Stoics, is to self-preservation, because nature from the outset endears it to itself, as Chrysippus affirms in the first book of his work *On Ends:* his words are, "The dearest thing to every animal is its own constitution and its consciousness thereof"; for it was not likely that nature should estrange the living thing from itself or that she should leave the creature she has made without either estrangement from or affection for its own constitution. We are forced then to conclude that nature in constituting the animal made it near and dear to itself; for so it comes to repel all that is injurious and give free access to all that is serviceable or akin to it.

As for the assertion made by some people that pleasure is the object to which the first impulse of animals is directed, it is shown by the Stoics to be false. For pleasure, if it is really felt, they declare to be a by-product, which never comes until nature by itself has sought and found the means suitable to the animal's existence or constitution; it is an aftermath comparable to the condition of animals thriving and plants in full bloom. And nature, they say, made no difference originally between plants and animals, for she regulates the life of plants too, in their case without impulse and sensation, just as also certain processes go on of a vegetative kind in us. But when in the case of animals impulse has been superadded, whereby they are enabled to go in quest of their proper aliment, for them, say the Stoics, Nature's rule is to follow the direction of impulse. But when reason by way of a more perfect leadership has been bestowed on the beings we call rational, for them life according to reason rightly becomes the natural life. For reason supervenes to shape impulse scientifically.

This is why Zeno was the first (in his treatise *On the Nature of Man*) to designate as the end "life in agreement with nature" (or living agreeably to nature), which is the same as a virtuous life, virtue being the goal towards which nature guides us. So too Cleanthes in his treatise *On Pleasure,* as also Posidonius, and Hecato in his work *On Ends.* Again, living virtuously is equivalent to living in accordance with experience of the actual course of nature, as Chrysippus says in the first book of his *De finibus;* for our individual natures are parts of the nature of the whole universe. And this is why the end may be defined as life in accordance with nature, or, in other words, in accordance with our own human nature as well as that of the universe, a life in which we refrain from every action forbidden by the law common to all things, that is to say, the right reason which pervades all things, and is identical with this Zeus, lord and ruler of all that is. And this very thing constitutes the virtue of the happy man and the smooth current of life, when all actions promote the harmony of the spirit dwelling in the individual man with the will of him who orders the universe. Diogenes then expressly declares the end to be to act with good reason in the selection of what is natural. Archedemus says the end is to live in the performance of all befitting actions.

By the nature with which our life ought to be in accord, Chrysippus understands both universal nature and more particularly the nature of man, whereas Cleanthes takes

Reprinted by permission of the publishers and the Loeb Classical Library from Diogenes Laertius, *Lives of Eminent Philosophers,* Volume II, translated by R.D. Hicks (Cambridge, MA: Harvard University Press, 1925). Copyright © 1925 by Harvard University Press.

The Painted Porch or *Stoa Poikile* of Athens where Zeno of Citium first taught (as reconstructed). *(UPI/Bettmann)*

the nature of the universe alone as that which should be followed, without adding the nature of the individual.

And virtue, he holds, is a harmonious disposition, choice-worthy for its own sake and not from hope or fear or any external motive. Moreover, it is in virtue that happiness consists; for virtue is the state of mind which tends to make the whole of life harmonious. When a rational being is perverted, this is due to the deceptiveness of external pursuits or sometimes to the influence of associates. For the starting-points of nature are never perverse.

*   *   *

They hold the emotions to be judgements, as is stated by Chrysippus in his treatise *On the Passions:* avarice being a supposition that money is a good, while the case is similar with drunkenness and profligacy and all the other emotions.

And grief or pain they hold to be an irrational mental contraction. Its species are pity, envy, jealousy, rivalry, heaviness, annoyance, distress, anguish, distraction. Pity is grief felt at undeserved suffering; envy, grief at others' prosperity; jealousy, grief at the possession by another of that which one desires for oneself; rivalry, pain at the possession by another of what one has oneself. Heaviness or vexation is grief which weighs us down, annoyance that which coops us up and straitens us for want of room, distress a pain brought on by anxious thought that lasts and increases, anguish painful grief, distraction irrational grief, rasping and hindering us from viewing the situation as a whole.

Fear is an expectation of evil. Under fear are ranged the following emotions: terror, nervous shrinking, shame, consternation, panic, mental agony. Terror is a fear which produces fright; shame is fear of disgrace; nervous shrinking is a fear that one will have to act; consternation is fear due to a presentation of some unusual occurrence; panic is fear with pressure exercised by sound; mental agony is fear felt when some issue is still in suspense.

Desire or craving is irrational appetency, and under it are ranged the following states: want, hatred, contentiousness, anger, love, wrath, resentment. Want, then, is a craving when it is baulked and, as it were, cut off from its object, but kept at full stretch and attracted towards it in vain. Hatred is a growing and lasting desire or craving that it should go ill with somebody. Contentiousness is a craving or desire connected with partisanship; anger a craving or desire to punish one who is thought to have done you an undeserved injury. The passion of love is a craving from which good men are free; for it is an effort to win affection due to the visible presence of beauty. Wrath is anger which has long rankled and has become malicious, waiting for its opportunity, as is illustrated by the lines:*

> Even though for the one day he swallow his anger, yet doth he still keep his displeasure thereafter in his heart, till he accomplish it.

Resentment is anger in an early stage.

Pleasure is an irrational elation at the accruing of what seems to be choice-worthy; and under it are ranged ravishment, malevolent joy, delight, transport. Ravishment is pleasure which charms the ear. Malevolent joy is pleasure at another's ills. Delight is the mind's propulsion to weakness, its name in Greek ⟨terpsis⟩ being akin to ⟨trepsis⟩ or turning. To be in transports of delight is the melting away of virtue.

And as there are said to be certain infirmities in the body, as for instance gout and arthritic disorders, so too there is in the soul love of fame, love of pleasure, and the like. By infirmity is meant disease accompanied by weakness; and by disease is meant a fond imagining of something that seems desirable. And as in the body there are tendencies to certain maladies such as colds and diarrhea, so it is with the soul, there are tendencies like enviousness, pitifulness, quarrelsomeness, and the like.

Also they say that there are three emotional states which are good, namely, joy, caution, and wishing. Joy, the counterpart of pleasure, is rational elation; caution, the counterpart of fear, rational avoidance; for though the wise man will never feel fear, he will yet use caution. And they make wishing the counterpart of desire (or craving), inasmuch as it is rational appetency. And accordingly, as under the primary passions are classed certain others subordinate to them, so too is it with the primary eupathies or good emotional states. Thus under wishing they bring well-wishing or benevolence, friendliness, respect, affection; under caution, reverence and modesty; under joy, delight, mirth, cheerfulness.

Now they say that the wise man is passionless, because he is not prone to fall into such infirmity. But they add that in another sense the term apathy is applied to the bad man, when, that is, it means that he is callous and relentless. Further, the wise man is said to be free from vanity; for he is indifferent to good or evil report. However, he is not alone in this, there being another who is also free from vanity, he who is ranged among the rash, and that is the bad man. Again, they tell us that all good men are aus-

*Iliad, I. 81, 82.

tere or harsh, because they neither have dealings with pleasure themselves nor tolerate those who have. The term harsh is applied, however, to others as well, and in much the same sense as a wine is said to be harsh when it is employed medicinally and not for drinking at all.

Again, the good are genuinely in earnest and vigilant for their own improvement, using a manner of life which banishes evil out of sight and makes what good there is in things appear. At the same time they are free from pretence; for they have stripped off all pretence or "make-up" whether in voice or in look. Free too are they from all business cares, declining to do anything which conflicts with duty. They will take wine, but not get drunk. Nay more, they will not be liable to madness either; not but what there will at times occur to the good man strange impressions due to melancholy or delirium, ideas not determined by the principle of what is choice-worthy but contrary to nature. Nor indeed will the wise man ever feel grief; seeing that grief is irrational contraction of the soul, as Apollodorus says in his *Ethics*.

*   *   *

It is also their doctrine that amongst the wise there should be a community of wives with free choice of partners, as Zeno says in his *Republic* and Chrysippus in his treatise *On Government* [and not only they, but also Diogenes the Cynic and Plato]. Under such circumstances we shall feel paternal affection for all the children alike, and there will be an end of the jealousies arising from adultery. The best form of government they hold to be a mixture of democracy, kingship, and aristocracy (or the rule of the best).

Such, then, are the statements they make in their ethical doctrines, with much more besides, together with their proper proofs: let this, however, suffice for a statement of them in a summary and elementary form.

PHYSICS

Their physical doctrine they divide into sections (1) about bodies; (2) about principles; (3) about elements; (4) about the gods; (5) about bounding surfaces and space whether filled or empty. This is a division into species; but the generic division is into three parts, dealing with (i) the universe; (ii) the elements; (iii) the subject of causation.

The part dealing with the universe admits, they say, of division into two: for with one aspect of it the mathematicians also are concerned, in so far as they treat questions relating to the fixed stars and the planets, *e.g.* whether the sun is not just so large as it appears to be, and the same about the moon, the question of their revolutions, and other inquiries of the same sort. But there is another aspect or field of cosmological inquiry, which belongs to the physicists alone: this includes such questions as what the substance of the universe is, whether the sun and the stars are made up of forms and matter, whether the world has had a beginning in time or not, whether it is animate or inanimate, whether it is destructible or indestructible, whether it is governed by providence, and all the rest. The part concerned with causation, again, is itself subdivided into two. And in one of its aspects medical inquiries have a share in it, in so far as it involves investigation of the ruling principle of the soul and the phenomena of soul, seeds, and the like. Whereas the other part is claimed by the mathematicians also, *e.g.* how vision is to be explained, what causes the image on the mirror, what is the origin of clouds, thunder, rainbows, halos, comets, and the like.

They hold that there are two principles in the universe, the active principle and the passive. The passive principle, then, is a substance without quality, *i.e.* matter, whereas the active is the reason inherent in this substance, that is God. For he is everlasting and is the artificer of each several thing throughout the whole extent of matter. This doctrine is laid down by Zeno of Citium in his treatise *On Existence,* Cleanthes in his work *On Atoms,* Chrysippus in the first book of his *Physics* towards the end, Archedemus in his treatise *On Elements,* and Posidonius in the second book of his *Physical Exposition.* There is a difference, according to them, between principles and elements; the former being without generation or destruction, whereas the elements are destroyed when all things are resolved into fire. Moreover, the principles are incorporeal and destitute of form, while the elements have been endowed with form.

Body is defined by Apollodorus in his *Physics* as that which is extended in three dimensions, length, breadth, and depth. This is also called solid body. But surface is the extremity of a solid body, or that which has length and breadth only without depth. That surface exists not only in our thought but also in reality is maintained by Posidonius in the third book of his *Celestial Phenomena.* A line is the extremity of a surface or length without breadth, or that which has length alone. A point is the extremity of a line, the smallest possible mark or dot.

God is one and the same with Reason, Fate, and Zeus; he is also called by many other names. In the beginning he was by himself; he transformed the whole of substance through air into water, and just as in animal generation the seed has a moist vehicle, so in cosmic moisture God, who is the seminal reason of the universe, remains behind in the moisture as such an agent, adapting matter to himself with a view to the next stage of creation. Thereupon he created first of all the four elements, fire, water, air, earth. They are discussed by Zeno in his treatise *On the Whole,* by Chrysippus in the first book of his *Physics,* and by Archedemus in a work *On Elements.* An element is defined as that from which particular things first come to be at their birth and into which they are finally resolved. The four elements together constitute unqualified substance or matter. Fire is the hot element, water the moist, air the cold, earth the dry. Not but what the quality of dryness is also found in the air. Fire has the uppermost place; it is also called aether, and in it the sphere of the fixed stars is first created; then comes the sphere of the planets, next to that the air, then the water, and lowest of all the earth, which is at the centre of all things.

The term universe or cosmos is used by them in three senses: (1) of God himself, the individual being whose quality is derived from the whole of substance; he is indestructible and ingenerable, being the artificer of this orderly arrangement, who at stated periods of time absorbs into himself the whole of substance and again creates it from himself. (2) Again, they give the name of cosmos to the orderly arrangement of the heavenly bodies in itself as such; and (3) in the third place to that whole of which these two are parts. Again, the cosmos is defined as the individual being qualifying the whole of substance, or, in the words of Posidonius in his elementary treatise on *Celestial Phenomena,* a system made up of heaven and earth and the natures in them, or, again, as a system constituted by gods and men and all things created for their sake. By heaven is meant the extreme circumference or ring in which the deity has his seat.

The world, in their view, is ordered by reason and providence: so says Chrysippus in the fifth book of his treatise *On Providence* and Posidonius in his work *On the Gods,* book iii.—inasmuch as reason pervades every part of it, just as does the soul in us. Only there is a difference of degree; in some parts there is more of it, in others less. For through some parts it passes as a "hold" or containing force, as is the case with our bones and sinews; while through others it passes as intelligence, as in the ruling part of the soul. Thus, then, the whole world is a living being, endowed with soul and reason, and having aether for its ruling principle: so says Antipater of Tyre in the eighth book of his treatise *On the Cosmos.* Chrysippus in the first book of his work *On Providence* and Posidonius in his book *On the Gods* say that the heaven, but Cleanthes that the sun, is the ruling power of the world. Chrysippus, however, in the course of the same work gives a somewhat different account, namely, that it is the purer part of the aether; the same which they declare to be preeminently God and always to have, as it were in sensible fashion, pervaded all that is in the air, all animals and plants, and also the earth itself, as a principle of cohesion.

The world, they say, is one and finite, having a spherical shape, such a shape being the most suitable for motion, as Posidonius says in the fifth book of his *Physical Discourse* and the disciples of Antipater in their works on the Cosmos. Outside of the world is diffused the infinite void, which is incorporeal. By incorporeal is meant that which, though capable of being occupied by body, is not so occupied. The world has no empty space within it, but forms one united whole. This is a necessary result of the sympathy and tension which binds together things in heaven and earth. Chrysippus discusses the void in his work *On Void* and in the first book of his *Physical Sciences;* so too Apollophanes in his *Physics,* Apollodorus, and Posidonius in his *Physical Discourse,* book ii. But these, it is added [*i.e.* sympathy and tension], are likewise bodies.

Time too is incorporeal, being the measure of the world's motion. And time past and time future are infinite, but time present is finite. They hold that the world must come to an end, inasmuch as it had a beginning, on the analogy of those things which are understood by the senses. And that of which the parts are perishable is perishable as a whole. Now the parts of the world are perishable, seeing that they are transformed one into the other. Therefore the world itself is doomed to perish. Moreover, anything is destructible if it admits of deterioration; therefore the world is so, for it is first evaporated and again dissolved into water.

The world, they hold, comes into being when its substance has first been converted from fire through air into moisture and then the coarser part of the moisture has condensed as earth, while that whose particles are fine has been turned into air, and this process of rarefaction goes on increasing till it generates fire. Thereupon out of these elements animals and plants and all other natural kinds are formed by their mixture. The generation and the destruction of the world are discussed by Zeno in his treatise *On the Whole,* by Chrysippus in the first book of his *Physics,* by Posidonius in the first book of his work *On the Cosmos,* by Cleanthes, and by Antipater in his tenth book *On the Cosmos.* Panaetius, however, maintained that the world is indestructible.

The doctrine that the world is a living being, rational, animate and intelligent, is laid down by Chrysippus in the first book of his treatise *On Providence,* by Apollodorus in his *Physics,* and by Posidonius. It is a living thing in the sense of an animate substance endowed with sensation; for animal is better than non-animal, and nothing is better than the world, ergo the world is a living being. And it is endowed with soul, as is clear from our several souls being each a fragment of it. Boëthus, however, denies that the world is a living thing. The unity of the world is maintained by Zeno in his treatise *On the Whole,* by Chrysippus, by Apollodorus in his *Physics,* and by Posidonius in the first book of his *Physical Discourse.* By the totality of things, the All, is meant, according to Apollodorus, (1) the world, and in another sense (2) the system composed of the world and the void outside it. The world then is finite, the void infinite.

Of the stars some are fixed, and are carried round with the whole heaven; others, the wandering stars or planets, have their special motions. The sun travels in an oblique path through the zodiac. Similarly the moon travels in a spiral path. The sun is pure fire:

so Posidonius in the seventh book of his *Celestial Phenomena*. And it is larger than the earth, as the same author says in the sixth book of his *Physical Discourse*. Moreover it is spherical in shape like the world itself according to this same author and his school. That it is fire is proved by its producing all the effects of fire; that it is larger than the earth by the fact that all the earth is illuminated by it; nay more, the heaven beside. The fact too that the earth casts a conical shadow proves that the sun is greater than it. And it is because of its great size that it is seen from every part of the earth.

The moon, however, is of a more earthy composition, since it is nearer to the earth. These fiery bodies and the stars generally derive their nutriment, the sun from the wide ocean, being a fiery kindling, though intelligent; the moon from fresh waters, with an admixture of air, close to the earth as it is: thus Posidonius in the sixth book of his *Physics;* the other heavenly bodies being nourished from the earth. They hold that the stars are spherical in shape and that the earth too is so and is at rest; and that the moon does not shine by her own light, but by the borrowed light of the sun when he shines upon her.

An eclipse of the sun takes place when the moon passes in front of it on the side towards us, as shown by Zeno with a diagram in his treatise *On the Whole*. For the moon is seen approaching at conjunctions and occulting it and then again receding from it. This can best be observed when they are mirrored in a basin of water. The moon is eclipsed when she falls into the earth's shadow: for which reason it is only at the full moon that an eclipse happens [and not always then], although she is in opposition to the sun every month; because the moon moves in an oblique orbit, diverging in latitude relatively to the orbit of the sun, and she accordingly goes farther to the north or to the south. When, however, the moon's motion in latitude has brought her into the sun's path through the zodiac, and she thus comes diametrically opposite to the sun, there is an eclipse. Now the moon is in latitude right on the zodiac, when she is in the constellations of Cancer, Scorpio, Aries and Taurus: so Posidonius and his followers tell us.

The deity, say they, is a living being, immortal, rational, perfect or intelligent in happiness, admitting nothing evil [into him], taking providential care of the world and all that therein is, but he is not of human shape. He is, however, the artificer of the universe and, as it were, the father of all, both in general and in that particular part of him which is all-pervading, and which is called many names according to its various powers. They give the name Dia ⟨*Dia*⟩ because all things are due to ⟨*dia*⟩ him; Zeus ⟨*Zana*⟩ in so far as he is the cause of life ⟨*zan*⟩ or pervades all life; the name Athena is given, because the ruling part of the divinity extends to the aether; the name Hera marks its extension to the air; he is called Hephaestus since it spreads to the creative fire; Poseidon, since it stretches to the sea; Demeter, since it reaches to the earth. Similarly men have given the deity his other titles, fastening, as best they can, on some one or other of his peculiar attributes.

The substance of God is declared by Zeno to be the whole world and the heaven, as well as by Chrysippus in his first book *Of the Gods,* and by Posidonius in his first book with the same title. Again, Antipater in the seventh book of his work *On the Cosmos* says that the substance of God is akin to air, while Boëthus in his work *On Nature* speaks of the sphere of the fixed stars as the substance of God. Now the term Nature is used by them to mean sometimes that which holds the world together, sometimes that which causes terrestrial things to spring up. Nature defined as a force moving of itself, producing and preserving in being its offspring in accordance with seminal principles within definite periods, and effecting results homogeneous with their sources. Nature, they hold, aims both at utility and at pleasure, as is clear from the analogy of human craftsmanship. That all things happen by fate or destiny is maintained by Chrysippus in his treatise *De fato,* by Posidonius in his *De fato,* book ii., by Zeno and by Boëthus in his *De fato,* book i. Fate is defined as an endless chain of causation, whereby things are, or as the reason or formula by which the world goes on. What is more, they say that divination in all its forms is a real and substantial fact, if there is really Providence. And they prove it to be actually a science on the evidence of certain results: so Zeno, Chrysippus in the second book of his *De divinatione,* Athenodorus, and Posidonius in the second book of his *Physical Discourse* and the fifth book of his *De divinatione.* But Panaetius denies that divination has any real existence.

The primary matter they make the substratum of all things: so Chrysippus in the first book of his *Physics,* and Zeno. By matter is meant that out of which anything whatsoever is produced. Both substance and matter are terms used in a twofold sense according as they signify (1) universal or (2) particular substance or matter. The former neither increases nor diminishes, while the matter of particular things both increases and diminishes. Body according to them is substance which is finite: so Antipater in his second book *On Substance,* and Apollodorus in his *Physics.* Matter can also be acted upon, as the same author says, for if it were immutable, the things which are produced would never have been produced out of it. Hence the further doctrine that matter is divisible *ad infinitum.* Chrysippus says that the division is not *ad infinitum,* but itself infinite; for there is nothing infinitely small to which the division can extend. But nevertheless the division goes on without ceasing.

Hence, again, their explanation of the mixture of two substances is, according to Chrysippus in the third book of his *Physics,* that they permeate each other through and through, and that the particles of the one do not merely surround those of the other or lie beside them. Thus, if a little drop of wine be thrown into the sea, it will be equally diffused over the whole sea for a while and then will be blended with it.

Also they hold that there are daemons ⟨*daimones*⟩ who are in sympathy with mankind and watch over human affairs. They believe too in heroes, that is, the souls of the righteous that have survived their bodies.

Of the changes which go on in the air, they describe winter as the cooling of the air above the earth due to the sun's departure to a distance from the earth; spring as the right temperature of the air consequent upon his approach to us; summer as the heating of the air above the earth when he travels to the north; while autumn they attribute to the receding of the sun from us. As for the winds, they are streams of air, differently named according to the localities from which they blow. And the cause of their production is the sun through the evaporation of the clouds. The rainbow is explained as the reflection of the sun's rays from watery clouds or, as Posidonius says in his *Meteorology,* an image of a segment of the sun or moon in a cloud suffused with dew, which is hollow and visible without intermission, the image showing itself as if in a mirror in the form of a circular arch. Comets, bearded stars, and meteors are fires which arise when dense air is carried up to the region of aether. A shooting star is the sudden kindling of a mass of fire in rapid motion through the air, which leaves a trail behind it presenting an appearance of length. Rain is the transformation of cloud into water, when moisture drawn up by the sun from land or sea has been only partially evaporated. If this is cooled down, it is called hoar-frost. Hail is frozen cloud, crumbled by a wind; while snow is moist matter from a cloud which has congealed: so Posidonius in the eighth book of his *Physical Discourse.* Lightning is a kindling of clouds from being rubbed together or being rent by wind, as Zeno says in his treatise *On the Whole;* thunder the noise these clouds make when they rub against each other or burst. Thunderbolt is the term used when the fire is violently kindled and hurled to the ground with great force as the clouds grind against each other or are torn by the wind. Others say that it is a compression of fiery air descending with great force. A typhoon is a great and violent thunderstorm whirlwindlike, or a whirlwind of smoke from a cloud that has burst. A "prester" is a cloud rent all round by the force of fire and wind. Earthquakes, say they, happen when the wind finds its way into, or is imprisoned in, the hollow parts of the earth: so Posidonius in his eighth book; and some of them are tremblings, others openings of the earth, others again lateral displacements, and yet others vertical displacements.

They maintain that the parts of the world are arranged thus. The earth is in the middle answering to a centre; next comes the water, which is shaped like a sphere all round it, concentric with the earth, so that the earth is in water. After the water comes a spherical layer of air. There are five celestial circles: first, the arctic circle, which is always visible; second, the summer tropic; third, the circle of the equinox; fourth, the winter tropic; and fifth, the antarctic, which is invisible to us. They are called parallel, because they do not incline towards one another; yet they are described round the same centre. The zodiac is an oblique circle, as it crosses the parallel circles. And there are five terrestrial zones: first, the northern zone which is beyond the arctic circle, uninhabitable because of the cold; second, a temperate zone; a third, uninhabitable because of great heats, called the torrid zone; fourth, a counter-temperate zone; fifth, the southern zone, uninhabitable because of its cold.

Nature in their view is an artistically working fire, going on its way to create; which is equivalent to a fiery, creative, or fashioning breath. And the soul is a nature capable of perception. And they regard it as the breath of life, congenital with us; from which they infer first that it is a body and secondly that it survives death. Yet it is perishable, though the soul of the universe, of which the individual souls of animals are parts, is indestructible. Zeno of Citium and Antipater, in their treatises *De anima,* and Posidonius define the soul as a warm breath; for by this we become animate and this enables us to move. Cleanthes indeed holds that all souls continue to exist until the general conflagration; but Chrysippus says that only the souls of the wise do so.

They count eight parts of the soul: the five senses, the generative power in us, our power of speech, and that of reasoning. They hold that we see when the light between the visual organ and the object stretches in the form of a cone: so Chrysippus in the second book of his *Physics* and Apollodorus. The apex of the cone in the air is at the eye, the base at the object seen. Thus the thing seen is reported to us by the medium of the air stretching out towards it, as if by a stick.

We hear when the air between the sonant body and the organ of hearing suffers concussion, a vibration which spreads spherically and then forms waves and strikes upon the ears, just as the water in a reservoir forms wavy circles when a stone is thrown into it. Sleep is caused, they say, by the slackening of the tension in our senses, which affects the ruling part of the soul. They consider that the passions are caused by the variations of the vital breath.

Semen is by them defined as that which is capable of generating offspring like the parent. And the human semen which is emitted by a human parent in a moist vehicle is mingled with parts of the soul, blended in the same ratio in which they are present in the parent. Chrysippus in the second book of his *Physics* declares it to be in substance identical with vital breath or spirit. This, he thinks, can be seen from the seeds cast into the earth, which, if kept till they are old, do not germinate, plainly because their fertility has evaporated. Sphaerus and his followers also maintain that semen derives its origin from the whole of the body; at all events every part of the body can be reproduced from it. That of the female is according to them sterile, being, as Sphaerus says, without tension, scanty, and watery. By ruling part of the soul is meant that which is most truly soul proper, in which arise presentations and impulses and from which issues rational speech. And it has its seat in the heart.

Such is the summary of their Physics which I have deemed adequate.

HYMN TO ZEUS

O God most glorious, called by many a name,
Nature's great King, through endless years the same;
Omnipotence, who by thy just decree
Controllest all, hail, Zeus, for unto thee
Behooves thy creatures in all lands to call.
We are thy children, we alone, of all
On earth's broad ways that wander to and fro,
Bearing thine image whereso'er we go.
Wherefore with songs of praise thy power I will forth show
Lo! yonder Heaven, that round the earth is wheeled,
Follows thy guidance, still to thee doth yield
Glad homage; thine unconquerable hand
Such flaming minister, the levin brand,
Wieldeth, a sword two-edged, whose deathless might
Pulsates through all that Nature brings to light;
Vehicle of the universal Word, that flows
Through all, and in the light celestial glows
Of stars both great and small. A King of Kings
Through ceaseless ages, God, whose purpose brings
To birth, whate'er on land or in the sea
Is wrought, or in high heaven's immensity;
Save what the sinner works infatuate.
Nay, but thou knowest to make crooked straight:
Chaos to thee in order: in thine eyes
The unloved is lovely, who didst harmonize
Things evil with things good, that there should be
One Word through all things everlastingly.
One Word—whose voice alas! the wicked spurn;
Insatiate for the good their spirits yearn:
Yet seeing see not, neither hearing hear
God's universal law, which those revere,
By reason guided, happiness who win.
The rest, unreasoning, diverse shapes of sin
Self-prompted follow: for an idle name
Vainly they wrestle in the lists of fame:
Others inordinately riches woo,
Or dissolute, the joys of flesh pursue.
Now here, now there they wander, fruitless still,

"The Hymn of Cleanthes" from James Adams, *The Vitality of Platonism* (Cambridge, England: Cambridge University Press, 1911). Reprinted by permission.

Forever seeking good and finding ill.
Zeus the all-bountiful, whom darkness shrouds,
Whose lightning lightens in the thunder-clouds;
Thy children save from error's deadly away:
Turn thou the darkness from their souls sway:
Vouchsafe that unto knowledge they attain;
For thou by knowledge art made strong to reign
O'er all, and all things rulest righteously.
So by thee honoured, we will honour thee,
Praising thy works continually with songs,
As mortals should; nor higher meed belongs
E'en to the gods, than justly to adore
The universal law for evermore.

EPICTETUS
ca. A.D. 50–ca. 130

Epictetus was born a slave in Hierapolis, a small town in Phrygia, Asia Minor (in present-day Turkey). His master was Epaphroditus, a member of Emperor Nero's personal staff in Rome. As was often done at that time, Epaphroditus saw to it that Epictetus had a good education, sending him to study with the Roman Stoic, Rufus. Epictetus gained his freedom sometime after the death of the emperor in A.D. 68 and began to teach philosophy in Rome. In A.D. 89 or 93 Emperor Domitian expelled all philosophers from Rome. Domitian seems to have been especially angry with the Stoics for teaching that sovereignty comes from God and is for the benefit of the people. (Epictetus' reported claim that he had the same regard for the emperor as for his water-pot could not have helped.) Epictetus moved to Nicropolis in Epirus (northwestern Greece), where he established a thriving Stoic school and lived a simple life with few material goods. As an old man he married so that he could adopt a child who otherwise would have been "exposed," that is, left to die. Those whom he taught described him as a humble, charitable man of great moral and religious devotion.

Epictetus never wrote anything, but one of his admiring students, Arrian, composed eight *Discourses* based on Epictetus' lectures, along with a summary of the great man's thought, the *Encheiridion* (or *Manual*). The *Encheiridion,* given here complete in the W.A. Oldfather translation, builds on the early Stoa's concept of *logos*. Since the *logos* or natural law permeates everything, it provides us with moral intuition, so all persons have the capacity for virtue. But in order to live the moral life, one must apply these intuitions to specific cases. Education is necessary if we are to learn how to properly connect moral insights with life. We must begin by recognizing the fact that we cannot change events that happen to us, but we can change our attitude toward those events. To accomplish this and achieve the good life, we must go through three stages. First, we must order our desires and overcome our fears. Next, we must perform our duties—in whatever role fate has given us. Finally, we must think clearly and judge accurately. Only then will we be successful in ordering our desires and performing our duties; only then will we gain inner tranquillity.

Despite Emperor Domitian's condemnation, Stoicism had a special appeal to the Roman mind. The Romans were not much interested in the speculative and theoretical content of Zeno's early Stoa. Instead, in the austere moral emphasis of Epictetus, with his concomitant stress on self-control and superiority to pain, the Romans found an ideal for the wise man, while the Stoic description of natural law provided a basis for Roman law. One might say that the pillars of republican Rome tended to be Stoical, even if some Romans had never heard of Stoicism.

*   *   *

For works on the Stoics in general, which include Epictetus, see the introductory material on the Early Stoa on pages 399–400. For a volume specifically on Epictetus, see John Bonforte, *The Philosophy of Epictetus* (New York: Philosophical Library, 1955). Iason Xenakis, *Epictetus: Philosopher-Therapist* (The Hague, Netherlands: Martinus Nijhoff, 1969), makes an interesting application of Epictetus; while W.A. Oldfather, *Contributions Towards a Bibliography of Epictetus* (Urbana: University of Illinois Press, 1927; supplement, 1952), furnishes a bibliography. For a study of Epictetus' star pupil, see Philip A. Stadter, *Arrian of Nicomedia* (Chapel Hill: University of North Carolina Press, 1980).

ENCHEIRIDION (Manual)

1. Some things are under our control, while others are not under our control. Under our control are conception, choice, desire, aversion, and in a word, everything that is our own doing; not under our control are our body, our property, reputation, office and, in a word, everything that is not our own doing. Furthermore, the things under our control are by nature free, unhindered, and unimpeded; while the things not under our control are weak, servile, subject to hindrance, and not our own. Remember, therefore, that if what is naturally slavish you think to be free, and what is not your own to be your own, you will be hampered, will grieve, will be in turmoil, and will blame both gods and

men; while if you think only what is your own to be your own, and what is not your own to be, as it really is, not your own, then no one will ever be able to exert compulsion upon you, no one will hinder you, you will blame no one, will find fault with no one, will do absolutely nothing against your will, you will have no personal enemy, no one will harm you, for neither is there any harm that can touch you.

With such high aims, therefore, remember that you must bestir yourself with no slight effort to lay hold of them, but you will have to give up some things entirely, and defer others for the time being. But if you wish for these things also, and at the same time for both office and wealth, it may be that you will not get even these latter, because you aim also at the former, and certainly you will fail to get the former, which alone bring freedom and happiness.

Make it, therefore, your study at the very outset to say to every harsh external impression, "You are an external impression and not at all what you appear to be." After that examine it and test it by these rules which you have, the first and most important of which is this: Whether the impression has to do with the things which are under our control, or with those which are not under our control; and, if it has to do with some one of the things not under our control, have ready to hand the answer, "It is nothing to me."

2. Remember that the promise of desire is the attainment of what you desire, that of aversion is not to fall into what is avoided, and that he who fails in his desire is unfortunate, while he who falls into what he would avoid experiences misfortune. If, then, you avoid only what is unnatural among those things which are under your control, you will fall into none of the things which you avoid; but if you try to avoid disease, or death, or poverty, you will experience misfortune. Withdraw, therefore, your aversion from all the matters that are not under our control, and transfer it to what is unnatural among those which are under our control. But for the time being remove utterly your desire; for if you desire some one of the things that are not under our control you are bound to be unfortunate; and, at the same time, not one of the things that are under our control, which it would be excellent for you to desire, is within your grasp. But employ only choice and refusal, and these too but lightly, and with reservations, and without straining.

3. With everything which entertains you, is useful, or of which you are fond, remember to say to yourself, beginning with the very least things, "What is its nature?" If you are fond of a jug, say, "I am fond of a jug"; for when it is broken you will not be disturbed. If you kiss your own child or wife, say to yourself that you are kissing a human being; for when it dies you will not be disturbed.

4. When you are on the point of putting your hand to some undertaking, remind yourself what the nature of that undertaking is. If you are going out of the house to bathe, put before your mind what happens at a public bath—those who splash you with water, those who jostle against you, those who vilify you and rob you. And thus you will set about your undertaking more securely if at the outset you say to yourself, "I want to take a bath, and, at the same time, to keep my moral purpose in harmony with nature." And so do in every undertaking. For thus, if anything happens to hinder you in your bathing, you will be ready to say, "Oh, well, this was not the only thing that I wanted, but I wanted also to keep your moral purpose in harmony with nature; and I shall not so keep it if I am vexed at what is going on."

5. It is not the things themselves that disturb men, but their judgements about these things. For example, death is nothing dreadful, or else Socrates too would have thought so, but the judgement that death is dreadful, *this* is the dreadful thing. When, therefore, we are hindered, or disturbed, or grieved, let us never blame anyone but ourselves, that means, our own judgements. It is the part of an uneducated person to blame

others where he himself fares ill; to blame himself is the part of one whose education has begun; to blame neither another nor his own self is the part of one whose education is already complete.

6. Be not elated at any excellence which is not your own. If the horse in his elation were to say, "I am beautiful," it could be endured; but when you say in your elation, "I have a beautiful horse," rest assured that you are elated at something good which belongs to a horse. What then, is your own? The use of external impressions. Therefore, when you are in harmony with nature in the use of external impressions, then be elated; for then it will be some good of your own at which you will be elated.

7. Just as on a voyage, when your ship has anchored, if you should go on shore to get fresh water, you may pick up a small shell-fish or little bulb on the way, but you have to keep your attention fixed on the ship, and turn about frequently for fear lest the captain should call; and if he calls, you must give up all these things, if you would escape being thrown on board all tied up like the sheep. So it is also in life: If there be given you, instead of a little bulb and a small shell-fish, a little wife and child, there will be no objection to that; only, if the Captain calls, give up all these things and run to the ship, without even turning around to look back. And if you are an old man, never even get very far away from the ship, for fear that when He calls you may be missing.

8. Do not seek to have everything that happens happen as you wish, but wish for everything to happen as it actually does happen, and your life will be serene.

9. Disease is an impediment to the body, but not to the moral purpose, unless that consents. Lameness is an impediment to the leg, but not to the moral purpose. And say this to yourself at each thing that befalls you; for you will find the thing to be an impediment to something else, but not to yourself.

10. In the case of everything that befalls you, remember to turn to yourself and see what faculty you have to deal with it. If you see a handsome lad or woman, you will find continence the faculty to employ here; if hard labour is laid upon you, you will find endurance; in this fashion, your external impressions will not run away with you.

11. Never say about anything, "I have lost it," but only "I have given it back." Is your child dead? It has been given back. Is your wife dead? She has been given back. "I have had my farm taken away." Very well, this too has been given back. "Yet it was a rascal who took it away." But what concern is it of yours by whose instrumentality the Giver called for its return? So long as He gives it to you, take care of it as of a thing that is not your own, as travellers treat their inn.

12. If you wish to make progress, dismiss all reasoning of this sort: "If I neglect my affairs, I shall have nothing to live on." "If I do not punish my slave-boy he will turn out bad." For it is better to die of hunger, but in a state of freedom from grief and fear, than to live in plenty, but troubled in mind. And it is better for your slave-boy to be bad than for you to be unhappy. Begin, therefore, with the little things. Your paltry oil gets spilled, your miserable wine stolen; say to yourself, "This is the price paid for a calm spirit, this the price for peace of mind." Nothing is got without a price. And when you call your slave-boy, bear in mind that it is possible he may not heed you, and again, that even if he does heed, he may not do what you want done. But he is not in so happy a condition that your peace of mind depends upon him.

13. If you wish to make progress, then be content to appear senseless and foolish in externals, do not make it your wish to give the appearance of knowing anything; and if some people think you to be an important personage, distrust yourself. For be assured that it is no easy matter to keep your moral purpose in a state of conformity with nature, and, at the same time, to keep externals; but the man who devotes his attention to one of these two things must inevitably neglect the other.

14. If you make it your will that your children and your wife and your friends should live forever, you are silly; for you are making it your will that things not under your control should be under your control, and that what is not your own should be your own. In the same way, too, if you make it your will that your slave-boy be free from faults, you are a fool; for you are making it your will that vice be not vice, but something else. If, however, it is your will not to fail in what you desire, this is in your power. Wherefore, exercise yourself in that which is in your power. Each man's master is the person who has the authority over what the man wishes or does not wish, so as to secure it, or take it away. Whoever, therefore, wants to be free, let him neither wish for anything, nor avoid anything, that is under the control of others; or else he is necessarily a slave.

15. Remember that you ought to behave in life as you would at a banquet. As something is being passed around it comes to you; stretch out your hand and take a portion of it politely. It passes on; do not detain it. Or it has not come to you yet; do not project your desire to meet it, but wait until it comes in front of you. So act toward children, so toward a wife, so toward office, so toward wealth; and then some day you will be worthy of the banquets of the gods. But if you do not take these things even when they are set before you, but despise them, then you will not only share the banquet of the gods, but share also their rule. For it was by so doing that Diogenes and Heracleitus, and men like them, were deservedly divine and deservedly so called.

16. When you see someone weeping in sorrow, either because a child has gone on a journey, or because he has lost his property, beware that you be not carried away by the impression that the man is in the midst of external ills, but straightway keep before you this thought: "It is not what has happened that distresses this man (for it does not distress another), but his judgement about it." Do not, however, hesitate to sympathize with him so far as words go, and, if occasion offers, even to groan with him; but be careful not to groan also in the centre of your being.

17. Remember that you are an actor in a play, the character of which is determined by the Playwright: if He wishes the play to be short, it is short; if long, it is long; if He wishes you to play the part of a beggar, remember to act even this role adroitly; and so if your role be that of a cripple, an official, or a layman. For this is your business, to play admirably the role assigned you; but the selection of that rôle is Another's.

18. When a raven croaks inauspiciously, let not the external impression carry you away, but straightway draw a distinction in your own mind, and say, "None of these portents are for me, but either for my paltry body, or my paltry estate, or my paltry opinion, or my children, or my wife. But for me every portent is favourable, if I so wish; for whatever be the outcome, it is within my power to derive benefit from it."

19. You can be invincible if you never enter a contest in which victory is not under your control. Beware lest, when you see some person preferred to you in honour, or possessing great power, or otherwise enjoying high repute, you are ever carried away by the external impression, and deem him happy. For if the true nature of the good is one of the things that are under our control, there is no place for either envy or jealousy; and you yourself will not wish to be a praetor, or a senator, or a consul, but a free man. Now there is but one way that leads to this, and that is to despise the things that are not under our control.

20. Bear in mind that it is not the man who reviles or strikes you that insults you, but it is your judgement that these men are insulting you. Therefore, when someone irritates you, be assured that it is your own opinion which has irritated you. And so make it your first endeavour not to be carried away by the external impression; for if once you gain time and delay, you will more easily become master of yourself.

Theater at Ephesus, Turkey, built A.D. 41–117. In theaters like this, with a capacity for more than eighteen thousand spectators, Greek playwrights presented all-day festivals of drama on every phase of Greek life from the tragic to the comic. It is not surprising that Epictetus uses the image of the play and the playwright to make his point. *(Gian Berto Vanni/Art Resource)*

21. Keep before your eyes day by day death and exile, and everything that seems terrible, but most of all death; and then you will never have any abject thought, nor will you yearn for anything beyond measure.

22. If you yearn for philosophy, prepare at once to be met with ridicule, to have many people jeer at you, and say, "Here he is again, turned philosopher all of a sudden," and "Where do you suppose he got that high brow?" But do you not put on a high brow, and do you so hold fast to the things which to you seem best, as a man who has been assigned by God to this post; and remember that if you abide by the same principles, those who formerly used to laugh at you will later come to admire you, but if you are worsted by them, you will get the laugh on yourself twice.

23. If it should ever happen to you that you turn to externals with a view to pleasing someone, rest assured that you have lost your plan of life. Be content, therefore, in everything to be a philosopher, and if you wish also to be taken for one, show to yourself that you are one, and you will be able to accomplish it.

24. Let not these reflections oppress you: "I shall live without honour, and be nobody anywhere." For, if lack of honour is an evil, you cannot be in evil through the instrumentality of some other person, any more than you can be in shame. It is not your business, is it, to get office, or to be invited to a dinner-party? Certainly not. How, then, can this be any longer a lack of honour? And how is it that you will be "nobody anywhere," when you ought to be somebody only in those things which are under your control, wherein you are privileged to be a man of the very greatest honour? But your

friends will be without assistance? What do you mean by being "without assistance"? They will not have paltry coin from you, and you will not make them Roman citizens. Well, who told you that these are some of the matters under our control, and not rather things which others do? And who is able to give another what he does not himself have? "Get money, then," says some friend, "in order that we too may have it." If I can get money and at the same time keep myself self-respecting, and faithful, and high-minded, show me the way and I will get it. But if you require me to lose the good things that belong to me, in order that you may acquire the things that are not good, you can see for yourselves how unfair and inconsiderate you are. And which do you really prefer? Money, or a faithful and self-respecting friend? Help me, therefore, rather to this end, and do not require me to do those things which will make me lose these qualities.

"But my country," says he, "so far as lies in me, will be without assistance." Again I ask, what kind of assistance do you mean? It will not have loggias or baths of your providing. And what does that signify? For neither does it have shoes provided by the blacksmith, nor has it arms provided by the cobbler; but it is sufficient if each man fulfil his own proper function. And if you secured for it another faithful and self-respecting citizen, would you not be doing it any good? "Yes." Very well, and then you also would not be useless to it. "What place, then, shall I have in the State?" says he. Whatever place you can have, and at the same time maintain the man of fidelity and self-respect that is in you. But if, through your desire to help the State, you lose these qualities, of what good would you become to it, when in the end you turned out to be shameless and unfaithful?

25. Has someone been honoured above you at a dinner-party, or in salutation, or in being called in to give advice? Now if these matters are good, you ought to be happy that he got them; but if evil, be not distressed because you did not get them; and bear in mind that, if you do not act the same way that others do, with a view to getting things which are not under our control, you cannot be considered worthy to receive an equal share with others. Why, how is it possible for a person who does not haunt some man's door, to have equal shares with the man who does? For the man who does not do escort duty, with the man who does? For the man who does not praise, with the man who does? You will be unjust, therefore, and insatiable, if, while refusing to pay the price for which such things are bought, you want to obtain them for nothing. Well, what is the price for heads of lettuce? An obol, perhaps. If, then, somebody gives up his obol and gets his heads of lettuce, while you do not give your obol, and do not get them, do not imagine that you are worse off than the man who gets his lettuce. For as he has his heads of lettuce, so you have your obol which you have not given away.

Now it is the same way also in life. You have not been invited to somebody's dinner-party? Of course not; for you didn't give the host the price at which he sells his dinner. He sells it for praise; he sells it for personal attention. Give him the price, then, for which it is sold, if it is to your interest. But if you wish both not to give up the one and yet to get the other, you are insatiable and a simpleton. Have you, then, nothing in place of the dinner? Indeed you have; you have not had to praise the man you did not want to praise; you have not had to put up with the insolence of his doorkeepers.

26. What the will of nature is may be learned from a consideration of the points in which we do not differ from one another. For example, when some other person's slave-boy breaks his drinking-cup, you are instantly ready to say. "That's one of the things which happen." Rest assured, then, that when your own drinking-cup gets broken, you ought to behave in the same way that you do when the other man's cup is broken. Apply now the same principle to the matters of greater importance. Some other person's child or wife has died; no one but would say, "Such is the fate of man." Yet

when a man's own child dies, immediately the cry is, "Alas! Woe is me!" But we ought to remember how we feel when we hear of the same misfortune befalling others.

27. Just as a mark is not set up in order to be missed, so neither does the nature of evil arise in the universe.

28. If someone handed over your body to any person who met you, you would be vexed; but that you hand over your mind to any person that comes along, so that, if he reviles you, it is disturbed and troubled—are you not ashamed of that?

29. In each separate thing that you do, consider the matters which come first and those which follow after, and only then approach the thing itself. Otherwise, at the start you will come to it enthusiastically, because you have never reflected upon any of the subsequent steps, but later on, when some difficulties appear, you will give up disgracefully. Do you wish to win an Olympic victory? So do I, by the gods! for it is a fine thing. But consider the matters which come before that, and those which follow after, and only when you have done that, put your hand to the task. You have to submit to discipline, follow a strict diet, give up sweet cakes, train under compulsion, at a fixed hour, in heat or in cold; you must not drink cold water, nor wine just whenever you feel like it; you must have turned yourself over to your trainer precisely as you would to a physician. Then when the contest comes on, you have to "dig in" beside your opponent, and sometimes dislocate your wrist, sprain your ankle, swallow quantities of sand, sometimes take a scourging, and along with all that get beaten. After you have considered all these points, go on into the games, if you still wish to do so; otherwise, you will be turning back like children. Sometimes they play wrestlers, again gladiators, again they blow trumpets, and then act a play. So you too are now an athlete, now a gladiator, then a rhetorician, then a philosopher, yet with your whole soul nothing; but like an ape you imitate whatever you see, and one thing after another strikes your fancy. For you have never gone out after anything with circumspection, nor after you had examined it all over, but you act haphazard and half-heartedly.

In the same way, when some people have seen a philosopher and have heard someone speaking like Euphrates (though, indeed, who can speak like him?), they wish to be philosophers themselves. Man, consider first the nature of the business, and then learn your own natural ability, if you are able to bear it. Do you wish to be a contender in the pentathlon, or a wrestler? Look to your arms, your thighs, see what your loins are like. For one man has a natural talent for one thing, another for another. Do you suppose that you can eat in the same fashion, drink in the same fashion, give way to impulse and to irritation, just as you do now? You must keep vigils, work hard, abandon your own people, be despised by a paltry slave, be laughed to scorn by those who meet you, in everything get the worst of it, in honour, in office, in court, in every paltry affair. Look these drawbacks over carefully, if you are willing at the price of these things to secure tranquillity, freedom and calm. Otherwise, do not approach philosophy; don't act like a child—now a philosopher, later on a tax-gatherer, then a rhetorician, then a procurator of Caesar. These things do not go together. You must be one person, either good or bad; you must labour to improve either your own government principle or externals; you must work hard either on the inner man, or on things outside; that is, play either the rôle of a philosopher or else that of a layman.

30. Our duties are in general measured by our social relationships. He is a father. One is called upon to take care of him, to give way to him in all things, to submit when he reviles or strikes you. "But he is a bad father." Did nature, then, bring you into relationship with a *good* father? No, but simply with a father. "My brother does me wrong." Very well, then, maintain the relation that you have toward him; and do not consider what he is doing, but what you will have to do, if your moral purpose is to be in har-

mony with nature. For no one will harm you without your consent; you will have been harmed only when you think you are harmed. In this way, therefore, you will discover what duty to expect of your neighbour, your citizen, your commanding officer, if you acquire the habit of looking at your social relations with them.

31. In piety towards the gods, I would have you know, the chief element is this, to have right opinions about them—as existing and as administering the universe well and justly—and to have set yourself to obey them and to submit to everything that happens, and to follow it voluntarily, in the belief that it is being fulfilled by the highest intelligence. For if you act in this way, you will never blame the gods, nor find fault with them for neglecting you. But this result cannot be secured in any other way than by withdrawing your idea of the good and the evil from the things which are not under our control, and placing it in those which are under our control, and in those alone. Because, if you think any of those former things to be good or evil, then, when you fail to get what you want and fall into what you do not want, it is altogether inevitable that you will blame and hate those who are responsible for these results. For this is the nature of every living creature, to flee from and to turn aside from the things that appear harmful, and all that produces them, and to pursue after and to admire the things that are helpful, and all that produces them. Therefore, it is impossible for a man who thinks that he is being hurt to take pleasure in that which he thinks is hurting him, just as it is also impossible for him to take pleasure in the hurt itself. Hence it follows that even a father is reviled by a son when he does not give his child some share in the things that seem to be good; and this it was which made Polyneices and Eteocles enemies of one another, the thought that the royal power was a good thing. That is why the farmer reviles the gods, and so also the sailor, and the merchant, and those who have lost their wives and their children. For where a man's interest lies, there is also his piety. Wherefore, whoever is careful to exercise desire and aversion as he should, is at the same time careful also about piety. But it is always appropriate to make libations, and sacrifices, and to give of the firstfruits after the manner of our fathers, and to do all this with purity, and not in a slovenly or careless fashion, nor, indeed, in a miserly way, nor yet beyond our means.

32. When you have recourse to divination, remember that you do not know what the issue is going to be, but that you have come in order to find this out from the diviner; yet if you are indeed a philosopher, you know, when you arrive, what the nature of it is. For if it is one of the things which are not under our control, it is altogether necessary that what is going to take place is neither good nor evil. Do not, therefore, bring to the diviner desire or aversion, and do not approach him with trembling, but having first made up your mind that every issue is indifferent and nothing to you, but that, whatever it may be, it will be possible for you to turn it to good use, and that no one will prevent this. Go, then, with confidence to the gods as to counsellors; and after that, when some counsel has been given you, remember whom you have taken as counsellors, and whom you will be disregarding if you disobey. But go to divination as Socrates thought that men should go, that is, in cases where the whole inquiry has reference to the outcome, and where neither from reason nor from any other technical art are means vouchsafed for discovering the matter in question. Hence, when it is your duty to share the danger of a friend or of your country, do not ask of the diviner whether you ought to share that danger. For if the diviner forewarns you that the omens of sacrifice have been unfavourable, it is clear that death is portended, or the injury of some member of your body, or exile; yet reason requires that even at this risk you are to stand by your friend, and share the danger with your country. Wherefore, give heed to the greater diviner, the Pythian Apollo, who cast out of his temple the man who had not helped his friend when he was being murdered.

33. Lay down for yourself, at the outset, a certain stamp and type of character for yourself, which you are to maintain whether you are by yourself or are meeting with people. And be silent for the most part, or else make only the most necessary remarks, and express these in few words. But rarely, and when occasion requires you to talk, talk, indeed, but about no ordinary topics. Do not talk about gladiators, or horse-races, or athletes, or things to eat or drink—topics that arise on all occasions; but above all, do not talk about people, either blaming, or praising, or comparing them. If, then, you can, by your own conversation bring over that of your companions to what is seemly. But if you happen to be left alone in the presence of aliens, keep silence.

Do not laugh much, nor at many things, nor boisterously.

Refuse, if you can, to take an oath at all, but if that is impossible, refuse as far as circumstances allow.

Avoid entertainments given by outsiders and by persons ignorant of philosophy; but if an appropriate occasion arises for you to attend, be on the alert to avoid lapsing into the behaviour of such laymen. For you may rest assured, that, if a man's companion be dirty, the person who keeps close company with him must of necessity get a share of his dirt, even though he himself happens to be clean.

In things that pertain to the body take only as much as your bare need requires, I mean such things as food, drink, clothing, shelter, and household slaves; but cut down everything which is for outward show or luxury.

In your sex-life preserve purity, as far as you can, before marriage, and, if you indulge, take only those privileges which are lawful. However, do not make yourself offensive, or censorious, to those who do indulge, and do not make frequent mention of the fact that you do not yourself indulge.

If someone brings you word that So-and-so is speaking ill of you, do not defend yourself against what has been said, but answer, "Yes, indeed, for he did not know the rest of the faults that attach to me; if he had, these would not have been the only ones he mentioned."

It is not necessary, for the most part, to go to the public shows. If, however, a suitable occasion ever arises, show that your principal concern is for none other than yourself, which means, wish only for that to happen which does happen, and for him only to win who does win; for so you will suffer no hindrance. But refrain utterly from shouting, or laughter at anyone, or great excitement. And after you have left, do not talk a great deal about what took place, except in so far as it contributes to your own improvement; for such behaviour indicates that the spectacle has aroused your admiration.

Do not go rashly or readily to people's public reading, but when you do go, maintain your own dignity and gravity, and at the same time be careful not to make yourself disagreeable.

When you are about to meet somebody, in particular when it is one of those men who are held in very high esteem, propose to yourself the question, "What would Socrates or Zeno have done under these circumstances?" and then you will not be at a loss to make proper use of the occasion. When you go to see one of those men who have great power, propose to yourself the thought that you will not find him at home, that you will be shut out, that the door will be slammed in your face, that he will pay no attention to you. And if, despite all this, it is your duty to go, go and take what comes, and never say to yourself, "It was not worth all the trouble." For this is characteristic of the layman, that is, a man who is vexed at externals.

In your conversation avoid making mention at great length and excessively of your own deeds or dangers, because it is not as pleasant for others to hear about your adventures, as it is for you to call to mind your own dangers.

Avoid also raising a laugh, for this is a kind of behaviour that slips easily into vulgarity, and at the same time is calculated to lessen the respect which your neighbours have of you. It is dangerous also to lapse into foul language. When, therefore, anything of the sort occurs, if the occasion be suitable, go even so far as to reprove the person who has made such a lapse; if, however, the occasion does not arise, at all events show by keeping silence, and blushing, and frowning, that you are displeased by what has been said.

34. When you get an external impression of some pleasure, guard yourself, as with impressions in general, against being carried away by it; nay, let the matter wait upon your leisure, and give yourself a little delay. Next think of the two periods of time, first, that in which you will enjoy your pleasure, and second, that in which, after the enjoyment is over, you will later repent and revile your own self; and set over against these two periods of time how much joy and self-satisfaction you will get if you refrain. However, if you feel that a suitable occasion has arisen to do the deed, be careful not to allow its enticement, and sweetness, and attractiveness to overcome you; but set over against all this the thought, how much better is the consciousness of having won a victory over it.

35. When you do a thing which you have made up your mind ought to be done, never try not to be seen doing it, even though most people are likely to think unfavourably about it. If, however, what you are doing is not right, avoid the deed itself altogether; but if it is right, why fear those who are going to rebuke you wrongly?

36. Just as the propositions, "It is day," and "it is night," are full of meaning when separated, but meaningless if united; so also, granted that for you to take the larger share at a dinner is good for your body, still, it is bad for the maintenance of the proper kind of social feeling. When, therefore, you are eating with another person, remember to regard, not merely the value for your body of what lies before you, but also to maintain your respect for your host.

37. If you undertake a role which is beyond your powers, you both disgrace yourself in that one, and at the same time neglect the role which you might have filled with success.

38. Just as you are careful, in walking about, not to step on a nail or to sprain your ankle, so be careful also not to hurt your governing principle. And if we observe this rule in every action, we shall be more secure in setting about it.

39. Each man's body is a measure for his property, just as the foot is a measure for his shoe. If, then, you abide by this principle, you will maintain the proper measure, but if you go beyond it, you cannot help but fall headlong over a precipice, as it were, in the end. So also in the case of your shoe; if once you go beyond the foot, you get first a gilded shoe, then a purple one, then an embroidered one. For once you go beyond the measure there is no limit.

40. Immediately after they are fourteen, women are called "ladies" by men. And so when they see that they have nothing else but only to be the bedfellows of men, they begin to beautify themselves, and put all their hopes in that. It is worthwhile for us to take pains, therefore, to make them understand that they are honoured for nothing else but only for appearing modest and self-respecting.

41. It is a mark of an ungifted man to spend a great deal of time in what concerns his body, as in much exercise, much eating, much drinking, much evacuating of the bowels, much copulating. But these things are to be done in passing; and let your whole attention be devoted to the mind.

42. When someone treats you ill or speaks ill of you, remember that he acts or speaks thus because he thinks it is incumbent upon him. That being the case, it is im-

possible for him to follow what appears good to you, but what appears good to himself; whence it follows that, if he gets a wrong view of things, the man that suffers is the man that has been deceived. For if a person thinks a true composite judgement to be false, the composite judgement does not suffer, but the person who has been deceived. If, therefore, you start from this point of view, you will be gentle with the man who reviles you. For you should say on each occasion, "He thought that way about it."

43. Everything has two handles, by one of which it ought to be carried and by the other not. If your brother wrongs you, do not lay hold of the matter by the handle of the wrong that he is doing, because this is the handle by which the matter ought not to be carried; but rather by the other handle—that he is your brother, that you were brought up together, and then you will be laying hold of the matter by the handle by which it ought to be carried.

44. The following statements constitute a *non sequitur:* "I am richer than you are, therefore I am superior to you"; or, "I am more eloquent than you are, therefore I am superior to you." But the following conclusions are better: "I am richer than you are, therefore my property is superior to yours"; or, "I am more eloquent than you are, therefore my elocution is superior to yours." But *you* are neither property nor elocution.

45. Somebody is hasty about bathing; do not say that he bathes badly, but that he is hasty about bathing. Somebody drinks a good deal of wine; do not say that he drinks badly, but that he drinks a good deal. For until you have decided what judgement prompts him, how do you know that what he is doing is bad? And thus the final result will not be that you receive convincing sense-impressions of some things, but give your assent to others.

46. On no occasion call yourself a philosopher, and do not, for the most part, talk among laymen about your philosophic principles, but do what follows from your principles. For example, at a banquet do not say how people ought to eat, but eat as a man ought. For remember how Socrates had so completely eliminated the thought of ostentation, that people came to him when they wanted him to introduce them to philosophers, and he used to bring them along. So well did he submit to being overlooked. And if talk about some philosophic principle arises among laymen, keep silence for the most part for there is great danger that you will spew up immediately what you have not digested. So when a man tells you that you know nothing, and you, like Socrates, are not hurt, then rest assured that you are making a beginning with the business you have undertaken. For sheep, too, do not bring their fodder to the shepherds and show how much they have eaten, but they digest their food within them, and on the outside produce wool and milk. And so do you, therefore, make no display to the laymen of your philosophical principles, but let them see the results which come from these principles when digested.

47. When you have become adjusted to simple living in regard to your bodily wants, do not preen yourself about the accomplishment; and so likewise, if you are a water-drinker, do not on every occasion say that you are a water-drinker. And if ever you want to train to develop physical endurance, do it by yourself and not for outsiders to behold; do not throw your arms around statues, but on occasion, when you are very thirsty, take cold water into your mouth, and then spit it out, without telling anybody.

48. This is the position and character of a layman: He never looks for either help or harm from himself, but only from externals. This is the position and character of the philosopher: He looks for all his help or harm from himself.

Signs of one who is making progress are: He censures no one, praises no one, blames no one, finds fault with no one, says nothing about himself as though he were somebody or knew something. When he is hampered or prevented, he blames himself.

And if anyone compliments him, he smiles to himself at the person complimenting; while if anyone censures him, he makes no defence. He goes about like an invalid, being careful not to disturb, before it has grown firm, any part which is getting well. He has put away from himself his every desire, and has transferred his aversion to those things only, of what is under our control, which are contrary to nature. He exercises no pronounced choice in regard to anything. If he gives the appearance of being foolish or ignorant he does not care. In a word, he keeps guard against himself as though he were his own enemy lying in wait.

49. When a person gives himself airs because he can understand and interpret the books of Chrysippus, say to yourself, "If Chrysippus had not written obscurely, this man would have nothing about which to give himself airs."

But what is it I want? To learn nature and to follow her. I seek, therefore, someone to interpret her; and having heard that Chrysippus does so, I go to him. But I do not understand what he has written; I seek, therefore, the person who interprets Chrysippus. And down to this point there is nothing to justify pride. But when I find the interpreter, what remains is to put his precepts into practice; this is the only thing to be proud about. If, however, I admire the mere act of interpretation, what have I done but turned into a grammarian instead of a philosopher? The only difference, indeed, is that I interpret Chrysippus instead of Homer. Far from being proud, therefore, when somebody says to me, "Read me Chrysippus," I blush the rather, when I am unable to show him such deeds as match and harmonize with his words.

50. Whatever principles are set before you, stand fast by these like laws, feeling that it would be impiety for you to transgress them. But pay no attention to what somebody says about you, for this is, at length, not under your control.

51. How long will you still wait to think yourself worthy of the best things, and in nothing to transgress against the distinctions set up by the reason? You have received the philosophical principles which you ought to accept, and you have accepted them. What sort of a teacher, then, do you still wait for, that you should put off reforming yourself until he arrives? You are no longer a lad, but already a full-grown man. If you are now neglectful and easy-going, and always making one delay after another, and fixing first one day and then another, after which you will pay attention to yourself, then without realizing it you will make no progress, but, living and dying, will continue to be a layman throughout. Make up your mind, therefore, before it is too late, that the fitting thing for you to do is to live as a mature man who is making progress, and let everything which seems to you to be best be for you a law that must not be transgressed. And if you meet anything that is laborious, or sweet, or held in high repute, or in no repute, remember that now is the contest, and here before you are the Olympic games, and that it is impossible to delay any longer, and that it depends on a single day and a single action, whether progress is lost or saved. This is the way Socrates became what he was, by paying attention to nothing but his reason in everything that he encountered. And even if you are not yet a Socrates, still you ought to live as one who wishes to be a Socrates.

52. The first and most necessary division in philosophy is that which has to do with the application of the principles, as, for example, Do not lie. The second deals with the demonstrations, as, for example, How comes it that we ought not to lie? The third confirms and discriminates between these processes, as, for example, How does it come that this is a proof? For what is a proof, what is logical consequence, what contradiction, what truth, what falsehood? Therefore, the third division is necessary because of the second, and the second because of the first; while the most necessary of all, and the one in which we ought to rest, is the first. But we do the opposite; for we spend our time in the third division, and all our zeal is devoted to it, while we utterly neglect the first.

Wherefore, we lie, indeed, but are ready with the arguments which prove that one ought not to lie.

53. Upon every occasion we ought to have the following thoughts at our command:

Lead thou me on, O Zeus, and Destiny,
To that goal long ago to me assigned.
I'll follow and not falter; if my will
Prove weak and craven, still I'll follow on.—Cleanthes

"Whoso has rightly with necessity complied, We count him wise, and skilled in things divine."—Euripides

"Well, O Crito, if so it is pleasing to the gods, so let it be."—Socrates [*Crito,* 43D]

"Anytus and Meletus can kill me, but they cannot hurt me."—Socrates [*Apology,* 30C]

Lucretius

ca. 99–55 B.C.

Virtually nothing is known of Titus Lucretius Carus except his famous poem, *De Rerum Natura (On the Nature of Things)*. According to a secondhand report, he was driven insane by a love potion and eventually committed suicide. Apart from this, our knowledge of his life can be gained only from his poem. From internal evidence it seems he came from a wealthy Roman family and that he did some travelling. He also seems to have intentionally avoided the social and political upheavals of his day.

In his poem Lucretius embraces and expounds the philosophy of Epicurus. In particular he develops his master's atomistic materialism. Lucretius holds that in all nature there are only atoms moving in a void. (Actually, Lucretius wrote in Latin and did not use the Greek word <atom>; his word was *primordia,* "first-beginnings.") As these atoms fall downward in empty space, some swerve from their course and collide with others. These collisions lead to the world as we experience it.

Lucretius uses this theory to explain human activity as well. The human soul is made up of very fine atoms, and free will is simply the result of a "swerve" of atoms. Sensation occurs when thin films or "idols" (i.e., images) are thrown off from objects and, entering us through our sense organs, jostle the atoms of the mind. Consciousness is also explained atomistically as the motion of our soul atoms.

Book Three of the *De Rerum Natura* is reprinted here in the Martin Ferguson

Smith translation. In this selection, Lucretius explains that his atomistic theory teaches that death is simply the cessation of sensation and consciousness: ". . . death is nothing to us, it matters not one jot, . . . when we shall no longer be, when the parting shall have come about between body and spirit from which we are compacted into one whole, then sure enough nothing at all will be able to happen to us, who will then no longer be. . . ." There is no afterlife to fear, no immortality to be sought: Death awaits everyone and is final.

* * *

On the Nature of Things is noted as much for its literary qualities as for its philosophy, and numerous books have been written about Lucretius' hexameter verse. John Masson, *Lucretius, Epicurean and Poet* (London: Murray, 1907–1909); George Santayana, *Three Philosophical Poets: Lucretius, Dante, and Goethe* (Cambridge, MA: Harvard University Press, 1910); and Henri Bergson, *The Philosophy of Poetry: The Genius of Lucretius,* translated by Wade Baskin (New York: Philosophical Library, 1959), consider Lucretius as both philosopher and poet. For a general explication of Lucretius' philosophy, see George Depue Hadzsits, *Lucretius and His Influence* (New York: Longmans, Green and Co., 1935); E.J. Kenney, *Lucretius* (Oxford: Oxford University Press, 1977); and Diskin Clay, *Lucretius and Epicurus* (Ithaca, NY: Cornell University Press, 1983). David Konstan, *Some Aspects of Epicurean Psychology* (Leiden, Netherlands: Brill, 1973), and James H. Nichols, Jr., *Epicurean Political Philosophy: The De Rerum Natura of Lucretius* (Ithaca, NY: Cornell University Press, 1976), are specialized studies; while Cosmo Alexander Gordon, *A Bibliography of Lucretius* (1962; reprinted Winchester, Hampshire, England: St. Paul's Bibliographies, 1985), provides a bibliography.

ON THE NATURE OF THINGS (in part)

BOOK THREE

O you who first amid so great a darkness were able to raise aloft a light so clear, illumining the blessings of life, you I follow, O glory of the Grecian race,* and now on the marks you have left I plant my own footsteps firm, not so much desiring to be your rival, as for love, because I yearn to copy you: for why should a swallow vie with swans, or what could a kid with its shaking limbs do in running to match himself with the strong horse's vigour? You are our father, the discoverer of truths, you supply us with a father's precepts, from your pages, illustrious man, as bees in the flowery glades sip all

*Epicurus.

Reprinted by permission of the publishers and the Loeb Classical Library from Lucretius, *De Rerum Natura,* translated by W.H.D. Rouse, revised by Martin Ferguson Smith (Cambridge, MA: Harvard University Press, 1975). Copyright © 1975 by Harvard University Press.

the sweets, so we likewise feed on all your golden words, your words of gold, ever most worthy of life eternal. For as soon as your reasoning begins to proclaim the nature of things revealed by your divine mind, away flee the mind's terrors, the walls of the world open out, I see action going on throughout the whole void: before me appear the gods in their majesty, and their peaceful abodes, which no winds ever shake nor clouds besprinkle with rain, which no snow congealed by the bitter frost mars with its white fall, but the air ever cloudless encompasses them and laughs with its light spread wide abroad. There moreover nature supplies everything, and nothing at any time impairs their peace of mind. But contrariwise nowhere appear the regions of Acheron; yet the earth is no hindrance to all being clearly seen, whatsoever goes on below under our feet throughout the void. Thereupon from all these things a sort of divine delight gets hold upon me and a shuddering, because nature thus by your power has been so manifestly laid open and uncovered in every part.

[31] And since I have shown of what kind are the beginnings of all things, and in how varying and different shapes they fly of their own accord driven in everlasting motion, and how all things can be produced from these, following next upon this the nature of mind and spirit must now clearly be explained in my verses, and that fear of Acheron be sent packing which troubles the life of man from its deepest depths, suffuses all with the blackness of death, and leaves no delight clean and pure. For when men often declare that disease and a life of infamy are more to be feared than the bottomless Pit of death, and that they know the nature of the soul to be that of blood or even air if their whim so direct, and that they have no need of our reasoning, what follows will show you that they make all these boasts in vainglory rather than because the fact itself is established. These same men, driven from their native land and banished far from the sight of men, stained with some disgraceful charge, in short afflicted with all tribulations, yet live; and in spite of all, wherever the wretches go they sacrifice to their ancestors, and slay black cattle, and send down oblations to the departed ghosts, and in their bitter days direct their minds far more eagerly to superstition. Thus it is more useful to scrutinize a man in danger or peril, and to discern in adversity what manner of man he is: for only then are the words of truth drawn up from the very heart, the mask is torn off, the reality remains.

[59] Moreover, avarice and the blind lust of distinction, which drive wretched men to transgress the bounds of law, and sometimes by sharing and scheming crime to strive night and day with exceeding toil to climb the pinnacle of power, these sores of life in no small degree are fed by the fear of death. For in general degrading scorn and bitter need are seen to be far removed from sweetness and stability of life, and a lingering as it were before the gates of death; from which men desiring to escape afar and to remove themselves far away, driven by false terror, amass wealth by civil bloodshed and greedily multiply riches, piling murder upon murder; cruelly they rejoice at the mournful death of a brother, they hate and they fear a kinsman's hospitality.

[74] In like manner and through the same fear, they are often consumed with envy that before their very eyes he is clothed in power, he is the sight of the town, who parades in shining pomp, while they complain that they themselves are wallowing in darkness and mire. Some wear out their lives for the sake of a statue and a name. And often it goes so far, that for fear of death men are seized by hatred of life and of seeing the light, so that with sorrowing heart they devise their own death, forgetting that this fear is the fountain of their cares: it induces one man to violate honour, another to break the bonds of friendship, and in a word to overthrow all natural feeling; for often before now men have betrayed fatherland or beloved parents in seeking to avoid the regions of Acheron. For as children tremble and fear everything in the blind darkness, so we in the

light sometimes fear what is no more to be feared than the things that children in the dark hold in terror and imagine will come true. This terror, therefore, and darkness of the mind must be dispersed, not by rays of the sun nor the bright shafts of daylight, but by the aspect and law of nature.

[94] First I say that the mind, which we often call the intelligence, in which is situated the understanding and the government of life, is a part of man, no less than hands and feet and eyes are parts of the whole living being.

[98] [However, some philosophers have thought] that the feeling of the mind is not situated in any fixed part, but that it is a sort of vital condition of the body, called harmony by the Greeks, which makes us live endowed with feeling, although the intelligence is not situated in any part; as when the body is often said to have good health, and yet this health is no part of the healthy creature. Thus they do not place the feeling of the mind in any fixed part; and in this they seem to me to wander very far astray. For indeed the body which we can see plain before us is often sick, although we are yet happy in the other part which lies hidden; and again it often happens that the contrary is true in its turn, when one wretched in mind is happy in all his body, not otherwise than if the sick man's foot gives him pain when there is no pain meanwhile in the head. Besides, when the frame is given over to soft sleep, and the body lies outspread heavy and without sensation, there is yet something in us which at that time is agitated in many ways, and admits into itself all the motions of joy and cares of the heart, which have no meaning.

[117] Next, that you may recognize that the spirit also lies within the frame and that it is not harmony that causes the body to feel, firstly it happens that if a great part of the body be taken away, yet life often remains in our frame; and again when a few particles of heat have dispersed abroad and air is driven out through the mouth, the same life in a moment deserts the veins and leaves the bones; so that from this you may recognize that not all particles have a like function or support life equally, but rather that those which are seeds of wind and warming heat see to it that life lingers in the frame. There is therefore within the body itself a heat and a vital wind which deserts our frame on the point of death.

[130] Therefore, since the nature of the mind and spirit has been found to be in some way a part of the man, give back the name of harmony, brought down to musicians from high Helicon, or perhaps the musicians themselves drew it from some other source and applied it to that which then lacked a name of its own. Be that how it may, let them keep it; do you now learn what else I have to say.

[136] Next, I say that mind and spirit are held in conjunction together and compound one nature in common, but that the head so to speak and lord over the whole body is the understanding which we call mind and intelligence. And this has its abiding place in the middle region of the breast. For in this place throbs terror and fear, hereabouts is melting joy: here therefore is the intelligence and the mind. The rest of the spirit, dispersed abroad through the whole body, obeys and is moved according to the will and working of the intelligence. This alone by itself has sense, alone for itself rejoices, when nothing affects either spirit or body at the same time. And just as when head or eye is hurt by an attack of pain in us we are not tormented in the whole of our body, so the mind sometimes is hurt by itself, and is eager with joy, when the rest of the spirit throughout the limbs and frame is not stirred by any new sensation. But when the intelligence is moved by more vehement fear, we see the whole spirit throughout the frame share in the feeling: sweatings and pallor hence arise over the whole body, the speech falters, the voice dies away, blackness comes before the eyes, a sounding is in the ears, the limbs give way beneath; in a word we often see men fall to the ground for

mental terror; so that everyone may easily recognize from this that the spirit is conjoined with the mind, and when this has been smitten by the mind's power, straightway it strikes and drives forward the body.

[161] This same reasoning teaches that the nature of mind and spirit is bodily; for when it is seen to drive forward the limbs, to arouse the body from sleep, to change the countenance, to guide and steer the whole man, and we see that none of these things can be done without touch, and further that there is no touch without body, must we not confess that mind and spirit have a bodily nature? Besides you perceive the mind to suffer along with the body, and to share our feeling in the body. If the grim force of a weapon driven deep to the dividing of bones and sinews fails to hit the life, yet a languor follows and a blissful fall to the ground, and upon the ground a turmoil that comes about in the mind, and sometimes a kind of hesitating desire to rise. Therefore the nature of the mind must be bodily, since it suffers by bodily weapons and blows.

[177] Now I shall go on to explain to you, of what kind of body this mind is, and of what it is formed. First I say that it is exceedingly delicate and formed of exceedingly minute particles. That this is so, you may consider the following points to convince you. Nothing is seen to be done so swiftly as the mind determines it to be done and does its own first act; therefore the mind bestirs itself more quickly than any of these things which are seen plain before our eyes. But that which is so readily moved must consist of seeds exceedingly rounded and exceedingly minute, that they may be moved when touched by a small moving power. For water moves and flows with so very small a moving power because it is made of small rolling shapes. But on the other hand the nature of honey has more cohesion, its fluid is more sluggish, and its movement more tardy; for the whole mass of its matter coheres more closely, assuredly because it is not made of bodies so smooth or so delicate and round. For a checked and light breath of air can make, as you may see, a high heap of poppy-seed slip down from the top; but contrariwise it cannot stir a pile of stones or wheat-ears. So, according as bodies are extremely small and smooth, they have power of motion; but contrariwise, whatever is found to be more weighty and rough is by so much the more stable. Now, therefore, since the nature of the mind has been found to be moved with unusual ease, it must consist of bodies exceedingly small and smooth and round. If this be known to you, my good friend, it will be found of advantage in many ways, and you will call it useful.

[208] Another thing also makes clear of how fine a texture it is, and in how small a space it might be contained if it could be gathered together; namely that as soon as death's peaceful calm has taken possession of a man, when mind and spirit have departed, you could not perceive any jot or tittle to be diminished from the body whether in look or in weight: death presents all, except vital sense and warming heat. Accordingly the whole spirit must consist of very small seeds, being interlaced through veins, flesh, and sinews, since, when the whole has already departed from all the body, nevertheless the outward contour of the limbs presents itself undiminished, nor is one jot of the weight lacking; just as happens when the bouquet of wine has vanished, or when the sweet breath of ointment has dispersed into the air, or when the flavour has passed from a substance, and yet the thing itself does not seem any smaller to the eye for all that, nor is anything lost in the weight, because assuredly many minute seeds compose the flavour and the smell in the whole substance of the things. Therefore again and again I say, we may understand the substance of mind and spirit to be made of very minute seeds, since in departing it takes nothing from the weight.

[231] But we must not believe this nature to be single. For a kind of thin breath mixed with heat leaves the dying, and the heat, moreover, draws air with it. Nor is there any heat which is not mixed with air; for since its nature is rarefied, many first-

a.

b.

c.

d.

Roman Construction

The Romans were masters of practical construction. Many of their greatest architectural feats were devoted to transportation, commerce, and amusement (not unlike today).

a. The Roman Forum. Artist's Reconstruction. The Forum was the primary market and meeting place in Rome. *(Library of Congress/Instructional Resources Corp.)*

b. Appian Way. The Romans built excellent roads to places as far away as Britain. The roads were constructed of six inches of lava on top of twelve inches of gravel on top of nine inches of small stones on top of ten to twenty inches of large stones. The result was a solid thoroughfare that the army could use in all weather. *(Italian Tourist Office)*

c. Aqueduct. Aqueducts were used to bring water into the cities of the Empire. This one, in Spain, is still in use. *(Joelle Burrows)*

d. Circus Flaminius. Huge stadiums such as this one allowed for chariot races, horse races, and other spectacles. Admission was free and over 100,000 people would often attend. *(Library of Congress)*

beginnings of air must be moving through it. Already, therefore, the nature of the mind is found to be threefold; yet all these three together are not enough to produce feeling, since the mind cannot admit that any of these can produce sense-bringing motions and the thoughts which a man revolves in his mind. A fourth nature must therefore be added to these; this is entirely without name; nothing exists more easily moved and more thin than this, or made of elements smaller and smoother; and this first distributes the sense-giving motions through the limbs. For this is first set in motion, being composed of small shapes; after that, heat takes on the movement, and the unseen power of wind, then the air; after which all is set in movement, the blood is agitated, the flesh is all thrilled through with feeling, last is communicated to bone and marrow it may be: the pleasure, it may be the opposite excitement. Nor is it easy for pain to soak through thus far, or any violent mischief, without throwing all into so great a riot that no place is left for life, and the particles of spirit flee abroad through all the pores of the body. But usually there is an end to the movement almost at the surface of the body; on this account we are strong enough to retain life.

[258] Now when I long to explain how these things are intermingled and in what ways they are arranged so as to be active, I am drawn away against my will by the poverty of our mother tongue; but notwithstanding I will touch upon the chief points, so far as I can.

[262] The first-beginnings of the elements so interpenetrate one another in their motions that no single element can be separated off nor can its power act divided from the rest by space, but they are, as it were, the many forces of a single body. Just as in the flesh of any living creature there is a scent and a certain heat and flavour, and yet from all these is made one body grown complete: so heat and air and the unseen power of wind commingled form one nature along with that quickly moving force, which from itself distributes amongst them the beginning of motion, whence first the sense-bringing motion arises spreading through the flesh. For this nature lies deep down, hidden in the most secret recess, and there is nothing in our body more deeply seated than this; and it is itself furthermore the spirit of the whole spirit. Just as commingled in our frame and in all our body the force of mind and the power of spirit lies hidden, because it is composed of small and scanty elements: so, I tell you, this force without name composed of minute particles lies hid, and is furthermore itself as it were spirit of the whole spirit and lords it in all the body. In like manner it is necessary that wind and air and heat interact commingled throughout the frame, one element yielding place to another or rising pre-eminent in such a way that a unity be seen to be made of all, or else heat and wind apart and the power of air apart would destroy and dissipate the sensation by being separated.

[288] The mind has also that heat, which it takes on when it boils in wrath and fire flashes more fiercely from the eyes; it has also abundance of that cold wind, fear's comrade, which makes the limbs shiver and stirs the frame; it has too that quietude of calm air which comes about when the heart is tranquil and the countenance serene. But there is more of the hot in those creatures whose bitter hearts and angry minds easily boil up in wrath. A notable instance of this is the violent fury of the lion, which so often bursts his breast with roaring and growling, nor can he find room in his heart for the storm of passion. But the cold mind of the stag has more of wind, and more speedily sends currents of cold breath through his flesh, which cause a tremulous movement to pervade the limbs. But the nature of the cow lives more by the peaceful air; never overmuch excited by the smoky torch of wrath which when applied spreads a shade of blinding darkness around, never pierced and frozen with cold shafts of fear: she stands between the two, stags and wild lions.

[307] So also is it in the race of men: although training may bring some to an equal outside polish, yet it leaves there those original traces of the character of each mind. And we must not suppose that faults can be torn up by the roots, so that one man will not too readily run into bitter anger, another be attacked somewhat too soon by fear, a third put up with an affront more meekly than he should. And in many other respects the various natures of men must differ, and the habits that follow from them; I cannot now set forth the hidden causes of these, nor find names enough to fit the shapes assumed by the first-beginnings from which arises this variety in things. One thing I see that I can affirm in this regard is this: so trivial are the traces of different natures that remain, beyond reason's power to expel, that nothing hinders our living a life worthy of gods.

[323] This nature then is contained by the whole body, and is itself the body's guardian and source of its existence, for they cling together with common roots, and manifestly they cannot be torn asunder without destruction. Just as it is not easy to tear out the scent from lumps of frankincense, without its very nature being destroyed: so it is not easy to draw out mind and spirit from the whole body, without the dissolution of all. So interwoven are their elements from their first origin in the life which they live together; and we see that neither body nor mind has the power to feel singly without the other's help, but by common motions proceeding from both conjointly sensation is kindled for us in our flesh.

[337] Besides, a body is never born by itself, nor grows by itself, nor is it seen to last long after death. For it is not as when the liquid of water often throws off the heat which has been given to it, and yet is not itself torn to pieces for that reason, but remains uninjured; not thus, I say, can the frame endure disruption apart from the spirit which has left it; but it is utterly undone, torn to pieces, and rots away. From the first moment of life, the interdependent contacts of body and spirit, while yet laid away in the mother's body and womb, so learn the vital motions, that disruption apart cannot be without their ruin and damage; so that you may see that, since conjunction is necessary to their existence, so also theirs must be a joint nature.

[350] Furthermore, if anyone denies that body can feel, and believes that it is the spirit mingled throughout with the body that takes on that motion which we name feeling, he fights against things that are quite manifest and true. For who will ever explain what it is for the body to feel, unless it be what experience has openly shown and taught us? "But the spirit gone, the body lacks feeling in every part." Yes, for it loses that which in life was not its own property; as there are many other things that it loses when it is driven from life.

[359] Moreover, to say that the eyes can discern nothing, but that the mind looks out through them as through open portals, is difficult, when their own feeling leads us to the opposite conclusion; for it is their feeling that draws us and pushes us on to the very eyeballs; especially since we are often unable to perceive glaring objects because our bright eyes are hindered by the brightness, which never happens with portals; for an open door through which we look out ourselves never receives any annoyance. Besides, if our eyes act as portals, why then take the eyes away, and it is obvious that the mind should perceive things all the better with doors, posts and all, removed.

[370] There is another thing, laid down by the revered judgement of the great Democritus, to which you could never assent: that the first-beginnings of body and of soul are placed one beside one alternately in pairs, and so link the frame together. For, as the elements of spirit are much smaller than those which compose our body and flesh, so they are fewer also in number and are dispersed at rare intervals through the frame; so that at least you may safely say that the first-beginnings of spirit lie at such inter-

vals apart as equal the smallest things which falling upon us are able to awaken sense-bringing motions in our body. For sometimes we do not feel dust clinging to the body, or chalk* shaken on us settling on our limbs, nor do we feel the impact of a mist by night, or a spider's gossamer threads when we are caught in their net as we go along, nor the flimsy vesture of the same creature falling upon our head, nor birds' feathers or flying thistle-down, which are so exceeding light that they usually find it a heavy task to fall, nor the progress of every creeping thing, nor each of the footsteps that gnats and suchlike place on our body: so true is it that many particles must be moved in us, before the seeds of spirit mingled with our bodies throughout our frame begin to feel that the first-beginnings** have been struck, and before they can go buffeting over such great intervals, run together, meet together, and leap apart in turn.

[396] And the mind is more potent in holding fast the barriers of life, and has more dominance over life, than the spirit's force. For without the mind and intelligence no particle of the spirit can abide in the frame for an instant, but readily follows after it, and departs into the air, and leaves the limbs cold in the chill of death. But he remains in life to whom the mind and intelligence remains. He may be a mutilated trunk dismembered all about, the spirit removed all around and separated from the limbs, yet he lives and breathes the vital air. Deprived of a great part of the spirit, if not of all, yet he lingers and clings to life; just as when the eye is lacerated all round, if the pupil remains unhurt, there abides the lively power of seeing, provided you do not mangle the whole eyeball and cut round the pupil and leave that isolated; for that will not be done without destroying them both. But if that tiny spot in the middle of the eye is eaten through, in a trice the light is out and darkness follows, even though the radiant orb is otherwise unharmed. Such is the alliance by which spirit and mind are forever bound.

[417] Listen now: that you may be able to recognize that the minds and light spirits of living creatures are born and are mortal, I shall proceed to set forth verses worthy of your character, long sought out and found with delightful toil. Be so good as to apply both these names to one thing; and when for example I speak of spirit, showing it to be mortal, believe me to speak also of mind, inasmuch as it is one thing and a combined nature.

[425] First of all, since I have shown it to be delicate and composed of minute particles and elements much smaller than the flowing liquid of water or cloud or smoke—for it surpasses these far in quickness, and moves if touched by a more delicate cause, inasmuch as it is moved by images of smoke and mist, as for example when sunk in sleep we perceive altars exhale their steam on high and send up smoke (for without doubt these are images borne to us)—now, therefore, since, when vessels are shattered, you perceive the water flowing out on all sides and the liquid dispersing, and since mist and smoke disperse abroad into the air, believe that the spirit also is spread abroad and passes away far more quickly, and is more speedily dissolved into its first bodies, as soon as it has departed withdrawn from the limbs of a man. In fact if the body, which is in a way its vessel, cannot contain it, when once broken up by any cause and rarefied by the withdrawal of blood from the veins, how could you believe that it could be contained by any air, which is a more porous container than our body?

[445] Besides, we feel that the mind is begotten along with the body, and grows up with it, and with it grows old. For as toddling children have a body infirm and tender, so a weak intelligence goes with it. Next, when their age has grown up into robust

*[Chalk was used as a cosmetic and for bleaching clothes.]
**[The body-atoms.]

strength, the understanding too and the power of the mind is enlarged. Afterwards, when the body is now wrecked with the mighty strength of time, and the frame has succumbed with blunted strength, the intellect limps, the tongue babbles, the intelligence totters, all is wanting and fails at the same time. It follows therefore that the whole nature of the spirit is dissolved abroad, like smoke, into the high winds of the air, since we see it begotten along with the body, and growing up along with it, and as I have shown, falling to pieces at the same time worn out with age.

[459] Add to this that, just as the body itself is liable to awful diseases and harsh pain, so we see the mind liable to anxious care and grief and fear; therefore it follows that the mind also partakes of death.

[463] Moreover, in bodily diseases the mind often wanders astray; for it is demented and talks deliriously, and at times is carried by heavy lethargy into the deep everlasting sleep with eyes drooping and dejected head, from which it can neither catch the voices nor recognize the looks of those who stand round calling it back to life, their faces and cheeks bedewed with tears. Therefore you must confess that the mind also is dissolved, since the contagion of disease penetrates within it; for both pain and disease are makers of death, as we have been well taught by the perishing of many before now.

[476] Moreover, when the piercing power of wine has penetrated into a man, and its fire has been dispersed abroad, spreading through the veins, why does heaviness come upon the limbs, why are his legs impeded, why does he stagger, his tongue grow tardy, his mind soaked, his eyes swim, noise and hiccups and brawls burst out, and all the rest of such things follow, why is this, I say, unless it be that the vehement fury of wine is accustomed to confuse the spirit while yet in the body? But if anything can be confused and impeded, this indicates that, if some cause a little more compelling should penetrate, the thing would perish, and be robbed of its future life.

[487] Moreover, we have often seen someone constrained on a sudden by the violence of disease, who, as if struck by a thunderbolt, falls to the ground, foams at the mouth, groans and shudders, raves, grows rigid, twists, pants irregularly, outwearies himself with contortions; assuredly because the spirit, torn asunder by the violence of the disease throughout the frame, is in turmoil and foams, just as in the salt sea the waves boil under the mighty strength of the winds. Further, groans are forced out, because the limbs are afflicted with pain, and in general because seeds of voice are ejected and rush forth from the mouth in a mass, where they have been, as it were, accustomed to pass, where is the established highroad. There is raving, because the strength of mind and spirit is set in a turmoil and, as I have shown, divided apart and separated up and drawn asunder by that same poison. Next, when the cause of the disease has already turned back, and the corroding humour of the diseased body has returned to its secret haunts, then first, staggering as it were, the man rises, and by degrees comes back to his full senses and receives back his spirit. Since, therefore, the mind and spirit are tossed about by so great diseases in the very body itself, and are miserably torn asunder and distressed, why do you believe that the same without body, in the open air, amidst mighty winds, are able to live?

[510] And since we see that the mind, like a sick body, can be healed and changed by medicine, this also foreshows that the mind has a mortal life. For it is necessary to add parts or transpose them or draw away at least some tittle from the whole, whenever anyone attempts and begins to alter the mind or indeed to change any other nature whatever. But that which is immortal does not permit its parts to be transposed, or anything to be added, or one jot to ebb away; for whatever by being changed passes outside its own boundaries, at once that is death for that which was before. Therefore, if the mind is sick, it gives indications of mortality, as I have shown, or if it is changed by medicine:

so completely is the truth seen to combat false reasoning, and to cut off its retreat as it flies, and to convict falsehood by a double refutation.

[526] Furthermore, we often see a man pass away by degrees, and limb by limb lose the sensation of life: first the toes of the feet grow livid, and the nails, next die feet and legs, afterwards over the other limbs go creeping the cold footsteps of death. Since in this case the substance of the spirit is divided and passes away and does not issue forth whole at one time, it must be held to be mortal. But if by any chance you think that it can of its own accord pull itself inwards through the limbs and draw together its portions into one place, and that is how it withdraws sensation from all the limbs, then the place into which all that quantity of spirit is gathered together ought to seem more sensitive; but since this place is nowhere to be found, undoubtedly, as I said before, the spirit is torn to pieces and dispersed abroad, perishes therefore. Moreover, if I had the whim after all to concede a falsehood, and to grant you that the spirit might be concentrated in the body of those who are leaving the daylight by dying piecemeal, yet you must confess the spirit to be mortal, for it does not matter whether it passes away dispersed abroad through the air, or draws in its parts upon itself and grows dull, seeing that more and more sensation leaves the whole man on all sides, and on all sides less and less of life remains.

[548] And since the mind is one part of a man, which abides planted in a fixed place, just as eyes and ears are and all the other organs of sense that govern life; and just as hand or eye or nose separated from us can neither feel nor be, but rather are soon dissolved in putrefaction, so the mind cannot be by itself without body or without the man himself, which body seems to be a kind of vessel for it or any other similitude you may choose for a closer conjunction, since in fact the body does cling closely to it.

[558] Furthermore, the quickened power of body and mind have vigour and enjoy life only in close conjunction together; for neither can the nature of the mind show vital motions alone by itself without the body, nor again deprived of the spirit can the body endure and use the senses. To be sure, just as the eye torn from its roots cannot by itself distinguish anything apart from the whole body, so it is seen that mind and spirit can do nothing alone. Undoubtedly because their first-beginnings are held in by the whole body, commingled throughout veins and flesh, sinews and bones, and cannot leap freely apart through wide intervals: for this reason, when shut in together, they make those sense-giving motions, which they cannot make outside the body when cast forth into the winds of the air after death, because they are not held in as before. For air will be a body and a living creature, if the spirit shall be able to keep itself together, and to confine itself to those motions which before it used to make in the sinews and in the body itself. Therefore again and again I say, when all the covering of the body is broken up, and the breath of life is cast forth out, you must confess that the sensations of the mind are dissolved, and the spirit too, since the two exist by union.

[580] Again, since the body cannot endure tearing apart from the spirit without putrefying with a loathsome stench, why do you doubt that the strength of the spirit, after gathering together from its depths and inmost recesses, has oozed out already dispersed abroad like smoke, and that the reason why the body changing and crumbling in such ruin has collapsed altogether, is that its foundations to their inmost recesses have been moved from their place while the spirit was oozing out all through the limbs and through all the meandering passages and pores that are in the body? So that in many ways you may learn that the spirit was scattered abroad when it went out through the limbs, and had been torn all apart within the body itself, before it glided out and swam into the winds of the air. Moreover, while the spirit still moves about within the bounds of life, nevertheless, when weakened by some cause or other, it often appears to wish to

depart and to be released from the whole body, and the countenance appears to grow languid as at the last hour, and all the limbs to relax and droop from the bloodless body. This is what happens when the phrase is used "the mind fails" or "the spirit faints": when all is trepidation, and all those present desire to pull back again the last bond of life. For at that time the intelligence and all the power of the spirit are shaken altogether, and these fail together with the body itself, so that a slightly more serious cause could dissolve them. Why then after all do you doubt that, when driven without the body, weak, outside, in the open, without a covering, the spirit could not only not endure through all time, but could not last even for the smallest space?

[607] It is evident that no one in dying feels his soul go forth from the whole body intact, nor rise first to the throat and then pass up to the gullet; rather he feels it fail in the particular region where it is located, as he knows his other senses to be dispersing abroad each in its own part. But if our intelligence were immortal, in dying it would not so much complain of dispersing abroad, but rather of passing out and quitting its [skin], like a snake.

[615] Again, why are the mind's intelligence and understanding never produced in the head or feet or hands, but abide in one sole position and fixed region in all men, if not because fixed positions are assigned to each thing for its birth and a place where it may endure when made, with its manifold limbs being arranged in such a way that their order is never reversed? So surely one thing follows another; neither is flame accustomed to be produced from streams, nor frost in fire.

[624] Besides, if the nature of the spirit is immortal and can feel when separated from our body, we must, I think, assume that it is endowed with the five senses; in no other way can we imagine the spirits below to be wandering in Acheron. Painters therefore, and the earlier generations of writers, have introduced the spirits thus provided with senses. But apart from the body there can never be either eyes or nose or hand by itself for the spirit, nor tongue apart from the body, nor ears; therefore spirits by themselves cannot either have sensation or exist.

[634] And since we feel that vital sense inheres in the whole body, and see that it is the whole that is animated, if suddenly some force with a swift blow shall cut the body through the middle so as to sever the two parts asunder, there is no doubt that the spirit also will be sundered apart and cleft apart and cut apart with the body. But that which is cleft and divided into parts assuredly renounces all claim to be everlasting.

[642] They tell how scythed chariots,* reeking with indiscriminate slaughter, often shear off a limb so suddenly that it is seen to quiver on the ground when it falls shorn from the trunk, although the man's mind and strength can feel no pain, from the swiftness of the blow, and at the same time because the mind is absorbed in the ardour of battle; with what is left of his body he pursues battle and blood, and does not observe that his left arm, it may be, with its shield has been carried off amidst the horses by the wheels and their ravening scythes, or another that his right arm has fallen while he climbs and presses on. Then another essays to rise with a leg lost, while the dying foot hard by on the ground twitches its toes. Even the head shorn off from the hot and living trunk retains on the ground the look of life and its open eyes, until it has rendered up all that is left of the spirit.

[657] Moreover, when you see a serpent with flickering tongue, menacing tail, long body, if it please you to cut up both parts with your steel into many pieces, you will see all the parts cut away writhing separately while the wound is fresh, and bespattering

---

*[War-chariots with scythes (blades) attached to the wheels.]

the earth with gore, and the fore part turning back and seeking to gnaw itself, that by its bite it may assuage the burning pain of the wound which struck it. Shall we say then that there is a whole spirit in each of these fractions? But in that way it will follow that one living creature had many spirits in its body. Therefore that spirit which was one has been divided apart together with the body; and so each must be considered mortal, since each alike is cut asunder into many parts.

[670] Besides, if the nature of the spirit is immortal and creeps into the body as we are born, why can we not remember also the time that has passed before, and why do we keep no traces of things done? For if the power of the mind has been so greatly changed that it has lost all recollection of things done, that, I think, is not far removed from death. Therefore you must confess that the spirit that was before has perished, and that which now is has now been made.

[679] Besides, if the body is already complete when the quickened power of the mind is accustomed to be introduced into us, at the moment when we are born and when we enter the threshold of life, it ought not so to live that it should be seen to grow with the body and together with the frame in the very blood, but it should live alone by itself as it might be in a cage, while nevertheless all the body should be full of streams of sensation. Therefore again and again I say that spirits must not be considered to be without beginning or free from the law of death. For we must not believe that they could have been so closely connected with our bodies if they had been introduced from without, when experience manifestly proves the clean contrary; for the spirit is so closely connected with the body through all the veins, flesh, sinews, and bones that even the teeth feel like the rest, as their aching proves, and the twinge of cold water, and the crunching of rough grit, when it has got into them out of bread; and since they are so closely connected, it is clear that they are not able to emerge intact and loosen themselves away whole from all the sinews and bones and joints.

[698] But if by any chance you think that the spirit is accustomed to creep in from without and so to ooze through our frame, so much the more will it perish, being interfused with the body; for that which permeates is dissolved, perishes therefore. The spirit is distributed through all the pores of the body; just as food, while it is being dispersed into all the members and limbs, perishes and supplies, another nature from its substance, so spirit and mind, even though they enter whole into a new body, yet in permeating it are dissolved, while the particles are being dispersed through all the pores, as we may call them, into the limbs, those particles that compose this mind which now lords it in our body, born of that mind which perished at the time when it was distributed through the limbs. Therefore the spirit is seen to be neither without a birthday nor without death.

[713] Again, do any seeds of spirit remain or not in the lifeless body? Now if any are left and are in it, it will be impossible rightly to consider the spirit immortal, since it has gone away diminished by the loss of some parts. But if it has departed and fled forth with its component parts so intact that it has left in the body no particles of itself, how do corpses exhale worms from flesh already grown putrid,* whence comes all the great mass of living creatures, boneless and bloodless, that surge through the swelling limbs? Now if you believe by any chance that spirits can creep into the worms from without and come one by one into the bodies, if you do not ponder why many thousands of spirits gather together where one has gone away, here is a question that it seems worthwhile

---

*[Lucretius is reflecting the popular belief of his time that worms are spontaneously generated from dead flesh.]

to ask and to bring under examination, whether in fact the spirits go a-hunting for all the seeds of little worms and themselves make them a habitation, or whether they creep as it were into bodies already formed. But there is no answer to the question why they should make bodies themselves, or why they should take that trouble. For, when they are without bodies, they are not plagued with disease as they fly about, or with cold and hunger; for it is the body rather that is troubled through susceptibility to these infirmities, and the mind suffers many maladies by contact with it. Grant, however, that it be as useful as you will that these make them a body to enter: but how they can, there is no way to be seen. Spirits therefore do not make themselves bodies and limbs. Nor is there any possibility that they creep into bodies already made; for they will not be able to conjoin themselves closely together with these, nor will harmony be established through community of sensation.

[741] Furthermore, why does bitter fury go with the sullen breed of lions, why craft with foxes, why is the instinct of flight transmitted to deer from their fathers, the father's timidity impelling their limbs, why are all other qualities of this sort generated in the body and the character from the beginnings of life, if not because in each seed and breed its own fixed power of mind grows along with each body? But if it were immortal, and accustomed to pass from body to body, living creatures would show confused habits: the dog of Hyrcanian breed* would often flee before the horned stag's onset; the hawk would tremble, flying through the air from the advancing dove; men would lack reason, the wild generations of wild beasts would have it.

[754] For it is based on false reasoning to say that an immortal spirit is altered by a change of body; for that which changes is dissolved, therefore perishes. The parts of the spirit are transposed, and move from their position; therefore they must be capable of being dissolved also through the frame, to perish at last one and all with the body.

[760] But if they say that the spirits of men always pass into men's bodies, I will still ask why a foolish spirit can be made of a wise one, why no child is ever prudent, and no foal ever so accomplished as the horse of powerful strength. No doubt they will take refuge in saying that in a tender body the mind becomes tender. But even if this is so, you must confess that the spirit is mortal, since being changed so completely throughout the body it loses its former life and feeling.

[769] Or how will the power of the mind be able to grow strong together with any given body and attain the longed-for flowering of life, unless it shall be its partner in the first origin? Or why does it wish to issue forth from a frame grown old? Does it fear to remain imprisoned in a putrefying corpse, fear lest its house, worn out with the long lapse of years, fall in upon it? But there are no dangers for the immortal.

[776] Again, to suppose that spirits stand ready for the amours and the parturition of wild beasts is plainly too ridiculous—immortal spirits awaiting mortal frames in number numberless, and struggling together in hot haste which first and foremost shall creep in unless perhaps the spirits have contracts so arranged, that the spirit which comes flying up first may creep in first, and they need not come to blows one whit.

[784] Again, a tree cannot grow in the sky, nor clouds be in the deep sea, nor fish live in the fields, nor can blood be in sticks nor sap in rocks. It is fixed and arranged where each thing is to grow and have its being. So the nature of the mind cannot arise alone without body, nor exist far from sinews and blood. But if it could do this, the power of the mind itself could much more easily be in the head or shoulders or the heels of the feet, and be born in any part, and at least remain in the same man, the same ves-

---

*[The dogs of Hyrcania, on the southeast shore of the Caspian Sea, were noted for their ferocity.]

sel. But since even in our body there is seen to be a fixed rule and ordinance in what place mind and spirit may exist and grow apart, so much the more must we deny that they can endure and be produced wholly outside the body. Therefore, when the body has perished, you must confess that the spirit has passed away, torn to pieces throughout the body.

[800] In fact, to yoke mortal with immortal, and to think that they can be partners in feeling and act upon each other, is folly; for what can be considered more discordant, more contradictory or inconsistent, than that what is mortal can be yoked together in combination with immortal and imperishable, to weather furious storms!

[808] Besides, whatever bodies abide everlasting must, either, being of solid structure, reject blows and allow nothing to penetrate them that could dissever asunder the close-joined parts within, as the particles of matter are, the nature of which we have shown before; or else the reason why they can endure through all time must be that they are free from assaults, as the void is, which remains untouched and is not a whit affected by blows; or again because there is no extent of space around into which things can as it were disperse and dissolve, as the sum of all sums* is eternal, and there is no place without it into which its elements may escape, nor bodies to fall upon it and dissolve it asunder with a strong blow.

[819] But if possibly the reason why the spirit is to be held immortal is rather this, that it is sheltered and protected by the forces of life, either because nothing comes at all that is hostile to its existence, or because all that does come goes back, in some way repulsed before we can perceive what harm it does, [experience manifestly shows that this cannot be true.] For not to mention that it sickens along with bodily disease, something often comes that torments it about the future, keeps it miserable in fear, wearies it with anxiety, and, when there has been evil done in the past, its sins bring remorse. Add madness which is peculiar to the mind, and forgetfulness of all things, add that it is drowned in the black waters of lethargy.

[830] Therefore death is nothing to us, it matters not one jot, since the nature of the mind is understood to be mortal; and as in time past we felt no distress, while from all quarters the Carthaginians were coming to the conflict, when the whole world, shaken by the terrifying tumult of war, shivered and quaked under the lofty and breezy heaven, and was in doubt under which domination all men were destined to fall by land and sea;** so, when we shall no longer be, when the parting shall have come about between body and spirit from which we are compacted into one whole, then sure enough nothing at all will be able to happen to us, who will then no longer be, or to make us feel, not if earth be commingled with sea and sea with sky.

[843] And grant for the moment that the nature of mind and power of spirit does feel after it has been torn away from our body, yet that is nothing to us, who by the welding and wedding together of body and spirit exist compacted into one whole. Even if time should gather together our matter after death and bring it back again as it is now placed, and if once more the light of life should be given to us, yet it would not matter one bit to us that even this had been done, when the recollection of ourselves has once been broken asunder. And even now we are not concerned at all about any self which we have been before, nor does any anguish about it now touch us. For when you look back upon all the past expanse of measureless time, and think how various are the motions of matter, you may easily come to believe that these same seeds of which now we

---

*[The universe.]
**[Referring to the Second Punic War (218–201 B.C.).]

consist have been often before placed in the same arrangement they now are in. And yet we cannot call that back by memory; for in between has been cast a stoppage of life, and all the motions have wandered and scattered afar from those sensations.

[862] For, if by chance anyone is to have misery and pain in the future, he must himself also exist then in that time to be miserable. Since death takes away this possibility, and forbids him to exist for whom these inconveniences may be gathered together, we may be sure that there is nothing to be feared after death, that he who is not cannot be miserable, that it makes not one jot of difference whether or not he has ever been born, when death the immortal has taken away his mortal life.

[870] Accordingly, when you see a man resenting his fate, that after death he must either rot with his body laid in the tomb, or perish by fire or the jaws of wild beasts, you may know that he rings false, and that deep in his heart is some hidden sting, although himself he deny the belief in any sensation after death. He does not, I think, admit what he professes to admit, nor the premise from which his profession is derived; he does not wholly uproot and eject himself from life, but unknown to himself he makes something of himself to survive. For when anyone in life anticipates that birds and beasts will mangle his body after death, he pities himself; for he does not distinguish himself from that thing, he does not separate himself sufficiently from the body there cast out, he imagines himself to be that and, standing beside it, infects it with his own feeling. Hence he resents that he was born mortal, and does not see that in real death there will be no other self that could live to bewail his perished self, or stand by to feel pain that he lay there lacerated or burning. For if after death it is an evil to be mauled by the jaws and teeth of wild beasts, I do not see how it should not be unpleasant to be laid upon the fire and to shrivel in the hot flames, or to be packed in honey and stifled, and to be stiff with cold lying upon a slab of cold marble, or to be buried and crushed under a weight of superimposed earth.

[894] "No longer now will your happy home give you welcome, no longer will your best of wives; no longer will your sweet children race to win the first kisses, and thrill your heart to its depths with sweetness. You will no longer be able to live in prosperity, and to protect your own. Poor man, poor man!" they say, "one fatal day has robbed you of all these prizes of life." But they do not go on to add: "No longer too does any craving possess you for these things." If they could see this clearly in mind and so conform their speech, they would free themselves from great anguish and fear of mind.

[904] "Yes, you, as you now lie in death's quiet sleep, so you will be for all time that is to come, removed from all distressing pains; but we beside you, as you lay burnt to ashes on the horrible pyre, have bewailed you inconsolably, and that everlasting grief no time shall take from our hearts." Of such a speaker then we may well ask, if all ends in sleep and quiet rest, what bitterness there is in it so great that one could pine with everlasting sorrow.

[912] This also is the way among men, when they have laid themselves down at table and hold goblets in their hands and shade their brows with garlands, that they often say from their hearts: "Short enjoyment is given to poor mankind; soon it will be gone, and none will ever be able to recall it." As if after death their chief trouble will be to be miserably consumed and parched by a burning thirst, or a craving possess them for some other thing! In fact, no one feels the want of himself and his life when both mind and body alike are quiet in sleep; for all we care that sleep might be everlasting, and no craving for ourselves touches us at all; and yet those first-beginnings dispersed through our body are not straying far from sense-giving motions at the time when a man, startled from sleep, gathers himself together. Death therefore must be thought of much less moment to us, if there can be anything less than what we see to be nothing; for a greater

dispersion of the disturbed matter takes place at death, and no one awakens and rises whom the cold stoppage of life has once overtaken.

[931] Besides, suppose that nature should suddenly utter a voice, and thus take her turn to upbraid one of us: "What ails you so, O mortal, to indulge overmuch in sickly lamentations? Why do you groan aloud and weep at death? For if your former life now past has been to your liking, if it is not true that all your blessings have been gathered as it were into a riddled jar, and have run through and been lost without gratification, why not, like a banqueter fed full of life, withdraw with contentment and rest in peace, you fool? But if all that you have enjoyed has been spilt out and lost, and if you have a grudge at life, why seek to add more, only to be miserably lost again and to perish wholly without gratification? Why not rather make an end of life and trouble? For there is nothing else I can devise and invent to please you: everything is always the same. If your body is not already withering with years and your limbs worn out and languid, yet everything remains the same, even if you shall go on to outlive all generations, and even more if you should be destined never to die." What have we to answer, but that nature urges against us a just charge and in her plea sets forth a true case?

[952] But if in this regard some older man, well stricken in years, should make complaint, wretchedly; bewailing his death more than he ought, would she not have reason to cry more loudly still and to upbraid in bitter words? "Away, away with your tears, ruffian, check your lamentations! All life's prizes you have enjoyed and now you wither. But because you always crave what you have not, and condemn what you have, life has slipped by for you incomplete and ungratifying, and death stands by your head unexpected, before you can retire glutted and full of the feast. But now in any case dismiss all that does not befit your age, and with equanimity, come now, yield to your years: thus it must be." She would be right, I think, to bring her charge, right to upbraid and reproach. For the old order always passes, thrust out by the new, and one thing has to be made afresh from others; but no one is delivered into the pit of black Tartarus: matter is wanted, that coming generations may grow; and yet they all, when their life is done, will follow you, and so, no less than you, these generations have passed away before now, and will continue to pass away. So one thing will never cease to arise from another, and no man possesses life in freehold—all as tenants. Look back also and see how the ages of everlasting time past before we were born have been to us nothing. This therefore is a mirror which nature holds up to us, showing the time to come after we at length shall die. Is there anything horrible in that? Is there anything gloomy? Is it not more peaceful than any sleep?

[978] And assuredly whatsoever things are fabled to exist in deep Acheron, these all exist for us in this life. There is no wretched Tantalus, as the story goes, fearing the great rock that hangs over him in the air and frozen with vain terror; rather it is in this life that the fear of gods oppresses mortals without cause, and the fall they fear is any that chance may bring.

[984] No Tityos lying in Acheron is rummaged by winged creatures, nor assuredly can they find in eternity anything at all to dig for deep in that vast breast. Wide as you will, let that huge body be spread forth, enough to cover not nine acres only with the outstretched limbs, but the whole globe of earth: yet he will not be able to bear pain forever, nor to provide food from his own body always. But Tityos is here among us, the man who, as he lies in love, is torn by winged creatures and devoured by agonizing anguish or rent by anxieties through some other passion.

[995] Sisyphus also appears in this life before our eyes, athirst to solicit from the people the lictor's rods and cruel axes, and always retiring defeated and full of gloom: for to solicit power, an empty thing, which is never granted, and always to endure hard

toil in the pursuit of it, this is to push laboriously up a hill the rock that still rolls down again from the very top, and in a rush recovers the levels of the open plain.

[1003] Then to be always feeding an ungrateful mind, yet never able to fill and satisfy it with good things—as the seasons of the year do for us when they come round bringing their fruits and manifold charms, yet we are never filled with the fruits of life—this, I think, is meant by the tale of the damsels* in the flower of their age pouring water into a riddled urn, which, for all their trying, can never be filled.

[1011] Cerberus** also and the Furies and the withholding of light, and Tartarus belching horrible fires from his throat—these neither exist anywhere nor in truth can exist. But in this life there is fear of punishment for evil deeds, fear as notorious as the deeds are notorious, and atonement for crime—prison, and the horrible casting down from the Rock, stripes, executioners, condemned cell, pitch, red-hot plates, firebrands; and even if these are absent, yet the guilty conscience, terrified before anything can come to pass, applies the goad and scorches itself with whips, and meanwhile does not see where can be the end to its miseries or the final limit to its punishment, and fears that these same afflictions may become heavier after death. The fool's life at length becomes a hell on earth.

[1024] This thought also you may at times address to yourself: "Even good Ancus*** has closed his eyes on the light, who was better than you, unconscionable man, in many ways. After him many other kings and potentates have fallen, who ruled over great nations. Even he† himself, who once paved a road across the great sea for his armies to pass over the deep, and taught them to walk on foot over the salt bays, and despised the roarings of the ocean as he trampled upon it with his cavalry, he also was robbed of the light and poured his spirit out of a dying body. The son of the house of Scipio, thunderbolt of war, terror of Carthage, gave his bones to the earth as though he had been the humblest menial. Add the inventors in the worlds of science and beauty, add the companions of the Heliconian maids,†† whose one and only king, Homer, has been laid to rest in the same sleep with all the others. Democritus again, when ripe old age warned him that the recording motions of his mind were beginning to fail, of his own free will himself offered his head to death. Epicurus himself died when the light of life had run its course, he whose intellect surpassed humanity, who quenched the light of all as the risen sun of heaven quenches the stars. And will you hesitate, will you be indignant to die? You whose life is now all but dead though you live and see, you who waste the greater part of your time in sleep, who snore open-eyed and never cease to see dreams, who bear with you a mind plagued with vain terror, who often cannot discover what is amiss with you, when you are oppressed, poor drunken wretch by a host of cares on all sides, while you wander drifting on the wayward tides of impulse!"

[1063] Just as men evidently feel that there is a weight on their minds which wearies with its oppression, if so they could also recognize from what causes it comes, and what makes so great a mountain of misery to lie on their hearts, they would not so live their lives as now we generally see them do, each ignorant what he wants, each seeking always to change his place as if he could drop his burden. The man who has been bored to death at home often goes forth from his great mansion, and then suddenly returns because he feels himself no better abroad. Off he courses, driving his Gallic ponies to his

---

*[The Danaids.]

**[The monstrous watchdog at the entrance to the lower world.]

***[According to legend, the fourth king of Rome.]

†[Xerxes, who in 480 B.C. built a pontoon bridge over the Hellespont.]

††[The Muses.]

country house in headlong haste, as if he were bringing urgent help to a house on fire. The moment he has reached the threshold of the house, he yawns, or falls into heavy sleep and seeks oblivion, or even makes haste to get back and see the city again. Thus each man tries to flee from himself, but to that self, from which of course he can never escape, he clings against his will, and hates it, because he is a sick man that does not know the cause of his complaint; for could he see that well, at once each would throw his business aside and first study to learn the nature of things, since the matter in doubt is not his state for one hour, but for eternity, in what state mortals must expect all time to be passed which remains after death.

[1076] Besides, what is this great and evil lust of life that drives us to be so greatly agitated amidst doubt and peril? There is an end fixed for the life of mortals, and death cannot be avoided, but die we must. Again we move and have our being always amidst the same things, and by living we cannot forge for ourselves any new pleasure; but while we have not what we crave, that seems to surpass all else; afterwards, when we have attained that, we crave something else; one unchanging thirst of life fills us and our mouths are forever agape. And it is uncertain what fortune the next years may bring, what chance has in store, what end awaits us. And by protracting life we do not deduct one jot from the duration of death, nor are we able to diminish that, so as to leave perhaps a shorter time after our taking off. Therefore you may live to complete as many generations as you will: nevertheless that everlasting death will still be waiting, and no less long a time will he be no more, who has made an end of life with to-day's sun, than he who fell many a month and year before.

Marcus Aurelius
A.D. 121–180

Marcus Aurelius was born to a patrician family of Rome. Following the death of his parents, he was raised by his grandfather and eventually adopted by the future emperor, Aurelius Antonius. While still a boy, he became a Stoic, giving himself fully to the study and practice of Stoicism. Following the death of Aurelius Antonius in 161, Marcus Aurelius became emperor of Rome. By nature a gentle and peace-loving man, he nevertheless spent most of his reign fighting in campaigns against the barbarians on the borders of the empire. He was also forced to deal with an epidemic of the plague, a revolt by one of his generals, the death of four of his five sons, and a perceived threat from the new religion, Christianity. Yet as eighteenth-century historian Edward Gibbon explains in *The Decline and Fall of the Roman Empire:*

> His life was the noblest commentary on the precepts of Zeno [of Citium—founder of Stoicism]. He was severe to himself, indulgent to the imperfections of others, just and beneficent to all mankind. He regretted that Avidius Cassius, who excited a rebellion in Syria, had disappointed him, by a voluntary death, of the pleasure of converting an enemy into a friend; and he justified the sincerity of that sentiment, by moderating the zeal of the senate against the adherents of the traitor. War he detested, as the disgrace and calamity of human nature, but when the necessity of a just defence called upon him to take up arms, he readily exposed his person to eight winter campaigns on the frozen banks of the Danube, the severity of which was at last

fatal [he died in 180] to the weakness of his constitution. His memory was revered by a grateful posterity, and above a century after his death, many persons preserved the image of Marcus [Aurelius], among those of their household gods.

While on his miliary campaigns, Marcus Aurelius wrote a book of disconnected reflections on life known as the *Meditations.* These *Meditations* reflect a Stoic acceptance of nature and of the need for self-control in the face of adversity. As a practical Roman, Marcus Aurelius was not interested in the metaphysical materialism of the early Stoa. Instead, he stressed the need for active benevolence and the acceptance of divine providence, or fate. Touching on several topics, the passage here, translated by George Long, includes Marcus Aurelius' claim that apparent evil is actually a part of the overall good of the universe. As Alexander Pope *(Essay on Man)* was to say fifteen hundred years later,

All Nature is but Art, unknown to thee;
All Chance, Direction, which thou canst not see;
All Discord, Harmony, not understood;
All partial Evil, universal Good:
And, spite of Pride, in erring Reason's spite,
One truth is clear, "Whatever IS, is RIGHT."

* * *

The standard study of Marcus Aurelius is F.W. Bussell, *Marcus Aurelius and the Later Stoics* (Edinburgh: T. & T. Clark, 1910). A.S.L. Farquharson, *Marcus Aurelius, His Life and His World,* edited by D.A. Rees (Oxford: Basil Blackwell, 1951), and Anthony R. Birley, *Marcus Aurelius* (Boston: Little, Brown, 1966), are also helpful general studies. E.R. Dodds, *Pagan and Christian in an Age of Anxiety* (Cambridge: Cambridge University Press, 1965), examines the culture in which Marcus Aurelius lived and wrote; while Henry D. Sedgwick, *Marcus Aurelius* (New Haven, CT: Yale University Press, 1922), and Anthony Richard Birley, *Marcus Aurelius: A Biography* (London: Batsford, 1987), provide general biographies. For commentaries on the *Meditations* see the classic, A.S.L. Farquharson, ed., *The Meditations of the Emperor Marcus Antonius* (Oxford: Clarendon Press, 1944), and the more recent R.B. Rutherford, *The Meditations of Marcus Aurelius: A Study* (Oxford: Oxford University Press, 1989).

MEDITATIONS (in part)

BOOK SEVEN

What is badness? It is that which thou hast often seen. And on the occasion of everything which happens keep this in mind, that it is that which thou hast often seen. Everywhere up and down thou wilt find the same things, with which the old histories are filled, those of the middle ages and those of our own day; with which cities and houses are filled now. There is nothing new: all things are both familiar and short-lived.

2. How can our principles become dead, unless the impressions (thoughts) which correspond to them are extinguished? But it is in thy power continuously to fan these thoughts into a flame. I can have that opinion about anything, which I ought to have. If I can, why am I disturbed? The things which are external to my mind have no relation at all to my mind.—Let this be the state of thy affects, and thou standest erect. To recover thy life is in thy power. Look at things again as thou didst use to look at them; for in this consists the recovery of thy life.

3. The idle business of show, plays on the stage, flocks of sheep, herds, exercises with spears, a bone cast to little dogs, a bit of bread into fish-ponds, labourings of ants and burden-carrying, runnings about of frightened little mice, puppets pulled by strings—all alike. It is thy duty then in the midst of such things to show good humour and not a proud air; to understand however that every man is worth just so much as the things are worth about which he busies himself.

4. In discourse thou must attend to what is said, and in every movement thou must observe what is doing. And in the one thou shouldst see immediately to what end it refers, but in the other watch carefully what is the thing signified.

5. Is my understanding sufficient for this or not? If it is sufficient, I use it for the work as an instrument given by the universal nature. But if it is not sufficient, then either I retire from the work and give way to him who is able to do it better, unless there be some reason why I ought not to do so; or I do it as well as I can, taking to help me the man who with the aid of my ruling principle can do what is now fit and useful for the general good. For whatsoever either by myself or with another I can do, ought to be directed to this only, to that which is useful and well suited to society.

6. How many after being celebrated by fame have been given up to oblivion; and how many who have celebrated the fame of others have long been dead.

7. Be not ashamed to be helped; for it is thy business to do thy duty like a soldier in the assault on a town. How then, if being lame thou canst not mount up on the battlements alone, but with the help of another it is possible?

8. Let not future things disturb thee, for thou wilt come to them, if it shall be necessary, having with thee the same reason which now thou usest for present things.

9. All things are implicated with one another, and the bond is holy; and there is hardly anything unconnected with any other thing. For things have been co-ordinated, and they combine to form the same universe (order). For there is one universe made up of all things, and one God who pervades all things, and one substance, and one law, one common reason in all intelligent animals, and one truth; if indeed there is also one perfection for all animals which are of the same stock and participate in the same reason.

10. Everything material soon disappears in the substance of the whole; and everything formal (causal) is very soon taken back into the universal reason; and the memory of everything is very soon overwhelmed in time.

11. To the rational animal the same act is according to nature and according to reason.

12. Be thou erect, or be made erect.

13. Just as it is with the members in those bodies which are united in one, so it is with rational beings which exist separate, for they have been constituted for one co-operation. And the perception of this will be more apparent to thee, if thou often sayest to thyself that I am a member ⟨melos⟩ of the system of rational beings. But if (using the letter r) thou sayest that thou art a part ⟨meros⟩ thou dost not yet love men from thy heart; beneficence does not yet delight thee for its own sake; thou still doest it barely as a thing of propriety, and not yet as doing good to thyself.

Dying Gaul, a Roman copy after a bronze original of ca. 225 B.C. While
the original statue depicts a casualty inflicted by the troops of Attalus I of
Pergamon (241–197 B.C.), Marcus Aurelius, despite his pacifist
philosophy, also led his troops against the barbarian Gauls. *(Alinari-
Scala/Art Resource)*

14. Let there fall externally what will on the parts which can feel the effects of
this fall. For those parts which have felt will complain, if they choose. But I, unless I
think that what has happened is an evil, am not injured. And it is in my power not to
think so.

15. Whatever anyone does or says, I must be good, just as if the gold, or the
emerald, or the purple were always saying this, Whatever anyone does or says, I must
be emerald and keep my colour.

16. The ruling faculty does not disturb itself; I mean, does not frighten itself or
cause itself pain. But if anyone else can frighten or pain it, let him do so. For the faculty
itself will not by its own opinion turn itself into such ways. Let the body itself take care,
if it can, that it suffer nothing, and let it speak, if it suffers. But the soul itself, that which
is subject to fear, to pain, which has completely the power of forming an opinion about
these things, will suffer nothing, for it will never deviate into such a judgement. The
leading principle in itself wants nothing, unless it makes a want for itself; and therefore
it is both free from perturbation and unimpeded, if it does not disturb and impede itself.

17. *Eudaemonia* (happiness) is a good daemon, or a good thing. What then art
thou doing here, O imagination? Go away, I entreat thee by the gods, as thou didst
come, for I want thee not. But thou art come according to thy old fashion. I am not angry with thee: only go away.

18. Is any man afraid of change? Why what can take place without change? What
then is more pleasing or more suitable to the universal nature? And canst thou take a
bath unless the wood undergoes a change? And canst thou be nourished, unless the food

undergoes a change? And can anything else that is useful be accomplished without change? Dost thou not see then that for thyself also to change is just the same, and equally necessary for the universal nature?

19. Through the universal substance as through a furious torrent all bodies are carried, being by their nature united with and cooperating with the whole, as the parts of our body with one another. How many a Chrysippus, how many a Socrates, how many an Epictetus has time already swallowed up? And let the same thought occur to thee with reference to every man and thing.

20. One thing only troubles me, lest I should do something which the constitution of man does not allow, or in the way which it does not allow, or what it does not allow now.

21. Near is thy forgetfulness of all things; and near the forgetfulness of thee by all.

22. It is peculiar to man to love even those who do wrong. And this happens, if when they do wrong it occurs to thee that they are kinsmen, and that they do wrong through ignorance and unintentionally, and that soon both of you will die; and above all, that the wrong-doer has done thee no harm, for he has not made thy ruling faculty worse than it was before.

23. The universal nature out of the universal substance, as if it were wax, now moulds a horse, and when it has broken this up, it uses the material for a tree, then for a man, then for something else; and each of these things subsists for a very short time. But it is no hardship for the vessel to be broken up, just as there was none in its being fastened together.

24. A scowling look is altogether unnatural; when it is often assumed, the result is that all comeliness dies away, and at last is so completely extinguished that it cannot be again lighted up at all. Try to conclude from this very fact that it is contrary to reason. For if even the perception of doing wrong shall depart, what reason is there for living any longer?

25. Nature which governs the whole will soon change all things which thou seest, and out of their substance will make other things, and again other things from the substance of them, in order that the world may be ever new.

26. When a man has done thee any wrong, immediately consider with what opinion about good or evil he has done wrong. For when thou hast seen this, thou wilt pity him, and wilt neither wonder nor be angry. For either thou thyself thinkest the same thing to be good that he does or another thing of the same kind. It is thy duty then to pardon him. But if thou dost not think such things to be good or evil, thou wilt more readily be well disposed to him who is in error.

27. Think not so much of what thou hast not as of what thou hast: but of the things which thou hast select the best, and then reflect how eagerly they would have been sought, if thou hadst them not. At the same time however take care that thou dost not through being so pleased with them accustom thyself to overvalue them, so as to be disturbed if ever thou shouldst not have them.

28. Retire into thyself. The rational principle which rules has this nature, that it is content with itself when it does what is just, and so secures tranquillity.

29. Wipe out the imagination. Stop the pulling of the strings. Confine thyself to the present. Understand well what happens either to thee or to another. Divide and distribute every object into the causal (formal) and the material. Think of thy last hour. Let the wrong which is done by a man stay there where the wrong was done.

30. Direct thy attention to what is said. Let thy understanding enter into the things that are doing and the things which do them.

31. Adorn thyself with simplicity and modesty and with indifference towards the things which lie between virtue and vice. Love mankind. Follow God. The poet says that Law rules all.—And it is enough to remember that Law rules all.

32. About death: Whether it is a dispersion, or a resolution into atoms, or annihilation, it is either extinction or change.

33. About pain: The pain which is intolerable carries us off; but that which lasts a long time is tolerable; and the mind maintains its own tranquillity by retiring into itself, and the ruling faculty is not made worse. But the parts which are harmed by pain, let them, if they can, give their opinion about it.

34. About fame: Look at the minds of those who seek fame, observe what they are, and what kind of things they avoid, and what kind of things they pursue. And consider that as the heaps of sand piled on one another hide the former sands, so in life the events which go before are soon covered by those which come after.

35. From Plato: The man who has an elevated mind and takes a view of all time and of all substance, dost thou suppose it possible for him to think that human life is anything great? It is not possible, he said.—Such a man then will think that death also is no evil.—Certainly not.*

36. From Antisthenes: It is royal to do good and to be abused.

37. It is a base thing for the countenance to be obedient and to regulate and compose itself as the mind commands, and for the mind not to be regulated and composed by itself.

38. It is not right to vex ourselves at things,
    For they care nought about it.**

39. To the immortal gods and us give joy.

40. Life must be reaped like the ripe ears of corn:
    One man is born; another dies.

41. If gods care not for me and for my children,
    There is a reason for it.

42. For the good is with me, and the just.

43. No joining others in their wailing, no violent emotion.

44. From Plato: But I would make this man a sufficient answer, which is this: Thou sayest not well, if thou thinkest that a man who is good for anything at all ought to compute the hazard of life or death, and should not rather look to this only in all that he does, whether he is doing what is just or unjust, and the works of a good or a bad man.***

45. For thus it is, men of Athens, in truth: wherever a man has placed himself thinking it the best place for him, or has been placed by a commander, there in my opinion he ought to stay and to abide the hazard, taking nothing into the reckoning, either death or anything else, before the baseness of deserting his post.†

46. But, my good friend, reflect whether that which is noble and good is not something different from saving and being saved; for as to a man living such or such a time, at least one who is really a man, consider if this is not a thing to be dismissed from the thoughts: and there must be no love of life: but as to these matters a man must intrust them to the deity and believe what the women say, that no man can escape his destiny, the next inquiry being how he may best live the time that he has to live.††

---

*Republic, 486.
**Numbers 38, 40–42, 50–51 are all fragments of plays by Euripides.
***Apology, 28.
†Ibid.
††Plato, Gorgias, 512.

47. Look round at the courses of the stars, as if thou wert going along with them; and constantly consider the changes of the elements into one another; for such thoughts purge away the filth of the terrene life.

48. This is a fine saying of Plato: That he who is discoursing about men should look also at earthly things as if he viewed them from some higher place; should look at them in their assemblies, armies, agricultural labours, marriages, treaties, births, deaths, noise of the courts of justice, desert places, various nations of barbarians, feasts, lamentations, markets, a mixture of all things and an orderly combination of contraries.

49. Consider the past; such great changes of political supremacies. Thou mayest foresee also the things which will be. For they will certainly be of like form, and it is not possible that they should deviate from the order of the things which take place now: accordingly to have contemplated human life for forty years is the same as to have contemplated it for ten thousand years. For what more wilt thou see?

50. That which has grown from the earth to the earth,
    But that which has sprung from heavenly seed,
    Back to the heavenly realms returns.

This is either a dissolution of the mutual involution of the atoms, or a similar dispersion of the unsentient elements.

51. With food and drinks and cunning magic arts
    Turning the channel's course to 'scape from death.
    The breeze which heaven has sent
    We must endure, and toil without complaining.

52. Another may be more expert in casting his opponent; but he is not more social, nor more modest, nor better disciplined to meet all that happens, nor more considerate with respect to the faults of his neighbours.

53. Where any work can be done conformably to the reason which is common to gods and men, there we have nothing to fear: for where we are able to get profit by means of the activity which is successful and proceeds according to our constitution, there no harm is to be suspected.

54. Everywhere and at all times it is in thy power piously to acquiesce in thy present condition, and to behave justly to those who are about thee, and to exert thy skill upon thy present thoughts, that nothing shall steal into them without being well examined.

55. Do not look around thee to discover other men's ruling principles, but look straight to this, to what nature leads thee, both the universal nature through the things which happen to thee, and thy own nature through the acts which must be done by thee. But every being ought to do that which is according to its constitution; and all other things have been constituted for the sake of rational beings, just as among irrational things the inferior for the sake of the superior, but the rational for the sake of one another.

The prime principle then in man's constitution is the social. And the second is not to yield to the persuasions of the body, for it is the peculiar office of the rational and intelligent motion to circumscribe itself, and never to be overpowered either by the motion of the senses or of the appetites, for both are animal; but the intelligent motion claims superiority and does not permit itself to be overpowered by the others. And with good reason, for it is formed by nature to use all of them. The third thing in the rational constitution is freedom from error and from deception. Let then the ruling principle holding fast to these things go straight on, and it has what is its own.

56. Consider thyself to be dead, and to have completed thy life up to the present time; and live according to nature the remainder which is allowed thee.

57. Love that only which happens to thee and is spun with the thread of thy destiny. For what is more suitable?

58. In everything which happens keep before thy eyes those to whom the same things happened, and how they were vexed, and treated them as strange things, and found fault with them: and now where are they? Nowhere. Why then dost thou too choose to act in the same way? And why dost thou not leave these agitations which are foreign to nature, to those who cause them and those who are moved by them? And why art thou not altogether intent upon the right way of making use of the things which happen to thee? For then thou wilt use them well, and they will be a material for thee to work on. Only attend to thyself, and resolve to be a good man in every act which thou doest: and remember . . .

59. Look within. Within is the fountain of good, and it will ever bubble up, if thou wilt ever dig.

60. The body ought to be compact, and to show no irregularity either in motion or attitude. For what the mind shows in the face by maintaining in it the expression of intelligence and propriety, that ought to be required also in the whole body. But all of these things should be observed without affectation.

61. The art of life is more like the wrestler's art than the dancer's, in respect of this, that it should stand ready and firm to meet onsets which are sudden and unexpected.

62. Constantly observe who those are whose approbation thou wishest to have, and what ruling principles they possess. For then thou wilt neither blame those who offend involuntarily, nor wilt thou want their approbation, if thou lookest to the sources of their opinions and appetites.

63. Every soul, the philosopher says, is involuntarily deprived of truth; consequently in the same way it is deprived of justice and temperance and benevolence and everything of the kind. It is most necessary to bear this constantly in mind, for thus thou wilt be more gentle towards all.

64. In every pain let this thought be present, that there is no dishonour in it, nor does it make the governing intelligence worse, for it does not damage the intelligence either so far as the intelligence is rational or so far as it is social. Indeed in the case of most pains let this remark of Epicurus aid thee, that pain is neither intolerable nor everlasting, if thou bearest in mind that it has its limits, and if thou addest nothing to it in imagination: and remember this too, that we do not perceive that many things which are disagreeable to us are the same as pain, such as excessive drowsiness, and the being scorched by heat, and the having no appetite. When then thou art discontented about any of these things, say to thyself, that thou art yielding to pain.

65. Take care not to feel towards the inhuman, as they feel towards men.

66. How do we know if Telauges was not superior in character to Socrates? For it is not enough that Socrates died a more noble death, and disputed more skilfully with the sophists, and passed the night in the cold with more endurance, and that when he was bid to arrest Leon of Salamis, he considered it more noble to refuse, and that he walked in a swaggering way in the streets*—though as to this fact one may have great doubts if it was true. But we ought to inquire, what kind of a soul it was that Socrates possessed, and if he was able to be content with being just towards men and pious towards the gods, neither idly vexed on account of men's villainy, nor yet making himself a slave to any man's ignorance, nor receiving as strange anything that fell to his share

*Cf. Aristophanes, *Clouds,* 363.

out of the universal, nor enduring it as intolerable, nor allowing his understanding to sympathize with the affects of the miserable flesh.

67. Nature has not so mingled the intelligence with the composition of the body, as not to have allowed thee the power of circumscribing thyself and of bringing under subjection to thyself all that is thy own; for it is very possible to be a divine man and to be recognised as such by no one. Always bear this in mind; and another thing too, that very little indeed is necessary for living a happy life. And because thou hast despaired of becoming a dialectician and skilled in the knowledge of nature, do not for this reason renounce the hope of being both free and modest and social and obedient to God.

68. It is in thy power to live free from all compulsion in the greatest tranquillity of mind, even if all the world cry out against thee as much as they choose, and even if wild beasts tear in pieces the members of this kneaded matter which has grown around thee. For what hinders the mind in the midst of all this from maintaining itself in tranquillity and in a just judgement of all surrounding things and in a ready use of the objects which are presented to it, so that the judgement may say to the thing which falls under its observation: This thou art in substance (reality), though in men's opinion thou mayest appear to be of a different kind; and the use shall say to that which falls under the hand: Thou art the thing that I was seeking; for to me that which presents itself is always a material for virtue both rational and political, and in a word, for the exercise of art, which belongs to man or God. For everything which happens has a relationship either to God or man, and is neither new nor difficult to handle, but usual and apt matter to work on.

69. The perfection of moral character consists in this, in passing every day as the last, and in being neither violently excited nor torpid nor playing the hypocrite.

70. The gods who are immortal are not vexed because during so long a time they must tolerate continually men such as they are and so many of them bad; and besides this, they also take care of them in all ways. But thou, who art destined to end so soon, art thou wearied of enduring the bad, and this too when thou art one of them?

71. It is a ridiculous thing for a man not to fly from his own badness, which is indeed possible, but to fly from other men's badness, which is impossible.

72. Whatever the rational and political (social) faculty finds to be neither intelligent nor social, it properly judges to be inferior to itself.

73. When thou hast done a good act and another has received it, why dost thou look for a third thing besides these, as fools do, either to have the reputation of having done a good act or to obtain a return?

74. No man is tired of receiving what is useful. But it is useful to act according to nature. Do not then be tired of receiving what is useful by doing it to others.

75. The nature of the All moved to make the universe. But now either everything that takes place comes by way of consequence or continuity; or even the chief things towards which the ruling power of the universe directs its own movement are governed by no rational principle. If this is remembered it will make thee more tranquil in many things.

Pyrrho *ca. 360–ca. 270 B.C.*
and
Sextus Empiricus *A.D. third century*

Pyrrho was born in the town of Elis on the Greek Peloponnesus. He joined the expedition of Alexander the Great to India and there met several of the learned magi of the East. Following Alexander's death in 323 B.C., Pyrrho returned to Elis and spent the rest of his life teaching there.

Pyrrho was greatly influenced by the Democritean notion that the world is not as our sense perceptions would lead us to believe. According to Pyrrho, we can know only appearances relative to each person—there is no way we can know things as they really are. This means that any statement we might make about reality can be opposed by an equally valid statement that contradicts it. Given this inability to know which assertion is true, Pyrrho said we should develop an attitude of suspended judgment ⟨*epoche*⟩ and thus gradually attain "unperturbedness" or "quietude" ⟨*ataraxia*⟩. This claimed inability to know came to be called "Skepticism."

Pyrrho left no writings, but his philosophy is well represented by the works of the third-century A.D. author Sextus Empiricus. Little is known about this writer other than that he was apparently a Greek physician, that he was the head of a Skeptical school in some major city, and that he wrote the *Outlines of Pyrrhonism*. The selection reprinted here, in the R.G. Bury translation, begins by dividing philosophers into three categories: "Dogmatists," who claim to know the truth; those inheritors of Plato's Academy such as Carneades, who made the opposite dogmatic claim that no truth is possible; and the Pyrrhoist skeptics, who suspend judgment while looking for the truth. Sextus Empiricus goes on to explain the nature of such a suspension of judgment and concludes with a discussion of how this suspension leads to "quietude." In the process of his explication, Sextus avoids self-refutation by explaining that he is not describing what is really true (which would be dogmatism), but only how things *appear* to him to be.

As for its impact, elements of Pyrrhoist skepticism are echoed in Hegel's concept of the dialectic (with the claim that every statement can be contradicted by its opposite) and in Husserl's use of ⟨*epoche*⟩. Thinkers such as Montaigne, Hume, and Santayana have used skepticism to attack the dogmatic philosophies of their day. While it has rarely been an established school of thought, skepticism has raised questions for all systematic philosophers since the time of Pyrrho.

* * *

For general accounts of Greek skepticism, see Mary Mills Patrick, *The Greek Skeptics* (New York: Columbia University Press, 1929); Charlotte L. Stough, *Greek Skepticism: A Study in Epistemology* (Berkeley: University of California Press, 1969); Leo Groarke, *Greek Scepticism: Anti-Realist Trends in Ancient Thought* (Montreal: McGill-Queen's University Press, 1990); and a collection of essays, Malcolm Schofield, Myles Burnyeat, and Jonathan Barnes, eds., *Doubt and Dogmatism: Studies in Hellenistic Epistemology* (Oxford: Clarendon Press, 1979). For a work specifically on Sextus Empiricus, see Mary Mills Patrick, *Sextus Empiricus and Greek Scepticism* (Cambridge: D. Bell, 1899). Edwyn Robert Bevan, *Stoics and Skeptics* (Oxford: Clarendon Press, 1913), provides a comparison with the Stoics, while Benson Mates, *Stoic Logic* (Berkeley: University of California Press, 1953), includes a section on Sextus Empiricus' contribution to the field of logic.

OUTLINES OF PYRRHONISM (in part)

BOOK I

Chapter 1. Of the Main Difference Between Philosophic Systems

The natural result of any investigation is that the investigators either discover the object of their search or deny that it is discoverable and confess it to be inapprehensible or persist in their search. So, too, with regard to the objects investigated by philosophy, this is probably why some have claimed to have discovered the truth, others have asserted that

Reprinted by permission of the publishers and the Loeb Classical Library from Sextus Empiricus, *Outlines of Pyrrhonism,* Book I, translated by Rev. R.G. Bury (Cambridge, MA: Harvard University Press, 1933). Copyright © 1933 by Harvard University Press.

it cannot be apprehended, while others again go on inquiring. Those who believe they have discovered it are the "Dogmatists," specially so called—Aristotle, for example, and Epicurus and the Stoics and certain others; Cleitomachus and Carneades and other Academics treat it as inapprehensible; the Sceptics keep on searching. Hence it seems reasonable to hold that the main types of philosophy are three—the Dogmatic, the Academic, and the Sceptic. Of the other systems it will best become others to speak: our task at present is to describe in outline the Sceptic doctrine, first premising that of none of our future statements do we positively affirm that the fact is exactly as we state it, but we simply record each fact, like a chronicler, as it appears to us at the moment.

Chapter 2. Of the Arguments of Scepticism

Of the Sceptic philosophy one argument (or branch of exposition) is called "general," the other "special." In the general argument we set forth the distinctive features of Scepticism, stating its purport and principles, its logical methods, criterion, and end or aim; the "Tropes," also, or "Modes," which lead to suspension of judgment, and in what sense we adopt the Sceptic formulae, and the distinction between Scepticism and the philosophies which stand next to it. In the special argument we state our objections regarding the several divisions of so-called philosophy. Let us, then, deal first with the general argument, beginning our description with the names given to the Sceptic School.

Chapter 3. Of the Nomenclature of Scepticism

The Sceptic School, then, is also called "Zetetic" from its activity in investigation and inquiry, and "Ephectic" or Suspensive from the state of mind produced in the inquirer after his search, and "Aporetic" or Dubitative either from its habit of doubting and seeking, as some say, or from its indecision as regards assent and denial, and "Pyrrhonean" from the fact that Pyrrho appears to us to have applied himself to Scepticism more thoroughly and more conspicuously than his predecessors.

Chapter 4. What Scepticism Is

Scepticism is an ability, or mental attitude, which opposes appearances to judgements in any way whatsoever, with the result that, owing to the equipollence of the objects and reasons thus opposed, we are brought firstly to a state of mental suspense and next to a state of "unperturbedness" or quietude. Now we call it an "ability" not in any subtle sense, but simply in respect of its "being able." By "appearances" we now mean the objects of sense-perception, whence we contrast them with the objects of thought or "judgements." The phrase "in any way whatsoever" can be connected either with the word "ability," to make us take the word "ability," as we said, in its simple sense, or with the phrase "opposing appearances to judgements"; for inasmuch as we oppose these in a variety of ways—appearances to appearances, or judgements to judgements, or *alternando* appearances to judgements,—in order to ensure the inclusion of all these antitheses we employ the phrase "in any way whatsoever." Or, again, we join "in any way whatsoever" to "appearances and judgements" in order that we may not have to inquire how the appearances appear or how the thought-objects are judged, but may take these terms in the simple sense. The phrase "opposed judgements" we do not employ in the sense of negations and affirmations only but simply as equivalent to "conflicting judgements." "Equipollence" we use of equality in respect of probability and improbability, to indicate that no one of the conflicting judgements takes precedence of any other as being more probable. "Suspense" is a state of mental rest owing to which we neither deny nor affirm anything. "Quietude" is an untroubled and tranquil condition of soul. And how quietude enters the soul along with suspension of judgement we shall explain in our chapter (XII.) "Concerning the End."

Chapter 5. Of the Sceptic

In the definition of the Sceptic system there is also implicitly included that of the Pyrrhonean philosopher: he is the man who participates in this "ability."

Chapter 6. Of the Principles of Scepticism

The originating cause of Scepticism is, we say, the hope of attaining quietude. Men of talent, who were perturbed by the contradictions in things and in doubt as to which of the alternatives they ought to accept, were led on to inquire what is true in things and what false, hoping by the settlement of the question to attain quietude. The main basic principle of the Sceptic system is that of opposing to every proposition an equal proposition; for we believe that as a consequence of this we end by ceasing to dogmatize.

Chapter 7. Does the Sceptic Dogmatize?

When we say that the Sceptic refrains from dogmatizing we do not use the term "dogma," as some do, in the broader sense of "approval of a thing" (for the Sceptic gives assent to the feelings which are the necessary results of sense-impressions, and he would not, for example, say when feeling hot or cold "I believe that I am not hot or cold"); but we say that "he does not dogmatize" using "dogma" in the sense, which some give it, of "assent to one of the non-evident objects of scientific inquiry"; for the Pyrrhonean philosopher assents to nothing that is non-evident. Moreover, even in the act of enunciating the Sceptic formulae concerning things non-evident—such as the formula "No more (one thing than another)," or the formula "I determine nothing," or any of the others which we shall presently mention,—he does not dogmatize. For whereas the dogmatizer posits the things about which he is said to be dogmatizing as really existent, the Sceptic does not posit these formulae in any absolute sense; for he conceives that, just as the formula "All things are false" asserts the falsity of itself as well as of everything else, as does the formula "Nothing is true," so also the formula "No more" asserts that itself like all the rest, is "No more this than that," and thus cancels itself along with the rest. And of the other formulae we say the same. If then, while the dogmatizer posits the matter of his dogma as substantial truth, the Sceptic enunciates his formulae so that they are virtually canceled by themselves, he should not be said to dogmatize in his enunciation of them. And, most important of all, in his enunciation of these formulae he states what appears to himself and announces his own impression in an undogmatic way, without making any positive assertion regarding the external realities.

Chapter 8. Has the Sceptic a Doctrinal Rule?

We follow the same lines in replying to the question "Has the Sceptic a doctrinal rule?" For if one defines a "doctrinal rule" as "adherence to a number of dogmas which are dependent both on one another and on appearances," and defines "dogma" as "assent to a non-evident proposition," then we shall say that he has not a doctrinal rule. But if one defines "doctrinal rule" as "procedure which, in accordance with appearance, follows a certain line of reasoning, that reasoning indicating how it is possible to seem to live rightly (the word 'rightly' being taken, not as referring to virtue only, but in a wider sense) and tending to enable one to suspend judgement," then we say that he has a doctrinal rule. For we follow a line of reasoning which, in accordance with appearances, points us to a life conformable to the customs of our country and its laws and institutions, and to our own instinctive feelings.

Chapter 9. Does the Sceptic Deal with Physics?

We make a similar reply also to the question "Should the Sceptic deal with physical problems?" For while, on the one hand, so far as regards making firm and positive assertions about any of the matters dogmatically treated in physical theory, we do not deal with physics; yet, on the other hand, in respect of our mode of opposing to every proposition an equal proposition and of our theory of quietude we do treat of physics. This, too, is the way in which we approach the logical and ethical branches of so-called "philosophy."

Chapter 10. Do the Sceptics Abolish Appearances?

Those who say that "the Sceptics abolish appearances," or phenomena, seem to me to be unacquainted with the statements of our School. For, as we said above, we do not overthrow the affective sense-impressions which induce our assent involuntarily; and these impressions are "the appearances." And when we question whether the underlying object is such as it appears, we grant the fact that it appears, and our doubt does not concern the appearance itself but the account given of the appearance,—and that is a different thing from questioning the appearance itself. For example, honey appears to us to be sweet (and this we grant, for we perceive sweetness through the senses), but whether it is also sweet in its essence is for us a matter of doubt, since this is not an appearance but a judgement regarding the appearance. And even if we do actually argue against the appearances, we do not propound such arguments with the intention of abolishing appearances, but by way of pointing out the rashness of the Dogmatists; for if reason is such a trickster as to all but snatch away the appearances from under our very eyes, surely we should view it with suspicion in the case of things non-evident so as not to display rashness by following it.

Chapter 11. Of the Criterion of Scepticism

That we adhere to appearances is plain from what we say about the Criterion of the Sceptic School. The word "Criterion" is used in two senses: in the one it means "the standard regulating belief in reality or unreality," (and this we shall discuss in our refutation); in the other it denotes the standard of action by conforming to which in the conduct of life we perform some actions and abstain from others; and it is of the latter that we are now speaking. The criterion, then, of the Sceptic School is, we say, the appearance, giving this name to what is virtually the sense-presentation. For since this lies in feeling and involuntary affection, it is not open to question. Consequently, no one, I suppose, disputes that the underlying object has this or that appearance; the point in dispute is whether the object is in reality such as it appears to be.

Adhering, then, to appearances we live in accordance with the normal rules of life, undogmatically, seeing that we cannot remain wholly inactive. And it would seem that this regulation of life is fourfold, and that one part of it lies in the guidance of Nature, another in the constraint of the passions, another in the tradition of laws and customs, another in the instruction of the arts. Nature's guidance is that by which we are naturally capable of sensation and thought; constraint of the passions is that whereby hunger drives us to food and thirst to drink; tradition of customs and laws, that whereby we regard piety in the conduct of life as good, but impiety as evil; instruction of the arts, that whereby we are not inactive in such arts as we adopt. But we make all these statements undogmatically.

Chapter 12. What Is the End of Scepticism?

Our next subject will be the End of the Sceptic system. Now an "End" is "that for which all actions or reasonings are undertaken, while it exists for the sake of none"; or, otherwise, "the ultimate object of appetency." We assert still that the Sceptic's End is quietude in respect of matters of opinion and moderate feeling in respect of things unavoidable. For the Sceptic, having set out to philosophize with the object of passing judgement on the sense-impressions and ascertaining which of them are true and which false, so as to attain quietude thereby, found himself involved in contradictions of equal weight, and being unable to decide between them suspended judgement; and as he was thus in suspense there followed, as it happened, the state of quietude in respect of matters of opinion. For the man who opines that anything is by nature good or bad is forever being disquieted: when he is without the things which he deems good he believes himself to be tormented by things naturally bad and he pursues after the things which are, as he thinks, good; which when he has obtained he keeps falling into still more perturbations because of his irrational and immoderate elation, and in his dread of a change of fortune he uses every endeavour to avoid losing the things which he deems good. On the other hand, the man who determines nothing as to what is naturally good or bad neither shuns nor pursues anything eagerly; and, in consequence, he is unperturbed.

The Sceptic, in fact, had the same experience which is said to have befallen the painter Apelles. Once, they say, when he was painting a horse and wished to represent in the painting the horse's foam, he was so unsuccessful that he gave up the attempt and flung at the picture the sponge on which he used to wipe the paints off his brush, and the mark of the sponge produced the effect of a horse's foam. So, too, the Sceptics were in hopes of gaining quietude by means of a decision regarding the disparity of the objects of sense and of thought, and being unable to effect this they suspended judgement; and they found that quietude, as if by chance, followed upon their suspense, even as a shadow follows its substance. We do not, however, suppose that the Sceptic is wholly untroubled; but we say that he is troubled by things unavoidable; for we grant that he is old at times and thirsty, and suffers various affections of that kind. But even in these cases, whereas ordinary people are afflicted by two circumstances,—namely, by the affections themselves and in no less a degree, by the belief that these conditions are evil by nature,—the Sceptic, by his rejection of the added belief in the natural badness of all these conditions, escapes here too with less discomfort. Hence we say that, while in regard to matters of opinion the Sceptic's End is quietude, in regard to things unavoidable it is "moderate affection." But some notable Sceptics have added the further definition "suspension of judgement in investigations."

Chapter 13. Of the General Modes Leading to Suspension of Judgment

Now that we have been saying that tranquillity follows on suspension of judgement, it will be our next task to explain how we arrive at this suspension. Speaking generally, one may say that it is the result of setting things in opposition. We oppose either appearances to appearances or objects of thought to objects of thought or *alternando*. For instance, we oppose appearances when we say "The same tower appears round from a distance, but square from close at hand"; and thoughts to thoughts, when in answer to him who argues the existence of Providence from the order of the heavenly bodies we oppose the fact that often the good fare ill and the bad fare well, and draw from this the inference that Providence does not exist. And thoughts we oppose to appearances, as when Anaxagoras countered the notion that snow is white with the argument, "Snow is frozen water, and water is black; therefore snow also is black." With a different idea we oppose things present sometimes to things present, as in the foregoing examples, and sometimes to things past or future, as, for instance, when someone propounds to us a theory which we are unable to refute, we say to him in reply, "Just as, before the birth of the founder of the School to which you belong, the theory it holds was not as yet apparent as a sound theory, although it was really in existence, so likewise it is possible that the opposite theory to that which you now propound is already really existent, though not yet apparent to us, so that we ought not as yet to yield assent to this theory which at the moment seems to be valid."

But in order that we may have a more exact understanding of these antitheses I will describe the Modes by which suspension of judgement is brought about, but without making any positive assertion regarding either their number or their validity; for it is possible that they may be unsound or there may be more of them than I shall enumerate.

Chapter 14. Concerning the Ten Modes

The usual tradition amongst the older Sceptics is that the "modes" by which "suspension" is supposed to be brought about are ten in number; and they also give them the synonymous names of "arguments" and "positions." They are these: the first, based on the variety in animals; the second, on the differences in human beings; the third, on the different structures of the organs of sense; the fourth, on the circumstantial conditions; the fifth, on positions and intervals and locations; the sixth, on intermixtures; the seventh, on the quantities and formations of the underlying objects; the eighth, on the fact of relativity; the ninth, on the frequency or rarity of occurrence; the tenth, on the disciplines and customs and laws, the legendary beliefs and the dogmatic convictions. This order, however, we adopt without prejudice.

*   *   *

Chapter 15. Of the Five Modes

The later Sceptics hand down Five Modes leading to suspension, namely these: the first based on discrepancy, the second on regress *ad infinitum,* the third on relativity, the fourth on hypothesis, the fifth on circular reasoning. That based on discrepancy leads us to find that with regard to the object presented there has arisen both amongst ordinary people and amongst the philosophers an interminable conflict because of which we are unable either to choose a thing or reject it, and so fall back on suspension. The Mode based upon regress *ad infinitum* is that whereby we assert that the thing adduced as a proof of the matter proposed needs a further proof, and this again another, and so on *ad infinitum,* so that the consequence is suspension, as we possess no starting-point for our argument. The Mode based upon relativity, as we have already said, is that whereby the object has such or such an appearance in relation to the subject judging and to the concomitant percepts, but as to its real nature we suspend judgement. We have the Mode based on hypothesis when the Dogmatists, being forced to recede *ad infinitum,* take as their starting-point something which they do not establish by argument but claim to assume as granted simply and without demonstration. The Mode of circular reasoning is the form used when the proof itself which ought to establish the matter of inquiry requires confirmation derived from that matter; in this case, being unable to assume either in order to establish the other, we suspend judgement about both.

That every matter of inquiry admits of being brought under these Modes we shall show briefly in this way. The matter proposed is either a sense-object or a thought-object, but whichever it is, it is an object of controversy; for some say that only sensibles are true, others only intelligibles, others that some sensible and some intelligible objects are true. Will they then assert that the controversy can or cannot be decided? If they say it cannot, we have it granted that we must suspend judgement; for concerning matters of dispute which admit of no decision it is impossible to make an assertion. But if they say that it can be decided, we ask by what is it to be decided. For example, in the case of the sense-object (for we shall base our argument on it first), is it to be decided by a sense-object or a thought-object? For if they say by a sense-object, since we are inquiring about sensibles that object itself also will require another to confirm it; and if that too is to be a sense-object, it likewise will require another for its confirmation, and so on *ad infinitum.* And if the sense-object shall have to be decided by a thought-object, then, since thought-objects also are controverted, this being an object of thought will need examination and confirmation. Whence then will it gain confirmation? If from an intelligible object, it will suffer a similar regress *ad infinitum;* and if from a sensible object, since an intelligible was adduced to establish the sensible and a sensible to establish the intelligible, the Mode of circular reasoning is brought in.

If, however, our disputant, by way of escape from this conclusion, should claim to assume as granted and without demonstration some postulate for the demonstration of the next steps of his argument, then the Mode of hypothesis will be brought in, which allows no escape. For if the author of the hypothesis is worthy of credence, we shall be no less worthy of credence every time that we make the opposite hypothesis. Moreover, if the author of the hypothesis assumes what is true he causes it to be suspected by assuming it by hypothesis rather than after proof; while if it is false, the foundation of his argument will be rotten. Further, if hypothesis conduces at all to proof, let the subject of inquiry itself be assumed and not some other thing which is merely a means to establish the actual subject of the argument; but if it is absurd to assume the subject of inquiry, it will also be absurd to assume that upon which it depends.

It is also plain that all sensibles are relative; for they are relative to those who have the sensations. Therefore it is apparent that whatever sensible object is presented can easily be referred to one of the Five Modes. And concerning the intelligible object we argue similarly. For if it should be said that it is a matter of unsettled controversy, the necessity of our suspending judgement will be granted. And if, on the other hand, the controversy admits of decision, then if the decision rests on an intelligible object we shall be driven to the regress *ad infinitum,* and to circular reasoning if it rests on a sensible; for since the sensible again is controverted and cannot be decided by means of itself because of the regress *ad infinitum,* it will require the intelligible object, just as also the intelligible will require the sensible. For these reasons, again, he who assumes anything by hypothesis will be acting illogically. Moreover, objects of thought, or intelligibles, are relative; for they are so named on account of their relation to the person thinking, and if they had really possessed the nature they are said to possess, there would have been no controversy about them. Thus the intelligible also is referred to the Five Modes, so that in all cases we are compelled to suspend judgement concerning the object presented.

Such then are the Five Modes handed down amongst the later Sceptics; but they propound these not by way of superseding the Ten Modes, but in order to expose the rashness of the Dogmatists with more variety and completeness by means of the Five in conjunction with the Ten.

PLOTINUS
ca. A.D. 204–270

The last great school of Greek philosophy was Neoplatonism, and its most famous representative was Plotinus, born in
Lykopolis, Egypt in A.D. 204. In his late
twenties, Plotinus began to study in
Alexandria with Ammonius Saccas, a
shadowy figure who was also the teacher
of the theologian Origen. After eleven
years with Ammonius, Plotinus joined an
expedition to Persia to learn Persian and
Indian wisdom. The trek proved unsuccessful and Plotinus moved to Rome.
There he established a school of philosophy and a friendship with the emperor
Gallenius. At one point he sought permission to found a city based on Plato's
Republic, but the plan came to naught.
He stayed in Rome, teaching and writing,
until the death of the emperor in 268. He
then moved to the home of a friend
where he died in 270, apparently from
leprosy.

Developing Plato's dualistic understanding of reality, Plotinus taught that
true reality lies "beyond" the physical
world. This "reality beyond reality" has
no limits and so cannot be described by
words, since words invariably have limits.
Plotinus, again borrowing from Plato,
calls this ultra-reality the "Good" or the
"One." The One/Good has no limits and is
so supremely rich that it overflows or
"emanates" to produce "Intellectual-Principle" or "Divine Mind" *<Nous>*. This Intellectual-Principle, in turn, overflows and
"Divine-Soul" emanates from it. This process continues as Divine-Soul generates
the material world. The lowest level of

463

emanation, at the furthest extreme from the One/Good, is the utter formlessness and unreality of matter.

The goal of philosophy is to awaken individuals to the reality beyond the material world. But philosophy alone cannot take a person to the highest reality of the One. Only in mystical experience can an individual unite with the One. Plotinus himself claimed to have achieved such a union four times during his life.

Plotinus' writings were edited by one of his pupils, Porphyry, in the form of six groups of nine "Tractates" (treatises), published as the so-called *Enneads* (from the Greek word for "nine"). The selections given here, in the A.H. Armstrong translation, begin with the Treatise on Beauty. This Tractate explains how the ascent of the soul to the One/Good is dependent on the beauty of soul, a godlike disposition. Plotinus' description parallels the ascending dialectic in Plato's *Symposium* (210ᵃ). The second selection discusses the three "hypostases," or stages—the One/Good, the Intellectual-Principle, and the World-Soul—explaining how each is generated from the one above. The final selection is thought to have been written late in Plotinus' life and gives a detailed description of the soul's ascent to ecstatic union. At the end of this tractate, Plotinus, in order to represent the One/Good, borrows Plato's image of the sun from the Myth of the Cave.

Neoplatonism, with its emphasis on the otherworldly and the need for escape from the physical world, was the perfect philosophy for the chaotic final days of the Roman Empire. Plotinus' thought had a profound influence on Christian thought, especially on St. Augustine. Indeed, if St. Thomas is considered an Aristotelian, St. Augustine may be called a Neoplatonist. Many later thinkers, such as Eckhart, Nicolas of Cusa, Comenius, Boehme, Hegel, and Schelling, also had their philosophy molded by Neoplatonist doctrines.

* * *

Joseph Katz, *Plotinus' Search for the Good* (New York: King's Crown Press, 1950), and Émile Bréhier, *The Philosophy of Plotinus,* translated by Joseph Thomas (Chicago: University of Chicago Press, 1958) are good introductions to the study of Plotinus. For more advanced studies, see A.H. Armstrong, *The Architecture of the Intelligible Universe in the Philosophy of Plotinus* (Cambridge: Cambridge University Press, 1940), and J.M. Rist, *Plotinus: The Road to Reality* (Cambridge: Cambridge University Press, 1967). E.R. Dodds, *Select Passages Illustrating Neoplatonism,* translated by E.R. Dodds (New York: Macmillan, 1923) provides a topical guide to the key ideas in the *Enneads;* while Dominic J. O'Meara, *Plotinus: An Introduction to the Enneads* (Oxford: Oxford University Press, 1993), discusses specific important passages. For specialized topics related to Plotinus see B.A.G. Fuller, *The Problem of Evil in Plotinus* (Cambridge: Cambridge University Press, 1912); Philip Merlan, *From Platonism to Neoplatonism* (The Hague, Netherlands: Martinus Nijhoff, 1953); John M. Rist, *Eros and Psyche: Studies in Plato, Plotinus, and Origen* (Toronto: University of Toronto Press, 1964); and Andreas Graeser, *Plotinus and the Stoics: A Preliminary Study* (Leiden, Netherlands: Brill, 1972). Finally, for discussions of Neoplatonism as a school, see Thomas Whittaker, *The Neo-Platonists* (Cambridge: Cambridge University Press, 1918); Arthur O. Lovejoy, *The Great Chain of Being* (Cambridge, MA: Harvard University Press, 1936); R.T. Wallis, *Neoplatonism* (London:

Duckworth, 1972); and the collection of essays, R. Baine Harris, ed., *The Structure of Being: A Neoplatonic Approach* (Norfolk, VA: International Society for Neoplatonic Studies, 1982).

ENNEADS (in part)

FIRST ENNEAD, SIXTH TRACTATE: BEAUTY

1. Beauty is mostly in sight, but it is to be found too in things we hear, in combinations of words and also in music, and in all music [not only in songs]; for tunes and rhythms are certainly beautiful: and for those who are advancing upwards from sense-perception ways of life and actions and characters and intellectual activities are beautiful, and there is the beauty of virtue. If there is any beauty prior to these, this discussion will reveal it.

Very well then, what is it which makes us imagine that bodies are beautiful and attracts our hearing to sounds because of their beauty? And how are all the things which depend on soul beautiful? Are they all made beautiful by one and the same beauty or is there one beautifulness in bodies and a different one in other things? And what are they, or what is it? Some things, bodies for instance, are not beautiful from the nature of the objects themselves, but by participation, others are beauties themselves, like the nature of virtue. The same bodies appear sometimes beautiful, sometimes not beautiful, so that their being bodies is one thing, their being beautiful another. What is this principle, then, which is present in bodies? We ought to consider this first. What is it that attracts the gaze of those who look at something, and turns and draws them to it and makes them enjoy the sight? If we find this perhaps we can use it as a stepping-stone and get a sight of the rest. Nearly everyone says that it is good proportion of the parts to each other and to the whole, with the addition of good colour, which produces visible beauty, and that with the objects of sight and generally with everything else, being beautiful is being well-proportioned and measured. On this theory nothing single and simple but only a composite thing will have any beauty. It will be the whole which is beautiful, and the parts will not have the property of beauty by themselves, but will contribute to the beauty of the whole. But if the whole is beautiful the parts must be beautiful too; a beautiful whole can certainly not be composed of ugly parts; all the parts must have beauty. For these people, too, beautiful colours, and the light of the sun as well, since they are simple and do not derive their beautifulness from good proportion, will be excluded from beauty And how do they think gold manages to be beautiful? And what makes lightning in the night and stars beautiful to see? And in sounds in the same way the simple will be banished, though often in a composition which is beautiful as a whole each separate sound is beautiful. And when, though the same good proportion is there all the time, the same face sometimes appears beautiful and sometimes does not, surely we must say that being beautiful is something else over and above good proportion, and good proportion is beautiful because of something else? But if when these people pass on to ways of life and beautiful expressions of thought they allege good proportion as the cause of beauty in these too, what can be meant by good proportion in beautiful ways of life or laws or studies or branches of knowledge? How can speculations be well-proportioned in relation to each other? If it is because they agree, there can be con-cord and agreement between bad ideas. The statement that "righteousness is a fine sort of silliness" agrees with and is in tune with the saying that "morality is stupidity"; the two fit perfectly. Again, every sort of virtue is a beauty of the soul, a truer beauty than those mentioned before; but how is virtue well-proportioned? Not like magnitudes or a number. We grant that the soul has several parts, but what is the formula for the com-position or mixture in the soul of parts or speculations? And what [on this theory], will the beauty of the intellect alone by itself be?

2. So let us go back to the beginning and state what the primary beauty in bodies really is. It is something which we become aware of even at the first glance; the soul speaks of it as if it understood it, recognises and welcomes it and as it were adapts itself to it. But when it encounters the ugly it shrinks back and rejects it and turns away from it and is out of tune and alienated from it. Our explanation of this is that the soul, since it is by nature what it is and is related to the higher kind of reality in the realm of being, when it sees something akin to it or a trace of its kindred reality, is delighted and thrilled and returns to itself and remembers itself and its own possessions. What likeness, then, is there between beautiful things here and There? If there is a likeness, let us agree that they are alike. But how are both the things in that world and the things in this beautiful? We maintain that the things in this world are beautiful by participating in form; for ev-ery shapeless thing which is naturally capable of receiving shape and form is ugly and outside the divine formative power as long as it has no share in formative power and form. This is absolute ugliness. But a thing is also ugly when it is not completely dom-inated by shape and formative power, since its matter has not submitted to be com-pletely shaped according to the form. The form, then, approaches and composes that which is to come into being from many parts into a single ordered whole; it brings it into a completed unity and makes it one by agreement of its parts; for since it is one it-self, that which is shaped by it must also be one as far as a thing can be which is com-posed of many parts. So beauty rests upon the material thing when it has been brought into unity, and gives itself to parts and wholes alike. When it comes upon something that is one and composed of like parts it gives the same gift to the whole; as sometimes art gives beauty to a whole house with its parts, and sometimes nature gives beauty to a single stone. So then the beautiful body comes into being by sharing in a formative power which comes from the divine forms.

3. The power ordained for the purpose recognises this, and there is nothing more effective for judging its own subject-matter, when the rest of the soul judges along with it; or perhaps the rest of the soul too pronounces the judgement by fitting the beautiful body to the form in itself and using this for judging beauty as we use a ruler for judging straightness. But how does the bodily agree with that which is before body? How does the architect declare the house outside beautiful by fitting it to the form of house within him? The reason is that the house outside, apart from the stones, is the inner form di-vided by the external mass of matter, without parts but appearing in many parts. When sense-perception, then, sees the form in bodies binding and mastering the nature op-posed to it, which is shapeless, and shape riding gloriously upon other shapes, it gathers into one that which appears dispersed and brings it back and takes it in, now without parts, to the soul's interior and presents it to that which is within as something in tune

with it and fitting it and dear to it; just as when a good man sees a trace of virtue in the young, which is in tune with his own inner truth, the sight delights him. And the simple beauty of colour comes about by shape and the mastery of the darkness in matter by the presence of light which is incorporeal and formative power and form. This is why fire itself is more beautiful than all other bodies, because it has the rank of form in relation to the other elements; it is above them in place and is the finest and subtlest of all bodies, being close to the incorporeal. It alone does not admit the others; but the others admit it for it warms them but is not cooled itself; it has colour primarily and all other things take the form of colour from it. So it shines and glitters as if it was a form. The inferior thing which becomes faint and dull by the fire's light, is not beautiful any more, as not participating in the whole form of colour. The melodies in sounds, too, the imperceptible ones which make the perceptible ones, make the soul conscious of beauty in the same way, showing the same thing in another medium. It is proper to sensible melodies to be measured by numbers, not according to any and every sort of formula but one which serves for the production of form so that it may dominate. So much, then, for the beauties in the realm of sense, images and shadows which, so to speak, sally out and come into matter and adorn it and excite us when they appear.

4. But about the beauties beyond, which it is no more the part of sense to see, but the soul sees them and speaks of them without instruments—we must go up to them and contemplate them and leave sense to stay down below. Just as in the case of the beauties of sense it is impossible for those who have not seen them or grasped their beauty—those born blind, for instance,—to speak about them, in the same way only those can speak about the beauty of ways of life who have accepted the beauty of ways of life and kinds of knowledge and everything else of the sort; and people cannot speak about the splendour of virtue who have never even imagined how fair is the face of justice and moral order; "neither the evening nor the morning star are as fair." But there must be those who see this beauty by that with which the soul sees things of this sort, and when they see it they must be delighted and overwhelmed and excited much more than by those beauties we spoke of before, since now it is true beauty they are grasping. These experiences must occur whenever there is contact with any sort of beautiful thing, wonder and a shock of delight and longing and passion and a happy excitement. One can have these experiences by contact with invisible beauties, and souls do have them, practically all, but particularly those who are more passionately in love with the invisible, just as with bodies all see them, but all are not stung as sharply, but some, who are called lovers, are most of all.

5. Then we must ask the lovers of that which is outside sense "What do you feel about beautiful ways of life, as we call them, and beautiful habits and well-ordered characters and in general about virtuous activities and dispositions and the beauty of souls? What do you feel when you see your own inward beauty? How are you stirred to wild exultation, and long to be with yourselves, gathering your selves together away from your bodies?" For this is what true lovers feel. But what is it which makes them feel like this? Not shape or colour or any size, but soul, without colour itself and possessing a moral order without colour and possessing all the other light of the virtues; you feel like this when you see, in yourself or in someone else, greatness of soul, a righteous life, a pure morality, courage with its noble look, and dignity and modesty advancing in a fearless, calm and unperturbed disposition, and the godlike light of intellect shining upon all this. We love and delight in these qualities, but why do we call them beautiful? They exist and appear to us and he who sees them cannot possibly say anything else except that they are what really exists. What does "really exists" mean? That they exist as beauties. But the argument still requires us to explain why real beings

make the soul lovable. What is this kind of glorifying light on all the virtues? Would you like to take the opposites, the uglinesses in soul, and contrast them with the beauties? Perhaps a consideration of what ugliness is and why it appears so will help us to find what we are looking for. Suppose, then, an ugly soul, dissolute and unjust, full of all lusts, and all disturbance, sunk in fears by its cowardice and jealousies by its pettiness, thinking mean and mortal thoughts as far as it thinks at all, altogether distorted, loving impure pleasures, living a life which consists of bodily sensations and finding delight in its ugliness. Shall we not say that its ugliness came to it as a "beauty" brought in from outside, injuring it and making it impure and "mixed with a great deal of evil," with its life and perceptions no longer pure, but by the admixture of evil living a dim life and diluted with a great deal of death, no longer seeing what a soul ought to see, no longer left in peace in itself because it keeps on being dragged out, and down, and to the dark? Impure, I think, and dragged in every direction towards the objects of sense, with a great deal of bodily stuff mixed into it, consorting much with matter and receiving a form other than its own it has changed by a mixture which makes it worse; just as if anyone gets into mud or filth he does not show any more the beauty which he had what is seen is what he wiped off on himself from the mud and filth; his ugliness has come from an addition of alien matter, and his business, if he is to be beautiful again, is to wash and clean himself and so be again what he was before. So we shall be right in saying that the soul becomes ugly by mixture and dilution and inclination towards the body and matter. This is the soul's ugliness, not being pure and unmixed, like gold, but full of earthiness; if anyone takes the earthy stuff away the gold is left, and is beautiful, when it is singled out from other things and is alone by itself. In the same way the soul too, when it is separated from the lusts which it has through the body with which it consorted too much, and freed from its other affections, purged of what it gets from being embodied, when it abides alone has put away all the ugliness which came from the other nature.

6. For, as was said in old times, self-control, and courage and every virtue, is a purification, and so is even wisdom itself. This is why the mysteries are right when they say riddlingly that the man who has not been purified will lie in mud when he goes to Hades, because the impure is fond of mud by reason of its badness; just as pigs, with their unclean bodies, like that sort of thing. For what can true self-control be except not keeping company with bodily pleasures, but avoiding them as impure and belonging to something impure? Courage, too, is not being afraid of death. And death is the separation of body and soul; and a man does not fear this if he welcomes the prospect of being alone. Again, greatness of soul is despising the things here and wisdom is an intellectual activity which turns away from the things below and leads the soul to those above. So the soul when it is purified becomes form and formative power, altogether bodiless and intellectual and entirely belonging to the divine, whence beauty springs and all that is akin to it. Soul, then, when it is raised to the level of intellect increases in beauty. Intellect and the things of intellect are its beauty, its own beauty and not another's, since only then [when it is perfectly conformed to intellect] is it truly soul. For this reason it is right to say that the soul's becoming something good and beautiful is its being made like to God, because from Him come beauty and all else which falls to the lot of real beings. Or rather, beautifulness is reality, and the other kind of thing is the ugly, and this same is the primary evil; so for God the qualities of goodness and beauty are the same, or the realities, the good and beauty. So we must follow the same line of enquiry to discover beauty and goodness, and ugliness and evil. And first we must posit beauty which is also the good; from this immediately comes intellect, which is beauty; and soul is given beauty by intellect. Everything else is beautiful by the shaping of soul, the beau-

ties in actions and in ways of life. And soul makes beautiful the bodies which are spoken of as beautiful; for since it is a divine thing and a kind of part of beauty, it makes everything it grasps and masters beautiful, as far as they are capable of participation.

7. So we must ascend again to the good, which every soul desires. Anyone who has seen it knows what I mean when I say that it is beautiful. It is desired as good, and the desire for it is directed to good, and the attainment of it is for those who go up to the higher world and are converted and strip off what we put on in our descent; (just as for those who go up to the celebrations of sacred rites there are purifications, and strippings off of the clothes they wore before, and going up naked) until, passing in the ascent all that is alien to the God, one sees with one's self alone That alone, simple, single and pure, from which all depends and to which all look and are and live and think for it is cause of life and mind and being. If anyone sees it, what passion will he feel, what longing in his desire to be united with it, what a shock of delight! The man who has not seen it may desire it as good, but he who has seen it glories in its beauty and is full of wonder and delight, enduring a shock which causes no hurt, loving with true passion and piercing longing; he laughs at all other loves and despises what he thought beautiful before; it is like the experience of those who have met appearances of gods or spirits and do not any more appreciate as they did the beauty of other bodies. "What then are we to think, if anyone contemplates the absolute beauty which exists pure by itself, uncontaminated by flesh or body, not in earth or heaven, that it may keep its purity?" All these other things are external additions and mixtures and not primary, but derived from it. If then one sees That which provides for all and remains by itself and gives to all but receives nothing into itself, if he abides in the contemplation of this kind of beauty and rejoices in being made like it, how can he need any other beauty? For this, since it is beauty most of all, and primary beauty, makes its lovers beautiful and lovable. Here the greatest, the ultimate contest is set before our souls; all our toil and trouble is for this, not to be left without a share in the best of visions. The man who attains this is blessed in seeing that "blessed sight," and he who fails to attain it has failed utterly. A man has not failed if he fails to win beauty of colours or bodies, or power or office or kingship even, but if he fails to win this and only this. For this he should give up the attainment of kingship and of rule over all earth and sea and sky, if only by leaving and overlooking them he can turn to That and see.

8. But how shall we find the way? What method can we devise? How can one see the "inconceivable beauty" which stays within in the holy sanctuary and does not come out where the profane may see it? Let him who can, follow and come within, and leave outside the sight of his eyes and not turn back to the bodily splendours which he saw before. When he sees the beauty in bodies he must not run after them; we must know that they are images, traces, shadows, and hurry away to that which they image. For if a man runs to the image and wants to seize it as if it was the reality (like a beautiful reflection playing on the water, which some story somewhere, I think, said riddlingly a man wanted to catch and sank down into the stream and disappeared) then this man who clings to beautiful bodies and will not let them go, will, like the man in the story, but in soul, not in body, sink down into the dark depths where intellect has no delight, and stay blind in Hades, consorting with shadows there and here. This would be truer advice "Let us fly to our dear country." What then is our way of escape, and how are we to find it? We shall put out to sea, as Odysseus did, from the witch Circe or Calypso—as the poet says (I think with a hidden meaning)—and was not content to stay though he had delights of the eyes and lived among much beauty of sense. Our country from which we came is there, our Father is there. How shall we travel to it, where is our way of escape? We cannot get there on foot; for our feet only carry us everywhere in this world, from

one country to another. You must not get ready a carriage, either, or a boat. Let all these things go, and do not look. Shut your eyes, and change to and wake another way of seeing, which everyone has but few use.

9. And what does this inner sight see? When it is just awakened it is not at all able to look at the brilliance before it. So that the soul must be trained, first of all to look at beautiful ways of life then at beautiful works, not those which the arts produce, but the works of men who have a name for goodness: then look at the souls of the people who produce the beautiful works. How then can you see the sort of beauty a good soul has? Go back into yourself and look; and if you do not yet see yourself beautiful, then, just as someone making a statue which has to be beautiful cuts away here and polishes there and makes one part smooth and clears another till he has given his statue a beautiful face, so you too must cut away excess and straighten the crooked and clear the dark and make it bright, and never stop "working on your statue" till the divine glory of virtue shines out on you, till you see "self-mastery enthroned upon its holy seat." If you have become this, and see it, and are at home with yourself in purity, with nothing hindering you from becoming in this way one, with no inward mixture of anything else, but wholly yourself, nothing but true light, not measured by dimensions, or bounded by shape into littleness, or expanded to size by unboundedness, but everywhere unmeasured, because greater than all measure and superior to all quantity; when you see that you have become this, then you have become sight; you can trust yourself then; you have already ascended and need no one to show you; concentrate your gaze and see. This alone is the eye that sees the great beauty. But if anyone comes to the sight blear-eyed with wickedness, and unpurified, or weak and by his cowardice unable to look at what is very bright, he sees nothing, even if someone shows him what is there and possible to see. For one must come to the sight with a seeing power made akin and like to what is seen. No eye ever saw the sun without becoming sun-like, nor can a soul see beauty without becoming beautiful. You must become first all godlike and all beautiful if you intend to see God and beauty. First the soul will come in its ascent to intellect and there will know the Forms, all beautiful, and will affirm that these, the Ideas, are beauty; for all things are beautiful by these, by the products and essence of intellect. That which is beyond this we call the nature of the Good, which holds beauty as a screen before it. So in a loose and general way of speaking the Good is the primary beauty; but if one distinguishes the intelligibles [from the Good] one will say that the place of the Forms is the intelligible beauty, but the Good is That which is beyond, the "spring and origin" of beauty; or one will place the Good and the primal beauty on the same level in any case, however, beauty is in the intelligible world.

* * *

FIFTH ENNEAD, FIRST TRACTATE: ON THE THREE PRIMARY HYPOSTASES

1. What is it, then, which has made the souls forget their father, God, and be ignorant of themselves and him, even though they are parts which come from his higher world and altogether belong to it? The beginning of evil for them was audacity and coming to birth and the first otherness and the wishing to belong to themselves. Since they were clearly delighted with their own independence, and made great use of self-movement,

running the opposite course and getting as far away as possible, they were ignorant even that they themselves came from that world; just as children who are immediately torn from their parents and brought up far away do not know who they themselves or their parents are. Since they do not any more see their father or themselves, they despise themselves through ignorance of their birth and honour other things, admiring everything rather than themselves, and, astonished and delighted by and dependent on these [earthly] things, they broke themselves loose as far as they could in contempt of that from which they turned away; so that their honour for these things here and their contempt for themselves is the cause of their utter ignorance of God. For what pursues and admires something else admits at the same time its own inferiority; but by making itself inferior to things which come into being and perish and considering itself the most contemptible and the most liable to death of all the things which it admires it could not possibly have any idea of the nature and power of God. One must therefore speak in two ways to men who are in this state of mind, if one is going to turn them round to what lies in the opposite direction and is primary, and to lead them up to that which is highest, one, and first. What, then, are these two ways? One shows how contemptible are the things now honoured by the soul, and this we shall develop more amply elsewhere, but the other teaches and reminds the soul how high its birth and value are, and this is prior to the other one and when it is clarified will also make the other obvious. This is what we must speak about now; it is close to the subject of our investigation and will be useful for that other discourse. For that which investigates is the soul, and it should know what it is as an investigating soul, so that it may learn first about itself, whether it has the power to investigate things of this kind, and if it has an eye of the right kind to see them, and if the investigation is suitable for it. For if the objects are alien, what is the point? But if they are akin, the investigation is suitable and discovery is possible.

2. Let every soul, then, first consider this, that it made all living things itself, breathing life into them, those that the earth feeds and those that are nourished by the sea, and the divine stars in the sky; it made the sun itself, and this great heaven, and adorned it itself, and drives it round itself, in orderly movement; it is a nature other than the things which it adorns and moves and makes live; and it must necessarily be more honourable than they, for they come into being or pass away when the soul leaves them or grants life to them, but soul itself exists for ever because "it does not depart from itself." This is how soul should reason about the manner in which it grants life in the whole universe and in individual things. Let it look at the great soul, being itself another soul which is no small one, which has become worthy to look by being freed from deceit and the things that have bewitched the other souls, and is established in quietude. Let not only its encompassing body and the body's raging sea be quiet, but all its environment: the earth quiet, and the sea and air quiet, and the heaven itself at peace. Into this heaven at rest let it imagine soul as if flowing in from outside, pouring in and entering it everywhere and illuminating it: as the rays of the sun light up a dark cloud, and make it shine and give it a golden look, so soul entering into the body of heaven gives it life and gives it immortality and wakes what lies inert. And heaven, moved with an everlasting motion by the wise guidance of soul, becomes a "fortunate living being" and gains its value by the indwelling of soul; before soul it was a dead body, earth and water, or rather the darkness of matter and non-existence, and "what the gods hate," as a poet says. The power and nature of soul will become still clearer and more obvious if one considers here how it encompasses the heaven and drives it by its own acts of will. For soul has given itself to the whole magnitude of heaven, as far as it extends, and every stretch of space, both great and small, is ensouled; one body lies in one place and one in another, and one is here and another there; some are separated by being in oppo-

site parts of the universe, and others in other ways. But soul is not like this and it is not by being cut up that it gives life, by a part of itself for each individual thing, but all things live by the whole, and all soul is present everywhere, made like to the father who begat it in its unity and its universality. And by its power the heaven is one, though it is multiple with one part in one place and one in another, and our universe is a god by the agency of this soul. And the sun also is a god because it is ensouled, and the other heavenly bodies, and we, if we are in any way divine, are so for this reason: for "corpses are more throwable away than dung." But that which is for the gods the cause of their being gods must necessarily be a divinity senior to them. But our soul is of the same kind, and when you look at it without its accretions and take it in its purified state you will find that very same honourable thing which [we said] was soul, more honourable than everything which is body. For all bodily things are earth; and even if they are fire, what would its burning principle be [but soul]? And the same is true of all things compounded of these, even if you add water to them, and air as well. But if the bodily is worth pursuing because it is ensouled, why does one let oneself go and pursue another? But by admiring the soul in another, you admire yourself.

3. Since the soul is so honourable and divine a thing, be sure already that you can attain God by reason of its being of this kind, and with this as your motive ascend to him: in all certainty you will not look far; and the stages between are not many. Grasp then the soul's upper neighbour, more divine than this divine thing, after which and from which the soul comes. For, although it is a thing of the kind which our discussion has shown it to be, it is an image of Intellect; just as a thought in its utterance is an image of the thought in soul, so soul itself is the expressed thought of Intellect, and its whole activity, and the life which it sends out to establish another reality; as fire has the heat which remains with it and the heat which it gives. But one must understand that the activity on the level of Intellect does not flow out of it, but the external activity comes into existence as something distinct. Since then its existence derives from Intellect soul is intellectual, and its intellect is in discursive reasonings, and its perfection comes from Intellect, like a father who brings to maturity a son whom he begat imperfect in comparison with himself. Soul's establishment in reality, then, comes from Intellect and its thought becomes actual in its seeing of Intellect. For when it looks into Intellect, it has within it and as its own what it thinks in its active actuality. And we should call these alone activities of the soul, all it does intellectually and which spring from its own home; its inferior activities come from elsewhere and belong to a soul of this inferior kind. Intellect therefore makes soul still more divine by being its father and by being present to it; for there is nothing between but the fact that they are different, soul as next in order and as the recipient, Intellect as the form; and even the matter of Intellect is beautiful, since it has the form of Intellect and is simple. But what Intellect is like is clear from this very fact that it is superior to soul which is of such great excellence.

4. But one might see this also from what follows: if someone admires this perceptible universe, observing its size and beauty and the order of its everlasting course, and the gods in it, some of whom are seen and some are invisible, and the spirits, and all animals and plants, let him ascend to its archetypal and truer reality and there see them all intelligible and eternal in it, in its own understanding and life; and let him see pure Intellect presiding over them, and immense wisdom, and the true life of Kronos, a god who is fullness and intellect. For he encompasses in himself all things immortal, every intellect, every god, every soul, all for ever unmoving. For why should it seek to change when all is well with it? Where should it seek to go away to when it has everything in itself? But it does not even seek to increase, since it is most perfect. Therefore all things in it are perfect, that it may be altogether perfect, having nothing which is not so, hav-

ing nothing in itself which does not think; but it thinks not by seeking but by having. Its blessedness is not something acquired, but all things are in eternity, and the true eternity, which time copies, running round the soul, letting some things go and attending to others. For around Soul things come one after another: now Socrates, now a horse, always some one particular reality; but Intellect is all things. It has therefore everything at rest in the same place, and it only is, and its "is" is for ever, and there is no place for the future for then too it is—or for the past—for nothing there has passed away—but all things remain stationary for ever, since they are the same, as if they were satisfied with themselves for being so.

But each of them is Intellect and Being, and the whole is universal Intellect and Being, Intellect making Being exist in thinking it, and Being giving Intellect thinking and existence by being thought. But the cause of thinking is something else, which is also cause of being; they both therefore have a cause other than themselves. For they are simultaneous and exist together and one does not abandon the other, but this one is two things, Intellect and Being and thinking and thought, Intellect as thinking and Being as thought. For there could not be thinking without otherness, and also sameness. These then are primary, Intellect, Being, Otherness, Sameness; but one must also include Motion and Rest. One must include movement if there is thought, and rest that it may think the same; and otherness, that there may be thinker and thought; or else, if you take away otherness, it will become one and keep silent; and the objects of thought, also, must have otherness in relation to each other. But one must include sameness, because it is one with itself, and all have some common unity; and the distinctive quality of each is otherness. The fact that there are several of these primaries makes number and quantity; and the particularity of each makes quality, and from these as principles everything else comes.

5. This god, then, which is over the soul, is multiple; and soul exists among the intelligible realities in close unity with them, unless it wills to desert them. When it has come near then to him and, in a way, become one with him, it lives for ever. Who is it, then, who begat this god? The simple god, the one who is prior to this kind of multiplicity, the cause of this one's existence and multiplicity, the maker of number. For number is not primary: the One is prior to the dyad, but the dyad is secondary and, originating from the One, has it as definer, but is itself of its own nature indefinite; but when it is defined, it is already a number, but a number as substance; and soul too is a number. For masses and magnitudes are not primary: these things which have thickness come afterwards, and sense-perception thinks they are realities. Even in seeds it is not the moisture which is honourable, but what is unseen: and this is number and rational principle. Therefore what is called number in the intelligible world and the dyad are rational principles and Intellect; but the dyad is indefinite when one forms an idea of it by what may be called the substrate, but each and every number which comes from it and the One is a form, as if Intellect was shaped by the numbers which came to exist in it; but it is shaped in one way by the One and in another by itself, like sight in its actuality; for intellection is seeing sight, and both are one.

6. How then does it see, and whom does it see? And how did it come into existence at all and arise from the One so as to be able to see? For the soul now knows that these things must be, but longs to answer the question repeatedly discussed also by the ancient philosophers, how from the One, if it is such as we say it is, anything else, whether a multiplicity or a dyad or a number, came into existence, and why it did not on the contrary remain by itself, but such a great multiplicity flowed from it as that which is seen to exist in beings, but which we think it right to refer back to the One. Let us speak of it in this way, first invoking God himself, not in spoken words, but stretching

ourselves out with our soul into prayer to him, able in this way to pray alone to him alone. The contemplator, then, since God exists by himself as if inside the temple, remaining quiet beyond all things, must contemplate what correspond to the images already standing outside the temple, or rather that one image which appeared first; and this is the way in which it appeared: everything which is moved must have some end to which it moves. The One has no such end, so we must not consider that it moves. If anything comes into being after it, we must think that it necessarily does so while the One remains continually turned towards itself. When we are discussing eternal realities we must not let coming into being in time be an obstacle to our thought; in the discussion we apply the word "becoming" to them in attributing to them causal connection and order, and must therefore state that what comes into being from the One does so without the One being moved: for if anything came into being as a result of the One's being moved, it would be the third starting from the One, not the second, since it would come after the movement. So if there is a second after the One it must have come to be without the One moving at all, without any inclination or act of will or any sort of activity on its part. How did it come to be then, and what are we to think of as surrounding the One in its repose? It must be a radiation from it while it remains unchanged, like the bright light of the sun which, so to speak, runs round it, springing from it continually while it remains unchanged. All things which exist, as long as they remain in being, necessarily produce from their own substances, in dependence on their present power, a surrounding reality directed to what is outside them, a kind of image of the archetypes from which it was produced: fire produces the heat which comes from it; snow does not only keep its cold inside itself. Perfumed things show this particularly clearly. As long as they exist, something is diffused from themselves around them, and what is near them enjoys their existence. And all things when they come to perfection produce; the One is always perfect and therefore produces everlastingly; and its product is less than itself. What then must we say about the most perfect? Nothing can come from it except that which is next greatest after it. Intellect is next to it in greatness and second to it: for Intellect sees it and needs it alone; but it has no need of Intellect; and that which derives from something greater than Intellect is intellect, which is greater than all things, because the other things come after it: as Soul is an expression and a kind of activity of Intellect, just as Intellect is of the One. But soul's expression is obscure—for it is a ghost of Intellect—and for this reason it has to look to Intellect; but Intellect in the same way has to look to that god, in order to be Intellect. But it sees him, not as separated from him, but because it comes next after him, and there is nothing between, as also there is not anything between soul and Intellect. Everything longs for its parent and loves it, especially when parent and offspring are alone; but when the parent is the highest good, the offspring is necessarily with him and separate from him only in otherness.

7. But we say that Intellect is an image of that Good; for we must speak more plainly; first of all we must say that what has come into being must be in a way that Good, and retain much of it and be a likeness of it, as light is of the sun. But Intellect is not that Good. How then does it generate Intellect? Because by its return to it it sees: and this seeing is Intellect. For that which apprehends something else is either sense-perception or intellect; (sense-perception is a line etc.) but the circle is of a kind which can be divided; but this [intellectual apprehension] is not so. There is One here also, but the One is the productive power of all things. The things, then, of which it is the productive power are those which Intellect observes, in a way cutting itself off from the power; otherwise it would not be Intellect. For Intellect also has of itself a kind of intimate perception of its power, that it has power to produce substantial reality. Intellect, certainly, by its own means even defines its being for itself by the power which comes

from the One, and because its substance is a kind of single part of what belongs to the One and comes from the One, it is strengthened by the One and made perfect in substantial existence by and from it. But Intellect sees, by means of itself, like something divided proceeding from the undivided, that life and thought and all things come from the One, because that God is not one of all things; for this is how all things come from him, because he is not confined by any shape; that One is one alone: if he was all things, he would be numbered among beings. For this reason that One is none of the things in Intellect, but all things come from him. This is why they are substances; for they are already defined and each has a kind of shape. Being must not fluctuate, so to speak, in the indefinite, but must be fixed by limit and stability; and stability in the intelligible world is limitation and shape, and it is by these that it receives existence. "Of this lineage" is this Intellect of which we are speaking, a lineage worthy of the purest Intellect, that it should spring from nowhere else but the first principle, and when it has come into existence should generate all realities along with itself, all the beauty of the Ideas and all the intelligible gods; and it is full of the beings which it has generated and as it were swallows them up again, by keeping them in itself and because they do not fall out into matter and are not brought up in the house of Rhea; as the mysteries and the myths about the gods say riddlingly that Kronos, the wisest god, before the birth of Zeus took back and kept within himself all that he begat, and in this way is full and is Intellect in satiety; and after this they say he begat Zeus who is then his Koros [that is, boy and satiety]; for Intellect generates soul, since it is perfect Intellect. For since it was perfect it had to generate, and not be without offspring when it was so great a power. But its offspring could not be better than it (this is not so even here below) but had to be a lesser image of it, and in the same way indefinite, but defined by its parent and, so to speak, given a form. And the offspring of Intellect is a rational form and an existing being, that which thinks discursively; it is this which moves round Intellect and is light and trace of Intellect and dependent on it, united to it on one side and so filled with it and enjoying it and sharing in it and thinking, but, on the other side, in touch with the things which came after it, or rather itself generating what must necessarily be worse than soul; about these we must speak later. This is as far as the divine realities extend.

8. This is the reason why Plato says that all things are threefold "about the king of all"—he means the primary realities—and "the second about the second and the third about the third." But he also says that there is a "father of the cause," meaning Intellect by "the cause": for Intellect is his craftsman; and he says that it makes Soul in that "mixing-bowl" he speaks of. And the father of Intellect which is the cause he calls the Good and that which is beyond Intellect and "beyond being." And he also often calls Being and Intellect Idea: so Plato knew that Intellect comes from the Good and Soul from Intellect. And [it follows] that these statements of ours are not new; they do not belong to the present time, but were made long ago, not explicitly, and what we have said in this discussion has been an interpretation of them, relying on Plato's own writings for evidence that these views are ancient. And Parmenides also, before Plato, touched on a view like this, in that he identified Being and Intellect and that it was not among things perceived by the senses that he placed Being, when he said "Thinking and Being are the same." And he says that this Being is unmoved—though he does attach thinking to it—taking all bodily movement from it that it may remain always in the same state, and likening it to "the mass of a sphere," because it holds all things in its circumference and because its thinking is not external, but in itself. But when he said it was one, in his own works, he was open to criticism because this one of his was discovered to be many. But Parmenides in Plato speaks more accurately, and distinguishes from each other the first One, which is

The School of Plato, Roman Mosaic, n.d. The Platonism of late antiquity (and the Middle Ages) was strongly influenced by Plotinus' development and modification of Plato's thought. *(Art Resource)*

more properly called One, and the second which he calls "One-Many" and the third, "One and Many." In this way he too agrees with the doctrine of the three natures.

9. And Anaxagoras also, when he says that Intellect is pure and unmixed, posits that the first principle is simple and that the One is separate, but he neglects to give an accurate account because of his antiquity. Heraclitus also knows that the one is eternal and intelligible: for bodies are always coming into being and flowing away. And for Empedocles Strife divides, but Love is the One—he too makes it incorporeal—and the elements serve as matter. Later, Aristotle makes the first principle separate and intelligible, but when he says that it knows itself, he goes back again and does not make it the first principle; and by making many other intelligible realities, as many as the heavenly spheres, that each particular intelligible may move one particular sphere, he describes the intelligible world in a different way from Plato, making a probable assumption which has no philosophical necessity. But one might doubt whether it is even probable:

for it would be more probable that all the spheres, contributing their several movements to a single system, should look to one principle, the first. And one might enquire whether Aristotle thinks that the many intelligibles derive from one, the first, or whether there are many primary principles in the intelligible world; and if they derive from one, the situation will clearly be analogous to that of the heavenly spheres in the sense-world, where each contains the other and one, the outermost, dominates; so that there too the first would contain the others and there will be an intelligible universe; and, just as here in the sense-world the spheres are not empty, but the first is full of heavenly bodies and the others have heavenly bodies in them, so there also the moving principles will have many realities in them, and the realities there will be truer. But if each is primary principle, the primary principles will be a random assembly; and why will they be a community and in agreement on one work, the harmony of the whole universe? And how can the perceptible beings in heaven be equal in number to the intelligible movers? And how can the intelligibles even be many, when they are incorporeal, as they are, and matter does not divide them? For these reasons those of the ancient philosophers who took up positions closest to those of Pythagoras and his successors (and Pherecydes) held closely to this nature; but some of them worked out the idea fully in their own writings, others did not do so in written works but in unwritten group discussions, or left it altogether alone.

10. It has been shown that we ought to think that this is how things are, that there is the One beyond being, of such a kind as our argument wanted to show, so far as demonstration was possible in these matters, and next in order there is Being and Intellect, and the nature of Soul in the third place. And just as in nature there are these three of which we have spoken, so we ought to think that they are present also in ourselves. I do not mean in [ourselves as] beings of the sense-world—for these three are separate from the things of sense]—but in [ourselves as] beings outside the realm of sense-perception; "outside" here is used in the same sense as those realities are also said to be "outside" the whole universe: so the corresponding realities in man are said to be "outside," as Plato speaks of the "inner man." Our soul then also is a divine thing and of a nature different [from the things of sense], like the universal nature of soul; and the human soul is perfect when it has intellect; and intellect is of two kinds, the one which reasons and the one which makes it possible to reason. Now this reasoning part of the soul, which needs no bodily instrument for its reasoning, but preserves its activity in purity in order that it may be able to engage in pure reasoning, one could without mistake place, as separate and unmixed with body, in the primary intelligible realm. I or we should not look for a place in which to put it, but make it exist outside all place. For this is how it is by itself and outside and immaterial, when it is alone and retains nothing from the nature of body. This is the reason why Plato says of the universe also that the craftsman wrapped the soul round it "from outside," indicating the part of the soul which remains in the intelligible; and he said obscurely about us that the soul is "on top in the head." And his exhortation to separate ourselves is not meant in a spatial sense—this [higher part] of soul is naturally separated—but refers to our not inclining to the body, and to our not having mental images, and our alienation from the body—if by any chance one could make the remaining form of soul ascend, and take along with us to the heights that of it which is established here below, which alone is the craftsman and modeller of the body and is actively concerned with it.

11. Since, then, there exists soul which reasons about what is right and good, and discursive reasoning which enquires about the rightness and goodness of this or that particular thing, there must be some further permanent rightness from which arises the discursive reasoning in the realm of soul. Or how else would it manage to reason? And

if soul sometimes reasons about the right and good and sometimes does not, there must be in us Intellect which does not reason discursively but always possesses the right, and there must be also the principle and cause and God of Intellect. He is not divided, but abides, and as he does not abide in place he is contemplated in many beings, in each and every one of those capable of receiving him as another self, just as the centre of a circle exists by itself, but every one of the radii in the circle has its point in the centre and the lines bring their individuality to it. For it is with something of this sort in ourselves that we are in contact with god and are with him and depend upon him; and those of us who converge towards him are firmly established in him.

12. Why then, when we have such great possessions, do we not consciously grasp them, but are mostly inactive in these ways, and some of us are never active at all? They are always occupied in their own activities, Intellect, and that which is before Intellect, always in itself, and soul, which is in this sense "ever-moving." For not everything which is in the soul is immediately perceptible, but it reaches us when it enters into perception; but when a particular active power does not give a share in its activity to the perceiving power, that activity has not yet pervaded the whole soul. We do not therefore yet know it, since we are accompanied by the perceptive power and are not a part of soul but the whole soul. And further, each soul-part, since it is always living, always exercises its own activity by itself; but the discovery of it comes when sharing with the perceptive power and conscious awareness takes place. If then there is to be conscious apprehension of the powers which are present in this way, we must turn our power of apprehension inwards, and make it attend to what is there. It is as if someone was expecting to hear a voice which he wanted to hear and withdrew from other sounds and roused his power of hearing to catch what, when it comes, is the best of all sounds which can be heard; so here also we must let perceptible sounds go (except in so far as we must listen to them) and keep the soul's power of apprehension pure and ready to hear the voices from on high.

*   *   *

FIFTH ENNEAD, THIRD TRACTATE:
ON THE KNOWING HYPOSTASES
AND THAT WHICH IS BEYOND

[12. cont.] But the One, as it is beyond Intellect, so is beyond knowledge, and as it does not in any way need anything, so it does not even need knowing; but knowing has its place in the second nature. For knowing is one thing; but that is one without the thing; for if it is one thing it would not be the absolute One: for "absolute" comes before "something."

13. It is, therefore, truly ineffable: for whatever you say about it, you will always be speaking of a "something." But "beyond all things and beyond the supreme majesty of Intellect" is the only one of all the ways of speaking of it which is true; it is not its name, but says that it is not one of all things and "has no name," because we can say nothing of it: we only try, as far as possible, to make signs to ourselves about it. But when we raise the difficulty "Then it has no perception of itself and is not even conscious of itself and does not even know itself," we should consider that by saying this we are turning ourselves round and going in the opposite direction. I or we are making it many when we make it object of knowledge and knowledge, and by attributing

thought to it we make it need thought: even if thought goes intimately with it, thought will be superfluous to it. I or in general thought seems to be an intimate consciousness of the whole when many parts come together in the same thing; [this is so] when a thing knows itself, which is knowing in the proper sense: each single part is just itself and seeks nothing; but if the thinking is of what is outside, the thoughts will be deficient, and not thought in the proper sense. But that which is altogether simple and self-sufficient needs nothing; but what is self-sufficient in the second degree, but needs itself, this is what needs to think itself; and that which is deficient in relation to itself achieves self-sufficiency by being a whole, with an adequacy deriving from all its parts, intimately present to itself and inclining to itself. For intimate self-consciousness is a consciousness of something which is many: even the name bears witness to this. And thinking, which is prior, turns inward to Intellect which is obviously multiple; for even if it only says this, "I am existent," it says it as a discovery, and says it plausibly, for existence is multiple: since if it concentrated its gaze on itself as something simple and said "I am existent," it would not attain either itself or existence. For it does not mean something like a stone by existence, when it is speaking the truth, but says many things in one word. For this being—which is meant to be real being and not what has a trace of being, which would not even be called being because of this trace, but is as image to archetype—contains many things. Well, then, will not each of these many things be thought? Now if you want to grasp the "isolated and alone," you will not think; but absolute being is multiple in itself, and if you speak of something else, being contains it. But if this is so, if anything is the simplest of all, it will not possess thought of itself: for if it is to possess it, it will possess it by being multiple. It is not therefore thought, nor is there any thinking about it.

14. How then do we ourselves speak about it? We do indeed say something about it, but we certainly do not speak it, and we have neither knowledge or thought of it. But if we do not have it in knowledge, do we not have it at all? But we have it in such a way that we speak about it, but do not speak it. For we say what it is not, but we do not say what it is: so that we speak about it from what comes after it. But we are not prevented from having it, even if we do not speak it. But just as those who have a god within them and are in the grip of divine possession may know this much, that they have something greater within them, even if they do not know what, and from the ways in which they are moved and the things they say get a certain awareness of the god who moves them, though these are not the same as the mover; so we seem to be disposed towards the One, divining, when we have our intellect pure, that this is the inner intellect, which gives substance and everything else which belongs to this level, but that he is not only of a kind not to be these, but something higher than what we call "being," but is more and greater than anything said about him, because he is higher than speech and thought and awareness; he gives us these, but he is not these himself.

15. But how does he give them? By having them, or by not having them? But how did he give what he does not have? But if he has them, he is not simple; if he does not have them, how does the multiplicity come from him? One might perhaps grant that he gives one simple thing from himself—yet there would be room for enquiry how this could come from the absolute One; but all the same one can speak of the radiance from him, as from a light—but how can he give many things? Now what comes from him could not be the same as himself. If then it is not the same, it cannot of course be better: for what could be better than the One or in any way transcend him? It must then be worse; and this means more deficient. When then is more deficient than the One? That which is not one; it is therefore many; but all the same it aspires to the One: so it is a one–many. For all that is not one is kept in being by the one, and is what it is by this

"one": for if it had not become one, even though it is composed of many parts, it is not yet what one would call "itself." And if it is possible to say of each individual part what it is, one says it because each of them is one and it is it because of this very fact. But that which does not already have many parts in itself is not one by participation in the One, but is the One itself, not the "one" predicated of something else but because it is this One from which, somehow, the others derive their oneness, some [in a greater degree] because they are near and others [in a lesser degree] because they are far away. For that which comes immediately after it shows clearly that it is immediately after it because its multiplicity is a one-everywhere; for although it is a multiplicity it is at the same time identical with itself and there is no way in which you could divide it, because "all things are together"; for each of the things also which come from it, as long as it participates in life, is a one–many: for it cannot reveal itself as a one–all. But [Intellect] does reveal itself as a one–all, because it comes after the origin: for its origin is really one and truly one. But that which comes after the origin is, somehow, under the pressure of the One, all things by its participation in the One, and each and every part of it is both all and one. What then are "all things"? All things of which that One is the principle. But how is that One the principle of all things? Is it because as principle it keeps them in being, making each one of them exist? Yes, and because it brought them into existence. But how did it do so? By possessing them beforehand. But it has been said that in this way it will be a multiplicity. But it had them in such a way as not to be distinct: they are distinguished on the second level, in the rational form. For this is already actuality; but the One is the potency of all things. But in what way is it the potency? Not in the way in which matter is said to be in potency, because it receives: for matter is passive; but this [material] way of being a potency is at the opposite extreme to making. How then does the One make what it does not have? It does not do it casually, nor reflecting on what it will make, but all the same it will make. Now it has been said that, if anything comes from the One, it must be something different from it; and in being different, it is not one: for if it was, it would be that One. But if it is not one, but two, it must necessarily also be many: for it is already the same and different and qualified and all the rest. And that what comes from the One is certainly not one, may be taken as demonstrated; but it is worth querying the proposition that it is a multiplicity, and a multiplicity of the sort which is observed in what comes after it; and the necessity of there being anything after the One remains to be enquired into.

16. It has been said elsewhere that there must be something after the first, and in a general way that it is power, and overwhelming power; and the point has also been made that this is to be believed on the evidence of all other things, because there is nothing, even among the things on the lowest level, which does not have power to produce. But we now have to add this further point, that, since in things which are generated it is not possible to go upwards but only to go downwards and move further towards multiplicity, the principle of each group of things is simpler than they are themselves. Therefore that which makes the world of sense could not be a world of sense itself, but must be an intellect and an intelligible world; and that which is before this and generates it could not be intellect or an intelligible world, but simpler than intellect and simpler than an intelligible world. For many does not come from many, but this [intelligible] many comes from what is not many: for this would not be the principle if it was also many itself, but something else before it. There must therefore be a concentration into a real one outside all multiplicity and any ordinary sort of simplicity, if it is to be really simple. But how is what comes from it a multiple and universal rational form, when it is obviously not a rational form? And if it is not this why does rational form come not from rational form [but something else]? And how does what is like the Good come from the